Maltese Society
A Sociological Inquiry

Maltese Society
A Sociological Inquiry

edited by

Ronald G. Sultana
Godfrey Baldacchino

First published in 1994
by Mireva Publications of
Tower Street, Msida, Malta. MSD 06.
Typeset and paged on
New Century Schoolbook 10/12 pt by
MirevaSet, Msida, Malta.
Produced by Evan Cumbo.
Printed and bound by
Gutenberg Press,
Żabbar, Malta.

International Standard Book Number

1-870579-24-0

All rights reserved. No part of this publication may be produced or transmitted in any form or by any means electronical, mechanical, photocopying, recording or otherwise, or stored in any retrieval system of any nature without the written permission of the copyright holder and the publisher, application for which shall be made to the publisher.

© Mireva Publications
1994

Editors' Note
Disclaimer

Opinions expressed in this publication are those of the authors and need not necessarily reflect those of the editors.

 Every year, the book industry all over the world, consumes millions of tons of printing paper. This means that book production is directly responsible for the destruction of hundreds of thousands of trees and the consumption of billions of litres of water.

Every year, the book industry produces enormous amounts of wastes and air-polluting effluents.

By using recycled paper Mireva Publications is expressing its commitment to use natural resources wisely and to protect the environment. Therefore by choosing a Mireva Publication you are opting for an enhanced quality of life – both intellectually and environmentally.

Table of Contents

Notes on Contributors	xi
Acknowledgements	xxiii
Foreword	
Anthony Giddens	xxvii

1. Introduction: Sociology and Maltese Society: The Field and its Context   1

Part 1: Dependence and Social Stratification   23

2. Perspectives on Class in Malta
   Ronald G. Sultana   27
3. 'That Favourite Dream of the Colonies': Industrialization, Dependence and the Limits of Development Discourse in Malta
   Mario Vella   55
4. The Visibility and Invisibility of Women
   Pauline Miceli   79
5. Maltese Political Parties and Political Modernization
   Godfrey A. Pirotta   95

Part 2: Distinction and Differentiation   113

6. Language and Class In Malta
   Lydia Sciriha   117
7. The Social Prestige of Residential Areas
   David M. Boswell   133
8. Towards a Sociology of Consumption in Malta
   Ronald G. Sultana   163

9 Cancer in Malta: Trends in Mortality and Incidence Rates of Lung and Breast Cancer
   Yana Mintoff Bland   187

10 The Maltese Community in Metro Toronto: Invisible Identity/ies
   Carmel Borg & Peter Mayo   211

Part 3: Continuity and Change   225

11 The Maltese Family in the Context of Social Change
   Carmel Tabone   229

12 Values for Malta's Future: Social Change, Values and Social Policy
   Anthony M. Abela   253

13 *Festa Partiti*: Parish Competition and Conflict
   Jeremy Boissevain   271

14 Secularization
   Carmel Tabone   285

15 Television and its Viewers: The Case of Soap Opera
   Mary Anne Lauri   301

16 Schooling and Socialization: Rituals, Symbols and Hidden Messages in a Private School
   Emmanuel Mifsud   323

17 The Impact of Tourism in Malta: Cultural Rupture or Continuity?
   Joe Inguanez   343

Part 4: Control and Resistance   353

18 As We Sit Together, Should We Use the Phone? A Research Agenda for the Study of Media in Malta
   Saviour Chircop   357

19 Gossip: A Means of Social Control
   Sibyl O'Reilly Mizzi   369

20 Absenteeism: Deviance, Resistance and Contestation
   Denise Chircop   383

21	A Politician and His Audience: Malta's Dom Mintoff *Jeremy Boissevain*	409
22	Rock Music and Counter-Culturalism in Malta *Albert Bell*	421
23	Privatization: Policy and Politics *Mary Darmanin*	441

Part 5: Work and Production Relations — 457

24	A Labour Market in Transition *E.P. Delia*	461
25	Maltese Orientations To Work *Edward L. Zammit*	483
26	Worker Cooperatives in Malta: Between Self-Help and Subsidy *Godfrey Baldacchino*	505
27	School Children in Malta's Twilight Economy *Ronald G. Sultana*	521
28	The Locus and Distribution of Power: The Phoenicia Hotel Dispute *Alfred Grixti*	537
29	Threads For Survival: Workplace Relations in a Clothing Firm *Benny Borg Bonello*	553
30	Workers' Participation and the Control of Labour *Godfrey Baldacchino*	573

Part 6: Deviance and Social Problems — 591

31	Outsiders *Maureen Cole*	595
32	Substance Abuse: Focus on Alcohol *Alexander M. Baldacchino*	617
33	Patterns of Crime *Michael Tanti Dougall*	635

34 The Maltese Elderly: From Institutionalization to
    Active Participation in the Community
    Joseph Troisi 655
35 Drug Abuse Among School Children
    Anthony M. Abela 669
36 Land Use: An Account of Environmental Stewardship
    Edward A. Mallia 685

Index 707

Notes on Contributors

Abela Anthony M. holds a B.A. (Hons.) degree from the University of Malta, a S.T.B. from the Gregorian University of Rome, an M.Th. from the Centre Sevres (Paris), an M.A. from Loyola University (Chicago) and a D.Phil. from Oxford University. He is the author of *Transmitting Values in European Malta: A Study in the Contemporary Values of Modern Society* (Jesuit Publications & Editrice Pontificia Università Gregoriana, 1991), *Changing Youth Culture in Malta* (Jesuit Publications, 1992), and *Shifting Family Values in Malta* (Discern, 1994). Abela has also published a number of articles in *Problemi ta' Llum*, *La Civiltà Cattolica* and *Melita Teologica*. He is a lecturer in social policy at the University of Malta, where he is also Director of the Institute of Social Welfare.

Baldacchino Alexander Mario holds an M.D. degree from the University of Malta, and a Diploma in Addictive Behaviour from the University of London. He is currently following an M.Phil. course in Psychiatry at the University of Edinburgh, and works as a Registrar in Psychiatry in the South-East Scotland Postgraduate Training Scheme. Prior to that he worked in Malta for a number of years in the field of drug prevention. He has authored *Medical Advisor – On Line* (Commonwealth Secretariat Training Package) and has published articles in the *British Journal of Addiction* and the *Pharmaceutical Journal*. His main research interests are in childhood sexual abuse, and he has been a consultant for the Commonwealth Secretariat in India on drug related issues.

Baldacchino Godfrey holds a B.A. (Gen.) and a PGCE from the University of Malta, an M.A. from the Hague, and a Ph.D. from the University of Warwick. He is Research Officer at the Workers' Participation Development Centre and a visiting lecturer in the Department of Public Policy at the University of Malta. He served as Visiting Research Fellow at the University of the West Indies, Barbados Campus as a beneficiary of a Commonwealth Secretariat Academic Exchange Fellowship (1992). He has published widely in the fields of industrial relations, workplace democracy and education, and his articles have appeared in *Development and Change, Economic and Industrial Democracy, Tourism Management, Hyphen, Education*, and the *Economics and Social Studies*. He is the author of *Il-Partecipazzjoni fit-Tarzna: Kif Jaħsibha l-Ħaddiem* (WPDC, 1984), *Introducing Social Studies* (PEG, 1988; revised, 1991) and *Worker Cooperatives with Particular Reference to Malta* (The Hague, 1990). Dr Baldacchino is a member of the Board of Cooperatives.

Bell Albert is a graduate in Psychology and Social Studies from the University of Malta, and is currently reading for an MA in sociology at the same University. His main research interests are in youth culture and sociology of youth deviance, and he was recently appointed an assistant lecturer at the University of Malta's Institute for Forensic Studies.

Borg Carmel holds a B.Ed. (Hons.) degree from the University of Malta, and an M.Ed. from the Ontario Insitute for Studies in Education. He is currently a Ph.D. student in the department of Curriculum Studies at OISE. He has published articles in a number of international journals, including *Convergence, Canadian Journal of Education, McGill Journal of Education*, and *Trans/Forms*.

Borg Bonello Benny holds a B.A. (Hons.) in Public Administration and an M.A. in Industrial Relations from the University of Warwick. He is a Laboratory Manager at the University of Malta, and his main research interests are in the sociology of work and consumer protection.

Boissevain Jeremy is a professor of social anthropology at the University of Amsterdam. After obtaining his B.A. (Haverford, USA), he directed the CARE programme in the Philippines, Japan, India and Malta. In 1962 he was granted a Ph.D. in social anthropology by the London School of Economics and Political Science. He subsequently taught at the universities of Montreal and Sussex and has held visiting appointments at the Universities of Sussex, New York (Stony Brook), Columbia, Massachusetts (Amherst) and Malta, where he is currently visiting professor. His research has focused on local power relations, immigrant adjustment, immigrant entrepreneurs and, currently, ritual change and the impact of tourism. The author of more than 40 published articles, his works in English include *Saints and Fireworks: Religion and Politics in Rural Malta* (Athlone Press, 1965, 1969; Progress Press 1993), *Hal Farrug: A Village in Malta* (Holt, Rinehart & Winston, 1969, 1980), *The Italians of Montreal: Immigrant Adjustment in a Plural Society* (Information Canada, 1970), and *Friends of Friends: Networks, Manipulators and Coalitions* (Basil Blackwell, 1974). He also co-edited *Network Analysis* (Mouton, 1973), *Beyond the Community: Social Process in Europe* (Netherlands Ministry of Education and Science, 1973), *Ethnic Challenge: The Politics of Ethnicity in Europe* (Herodot, 1984), and *Dutch Dilemmas: Anthropologists look at the Netherlands* (Van Gorcum, 1989). He is the editor of *Revitalizing European Rituals* (Routledge, 1992) and is currently editing a collection on reactions to tourism in Europe. Besides his writing in English, his work appeared in Dutch, French, Italian, Spanish and Japanese.

Boswell David M. is professor of social policy at the Open University, Milton Keynes (UK). He served as visiting professor of sociology at the University of Malta between 1976 and 1980. He is co-editor and co-author of various books published by Open University Press, including *Models of Social Class* (1976), *The Organizational Practice of Residential Care* (1978) and *Health and Disease* (1985). His current research interests are in the area of sociology of health.

Chircop Denise holds a first class B.Ed. (Hons.) from the University of Malta, and is currently reading for a Masters degree, with a focus on adult education and women's studies at the University of Firenze, Italy. She is active in a number of youth organizations, and a founder member of the Moviment Edukazzjoni Umana.

Chircop Saviour is the Director of the Centre for Communications Technology and the Head of Department of Communications and Instructional Technology at the University of Malta. He obtained his Ph.D. from Syracuse University (USA) and his current research interests are in the theory of evaluation, research methods and instructional design. He was awarded the Marsia Guttengag Award by the American Evaluation Association in 1991.

Cole Maureen is a B.A. (Gen.) graduate of the University of Malta, having also studied at Monash University, Melbourne, Australia. She is currently an Assistant Lecturer in Social Work at the Institute of Social Welfare, the University of Malta. Between 1983 and 1988 she was employed as a social worker with CARITAS (Malta), and since 1983 she has participated in a number of initiatives aimed at training and empowering users and volunteers in the social welfare sector. In 1984 she co-organized an exchange conference in collaboration with *Social Work Today*, the Journal of the British Association of Social Workers. She was a member of the core team during the launching of an Action Research Project on and for the Handicapped, a member of the Organizing and Scientific Committee responsible for an International Conference entitled 'The Care and Education of Disabled Children – A Multi-disciplinary Approach', and is currently a member of the Bioethics Consultative Committee, a member of the Maltese Association of Social Workers, and a Voluntary Collaborator in the Centre for Faith and Justice.

Darmanin Mary holds B.A. (Hons.) from the University of Malta, an MA. Soc. Lit. from the University of Essex (UK) and a Ph.D. from the University of Wales College of Cardiff. She is a senior lecturer in sociology in the Department of Foundations in Education (Faculty of Education) and the Department of Sociology (Faculty of Arts). She has contributued chapters to edited collections of books both in Malta and abroad, and published a number of articles in international journals such as the *British Journal of Sociology of Education*, *Gender and Education* and *International Studies in Sociology of Education*. She is on the Board of international editors of the latter journal and was guest editor of the Faculty of Education's journal, with a special issue on gender in 1992. Early research interests include primary schooling and classroom interaction, teachers' unionization, and gender in education. Currently she is working on policy making using life history methodology to study the subjective and objective careers of policy makers.

Delia Emmanuel Paul holds a B.A. (Hons) and an M.A. degree in economics from the University of Malta, and an M.Litt. from the University of Oxford. He has authored a number of books, including *Taxation: An Evaluation* (Chamber of Commerce, 1981), *Focus on Aspects of the Maltese Economy* (Midsea Books, 1978), *The Currency Basket* (COPE, 1986), *The Task Ahead: Dimensions, Ideologies and Policies* (COPE, 1987), and *The Welfare Gap and Pensions in Malta* (Chamber of Commerce, 1993), apart from numerous articles. His main research activities are in policy-oriented fields such as demography, fiscal and monetary policy, and welfare and income distribution. He is the Head of Department of Economics at the University of Malta, a Director of the Central Bank of Malta, and a member of the Public Service Reform Commission as well as of the Malta Council for Economic Development. He is a consultant for the FAO on a Malta Case Study on Nutrition.

Giddens Anthony is Professor of Sociology at the University of Cambridge. He is the author of many works including *The Consequences of Modernity* (1991), *Modernity and Self-Identity* (1991), *The Transformation of Intimacy* (1992) and *Sociology* (2e. 1993), a widely used undergraduate text.

Grixti Alfred holds a B.Educ (Hons.) degree from the University of Malta, and a Diploma in Social Studies as well as an M.Sc. in Management from the University of Oxford. He has published in *Society*, and is a regular contributor to *L-Orizzont*. His main research interests are in trade unions and human resource management. He is currently a secondary school teacher, and is the Education Secretary for the Malta Labour Party. He was formerly General Secretary of the Federazzjoni Għaqdiet taż-Żgħazagħ Maltin, and President of the Maltese Young Socialists.

Inguanez Joe holds a Lic.Sc.Soc from the Gregorian University (Rome) and a Ph.D. from Goldsmiths College, University of London. He is the Head of Department of Sociology at the Univesity of Malta, and a member of the British Sociological Association, the American Sociological Association, the International Association for Impact Assessment, the International Association of Tourism Experts, and of the Associazione Sociologici del Mediterraneo. He has contributed chapters to books on sociology of tourism and of church structures, as well as articles to the journal *Sociologica Urbana e Rurale*. His current interests are in the sociology of tourism, in social change and development, and in symbolic interaction theory. He is a member of the Diocesan Representative Council.

Lauri Mary Anne holds a B.A. (Hons.) in Psychology from the University of Malta and an M.Sc. in Social Psychology from the University of London. She co-authored the third edition of a secondary school textbook on Media Studies, and is currently reading for a doctorate at the University of London. Lauri is an assistant lecturer in the Department of Psychology at the University of Malta.

Mallia Edward A. holds a B.Sc. from the University of Malta, and an M.A., a D.Phil. and a PGCE from the University of Oxford. He is the author of forty articles which have been published in astrophysical journals, and his main research interests are in alternative and renewable energy sources and in environmental physics. He is an Associate Professor at the University of Malta, where he is the Head of the Department of Physics and the Dean of the Faculty of Science.

Mayo Peter holds first degrees in Education (University of Malta) and English (University of London), a Masters degree (University of Alberta) and a doctorate (OISE/University of Toronto) in Sociology of Education. He is the author of *The National Museum of Fine Arts* (Midsea Books, 1994), and of a number of articles on adult education which have been published in books and journals such as the *International Journal of Lifelong Education, Language and Education, Studies in the Education of Adults*, and *Adults Learning*. He is a lecturer in the Faculty of Education and co-ordinates the Diploma in Education (Adult) course.

Miceli Pauline has a Diploma in Writing for Children and Teenagers from the Institute of Children's Literature, Connecticut USA, and has followed a Certificate Course in Personal and Social Education at the University of Malta. She is the author of two books for children, *L-Avventuri ta' Heliks* (Bugelli, 1990) and *Il-Kewkba* ta' *Debra u Stejjer Oħra* (Sensiela Kotba Soċjalisti, 1993), as well as a book on women in Malta entitled *Maria-Eva* (SKS, 1991). Miceli has fifteen years' experience in the production of educational radio programmes, and is currently employed as a teacher.

Mifsud Emmanuel hold a B.Ed. (Hons.) degree from the University of Malta, and is currently reading for an M.Ed. His main interests are in the sociology of education, particularly on privatization policies and their effects on education. He has published two books of short stories entitled *Stejjer ta' Nies Koroh* (1991) and *Ktieb tas-Sibt Filgħaxija* (1993), besides directing a number of dramatic pieces for conventional and street theatre. He is currently a teacher.

Mintoff Bland Yana is the Administrator of the Foundation for a Compassionate Society based in Austin, Texas (USA). She is the co-founder and President of the Association of Women of the Mediterranean Region. She graduated B.A. Economics (Exeter), and M.Sc. Economics and Ph.D. Queen Mary's College (London, UK). She has worked for Malta Counter Trade as well as a lecturer in economics at the University of Malta. Her research and publications have focused on the sociology of health. She has published on cancer in the Mediterranean, workers' participation and the new technology, the war economy and women's oppression.

O'Reilly Mizzi Sibyl holds a Masters and doctoral degrees in anthropology from the State University of New York at Stonybrook. She is currently a visiting lecturer in the Department of Anthropology at the University of Malta. Her main research interests are in women in the Mediterranean, and she has written extensively on this subject and contributed chapters to various books. She is the author of *Women in Senglea: The Changing Role of Urban, Working-Class Women in Malta* (1981), and is a consultant to various women's groups, including the National Council of Women.

Pirotta Godfrey A. holds a Diploma in Social Studies from the University of Oxford (UK), a B.A. (Hons.) Politics from the University of Reading (UK), a Postgraduate Certificate in Education (University of Malta), and a Ph.D. from the University of Bath

(UK). He has authored several articles in the field of politics in such journals as *Economic and Social Studies*, and has contributed chapters in the same field to a number of books. His main research interest is in Public Service Reform and in Local Council Development. Dr Pirotta currently lectures in the Department of Public Policy, Coordinator of the Diploma in Political Studies, and Board Member of the Worker's Participation Development Centre. In 1971 he founded the Consumer Protection Association, and between 1978 and 1981 he was Chairman of the Editorial Board of *Il-Ħsieb*.

Sciriha Lydia holds a B.A.(Gen.) degree and a Post-Graduate Certificate in Education from the University of Malta, and an M.A. in Linguistics and a Ph.D. from the University of Victoria, British Columbia, Canada. Her main research interests are in the fields of sociolinguistics, psycholinguistics, discourse analysis and English phonology, and has published in this area in a number of academic journals including the *Journal of Maltese Studies and Contrastive Linguistics*. Sciriha is a senior lecturer at the University of Malta and is the Director of the University's Language Laboratory Complex.

Sultana Ronald G. is a senior lecturer in the Department of Foundations in Education (Faculty of Education) and in the Department of Sociology (Faculty of Arts). He is the founder and co-ordinator of the Comparative Education Programme, and University Senate representative on the International Social Sciences Institute. He is the author of over 40 book chapters and articles published in different scholarly journals, including the *British Journal of Sociology of Education*, *Qualitative Studies in Education*, and the *International Studies in Sociology of Education*. He is the executive editor of the journal *Education* (Malta), and a member of several editorial boards including those of the *McGill Journal of Education*, the *International Journal of Educational Development*, *Teaching in Higher Education*, and *Taboo: International Journal of Education and Culture*. Sultana has edited *Themes in Education: A Maltese Reader* (Mireva Publications, 1991), and *Ġenituri u Għalliema għal Edukazzjoni Aħjar* (Mireva Publications, 1994) and authored *Education and National Development: Historical and Critical Perspectives on Vocational Schooling* *in Malta* (Mireva, 1992). His main research interests are in the political economy of education, and is currently directing a national analysis of the class structure in Malta. He was a Fulbright Scholar at Stanford University (Palo Alto, USA) in 1990 and Distinguished Visiting Scholar at the Victoria University of Technology (Melbourne, Australia) in 1993.

Tabone Carmel graduated with an S.Th.L. from St Thomas Aquinas College, Rabat (Malta), an S.Th.Lic. (Moral Theology) and an Sc.Soc.D. from the Pontifical University St Thomas Aquinas, Angelicum (Rome). He is a lecturer in sociology in the Department of Public Policy and in the Department of Sociology, Chairman of the Family Study and Research Project of the Ministry for Home Affairs and Social Development, member of the Commission for the Advancement of Women and Editor of the *Mediterranean Social Sciences Network Journal*. His main research interests are in sociology of development and sociology of religion, and is the author of *Secularization of the Family in Changing Malta* (Dominican Publications, 1987) and of a series of articles in local journals on issues dealing with family, religion and development.

Tanti Dougall Michael holds a B.A., a B.Ed. (Hons.) and an LL.D. from the University of Malta. He is currently following a Diploma course in Canonical Marriage Cases Jurisprudence and Procedure, and is editor of *Id-Dritt*, a Law journal to which he regularly contributes articles. His main research interest is in the sociology of law, currently teaches sociology at a sixth form level, and is a visiting lecturer at the University of Malta. He is a founder-member of the University Student Teachers' Association, of the Human Rights Research Unit, and President of the Law Society.

Troisi Joseph holds a B.A. (Hons.) degree, an M.Th., an M.A. (Phil.), as well as a masters and a doctorate in sociology. He is a senior lecturer in Sociology at the Institute of Gerontology at the University of Malta. He is a member of the Committee of Experts on Varieties of Welfare Provision and Dependent Old People, Directorate of Social and Economic Affairs (Council of Europe), as well as of the International Project of Sociological Research of the Scientific Institute, Oasi Maria SS, Troina. He is also Research Consultant at the Centre for Social Research, Social Action Movement, Malta. He has served as Programme Manager and Coordinator of the International Institute on Ageing (United Nations-Malta). For a number of years he was Assistant Director of the Department of Research and Publications of the Indian Social Institute, New Delhi, India and Associate Editor of *Social Action*, a quarterly review of social trends. He has taught sociology at the Universities of Delhi, Poona, Madras, Manila and served as Visiting Professor at the Gregorian University, Rome. Troisi is the author of *The Role of the Maltese Elderly in the Community*; *Full Participation and Equality of the Disabled: Myth or Reality*; *Tribal Religion, Religious Beliefs and Practices among the Santals*; *Readings in Tribal Life: The Santals, A work in Ten Volumes*; *The Santals: A Classified and Annotated Bibliography*. He has also published a number of articles in scholarly journals internationally, and contributed to various books in the fields of the social sciences.

Vella Mario holds degrees in philosophy from the University of Malta and sociology from the London School of Economics and Political Science. He obtained a doctorate in political economy from the Humboldt University in Berlin. He is the author of a number of articles on the sociology of development, and is the author of *Reflections in a Canvas Bag: Beginning Philosophy between Politics and History* (PEG, 1989). Dr Vella is currently the President of the Malta Labour Party.

Zammit Edward L. holds a B.A. and a Ph.L. from Loyola University (Chicago, USA) and a M.Litt. and a D.Phil. from Eton College, Oxford University (UK). He is the author of *A Colonial Inheritance: Maltese Perceptions of Work, Power and Class Structure with reference to the Labour Movement*, (Malta University Press, 1984), and editor of *Workers' Participation in Malta – Options for Future Policy* (WPDC, 1989) and *Trejd Unjoniżmu f'Malta: Ħarsa Lura u 'l Quddiem* (WPDC-FES, 1993). He is the author of a number of articles, the most recent appearing in the *Concise Encyclopaedia of Participation and Co-Management* (edited by G. Gzell, de Gruyter Press, 1992) and *European Labour Unions* (edited by J. Campbell, Greenwood Press, 1992). His main research interests are in the field of the sociology of work, industrial relations, workers' participation and human resource development. Zammit is the Head of the University of Malta's Department of Public Policy and the Director of the Workers' Participation Development Centre. He is the Chairperson of the Malta Cooperatives Board, member of the 'Trade Unions and Democratic Participation' Research Group (ETUC/CFDT), and Visiting Professor at the Institute of Social Studies, The Hague (1983-88) and the University of Augsburg (1994).

Acknowledgements

Abela, Anthony M. – 'Values for Malta's future: Social change, values and social policy'. This paper is a revised version of an address to the General Council of the Nationalist Party, and was first published in *Problemi ta' Llum*, October 1992, and in *La Civiltà Cattolica*, quaderno 3429, 1 Maggio 1993.

Abela, Anthony M. – 'Drug abuse among school children'. This paper is a revised and extended version of a preliminary report presented to Caritas (Malta) on March 28, 1992. An abridged Maltese version of this paper was published in *Problemi ta' Llum*, June 1992, pp. 145-51.

Baldacchino, Godfrey – 'Worker cooperatives in Malta: Between self-help and subsidy'. The author is grateful to Romeo A. Formosa, Saviour Rizzo and Joe Saliba for commenting on an earlier draft of this paper. He would also like to thank the Board of Cooperatives for providing the statistics reproduced in tabular form. Acknowledgements are also due to the Hon. Dr. Joe Cassar, Parliamentary Secretary responsible for cooperative affairs, for his assistance in tracing press items referring to local cooperative initiatives prior to the enactment of any supportive legislation. Responsibility for the contents of this article remains, however, solely of the author.

Baldacchino, Godfrey – 'Workers' participation and the control of labour'. The author would like to thank Benny Borg Bonello and Saviour Rizzo for their comments on an earlier draft of this paper. The author would also like to point out that the views and opinions expressed in this paper are his own and not necessarily those of the Workers' Participation Development Centre of the University of Malta.

Boissevain, Jeremy – 'A politician and his audience: Malta's Dom Mintoff'. This discussion, accompanied by translated excerpts of Mintoff's speech, was first presented to a colloquium on

'Politicians and their Public' at the Harlow (Essex) campus of the Memorial University of Newfoundland, September 5th-9th, 1976. Dom Mintoff was no longer Prime Minister when it was finally published (cf. Boissevain 1986). The present article is a shortened version of the 1986 publication. The author would like to thank Robert Paine, Kola Muscat, Les Collins, Bertus Hendriks, Jojada Verrips, Kitty Verrips, Peter Serracino-Inglott, Jean Killick, Gemma Cachia, Edward Zammit, Hannie Hoekstra, Anne Busuttil, Lawrence Ancilleri, Inga Boissevain and Ronald G. Sultana for their help in various ways. Shortcomings are, of course, strictly the responsibility of the author.

Boissevain, Jeremy – *'Festa partiti*: Parish competition and conflict'. An earlier version of this paper was published in Victor Mallia-Milanes (ed.), *The British Colonial Experience 1800-1964: The Impact on Maltese Society*, (Malta, Mireva Publications, 1988).

Borg, Carmel & **Mayo**, Peter – 'The Maltese community in Metro Toronto: Invisible identity/ies' would like to thank Jennifer Camilleri, Aoi Okuno and Toni Xerri, besides the two editors of this volume, for responding critically to earlier drafts of the text. The first draft of this paper was written when both authors were full time Ph.D. candidates at the Ontario Institute for Studies in Education, the University of Toronto's graduate school of education. Substantial parts of this work have appeared in another paper, this time consisting of a proposal for a community adult education programme among the Maltese in Toronto. The latter paper, coauthored with Jennifer Camilleri, is included in the Proceedings of the 12th Annual Conference of the Canadian Association for the Study of Adult Education, Ottawa, Canada, 1993.

Boswell, David M. – 'The social prestige of residential areas'. The author acknowledges the influence of David Glass at the London School of Economics and Political Science (LSE), Clyde Mitchell in Central Africa and Manchester, and the sociologists of Nuffield College for nurturing an interest in and familiarity with concepts of social prestige and social status as well as social stratification. Also acknowledged are small research grants from The Nuffield Foundation and the research committees of the

Open University, and study facilities at Nuffield College during the analysis of this material. Several colleagues from the OU as well as from the Department of Social Studies at the University of Malta helped with various stages of the project which was undertaken as an exercise in research methods for students of the full and part-time Maltese BA programme in 1979. Much of the computation of the social distance data is owed to Clyde Mitchell and to Caroline Hawkridge who managed to set up this substantial file. John Hunt drew the figures.

Cole, Maureen – 'Outsiders'. An earlier version of this paper appeared in Maltese under the title *L-Imwarrbin* in *Malta Illum ...u Forsi Għada: Analiżi tar-Realtà Socjali Maltija*, Kummissjoni Ġustizzja u Paċi, Malta, Veritas Press, 1991.

Darmanin, Mary – 'Privatization: policy and politics'. The author would like to thank Mr J. Grima, librarian of the Central Bank of Malta for allowing her to make use of the Library's excellent print media collection. She would also like to thank the editors for their stimulating critique and useful suggestions on an earlier draft of this paper.

Mintoff Bland, Yana – 'Cancer and health inequalities in Malta'. An earlier version appeared in the *Economic and Social Studies*, vol. 5, 1989/1990.

Sultana, Ronald G. – 'Perspectives on class in Malta'. An earlier version was published in the *Journal of Economics and Social Studies*, vol. 5, 1989/1990.

Tabone, Carmel – 'The Maltese family in the context of social change' wishes to thank Godfrey Baldacchino for his comments and Charles Briffa for translating extracts of this paper from a previous work which had appeared in Maltese. See Tabone (1991).

Tanti Dougall, Michael – 'Patterns of crime'. The author would like to thank the Commissioner of Police, Mr George Grech, the Commander of the Police Academy, Mr Anthony Mifsud Tomasi, Superintendent Angelo Farrugia and the staff of the Data

Processing Branch under the responsibility of Inspector Rita Criminale, without whose support and co-operation it would not have been possible to acquire the necessary data.

Foreword

Anthony Giddens

Along with the social world itself, sociology has changed enormously over the past two decades. The intensifying of globalizing influences has drawn every society increasingly into an international division of labour, while the relentless spread of the electronic media has penetrated all corners of the earth. The impact of globalization has been paradoxical, however. Along with the development of large-scale global systems has gone the emergence of local nationalisms and the development of local cultural identities. These processes have to be seen as causally bound up with one another: globalization intrudes into, and alters structures of day-to-day life, at the same time as those structures of day-to-day life have an impact upon the larger social world. Together with technological changes affecting the workplace, transformations in the nature of industrial and business organizations, and changes affecting gender and the family in dramatic ways, the landscapes of social life are becoming altered everywhere.

In many societies major processes of de-traditionalization are occurring today as a result of the changes just described. Tradition survives everywhere, but changes its character as local traditions are forced into contact with wider cosmopolitan influences. Traditions are increasingly compelled to justify themselves in the face of alternative ways of life. In some contexts, this leads to the reaffirmation, even the reinvention of tradition; in others long-established traditions fade away. One should not understand this process simply in relation to religion or other 'grand traditions'. Traditional modes of behaviour associated with gender and the family, for instance, are now under great strain, partly as a result of active challenges to them. Here as in other domains there is a tangled web of tradition and modernity.

The chapters of this rich and comprehensive book indicate the importance of all these changes in Maltese society today. The volume gives ample evidence of the fruitfulness of Maltese sociology and also shows that it is in the forefront of sociological research and thinking. The articles range over many aspects of Maltese life, formal and informal. As such, they provide a very comprehensive picture of Maltese social organization. Much more than this, however, they allow the reader to integrate the study of specific contexts of Maltese society with the larger trends affecting the social world everywhere.

New trends: new forms of sociology – this book is full of examples of this connection. As the authors of the introductory paper demonstrate, sociology today is a narrative alert to the conditions of its own production and distribution. Sociologists have to give due attention to the soundness of their research procedures and the validity of their interpretations. Yet sociology, more than the other social sciences, goes 'behind the scenes' to uncover hidden dimensions of power, stratification and ideology. In so doing, it helps to introduce into discourse and practical action the very findings with which it comes up and the theories propagated to make sense of them. This reflexive component of sociology is integral to its very nature. Sociology hence calls for a distinctive blend of hard-headed research and imaginative theoretical construction. Many social practices and ideas which appear to be natural, are disclosed by sociological inquiry to be social and cultural. Yet this very disclosure can alter the field of action itself, leading those involved in it to view their circumstances in a new way and perhaps alter the very character of their activities. As the authors of the various chapters of the book demonstrate with great insight, an awareness of these considerations can be used to reconstruct an overall vision for sociology as applied to Maltese society.

The theme of globalization is discussed in a perceptive and sensitive way in several of the chapters of the book. Malta cannot be studied, it is demonstrated over and over again, as though it were an isolated unit. It is part of a wider global society and the influence of the wider global order appears almost everywhere. Thus Mario Vella discusses the position of Malta, as a post-colonial order, within the context of global development patterns. The idea of 'development' today has become as problematic and controversial as have other key concepts in sociological thought. However, unless the analysis of Maltese society is situated in the context of these debates, it will be impossible to understand its own distinct characteristics, let alone relate these satisfactorily to the turbulence affecting the global order.

Globalization also enters as an important theme in articles by Sultana on consumption, Borg and Mayo on Maltese communities in Toronto, Abela's study of Maltese values, Lauri on the influence of television and Mallia's discussion of the environment. The trend towards consumerism is a world-wide one, all the more so now that the 'alternative' type of production order represented by the Soviet Union and the East European societies has become dissolved. Malta is not yet a 'consumer society' in the same sense as the countries of Western Europe, but consumerism eats into old ways of life and undermines them at the same time as it tends to create homogenizing processes of a transnational sort. Consumerism nowhere triumphs in unalloyed form, however; it breeds diverse forms of opposition, including the deliberate attempt to sustain or reconstruct local traditions and customs.

The pleasures and special perils of living in a small country are well exposed in the contribution from Borg and Mayo, but in a 'reverse context'. Maltese immigrants living in a large urban community in North America experience particular difficulties in asserting an ethnic identity which to other members of the surrounding urban community appears insignificant and about which they know little or nothing. The characteristics accorded to Malta by other, 'larger' states – such that it is a society on the 'periphery' of Europe – here come back to haunt those far from their homeland. On the other hand, the experience of marginalization is not just accepted passively; one response is a forceful assertion of the importance of Maltese identity in an alien cultural context.

There is a danger here that the values which the expatriate Maltese community asserts may simultaneously be becoming transcended in the land of origin, as Abela's analysis indicates. Maltese society, he shows, has retained an important core of its traditional and religious values. Yet these values are subject to tensions and to change. New ideas and attitudes, in some part reflecting those found elsewhere, appear.

Television obviously plays a part in globalization, the transformation of local cultures and the creation of novel cultural diasporas. Many millions of people throughout the world now watch the same TV programmes, although as students of media point out, they certainly do not always interpret or react to them in the same way. Soap operas, discussed by Mary Anne Lauri, are among the most popular of all television productions everywhere. Soap opera, some have suggested, is the modern, or post-modern, equivalent to myth: it confirms basic aspects of human existence and weaves them into a cogent narrative. The influence of soap operas upon local culture, however, is not easy to ascertain. Most people probably read soap operas through the frameworks of their local experience and thereby create their own sense of 'familiarity'. Since viewers know soap operas to be soap operas, it is not clear that even those who are most involved with the genre change their lives in a significant way as a result of exposure to them; rather, diverse motives such as temporary escape from the pressures of everyday life, involvement in the story or plain enjoyment – figure as important.

No society, no matter how geographically distinct it might be, can escape the ravages inflicted by modern industrial development upon the environment. The study of the environment is a global theme par excellence. At the same time, as in other areas of study, pollution and other forms of environmental degradation take on specific characters in particular areas, and Malta is no exception. Malta has had an influence upon the global discussion of environmental issues, but somewhat paradoxically this has meant that local environmental regulation has not been as thorough as one might expect. Environmental issues and problems in Malta have been brought before much more by the activity of organizations outside the sphere of government than by the government authorities themselves. Some forms of industrial production, such as quarrying, have had devastating effects upon the landscape.

The other side of globalization, as mentioned above, is the transformation of everyday life and the reorganization of local social systems. The book contains an abundance of sources showing the radical nature of the changes now affecting day-to-day life in the various contexts of Maltese society and the conflicting entanglements of tradition and modernity. All societies are stratified and all societies are systems of power. A number of important contributions to the volume explore the relations between class, inequality and power, seeing these in relation to the social transitions now taking place. The class map of Malta is changing, in ways roughly similar to those found in other comparable societies. Class structure has today become complex and various tensions exist between the old and new middle classes as well as within elite groups. While there is not at the moment a distinct 'underclass', such as is found in the United States or some of the European countries, the increasingly pervasive influence of market philosophies, Sultana concludes, could point in this direction.

The relations between gender, inequality and power, and indeed the issue of gender more generally, have emerged as fundamental problems in sociological analysis in the present day. For many years, as in other disciplines, women were effectively treated as invisible in sociological thinking and research. Recent years, however, have seen an enormous upsurge of research and theory concerned with women's position in society and with the nature of patriarchal domination. In Malta, Miceli shows, women continue to be radically under-represented in the higher echelons of power. At the lower levels of the stratification system, on the other hand, a growing number of women live in poverty. Separated and widowed women in Malta, as in the United States and Western Europe, form the largest group of the 'new poor'. Their plight is not fully appreciated, partly because official statistics concentrate upon families and family households. Women who do manage to forge a successful career still face fundamental dilemmas if they wish at the same time to raise a family, because of the strong expectation that women are responsible for child-care and domestic chores. In Malta, of course, the teachings of the Catholic church still have a strong effect upon gender identity and differentials.

Assertion of a need for autonomy on the part of women is one among several factors affecting the Maltese family, as Carmel Tabone demonstrates. Traditional Maltese family forms are still very much alive. Unity and duty, coupled to the notions of family honour, are central features of more traditional modes of family life. The growth of new forms of consumerism and individualism, affecting the position of both women and men, is serving to alter preexisting family structures. As elsewhere, rather than today speaking of the 'Maltese family' we have to recognize the existence of a diversity of family types.

Patterns of work, together with modes of non-work activity, are in the present-day also experiencing major transitions. Changes in the labour market, for instance, discussed by E.P. Delia, reflect and reciprocally influence the transformations happening in respect of gender and the family. A smaller proportion of women are in the paid labour force than in the societies of Western Europe. Likely increase in female participation in the labour force, however, will produce important tensions affecting the male role of breadwinner. But male employment is also increasingly affected by the decline in the number of 'life-time' jobs. Diminishing opportunities provided in the state sector also can be expected to exert strong pressures upon the labour force in private industry.

Labour in Malta remains powerful, as Godfrey Baldacchino makes clear. Patterns of compliance and control, nonetheless, have changed and are changing. Malta has a highly unionized labour force and various forms of worker participation in industry have been experimented with. Moves to industrial democracy for the most part have broken down. Yet new forms of participatory mechanisms, influenced less by the rhetoric of industrial democracy and more by new managerial ideas of the empowerment of the workers, job enlargement, quality circles and so forth have arisen. It is too early to say whether these will lead to some enduring patterns of real democratization in the industrial sphere. In so far as they are backed by the unions, they might however provide a basis for the extension of various other structures relevant to the welfare of labour – such as work, education, health and safety in industry.

Malta has its own deprived groups, outsiders and marginalized sectors. In the 'twilight zone' of the economy, various forms of child labour are to be found. In tourism and other industries, under-age children have played a significant part in the marginal labour force. Young people on the whole are prepared to work for much lower wages than their adult counterparts. While some kinds of work taken on by children are transitory and perhaps prepare them for future, quite different, forms of work experience, others become trapped in poorly-paid sectors of the labour market with little chance of self-improvement. They are made the more vulnerable because, working illegally, they have no form of organized representation.

Child labour may perhaps make some people outsiders, by marginalizing them at an early age. But the 'outsiders' in Maltese society do not only consist of those who do not manage to make secure careers for themselves in an unorthodox fashion. Maureen Cole's paper considers the experience of gay men and women, together with the victims of family violence as outsiders. Maltese social attitudes have proved resistant to the sorts of sexual liberation movements that have elsewhere made a major impact; homosexuals, therefore, have to struggle against more entrenched homophobic attitudes than elsewhere. One of the main reasons for this seems to be the continuing relative strength of the traditional family, together with the strong disapproval of homosexuality coming from the Catholic church. The same influences have probably limited the degree to which violence within the family, and child sexual abuse, have been brought to light to a degree comparable to that found in other countries.

In modern societies no outsiders can be wholly 'outside'; conversely, many activities which seem to be marginal and 'deviant' interlace closely with activities followed by the majority. An example is to be found in attitudes towards 'drugs' and 'drug abuse'. Drug users are widely condemned by reference to a demand for a return to traditional family values and restraints. Yet alcohol is a drug, and a harmful one, consumed as a normal, part of life by many people. A good case can be made for saying that alcohol abuse is a vastly more important social problem than 'illicit drugs'.

Malta may be a small society, but this is a big book; big not only in terms of its admirable comprehensiveness, but in terms of the contribution it represents. Probably for the first time, Maltese society is offered a thorough-going account of its institutions and social organization. This book is of enormous value in that context, but it is also significant upon a much more general scale. It is, in other words, a major contribution to sociology in general and a valuable comparative resource for those familiar with the institutions of other societies.

1

Introduction

*Sociology and Maltese Society:
The Field and its Context*

Defining Sociology

It seems to be the destiny of a people to reflect upon itself, to look at itself critically, comparing itself, in space and time, with the fortunes and misfortunes of others. This it does in a myriad of ways and for different reasons. Occasionally narratives about the identity of a nation are woven popularly, with 'folk sociology' – encapsulated in sayings and proverbs – providing images reflecting fears, hopes, knowledge about how the system works, or about how to work the system. At other times, narratives are developed more formally, on command even, to celebrate particular events, to highlight landmarks of historical development, or to applaud or decry the ruler or the ruled, the rebellious or the domesticated.

In all instances, these self-definitions are social constructions of identity. They are never innocent, never uni-dimensional, always tenuously balancing competing definitions of the same situation, reflecting as they do the necessarily conflictual nature of the social formation which gave rise to them in the first place.

This book purports to be about 'Maltese society', and hence is yet another narrative the ambition of which is to enlighten readers about key themes and processes that make Malta different – and occasionally similar – to, say, Fiji, Tunisia, or the United Kingdom. The title of the book goes on to specify that this particular narrative is the result of 'Sociological Inquiry', which would seem to imply that the collection of readings would have been different, and would have provided other kinds of insights, had it been based on philosophical, literary, anthropological or historical inquiry, to mention only four other disciplines.

It thus becomes important to define the way the word 'sociology' is being used in this book. For this word in itself, apparently delimiting a special and specific disciplinary world, with clearcut boundaries framed around a 'department' or 'school' of sociology, has its own history and its own narrative. In its infancy, sociology had to construct these frontiers in order to carve out for itself a legitimate space in the status-conscious knowledge gate-keeper of an institution commonly referred to as 'University'. Sociologists had to prove themselves in an enclave of the old sciences, and they set about doing this by adopting the criteria of the natural sciences: empiricism, positivism, the development of a special jargon and of methodologies of research which purported to be precise, systematic, reflective of the essentially real.

That social context for the production of sociological discourse has changed, and today sociology is not only recognized but, when it is exercised with imagination, also feared. For sociology is a special kind of narrative, one that promises to uncover the hidden principles that make societies tick, much as psychoanalysis, for instance, promises to lay bare the deeper workings of the soul, where motives for being and acting are submerged. It explores the ways in which private, institutional and even large group meaning- and decision-making are far from being free from constraints, including the determining influences of national and international politics; it suggests that the concept of the wage is an exploitative measure rather more than a just day's reward for a day's work; it reveals that schooling, rather than enhancing social mobility through meritocracy, is itself a key instrument in the reproduction of inequality from one generation to the next; it shows how language and other cultural and communicative tools are used to position others in subordinate roles; it teases out the difference between the declared values of groups, and the principles organizing their behaviour; it shows how participation in daily interactive rituals, such as gossip or celebrations, carries deeper meanings and fulfils needs that reach beyond those that are evident at the surface of the activity; it discriminates between social problems and their incarnation in real people, in order to argue that systems rather than victims – the unemployed, the poor, the depressed housebound wife, the deprived – are to blame; it exposes the textuality of everyday lives, what it means to be marginalized, to be female, to be in positions of power or of subordination, linking that experiential world with the macro structures (on) which it feeds.

In other words, sociology shows up bigotry and power-play when these are hidden under genteel manners, consensual discourse, or flourishes of good will. It does so in order to drive a wedge between the illusory and self-deluding and the 'real', the intended and unintended consequences of human action.

Sociologists are therefore called to exercise a special kind of imagination as they look at what, for many, is an apparently 'natural' way in which people live together, share resources, and somehow survive on planet earth. It is the task of sociologists to first make this 'reified' picture of 'reality' the object of their intense inquiry. They then ask a series of questions which dart through the very seams of this 'totality', in order to explore the whys and the wherefores of a particular social formation. By comparing a specific society with others across time and space, they can show up the constructed nature of the current state of affairs, and to argue that, if people elsewhere and/or at different points in time acted differently, then there are no grounds to argue that one mode of being is more 'natural' than another. No male, for instance, can argue that it is 'natural' for men to be in privileged positions, if he is aware of the historical and anthropological embeddedness of his views. In addition to that, if we recognize society as an accomplishment rather than as a 'thing', it obviously follows that people do have the option – conditioned though this may be by a great many elements – to organize and reorganize society differently.

And this leads us to a consideration of the final task of sociologists, who (generally) seek to offer alternative visions and alternative bases for human solidarity – which does not mean, of course, that all sociologists are engaged in the latter project. For sociology, like many other narratives, can be used to serve its masters, to legitimate rather than question social forms, to hide behind a language of 'science', 'objectivity', and 'neutrality' (or more recently, 'playfulness').

Sociology can then be said to be an exercise of deconstruction and reconstruction. It unpackages reality, as handed down by families and other socializing institutions to offsprings and new generations. It refuses to accept such 'reality' as natural, god-given, sacrosanct, inevitable. Rather, it strives to disclose its key patterns and organizing principles. Sociology builds upon common-sense understandings of situations to pose such questions as: Why do these people stay together? How are they socialized into accepting certain definitions of situations? In whose interests do particular ways of being together work? Who has power and how did that group obtain it? Why do others who have less power (and/or wealth, status, life-chances) allow the situation to remain as it is? When does conflict arise? How is it managed? Who mediates between different groups with different interests?

Sociology, therefore, asks dangerous questions and is a dangerous occupation, for its very calling is to reflect critically on society, to make the familiar strange, to extraordinarily re-experience the ordinary. While one could argue that many other disciplines would also recognize this critical reflection as their reason for being, sociology engages in this exercise in a very particular way. Our understanding of sociology is that it looks at social formations *empirically*, *theoretically*, and *interpretatively*. All three ways are important, and neither of the three would be sufficient on its own, in our view, to create a good sociological narrative.

The latter has to be *empirical*, that is it uses data collecting methodologies reflexively, ever aware of the pitfalls, limitations and problematic assumptions as well as politics of each, be these sophisticated, number-crunching quantitative tools – where the geography of the terrain of the problem is outlined – or less precise but more personalized, if less immediately generalizable, qualitative data – where the more intimate details of that problematic terrain are explored.

We recognize that sociological narratives can also be *abstract/ theoretical*, and need not necessarily be directly engaged in reporting or processing empirical data. Such narratives are instruments of critique and understanding. They are therefore necessarily influenced by the contexts which give rise to them and on which they are brought to bear. Nevertheless, they are not reducible to those contexts and can have powerful generalizable currency – in recognition that there is nothing more practical than a good theory. The best sociology for us, therefore, is grounded in data yet theoretically sophisticated. It is not enough to present data on social formations, for that can easily be reduced to the sort of statistical 'head hunting' justly decried by the Frankfurt School theorists in postwar America, and which today parades under different guises, commonly known as 'market research'.

The recognition of the *interpretative* nature of sociology places us in a critical and humble stance in the interstices between micro empirical narratives and macro grand theoretical narratives, between the realm of the particularistic on the one hand and overarching explanations on the other. The awareness of the textuality of everyday life, of the different interpretations of social 'reality', encourages an open-minded, non-dogmatic engagement with narratives. The privileging of one totalizing discourse which presumes to represent 'the truth', has historically been a boon to certain social groupings and a bane to others. Truth-claiming is thus exposed by the sociological imagination to be another manifestation of the social exercise of power. On the other hand, we position ourselves against the kind of postmodern discourses that are currently gaining popularity, where, in celebrating individualism, reality becomes multi-referential and relative. Each narrative becomes, therefore, a playful acknowledgement of difference, with the result that not only meaning but solidarity is fragmented. We are therefore in favour of breaking the 'hermeneutic circle', the paralyzing belief that all social representations are equally legitimate, irreducible to any substance. An awareness of other discourses and narratives positions us in such a way as to learn, in humility, about the experiences of others, and hence to transcend our 'horizons of prejudices'. It remains nevertheless important, in post-modern as in modern times, to construct an action and policy driven agenda, a new 'arch of social dreaming' where, to echo one of the founders of sociology, Karl Marx, we move away from merely interpreting the world to imagining a world as it could and should be, and to struggle collectively in giving birth to that kind of world.

The Field

This is not the first sociological narrative of the Maltese Islands. There have been pioneering efforts which have looked at some of the classic themes associated with the sociological enterprise, and the work of these pioneers – of David Boswell, Mario Vassallo, Edward Zammit – are either directly or indirectly represented in this text. The many references to their writings by other authors indicate the debt local sociology owes to these early efforts.

But this particular narrative has been characterized by fragmentation, and has not been developed systematically. As a result, sociology in Malta has suffered a number of ills. These include the lack of an overall vision for sociology, of a planned research programme to tackle specific themes in an incremental manner, and of critical, creative dialogue among those researching and writing in the social sciences. There have been neither serious debates nor serious conflicts, a clear sign, prevalent in practically all other fields in Malta, that all is not well with the intellectual endeavours in this small island state. Of course, one needs a critical mass of intellectuals in order to develop the kind of debates and discussions that push a field forward. But even when this could have been achieved, through inter-disciplinary means – and the study of society is and should be nothing if not inter-disciplinary – that critical mass has not been formed. This collection of readings sets out to address these failings and weaknesses, with the hope that the professional association of students of society of all ages will lead to the kinds of deliberation which sociology elsewhere has led to.

In the first place, therefore, the book organizes data of a sociological nature around six key generative themes. The outlines of the field of sociology are thus set out in such a way as to include and report on research already carried out, and to point out lacunae where these exist. The organization of the book around themes leads to direct and indirect debate about the field of sociology by those who are centrally or more marginally engaged with the analysis of the local social formation.

Furthermore, this text has facilitated the commissioning of research specifically aimed at addressing some of the lacunae identified. The book in fact has itself become one such opportunity to launch new research projects, or to encourage young authors to present, in an article form, research they had recently carried out.

Lacunae still exist, and the politics of absence − that is, the identification of the themes which fail to appear in this book − is of sociological interest in its own right. Each generative theme has its own particular absences, and some of these absences are particularly striking. With reference to social stratification, for instance, we have, as yet, no empirical study of the class structure of Maltese society, or of the loci of power and of how influence is wielded. We know next to nothing about social mobility or lack of it, and very little empirical work has been done in terms of analysis of the State. Few have dared to systematically address the hegemony of the Catholic Church in Malta, the distribution of wealth among various groups, or the principles of cultural inclusion and exclusion which are exercised locally.

Ralf Dahrendorf's comment during an address he recently gave at the University of Malta is particularly relevant, it seems to us, to the local state of sociology. Dahrendorf noted that investigative journalism had taken a feather out of sociology's cap, since it has tended to uncover and report society's wheelings and dealings much more effectively and efficiently. Sociologists came later, dragging their feet, perhaps like vultures to the day's pickings, operating their often unwieldy models and even more outlandish language, losing in punch and immediacy what they might have gained in sophistication.

Over and above the substantive themes raised by the readings, there are other central concerns of sociology which cut across the issues raised. Transversal themes which have generated heated debate in the field of sociology can be referred to in their most cryptic form through pithy opposites, including: structure vs. agency; determinism vs. freedom; consensus vs. conflict; reproduction vs.

transformation. Each substantive theme addressed in this book necessarily engages with these transversal themes, to ask about the extent to which people are free to make society in conditions which are not of their own making, to ask whether the current state of affairs responds to the needs and satisfies the interests of all, and to argue for social stasis or for change. Not all papers leave their micro context to theorize self-consciously about their contribution to the key debates in the field of sociology, but students of that macro context will find much that is helpful in the substantive data and issues raised in the readings.

The Context

If this volume strives to repropose the fascinating weave of the Maltese social fabric not as a fact but as a problem, then it cannot fail to go without a critical gaze at local social interpreters and their disciplinary heritage. It is these who are defining the problem in the first instance. The book's endeavour needs therefore to go beyond being a mere collection of essays: what is distinctly local, in Malta as elsewhere, is after all not an objective given, a social thing which has a life and autonomy of its own. The constitution of Maltese society comes to us as a particular interpretation of the social universe. There is a sociological cadre, craft and tradition in place which has authoritatively defined and shaped the subject matter. We cannot therefore fail to ask ourselves: what has been the social context for the production of such sociological discourse? If we are talking in terms of a Maltese social fabric, who indeed are those who have woven the cloth and determined its weave?

This concern is none other than the search for an ontological framework – by this we mean a tentative coming to grips not only with the nature of answers but with that of the questions which preceeded and preempted them in the first place. This is equivalent to the search for those fundamental, influential parameters and variables whose relationship suggests conceptually valid explanations for the manner in which Maltese society has, and has not, been defined.

Obviously, we must declare up front that such a project is by its very nature partial and incomplete: it cannot avoid rendering simplistic the complex interplay of a multitude of variables; it may readily fail to ascribe particular parameters with the importance and centrality they may deserve within the overall relational architecture; it may fail outright to identify certain themes and thus render them injustice by total absence. These sins of omission and commission we cannot sincerely fail to commit to some extent, given also that we are ourselves party to the contemporary sociological cadre of the Maltese Islands hereunder being problematized. This apart from our invariable location within our own social and temporal predicament, as well as us being equipped with a particular intellectual, experiential and ideological baggage which filters and colours the way we see the world. The task in both its content and form thus stands to be challenged, rebuked and hopefully revised in accordance with the premises, procedures and revelations of further sociological questioning and answering. This is after all to be expected from a vibrant and vigorous sociological tradition.

Indeed, we owe it to the sociological inquiry of the past and present that this locale-specific framework can be proposed at all in its current format. We present it, in spite of its obvious limitations, as an exploratory heuristic device, prompting a set of organizing principles and interpretative schemes; these themselves bear the transversal orientation already explained and resorted to above. The ensuing narrative therefore suggests an answer to the crucial question posited earlier; supported, we hope, with the imaginative, grounded, critical and evaluative stance that we understand sociology to embrace and enthuse.

A Confluence of Within and Without

The quintessential aspects of the Maltese social formation which demand unpacking can be traced to a confluence of internal and external dynamics: the micro-status and insularity on one hand; its falling within the shadow of European influences and value systems on the other. It is this mosaical synthesis which, to our eyes, seems to best locate the current Maltese sociological community, as it does also define the main environmental factors impinging on Maltese social life.

The society's geographical parameters speak for themselves: a small, barren archipelago with a surface area of 316 square kilometres and a resident population of around 360,000. This implies a very small absolute figure for a nation state; but this is a relatively high statistic, given the resulting intense land use competition on the surface area available. The population density of the country is in fact one of the highest in the world.

This resource-poor limestone outcrop happens to lie astride the narrowest straits of the Mediterranean sea, a sensitive meeting place of cultures, religions and empires. The Maltese Islands lie 90 km south of European Sicily and 290 km to the north and east of African Tunisia and Libya, while being almost equidistant from the Straits of Gibraltar and Alexandria, Egypt. This central location in this ebullient context can perhaps be summarily described as a fortunate fortuity.

With the islands boasting naturally deep and sheltered harbours, they became, for all their inherent resource poverty, the coveted possession of several Mediterranean potentates who struggled for supremacy in this geo-politically sensitive theatre. The Carthaginians, the Romans, the Byzantines, the Arabs, the Normans, the various Royal Houses of Spain, the French and finally the British passed on the baton in successive waves of colonial rule.

The British Tradition...

The consequences of colonization for strategic (rather than economic or commercial) interests presented themselves in a local economic structure geared almost exclusively to the maintenance and furbishing of the foreign military/naval garrison. At a political, administrative and, in the course of time even cultural level, the British colonial rulers in particular successfully groomed a fortress culture which is a prerequisite for a secure fortress economy: the effective control of an 'unsinkable aircraft carrier' depended also on an indigenous population which harboured generally (though at times begrudgingly) positive dispositions towards its alien occupiers. Such inclinations went much further (in contrast to other British colonies) than the population's small, comprador élite.

This outlook was mainly engendered by virtue of the employment and social mobility which such an association promised and indeed delivered. The strategic interests of the island colony have since waned, following the granting of political independence in 1964 and the total dismantling of the fortress service economy by 1979. Yet, such a colonial legacy spills over into a variety of contemporary behaviour patterns. These include Western-inspired conspicuous consumption, a 'welcoming society' orientation which is amenable to a vibrant tourist economy as well as an educational, legal and general institutional set-up which draws heavy inspiration from the hallowed canons of metropolitan practice.

The implications of this modelling disposition on local sociological discourse and on the local sociological community which critiques it are particularly acute on two counts. The first is the affinity and role modelling with metropolitan, particularly British (which resolutely replaced Italian following the advent of the Second World War) but also increasingly American, academe. This is reproduced because of the constant traffic of personnel and ideas from these centres to the Maltese periphery. Foreign examiners, consultants, conference guest speakers and other imports are heavily drawn from the 'Am-Brit' camp. Secondly and what is perhaps more significant, aspiring Maltese academics pursue postgraduate studies and research in these same countries, returning to their Mediterranean homeland imbued with a corpus of knowledge, theory and techniques typically hailed as superior to anything local. The application of this corpus facilitates the vicious cycle of cultural cloning, given that it is also expected and requested by discerning peers and clientele. From amongst the crop of 'Am-Brit' Universities, the University of Oxford and its colleges stands out as the preferred pole of attraction for Maltese scholars in sociology and related disciplines.

...the Church of Rome...

There is a parallel strand to this narrative, similarly traced to historical developments and to a Western cultural inheritance. For while the (particularly British) colonial regime consolidated its control and legitimacy at the national level, a second European (or should one call it a multinational?) power-of-sorts was consolidating influence at the local, town and village level. The Roman Catholic Church, proudly tracing its presence on the Maltese Islands to the shipwreck of St. Paul in the year AD 60, survives to the present day as a (the most?) powerful social agent. It was during the period when, between 1530 and 1798,

Malta was administered as a buffer state by the Knights of St. John, a religious order, that the powers and privileges of the Church in Malta proliferated. And the consciously carved-out spheres of influence between church and state in the British period enabled the former to establish itself as an important referent to practically all social, including secular, events not falling within the national ambit.

Institutionally, the Church in Malta became even more intimately involved in the main events of the human life cycle – birth, marriage and death – at the same time transforming these rites of passage into social events: they stamp the individual's standing in the eyes of the community at different stages of maturation, and serve as opportunities for demonstrating and proclaiming social solidarity. Around three-quarters of the Maltese population attend Sunday Mass regularly and listen to weekly homilies from the pulpit. The parish priest remains a representative of village and community interests, an unofficial mayor in the absence – until now – of any other form of civil, local government. A considerable proportion of cultural artifacts – music, drama, poetry, prose, art and sculpture – invariably still carry a religious theme or contain undercurrents of the powerful role of the Catholic Church as a moulder and reproducer of specific values, affecting one's perception of reality and propriety.

This solid presence of the Catholic Church at the heart of Maltese social life is paralleled spatially by the central, dominant position of the parish church edifice proper, commanding the radial hub of all local towns and villages. Another curio reflects the same overbearing influence: the existence of one church or chapel for every square kilometre of the archipelago.

The Catholic Church operates among the rank and file as a powerful cultural force by virtue of a multitude of organizations. Notable among these are the Church schools. Run by nuns, priests and/or ecclesiastics, these schools educate today near to thirty per cent of the total formal school age population, from kindergarten to pre-University level. Access is keenly contested since they are popularly considered to provide a better education than the alternative state schools. (Ironically, church schools are in part financed by state subsidies). What constitutes better schooling is of course inherently problematic; but one outcome of this value orientation is that the most educationally motivated of the up and coming generation are groomed within a religious ethos which inculcates an ongoing, inter-generational loyalty to an often unquestioned, hegemonic dominance of the Catholic establishment in contemporary Maltese social life.

The University of Malta is the only local educational institution which is not subjected to a structural streaming between at least church and state sponsored education. Nevertheless, it is not exempted from the strong impact of the Church in Maltese social affairs. The University, the oldest in the British Commonwealth outside the United Kingdom, was actually a Jesuit College in 1769 when it was raised to the status of a general studies institution. The presence of priests, ex-priests and religious among the University's academic staff is particularly within, and at the helm of, the humanities departments. Appointments of academic members of staff within the Faculty of Theology remain subject to the endorsement of the Catholic Church authorities; and these find possibilities of interacting with other, nominally secular, faculties via courses dealing with ethical considerations. Hence an infusion of the Catholic Church's social doctrine onto campus curricula, with special reference to the sociological. The dove has not simply homed in on the owl's nest: is it there to roost?

One can perhaps agree to identify a socio-religious study of the Maltese Islands as the prototype of local sociological inquiry, carried out by a foreign priest in 1960. The first locally managed social research unit was probably a pastoral research services bureau set up in the late 1960s and directed by Benny Tonna, a diocesan priest; and the first chair in Sociology at the University of Malta was/is held by a priest, who eventually presented a doctorate on religion and social change in Malta.

The main point of reference for academic training and qualification for this population of mentors today is generally Rome, Italy. This follows because it is the site of Universities run by particular religious orders and which provide postgraduate and in-service training to the Maltese religious communities, just one hour flying time away. Universities in the United States (preferred particularly by Jesuits) and the Catholic University at Louvain, Belgium, are runners-up.

The interplay between the Anglo and the Roman Catholic traditions is thus posited as one powerful explanatory principle for the state and character of the contemporary Maltese social fabric; as much as the tale of the two cities, Rome and Oxford, reveals much about the island's sociological cadre. As editors of this collection, we appreciate the configuration of these two worlds of reference and their influence on our interpretation of events. Although neither of us has been to study at Oxford or Rome (yet), we have both pursued postgraduate training in British Universities; and we both resort heavily and often intuitively to British authors and theory for our inspiration. Our invitation to Anthony Giddens to contribute the 'Foreword' to this collection is in part an implicit acknowledgement of the relevance and pervasiveness of this connection, as well as of the importance of enhancing Maltese exposure within this tradition. At the same time, we have also spent many years of schooling in church-run schools; participated actively and enthusiastically in a number of catholic-inspired and church-spawned organizations; and we continue, in our different ways, to come to terms with the confluence of the secular and non-secular in our principles, pedagogies and general philosophy of life.

...and the Realm of Lilliput

The third strand towards an understanding of the Maltese social environment as fostering an idiosyncratic, culture-specific form of sociological discourse can be attributed to its unfolding within a society characterized by small size and small scale. Without implying geographical determinism, we can argue that Malta's qualification as an ex-colonial island microstate is likely to have firstly brought about peculiarly intensive cultural links with metropolitan imports; and secondly, facilitated the development of a social universe harbouring characteristics of a microstate syndrome.

Smallness is obviously a relative measure but the island archipelago scores as a very small, or micro, state irrespective of which parameter of size is resorted to – typically, land area, population size or gross domestic product. It appears that such a small-sized territory a stone's throw away from the European mainland has been a determining factor in persuading a number of foreign researchers into setting their sights on Malta for their fieldwork projects. The island state is in many ways a research haven, since it represents a total society, with its panoply of structures and processes, spread over a comfortable 300-odd square kilometres. Ironically, however, while praising Malta for being such a convenient laboratory for social investigation, most researchers have failed to question whether the smallness condition engenders its own dynamics. Even Maltese academics have proved by and large insensitive to an exploration of this qualification.

In a sense, Malta's lilliputian character robs even its very citizens of a home-grown reflexivity. As is typical of developing post-colonial states, there is in Malta an observable tendency to emulate and mimic the behaviour of foreign significant others. But such a history of tutelage appears bolstered by smallness and insularity since island microstates were very early on incorporated as bastions of Western maritime culture within the period of expansionist mercantile colonialism. For at least 2,000 years of Euro-Arab domination, the Maltese were subjected to continuous (sometimes intimate, and often weighty) interaction with colonial rulers, this being exacerbated by a relatively high population density. Hence the extent of colonial penetration was considerable in both duration and depth. Malta, like various other minuscule outposts of maritime empires scattered over the surface of the globe, was among the earliest territories to be colonized and among the last to be decolonized via the granting of political sovereignty. There was never any physical hinterland for the indigenous Maltese to retreat to. The country is thus an excellent example of the capacity of colonialism to effect an infiltration of culture to the point when it becomes endemic and thus, functionally attuned to fortress, strategic interests. This relatively thorough cloning orientation improves the unquestioned adoption of ascribed, given structures, principles and procedures – significantly those bearing the hallmark of erstwhile colonial masters. This is one reason why local social analysis, *inter alia*, may be somewhat impeded in its critical latitude by an excessive reliance on expatriate blueprints. These do not typically take small size into consideration.

And so, impervious to foreign observers and Maltese investigators, there is a stock of readily resorted to behaviour patterns which make perfect good sense in the local environment. Where they are identified, they often are summarily dismissed as deviant and improper, petty practices which refuse to abide to the dictates of grand doctrines. An inductive Maltese sociology would however suggest that it is the given doctrines which do not fit the practice and therefore require an overhaul. What follows is a reflexive interpretation of what appears to be distinctly and intimately Maltese, offspring of small size and the small scale dynamics that it engenders. At the same time, we hope you would agree, this perspective sheds new light and fosters an inspiring, novel conceptual framework towards an understanding of what makes Maltese society what it is.

It is here that one may propose a number of leitmotifs which collectively and in their complex interrelationship appear to capture the essentials of a microstate behaviour syndrome. These are intimacy, totality and monopoly.

Intimacy
The small size/scale environment ensures first of all a high degree of social visibility. Knowledge which elsewhere is either private or unavailable is quickly acquired, even inadvertently, and rapidly transformed into a public consumer good via the exchange of information and gossip. Such a high degree of transparent, interpersonal communication engenders a pervasive atmosphere of familiarity.

Most microstate inhabitants also grow up within an interdependent network where each person figures many times over. Nearly every social relationship serves a variety of interests, and many roles are played by relatively few individuals. The same persons are thus brought into contact over and over again in various activities, because each operates and meets the other on the basis of different roles held in the context of different role-sets; decisions and choices are therefore influenced by the relationships which individuals establish and cultivate with others in a repertoire of diverse social settings. Impersonal, non-person specific, standards of efficiency, performance and integrity cannot therefore fail to come into play, modified by the myriad relationships bringing the people concerned together. The overall suggestion is that the social space over which social relationships in small size/scale societies are particularistic, functionally diffuse, affectively charged and durable over time is wider than what obtains in other, larger societies. One expression of this is the greater probability in a small state of finding relatives working together.

This behaviour trait could result in the misuse and abuse, in a systemic sense, via friends of friends and kin of kin networks resulting from role multiplicity of system incumbents. The jaundiced, particularistic assessment of personal qualities could lead to situations where features such as loyalty, family background and political affiliation could totally override impersonal, legal-rational, universalistic attributes. And, given the absence of confidentiality and anonymity, inhabitants learn to manage intimacy: they get along, whether they like it or not, knowing that they are likely to renew and reinforce relationships with the same persons in a variety of settings over the course of a whole life span. There is therefore a high premium extracted from situations of open antagonism, since these tend to be emotionally charged, long lasting and with little avenues for escape or exit. The Maltese become thus adept at muting hostility, containing disagreement and avoiding disputes, a sophisticated mode of accommodation. Is this why the Maltese ask so few questions?

Totality
Social visibility and intimacy are not exclusively benign conditions, convincing attributes of a 'small is beautiful' stereotype. Microstate life could make one feel very hemmed in. It could feel like growing up in a straight jacket of community surveillance, given the dense psycho-social atmosphere. A small state government is also characteristically heavy and omnipresent and, as a result, omnipotent. Its extensive and aggrandized personality makes it party to every significant enterprise. Any state requires an irreducible amount of human and organizational infrastructure, a minimum critical mass. The smaller the country, therefore, the larger the state looms in its economy and society.

The condition approximates a Goffmanesque scenario of total institutions. Strategic, political reactions to such social claustrophobia include: a conscious, rigid adherence to role specificity; the screening and withholding of information; a cautious resort to 'baited breath' since everyone is a potential informant; an appeasement of power holders; all in all, much like a counterfeit society. Does not such a combination of action and reaction suggest an intriguing juxtaposition of face-to-face and back-to-back relationships?

Monopoly

Related to the incentive in keeping information to oneself is the ready tendency, within the small scale/size environment, of obtaining monopoly power. It is, after all, in every producer's interest to distort the market mechanism to one's net advantage, shifting preferably from a price-taker to a price-maker orientation where the milieu permits various degrees of differentiation. The cultivation of expertise is one technique towards such a monopoly orientation; and in the microstate setting, such an achievement can be almost spontaneous, even unavoidable, particularly if one is establishing oneself in a new domain of knowledge, product, competence or responsibility. As soon as an individual develops even a modest edge in an area of skill, study or research, s/he may find him/herself – we could add, to the great satisfaction of the person's ego – proclaimed as an expert and ascribed with authoritarian standing in that area by others. Expertise can be achieved thus almost by default. Presumptuousness may also pay dividends: because, sincerely, there may not be anyone around locally to challenge one's bluff or fragile claim to authority. The scale and indivisibility constraints – for example, there may be only one University on the small state but a fully fledged one at that – and the diversification of knowledge that the small territory needs to accommodate imply that one person (or even parts of one person) equals the society's total sum requirement of expertise in a particular field. It is thus relatively easy to become a big fish when one operates in a small pond, unless one takes the risk and challenge of testing the ocean deep. This would be possible by the regular exercise of quality matching, standard setting and sizing up through peer pressures forthcoming necessarily from abroad.

This phenomenon in a way finds ready expression in the state of the local social science community. The total number of social researchers is relatively very small, while the number of social issues (if they can at all be quantified) is as complex and multifarious as in any society. Hence a relative ease for an individual to carve out a niche of expertise(s). The temptation of achieving socially and/or self-proclaimed authority induces individuals to indulge in centrifugal adventures, locked within their own staunchly defended research pursuits, often in splendid isolation.

This is evidenced, for instance, in the rather scant cross referencing to collegial research and publications in the contributions to this volume; and to the excessive resort to self-referencing which (other than as vain intimations of glory) may be simply a stark recognition that there is no other work in the field to refer to locally other than one's own.

Constructing Maltese Society

The interplay of intimacy, totality and monopoly constitutes the germ of a microstate behaviour syndrome readily deployed by the Maltese as they go about constructing culture and society in their daily lives. By far the bulk of these nuances have remained only sketchily addressed by local sociological inquiry, the social investigators failing to obtain the right answers since, in many cases, they have not raised the pertinent questions.

And possibly consciously and purposely so. Take the case of a pioneering text on the multifunctionality of administrative incumbents in small states. The descriptions of the practices and implications of such role diversity and role enlargement are empirically explored and provide a useful contribution to the sparse literature on the allegedly distinct 'ecology' of small states. The prescriptive agenda and the urgency to reform however take precedence over the challenge of coming to grips with what is. The exercise is consumed by the imperative to transform and upgrade, and not towards a critical understanding. It fails to appreciate the rationale behind systemically subversive and organizationally erosive behaviour. It is as if there is a secret conspiracy not to go beyond, not to venture into the realm of Lilliputian interest maximizing individual behaviour. Such is not for foreign consumption; and we, of course, being Maltese, instinctively and experientially know all about it...

Such insider knowledge – termed by a contributor in this volume as the Mdina defence syndrome – is however not immune from sociological investigation. It had to be a non-Maltese to make one noteworthy inroad into this cluster of accommodational strategies, developing network theory essentially on the basis of social research undertaken in Malta. Functional networks of patronage are valuable assets for obtaining information and access to scarce resources for which there is likely to be the most savage competition. This is a conceptualization at home in a Catholic culture inhabited by intermediating saints. Such manipulations are also expressions of an individual, rather than a collective, route to goal satisfaction – possible reactions to the stifling prison scenario, a person avoiding where possible too close an association with others, where this is within his/her power to manage. The networking and coalition building is encouraged by encounters of individuals across different role-sets. Small size and scale foster cris-crossing webs of 'quasi-groups' which facilitate vital good turns by others and which subsequently call for a return of the compliment. This tacit principle of mutual obligation – a more elaborate and sophisticated variant of 'old boys' networks – enables microstate citizens to discover that the fulfilment of many hopes and the assuagement of many fears in life depends on the deployment of the brokerage function.

The brokerage concept suggests yet another, concluding observation about the Maltese societal make-up. The perennial threat of cultural engulfment may explain how this small island with a small population has nevertheless managed to develop and cultivate, over a millennium, its own distinct language. This, in spite of the fact that the island survives by virtue of economic cosmopolitanism, a rentier status brought about thanks to being at the hub of interactions of foreign cultures, tongues and commodity traffic. The likely explanation for this is that the Maltese language is representative of a cluster of behaviour patterns which found a rational reason for existence and reproduction because, not in spite, of the intense foreign activity on the island – a presence rendered even more stifling because of the ever-increasing tourist flows.

The Maltese – inherently multilingual and multicultural – have grown accustomed to operating in these two dimensions. There is on one hand the official, documented, public and transnational, the direct legacy of foreign domination. Its incorporation permits the tapping of foreign largesse, a 'friendly native' disposition, occupational mobility and emigration, as well as international credibility. English is thus the main language of international currency, apart from the symbol of prestigious cultural assimilation with the metropole. This in part explains the otherwise paradoxical resort to this volume on Maltese society written in an alien tongue.

The second realm is more private, microcosmic and intimate, characterized by the Maltese language and a behaviour pattern not readily decipherable and discernible to foreigners. This is an ancient cultural heritage, which has crystallized into a set of local customs, often unwritten traditional beliefs and values.

It appears unsound to interpret this interfacing as a dualism which begets a choice: a polarization of two mutually exclusive realities, demanding an uncompromising commitment to one world view and a brutal alienation from the other. It seems to be our politico-economic and socio-cultural destiny to play the catalysts and intermediaries, shifting from one world view to another and feeling at home in both. This is one dialectic at the heart of our Melitensian creative as well as critical impulse.

But, like so many elusive scarlet pimpernels, we are neither here nor there. This same predicament is bound to make it more difficult for us to declare and define who we are, as a people. This volume purports to tackle this issue by organizing a number of cameos of contemporary Maltese societal practices and observations. These, in their totality, suggest, without forcing the outcome, the first overall, albeit incomplete, vision of Maltese society. Concurrently, this is done in a manner which posits the subject matter as a problem, a void into which salvoes of research flares can be fired, illuminating what is (really) going on. In short, a sociological inquiry.

We, must thank the contributors of this volume for accepting to participate in this collective effort, for submitting their contributions in line with editorial recommendations, and for painstakingly conforming to the strict regime of deadlines such a project invariably necessitates. We are confident they would agree that the effort has been worthwhile, not only for the published product, but for the process of collegial dialogue and peer review which it engendered. May this serve as a foretaste of further collective efforts by the Maltese sociological community.

The Editors

part 1

dependence and social stratification

People can come together to form societies in a number of ways, and indeed, cross-cultural and historical studies attest to the variety of structures human beings have developed in order to live together and to satisfy individual and common needs. It is an unfortunate but historical reality that, most of the time, these social formations have shared one common feature despite their variety across time and space. This distinctive tendency has been the existence of hierarchical organisation. In other words, human societies tend to distribute their material and symbolic goods differentially, in such a way that particular groups are distinguished from others in terms of their relationship to wealth, power, status, and life-chances generally. In most human societies, these groups are differentiated from each other on the criteria of occupational roles, gender, age, race/ethnicity, religious belief, able-bodiedness, and so on.

Maltese society is no exception to this hierarchical organisation of people, and Sultana outlines the structure of the local pyramidal structure of power and resource allocation and distribution. He engages Marxist and Weberian sociological traditions in order to identify key groups and their respective influence in determining the boundaries of this class structure, as well as to construct a research agenda for future analysis of class, status and power in Malta. Vella's contribution provides a historical sociological perspective on the relations of power in the Maltese islands, stressing the linkage between international structures of production and exchange and the constraints these have imposed on political and economic activity in Malta with particular reference to economic development strategy. In other words, Vella reminds us that there is a larger pyramid in which the Maltese social formation is situated, and that in that pyramid, Malta occupies a very subordinate space.

Similarly subordinate, in both a local and international framework, are women. Miceli identifies the systematic discrimination against half of Malta's population, women, who are quite invisible in the world of power and politics. That world is almost exclusively populated by males who, at the head of Malta's political parties, have impacted on the social environment, constituting and infusing the local social formation with a set of distinct ideologies and vocabularies. The political parties themselves, as Pirotta argues, are as much a product of Maltese society as the latter is a product of their visions and agendas. The parties can be profitably appraised as agents of political mobilization which, in spite of policy divergences, generally reflected Malta's European vocation, and the country's dependent status in pursuit of such recognition.

2

Perspectives on Class in Malta

Ronald G. Sultana

Introduction

There exist a variety of approaches to defining 'class' but, as Joppke (1986, p. 55) points out, none of these approaches can avoid addressing, in a sympathetic or critical manner, 'the two main sociological traditions which – more or less in mutual rivalry – have shaped the discussion on class up to the present'. These are the Marxist[1] and Weberian[2] analyses of class. The

---

[1] The account of class developed by Karl Marx (b. 1818, d. 1883) can be analysed from the following selection of his writings: *The Economic and Philosophical Manuscripts of 1844*, *The German Ideology*, *The Poverty of Philosophy*, *The Manifesto of the Communist Party*, *The Eighteenth Brumaire of Louis Bonaparte*, *A Contribution to the Critique of Political Economy* and

former emphasizes the realm of production, and the latter that of consumption, in order to account for the different fortunes of different groups of people in a particular society (Sultana, 1990).

A Marxist Concept of Class

Marx argued that in human history, all the social formations that were set up were characterized by the leadership of a dominant group who, in different ways, exploited and oppressed other groups of people within the same society. According to Marx, this dominating-dominated relationship was above all an economic one, i.e. the group which had economic power, which owned the means of production, organized social life in such a way that they maintained their privilege, power and wealth. This economic relationship of dominance and exploitation was not always present and, importantly for Marx, it was possible – indeed imperative for those with a moral concern for justice – to imagine and bring about a classless society. Marx was mainly interested in analysing, explaining and envisaging a social formation which was more equal, just and humane than the society of his age, characterized by a capitalist mode of production.

According to Marx, while the industrial revolution had brought about with it the possibility of greater material wealth, the relations of production were organized in such a way that the hierarchical class divisions that existed between lord and serf in feudal relations of production were emphasised. In the capitalist social formation, people without property of their own – not owning the means of production (including tools, raw materials, industrial sites) – and having only their ability to work (labour power) to offer, sell this labour power to the capitalists (who own the means of production) in return for a wage (hence wage-

---

Capital (Vols. 1 and 3).

[2] The account of social class developed by Max Weber (b. 1864, d. 1920) can be analysed from the following selection of his writings: Economy and Society, vols. 1 and 2 and General Economic History.

labour). Marx argued that in a number of key ways, working for a wage was similar to the feudal rent imposed and appropriated by the feudal lord. This is because the capitalist does not give the real wage to his labourers, but underpays (extracts surplus value from) them to such an extent that profit can be registered. The industrial workers, like the serfs of the past, have to surrender a proportion of what is due to them in return for their labour to an industrial 'lord' who makes a comfortable living, so to speak, on the back of his workers. Thus, out of a working day of, say, ten hours, if the cost of providing a wage is recovered after six hours of work, the remaining or surplus value produced in four hours is appropriated by the capitalist and transformed into private profit. Miliband (1987, p. 327) notes that

> All societies need to appropriate a part of the product from the procedures for such purposes as the maintenance of the young, the sick and the old, investment for further production and later distribution, the provision of collective services, and so on. In a classless society, however, appropriation would occur only for those purposes.

In a class-based, capitalist society it is the capitalist who appropriates surplus value as profit, by virtue of ownership rights and privileged position.

Marx – and others such as Engels, Lenin and Kautsky who developed his thoughts – also argued that this exploitative wage relationship between capitalist and workers led to a conflict of interests between the two groups, or classes, of people. It is in the interest of workers to struggle together as a group – within the same factory against the factory owner, and with other workers in other factories nationally and internationally – against the capitalist class as a whole. In this way they can win for themselves higher wages, better conditions of work, more holidays, longer periods of rest during the working day, and a measure of control over the production process – in short, all those legitimate things which are not in the interest of the capitalist to concede.

While in feudal society, struggle against exploitation by lords was often fragmented – peasant revolts apart – due to the family-based economy, the situation in capitalist industrialist societies is different. For the factory and the city brought large numbers of workers together in the same place, and this made them become deeply aware of their condition not as individuals but as a group (hence 'class consciousness'). Such awareness of the unjust and inequitable state of affairs, argued Marx, would lead to class conflict and class struggle which would pave the way to an equal and just society where 'the free development of each is the condition for the free development of all', where people work 'according to ability' and receive 'according to their need'. In this new social formation, workers would produce to satisfy real needs, and citizens would be directly involved in direct democratic participation, decision-making, administration and problem-solving. As Giddens and Held (1982, pp. 6-7) note, such labour organization extends to the political sphere:

> The existence of parliaments and recognition of the formal right to organize political parties in the apparatus of bourgeois democracy permit the formation of labour parties that increasingly challenge the dominant order. Through such political mobilization the revolution is made – a process which Marx apparently believed would be a peaceful transition in certain countries with strong democratic traditions but more likely to involve violent confrontations elsewhere.

Pertinent to later discussions it is necessary to ask: 'How does the ruling class rule?' (Therborn, 1978). The ruling class not only controls (and generally owns) the means of production, but also the main means of communication and consent (Miliband, 1987, p. 329). In other words, as Gramsci (1971) has pointed out, the ruling class has an interest to establish its hegemony in society, i.e. a state of affairs whereby it is only their ideas, values and categories of thought – e.g. the belief that wage-labour is a fair exchange of money for labour, that profit is an indication of success, that ownership implies control – are in fact distributed and given legitimacy. Althusser (1971) notes that the ruling class tries to rule through engineering consent by using Ideological State Apparata such as schools, the churches and the media. It is only when these fail and that people see through common-sense ideas and realize that these are working against their own interest and in favour of the interests of others that the ruling class is obliged to use its Repressive State Apparata, among them the police and the military.

The above account of Marxist views on class has emphasised the division between the 'two great classes', the proletariat and the bourgeoisie. Marxist writers have, however, given importance also to gradations of social ranking or stratification in relation to these two basic classes. Keeping in mind that in this approach economic relationships form the basis of classes, workers who have different relationships to different sectors of the economic structure are also bound to fall within different social classes. Miliband (1987, pp. 330-3) for instance, distinguishes between the 'power élite', the bourgeoisie, the petty bourgeoisie, the working class and the 'underclass' in the pyramid that is constituted by modern class structures. This will be discussed in some detail as we come to describe the class structure in Malta.

A Weberian Conception of Class

Marx and his followers emphasised that for the truly human society to come about, different occupational groups had to forget and forgo their sectional interests in favour of presenting a stronger united front of proletariat against capitalists. The emphasis is on social relations of production. Not so for Weber who considered relations of production to be only one factor which led to a relationship of inequality, and that economic power was not necessarily, as it was for Marx, the overriding factor which determined political power or historical change. For Weber, the conflicts between states, ethnic communities and 'status groups' were at least as important as class conflict.

One way of understanding the thrust of Weber's analysis of class is to think of the economic system not in terms of those who own the means of production and those who do not, but rather as a market where occupational groups try to sell their skills or labour power. Those aggregates of individuals which have similar skills or work to 'sell' to employers constitute social classes, and these are not interested at all in overthrowing capitalism in favour of another economic system. Rather, as Weber portrays them, these occupational groups compete with each other in order to attract for themselves the best life chances, i.e. rewards and advantages, possible. Towards this end these different classes employ a variety of strategies, which, in the case of the traditional professions, for instance, include controlling access, through certification, of the number of people practising a particular skill so that what they have to offer remains scarce, and therefore the market is obliged to pay more for their services. According to Weber, these occupational groups are unable to take coordinated action on a class basis because they organize internally around two other poles of group solidarity, namely as 'status groups' and political parties. As Giddens and Held (1982, p. 10) point out,

> status groups are founded upon relationships of consumption rather than production and take the form of 'styles of life' that separate one group from another.

Occupational groups therefore share a variety of similar experiences and conditions at work, and tend to develop similar lifestyles. This fact tends to enhance intermarriage and the reproduction, from one generation to the next, of the same values, beliefs, and cultural practices. Weber also argues that groups can come together on bases other than economic relations or status by attaching themselves to a political party in order to defend and assert ethnic or nationalistic rights which do not necessarily coincide with either class membership or class interest.

The central concept used by Marx with reference to class, namely expropriation of the workers from control of the means of production, is for Weber an unavoidable and irreversible fact of life as a highly technological and modern society moves, irrevocably, towards bureaucratic forms of domination. In other words, for Weber the culprit, so to say, is not capitalism but industrialization. It is in the very nature of a bureaucracy that the ones in the lower echelons of an institution lose control over their work as this is devised for them by the ones in the upper echelons. In the Weberian approach to class, therefore, class struggle is not an attempt to move outside of the institutional rules and legal framework – in other words the rules of the social game – determined by a parliamentary system. Rather, it is 'another version of the eternal struggle for power between individuals and groups in human society' (Joppke, 1986, p. 56). Unlike Marx, Weber did not develop either an optimistic or a progressive vision for human society.

Defining Class

Both the Marxist and the Weberian approaches to class have their strengths and weaknesses. For the purpose of this article, it will be assumed that the explanatory power of class analysis can be heightened by a careful perusal of the tools provided by both traditions. The Marxist perspective helps us move away from seeing classes as merely groupings of people who share similar attributes such as occupation, income, life-style, et cetera. The Weberian approach allows us to understand more adequately the complexity of social inequality, i.e. the different gradations of rewards and consciousness in that large section of the population who are not capitalists. A working definition of social classes which draws on both perspectives and which should be kept in mind as we look at the structure of power relations in Malta is that of Anyon (1980) who, making reference to the work of key authors such as Wright (1978), Bourdieu and Passeron (1977) and Williams (1977) provides us with the following statement:

> One's occupation and income level contribute significantly to one's social class, but they do not define it. Rather, social class is a series of relationships. A person's social class is defined here by the way that person relates to the process in society by which goods, services and culture are produced. One relates to several aspects of the production process primarily through one's work. One has a relationship to the system of ownership, to other people (at work and society) and to the content and process of one's own productive activity. One's relationship to all these aspects of production determines one's social class; that is, all three relationships are necessary and none is sufficient for determining a person's relation to the process of production in society (Anyon, 1980, p. 68).

This definition should be kept in mind as we consider empirical and theoretical approaches to social class in Malta. The argument is that the data and perspectives currently available, while limited, do present us with an opportunity and a base from which to develop fresh research agendas in order to do justice to this crucial theme in sociology.

Social Class in Malta

Just like every other social formation you would care to mention, Malta has its own pattern of structured inequalities. The relations of domination and exploitation have, of course, changed as the archipelago passed from the hands of one ruler to another (see Zammit, 1984, pp. 7ff.). And so, any account of the contemporary local formation of class, gender and regional (if not racial) differences has to keep in mind a number of considerations which are peculiar to Malta. These would include our past colonial and present neo-colonial history, our small size, our geographic location, and the historic stronghold of the catholic church on the people.

Another crucial fact is that, as Baldacchino correctly points out (1988a), as a post-colonial society Malta still has an underdeveloped manufacturing industrial base and this involves a small percentage – never more than 10% – of the population of the Maltese islands. Furthermore, I would add that the industrial sector is characterized by small set-ups and this has a direct consequence on the kind of control exercised on labour as well as the responses that are likely to be made by workers. In 1988 89.5% of firms in manufacturing, quarrying and construction and non-manufacturing industries employed less than twenty people (Central Office of Statistics, 1991, p. 200). In our case, with the entrepreneur directly supervising the work and often labouring alongside his (or her) employees, we are more likely to find feudal patterns of labour relations, with the owner acting in paternalistic, often benevolent ways, assuming many social costs (such as refraining from firing workers in periods of slack production). There is therefore little foundation here for the development of a radical consciousness, unity and struggle in any Marxist sense.

Of historical importance too is the fact that for sixteen years – between 1971 and 1987 – Malta was governed by a Labour Party. For most of the period the Party was under the leadership of Dom Mintoff whose declared intention was the eradication of class differences. While this period is perhaps still too recent to attract adequate socio-political analysis, the beginnings of such an exercise can be found in Zammit (1984) and Vella (1989). In this context it is important to highlight a number of redistributive social measures introduced by the Labour Party (see Zammit, 1984, p. 63). These included

(1) the nationalization of a number of companies,
(2) a policy of granting annual cost of living increases and bonuses by a flat rather than a percentage rate, as well as
(3) encouraging initiatives in worker participation in a number of industrial set-ups.

The Labour government also narrowed wage differentials in the public sector from 15 to 5 times, and often referred to the terms 'social class' in its discourse, arguing for a necessity to construct an 'egalitarian society'. As Zammit (ibid., p. 63) points out, this was to be interpreted not in the 'complete levelling of incomes' but rather 'the removal of privileges' and the creation of a truly meritocratic society where the same opportunities existed for one and all. This required the creation of a welfare state so that those who started life in relatively underprivileged circumstances could be given support and help by the State in their competition for access to resources. It also required the eradication of

> snobbishness and similar forms of social exclusiveness which are still noticeable in Malta (ibid., p. 63).

It was work in all sectors of the economy which would be the basis of an economically successful and equitable Malta (ibid., pp. 59-60), and hence industriousness, rather than division between manual and non-manual workers, was what mattered.

Class Consciousness

There is no general consensus that class relations prevail in Malta. The question 'Are there classes in Malta?' could invite a number of responses, and even if a majority of citizens had to answer in the negative, this would still be a subjective statement. This is important in its own way, but it would certainly not represent all that there is to say about the matter. While Vassallo (1985) has argued that the question of class – in the economic sense – has been utilized by the Labour Party as a rhetorical strategy to attract people into its ranks, one can also consider the corollary of such a proposition. In other words, what I am suggesting is that in the sociological analysis of the structure of power and privilege in Malta it is far more important to ask:

> In whose interests does the denial of the existence of class work? Who stands to gain and who to lose by a belief that there is no structured inequality in the economic relations predominant in Malta?

It is helpful in this regard to note the distinction that Marxist sociologists draw between a 'class-of-itself' and a 'class-for-itself'.

In the first instance, classes objectively exist in as much as individuals and groups have different relationships to the economy. If these individuals and groups are aware of their subordinate and exploited status, and hence also of their lesser power to exert self-determination, lesser wealth, prestige, and life-chances generally relative to other groups, the objective class condition becomes 'class consciousness', in the sense that these groups are now appreciative of their objective social location. If they unite in order to struggle for social change in their own favour, we then have a 'class-for-itself', one which is ready to take action on its own behalf.

Boswell's (1982) research on occupational and residential prestige – or social worth – in Malta presents some interesting data on levels of status, if not class consciousness, locally. In his study of households in four urban localities in Malta – namely Senglea, Sliema, Fgura and Attard – he found that

> over sixty-five percent of the householders in each locality characterized their society as consisting of three or four social classes (ibid., p. 21).

Boswell (ibid., p. 45) therefore concludes that

> local householders have a clearly defined perception of their society mainly in terms of three social classes, irrespective of their own socio-economic characteristics; that the social status of occupations is very generally perceived in terms of a single hierarchy within which three large clusters may be discerned; that these clusters approximate to socio-economic groups which are further perceived in terms of occupations that are alike by reason of their education and skills, their associated income, their conditions of work, etc; and that this view of the occupational structure is maintained across the most established working-class and bourgeois, as well as the most personally socially mobile members of the urban population.

On the basis of these findings, Boswell notes that there is a highly developed perception of occupational status in Malta, and that this perception represents a very high degree of social consciousness as well as political involvement.

Zammit (1984, pp. 127ff.) presents a more detailed account regarding the perceptions of 'class' in Malta by interviewing a representative sample of 186 people. Taking 'social class' in the Weberian sense of 'grouping people who automatically share common characteristics', Zammit (ibid., p. 130) reports that 78%

of his sample recognized the existence of social class distinction in Malta, 3.2% denied its existence outright, and 18.8% 'failed to give a coherent answer or preferred not to express themselves on this matter'. Of the 78% who said that there were social classes in Malta, 60.8% had a hierarchical image of class divisions, a class structure composed of three or more 'classes' or 'strata' based upon the possession of objective attributes − namely education, occupation and wealth (30.1%) and upon interactional or prestige criteria (30.6%). The other 17.2% of those who held that classes exist in Malta generally saw two major classes divided in terms of access to power or wealth, or simply (or additionally) in terms of pure snobbery.

Supplementary data which Zammit collected from 23 Drydocks shop stewards and trade union activists confirm an overall view that it is only a minority who have class consciousness in terms of Marxist categories of 'class struggle' and 'class for itself'. Few indeed upheld a vision of a proletarian movement which would take over economic power through increased or total ownership of the means of production. For most of Zammit's respondents, society is not conflictual but harmonious, a conception which

> implies constant individual conflict in a situation of formal equality among the bulk of a population (Zammit, 1984, p. 134).

In other words, social members prefer individual − rather than collective or class-based − channels of interest satisfaction.

Of the minority who see Maltese society in terms of conflict, more of these were to be found among manual workers. Zammit (ibid., p. 136) also found that most of his respondents accepted the principle of income differentials 'provided that these are based on effort and ability'. Zammit thus concludes that 'the existence of social 'classes' is generally accepted as fair and legitimate − or, at any rate, a necessary fact of life' (ibid., p. 136). Consonant with such attitudes, it seems logical to assume that there is

> an overwhelming belief in the ability for upward mobility through individual rather than collective efforts (ibid., p. 138-9).

This assumption is in fact borne out by 90.5% of Zammit's respondents. In other words it is believed that the boundaries between classes − hence social mobility − can be overcome through merit and hard work, education for oneself and one's children, and patronage networks: in short, a combination of patronage and merit.

Both Boswell's and Zammit's research indicate high levels of social and status awareness among the Maltese, although this does not necessarily translate into 'class consciousness' or 'class action'. Indeed, if we follow Poulantzas (1974, p. 16), classes cannot be defined and grasped unless – and only when – seen in terms of struggle. Action on the part of economically subordinate groups in Malta would entail, as suggested earlier, unification and struggle not merely to gain higher social status and financial returns for their labour, but to transform the social relations of production. This would imply such practices as collective ownership of the means of production, the production for need rather than commodity exchange, and the development of a classless and stateless society based on the direct democratic participation of all citizens in decision-making, administration and problem-solving (Freeman-Moir et al., 1988).

This struggle would be aimed at abolishing class relations which, as Therborn (1986, p. 111) has argued, can be effectively achieved in one of two basic ways:

> either by abolishing owner-non-owner relations and making superordinate positions of management representative of the subordinates through elections of the former by the latter (and the possibly higher income of the former dependent on the choice of the latter); or by abolishing the vertical dimension of super- and subordinate and disproportionate rewards altogether. In most cases, the former would appear to be the most realistic alternative.

When we consider these goals in the light of organized working class struggle in Malta, it would be difficult to disagree with Zammit (1984), Vassallo (1985) and Vella (1989b) who, utilizing different theoretical tools, nevertheless all conclude that class struggle in the Marxist sense is either absent or incorporated within a welfare state approach. Even the movement towards worker participation in the management of industry could represent a sophisticated form of labour control (Baldacchino, 1988a, b).

Accounts of Class Formation and Structure in Malta: — A Critique of Two Opposing Views.

It has been argued above that there are objective as well as subjective accounts of class, and that the sociologist's major interest is in the former, although the latter is not without its particular importance. An account of class formation in Malta has still to be written. However, a number of authors – sociologists in the main – have pursued fieldwork and/or theorized about social class locally, engaging in Weberian and Marxist traditions when making their analyses.

A Weberian Approach to Class Relations in Malta

Vassallo (1979, p. 227), for instance, has argued that in the absence of 'social mobility studies and of statistics on the distribution and employment of wealth' in Malta, one cannot really speak of social class in a Marxist sense. He therefore subscribes

> to a view that upholds the existence of a stratification system based on 'status-groups', primarily but not exclusively related to educational achievement [...] rather than an economic power in the Marxist sense (ibid., p. 227, f.n. 59).

Vassallo (ibid. p. 64) argues – without, however, backing up his assertions with any empirical evidence – that access to education ensures the dissolution of traditional patterns of stratification. Thus, he writes (ibid., p. 64) that

> Inherited titles are no longer associated with authority, and the patronage patterns of the past, though still a force within politics, are generally disintegrating as children help their parents to reverse the consequences of ignorance and illiteracy.

Vassallo has reiterated this same view in a more recent paper (1989) where he specifically states his belief that, with the arrival of the 'new professions', the

> concept of 'class' in the Marxist sense is fast becoming irrelevant. It is being replaced by 'status groups' in the Weberian sense, and these are not necessarily income-based (ibid., p. 39).

Vassallo also proposes the view that rather than social class, the factor which leads to social stratification today is political patronage, whereby the political party in power ensures that the necessarily scarce resources of a small state such as Malta, are directed towards its adherents.

All in all, however, Vassallo believes that Malta is a meritocratic society and that what has brought this about is 'not exclusively but to a considerable extent...the diffusion of education' (1979, p.

64). He therefore concludes that any reference to contemporary class distinctions in Malta 'may generally be interpreted to be more of an attempt to politicize the issue, and legitimize the action of political leaders' (ibid., p. 227, f.n. 59; see also 1985).

There are a number of problems with Vassallo's analysis. It seems to me that he starts off with a personal preference for a Weberian account and then takes the presumed 'absence' of any evidence of class structure in the Marxist sense to confirm his personal bias by default. In so doing, he takes for granted as a fact that educational expansion leads unproblematically to social mobility; this is an untenable position as can be seen from the results of a number of local empirical studies which show that education reproduces and reinforces class differences (see Darmanin, 1989, 1991; Sultana, 1991, 1992). Vassallo's emphasis on meritocracy and social consensus fails to provide an explanatory framework to make sense of the power structure – based on economic relations – that prevail in contemporary Malta. His Weberian approach, however, does alert us to the possibility that power relations can be played out at different levels, some of these being outside the economic realm. Finally, however, it is Vassallo's failure to support his claims with any form of empirical evidence or research data – at least in his published works to date – that represents the most serious shortcoming of his particular thesis.

We will now turn to an analysis which places economic relations right at the heart of the Maltese power structure.

A Marxist Approach to Class Relations in Malta

As Miliband (1987, pp. 332-3) points out, Marxist class analysis involves
  (a) the detailed identification of the classes and subclasses which make up [a specific society] – in other words, the tracing of a 'social map' that is as detailed and accurate as possible and includes the many complexities which surround the nature of class;
  (b) class analysis must demonstrate the precise structures and mechanisms of domination and exploitation in [a society] and the different ways in which surplus labour is extracted, appropriated and allocated;

(c) class analysis must be concerned with the conflict between classes, pre-eminently between capital and the state on the one side and labour on the other, although it must also pay close attention to the pressures exercised by other classes and groupings, such as different sections of the petty bourgeoisie, or social movements with specific grievances and demands.

Vella has long been involved in a consideration of local class analysis along these lines (Sciberras and Vella, 1979; Vella, 1989a, 1989b). While Vella – or anyone else utilizing classical Marxist tools in order to throw light on the local situation – still has a long way to go to provide a detailed analysis of class structure in Malta, he does make a number of points which deserve to be highlighted.

Vella follows classical Marxist thought to argue that industry and industrialization (but not industrial capitalism) are not only important but necessary in order to provide the material wealth to feed, clothe, and shelter all the population. Such an industrialization will necessarily have to pass through a capitalist stage, i.e. the capitalist class will own the means of production and organize the relations of production to suit their immediate interests. Finally, industrialization, by bringing workers together in a condition of exploitation (i.e. extraction of surplus value), will lead to class consciousness and class struggle, which will lead to the working class taking over the means of production (factories, tools and economic capital generally).

This process did not, however, materialize in Malta. Vella argues that Malta – like other countries peripheral to highly developed capitalist countries – has not gone through a phase of industrialization as early or as thoroughly as other 'first world' nations. He attributes this mainly to the lack of a local entrepreneurial bourgeois class. The Maltese who did have capital, argues Vella, preferred to use it to buy and sell merchandise (hence merchant capital) rather than invest that capital in industrial development. The lack of this type of investment meant that feudal relations of production persisted in Malta – just as they did in southern Italy and Sicily for instance – right up to late this century. Thus, we find rich landowners (and Vella identifies the church as one) extracting feudal rent ('*il-qbiela*') from peasants. Since few industrial set-ups were developed, industrial workers consequently had little opportunity of getting together and of developing a trade union or class consciousness which could lead to some form of class struggle.

Vella further explains that practically the only industry to develop until after the second world war was shipbuilding. It is not surprising, he points out, that it is there that the most class-conscious of the proletariat are to be found. Vella argues that

> as often happens in societies with an underdeveloped bourgeoisie, the tasks of a national democratic revolution [have] to be carried out by movements that derive their strength from the working class. This has happened in Malta, beginning with the post-war years but more decisively after 1971 (Vella, 1989b, p. 165).

In other words, according to Vella, it fell to the Labour Movement to develop an industrial capitalism in Malta, which fact led to a number of contradictions, not least being that of inviting the working class in Malta to take up 'the tasks 'classically' implemented by the bourgeoisie' and then

> presenting to them state models that are quite compatible, if not necessary, to capitalism (including the welfare state) as either quasisocialism, or, worse, as a specifically national variant of socialism (ibid., p. 169).

This claim is, however, problematic, given the fact that direct state intervention during the labour administration was mainly in the service, not the manufacturing sector.

This historical and analytical sketch of the power struggle in Malta has led, according to Vella, to a specific class structure. Such a structure fits squarely within a contemporary formulation of class, provided by such Marxist authors as Miliband (1987). Miliband distinguishes between the two major groupings in society, i.e. the dominant and the subordinate classes. The former consists of the 'power élite' and the 'bourgeoisie'; the latter of the 'working class' and the 'underclass'. Between the ruling and the ruled classes lies the 'petty bourgeoisie'. It is clear that Vella has this sort of structure in mind as he attempts to describe local power relations. In the sections that follow, I will take up Miliband's (1987) description of the members of each particular class grouping, and substantiate this by drawing on relevant local sources where available.

A - The Dominant Class:

We can consider the dominant class in terms of both a 'power élite' and of a 'bourgeoisie'.

1. The 'power élite' is made up of those few people who 'control the few hundred largest industrial, financial and commercial enterprises in the private sector of the economy' (Miliband, 1987, p. 330) as well as those who

control the commanding positions in the state system − presidents, prime ministers and their immediate collaborators, the top people in the civil service, in the military and the police, in the judiciary and (at least in some systems, such as the American) in the legislature − and this element also includes people who control public or state enterprises and the media in the public sector (ibid., p. 330).[3]

Vella (1989b, p. 167) argues that in Malta there is a small industrialist capitalist class 'led by an emergent national bourgeoisie

---

[3] Work still needs to be done to identify the local power élite. While it is relatively easy to trace the networks of power in western countries through such publications as the 'Who Owns Whom' (published annually in the UK by Dun & Bradstreet), no such information is readily available in Malta. Urry (1989, p. 78) suggests that an analysis of the values of the property declared for death duty is 'the best estimate of wealth held in the form of land, houses, shares, factories and durable possessions', even though these declarations 'contain considerable inaccuracies as families try to minimize their declarations and hence their liability for paying such duties'. Such information can help us see more clearly the local patterns of the distribution of wealth, although it needs to be said that a problem specific to Malta is the large percentage of currency held in circulation − 50% of GNP in 1985, compared to 5-10% in many other countries in the same year (Briguglio, 1988, p. 94). This tendency − partly a strategy to evade taxation − effectively sabotages attempts to document the distribution of wealth through a perusal of official statistics. The only immediately available source of information about the local power élite comes from Manduca's (1987) *Who's Who* which gives details of the 'leading members' of the artistic, educational, banking, commercial, diplomatic, clerical, religious and military professions. It also provides limited information about the 'nobility'. This source is, however, limited in that it fails to inform the reader about the family origins of these individuals, or of the source of their power and/or wealth.

eager to demolish legal, political, cultural and other obstacles hindering the further development of modern manufacturing capitalism'. Spiteri (1989, p. 4), himself a Labour minister, has analysed various income and profit trends in gross domestic product and argues that the dominant class of local capitalists actually grew in numbers throughout the sixteen years of socialist administration. Spiteri also correctly points out that we need to distinguish between 'foreign' and 'local' or 'domestic' capitalists. This takes us into the realms of 'dependency theory' which argues (cf. Frank, 1978; Cardoso and Faletto, 1979) that in 'conditioned societies' (Carnoy and Samoff, 1990) such as ours is, any class analysis has to take into due consideration first the role of metropole capital, and secondly the kinds of allegiances and compromises reached by metropole capitalists and local ones so that wealth and other forms of power are distributed in directions previously agreed upon. Baldacchino (1993) has suggested that the structure of economic power in Malta is still dominated by a service, local, commercial élite, and he conjectures that

> the pinnacle of this local class structure [is] occupied by an organizational triumvirate enjoying significant inter-family connections and collusions, plus a very ample presence on a large number of company directorships and state appointed boards.

2. The 'bourgeoisie' has only a fraction of the power wielded by the élite, but is still part of the dominant class 'because its members do exercise a great deal of power and influence in economic, social, political and cultural terms, not only in society at large but in various parts of the state as well' (Miliband, 1987, p. 331).

There are business and professional elements in the bourgeoisie. In the first we find 'people who own and control a large number of medium-sized firms forming a vast scatter of very diverse enterprises, dwarfed by the corporate giants yet constituting a substantial part of total capitalist activity' (ibid., p. 330). In the other,

> a large professional class of men and women (mainly men), made up of lawyers, accountants, scientists, architects, doctors, middle-rank civil servants and military personnel, senior teachers and administrators in higher education, public relations experts, and many others (ibid., p. 330).

Perspectives on Class in Malta 45

While there are fractions and groupings within the dominant classes, 'they usually remain sufficiently cohesive to ensure that their common purposes are effectively defended and advanced... for whereas such people may disagree on what precisely they do want, they very firmly agree on what they do not want and this encompasses anything that might appear to them to threaten the structure of power, privilege and property of which they are the main beneficiaries' (ibid., p. 331). It is difficult to extract the size of this particular class as a percentage of the total Maltese work force, for Census occupational groupings (Central Office of Statistics, 1986) include a variety of other workers in their top employee category.[4]

---

[4]
The 1985 Census categorization of occupations is faulty and misleading in many ways. Among these limitations we can mention the fact that the allocation of economic status, despite the exhaustive instructions that were given to enumerators, depend to some extent on the exercise of judgement on the part of the enumerators, since it was not always possible to draw a well-defined interpretation between the different occupational classifications (Central Office of Statistics, 1986, p. 87). Vella (1989a, p. 11) furthermore notes that the category of salaried employees 'misleadingly includes a very small number of capitalists who appear as salaried employees of companies they control'. Despite these limitations, however, it provides a useful quantitative indication of the local occupational hierarchy, and therefore permits us to glimpse at the class structure in Malta, although of course, as has been pointed out in a number of places in this paper, the occupational structure is not the same as class structure. The Census (Central Office of Statistics, 1986, pp. 35-6) presents a hierarchical representation of employment status with all working members (105,293 persons) being classified under three categories, as follows:
  (a) Employers (2,315 persons, or 2.2% of total work force)
  (b) Own-account workers (10,695 persons, or 10.2% of total)
  (c) Employees (92,283 persons, or 87.6% of total).
The employees were then sub-divided into:
  (i) Professionals, technical and other related workers including professional scientists; doctors and dentists; architects, engineers and surveyors; qualified marine and aviation workers; University academics; qualified teachers (not kindergarten assistants); system analysts and computer programmers; lawyers, accountants (not book-keepers); members of religious orders; artists; librarians; qualified social workers; nurses (SEN [State Enrolled Nurses], SRN [State Registered Nurses] and higher grades); other para-medical workers (e.g. radiographers); other technicians (e.g. laboratory). These make up 7.7% (8,106 persons) of the total working population.
  (ii) Administrative, managerial and other related workers including

B - The 'Petty Bourgeoisie':

The 'petty bourgeoisie' – commonly known as the 'middle class' – lies between the dominating and subordinate classes, and while sharing many of the conditions of the latter class (e.g. lack of autonomy at work, dependence on wage), its loyalties vacillate between the two major classes depending on the stage of capital accumulation at a particular point in time. Unlike the capitalists and the working class – whose interests and allegiances are clearly demarcated and in oppositional, conflictual paths – the petty bourgeois oscillate between the two major classes depending on whether or not these groups experience capitalism as an external force. When economic conditions are favourable, then the allegiance of the petty bourgeoisie is towards the dominant or ruling class. When they are proletarianized, i.e. they experience more closely the conditions of life of the working class/es, then it is to these that their allegiance is addressed.

This class is composed of two distinct elements: 'first, a disparate range of small businessmen, shopkeepers, tradesmen and self-employed artisans' and

---

administrative and higher grades in the public service; consular staff; directors; managers in parastatal and private industry; officers of the Armed Forces; and Police (officer grade). These make up 5.2% (5,506 persons) of the total working population.

(iii) All executive, clerical and other related workers including executive and clerical officers in public service; stenographers and typists; punching and computing machine operators; bookkeepers and clerks of any kind; kindergarten assistants; nurses (unqualified) and other para-medical workers; transport despatchers; postmen; telephone operators; ship radio officers and flight guides; supervisors and foremen in industry; Police (below officer grade); draughtsmen and Works Technical Officers and assistants; unqualified marine and aviation workers. These make up 19.2% (20,229 persons) of the total working population.

(iv) Skilled and semi-skilled workers including drivers of machinery; non-clerical workers classified as Group D in public service; machine operators; shop assistants and services and catering workers. These make up 35% (36,921 persons) of the total working population.

(v) Unskilled workers, that is those who do not possess a basic knowledge of any trade or skill. These make up 20.4% (21,519 persons) of the total working population.

second, a large and constantly growing subclass of semi-professional, supervisory men and women engaged as salaried employees in capitalist enterprises, or in the administrative, welfare, control, coercive and service agencies of the state – social workers, local government officials, and the like (Miliband, 1987, pp. 332-3).

Vella, following Poulantzas and Baudelot and Establet, accords these so-called 'middle class' groups great importance and sees them as 'residues of pre-capitalist social formations and/or from earlier phases of development of capitalism itself' (Vella, 1989a, p. 10). He too distinguishes two subclasses within the local petty bourgeoisie, namely the traditional one consisting of 'small-scale production and ownership, independent craftsmen and traders, and – in the Maltese case – the small holding farmer' (Vella, 1989b, p. 170) and a new petty bourgeoisie 'made up of wage-earning groupings which, although 'produced' by capitalist development itself, do not perform productive labour, that is labour which directly produces surplus-value, which valorizes capital and is exchanged against capital' (ibid., p. 170). Vella argues that this group has grown in size, and includes employees such as office workers, business machine operators, engineers, accountants, researchers, etc. (1989a, p. 10).

Vella (ibid., p. 11) argues that both 'traditional' and 'new' petty bourgeois groups are affected by contemporary developments in the Maltese socio-political structure, quoting statistics from the 1985 census to show that while the former group is decreasing in number, the latter group is increasing.

C – *The Subordinate Class:*

We can consider the subordinate class in terms of both the 'working class' and the 'underclass'.
1. The 'working class' comprises by far the largest section of the population and is 'an extremely variegated, diverse class, divided on the basis of occupation, skill, gender, race, ethnicity, religion, ideology, etc.' (Miliband, 1987, p. 332). While in modern capitalist societies the industrial, manufacturing component of the working class is dwindling in numbers – largely due to technological innovation and changes in the labour process –

the working class as a whole, the people whose exclusive source of income is the sale of their labour power (or who mainly rely on transfer payments by the state), whose level of income puts them in the lower and lowest 'income groups', whose individual power and responsibility at work and beyond is low or virtually non-existent – this class of people has increased, not diminished over the years (ibid., p. 332).

Neither Vella nor any other local class analyst has provided any detailed account of the working class in Malta, although there are some interesting attempts in the writings of O'Reilly Mizzi (1981) for instance. Spiteri (1989) speaks of the working class in terms of those who depend on others for their living, i.e. those whom the wage renders dependent. This, however, is not enough. We need to distinguish between those who depend on a wage to make ends meet and those whose wage gives them access to a much larger share of financial and social resources. It would be useful in this context to make use of dual labour market theory (Addison and Siebert, 1979) which suggests that the labour market is divided (for the benefit of the capitalist) into several categories of occupations each with different criteria of hiring, paying, promotion, rules and behaviour. The essential division is between the primary and secondary sector, with very little economic mobility between the sectors. Jobs in the secondary sector are characterized by repetitive tasks, specific supervision and formalized work rules, low wage rates, poor working conditions and instability of employment. Such jobs lack a career structure and opportunities for promotion. The 'working class' would clearly fall into this secondary sector of a segmented labour market.

2. The 'underclass' is described by Miliband (1987, p. 333) as

issued from the working class and in some ways still part of it, yet also distinct from it: the more or less permanently unemployed, the members of the working class who are elderly, chronically sick or handicapped, and those unable for other reasons to find their way into the 'labour market'.

To Miliband's list one can add under-age workers whose activity in the 'twilight economy' renders them highly vulnerable to exploitation (cf. Sultana 1993). Again, no local author has given this class element much attention, partly, I would suggest, because the extensive welfare provisions put into place by a Labour government have guaranteed the basic necessities of life to all Maltese citizens (Tomorrow, 1984).[5] Despite a 4% unemployment rate – as a percentage of the labour supply in June 1993 (*Economic Trends*, June 1993) – there is little immediate sign of the rise of the 'new poor' that is so much in evidence in those countries – such as Britain, France and the United States – where unemployment is rife and where welfarism has come under attack. While the present Nationalist government has in some respects consolidated rather than dismantled the welfare system, its increasingly 'free market' approach to the economy and wage spiralling have resulted in an increase in the cost of living which could lead segments of the working class to experience conditions of poverty.

The above class account has its particular strengths in that the structure of power between the two major classes and the reasons for conflict between them emerge much more clearly. It displays the same weaknesses attributed generally to Marxist analyses, namely deterministic evolutionism (i.e. Malta must pass through a capitalist stage of development) and uni-causality (economic class relations are sufficient in themselves to explain structures of power). The account therefore fails to throw much light on how the different economic relations give rise to different life-styles and patterns of consumption. This is more satisfactorily achieved by Weberian approaches (e.g. Bourdieu, 1984), by interactionist perspectives which enter into the phenomenological

---

[5] Tabone (1987, p. 134) gives a list of these: the introduction of the national minimum wage and the compulsory payment of a yearly bonus to all workers as from 1975; the granting of parity of women's wages with those of men, in 1976; the compulsory grant of a cost of living increase to workers in the private sector and the payment of adult wage rates at the age of 18 as of 1977; the introduction of children's allowance in 1974; the regular increase of old age pensions, national insurance benefits and social assistance payments; the introduction of a national health scheme by which hospital services are freely available, and the provision of a large number of dwellings to solve the housing problem. Tabone, (ibid., p. 136) however also calculates that a family with more than three children and only one income would still find it difficult to cope with the cost of living.

fields of social actors, and by a culturalist rather than orthodox/ structuralist brand of Marxism as developed by Thompson (1968) – and subsequently by the members of the Centre for Contemporary Cultural Studies in Birmingham – who argue in favour of considering classes as both an economic and cultural formation. Thompson (1978) argues that

> it is impossible to give any theoretical priority to one aspect over the other ... what changes, as the mode of production and productive relations change, is the experience of living men and women.

Similarly missing from the above account is a direct reference to the place of the Church – still a leading institution despite political changes in post-feudal Malta (Koster, 1981) – within the contemporary hierarchy of wealth and power.

Coda

Class analysis in Malta has, as we have noted above, largely remained at an abstract theoretical level, divorced from empirical research which would strengthen the theory and sensitize the analysis to local peculiarities in the power structure. While this paper has set out to acknowledge some of the analyses that do exist, it is also necessary to chart the course for future work in class analysis by indicating some of the areas which need to be explored. Among these I would suggest the following:

(a) The documentation of the class-based nature of inequality in Malta, with a direct focus on the labour process and capitalist relations at work at the point of production.
(b) The acknowledgement of the determining constraints posed by national and international capitalism on the project of promoting equality.
(c) The analysis of class struggle and class mobilization as it has developed in Malta since the 19th century, and the particular forms it has taken in more recent history.
(d) The detailed definition and counting of present class forces from whose struggle some form of future social transformation is expected. This involves the demarcation of class boundaries in the attempt to develop our own class cartography.

(e) The analysis of political power and the State as manifestations of class power, giving due attention on the one hand to the bearing of capitalist powers upon state government, and to the relationships between class relations and state structure/state power configurations on the other.
(f) The use of class structures as raw materials in the process of modelling class voting and left-wing party strategies.
(g) The analysis of social mobility paths and patterns, and its incidence on an individual and group basis, as well as on an inter- and intra-generational one.
(h) The tapping of class consciousness, which would include a an analysis of class-differentiated behaviour and attitudes, and the relationship of these to status and prestige in Malta, and to life-chances generally.
(i) A concern not only with the workplace, property, markets, scarcity and economic equality but also, very much in the spirit of the Frankfurt School theorists, a focus on language, culture, discourse, communication, the individual, and non-economic power. This would lead to the social psychological investigation of the societal integration of individuals, and the cultural-theoretical analysis of the mode of operation of mass culture.

The fact that much of the above research agenda remains mostly untouched speaks eloquently of the lack of development in social science in Malta, and of the need for concerted action so that these gaps are filled so that the passage from the rhetoric to the practice of social justice and democracy is facilitated.

References:

Addison, J.T. & Siebert, W.S. (1979) *The Market for Labour: An Analytic Treatment*, Santa Monica, CA, Goodyear.

Althusser, L. (1971) *Lenin and Philosophy and other Essays*, London, New Left Books.

Anyon, J. (1980) 'Social class and the hidden curriculum of work', *Journal of Education* (Boston), vol. 162, 2.

Baldacchino, G. (1988a) 'The industrialisation of Malta: A historical analysis of the formation, control and response of labour', *Issues*, Malta, The New Economics Society.

Baldacchino, G. (1988b) 'Malta trade unionism at the crossroads: Problems and prospects within a historical context'. In *Malta's Changing Labour*

Market, Proceeding of a CIMIRA conference on 'Malta's changing labour market', February.
Baldacchino, G. (1993) 'Social class in Malta: Insights into a homegrown relationship with special reference to education', *Education* (Malta), vol. 5, 1.
Boswell, D.M. (1982) 'Patterns of occupational and residential area prestige in the Maltese conurbation'. Paper presented at the 10th World Congress of Sociology, Mexico City.
Bourdieu, P. (1984) *Distinction: A Social Critique of the Judgement of Taste*, Cambridge, MA, Harvard University Press.
Bourdieu, P. & Passeron, J.C. (1977) *Reproduction in Education, Society and Culture*, London, Sage.
Briguglio, L. (1988) *The Maltese Economy: A Macroeconomic Analysis*, Malta, David Moore Publications.
Cardoso, F.H. & Faletto, E. (1979) *Dependency and Development in Latin America*, Berkeley, CA, University of California Press.
Carnoy, M. & Samoff, J. (1990) *Education and Social Transition in the Third World*, Princeton, NJ, Princeton University Press.
Central Office of Statistics (1986) *Census 1985: vol. 1 – A Demographic Profile of Malta and Gozo*. Malta, Government Press.
Central Office of Statistics (1991) *Abstract of Annual Statistics 1988*, Malta, Government Press.
Central Office of Statistics (1990) *Economic Trends*, Malta.
Darmanin, M. (1990) 'Classroom practices and class pedagogies'. In Sultana, R.G. (ed.) *Themes in Education: A Maltese Reader*, Msida, Malta, Mireva Publications.
Darmanin, M. (1989) 'Sociological perspectives on schooling in Malta', Unpublished Ph.D. dissertation, University of Wales College, Cardiff.
Frank, A.G. (1978) *Dependent Accumulation and Underdevelopment*, New York, Monthly Review Press.
Freeman-Moir, J., Scott, A. & Lauder, H. (1988) 'Reformism or revolution: Liberalism and the metaphysics of democracy'. In Cole, M. (ed.) *Bowles and Gintis Revisited*, Lewes, Falmer Press.
Giddens, A. & Held, D. (eds) (1982) *Classes, Power and Conflict: Classical and Contemporary Debates*, California, University of California Press.
Gramsci, A. (1971) *Selections from the Prison Notebooks of Antonio Gramsci*. Hoare, Q. & Nowell-Smith, G. (eds), London, Lawrence and Wishart.
Joppke, C. (1986) 'The cultural dimensions of class formation and class struggle: On the social theory of Pierre Bourdieu', *Berkeley Journal of Sociology*, vol. 31.
Koster, A. (1981) *Prelates and Politicians in Malta: Changing Power-Balances between Church and State in a Mediterranean Island Fortress (1530-1976)*, Vijfhuizen, The Netherlands.
MacDonald, P. (1988) 'Historical school reform and the correspondence principle'. In Cole, M. (ed.) *Bowles and Gintis Revisited*, Lewes, Falmer Press.
Manduca, J. (ed.) (1987) *Malta Who's Who*, 7e. Malta, Progress Press.
Miliband, R. (1987) 'Class analysis'. In Giddens, A. & Turner, J. (eds) *Social Theory Today*, Cambridge, Polity Press.
Mizzi O'Reilly, S. (1981) *Women in Senglea: The Changing Role of Urban, Working-Class Women in Malta*, State University of New York, University Microfilms International.

Poulantzas, N. (1980) *State, Power, Socialism*, London, New Left Books.
Sciberras, L. & Vella, M. (1979) *Wara r-Repubblika: Versi*, Malta, K3.
Spiteri, L. (1989) 'St. George and the dragon: The changing fortunes of capitalists and dependents', *Society*, 2.
Sultana, R.G. (1990) 'Sociological Perspectives on Class in Malta', *Economic and Social Studies (New Series)*, vol. 5.
Sultana, R.G. (1991) 'Social class and educational achievement in Malta'. In Sultana, R.G. (ed.) *Themes in Education: A Maltese Reader*, Msida, Malta, Mireva Publications.
Sultana, R.G. (1992) *Education and National Development: Historical and Critical Perspectives on Vocational Schooling in Malta*, Msida, Malta, Mireva Publications.
Sultana, R.G. (1993) 'Practices and policies in child labour: Lessons from Malta', *British Journal of Education and Work*, vol. 6, 3.
Tabone, C. (1987) *The Secularization of the Family in Changing Malta*, Malta, Dominican Publications.
Therborn, G. (1986) 'Class analysis: history and defence'. In Himmelstrand, U. (ed.) *Sociology: From Crisis to Science?* Vol. 1, London, Sage.
Thompson, E.P. (1968) *The Making of the English Working Class*, Harmondsworth, Penguin.
Thompson, E.P. (1978) *The Poverty of Theory and Other Essays*, London, Merlin Press.
Tomorrow (1984) 'Is poverty extinct?' (March).
Townsend, P. (1979) *Poverty in the United Kingdom*, Harmondsworth, Penguin.
Urry, J. (1989) 'Social class in Britain'. In Cole, M. (ed.) *The Social Contexts of Schooling*, Lewes, Falmer Press.
Vassallo, M. (1979) *From Lordship to Stewardship: Religion and Social Change in Malta*, The Hague, Mouton.
Vassallo, M. (1985) 'L-elitiżmu fl-iskejjel privati: Realtà jew mit?' In *L-Edukazzjoni f'Pajjiżna*, Proceedings of a National Conference organized by the Nationalist Party, 14-16th February, Msida.
Vassallo, M. (1989) 'Professions: New and old'. In *Current and Future Trends in Higher Education*. Proceedings of a Conference organized by W.E.S.I.B. (March), Malta.
Williams, R. (1961) *The Long Revolution*, London, Chatto & Windus.
Vella, M. (1989a) 'Would you recognize the middle class if you saw it? Notes on certain Maltese social groups', *Society*, 2.
Vella, M. (1989b) *Reflections in a Canvas Bag*, Marsa, Malta, PEG.
Williams, R. (1977) *Marxism and Literature*, New York, Oxford University Press.
Wright, E.O. (1978) *Class, Crisis and the State*, London, New Left Books.
Wright, E.O. (1983) 'Giddens's Critique of Marxism', *New Left Review*, 138, March-April.
Zammit, E.L. (1984) *A Colonial Inheritance: Maltese Perceptions of Work, Power and Class Structure with reference to the Labour Movement*, Malta, Malta University Press.

3

'That Favourite Dream of the Colonies':
Industrialization, Dependence and the Limits of
Development Discourse in Malta

Mario Vella

The Uselessness of Essential Paradigms

The years 1971 and 1987 (which mark the beginning and the end of the Malta Labour Party's sixteen years in office) are invariably presented as moments of radical change in Maltese political economic policy. This paper questions the depth of that change and argues that the Maltese policy maker has never seriously questioned orthodox concepts of development. From this point of view, political economic policy since the Second World War has been characterized by a paradigmatic continuity of the concepts that underlie its various official formulations and its practical implementation. The ideologies of development to be found in Malta (ideologies which, we shall argue, are characterized by

a latent continuity beneath their manifest diver- sity) appear, in Germani's words, as '...hybrid, even paradoxical formulas from the point of view of the right-left dichotomy.'
This interpretative difficulty generally arises whenever we are faced with political forms which,

> ...despite their diverse and in many ways opposed variants, (...) we can subsume beneath the generic label of 'national-popular' movements, and which seem to represent the peculiar form of intervention into political life of those strata in the course of rapid mobilization in countries with delayed industrialization (1965, p. 157).

One may easily be tempted to portray the two mainstream political forces in Malta in the last half a century, the Labour Party and the Nationalist Party as, respectively, the left and right poles of a hypothetical political spectrum. From these 'ideal' or 'essential paradigms' – as Laclau (1977, p. 158) call them – one is also often tempted to infer, either according to a rationalist logic or to a 'common sense' one of association and evocation (ibid., pp. 7-12), opposite visions of social and economic development. In such a case, an unexplainable gap would appear between their operative discourse and action, on the one hand, and what they 'ought to be saying and doing' on the other. If we approach the problem in this fashion, we are bound to conclude that: 'We have here something difficult to understand within the experience of 19th century Europe' (Germani, 1965, p. 158).

This paper is built upon the position that ideological processes (whereby raw materials from a particular historical terrain are transformed in the process of transposition to another terrain) are 'unintelligible so long as ideological elements are pre-assigned to essential paradigms' (Laclau, 1977, p. 158) and that the 'scientific study of ideologies presupposes precisely the study of this kind of transformation' (ibid., p. 157).

The Dominant Paradigm: The Seminal Years

The paradigm of development that has dominated political economic discourse in Malta at least since the war is based on the following two assumptions: Firstly, that capitalist development is the only possible sort of development; and, secondly, that if this development is to be an industrial one it must be export-led and

'That Favourite Dream of the Colonies' 57

based mainly on wholly or partially foreign-owned enterprise.[1]

This paper is not concerned with the 'correctness' or otherwise of the social, economic and political values that underlie these assumptions.[2] It has been prompted by the comparative observation that in sharp contrast to the post-war intellectual history of other societies at the periphery of the world's industrial metropolises, Malta is characterized by the almost total absence of radical critiques of these assumptions. This observation is itself sociologically interesting. That it is itself long overdue enhances its sociological value. The Labour Party did for a while call itself 'socialist' and although never incorporating this into its statute, the latter does refer to its 'socialist democratic views and doctrine' (*Partit tal-Haddiema*, 1993, p. 3). However, the Party has never questioned capitalist development.[3] Indeed it has been argued that in the absence of a progressive national bourgeoisie able and willing to promote industrial development, and because the Nationalist Party was dominated by the interests of a merchant

---

[1] The 'common sense' objection that this is after all the only realistic perspective is of course sociologically untenable because it begs the question: what stated or unstated ideological premises have led to the systematic exclusion of 'utopian' elements from political discourse?

[2] 'In all but the very poorest Third World countries the belief in export-led industrialization fuelled by foreign investment and technology (hereafter ELIFFIT) has begun to challenge the other available strategies of development. Although more traditional development strategies, such as import substitution, varying degrees of autarky, or exporting primary products persist in practice, few countries continue to believe that they offer a realistic path to development. ...the ELIFFIT strategy represents a fundamental coming together of the interests of transnational corporations and some key élites in the countries of the Third World.' (Sklair, 1993, p. 1). The 'key élites' in the Maltese context deserve urgent sociological attention.

[3] The fact that 'soon after the launching of the Development Plan for Malta 1973-80 various sectors of the economy which were essential for development and which were under foreign control were gradually brought under Maltese ownership (...) banking, telecommunications, air and sea transport, broadcasting and oil importation and storage' (as the official Malta Handbook of 1984 proudly declared, p. 13) is quite compatible with, indeed in certain circumstances necessary for, capitalist development.

capital uninterested in if not downright opposed to industrialization, the task of promoting capitalist industrialization had to be taken up by the Labour movement (Vella & Sciberras, 1979, pp. 7-11; 1989, pp. 164-197).

It may be objected that as far as Labour and social democratic parties go (the MLP is a member of the social democratic and historically anticommunist Socialist International), reformist (as opposed to revolutionary) parties are the rule. The MLP in the seventies and early eighties, however, was distinguishable from mainstream (certainly European) social democracy and assumed a distinctly third-worldist stand with an active role in the Non-Aligned Movement, close relations with China, a trade reciprocity agreement with the Soviet Union and a special relationship with Libya.

This tendency would have suggested a more radical vision of development. This vision however never materialized. The MLP's notion of imperialism lacked any economic dimension. When the British bases were closed down in 1979, no authoritative voice within the Labour Party (nor any politically effective voice outside it) drew attention to the problem of economic imperialism and the role of foreign capital within it; the problem was not even broached as a hypothesis to be disproved.[4] References in development plans to 'dependence on outside forces' and to the desirability of local private initiative to match foreign investment in order to achieve more 'self-reliance' are duly balanced with references to the 'compensating benefits... derived from direct foreign investment' (Development Plan 1981-85, p. 63). Nor were they followed by effective practical initiatives and results, certainly not any that went beyond import substitution. This is more than simply saying that the Labour Party was not Marxist. After all, non-Marxist critiques of dependence had been circulating at least since the 1950s. A case in point being the work carried out within the framework of ECLA, the UN's Economic Commission for Latin America (United Nations, 1950). Growing around the work

---

[4] For an introduction to the literature on imperialism, see Barrat-Brown (1974), Owen & Sutcliffe (1972).

of Prebisch (e.g. Prebisch, 1959), the ECLA school has been criticized for its limitations, for example its historically unwarranted assumption that a progressive patriotic bourgeoisie in a peripheral setting would promote development and for its apparent inability to notice that sometimes import substitution can lead to greater dependence on the world's economic centres and to stagnation (see, for example Murga, 1971). At least, however, it did problematize the relationship between central and peripheral economies and attempted to explain what it saw as the functional nexus between the development of one and the underdevelopment of the other, at the level of trade.[5]

However narrow the political horizons of Prebisch's school may have appeared to its left critics and however similar some of its paradigmatic assumptions and policy options may have been to Labour's own economic policy in the 1970s and 1980s (for example import substitution), it contrasts radically with the MLP's vision of development – a vision that was essentially orthodox even in the seminal 1950s and may be located between the 'classical' (Lewis, 1955; Hicks, 1969) and the Keynesian (Knapp, 1969) world economic views (although the latter is objectively closer to the ECLA position) and is quite compatible

---

[5] There is a corpus of lively, often politically charged, debate that preceded mainly by authors working in Latin America, ran parallel to, interfaced with, and transcended the horizons of ECLA's discourse. Apart from the well known work of Frank (1971, 1975), see also as examples Cardoso & Faletto (1979) and dos Santos (1970). For an overall view see Oxaal et al. (1975) and Roxborough (1979). For a landmark critique of the limitations of Frank's loose notion of capitalism based not on relations of production but on the incorporation of an economy into the world market at the level of trade only, see Laclau (1977).

There is no evidence of sustained political or at least academic interest in their work in Malta where the sociology of development is certainly underdeveloped. Significantly the ideas expressed here unfolded over a number of years (beginning around 1974) outside of the context of the University of Malta with the exception of 1985-1987 when this author taught a public policy studies course with – towards the end of the period – the assistance of Edward Warrington. One student in the course, Mario Brincat, went on to post-graduate study and research in development sociology. Exceptional and noteworthy in these 'desert' conditions is the work of Godfrey Baldacchino (1992, 1993).

with the Rostowian 'stages' scheme.[6] As if to emphasise its disregard for economic dependence as opposed to politico-military dependence, the Labour government declared the 31st March, the day the last British serviceman left the islands, Freedom Day. It was also frequently qualified as 'the day when Malta achieved full freedom'.[7] There is no evidence of significant internal discussion in public[8] about the limits and nature of that freedom, about its economic boundaries. Nor is there evidence of a sustained and politically effective critique outside the MLP. Labour's rejoicing at the end of the colonial era seems to have precluded any reflection on the economics of neo-colonialism. This is surprising because in the 1960s, the leaders of the 'non-aligned' ex-colonies (a group with which the Labour leadership sought to identify itself) were greatly concerned with

> the survival of the colonial system in spite of formal recognition of independence in emerging countries, which became the victims of an indirect and subtle form of domination (O'Connor, 1970, p. 117).

One would have expected a national popular party such as the MLP, which had itself taken an uncompromising stand in 1964 against what it had considered a sham independence, to encourage discussion on the concept of neo-colonialism. Ironically one of the first British scholars who sought to understand the preoccupations of Asian and African leaders (who through the Francophone amongst them, had inherited the concept of neo-colonialism from the French left), was none other than the Oxford economist

---

[6] See Rostow, (1962); for a contemporary critique of his theory of growth see Baran & Hobsbawm (1961).

[7] See, for example, Sacco (1986, Chap. 26) which is entitled 'Il-Ħelsien shiħ – 31 ta' Marzu 1979' ['Full freedom – 31st March 1979]. Clearly, Freedom Day (31st March 1979) was meant to contrast with Independence Day (21st September 1964), traditionally regarded by the Maltese labour movement as a purely formal gesture on Britain's part and as the negation of full freedom.

[8] The possibility of an internal debate that never became public is not to be excluded. Historians have yet to tackle this subject.

Thomas Balogh. Together with Dudley Seers, then of Oxford's Institute of Statistics, he had only a few years previously co-operated in laying down the strategic foundations of Malta's future economic policy on the basis of export oriented foreign investment at first conceived in terms of integration with Britain. Balogh (1962) identified the following points of concern:
(a) the effect of capital investments and financial assistance controlled by former mother countries;
(b) continued economic dependence upon the latter; and
(c) integration into colonial economic blocs.

The seminal importance of early formulations of an export-led development strategy for Malta, a strategy dependent for its success on foreign investment, cannot be emphasised enough. Let us therefore now turn our attention to the period between the end of the war, when export-oriented industrialization was dismissed as a typical dream of the colonies, and Labour's electoral victory in 1971.

Industrial development was not considered as a serious possibility by British colonial administrators in the 1940s. Sir Wilfred Woods concluded that it did

> not seem reasonable to expect industrial development of sufficient magnitude to add materially to Malta's national income. The only possibility of such development which was suggested to me is that favourite dream of the colonies, the establishment of a motor car assembly factory to supply cars to a large adjacent territory. There seems to be no reason to expect anything of the sort and industrial development must be thought of in terms of minor accretions to the national wealth which it is important to encourage but from which much cannot be expected (Woods, 1946, pp. 1,7).

Woods did not exclude some industrial development but could not conceive this to go beyond small local market-oriented manufactures. He was convinced that in the last instance only 'the handling of wealth rather than its creation' could really 'flourish' in Malta. He observed that not only would such 'purely commercial operations' have nothing to do with exports but they would expand 'in proportion to the volume of imports, since a great part of such operations either originate in, or are dependent upon, import operations' (ibid.).

The efforts of Elias Zammit, founder of the Federation of Malta Industries, to press the colonial authorities to create conditions favourable to manufacturing contrasted sharply with Woods' skepticism but did not really go beyond a vision of local market led industrial development. 'It is imperative', Zammit lectured in 1949, 'that we should conceive a plan for a drive for new industries and improve and extend production to cut imports' (Zammit, 1949, p. 1).[9] While not excluding export industries, he did not consider them as a priority area (Zammit, 1950, p. 21).

It is in the 1950s that we find the first clear formulations of a strategy designed to establish favourable conditions for export-led industrial development. These formulations were to crystallize into an orthodoxy that dominated the developmental vision of the policy maker at least until 1987. It cannot be sufficiently emphasised that it was a policy-maker's orthodoxy, not the Maltese entrepreneur's orthodoxy. Orthodox business-sense continued to be the sense of merchant capital, the sense of importation and distribution, the sense of the Chamber of Commerce.

> ...to create new productive outlets for the Maltese population... to increase – even to sustain – the standard of life, which now depends so completely on the expenditure of the Imperial Government... Any such programme is dependent for success on the attraction to Malta of a number of overseas firms, especially British ones... The main attraction to Malta must be to firms with relatively large labour costs... There is a large body of intelligent and adaptable labour at wage levels which must (in the best of circumstances) remain below those of the United Kingdom for some time to come. This is the greatest attraction of Malta to overseas firms, and therefore it must play a big part in stimulating the birth of industrialization. In due course, the difference between wages in Malta and the United Kingdom would narrow, but by that time industrialization would have acquired a certain momentum (Balogh & Seers, 1955, pp. 25-26).

These passages, from Balogh and Seers' interim report of 1955 to the then Labour Prime Minister Dom Mintoff, contain all the elements of the 'new' vision: first, the necessity of industrial activity ('productive outlets'); secondly, the need to free the

---

[9] See also his inaugural address, Federation of Malta Industries, 17 June 1946; *Times of Malta* 22 August 1946; *Times of Malta* 2 November 1946.

Maltese economy from its dependence on British military spending; thirdly, the necessity of foreign industrial investment; fourthly, the need for wages to be lower in Malta than in those countries from which investment is expected ('the greatest attraction'). In terms of this vision, 'dependence' refers to Malta's almost complete economic reliance – direct and indirect – on British military presence. Economic reliance on foreign firms ('especially British ones') is not viewed as dependence; on the contrary, it is presented as the antidote to dependence. The improvement of 'the standard of life' of the Maltese is presented as the ultimate goal of economic policy but a limit is set to this improvement: 'wage levels... must remain below those of the United Kingdom for some time to come'. Balogh and Seers did not seem to share the enthusiasm of the Federation of Malta's Industries for the protection of local manufactures. Their support for protection was mild and qualified. Neither did they show any sympathy for the importers' lobby (ibid., para. 103). They were thinking of export-oriented foreign (mainly British) owned industries and none of these would be attracted to Malta's small market, no matter how well protected.

Their lack of enthusiasm for local-market based industry echoed the attitude of George Schuster in his report of 1950:

> It is to be noted that the Malta Government's chief weapon hitherto for the encouragement of industrial development has been the grant of monopolies for a period of years. I consider this to be a policy fraught with considerable dangers (quoted in Spiteri, 1969, p. 9).

Schuster & Scott's economic commission's report of 1957 began by assuming that the so-called 1955 Declaration implied 'a definite decision by the United Kingdom Government to back a positive policy for the economic development of Malta' (1957: no page numbers, para. 6). They stated clearly that 'success depends upon achieving industrial development' (ibid., para. 6). Schuster & Scott agreed with a memorandum presented to them by the Maltese Government pleading for British cooperation 'to attract substantial industrial enterprise to Malta' (ibid., para. 6.ii). They urged Britain to

> consider what would be the most effective way for enabling the Maltese Government to get into contact with British industrial concerns which might be interested (para. 6.ii).

They were equally clear concerning the price of labour:

> There is most urgent need to exercise restraint in demands for wage increases unrelated to increased productivity. Unless such restraint is exercised, Malta may price herself out of any possibility of developing new competitive industry (para. 6.vi.a).

The vision of export-led industrial development that emerged in the 1950s was a vision the contours of which were forced into focus by Britain's Defence White Paper of 1957 with its announcement of drastic cuts in British military spending. It culminated in the first five year development plan (1959-1964) and the enactment of the Aids to Industries Ordinance, both in 1959. The plan stressed the primacy of industry and specifically of export industry:

> Industry must be built up, and by, the very smallness of the home market, any significant industrial development must look largely to the highly competitive export markets in the United Kingdom and elsewhere, particularly in the Mediterranean and African markets. (...) Even so the task of winning export markets is formidable and will demand a high level of efficiency and productivity in relation to wage levels (quoted in Spiteri, 1969, p. 14).

The Aids to Industries Ordinance provided for a Board to process applications for assistance, that is, amongst others, grants and loans, tax-free holidays, exemption from customs duties for plant and equipment as well as raw materials and parts required for export manufactures. A revised version of the first development plan was published in 1961 listing the sort of projects that had, so far, been submitted for consideration: household and industrial textiles, plastic, building materials, motor vehicle assembly (the 'favourite dream'?), electronics, chrysanthemum cuttings, paints, children's wear, synthetic fabrics and steel rerolling. It announced that efforts were being made to encourage investment in semi-capital goods and to promote continental investment. It noted that it was

> ...a time when there have been many other countries, in all stages of development and in many cases with more natural assets, competing in the endeavour to build up local industries (quoted in Spiteri, 1969, p. 16).

Note the use of Rostowian terminology: W.W. Rostow's trend-setting *Stages of Growth: a Non Communist Manifesto*, appeared in the same year. Although the 'success' of the promotional effort is attributed to 'judicious advertising policy', to the advice given by the Industrial Development Board operating from London and the assistance offered to investors under the Ordinance, it follows from the reference to competition from countries with 'more natural assets' that the policy maker was aware that the low cost of labour must have had a determining influence on the investor's decision to locate in Malta.

In 1964, the second five year development plan was published. 'The long term aim', it stated, 'is to create a competitive economic structure largely oriented towards the export market' (para. 18). The creation of this structure would require 'outside help in terms of know-how, grants and loans' (para. 3) until such time as the economy would have reached

> the 'take-off' stage of development, when endogenous forces will be expected to support growth and lead the economy to eventual maturity (para. 3).

The dominance of the Rostowian paradigm – consecrated with the notion of 'take-off' – is now overt. The plan reiterated the point made by Balogh, Seers, Schuster & Scott, that development depended on exports which, in turn, depended on the competitivity of labour (para. 18). The Anglo-Maltese Joint Mission chaired by Lord Robens, reporting in the summer of 1967 in the wake of the previous year's decision by the British government to further run down its armed forces, pointed out that the target of 7,000 industrial new jobs by 1972 '...is not so much a forecast of what might be achieved, as a measure of the scale and the intensity of industrial promotion which Malta requires' (quoted in Spiteri, 1969, p. 18). The report tends to reduce the problem of attracting foreign direct investment to a technical question: promotional effectiveness and administrative efficiency. Having thus decided that the 'critical issue' (ibid.) is a technical one, the authors are able to sidestep the crucial problem of the profitability or otherwise of an industrial investment in a particular location and they do not, therefore, focus on what Balogh, Seers, Schuster & Scott, considered to be crucial, namely the attractiveness of the country's low priced labour to foreign investors. The technicist approach also enables one not to pose the social, economic but above all political problem of how to improve standards of living without repelling export-oriented foreign investment, assuming that development through export-oriented foreign investment is the only feasible development in the given circumstances.

Early in 1968, the long-awaited Malta Development Corporation (MDC) was set up through an act of parliament (Act No. XXVII of 1967). It thus replaced the Aids to Industries Board while still operating within the framework of the Aids to Industries Ordinance. A memo submitted by a public relations firm to the Corporation is indicative of the images and ideas circulating at the time:

> A willing and cheerful labour force, whose wages at the moment are lower than those in England and Northern Europe (but, in the main, higher than those in the Mediterranean littoral), is an asset (Impact Public Relations Ltd., 1968, pp. 195-6).

The Corporation's annual report of 1968 listed, amongst others, the following guiding criteria:
(a) to diversify the economy;
(b) to create male employment;
(c) to create exports in order to earn foreign currency;
(d) to increase import substitution in order to reduce expenditure of foreign currency' (pp. 3-4).

The third development plan (1969-1973) looked forward to a 'stage of autonomous growth' when 'economic development has been carried to the point where the economy has sufficient in-built resources to sustain future expansion without necessary recourse to outside aid' (para. 1.3). Noteworthy is the comment regarding dependence on foreign investment:

> A much higher proportion of Maltese capital should be invested in local productive enterprises, if only so that a greater part of... profits... will accrue to residents. (...) ...the mix of capital subscription must be less dependent on foreign finance than it has been (para. 1.8).

The MDC's birth was a confirmation of the choice of a development path based on foreign owned export led industry. This path has since then never been seriously questioned. Not only did the Labour administrations 1971-1987 not question this strategy, but it was under Labour that the strategy was implemented to such an extent that it changed the economy's structure from one almost totally dependent on British defence spending to one dependent on exports manufactured by foreign owned firms.

The Dominant Paradigm: A Quarter of a Century of Dependent Industrial Development

Writing in 1969, Lino Spiteri, at that time research officer for the Chamber of Commerce and eventually a minister of finance and trade in the 1981-1987 Labour government, noted the dangers of dependence on textile industries (Spiteri, 1969, pp. 33-39). He then proceeded beyond the narrow limits of this 'technical' notion of dependence. He argued that economic growth with a predominantly foreign-owned industry was 'unsafe'.

> A situation where local participation is low would be unsatisfactory because the benefits of industry remaining in Malta would be limited to employment earnings and taxes, as the bulk of realized profits, unless they are ploughed back, would find their way abroad (ibid., p. 48).

The argument is then taken still further: the participation of Maltese capital is necessary because foreign economic domination may eventually lead to local political dissatisfaction (ibid., p. 49). Such a clear cut position was unprecedented and probably unique in its clarity even in comparison to later texts. For example, when the 1981-1985 development plan speaks of 'the heavy bias of external effort in the existing industrial set up' (p. 63), there is no reference to political considerations. Spiteri's 1969 text is the exception that proves the rule. At the same time as Spiteri was writing this text, a process had begun, whereby eventually the continental industrialist would replace the high ranking British naval officer as the typical foreign VIP and manufacturing exports would replace British military expenditure as the main source of foreign earnings. A steady stream of, mainly German, fully foreign-owned industries were set up between 1968 and 1980, on average two a year. Domestic exports (f.o.b.) in 1980 stood at Lm 149 million, compared to Lm 9.1 million of 1970. Gross manufacturing output rose from Lm 38.8 million to Lm 248.5 million in the same period. Employment in manufacturing rose from 18,758 to 34,476. The manufacturing sector in 1980 was still dominated by textile, clothing and leather industries which accounted for 41.9 per cent of employment in manufacturing industry (COS, 1983, p. 147) and 54.5 per cent of total domestic exports (COS, 1981, pp. xii-xiii). Grech, in his study of the textile and clothing industry (1978) noted the exaggerated dependence of the Maltese economy on this sector (by then predominantly based on garments' manufacture) and a survey by the Malta Development Corporation (MDC, 1980) confirmed Grech's findings and noted the almost absolute dependence on

> factors that lie outside Malta based control... distribution and marketing networks, sourcing of fabric and other raw materials, promotion systems, ...strategic investment and operating decisions (ibid., p. 4).

It also noted that because of

> the relatively low investment outlay by way of capital equipment... it is possible for clothing firms to base plans on payback periods of three years or less, which makes them better able... to relocate quickly following even marginal changes in cost structures (ibid.).

It is pertinent to point out that, as at the end of 1979, 62.7 per cent of the shareholding of all aided manufacturing firms was foreign-owned; 51.4 per cent was owned by nationals of, or companies incorporated in, the EC, USA and Japan (MDC, 1980, p. 12). The survey spoke of 'an awareness of the need to make the economy progressively less dependent on clothing' (ibid.).

Note however the timidity of the language used. Firstly, the text seeks to avoid the dichotomy 'national-foreign' by using the notion of 'Malta based control' as opposed to control centres based outside Malta. The authors clearly wish to distance themselves from any nationalistic opposition to foreign investment. The owner's nationality, they are saying, is irrelevant: you could, presumably have a foreign-owned firm with Malta based control and a locally-owned one controlled from abroad. Note, on this issue, the contrast with Spiteri's text of 1969. Secondly, note the limited scope of the notion of dependence. It refers to none of the problems one finds in the literature on imperialism, neo-colonialism, dependence, unequal exchange; it does not refer to the exploitative character of foreign direct investment in a low wage environment. In fact not one question in the 11-page questionnaire refers to wages paid to operators.

The national minimum wage in 1980, and the average in this sector would not have been any higher, stood at Lm 22.88 per week plus an annual state bonus equivalent to Lm 1.76,9 weekly, that is Lm 0.62 per hour in all (US$ 1.74 at the 1980 rate of exchange). Inclusive of employer's social security contribution, the labour of a girl at a sewing machine would have cost her employer Lm0.67 or US$1.89 per hour exclusive of other incidental labour expenses (public holidays, vacation leave, sick leave, bonuses, company doctor, transport etc. estimated to range between 28 and 31 per cent of direct labour costs).

The advertisement that brought, in 1982, the Mexican girl Dolores to the border town of Ciudad Juarez:

> We need female workers. Older than 17, younger than 30, single and without children, minimum education primary school, maximum education secondary school, available for all shifts (Hilsum, 1982, p. 283)

sums up the requirements (with the exception of the night shift which would not have been officially allowed) of garments' producers in Malta in the 1960s, 1970s and 1980s. Dolores, as a *maquiladora* worker, in 1982 cost her US employer US$ 2.10 per hour inclusive of fringe benefits, US$ 1.45 less than the basic hourly wage in the US and about US$ 0.35 less than what the cost of the labour of an average Maltese garments' operator for her, possibly US, employer. The maquiladora industrialization programme (see Sklair, 1993) gave US investors roughly the same advantageous conditions offered by Maltese legislation at that time. 'The idea was to alleviate unemployment in Mexico and strengthen the economy, while enabling US transnationals to maximize profits' (Hilsum, 1982). To set the cost of labour in 1980 in its correct historical perspective, it must be borne in mind that between 1974, when it was first introduced, and the end of the decade, the minimum wage was increased 9 times beginning with Lm 10.38,5 a week (bonus included) or Lm 0.26 (US$ 0.69) per hour.[10] Already in 1969, Spiteri had noted the lower than average wages paid to the predominantly female labour in textiles and, linking this to the high import content/low value added nature of this industry, argued against a further expansion of the sector (Spiteri, 1969, pp. 38-9). Another 1960s reference to low wages and 'appalling' working conditions for female labour

---

[10] For a comparative perspective note that the average national minimum wage in Mexico in 1974 and 1980 respectively was US$ 0.44 and US$ 0.74. (Sklair, 1993, p. 38).

(especially outworkers) is to be found in a confidential report on Gozo by a UN expert (Hartley, 1968, pp. 7, 9, 23).[11]

Coming back to the 1971-1987 Labour governments: clearly they were caught between the pressing need to provide a decent standard of living to the people as well as to secure the fullest possible employment on the one hand, and the need to attract export-oriented industrial investment on the other. Eventually in 1982, under pressure from a recessionary global environment, the Labour government imposed a wages and prices freeze in an attempt to halt increasing unemployment whilst braking inflation. This, together with trade restrictions designed to encourage import substitution, enabled the opposition Nationalist Party to expand its mass base amongst the petty bourgeoisie and to make important inroads in the working class with electoral promises to end the wage freeze and abolish import restrictions. This tied up with the Nationalists' declared aim of taking Malta into the EC as a full member (an Association Agreement already existed since 1970).

Irrespective of the objective advantage and disadvantages of entry, and of the real chances of being accepted, the European goal had an important political function: to an electorate tired by the hardships brought about by the 'contradictions of export-led development' (Brincat, 1989) or 'throes of dependent lumpen-development' (Vella, 1989, p. 164) or 'contradictions of labour-led capitalist development' (ibid., p. 166), this European goal promised 'development' – conceived as the ability to adopt, without restrictions, metropolitan models of consumption. This without the need for the sacrifices implied (and already experienced) by Labour's attempt to export its way to development.

The Nationalist Party too may not be satisfactorily 'explained' in terms of any ideal paradigm. The increasing attractiveness of its discourse, especially in the 1980s, to sections of social classes as diverse as large scale importers critical of import restrictions, a frustrated new petty bourgeoisie eager to emulate metropolitan models of consumption, and private sector industrial workers

---

[11] See also Miceli Farrugia (1973, pp. 18, 21) and Meerdink & Schuiling (1984).

hard pressed by the wage freeze, cannot be idealistically deduced from any set principles (whether these principles are those associated with its historical origins and development, or those of its latest incarnation as a Christian Democrat party). Rather, they can only be satisfactorily understood through a concrete analysis of a concrete historical situation. Stated principles and names of parties are not in themselves 'causes' of concrete political 'effects'. They are merely attempts to impose unity on a diversity of interests brought together as actual or potential allies in a determinate situation. The resultant unitary discourse, therefore, is an 'effect' of concrete political 'causes'; it is the result of a process of transformation of various discursive elements corresponding to the diverse interests in the 'alliance' (see Vella, 1989, p. 166).

In the same way as the Nationalist governments of the 1960s adopted the strategy worked out under Labour in the 1950s for export-led development in a context dominated by foreign private enterprise and, consequently, increasing dependence on metropolitan economic centres, the post-1987 Nationalist governments retained the same basic model. Although they stressed the importance of the tertiary sector as opposed to industry and although manufacturing in 1990 accounted for 27 per cent of GDP at factor cost as compared to 33 per cent in 1980, it is difficult to imagine how it could be run down much further without serious balance of payments problems. In fact the importance of manufacturing exports evidently follows from the fact that whereas in 1990 revenue from these amounted to Lm 314 million, those from tourism stood at Lm 157.4 million.

Moreover, decreased dependence on manufacturing as such is no sign of a drawing nearer to a state of self-sustained growth. The opposite could equally well be the case. It is interesting to note that Serracino-Inglott (1980, pp. 27-28), writing in a Nationalist front publication, proposed a shift away from industry towards services. This he proposed partially on the grounds that Maltese industry was too dependent on foreign investment and external markets, as well as and its sensitivity to the changing structure of the world economy. That services, take tourism for example, are also dependent on foreign markets, are extremely sensitive to external conditions and will inevitably become dependent on foreign investment when the Maltese economy is deregulated and liberalized, is conveniently ignored. He argues, as abstractly as did the development plans published by Labour administrations, that whatever industry is left ought to diversify into specific market niches. He also, somewhat naïvely, argues that, within the framework of 'some sort of alliance between local firms and transnational enterprises', local firms should insist upon sharing in marketing and technological decisions. Lastly, he states that self-management should be progressively introduced in industry (that the private investor may beg to differ does not seem to matter). The present Nationalist administration has also stressed the importance of attracting small to medium-sized hi-tech as opposed to large traditional industries. Although the importance of textile, garments and footwear has continued its downward trend, and although electronic components have become the single most important export item, it must be noted that:

(a) all the marks of dependence that were observed of the textile and clothing sector towards the end of the 1970s are applicable to electronic production in Malta today (in fact the nature of the product accentuates the local plants' lack of autonomy); and

(b) the dangers of such a situation are more acute because electronic production is concentrated almost completely in one wholly-owned subsidiary (the Franco-Italian SGS-Thomson, formerly SGS-Ates, set up in Malta in 1981) exporting almost exclusively to (or through) one, the Italian, market.

In 1991, the so called electrical machinery sector (actually electronic components, a sector overwhelmingly dominated by SGS-Thomson) accounted for 55.2 per cent of all manufacturing exports. This company's exports alone today represent 35 per cent of the country's domestic exports (*The Sunday Times* 18 July 1993, p. 1)! Not surprisingly, Italy is now Malta's number one trade 'partner'. The high import content of locally manufactured electronic components is reflected in the very significant imports from Italy of electronic subcomponents.

Although the Nationalist government abolished the wage freeze, allowing wages to attempt to keep up with inflation, the consequent threat to the competitivity of exports pushed the Nationalist administration to work out an incomes' policy with the fragile consensus of unions and employers, whereby statutory wage increases are tied to official forecasts of cost of living increases. The government has abandoned import substitution as a complementary industrialization policy and has abolished import controls; a levy on selected imported goods has been set up as a transitional protective measure.

This policy change however, in view of the secondary role of the local market in Labour's overall economic policy, does not invalidate our thesis that the change in government has not modified the basic development model.

Between Discourse Analysis and Political Sociology: Interpretative Problems

In earlier work, I attempted to provide an outline of the cleavages and convergencies of interest that provide the social and political setting within which industrial development has been taking place since the Second World War (for example, Vella, 1989). The promoter of dependent capitalist development, I suggested, was an alliance between working class and an emerging national 'manufacturing' bourgeoisie interested in industrialization (an alliance represented at the political level by the Labour Party). This was counter-posed to a conservative social block (represented politically by the Nationalist Party) composed of a petty bourgeois mass base and dominated by a merchant 'import' bourgeoisie, much older, more powerful and more politically experienced than the 'manufacturing' one. I compared the 'backwardness' of the Maltese social formation to that of other southern European formations and attributed it to the historical absence of a local, national industrial bourgeoisie such as had led the rest of Europe into modernity and development in the late eighteenth, nineteenth and early twentieth century. This interpretation explained well the 'hybrid', to use Germani's term, character of Labour's discourse. The Labour Party (and the working class) have been cast into a role which in nineteenth century Europe had been reserved for the progressive national bourgeoisie and its political representatives, hence the 'contradictions of Labour led capitalist development' (Vella, 1979, 1989). This explanation has been interpreted, incorrectly I think, especially in view of my critique of the essentialist epistemology of Marxist orthodoxy (Vella, 1989, chap. 3) as 'orthodox Marxist' (Sultana, 1992, p. 419), probably because it 'justifies' Labour's promotion of capitalist industrialization and therefore its deviation from the 'ideal paradigm' of socialism, and because it seems to imply that an industrial capitalist phase of development was historically necessary. I hold to the basics of my view with one important reserve. I have overestimated the role of the manufacturing bourgeoisie in much the same way as some Latin American sociologists have overrated the progressive role of the manufacturing bourgeoisie in the struggle against the reactionary landowners. Chilcote & Edelstein (1974, p. 54) have remarked that 'theories relying on the national bourgeoisie... have been betrayed by history'. The proverbial lack of entrepreneurship and the political inefficacy of Maltese industrialists in the face of objective threats to their existence *qua* industrialists, as well as the close personal union between them and importers (enabling the former to metamorphose themselves back into the latter with relative ease), lead me to a reassessment of their role.

What little local private interest there has been in industrialization, an interest articulated by Elias Zammit and the Federation of Malta Industries which he founded in 1946 was mainly oriented towards import-substitution. Later, when restrictions on imports were imposed in the 70s and 80s, some importers did invest very modestly in industry but almost all of those who half-willingly did so, set up relatively low value-added import-substituting production units intended to assemble, mix or repackage into retail quantities those products that they had previously imported in immediately retailable form. When, following the Nationalist victory of 1987, policy began to change, those who lost the advantages of protection, went back – after token complaints – to the traditional line of their family business, importation and distribution, meanwhile probably buttressed by investments in the highly speculative property sector. The generally low value of their fixed investments in import substituting industry and the generally high profitability of producing for a captive and easily monopolizable market, explain the relative painlessness (for the entrepreneur) of reverting back to commerce or moving into other non-industrial sectors.

Only very few Maltese businessmen, alone or in joint ventures with foreign interests, have ever involved themselves in export-oriented industry; moreover most of these limited themselves to a particularly dependent mode of insertion into international markets, the CMT (Cut, Make and Trim). The CMT producer typically, but not exclusively, operates in the garments sector. Market trends do not really interest him or her: in fact, one rarely knows where one's goods are being sold and at what prices. The buyer provides material and design and pays according to an agreed rate based on an estimation of time required to cut, make and trim one garment. The overwhelming bulk of exporters in industry, accounting for the overwhelming bulk of exports, have been, and still are to date, totally foreign-owned firms. This was, after all, the vision of Malta's industrial future that began to emerge in the 1950s.

Perhaps closer attention to the Latin American experience would have reduced my optimism regarding the political 'progressiveness' and the entrepreneurial elan of local manufacturers in dependent peripheral economies. Latin American sociology has shown that manufacturers were not sufficiently independent from conservative agrarian and comprador interests to enable them to promote genuine development.[12] I failed to consider the hypothesis that Maltese manufacturers were insufficiently independent from importers to play an effective political role in the country's industrialization. The truth or falsity of this hypothesis will be determined by the concrete unfolding of history in the passage from the twentieth to the twenty-first century.

References

Baldacchino, G. (1992) 'Far better to serve in heaven than to reign in hell: The logic of incorporation in the European Communities by a very small developing country: Malta, a case study', unpublished paper for an international conference at the Institute of Island Studies, Prince Edward Island, Canada, September.

Baldacchino, G. (1993) 'Bursting the bubble: The pseudo-development strategies of microstates', *Development and Change*, vol. 24, 1.

---

[12] Veliz (1965, pp. 1-8) has noted that manufacturers have been coopted by traditional landed oligarchies. Zeitlin & Ratcliff (1975) emphasised the family ties between manufacturers and agrarian interests.

Balogh, T. (1962) 'The mechanism of neo-imperialism', *Oxford University Institute of Statistics Bullettin*, vol. 24, 3.
Balogh, T. & Seers, D. (1955) *The Economic Problems of Malta: An Interim Report (to the Prime Minister)*, Malta.
Baran, P. & Hobsbawm, E. (1961) 'The stages of economic growth', *Kyklos*, vol. XIV.
Barrat-Brown, M. (1974) *The Economics of Imperialism*, Harmondsworth, Penguin.
Brincat, M. (1989) 'The possibility, limits and contradictions of export-led development: Malta under the Labour administrations 1971-1987', unpublished MSc dissertation, London School of Economics and Political Science.
Chilcote, R.H. & Edelstein, J.C. (1974) *Latin America: The Struggle with Dependency and Beyond*, New York, Schenkman.
Cardoso, F.H. & Faletto, E. (1979) *Dependency and Development in Latin America*, Berkeley, CA, University of California Press.
Frank, A.G. (1971) *Capitalism and Underdevelopment in Latin America*, Harmondsworth, Penguin.
Frank, A.G. (1975) *On Capitalist Underdevelopment*, Oxford, Oxford University Press.
Germani, G. (1965) *Politica y Sociedad en una Epoca de Transicion*, Buenos Aires.
Government Publications: Development Plans from the First 1959-1964 to the Sixth 1986-1988; annual budget speeches; annual Economic Surveys; annual Abstract of Statistics.
Grech, J.C. (1978) *Threads of Dependence*, Malta, Malta University Press.
Hartley, A.W.M. (1968) *Light Industries in Gozo*, (Restricted report by United Nations Expert for the Government of Malta), Malta, November.
Hicks, J. (1969) *A Theory of Economic History*, Oxford, Oxford University Press.
Hilsum, L., 'Uncle Sam's jobs south of the border' (*The Guardian* 19 March, 1982) in O'Donnel, M. (ed.), *New Introductory Reader in Sociology*, Walton-on-Thames, Nelson, 1988.
Impact Public Relations Ltd. (1968) *Public Relations and Promotion: Proposals in Support of the Malta Development Corporation*, Malta, January.
Knapp, J.A. (1969) 'Vers une analyse Keynesienne des sous-developpement et des points de croissance', *Le Tiers Monde*, vol. 10, 37.
Laclau, E. (1977) *Politics and Ideology in Marxist Theory*, London, New Left Books.
Lewis, A. (1955) *Theory of Economic Growth*, London, Allen & Unwin.
Malta Development Corporation, Annual Reports, 1968-1991.
Malta Development Corporation (1980) *The Maltese Clothing Industry (in) Summer 1980: A Survey*, November.
Malta Development Corporation, promotional literature, eg. *Ile de Malte: La Rentabilité Retrouvée en Europe*, June 1978 and *Malta: A Profitable Proposition*, January 1988.
Meerdink, J. & Schuiling, M. (1984) 'I never have my hands empty: Gozitan outworkers', unpublished student paper for a seminar on Women and Development at the University of Leiden, The Netherlands.
Miceli Farrugia, M. (1973) 'Industrialization in Gozo: The Xewkija Industrial Estate', unpublished BA dissertation, Royal University of Malta.
Murga, F.A. (1971) 'Dependency: A Latin American view', *NACLA Newsletter*, vol. 4, February.

O'Connor, J. (1970) 'The meaning of economic imperialism' in Rhodes, R.I. (ed.), *Imperialism and Underdevelopment: A Reader*, New York, Monthly Review Press.
Owen, R.J. & Sutcliffe R.B. (eds) (1972) *Studies in the Theory of Imperialism*, London, Longman.
Oxaal, I., Barnett T. & Booth D. (eds) (1975) *Beyond the Sociology of Development*, London, Routledge & Kegan Paul.
Partit tal-Haddiema (1993) *Statut tal-Partit*, Malta, Marsa Press.
Prebisch, R. (1959) 'Commercial policy in underdeveloped countries', *American Economic Review*, vol. 49, 5.
Robens, Lord (1967) *Report of the Joint Mission for Malta*, July.
Rostow, W.W. (1962) *Stages of Growth. A non-Communist Manifesto*, Cambridge MA, Cambridge University Press.
Roxborough, I. (1979) *Theories of Underdevelopment*, London, Macmillan.
Sacco, R. (1986) *L-Elezzjonijiet Ġenerali 1849-1986: Il-Ġrajja Politika u Kostituzzjonali ta' Malta*, Valletta, Klabb Kotba Maltin.
Santos, T. dos (1970) 'The structure of dependence', *The American Economic Review*, vol. 60, 5.
Schuster, G. & Scott, W.D. (1957) *Malta: Report of the Economic Commission*, London, HMSO.
Serracino-Inglott, P. (1980) 'An alternative future for Malta', *AZAD-Perspektiv*, 13, October-December 1980; also in *IFDA Dossier* (International Federation of Development Alternatives), July-August 1980.
Sklair, L. (1991) *Sociology of the Global System*, London, Harvester.
Sklair, L. (1993) *Assembling for Development. The Maquila Industry in Mexico and the United States*, Center for US-Mexican Studies UCSD, San Diego.
Spiteri, L. (1969) *The Development of Industry in Malta*, Joint Consultative Council/Chamber of Commerce/Federation of Malta Industries/Employers' Association, Malta.
Sultana, R.G. (1992) *Education and National Development: Historical and Critical Perspectives in Vocational Schooling in Malta*, Malta, Mireva Publications.
United Nations, Economic Commission for Latin America (1950) *The Economic Development of Latin America and its Principal Problems*, New York.
Veliz, C. (ed.) (1965) *Obstacles to Change in Latin America*, Oxford, Oxford University Press.
Vella, M. (1989) *Reflections in a Canvas Bag: Beginning Philosophy between Philosophy and History. A Critical Assessment of Peter Serracino Inglott's Beginning Philosophy and Beyond*, Malta, PEG.
Vella, M. & Sciberras, L. (1979) 'Introduzzjoni politika' in *Wara ir-Repubblika: Versi*, Malta, K3.
Woods, W. (1946) *Report on the Finances of the Government of Malta*, London, HMSO.
Zammit, E. (1949) *An Outline for Industrial Development: Lecture delivered at the Headquarters of the Federation of Malta Industries*, Malta.
Zammit, E. (1950) *In Defence of Malta Industry: Lecture delivered at the Headquarters of the Federation of Malta Industries*, Malta.
Zeitlin, M. & Ratcliff, R.E. (1975) 'Research methods for the analysis of the internal structure of dominant classes: The case of landlords and capitalists in Chile', *Latin America Research Review*, vol. 10, Fall.

4

The Visibility and Invisibility of Women

Pauline Miceli

This paper tries to map out women's presence or absence in local social systems. It will focus on their continuing invisibility at the top of power institutions while pointing out their increasing numbers as consumers of social assistance. It argues that there is a relationship between gender, power and poverty, and concludes that self empowerment and the reconstruction of gender roles could make women's visibility in the future more equitable.

Introduction

The facts to be recited are part of the evidence available on the social positions of women and men in Malta. Some data are difficult to come by, and what is published or gathered by the sources is not always broken down by sex. This presents us with limitations when mapping the presence or absence of women in certain spheres. Therefore whenever possible I checked the sources available for an indication of gender. Statistics are helpful but on their own they do not mirror reality. For an analysis of the situation I will also draw on my own experiential information gathered through direct observation and participation in the media, where for a period I produced a daily women's programme on radio (1976-80), had a weekly page in a daily newspaper (*L-Orizzont*, 1980-92) and addressed women's issues in various public fora in the hope of raising local consciousness towards the status of women.

Reference will also be made to my work *Maria-Eva* (Miceli, 1991), written specifically to give an overview of the situation of women in contemporary Malta. The women chosen to tell their own stories cover ages from 16 to 69, lead a normal life and are not publicly known. Some were sought to shed light on particular social problems or situations such as drug dependence, marriage breakdown, teenage pregnancies and coping with the demands of career, family and politics. The first person accounts are based on semi-structured interviews. Unless specified, all data quoted refers to Malta.

The Social Factor

Women make up half the population of the Maltese Islands, and appear so in general demographic profiles. Their numbers in the 'female columns' increase, decrease or disappear completely in most data. However, changes in the marital status, sex and age structure of the population point to trends which could provide us with a framework. They could lead us to establish the changing role of women in society and to find out what is keeping us back from taking up new challenges. Considering for example the percentage distribution of population by marital status, we find that 41.7% of females and 43.2% of males are single, while 48.8% of women against 53.1% of men are married. Women also make up 55.5% of all those over the age of 60. There are also nearly three widowed women to every widower (COS, 1986, p. 66).

Through the twentieth century, in Malta as in developed countries, a complex network of services and benefits has grown around the widows' pensions, home care/help and Telecare services for the elderly, where the majority of users are women (unpublished statistics from Dept. of Care for the Elderly), maternity allowances, baby health clinics and women's health services. Women are now the major consumers partly because we live longer but also because of the ways in which state support, such as the family allowance granted to housewives and the widows' pension, is designed to substitute for husband's wages, presupposing women's exclusion from the labour market.

Moreover, the number of couples filing cases for separation cannot be ignored (*The Times*, 4 June 1991 p. 4). It is worth noting that the number of separated persons benefiting from social assistance from 1983 to 1991 increased by more than a third. The great majority of claimants are women as are those who fall under the miscellaneous heading covering unmarried mothers and women who are unable to earn a living (Department of Social Security, 1993). This information, sketchy as it may seem, is indicative of the inferior status of women. Only those who have no man to support them or have no other means of supporting themselves are eligible for social assistance. This money received works out to be much less than the minimum wage. Before a separated woman is granted any assistance, the Department exercises all the powers granted to it to make an estranged husband pay the wife alimony if it were decreed by the law courts.

Thus after marriage breakdown women may become visible among the poorest in society. But this may be just the tip of the iceberg of modern poverty.

Gender and Poverty

The assumption that women are dependent on the men with whom they live, and that this protects them from the experience of poverty, together render women invisible in both government and independent studies of poverty in Britain. I find that the same assumptions underlie social policy criteria in Malta. If being poor does not simply mean not having adequate material resources but also not having opportunities for independence and self-determination, then the structure of family and gender roles will make it much more difficult for women not to be poorer than men (Glendinning & Millar, 1991, p. 30).

Separated and widowed women in Malta as in Britain, are emerging as the largest 'problem group' (*sic*). When similar patterns resulted in studies of poverty in England in the early 60s, researchers attributed the situation as

> apparently not due to sex as such, but to difference in employment experience, past and present (Townsend & Wedderburn, 1965, p. 110).

Gender differences in poverty were visible in many studies of the early 70's but generally not remarked upon. Among those researchers who do acknowledge the high incidence of poverty among women in Britain little attempt is made to explain its causes (Fiegehen et al., 1977, p. 66). Explanation is so perfunctory that it simplistically attributes women's poverty to sex – to women being women – rather than to gender, that is to the economic and social processes which are constructed upon this basic biological distinction.

Another approach is to assume that although being a woman may increase the risk of poverty, in many instances being a woman actually decreases that risk: single women are poor because they do not have access to men's resources, but married women are apparently not poor because they do. For example Layard et al. (1978, p. 24) explain that low pay and household poverty are not correlated:

> the reason is of course that most of those on low hourly wages are married women, and married women are not usually poor.

The widespread failure to recognize the relationship between gender and poverty stems from the near universal use of aggregate living units as the basis on which information is collected and analysed. Aggregate units are defined as 'families', 'assessment units', 'tax units', or 'households'. Studies (for example National Censuses and Budgetary Surveys) using an aggregate rather than an individual basis obscure the particular circumstances of women in several ways. Women are not counted among the poor in Malta if household resources amount to more than those which make a person eligible for social assistance. A capital resources test and a weekly resources test[1] make up what is usually referred to as

---

[1] These tests refer to the total capital available as resources. By capital is meant not only liquid capital (money) but also includes property etc.

the means test: capital resources for a single person should not exceed Lm4,000 and for a married couple Lm7,000; the house of residence and the car are excluded. Weekly resources should not exceed the social assistance benefit one is claiming (Deparment of Social Security, 1993).

It is also assumed that there is a degree of equality in the distribution of resources within households. As a result no regard is paid to the dynamics of power and command over resources which are known to take place within households, especially in households which women share with male partners and/or children. In reality, the patriarchal structuring of conjugal relationships means that, within the household, men are likely to exercise greater control over whatever resources come into the household. For example, it is common in England, even in households where income is very limited, for men to retain some money for their own personal use, whether that is spent on alcohol, tobacco, or more expensive hobbies (Townsend, 1979; Graham, 1987).

Sibyl O'Reilly Mizzi who studied urban working-class women in Malta interprets her findings differently. She found that more than 50% of the women in all age categories interviewed for the study, were in charge of the family finances. Men keep an allowance to spend as they please, but after that all the family financial decisions regarding day-to-day running are made by the women (O'Reilly Mizzi, 1983, p. 201). Little evidence is available so far as to how women use any earnings or other sources of income of their own. My impression is that any extra money is much likely to be used for the benefit of other members of the household – on children's clothes, family holidays, redecorating or new furniture, for example.

Thus the aggregate base of all research has not only rendered women's poverty invisible; it has also feminized poverty by shifting indigence more squarely onto women's shoulders. Feminist researchers call for the reconstructing of research and social policy. They argue that only if women are also relieved of their present high levels of responsibility for domestic and caring work within the home can they have any chance of participating 'equally' in the labour market (Glendinning & Millar, 1991, p. 34). What is therefore needed is a simultaneous challenge to the conventional sexual division of labour within the home and in the labour market.

It is well recognized that the contemporary urban family/ household is constructed around a division of labour that defines certain kinds of work as domestic, unpaid and usually women's and other kinds as public, paid and usually men's. Women spend far more time on activities to maximize the benefits of their income through efficient consumption (shopping around, making rather than buying clothes) and other domestic tasks. Women are tied to places of consumption or care; homes, grocers, bazaars, household goods stores, open markets, vegetable trucks. They can be seen waiting outside school gates and doctrine classes, at the doctor's, school meetings, in religious and cultural segregated groups, visiting old relatives with their men waiting sheepishly out in the corridors. Yet again this time and effort spent for the conservation of resources is not given the amount of attention it deserves (O'Reilly Mizzi, 1981, p. 207).

Fertility and Paid Employment

Other important information relevant to our topic is the decline in fertility. One can observe that the Crude Birth Rate, which stood at 33 per thousand population in 1950 had dropped by over a fifth during the following decade. It came down to 16.3 by 1970 and retained this level since then. This is comparable to those of other European countries. Other information suggests that women are postponing child-bearing during the first years of marriage (COS, 1986, p. 17). This corresponds to more recent findings in relation to women's maternity and participation in paid employment in industry. Women make up only 30% of the total workforce. Within the 22-year-old age cohort, almost six out of every nine Maltese women are gainfully employed in full-time jobs. But the ratio drops sharply to just one in full-time employment out of nine when one considers the 30-year-old age cohort. Less than 3% of the total number of full-time employees working at industrial estates are mothers of children up to three years of age (W.P.D.C., 1992, p. 5).

So women seem to disappear from public life and the workplace to stay home raising children while men are busy consolidating their careers and promoting themselves to higher status positions. Childrearing is itself work and looms large in the sexual division of labour as a whole. The women workers interviewed for the previously-mentioned survey were in favour of having childcare centres for children below school-age irrespective of whether they considered giving up their job to stay home or not. More than half of the women said they wished the nurseries to be set up in their town or village and not close to their respective factory (W.P.D.C., 1992, p. 7). Meanwhile, the fewer the number of children the less the years a mother feels her full-time presence in the home is needed. Indeed there are indications that more married women with grown-up children are venturing out again into the workforce and public sphere even if this only means a few hours of voluntary work.

Education

Women's perception of themselves depends substantially on their level of education. Nevertheless educating women has always been regarded as essential for the family to better its standard of living. Education holds another pay off for women. It has helped change attitudes towards work and career after marriage. Despite the fact that more women than men are illiterate (COS, 1986, p. 80), the number of women attending university has steadily increased to almost 50% of the total student population (University of Malta, Students Information, Feb. 1993). However, women still outnumber men considerably in the fields of Education and Nursing, but are becoming more visible in Science, Medicine, Laws and Commerce. Theology remains a male domain. Parents seem to be encouraging daughters to further their studies and girls are taking up new challenges despite the sexism that is still rife in locally produced school textbooks (K.Għ.A.M., 1989).

However, teenage girls are less likely to proceed to higher education on reaching school-leaving age. They leave school to seek jobs. Half the women working full-time in the various factories spread over Malta's industrial estates are under 24 years of age. Women outnumber men in most enterprises operating from industrial estates. Yet it is women who occupy, almost without exception, the lowest jobs in the work hierarchy and secretarial posts. In contrast, men are spread more evenly along all the levels of the organization and continue to enjoy a near monopoly of posts at the managerial and supervisory levels (W.P.D.C., 1992, p. 6). The young factory girl I interviewed gives us an account of her schooling, her work and aspirations and provides us with the modern version of the old stereotype (Miceli, 1991, p. 14). Many young women still see marriage as their only future, with a few years of paid employment to help them save enough money to buy and furnish their dream house. Whether their dream is realized or not is another matter as other women in the same collection of stories recount.

The subject of women's participation in the labour market has been addressed by Darmanin (1992) among others. Information about women in part-time employment is difficult to gather partly because many do it illegally. The labour market constructed by capitalist industry and the state offers some low paid, low status, part-time jobs, and curiously enough most of the people recruited to these part-time jobs are women. Several schemes addressed mainly to women – involving clerical work and care of the elderly – were only recently introduced in Malta. This pattern of recruitment is justified by employers on the ground that married women only want part-time work because of their domestic responsibilities and only need low pay because theirs is a 'second-wage'. On the other hand, women have a heavier work-load at home, and this too is justified by husbands who state that this is so because the wives can only get part-time jobs (Connell, 1987, p. 135).

Therefore, in statistics, women are visible as those who on the whole attain a lower level of education, work in low status jobs for a number of years, get married, leave their jobs to raise children, are widowed and live longer on social security or assistance depending on the financial contributions of their husband. This suggests that women's status in Malta as elsewhere remains defined by their family functions, both actual and supposed, in a way that does not hold for men (Oakley, 1981, p. 297).

Power Structures

All political parties in Malta have, during these last years, committed themselves to women's equality. This is seen in their speeches and political manifestos of the last two elections. Amendments to the Civil Code to bring equality between the husband and wife in marriage have also recently been introduced. The husband is now no longer the head of the family with absolute authority over wife and children whom he had a duty to provide for and protect.

This old concept of patriarchal rule unfortunately prevails in the general mentality and law updating alone will not in itself empower women to make themselves visible in decision making positions. Despite the fact that the right to vote has been established since 1947, the year that Malta obtained self-government, and there is extensive participation in grass roots politics evident mostly in the months before general elections, women are nearly completely absent from the positions where policies are made, where real power resides. During the 1992 general elections, only one woman was elected to parliament out of a total of 238 men and 8 women who contested for the 65 seats. Our law courts boast of only one woman magistrate and other token women hold positions of power in trade unions, the business sector and executive boards.

Women are traditionally known to do volunteer work and it comes as a surprise to find that they are almost absent in official bodies. A look at the Directory of Voluntary Service Organizations, reveals that out of the 84 voluntary social organizations covering the needs of the elderly, the poor, the handicapped, alcoholics, battered women, and single mothers among others, only 26 women are listed as officials in the organizing body (Caritas, 1990). The general rule in Malta as elsewhere seems to be that where power is, there women are not.

Politics is an essential part of social life and a widespread one. A popular interpretation of women's absence from higher levels of politics is insufficient masculinization (Jacquette, 1974, p. xviii). Jacquette argues that if women were more like men (were more informed, had greater feelings of efficiency, were more involved in the real world) then the problem of female deviance from male norms of participation would be solved. According to this view, discrimination against women lies with women themselves. The general secretaries of the two main political parties I interviewed for this paper, seem to think likewise. They say that 'good' women do not come forward, that the situation of under representation will not change unless the women themselves decide to participate. They concede to the fact that family commitments are the greatest obstacles for women to enter politics. When asked about their own full time involvement, they admit that it occupies more than just a normal day's work. The wives shoulder the remaining responsibilities of home and children. They fear that women do not want to give up their full commitment to the family and are consequently blamed for staying out of politics. In her study of women living in Senglea, O'Reilly Mizzi found that men and women still operated in separate spheres and husband and wife had little interaction between them. Women do not encourage their husbands to help because they have strong feelings that the home and household is their responsibility, and that any encroachment would lessen their worth within the family (O'Reilly Mizzi, 1981, p. 88).

I tend to agree with O'Reilly Mizzi. Women do appear to be the main objectors for change. Witness how almost every public debate about women's rights provokes emotional arguments. Since women have been made to believe that their seat of power is in the home, they rightly feel threatened of losing control. Because power is control. It is a way of being, having and doing to the fullest extent. Power is also purpose. Its denial is annihilation. This is a human, not a gender based need. Therefore, one cannot expect women to give up their traditional power base if they themselves are not empowered to bring about change. Men will not give up any of the power which they hold in the public sphere as long as they keep thinking that sharing responsibility in the home means losing self-empowerment. In actual fact few women hold positions of power in the workplace. Moreover, it is interesting to note that married women tend to protect male authority – thus conforming to the patriarchal pattern of power – when in reality it is the women who control the household (O'Reilly Mizzi, 1981, p. 123). The same pattern reappears in a long series of sociological studies on families in different countries, together with the ideologies of masculine authority that support it (Connell, 1987, p. 122).

But the family as an institution might best be regarded now as the periphery rather than the core complex of power structures. We must distinguish the global or macro-relationship of power – where women are subordinated to men in society as a whole – from the local or micro-situation, that is, in particular households, particular workplaces, particular settings.

Given this scenario, combining the role of mother, homemaker and politician requires superhuman qualities and superwomen simply do not exist. There are no supermen either. Maltese women who have made it in politics are either single or enjoy massive support (Bestler, 1991). Agatha Barbara, the first woman to serve in parliament ever since women won the right to vote in 1947, and who was successful in all the elections until 1981, after which she was appointed President of Malta, expressed her belief – when interviewed by the present author – that the demands of politics and the family cannot be reconciled; therefore a woman has to choose between a family and a career in politics. Giovanna Debono, who stood for, and was elected in, the last two elections (1987, 1992) is a mother of two young children. She speaks of a great deal of support from her husband and her own family. But for a career woman who is also the breadwinner, and a mother of young children, politics become almost impossible. In the book *Maria-Eva* (Miceli, 1991, p. 115), Antoinette speaks about her experience of contesting two general elections unsuccessfully. She remains caught in a dilemma. She feels that problems cropping up in the family are essentially political and urge her to want to participate actively, but then, the demands of her profession, her family and politics are tiring her out so much that she's always thinking of quitting.

Political parties have at last realized that women can no longer be left out of decision-making structures. Carmen Sant, elected to parliament in 1987, was one who constantly spoke about the importance of introducing positive discrimination for women to encourage them to enter politics. (CIMIRA, 1989, p. 53) The *Alternattiva Demokratika* endorsed the quota system in its 1992 electoral manifesto. In its annual general meeting the Malta Labour Party amended its statute to stipulate that 20% of the delegates in its general conference should be women (*Rapport Konferenza Ġenerali, 1993*, p. 152). The Nationalist Party in government is allowing for a 20% representation of women in local councils.

However, power and political leadership are not confined to the public sphere. It would be misleading to say that women have not gained anything during these last decades even if our number in parliament has dwindled to one. Bright and ambitious women are making careers for themselves in law, medicine, banking and business. They are, as yet, few in number but they are the ones who will provide new models for other women, not least their own daughters.

The Church

When one considers that the vast majority of husbands and wives go to church regularly (Tabone, 1987, p. 217), that almost all children attend doctrine classes and sit through religion lessons and participate in religious activities in school, one cannot ignore the church's influence on the family and its teaching about the sexual division of labour. Christianity inherits from its historical past a fundamental contradiction in its views and treatment of one half of humanity, women. On the one hand, it teaches that all human beings, regardless of gender, class or ethnicity, are created by God and saved by Christ. In other words, salvation knows no distinction between human beings. On the other hand, Christian understanding of the nature of being, both of God and Christ and of humanity, has been cast in male generic terms. This has been used to subordinate women, both as members of humanity and as persons capable of exercising authority and representing God and Christ. Hence, the exclusion of women from ordained ministry, and indeed from all public leadership (Radford Ruether, 1991).

Also, women are presented with the model of the Virgin Mary to identify with; that of being silent, discreet and subordinate, always saying yes, the myth of the prototype of the eternal feminine which women have ceased to identify with (Lucchetti Bingemer, 1991). The messages received are those that women's place is in the home, dependent on and submissive to men.

It is not surprising that women feel that their life is their family and that they never thought about what they could do if they had not got married (Miceli, 1991, p. 57). Neither have they thought why maternal love is indispensable while paternal love is not. Or why many feel that love for home has an overriding powerful value and that women should dedicate themselves to the home and the family (Vassallo, 1983).

The Catholic magisterium now concedes to women the new arena of civil equality. This means that it also changes its previous teaching that women are unequal in nature to men. It declares itself to have 'always taught' that women are equal (Pastoral Letter, August 1991). But the Catholic Church has declared itself to be against the ordination of women priests and so women will remain invisible in the Church's hierarchy of power. Not one single nun let alone a lay woman occupies any of the numerous offices of the Curia (*Malta Year Book*, 1989).

Empowerment

Small children learn effortlessly about masculine power within the asymmetrical nuclear family. Father leaves the house each day as the family's representative in the public world and returns with proof, money, of the valuation of his labour. His status in the household and in society is clearly different from that of mother. In fact and paradoxically, dominance and nurturance are the two adult qualities that are most likely to make children identify with their parents (Bandura & Huston, 1981).

It is clearly demonstrable that high-achieving women come from backgrounds where in the course of growing up they learn that they can be strong, competent and successful – in a word, powerful – rather than the reverse. The family traits include a mother who is out of tune with domestic work and the conventional image of motherhood and a father who is emotionally warm, but seriously committed to his daughter's future in her own right. In her research regarding women of power, Rosalind Miles (1985) found that 40% of the mothers of these feminine achievers did not work, therefore suggesting that paid employment of the mother is not the key. She contends that more important was the mother's unconventional self-image, that is one that rejects the traditional wife and motherhood role. High achieving women, axiomatically, do not perceive themselves as full-time home-makers, and they learn this from their mothers.

Conclusion

Women's visibility or invisibility is a result of the interplay between structures in the family and the public sphere. While wage and career affect domestic power, domestic power affects the definition of the division of labour. In the public sphere, the power of men and the authority of masculinity are relatively concentrated. This pattern of power is more diffused or contested in the home.

For an equitable distribution of power, Connell (1987) suggests the reconstruction of household and sexual relationships based on thorough-going equality. This involves
(a) finding ways of equalizing economic resources and decision-making power;
(b) reconstructing relations between children and adults in the

teeth of the vast array of institutional and cultural arrangements that presuppose all early childcare is done by women; and

(c) re-working the sexual character and sexuality, emphasising the generation of energy, joys of being with children and pleasures of love between equals. Connell suggests the creation of 'liberated zones' – social spaces where a degree of sex equality has been achieved. These will provide the bases for politics of a wider scope.

Majorities matter if the process of social change is to come under conscious human control. Women will show up more at the poverty end of the spectrum if they continue to remain invisible at decision-making levels. But structures cannot be levered into new shapes without mutations of grassroot practice. And majorities do not fall from heaven. They have to be constructed around a radical programme of equality, a process where everyone has the political will to do so. This is not about abolishing gender but restructuring it.

References

Allen, S., Purcell, K., Waton, A., & Wood, S.(eds) (1985) *The Experience of Unemployment*, London, Macmillan.

Bandura, A. & Huston, A.C., (1981) 'Identification as a process of incidental learning' *Journal of Abnormal and Social Psychology*, vol. 63.

Bestler, A. (1991) 'Political participation of women in Malta' in Reimann, H. (ed.) Research on Malta: A German Perspective, *ABAKUS*, 13, Augsburg.

Central Office of Statistics, (1986) *Census '85 Vol. 1, A Demographic Review of Malta and Gozo*, Malta, Government Press.

CIMIRA (1989) *Women Mean Business* (mimeo).

Connell, R.W., (1987) *Gender and Power*, Stanford, CA, Stanford University Press.

Caritas (1990) *Direttorju tas-Servizzi Soċjali Volontarji ta' Malta*, CARITAS, Malta, Veritas Press.

Darmanin, M. (1992) 'The labour market of schooling: Maltese girls in education and economic planning', *Gender and Education*, vol. 4, 1.

Fiegehen, G., Lansley, P.S. & Smith, A.D. (1977) *Poverty and Progress in Britain 1953-1973*, Cambridge, Cambridge University Press.

Glendinning, C. & Millar, J. (1991) 'Poverty: the forgotten Englishwoman,' in Maclean M. & Groves, D.(eds) *Women's Issues in Social Policy*, London, Routledge.

Graham, H. (1987) 'Women's poverty and caring,' in Glendinning, C. & Millar, J. (eds) *Women and Poverty in Britain*, Brighton, Wheatsheaf Books.

Jacquette, J.S. (1974) *Introduction: Women in American Politics*, New York, Wiley International.
Kummissjoni għall-Avvanz tal-Mara (1989) *Studju fil-Qosor ta' Kotba Wżati fl-Iskejjel Primarji*, mimeo.
Layard, R., Piachaud, D. & Stewart, M. (1978) *The Causes of Poverty: Royal Commission on the Distribution of Income and Wealth*, Background Paper no. 5, London, HMSO.
Lucchetti Bingemer, M.C. (1991) 'Time and eternity: the eternal woman and the feminine face of God,' in Carr, A. & Schussler Fiorenza, E. (eds) *The Special Nature of Women?* London, SCM Press Ltd.
Malta Labour Party (1993) *Konferenza Ġenerali 1993*, Malta, Marsa Press.
Miceli, P. (1991) *Maria-Eva*, Malta, Sensiela Kotba Soċjalisti.
Miles, R. (1985) *Women and Power*, Great Britain, Futura Publications.
Oakley, A. (1981) *Subject Woman*, Great Britain, Fontana.
O'Reilly Mizzi, S. (1981) *Women in Senglea: The Changing Role of Urban Working-Class Women in Malta*, Ann Arbor, MI, University Microfilms International.
Pastoral Letter of the Bishops issued on the feast of *Santa Marija* (1991), Curia, August.
Radford Ruether, R. (1991) 'Women's difference and equal rights in the church,' in Carr, A. & Schussler Fiorenza, E. (eds) *The Special Nature of Women?* London, SCM Press Ltd.
Tabone, C. (1987) *The Secularization of the Family in Changing Malta*, , Malta, Dominican Publications.
Townsend, P. (1979) *Poverty in the United Kingdom*, Harmondsworth, Penguin.
Townsend, P. & Wedderburn, D. (1965) *The Aged in the Welfare State*, London, Bell.
Vassallo, M. (1983) *Report of the Pastoral Research Board Caritas on a Survey on the Family in Malta*.
Workers' Participation Development Centre (1992) *Women Workers in Industrial Estates: A Survey on their Needs and Facilities: A Report*, Malta, WPDC for The Commission for the Advancement of Women.

5

Maltese Political Parties and Political Modernization

Godfrey A. Pirotta

Introduction

Until fairly recently, political parties, in Europe as in Malta, have been the principal vehicles for political action. Through their activities and organization, they have provided the means by which popular interest and participation in politics could be achieved (Lane & Ersson, 1991, p. 102; Birch, 1970, p. 111). Various factors – in particular the widespread rise of professionally organized and managed pressure and lobbying groups – have led recently to a decline in the strength and influence of political parties. This is not to say that parties are no longer important to the politics of democratic societies for in the final analysis it is parties that govern; but merely to highlight the fact that, today, other secondary associations also play an important political role and are legitimate power-brokers and agenda setters in their own right. Nonetheless, as Blondel (1978, p. 1) has observed, political parties are still the principal means by which democracy, or at least a large measure of it, is maintained in modern politics and by which democracy from below and leadership from above can blend in our complex and changing world. Nor should one ignore the fact that it was political parties that gave practical expression and meaning to such commonly used concepts as choice and competition, rights and political equality, free association and political participation, representation and accountability.

Since their inception in Malta over one hundred years ago, political parties have come to exercise enormous hold and influence over the Maltese electorate. Every five years or so, during general elections, over ninety percent of those entitled to vote, although under no legal compulsion to do so, turn out to cast their vote in favour of one of the contending parties and its candidates. On election day, cloistered nuns have been known to abandon the seclusion of their convents to join with other voters at the polls. Other voters, sometimes only a few days from the grave, can also be seen being ferried, frequently of their own volition, from their sick beds to some polling station in order that they too may register a preference. Furthermore, tens of thousands of Maltese tend to flock to political meetings at which party leaders are usually the main speakers.

Existing hard evidence, small as this evidence is, indicates that, in Malta, voters and parties tend to be united by a rather strong bond. A survey of voters carried out in 1984 found, for example, that 55% of those questioned tended to see themselves as being close to a political party. In contrast, the percentage for Europe was only 39% (Gallup, 1984). This observation was subsequently confirmed by Abela in his sociological study of value transmission in Malta (Abela, 1991, p. 196). The author also found that the intensity of the Maltese sense of belonging to political parties was much greater than that for Europe. In contrast to Malta, the large majority of European respondents were found to be either fairly close to (31%), or merely sympathizers of (51%), political parties. Tabone, in his study of the Maltese family, found, for example, that 42% of the families interviewed had at least one member who was a card carrying member of a political party; that almost 72% buy a political newspaper (44% every day, 10% every Sunday, and 18% occasionally); and that 46% attend political meetings or other political manifestations (Tabone, 1987, pp. 144-5). But even more significant is the fact that just over 30% of the families interviewed openly admitted their readiness to obey their preferred political party always and in everything. This finding seems to emphasize the great loyalty which parties enjoy among a large strata of Maltese society – even, that is, when their instructions and directives go against the citizens' personal interests and opinions, or against the customs and traditions of Maltese society.

Indicators of Change

There are signs, however, that seem to suggest that the voter-party relationship is beginning to change. Baldacchino (1989) has argued, for example, that a degree of political de-freezing or re-structuring in traditional party loyalties has been witnessed in several West European states during the last decade or so. He attributes this process of realignment to the presence of an increasingly better-educated and affluent electorate which is beginning to give rise to a new political culture and which is now exerting new pressures on existing political structures. Such a shift may also be taking place in Malta and may be already influencing the political party environment. This thesis seems to enjoy, at least *prima facie*, some support from the result of the 1992 General Election which, for the first time in decades, saw one of the major parties – the Nationalist Party (PN) – gain a five percentage point lead over its post-war rival, the Malta Labour Party (MLP). Until recently the typical difference in votes which separated the two parties was a mere two per cent (Schiavone, 1992).

The ongoing controversy over the issue of political party participation in elections for local Councils, which were introduced in Malta for the first time in 1993, may also be taken as an indicator of change. A voter survey held over the issue of local Councils found, among other things, that 59% of those questioned wished to see political parties either barred from contesting local elections or voluntarily refraining from fielding candidates (MISCO, 1993). Only 21% 'agreed strongly' that parties should take part in the contest. 'A plague on both your houses' was how a Sunday newspaper interpreted the results of this survey (*The Malta Independent*, 9 May 1993). While its title may tend to exaggerate the growing divide between voters and parties, it does seem to express voter frustration at the way both major parties have, over the years, sought to monopolize every activity or project at the expense of individual citizen participation. Nonetheless, the findings of the survey seemed representative enough of voter opinion to induce the Malta Labour Party to refrain from nominating candidates for these elections (*L-Orizzont*, 12 June 1993). The results of the elections for the first twelve (out of sixty-seven) proposed Councils, held in November 1993, did partially vindicate the survey's findings. For while it is true that the Nationalist Party did gain an overall majority of Council seats, the overall majority of the votes cast were won by the independent candidates. Furthermore, 38% of those entitled to vote, despite the urging and the solicitations, stayed at home, while 9% of those who actually voted invalidated their votes (*The Sunday Times*, 21 November 1993).[1]

Further evidence of growing disenchantment with political parties, especially among young people and the more articulate of the population, may be discerned from the growing number of letters and articles in the Maltese press which seem to conclude that parties are somehow bad or harmful to Maltese society. One reason for this stems from the acute levels of polarization that have characterized Maltese politics for the best part of this century but which have been made worse by the way party competition was conducted during the 1980s. Another reason which might have served to strengthen this view may centre on the failure of both major parties, especially when in office, to discipline ministers and other party officials whenever alleged irregularities, sometimes of a very serious nature, are brought to light. In the view of many voters, this state of affairs contrasts sharply with that

---

[1] The Hunters & Trappers Association urged members to boycott council elections in protest against the way in which Government was allegedly giving in to pressure from the environmental lobby.

found in Europe and in nearby Italy where the *'tangenti'* affair – a term which has now been absorbed into daily Maltese linguistic usage – has resulted in the investigation, arrest, removal from office and/or imprisonment of several senior politicians, party officials and distinguished businessmen.

Nonetheless, it would be premature to try to infer from the above discussion that Maltese political parties are facing a crisis equal in scale to that being experienced by parties in Europe. Baldacchino (1989) may in fact be right in his assessment that, in Malta, similar developments lag behind those in Europe both in time and in momentum. But it is also true that political parties in Malta are no longer the sole political agenda setters and the number of instances when parties have had issues forced upon them, as in the case of environment-related issues, have increased.

The Argument

The future of Maltese political parties is not, however, the subject of this essay. Rather its concern is, in a sense, with their past. For parties do not exist in a vacuum and they are as much a product of Maltese society as the latter is a product of their vision and their activities. This paper, however, cannot on its own fill the void that exists in this sphere or indeed in the entire field of Maltese political sociology. What it seeks to do is to try and stimulate enough interest and debate in the hope that other studies will follow. It aims to do this by exploring, albeit in a general manner, the role played by Maltese political parties as agents of political modernization. This is an area of study which, like several others, has so far been neglected but which requires examination if we are to come to a better understanding of Maltese society.

The argument suggests that it was the pursuit of political modernization by different sets of Maltese élites that prompted the rise of Maltese political parties after 1880 and that it was this goal which conditioned both their development and their politics in later years. Therefore, the perspective which I offer below suggests that what mainly divided and set each group of local élites against each other, thereby giving rise to parties, was not a question of language but how each group defined the values and goals of political modernization and the strategies required to secure their interests and attain power.

This is not to say that language played no part but that language was not the *raison d'être* that gave meaning to local parties. Language was a banner which helped, for a time, to identify the respective emphasis of each élite group and the interests which each represented. It was as much a rallying factor as a means by which respective élite interests could be protected or promoted. The exaggerated attention which the language question has received from academics and non-academics has served, in the view of the author, principally to obscure rather than to explain the rise, role and impact that Maltese political parties have had on the entire social, economic and political environment of Malta. Even Frendo's (1979) excellent study of the issue does not adequately resolve some of the dilemmas which such a singular focus on the language question raises. For example, it does not quite explain why one set of élites should make the Italian language, instead of the Maltese, their basis for nationalism to the opposition of English, the language of the colonizer. After all, it has always been accepted that Maltese and not Italian was the language of those who identified themselves as Maltese. Furthermore, research does tend to stress that, in Malta, irredentist sentiments played a truly insignificant part.

In contrast, the perspective which I propose will allow the integration of a number of issues into the discussion, including the questions of race and colonial government. Space, of course, does not permit an indulgence in detail; but it is hoped nevertheless that the discussion will suffice to stimulate wider debate among interested academics.

The Characteristics of Modernity

Political modernization may be defined as the process by which traditional societies are induced to relinquish old authority structures and time-honoured customs and styles of life in order to achieve modernity. It is a process which, among other things, involves a political commitment to raise, to western standards, the social condition of the people, in terms of education, housing and health, to extend political participation, and to replace existing traditional authority systems through the development of key political institutions and conflict-resolving mechanisms, such as political parties, representative assemblies, impartial judiciaries, universal suffrage and secret ballots, capable of supporting participatory decision-making (Welch, 1971). It involves also the gradual diffusion of a political culture which places special emphasis on individual freedom, individual rights, political and legal equality, consent, choice, political tolerance, accountability and secularization (Apter, 1965).

All this is necessary because in a modernized society power is not the prerogative of one individual or one exclusive group, nor is it divinely-sanctioned. Power cannot be absolute for individuals enjoy certain inalienable rights which the state must guarantee and which allows individuals to exercise these rights free from government control or intervention. Rights, to be truly so, must belong to everyone without exception and the state must ensure that no individual or group of individuals are hindered or obstructed in the enjoyment of their rights, either through its own measures or those of other individuals or institutions. Where inalienable individual rights are concerned majority views cannot hold merely because they are the view of the majority. When individual, civic rights are thus respected, citizens are said to enjoy political and legal equality.

This also implies that a modernized society is a secular society. This is not, however, to be understood in the sense that religion has no place in the life of, or social significance for, individual members of society. Rather, religious leaders are not expected to wield political power and no single religious creed is allowed to dominate policy-making institutions thereby leading to discrimination against adherents of other, probably minority, religions or against non-believers. Religious authorities, of whatever denomination, are free to promote their religion, to conduct services and to speak freely on any issue; but they must do this mindful of the fact that others may – and have the right to – fundamentally disagree with their point of view and that the State has an obligation to protect and guarantee the rights of all its individual members. A modern secular society, therefore, is one which is normally characterized by mutual respect, social, religious and political tolerance, and the absence of political violence of any sort.

In a modernized political system, there is also nothing hereditary or permanent about political power. All government is said to rest, in the first instance, on the consent of the people. Power, therefore, is regarded as a trust. Those in whose hands it is vested are not only to be held accountable for its (ab)use but are also liable to be removed. Governments can be opposed legitimately and their measures and performance openly and publicly criticized. Furthermore, since the people have the right to remove and replace a government, in modern political systems people are also said to have choice. The latter finds its expression in the periodic election of representatives to Parliament, when candidates, normally sponsored or under the umbrella of a political party, compete for votes. The more the candidates and parties that take part in the electoral competition, the greater the choice enjoyed by the voters. Thus, in modernized political systems, the capture or retention of political power depends, by and large, on the ability of individual political parties to harness popular support at the polls on the basis of democratic competition, i.e. free, fair and open elections. It is for this reason that in so-called modern societies political parties are often seen as enshrining 'the competitive spirit' (Smith, 1972, p. 48) of these societies and Duverger was probably right in his conclusion that,

> on the whole, the development of political parties seems bound up with that of democracy' (Duverger, 1955, p. xx).

These then are the characteristics of what is held to be a modern political system and the process which must be travelled in order to attain it is known as political modernization. The emphasis here is on the notion of a process. This implies that a society cannot achieve modernity overnight but that there are stages, not necessarily time-defined, through which a modernizing society has to progress.

One may argue, rightly in my view, that what has been presented above amounts to a rather particularly ethnocentric view of political development for the latter has been fully equated with the process of development in the West. There are two points which I would like to raise in my defence. First, that the Western model of political development has come in for some strong criticism in the sense that modernization does not necessarily lead to economic growth and an equal distribution of social benefits.

Despite this, it remains the dominant model of political modernization. More so, since the collapse of the Soviet Union and its empire in Eastern Europe which has also rendered redundant (at least as far as popular opinion is concerned) Marxist alternatives to Western models of development. Furthermore, the Western model depends greatly on its doctrine of human rights which holds that these rights are universal and the very fact that most nations subscribe, at least in theory, to this doctrine enhances the dominant status enjoyed by this model.

The Maltese Identity

My second defence relates entirely to the case of Malta. Granted that the adopted model of political development is ethnocentric, given its overt Western origins, I submit that rather than creating problems for our analysis it is highly relevant. This is because the goals and values of Western society have nearly always been the goals and values of Maltese society and of its élites. European colonization has, of course, played an important part in this, allowing for certain integrative mechanisms – such as settlement, inter-marriage and imitation – to strike deep roots in Malta. Religion has both aided and abetted this integrative process for it served to place Malta on the European side of the religious, and geographical, divide between Christianity and Islam. Christianity has, after all, been one of the hallmarks or characteristics of all that defines Europe. Today, Maltese of all ages do not merely identify with most of what is European, be it culture, fashion or sport, as some non-Europeans do also; they also see themselves as Europeans. Perhaps more than ever before, their focus is strongly Europe-oriented.

Nonetheless, Malta's geographic location on the extreme periphery of Europe and the distinctly arab-based language of the inhabitants did not always readily lead to an outright endorsement of this view by the European powers that have colonized the islands. Not infrequently, therefore, Maltese claims to a European identity have been challenged though not quite fully rejected. The Order of St. John, for instance, whose members were recruited from the ranks of Europe's nobility and which ruled Malta from 1530 to 1798, consistently refused to allow members of Maltese noble families to join its ranks or to contemplate the setting up of a Maltese branch or langue. It did not, however, bar Maltese from joining its ecclesiastic community. The Maltese were, after all, Catholics. We also find, in this period of Maltese history, episodes in which the racial animosity displayed by some members of the Order of St John towards the Maltese was of such intensity that, quite often, the two communities found themselves on the brink of violent confrontation (e.g. Ryan, 1930, pp. 113-5).

The issue of Maltese racial identity also played a part – at times an important part – during the period of British rule. It was, for example, an issue which, for a time, served to obstruct schemes for Maltese migration to the British Dominions, such as Australia, which then favoured a 'Whites' only immigration policy (Attard, 1983, p. 46; Yorke, 1990). It also served to influence the ebb and flow that characterized Maltese political development in this period although, in the case of Malta, political and constitutional development was further complicated by the fact that the island was an important strategic British fortress. But the racial issue was never far from the surface, especially in the 19th century when it featured openly in official correspondence and internal colonial office minutes.[2] Indeed, the way colonial officials, governors or visiting Commissioners viewed the Maltese tended to have some bearing on how Maltese political affairs were conducted.

The evidence for this is well documented; for this reason, one solid example should suffice. It has often been noted by students of Maltese history that, in contrast with other crown colonies, a number of Maltese civil servants were already holding the office of Head of Department by the late 1830s and that by the 1920s nearly all such offices were in Maltese hands (e.g. Lee, 1972). Few have, however, commented on the fact that one of the principal arguments which had secured this reform was intimately concerned with the question of Maltese racial identity. 'The Maltese' John Austin and G.C. Lewis had reported, in support of their recommendation to have executive offices in the Maltese civil service opened to Maltese officers,

---

[2] For a thorough discussion and examples of this aspect see Pirotta (1991).

are an European and Christian community, and far superior in institutions, manners, science and arts to the most advanced of the Asiatic nations (Austin & Lewis, 1838).

While this appraisal did help to persuade British colonial officials to adopt and implement the proposed reform, one should note that the comparison resorted to by the Commissioners was not to Italy or some other European community but to the most advanced of the *Asiatic* nations. Relations between the local community and British officers serving in Malta were, it seems, at times complicated by the issue of race to the extent that the racial identity of the Maltese, not infrequently and under different guises, gave rise to public debate (Pirotta, 1991, Chapter 6).

There is evidence that strongly suggests that the issue of racial identity has left a lasting impression on the Maltese and that, even after independence, Maltese political thinking has remained conditioned by the experiences of past centuries. Witness to this is the way politicians, sections of the local press and some constituted bodies reacted to the *avis* on Malta's application to the European Community made public by the European Commission in July 1993. One local newspaper, for example, emphasised in one of its leader articles the fact that the Commission had declared that Malta had a 'right' (unlike Turkey or Morocco), to assert its vocation of membership of the EC, a right enjoyed only by those countries which are indisputably European (*The Sunday Times*, 4 July 1993). The Maltese Prime Minister too felt it necessary to stress that 'the Commission had made it clear that Malta had the qualifications for full membership' (*The Times*, 1 July 1993), one of the essential qualifications being Malta's Europeanness. But perhaps the most explicit statement in this connection was that made by the Maltese Institute of Directors. The *avis*, declared the Institute,

> confirms what has always been assumed in Malta but not always accepted outside it, namely that we are a European people living in a European country (*The Malta Independent*, 4 July 1993).

This discussion, as I hope to show, is not without significance for our examination of the modernizing role of Maltese political parties. Indeed, at this point, I would like to suggest that one of the factors that contributed towards the emergence of Maltese political parties in the latter part of the 19th century was occasioned by the pressing need, felt by local élites, to endeavour to steer Malta on the path of political modernization.

Modernization and Autonomy

It was the generally held view of the time, however, among Malta's élites that progress towards such political modernization was not possible until a large degree of autonomy in local affairs had been secured. Representative government was seen as the minimum form of autonomy if take-off into political development was to be achieved (Frendo, 1979; Pirotta, 1991). This view was based on the fact that existing and earlier forms of constitutions had failed to satisfy the aspirations of Malta's élites. Government, to all intents and purposes, had retained its military character and, with the intensification of superpower rivalry in the Mediterranean, Britain's military presence in Malta become more accentuated and intrusive. This is not to say that Malta's élites were in any way opposed to the employment opportunities and other benefits which came Malta's way as a consequence of the island's fortress role (Pirotta, 1991, Chapter 9). What Malta's élites complained of was that military interests tended to set, or dominate, the entire political and economic agenda in Malta, blocking and obstructing political development.

The issue took a new turn in the very early 1880s when Britain, determined to secure its strategic interests in the Mediterranean, resolved to embark on a policy which had, as its ultimate aim, the complete Anglicization of Malta. Henceforth, it was decided, English and not Italian was to become the language of education, administration and ultimately of culture in Malta. To achieve this aim as rapidly as possible, Maltese was to be given a settled alphabet and employed as the medium of instruction in the first years of a child's schooling. The intended reforms split Malta's élites in two, with one group, the *riformisti*, supporting them and a second group, the anti-*riformisti*, opposing them.

The *riformisti*, though not opposed to the idea of representative government, came to hold that, given the backward social and economic condition of the mass of the Maltese people, the time was not yet ripe for political development. What Malta required was development, yes, but of a social and economic kind. They believed that the use of Maltese (in lieu of Italian) in education would serve to extend the benefits of education to an ever-increasing number of Maltese. Knowledge of English would also unlock the door to employment opportunities at home and within the rest of the British Empire. They also held that the sooner the Maltese mastered the English language and came to adopt the values, habits and way of life of Britain (what they came to call, in the fashion of the times, the Mother Country), the sooner the Maltese would be allowed to adopt British-type political institutions (Lee, 1972; Frendo, 1979).

The stand adopted by the anti-riformisti was, as may be expected, opposed to this thesis. Anglicization, they argued, while clearly of economic benefit to certain classes, had British strategic interests at heart and would only serve to obstruct and retard Malta's political development. The Maltese, their argument ran, were not unmindful of British strategic interests. Hence, the issue as to what language they were to adopt in running their affairs was theirs to decide, since it was a purely local matter. Italian, they insisted, and not Maltese was the language of Malta for the Maltese were, as a people, of Italian descent. The Maltese language was no language at all and to impose it on the Maltese by such formal means as education would serve only to sever the Maltese nation from its rightful European heritage and culture. The elevation of Maltese to the status of a national language would thus hinder and not promote political modernization (Frendo, 1979, Chapter 2).

Stated like this, the position of the anti-*riformisti* or *nazionalisti* – as they eventually came to call themselves – seems at best perplexing and at worst anti-nationalist. Seen, however, in the context of racial identity and its intimate connection with existing doctrines of self-government, of self-determination in purely local affairs, the anti-*riformisti* platform gains greater coherence.

From a political point of view, the *nazionalisti* were right in resisting the elevation of Maltese to the status of a national language. Maltese was, and largely remains, an arab-based language. It is not a European tongue. Hence, to claim it as one's language is tantamount to renouncing one's Europeanness. It would be equivalent to admitting that the Maltese were not, racially or culturally, European. In that case, given the dominant European view that peoples that were not European by race were unfit for European institutions, the Maltese would either be refused representative government altogether or the prospect of it would be delayed indefinitely. What the Maltese 'required most was to be governed and not represented' (Bertram, 1930, p. 176), For the *nazionalisti*, this state of affairs was utterly unacceptable. They were no longer prepared to wait for representative government to simply come about. This explains Fortunato Mizzi's view, as the anti-*riformisti* leader, that the Maltese language was 'the curse of the country' (Frendo, 1979, p. 35) and that it was for the sake of 'patriotism' that its imposition should be resisted and Italian upheld.

Political or Economic Development?

Seen from this perspective, it would appear that what at least initially divided and set these two élite groups apart was their respective emphasis, one favouring as its foremost goal social and economic development, the other political development. The difference was, echoing Blondel's remarks (1978, p. 1) also a reflection of the dominant interests and aspirations of the respective blocks' popular base. The *riformisti* were essentially representing the new middle classes of importers, contractors and traders (who flourished on the presence of the large British garrison stationed in Malta), as well as the working classes who were mainly composed of drydocks and other Admiralty employees who constituted the bulk of the industrial labour force around the Grand Harbour (Zammit, 1984, p. 25, Note 48). No wonder therefore that their concern was primarily materialist and utilitarian, given that a pro-English platform permitted openings in social mobility for themselves and, with an institutionalized English curriculum at school, for their children. Bread and butter concerns were more immediate and enticing to them than the distant and somewhat alien pronouncements in favour of the granting of political concessions. Given the existing franchise limitations, such concessions would not have applied to most of them anyway. To the contrary, the anti-*riformisti* platform was closely akin to the traditional, professional-religious establishment. Their economic livelihood was less dependent on the British military machine; and their political agenda was also intent on preserving their socio-political status from upcoming social upstarts.

The onset of mass democracy in the past Second World War period sealed the fate of the pro-British 'liberals' as a truly independent political force and ensured the rise of the Malta Labour Party, the Island's first genuine mass party. Class politics rather than language now became the overt rallying banner with the consequence that by the late 1950s and early 1960s, a painless fusion between the two traditional and opposing élites was under way. This, I believe, is a point which has received scant attention from students of Maltese politics, and it does point to the notion that the language question was not all that it seemed to be. It was the Labour Party which, given its working-class base, inherited the materialist, utilitarian and ultimately secular perspective favouring English as a tool for development and Maltese as a mobilizing force. Labour's utilitarian but modernizing approach can best be identified with reference to two general but inextricably limited policy orientations. The first is the domestic aspect. For Labour nothing better epitomized the social and moral dimensions of a modern society than the creation of a welfare state. But the maintenance, rather than the establishment of such a state requires in a consistent manner enormous public funding which neither Malta's economic capacity nor fiscal potential could ever provide. Labour hoped that the second external dimension would remedy this. In the 1970s therefore, Labour set about rapidly decoupling Malta's economy from its dependency on a declining British defence budget, wresting Malta from the jurisdiction of NATO and actively promoting a neutral and non-aligned status for the Islands. It was a policy which aimed to open up for Malta the possibility of new markets, investments and financial aid from hitherto untapped sources, but notably from oil-rich Arab states (Pirotta, 1985). The price that Labour had to pay to achieve its policy aims, such as the championing of the Arab cause in international fora, the projection of the Maltese as a partly European partly Arab people, and the compulsory teaching of Arabic in Maltese secondary schools, served to re-open the racial identity issue. Nonetheless, the Nationalist Party, Labour's successor in office since 1987, despite its early move to reduce the status of Arabic in schools, has proved itself reluctant to jettison the economic opportunities raised by these connections notably because its stated aim of full membership of the European Community remains, as yet, a distant prospect.

But it remains all too easy to emphasize the differences rather than the similarities. The ultimate objective of political modernization substantially overshadows the policy divergences between the two main political parties in Malta. Priorities have, and still remain, disparate in a way which can perhaps be significantly explained by the diverging core social class support that each political party commands. But the pursuit of a decent quality of life, and the overtures to Europe as the model to be followed in achieving that quality of life, has never really subsided from the local political agenda, irrespective of the political élite in power.[3] Such an approach to Maltese political history is not only rewarding for highlighting the policy convergence across the political and ideological divide; it furthermore recasts, in a new light, the at times emotional and blown up issue surrounding the so-called language question as the catalyst of modern democratic political alignments in Malta.

A final note concerns one of the paradoxical outcomes of these political strategies and which is intimately related to the whole notion of political modernization, namely its democratic character. It may appear ironic that, in the at times slavish pursuit of 'development' in the institutionalized realm, with the espoused concerns for representative government and subsequently self-determination, there has been a disregard for certain values and attitudes which are as much an integral part of political modernity. Values such as tolerance, freedom of expression, the right to agree or disagree without coercion have not always been upheld by the parties involved. In recent years critical manifestations of this condition have also involved regrettable loss of life on three separate occasions. Perhaps, the extent and intensity of partisan political mobilization which Malta has seen over recent decades has at times led the parties to lose sight of their commonly valued goals of a modern, democratic – apart from a European – state.

---

[3] An examination of the electoral manifestos of Maltese political parties will reveal that all parties have consistently subscribed to the European model.

If one can refer at all to the appearance of a possible thaw or de-alignment from a rigid bi-partisan political cleavage, this could be indicative of how alert the Maltese electorate has become to the threat which acute polarity may pose to increasingly accepted and appreciated democratic freedoms and civic rights. The pursuit of a European dimension cannot proceed without a parallel concern for European values. And the Maltese electorate needs no convincing to the appeals of political modernization; such overtures are none other than a case of preaching to the converted. That we are European is now a fact of life; the bone of political party contention is the substance to be derived out of European values. It is over such a 'development' strategy that, both historically and contemporarily, the partisan battle lines are drawn.

References:

Abela, A.M. (1991) *Transmitting Values in European Malta*, Rome and Malta, Pontificia Universita Gregoriana and Malta Jesuit Publications.
Apter, D.E. (1965) *The Politics of Modernization*, Chicago, University of Chicago Press.
Attard, L.E. (1983) *Early Maltese Emigration: 1900-1914*, Valletta, Gulf Publishing.
Austin, J. & Lewis, G.C. (1838) *Report Relative to the Employment of Maltese in Executive Offices*, London, HMSO.
Baldacchino, G. (1988) 'The Dynamics of political restructuring in western Europe and Malta', *Hyphen*, vol. 6, 2.
Bertram, A. (1930) *The Colonial Service*, Cambridge, Cambridge University Press.
Birch, A.H. (1970) *The British System of Government*, 2e, London, George Allen & Unwin.
Blondel, J. (1978) *Political Parties: A Genuine Case for Discontent?*, London, Wildwood House.
Duverger, J. (1955) *Political Parties: Their Organisation and Activity in the Modern State*, (trans. by North, B. & North, R.), London, Methuen & Co.
Frendo, H. (1979) *Party Politics in a Fortress Colony: The Maltese Experience*, Valletta, Malta, Midsea Books.
GALLUP Ltd. Malta (1984) Gallup Sample Survey.
Lane, J. & Ersson, S.O. (1991) *Politics and Society in Western Europe*, 2e, London, Sage.
Lee, H.A. (1972) *Malta: 1813-1914. A Case Study in Constitutional and Strategic Development*, Valletta, Progress Press.
Malta Independent, The, (12 September, 1993) 'Avis: The key to Europe'.
MISCO (1993) Survey on Local Councils.

Pirotta, G.A. (1985) 'Malta's foreign policy after Mintoff', *Political Quarterly*, vol. 56, 2.
Pirotta, G.A. (1991) 'The administrative politics of a microstate: The Maltese public service 1800-1940', unpublished Ph.D. thesis, University of Bath.
Ryan, F.W. (1930) *The House of the Temple*, London, Burns Oates & Washbourne.
Smith, G. (1972) *Politics in Western Europe: A Comparative Analysis*, London, Heinemann Educational.
Tabone, C. (1987) *The Secularisation of the Family in Changing Malta*, Malta, Dominican Publications.
Schiavone, M.J.(1992) *L-Elezzjonijiet f'Malta: 1849-1992*, Malta, Pubblikazzjoni Indipendenza.
Welch, C. (ed.) (1971) *Political Modernization: A Reader in Comparative Political Change*, 2e, Belmont, CA, Wadsworth Publishing.
Yorke, B. (1990) *Empire and Race: The Maltese in Australia: 1881-1949*, Australia, New South Wales, Wales University Press.
Zammit, E.L. (1984) *A Colonial Inheritance: Work, Power and Class Structure with Reference to the Maltese Labour Movement*, Malta, Malta University Press.

part 2

distinction and differentiation

The pyramidal structure of any social formation is an achieved rather than a reified, 'natural' phenomenon. Groups or classes who, after successive historical battles in the fields of production of material and symbolic goods, have successfully occupied the upper echelons of a society, will tend to defend the privileges, wealth, and status they have acquired. In other words, they will use material and symbolic goods in order to socially position themselves close to some groups, and distant from others.

That positioning is achieved through a variety of ways. Sciriha, for instance, explores the way language is used as a positional good, so that despite the small size of the Maltese islands, particular and minor differences in articulation can become powerful and revealing indicators of class and status. Boswell extends this theme to the sphere of residential areas, and shows how patterns of land use by specific social groups lead to a highly developed perception of the different status and relative ranking of particular regions in Malta. In the same way, Sultana argues that it is not only language or residential areas that distinguish groups, but also a whole gamut of consumer goods. Consumption, especially as expressed in the fields of leisure and mass culture, is thus considered to be an important characteristic of contemporary Maltese society, where the use of material and symbolic goods attains a significance beyond the fulfilling of basic needs for food and shelter, and signals a social function in as much as it positions others in the social space.

The particular positioning which obtains within the pyramidal structure, and within the social and physical space, has specific and real material consequences on subordinate groups. Indeed, as Mintoff Bland shows, our very health and life chances are dependent on it, and it is not a coincidence that in Malta, the highest incidence of cancer is to be found in regions peopled in the main by manual, industrial wage-earners and their families.

Borg and Mayo consider another aspect of the repercussions of physical location on the inhabitants' status and well being generally. They in fact argue that the Maltese abroad suffer from a subordination and a particular kind of oppression consisting of the trivialization of small countries by ethnocentric individuals and institutions.

6

Language and Class in Malta

Lydia Sciriha

Introduction

In an often reproduced article, Fishman (1972, p. 45) argues that a sociological study of language

> focuses upon the entire gamut of language behaviour, including not only language usage per se but also language attitudes, overt behaviour toward language and toward language users.

Despite the small size of the Maltese islands, particular and minor differences in articulation have become powerful indicators of class and status. Such linguistic differences have been noted by Vassalli (1796), Stumme (1904), Aquilina (1959, 1961, '65, '66) and Aquilina & Isserlin (1981), even though these analyses generally failed to engage sociological or sociolinguistic theory in a rigorous manner.

The differential use of language in a stratified society is a key marker of 'cultural capital' (Bourdieu, 1984), and indeed language is used as a 'positional good' in order to create or close social distance. Knowing the varieties of Maltese (and of English), having the ability to discern which of these to use, to whom, when, and to what end (Fishman, 1972, p. 46) constitutes a veritable arsenal of linguistic capital which opens doors of opportunities in social, cultural, educational, political and financial spheres. The corollary to this holds true as well. Lack of such knowledge, discernment and ability in Maltese society is a definite handicap, and a narrow repertoire in sociolinguistic communicative competence has very real repercussions on the 'life chances' of any individual.

This chapter focuses on only one aspect of this problem, considering as it does, in the descriptive sociolinguistic tradition of Labov (1966), Trudgill (1974) and Hudson (1980) among others, some of the relations between language and class in Malta. It draws from a number of others studies carried out by the present author (Sciriha, 1986, 1990, '91, '92, Sciriha et al., 1992, Sciriha & Kmetova, 1992) in order to focus on two major sociolinguistic phenomena, namely:

(a) allophonic variation, manifested in the phonetic representation of certain Maltese dialects, which is in turn linked to social membership, and
(b) lexical alternation, which is a choice of words based on the social role played by each speaker in a given context.

It will be argued that not only does society construct language, but also that language constructs society, namely social relations.

Methodology

Sciriha's (1986) research was the first scientific project carried out in Malta to apply the sociolinguistic framework introduced by Labov (1966) in order to analyse how dialectal variations correlate with non-linguistic variables such as class, gender, age and context. The research analysed the dialectal variation of two diphthongs namely [au] ~ [ou] and [ai] ~ [ei] in initial, medial and final positions of the word. As an observer of the local scene, the author had noticed a particular phenomenon whereby these diphthongs were at times monophthongized (i.e. the diphthong is reduced to one vowel) by some speakers. In this survey, commonly used words which included the linguistic variables in question were used. For example, in Standard Maltese *għuda* is pronounced as either [ouda], or [auda]. In non-standard Maltese, this diphthong would be reduced to a monophthong as in [uːda].

During 1985, Sciriha personally interviewed, by means of a structured questionnaire, one hundred and seventy-six natives of eleven chosen areas: Senglea, Cospicua, Vittoriosa, Valletta, Sliema, Paola, Birkirkara, Ħamrun, Rabat, Żejtun and Mosta. There were equal numbers of males and females representing four age groups: Group 1: 13-19 years; Group 2: 20-36 years; Group 3: 37-55 years; and Group 4: over 55 years, with the informants hailing from the middle class and the working class. The informants were stratified according to their occupations. According to the classification of this study, the working class referred to respondents whose occupations were manual or non-clerical, and middle class if they had clerical or professional jobs. It should be noted that Zammit (1984) offers a similar classification but calls the working class and the middle class as manual and non-manual respectively. Students and housewives were ascribed the same class as their parents and their husbands respectively. This method of classification was in line with Levine & Crockett (1966) who also gauged housewives' social status by means of their husbands' occupations.

Since the author hypothesised that the acquisition of particular dialectal features depended on the length of stay of the individual in a village or a town, informants were not selected randomly but were specifically chosen from those who had been born and raised in the locality they lived in at the time they were interviewed. In addition, all of them had at least one parent who was a native of the same area. In view of the fact that informants who are under 18 years were an important element of this survey, the commonly used method of selecting informants from the electoral register listing had to be abandoned. As has been pointed out by Linn (1983) and Romaine (1982), stratified sampling is difficult to obtain in a sociolinguistic study of this nature. The sampling technique used was similar to the method of quota sampling which Linn (1983) described. The non-linguistic variables that were chosen were gender, age, class, dialect area and contextual styles (explained below). Respondents to the questionnaire were selected to represent each of the above categories.

Though the questionnaire was designed for fieldwork in Malta, the theoretical assumptions made were based on those of Labov (1966), who showed that linguistic variation in a speech community is not free but is determined by non-linguistic variables such as age, class, gender and social context. The latter variable was tested by means of three different styles elicited from the informants, namely a Word List style, a Reading Passage style, and a Speech style. Each of the contextual styles differed in the degree of formality.

In the Word List style, which is the most formal style, the informant's attention was concentrated on a single word at a time. The Reading Passage style is less formal than the Word List style because of the fact that the informant has to concentrate on more words. In this style, one is less on guard not to utter non-standard forms. The Speech style is the least formal of the previous two since informants are asked general questions.

The questionnaire consisted of five sections. In Section A, informants were asked to provide biographical data such as age, sex, birthplace, where they grew up, occupation or father's occupation or husband's occupations as well as whether one parent was native of the same area. Section B consisted of the Self-Evaluation test (S.V.). In this test, the interviewer read out three variant pronunciations of such key-words as *miegħi* and the informant was then asked to mark his/her pronunciation of the linguistic variable found in the key-word on the accompanying S.V. sheet. This section was done in order to test the informants' own evaluation of their speech. Section C was made up of the same key-words found in the Self-Evaluation test. These were the following sixteen words with the linguistic variable appearing in initial, medial and final position of the word: *għid* – say; *għira* – jealousy; *għuda* – wood; *Għuxa* – placename in Cottonera; *sebgħin* – seventy; *disgħin* – ninety; *mibgħuta* – sent; *mingħul* – devil; *tiegħi* – mine; *miegħi* – with me; *jidgħi* – he swears; *friegħi* – leaves; *tiegħu* – his; *miegħu* – with him; *baqgħu* – they remained, and *setgħu* – they could. Dummy words were also interspersed throughout the Word List, so that informants would not be so conscious of the repetition of the key-words found in the S.V. style. The Reading Passage in Section D was interspersed with the key-words found in the previous sections. The final section was the Speech Style.

A number of steps were involved in the analysis of the data. First of all, the data were transcribed phonetically from the tape recordings, as well as from the Self-Evaluation tests that the informants had filled in. In all, sixteen key-words having the diphthongs [au] ~ [ou] and [ai] ~ [ei] in either initial, or medial or final position were analysed. Percentages of monophthongization of the key-words were computed for all the styles used in the questionnaire and cross-tabulated with other variables such as age, class, gender, stylistic variation and locality.

Results of the Study

The results of the survey showed that monophthongization of the diphthongs under study was confined to four of the eleven chosen localities in Malta. Aquilina (1959; 1961; 1965) and Aquilina & Isserlin (1981) had noted that the dialectal feature of monophthongization was evident in the speech of Vittoriosa natives. The results of this study confirmed this. In addition, however, this study pointed out that this particular feature was generally prevalent among the natives of the Three Cities (Cospicua, Vittoriosa, and Senglea).

Moreover, monophthongization by these informants was not homogenous. There was considerable variation in the monophthongization of [au] ~ [ou] and [ai] ~ [ei] depending on the different positions of the diphthongs in the word. Cottonera and Paola informants, like others from the other seven areas, never monophthongized the linguistic variable [ai] ~ [ei], when this phonological feature surfaced in word-initial and word-medial positions. Monophthongization for the [au] ~ [ou] diphthong occurred in all positions of the word for some Cottonera and Paola informants. Of particular note was the fact that the percentages of monophthongization registered for the [au] ~ [ou] variable in final position of the word were higher than for that of the [ai] ~ [ei] variable in final position of the word. This is perhaps, indicative of a progressive decline in monophthongization of the [ai] ~ [ei]. After all, this diphthong was never monophthongized at the beginning (e.g. *għid* [i:t]) and in the middle (e.g. *sebgħin* [sebi:n] of the word. Aquilina & Isserlin (1981) noted that monophthongization surfaced when [ai] ~ [ei] is in medial position e.g. *ngħid* [ni:t] – I say. On the contrary, none of the informants in this study ever monophthongized the diphthong in the medial position as in Aquilina & Isserlin's example [ni:t].

Covariation of Monophthongization with Class and Contextual Style

Another goal which had been set in Sciriha (1986) was to establish whether there was any covariation of monophthongization with class and contextual style.

Monophthongization was shown to be definitely correlated with class especially, when the linguistic variable [ai] ~ [ei] was word-final and when [au] ~ [ou] was in initial, medial or final position of the word. Though the [au] ~ [ou] variable showed sharp class stratification in all three positions of the word, it was in word-final position that it showed its sharpest stratification. In fact, for final [au] ~ [ou] 44% of working class informants as opposed to 11% of middle-class informants monophthongized the diphthong. As regards the [ai] ~ [ei] variable in word-final position, the percentage of informants who monophthongized the diphthong in Cottonera was 36% for the working class and 6% for the middle class. A breakdown of the percentages of monophthongization showed that it was Cospicua natives who registered the highest percentages of monophthongization with 44% of the working class and 3% of the middle class displaying this dialectal feature. Out of the Three Cities, this dialectal feature seems to be on its way out in Senglea as the usage of this feature in this area is limited to 29% of the working class sample and 7% of the middle class sample.

However, differences were registered in the percentages of informants who monophthongized the diphthong when contextual style was covariated with class. As noted earlier, the [au] ~ [ou] variable showed sharp class stratification in all positions of the word. In sociolinguistic variation patterns noted by Labov (1966) and Trudgill (1983), less dialectal forms were used in the more formal styles. In the present author's study, the percentages of monophthongization also fluctuated according to the contextual style. Surprisingly, however, the working-class Cottonerans registered the highest percentages of monophthongization in the most formal style, namely the Word List style, and the lowest percentages in the Reading Passage. The middle-class informants' stylistic variation patterns tallied with Labov (1966).

Of particular interest was the fact that working-class natives of the Three Cities showed identical patterns of stylistic variation when word-final [au] ~ [ou] and [ai] ~ [ei] were considered. For these two linguistic variables, working-class Cottonerans consistently registered the highest percentages of monophthongization in the Word-List style and the lowest in the Reading Passage style. Middle class Cottonera natives differed from their working-class counterparts in their pattern of stylistic variation. In fact, for the middle-class informants, the percentages of monophthongization of word-final [au] ~ [ou] and [ai] ~ [ei] was the lowest, as Labov and Trudgill had discovered, in the most formal style, the Word List style; and monophthongization was higher in the Speech style, the least formal style of the three in question. Though there was covariation of class and context for word-final [au] ~ [ou] and [ai] ~ [ei] linguistic variables, there was no such pattern for word-initial and word-medial [au] ~ [ou] and [ai] ~ [ei]. Informants were consistent in the monophthongization of the diphthongs in these positions in all three styles. There was no stylistic variation pattern, unlike in word-final [au] ~ [ou] and [ai] ~ [ei]. As was noted in this study it was probably the case that informants had been made aware of the fact that the monophthongized word-final [au] ~ [ou] and [ai] ~ [ei] are socially stigmatized linguistic variables. Informants had told the author that they had often been ridiculed when they monophthongized the diphthongs word-finally but not word-initially and word-medially. As noted earlier there was no specific stylistic variation patterns for word-initial and word medial [au] ~ [ou] and [ai] ~ [ei]. This further emphasizes that it was only word-finally that the linguistic variables were socially stigmatized.

Other interesting facts emerged as regards the above-mentioned socially stigmatized linguistic variables. There were differences between the two classes. On the one hand, the Cottonera working class informants displayed a specific variation pattern, since they registered the highest percentages of monophthongization in the Word-List style and the lowest in the Reading Passage style. On the other hand, the middle-class Cottonera natives registered the lowest percentages of monophthongization in the Word List style and the highest in the Speech style. At first sight, the different but consistent stylistic variation patterns might seem to be the result of class differentiation. However, Paola working class informants displayed identical stylistic variation patterns to that of the middle-class Cottonera informants. In fact, the Word List style was the least monophthongized style and Speech style the most monophthongized.

Stylistic Variation and 'Dialectal Pride'

Had Paola working-class informants produced stylistic variation patterns similar to Cottonera working-class natives for the two socially stigmatized variables, then this pattern could easily have been interpreted as being a feature of Cottonera and Paola working-class informants only. However, Paola working-class natives did not display an identical stylistic variation pattern as Cottonera working-class natives. Consequently, Cottonera stylistic variation patterns cannot solely be attributed to class differentiation.

A possible reason for this variation is that working-class Cottonerans make a conscious effort to show how proud they are to be natives of the Three Cities, by using its dialectal features, especially in the most formal styles. Such a form of 'dialectal pride' may be the reason why the Word List style, the most formal style, was the most heavily monophthongized style. It was not that working-class Cottonerans were unaware of the standard forms of these linguistic variables. Had they not known, they would have been consistent in the percentages of monophthongization registered in all three styles. Moreover, it is hardly likely that these informants were not aware of their dialectal feature, considering that since most of them work, they were in contact with other people from different areas. They also knew that their dialect feature was not viewed favourably. Notwithstanding this fact, working-class Cottonera informants registered high percentages of the dialect feature in the most formal style. It seemed to be the case that using the dialect feature was their way of insisting that even though most non-Cottonerans laughed at what others had parochially and prescriptively dubbed as 'deformed' speech, Cottonera natives were proud of it. Their pride was furthermore emphasized by their use of the dialect feature frequently in the most formal style of all, thereby shocking the listener, who would have thought that Cottonera natives would restrict their dialect features to informal settings.

It is also evident that 'dialectal pride' owes its roots to the fact that most Cottonera informants had or had had both parents who were natives of Cottonera. In fact, 87.5% of Senglea informants had both parents from Cottonera; Vittoriosa informants had 75% and Cospicua informants 56%. No informant from Paola had parents from Cottonera. Thus, this study suggests that there is a direct correlation between dialectal features and class.

Sciriha (1992) delved deeper into one sector of language in order to see whether there was a similar correlation between lexical alternation and social class. This second study carried out in March 1992, analysed the forms of address in two distinctive geographic areas namely St Julians and Safi whose residents are reputedly of middle-class and working-class background respectively. The methodology was identical to the one followed in the previous study.

This survey was once again based on the principle adopted by sociolinguists that it is incorrect to attribute a dialect feature to a particular locality without rigorously checking who uses these features, when and why. In this paper, Sciriha pointed out that different levels of social relations amongst linguistic communities are maintained by the successful manipulation of language. Brown & Gilman (1960), Brown & Ford (1961), Ervin-Tripp (1972), Bates & Benigni (1975) and Lambert & Tucker (1976) had noted that different forms of address are effective tools in manifesting the relationship between speaker and addressee as well as in displaying the speaker's identity within the group. A point of interest in this context is the fact that the persons who hold power may manifest this by the address forms they give and those which they receive.

In this study the author focussed on the different forms of address within the Maltese extended family, specifically, the address forms used in communicating with parents-in-law. Preliminary observations in this area of research were extended over a period of five years, during which the author had informally asked her married and married-to-be students at the University of Malta which address forms they used when speaking with their parents-in-law. The students' responses ranged from the most formal Title Last Name (TLN) to the lesser formal First Name (FN). What was found particularly striking about the students' responses was that a number of them admitted that they resorted to strategies in which they avoided using any form of address to their parents-in-law. With reference to a similar context, Ervin-Tripp (1972, p. 228) had in fact noted that 'No naming is an outcome of uncertainty among these options'. In view of these students' responses, the present author decided to investigate, on the basis of empirical experience, whether it was merely uncertainty as to which address forms one should use or whether social factors were also at the root of this avoidance strategy.

One hundred and twenty subjects were interviewed by means of a questionnaire which was administered to a stratified random sample made up of sixty respondents from Safi and sixty from St Julians. Sciriha adopted the same classification as Linn (1983), so that the category 'manual worker' refers to informants of working-class extraction while the 'non-manual worker' category refers to middle-class informants. In the case of full-time housewives, Goldthorpe's (1969) strategy of ascribing class according to the housewife's husband's occupation was adopted.

As noted earlier, subjects were chosen from two distinctively opposite geo-social areas, Safi and St Julians. The small rural village of Safi in the southern part of Malta has a population of 1,323, and is predominantly working class. It is characterized by the fact that practically all inhabitants are native speakers of Maltese and that they speak Maltese with their family members and friends.

The other sixty informants were chosen from St Julians, a town of over 13,000 inhabitants. This town, situated on the north coast of Malta, is one of Malta's principal tourist resorts. Most of its inhabitants are of middle-class background. Before developing into a fully-fledged tourist resort, St Julians had a long standing British military presence. As a result of these factors, together with other social factors such as prestige (as noted in Sciriha, 1991), residents of St Julians interact with one another and with the tourists visiting the island in a variety of English known as Maltese English (Broughton, 1976).

Forms of Addressing Parents-in-Law

The results of this study regarding the use of address forms were correlated with four major independent variables, namely locality, gender, age and class.

Responses showed that the informants of both Safi and St Julians had a variety of terms to address their parents-in-law. There were eight different modes of address to the mother-in-law namely *ma*, *mamà*, mummy, *kunjata*, Title Last Name, First Name, *nanna* and Name Avoidance, of which the First Name was the form most commonly used (53.3%; N=120). There were 13.3% of the informants who did not use any form of address when interacting with their mother-in-law, whereas 10.8% used the term ma. The forms of address mamà, mummy, and kunjata were respectively used by 3.3%, 4.2% and 4.2% of the informants. However, if one considers mamà and mummy as a foreign variant of the form of address ma, one can conclude that 18.3% used ma followed by 13.3% who adopted Name Avoidance strategies.

The First Name form of address was more widespread in Safi than in St Julians; 66% of Safi respondents as opposed to the 40% in St Julians. On the other hand, the *ma* form of address was used almost equally in Safi and St Julians with 10% and 11.7% respectively. Name Avoidance was higher in St Julians than in Safi, totalling 18.3% and 8.3% respectively.

When analysing the different usages of *ma*, *mamà* and 'mummy', it surfaced that the *ma* form of address was roughly equally used in both localities under study with 10.8 % in Safi and 11.7% in St Julians. *Mamà*, the form of address of Italian origin was, however, more frequently used in St Julians with 5% using this mode of address as opposed to 1.7% of the informants from Safi. The English form of address 'mummy' was also more frequently used in St Julians than in Safi as 6.7% of the informants from St Julians used it as compared with 1.7% from Safi.

As regards the mode of addressing the father-in-law, informants similarly used eight modes of address. The forms of address are as follows: *pa, papà*, 'daddy', *kunjatu*, Title Last Name, First Name, *nannu* and Name Avoidance, of which the highest percentage of informants (53.3% N=120) use First Name. Safi residents used this mode of address nearly twice as much as St Julians informants with 68.3% as opposed to 38.3%. The second most used form of address – 13.3% of informants – was *pa*. This form of address was used slightly more in St Julians (15%) than in Safi (11.7%). There were 13.3% of informants who refrained from using any particular form of address with respect to the father-in-law, with the St Julians informants registering higher percentages (18.3%) of such usage than their Safi counterparts (8.3%). As was noted earlier this is the same pattern for the mothers-in-law.

Gender, age, occupation and to a lesser degree, locality seemed to have an important influence on the use of either of these three forms of address. In fact, in the use of the address form *pa*, females used this form more than their male counterparts (75% as compared to 25%). Moreover, a higher percentage of informants who were over 41 years of age (22%) used this form of address more than those who were in their twenties (10.3%) or in their thirties (7.5%). Class does not seem to have played any significant influence in the choice of *pa*. In fact, 13.3% of both the manual and non-manual workers used this form of address. However, manual workers used the First Name form of address significantly more than non-manual workers (66.7% as opposed to 40%), thus showing class stratification.

The *ma* form of address is used more by females than by males (15% as opposed to 6.7%). Moreover, informants who were over 41 years of age used this form of address more than those who were in their twenties (17.1% as opposed to 10.3%) and even less by those who were in their thirties (7.5%). The term *ma* was roughly used by both manual and non-manual workers. Manual workers used the First Name form of address significantly more than non-manual workers: 65% as opposed to 41.7%. This is similar to what has been noted with regard to the way these two classes used the *pa* form of address.

A total of 13.3% of the informants avoided using any form of address when speaking to their father-in-law. As noted earlier, Name Avoidance was more frequent in St Julians than in Safi. As one would expect in these cases, more females than males adopted this non-committal strategy (62.5% as opposed to 37.5%). Of particular note was the fact that class was an important variable as regards the no name form of address. Non-manual workers (68.8%) used this no name form of address more than manual workers (31.3%).

The overall results of the interviews with informants in both Safi and St Julians showed that there were different trends in the forms of addressing parents-in-law.

First Name emerged as the form of address that is predominantly used for both mother-in-law and father-in-law. Moreover, this address form was used mainly by informants who lived in Safi, rather than those who were living in St Julians. Males used this address form more than females.

The percentage of informants who used the *ma / pa* address form with their parents-in-law was also high, though there were different patterns of use between the Safi and St Julians residents. Interaction with parents-in-law was, to start with, more frequent with Safi informants than amongst those in St Julians. Compared with Safi respondents, residents of St Julians used the *ma/pa* or *mamà/papà* forms of address more frequently than the First Name when addressing their parents-in-law. This can be attributed to the fact that the *ma/pa* address form is more formal than the use of the First Name. It can also connote a lesser degree of solidarity amongst the addressers and addressees in St Julians. However, it is not only solidarity that might be a determining factor in the use of the First Name form as opposed to the *ma /pa*, *mama/papa* form. The fact that most of the users of the First Name form were males with manual jobs suggests that perhaps it is also a masculine trait.

The linguistic differences that surfaced in the use of forms of address between Safi informants as compared with those of St Julians, bear out the stark reality that the structure of Maltese society is in a state of flux. In other words, language and language use give us an insight into the change in social relations over time and space.

Conclusion

To conclude one might say that these studies have shown the interrelation between language and society, a relationship of mutual influence. As we have seen in the Cottonera study, a linguistic variation is used as a line of demarcation between one group and another involving an element of pride in those retaining the dialectal features. In the second study, a similar social distance is created by a very specific language use: forms of address. As much as language use can be influenced by social factors, there are occasions when language can have a dominant role in controlling social contexts.

References

Aquilina, J. (1959) *The Structure of Maltese: A Study in Mixed Grammar and Vocabulary*, Malta, Progress Press.
Aquilina, J. (1961) *Papers in Maltese Linguistics*, Malta, Progress Press.
Aquilina, J. (1965) *Teach Yourself Maltese*, London, The English Universities Press.
Aquilina, J. (1966) 'Maltese dialect survey', *Zeitschrift fur Mundartforschung*, Neue Folge, 3, 4.
Aquilina, J. & Isserlin, B.S.J. (1981) *A Survey of Contemporary Dialectal Maltese, Vol. 1: Gozo*, Leeds, Leeds University Press.

Bates, E. & Benigni, L. (1975) 'Rules for address in Italy: a sociological survey', *Language in Society*, vol. 4, 3.

Bourdieu, P. (1984) *Distinction: A Social Critique of the Judgement of Taste*, Harvard, Harvard University Press.

Broughton, G. (1976) 'The degree of proficiency to be aimed at in English in Maltese Schools'. Proceedings of Conference on Bilingual Education with reference to Malta, Malta, University of Malta.

Brown, R. & Ford, M. (1961) 'Address in American English' *Journal of Abnormal and Social Psychology*, vol. 62.

Brown, R. & Gilman, A. (1960) 'The pronouns of power and solidarity', *American Anthropologist*, vol. 4, 6.

Ellul, S. (1978) *A Case Study in Bilingualism: Code-switching Between Parents and their 12 year-old School Children in Malta*, Cambridge, Huntington Publishers.

Ervin-Tripp, S. (1972) 'On sociolinguistic rules: alternation and co-occurrence', in Gumperz, J. & Hymes, D. (eds), *Directions in Sociolinguistics: The Ethnography of Communication*, New York, Holt, Rinehart & Winston.

Fishman, J. A. (1972) 'The sociology of language', in Giglioli, P.P. (ed.) *Language and Social Context*, Harmondsworth, Penguin.

Goldthorpe, J.H., Lockwood, D., Beckhofer, F. & Platt, J. (1968, 1969) *The Affluent Worker in the Class Structure*, 3 vols, Cambridge, Cambridge University Press.

Hudson, R.A. (1980) *Sociolinguistics*, Cambridge, Cambridge University Press.

Labov, W. (1966) *The Social Stratification of English in New York City*, Washington DC, Centre for Applied Linguistics.

Lambert, W. & Tucker, G. (1976) *Tu, vous, usted: A Social Psychological Study of Address Patterns*, Rowley, MA, Newbury House.

Levine, L. & Crockett, H. (1966) 'Speech variation in a Piedmont community', in Lieberson, S. (ed.) *Explorations in Sociolinguistics*, The Hague, Mouton.

Linn, M. (1983) 'Information selection in dialectology', *American Speech*, vol. 58.

Romaine, S. (1982) *Sociolinguistic Variation in Speech Communities*, London, Edward Arnold.

Sciriha, L. (1986) 'A sociolinguistic study of monophthongization in Maltese'. unpublished Ph.D. thesis, University of Victoria, BC, Canada.

Sciriha, L. (1990) 'Language maintenance and language shift of the Maltese migrants in Canada', *Journal of Maltese Studies*, 19-20.

Sciriha, L. (1991) 'Sociolinguistic aspects of language use in Malta', *Proceedings of Conference on Languages of the Mediterranean*, Malta, Malta University Press.

Sciriha, L. (1992) 'The linguistic construction of social space: forms of addressing parents-in-law in Malta'. Paper presented at the Sociolinguistic Symposium 9, University of Reading.

Sciriha, L., Borg, A. & Mifsud, M. (1992) 'The position of Maltese in Malta'. *Proceedings of Experts' Meeting on Language Planning*, Malta, University of Malta.

Sciriha, L. & Kmetova, T. (1992) 'Why bother about those tenses?', *Contrastive Linguistics*, vol. 3.

Stumme, H. (1904) *Maltesische Studien, Eine Sammlung Prosaischer und Poetischer Texte in Maltesischer Sprache*, Leipzig.

Trudgill, P. (1974) *The Social Differentiation of English in Norwich*, Cambridge, Cambridge University Press.
Trudgill, P. (1983) *Sociolinguistics: An Introduction to Language and Society*, Harmondsworth, Penguin.
Vassalli, M.A. (1796) *Lexicon Melitense-Latino-Italum*, Rome, A. Fulgoni.
Zammit, E.L. (1984) *A Colonial Inheritance: Maltese Perceptions of Work, Power and Class Structure with Reference to the Labour Movement*, Malta, Malta University Press.

7

The Social Prestige of Residential Areas

David M. Boswell

A City State with a Shifting Population

Ruled by only two powers for almost half a millennium until Independence in 1964, the Knights of St. John from 1530 and the British from 1800, except for the brief Napoleonic occupation of 1798-1800, Malta's political history has been remarkably stable for islands so strategically placed in the central Mediterranean. Unlike many now depopulated islands, modern Malta has sustained both extensive emigration and a highly concentrated population density. In the late 1970s about two thirds of its 340,000 people lived in about one third of the main island's area, which in total barely exceeds 24 by 14 kilometres. By reason of their semitic and basically Arabic language, and unequivocal, enthusiastic Roman Catholic religion, the Maltese have a self-conscious identity which is neither Italian nor North African.

Ruled from the centre during the colonial era, Malta's single tier of government has been based on the proportional representation of several multi-member constituencies since 1921, with only Gozo sometimes having a separate administrative identity. But despite this demographic and political centralization in such a small area, characteristic of a city state, Maltese people are intensely parochial, loyal to their locality and often active in promoting its political, social and especially religious activities (Boissevain, 1965, 1969 and 1984). However, the particularities of locality are often fitted within a more generally defined framework of social prestige which is locality-based but associated with stereotypical assumptions about occupational distribution and party-political allegiances.

Maltese people often assess one another by reference to the virtually proverbial reputations of different localities. For centuries this has taken a form not unlike provincial France or Britain, but with a much smaller frame of reference because Malta's settlements can never be more than a few kilometres apart and are often only a few hundred metres away. But broader forms of categorization are superimposed on specific references, e.g. to the shrewdness of Gozitans or the roughness of people from Mqabba. Within the conurbation strong distinctions are drawn between the people on 'the other side' of the Grand Harbour in 'the Cottonera' cities of L-Isla, Birgu and Bormla, and the people on 'the Sliema side' whom the others call 'tal-Pepè', in reference to their snooty speech. The social implications of this were clearly demonstrated in social behaviour. In the 1970s, for example, young people from the three cities would spend their Saturday evenings mingling with those from other parts of the island beside the ruined Chalet (or pier) on Sliema's sea-front, whereas little could induce outsiders to set foot in the Cottonera towns, which they envisaged as a dangerous den of footpads, prostitutes and vicious political mountebanks – a source of much political posturing and legend. Now Paceville has replaced Sliema front for Malta's youth.

The urban concentration of population around the Grand Harbour was advanced by the Knights and under the British who developed the dockyard and built barracks on the northern side of the harbours, where substantial residential development provided both summer houses for the old-city residents and property to let to the British. After the Second World War this urban expansion continued with two major innovations, the first being the foundation of new towns, or rather garden-suburbs, at Santa Lucia and San Ġwann, and the second being the expansion and rebuilding of the larger villages throughout the island (see Harrison & Hubbard, 1950, and Richardson, 1964).

As people left Valletta or obtained certain sorts of job, so they settled on the Sliema side, whereas the post-war repopulation of the Cottonera is said to have introduced a poorer and socially more depressed working-class population than it had before its élite moved out. Mosta developed as a service centre and another major zone of British-rented accommodation and, after Independence, retired British settlers set the pattern for building detached villas in rural suburbs. This pattern was taken up by affluent Maltese followed by owner-occupiers redeveloping their villages. Meanwhile Floriana and Sliema have adopted some of the institutions and characteristics of governmental and private business districts respectively.

Although the 1985 census failed to ask the question, and the 1967 census publication was suppressed,[1] the pageproofs of the latter survive to provide the information necessary to review the pattern of internal migration in the previous decade. One sees the outflow of population from the inner harbour areas to the localities beyond them, the expansion of population in the rural centre and the coastal south-west of the island, and a reduction of population in the north, west and south which has subsequently been reversed by tourist and suburban development. Within this outflow, selective migration was to the higher status, northern sides of the harbours. Those in the dockyard towns generally moved out on their side of the harbour which only drew in other people from the adjacent locality i.e. Ħamrun (see Figure 1).

By 1979 there had been a substantial shift in the form of the Maltese economy. Although Government employment had been maintained, British defence establishments had been phased out, and the civilianized dockyard had turned to the maintenance of merchant shipping which had less call for skilled labour. The

---

[1] The corrected proof of the population volume of this census was withdrawn from publication by order of the new prime minister in 1971, but a copy is now lodged with Melitensia at the University of Malta library.

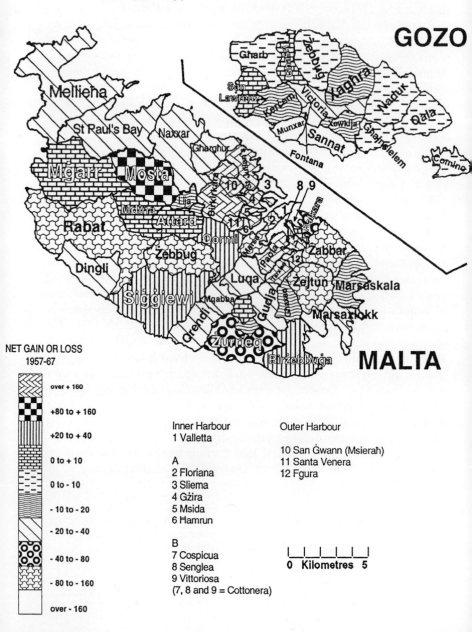

Figure 1. Net inter-locality flow of heads of households in Malta and Gozo, 1957-1967. (Note: Valletta is treated separately as the capital city.)

wholesale and retail trading of imports had lost some of its prominence. Package-tourism had largely replaced these as well as a variety of a few large and many often short-lived small manufacturing companies in new industrial estates on both sides of Marsa, between Tarxien and Żejtun, below San Ġwann, and on the Mosta plain (Metwally, 1977, Grech, 1978 and Malta Government, 1981). New and more jobs and a wider distribution of incomes enabled a larger proportion of the population to enjoy the social and residential mobility characteristic of consumer-orientated societies. Owing to external funding through the British military base, the Maltese population had already indulged in such mobility long before a local industrial base was developed. Meanwhile, this trend towards general urbanization was reinforced by the Government which embarked on major public-housing construction in most localities (Mifsud, 1983). By the end of the 1970s and since then, the sheer quantity of infilling, suburban construction, seaside resort development, and redevelopment for hotels and apartments in already built-up localities like Sliema, has eliminated many of the obvious rural boundaries between localities. It was in this context that the study sought to find out how Maltese people perceived their predominantly urban environment.[2] Although the survey was carried out in 1979 and its findings therefore refer to that period – a historic moment for Malta with the closure of the British defence base – there is no reason why it should not have been undertaken before or since then. What was significant was the emergence of a pattern, or several patterns, in the responses of residents. These trends were sufficiently robust as to respond to several different modes of analysis. This paper therefore seeks not only to discuss the patterns themselves but also to illustrate the method of data analysis utilized in the relation to the data.

---

[2] The study consisted of a social survey undertaken by university students as a training exercise. It was based on a ten per cent random sample of all households in Senglea, Fgura and Attard, and a seven and half per cent sample of those in Sliema excluding the commercial and hotel districts along the waterfronts, Rudolphe Street and what was then Prince of Wales Road (now Manwel Dimech Street). Interviews were conducted in the Easter vacation of 1979.

The Socio-economic Characteristics of the Respondents and their Experience of other Localities

The aim of this part of the study was to find out how urban Maltese people viewed the different localities on the island. Respondents were randomly sampled from the householders of residences in four localities selected because they typified aspects of urban settlement and migration within the island. Senglea is actually an old town built under the Order and developed by Maltese traders and the British dockyard in the nineteenth century. But, as a result of the Second World War, fifty-five per cent of its dwellings had to be reconstructed over the last thirty years. By contrast, Sliema was mainly built in the century before the war and only fourteen per cent built since then for Maltese domestic use. Ninety per cent of Fgura was built after the war and over sixty-four per cent since 1964. In Attard one found a dichotomy which was reflected in many responses, because twenty-eight per cent of the dwellings there dated from before the First World War – often farmers' dwellings, whereas fifty-four per cent were new villas built often initially for British settlers, since 1964.

Both Senglea and Sliema had ageing populations but the motivation of their young emigrants differed. Even if accommodation was available, Sengleans wanted to leave. But Sliema's offspring could not afford to stay even if they wanted to. By contrast Fgura and Attard had settled immigrant populations composed of middle-aged couples and their children, although Attard's householders were older, being mainly villagers and affluent villa-owners. In Fgura they were first-time buyers and tenants. In Senglea residences were generally rented from government or at prewar rent levels fixed by law, but in Sliema half were owner-occupied or decontrolled.[3] By contrast three quarters of households in Fgura

---

[3] Dwellings built before 1956 were statutorily held to pre-1939 rent levels thereby virtually socializing the older private rented sector. Although relaxed in 1980 the new controls were extended to cover most dwellings rented to Maltese citizens by specifying the permissible limits to rent increases and easing the conversion of such property to home ownership.

and Attard were owner-occupiers although only six per cent of the former and nearly half the latter lived in detached or semi-detached villas. Again this reflected their respective positions in the housing market and the sectoral pattern of migration from the two sides of the harbour. The differences were based on their levels of income: The latter were lowest in Senglea, highest in Sliema and most concentrated within a narrow central band in Fgura. But, even though remarkably low rentals were paid in controlled areas (half of Senglea and a quarter of Sliema paid less than Lm20 per year), there was a widespread desire to 'get on' by moving out, with places like Fgura being regarded as the stepping stone. As overcrowding declined, Senglea's average occupancy rate fell to those of Sliema and Attard, although the poorest conditions could still be found there. But in Fgura, with its young families, one found the highest occupancy rates despite the reduced birth rates in Malta since Independence.

One would expect a strong relationship between income, occupation and education and the types of housing, and therefore the residential localities, within a household's reach. Less than a third of Senglean householders had completed more than primary education and less than seven per cent of their children had stayed beyond the minimum school-leaving age. In the other three localities, at least eleven per cent of householders had stayed on at school, and in Attard almost half. Between a quarter and a half of their sons had stayed on to complete technical or A level education, in Fgura through government and in Sliema and Attard through private, fee-paying, church schools. But in Fgura far more children had failed to proceed beyond the minimum school-leaving age. Given that Fgura was seen as a social stepping stone, one could see education as one of the selectors in this process. This fact may explain why so many Fgura householders disliked their locality, an unusual response. They wanted to move on.

The relative ages of the four populations, and their different experience of British defence employment which had just ended, determined the proportion in gainful employment. Government and Malta Drydocks were the largest employers, with small-scale industry, commerce, and especially tourism filling some of the gap. By using general categories such as the British classification of manual and non-manual occupations by the Office of Population, Censuses and Statistics (OPCS), or Hope and Goldthorpe's

Figure 2. Age and sex of the total population in the households of the four sampled localities.

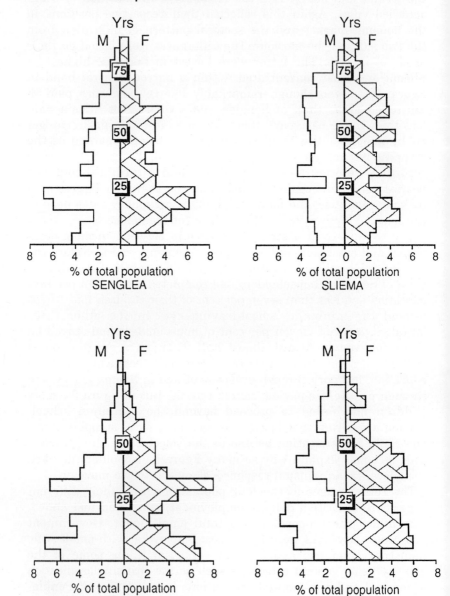

(1974) three-fold classification, the differences between the four localities were clear, once the householders who were housewives, mostly widows, had been removed (see Table 1 as well as Boswell, 1982). Only intermediate white-collar, sub-professional and supervisory occupations were relatively evenly spread between localities. On the other hand, it was clear that whenever people had moved out of town, their participation in the economy often changed as well. Although their experience of work reflected that of their parents, children's work patterns were different, primarily because, except in Attard, many fewer daughters than sons had a job. When they did work, however, young women were more often in non-manual occupations. Fgura's position was interstitial, having technicians and engineers, whereas Sliema and Attard had more professional and senior managerial employees, and many school teachers.

Table 1. General types of occupation of householders in the four sampled localities.

(Using OPCS Appendix B1 classification)

	Senglea %	Fgura %	Sliema %	Attard %
Non-manual	18.5	48.9	57.7	67.2
Manual	48.3	38.2	23.0	18.5
Armed Services not elsewhere included	8.0	3.5	3.8	1.4
Housewives without paid employment	16.5	6.2	14.2	4.3
Inadequately described	7.2	3.4	1.9	7.2
Total Number	**139**	**146**	**212**	**69**

(Using condensed form of Hope/Goldthorpe classification)

	Senglea %	Fgura %	Sliema %	Attard %
Service	9.4	33.6	33.5	46.4
Intermediate	28.1	23.3	34.4	29.0
Manual	38.8	33.6	16.0	13.0
Housewives, without paid employment	16.5	6.2	14.2	4.3
Inadequately described	7.2	3.4	1.9	7.2
Total Number	**139**	**146**	**212**	**69**

Figure 3. Current workplace of householders in the four sampled localities.

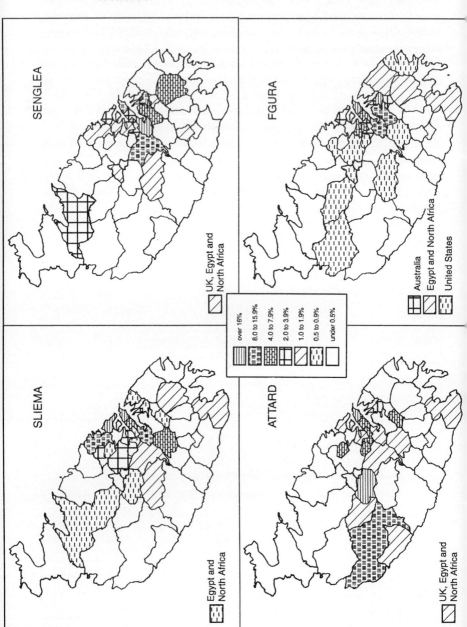

Although socio-economic criteria differentiated the localities, there was much that linked them. By far the most common was marriage, commonly a desire to live near the bride's family, or the need to move out to find one's own accommodation. But current contacts were maintained because most householders worked outside their locality (see Figure 3). In Fgura only ten per cent worked within it but in Sliema this exceeded seventeen per cent. Those from Sliema and Attard were two to three times as likely to work in Valletta because the capital was a centre of governmental, business and some professional work. Although government employment in particular took about twelve per cent of householders living in Fgura and Senglea to the other side of the harbour, especially to Floriana, over half their householders worked on their own side with less than ten per cent coming in from Sliema and Attard. Those from Sliema were more likely to work in the outer harbour areas including the airport.

Each locality except Fgura, had a high proportion of second-generation residents – over fifty per cent in Senglea and Sliema, and thirty five per cent in Attard, mainly local villagers. Even more parents lived in adjacent localities and this was also reflected in the location of children who had left home. What differed was the number of children who had emigrated abroad. These came mainly from the inner-urban core to the United Kingdom, although Fgura evidenced the more general Maltese pattern of emigration to Australia.

General Perceptions of the Social Prestige of Different Localities and the Methods Used to Assist their Analysis

Locality-specific patterns of experience of this sort may modify or reinforce any general status hierarchy of localities. In order to assess the latter, a set of twenty-four localities were selected from a potential Maltese total of about seventy. Most were in the inner and outer harbour regions that then formed most of the conurbation, with another eight selected from older villages in other parts of the island, holiday resorts then used by Maltese people, and areas with new villas. Each of the four sampled localities was included. Householders were given a randomly ordered set of place-name cards and asked to group them in up to five categories (from very high to very low status). They were

Figure 4. Mean status grading of residential localities in Malta as perceived by the householders of the four sampled localities (black and grey simply used for clarification).

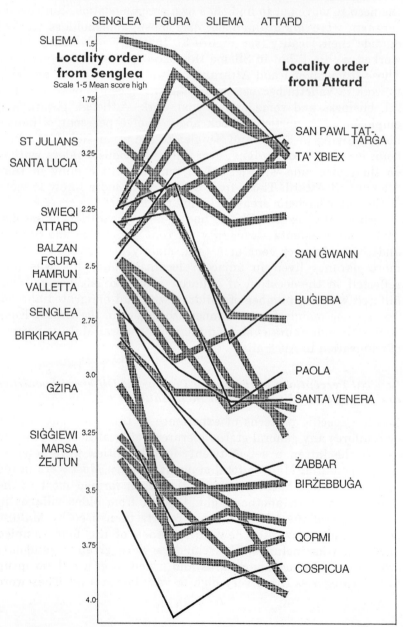

also asked where they would most and least like to live in Malta and which were the highest and lowest status parts of the locality in which they actually resided. The responses obtained have been subjected to a variety of different modes of statistical analysis, which have had the result of reinforcing each other and will be considered in ascending order of sophistication.

Figure 4 shows the mean status grading accorded to the set by each sampled locality. The overall pattern was fairly constant but some responses were locality-specific. With the notable exception of Sliema, Sengleans used a narrow range of the available scale but the position, for instance, of Ta' Xbiex, was in the same order even if awarded a different grade. More substantial differences in perception require explanation. Santa Lucia, a new town or garden suburb with public rentable housing, had high prestige for Sengleans who wanted to move out but was much more lowly placed by residents elsewhere. Senglea itself was only esteemed by Sengleans, but coupled with Cospicua at the bottom by everyone else. Gżira was probably elevated by Sengleans because of its position on the other side of the harbour, but despised by others because of its reputation as a red-light district.

Measures of centrality such as the mean grading of each locality's status offer rather crude guides to exploring the association between these variables. The use of 'space analysis' in sociology offers much more because the statistical procedures are more sensitive to patterns in the data. What may seem to be statistical juggling is actually a way of getting these methods of representing the data to fit them more closely, rather than forcing the data into the simple patterns required by the cruder measures. Space analysis is basically an extension of the two-dimensional scatter-diagram idea to a world of any number of dimensions that the investigator may conceive. An individual's position can be measured on a number of variables (or dimensions or factors) of interest to the researcher, which define a region in what may be termed a 'sociological space' (Loether & McTavish, 1974, Chap. 10). By adopting the notion of space, measures of distance and positions along the dimensions became conceivable and calculable. There are various methods for handling many variables simultaneously while describing and exploring this space. And one then has to use the insights gained to refine one's model of explaining what is going on sociologically.

One useful way of investigating data of this kind is factor analysis which is used when the correlations between the responses have already been obtained which represent a single measure of difference or distance between them. Factor analysis searches for a linear combination of variables, rather like multiple regression equations, in such a way that as much as possible of the variance between the original scored responses is explained. This line is called the 'factor' of the original matrix of scores. Generally more than one 'factor' is needed to explain this variance and the matrix can be rotated by 90° in any direction in order to take account of other 'factors' (see Loether & McTavish, 1974, Chapter 10). One factor often accounts for a substantial part of the variance but the rotation helps to explore further patterns. In this Maltese case, one may see the principal factor as representing a general status or prestige while others may reflect the assessment of localities in other, more specifically typifying ways. The extent to which the position of any locality was explained by one factor is indicated by its 'loading' weight or score.

Factor analysis of the combined responses from all four localities indicated a principal factor accounting for twenty per cent of the variance on which most of the localities were loaded with the notable exception of the seven most affluent and prestigious localities in the set. By rotating the matrix a wider spread of localities across the factors was obtained (see Table 2) which virtually reflects each type of urban settlement in Malta. Significantly loaded on the first factor were all the working-class towns in the set, those with the lowest educational and income levels in the 1967 Census and the highest levels of manual, industrial employment. Gżira was the main red-light district which survived the departure of the warships and the advent of tourism and the Libyan connection. Żabbar and Żejtun were urban villages closely associated with dockyard labour, new industrial estates and a reputation for rather riotous MLP organization. Valletta has been a source of major emigration and Ħamrun was a densely built thoroughfare adjacent to some of the poorest localities in the conurbation.

Although much less variance is explained by the other factors, two questions may be asked. Is there any pattern in the localities loaded on any factor? Does the most heavily loaded locality, at the top of each factor list, represent a model or ideal type for those which accompany it, such as one finds with occupational, ethnic and linguistic categories? In analyzing ethnicity and social distance, Mitchell (1974) indicated how ethnic groups in Central African towns assessed one another according to broad categories associated with a dominant tribe in each group as well as in terms of more specific sets of tribal hierarchies within each of these categories. Maltese people may adopt similar levels of categorization in assessing the social prestige of local residential areas. Some may act as lodestones for a cluster of similar places and mention of them may trigger a set of expectations and responses. Cospicua performed such a role on factor one. On factor two fell two new towns, the localities full of emigrants from the dockyard towns and two rapidly expanding seaside resorts used by the Maltese for second homes. Santa Lucia may be seen as a fairly good model for these. Similarly San Pawl tat-Tarġa was one of three of the most prestigious new and old residential districts that attracted people with high business and professional incomes. And three similarly prestigious old villages in the centre of the island were loaded together on factor four. The third, Lija, was not in the surveyed set anyway.

Table 2. Factor analysis of the householders' assessment of the social status of localities in Malta.
Varimax rotation of the factor matrix (with iterations) restricted to seven factors.

Factor 1	Factor 2	Factor 3	Factor 4	Factor 5	Factor 6	Factor 7
Cospicua .68	Santa Lucia .71	San Pawl tat-Tarġa .72	Balzan .83	Sliema .66	Siġġiewi .66	Santa Venera .47
Gżira .56	San Ġwann .58	Swieqi .66	Attard .72	St Julians .57	Żabbar .48	
Senglea .50	Fgura .57	Ta' Xbiex .51		Ta' Xbiex .35	Żejtun .46	
Valletta .49	Paola .56			Valletta .31	Qormi .42	
Marsa .45	Buġibba .43					
Ħamrun .41	Birżebbuġa .38					
Qormi .38						
Żejtun .37						
Żabbar .31						

(Birkirkara is omitted from any significant loading on any factor.)

Some localities appeared more than once which may indicate dichotomous patterns that are still explicable on the lines already suggested. All 'Sliema-side' harbour localities were loaded together on the fifth factor. Ta' Xbiex fits here as well as on factor three. But Valletta seemed to mean different things to different respondents – damp, dilapidation and overcrowded poverty to some, and the capital city, *Il-Belt*, to others whose business premises and town houses were located there. Loaded on factor six are the four large urban villages in the survey set, three of which had manual industrial populations, hence their loading on factor one as well. Siġġiewi had a much higher proportion of its population engaged full-time in agriculture. Two localities were isolated. Santa Venera was then one of the most recent areas of suburban infilling, and Birkirkara was one of the oldest large urban parishes in Malta with a largely unskilled manual working population, artisans in small enterprises and a high density of old buildings.

Factor analysis has often been used as if it represents clustering but it is based on Euclidian distance on *one* dimension at a time. Clustering techniques, such as hierarchical linkages, have the advantage of being based on all the dimensions as an overall distance. Both methods of analysis are attempts to discover and describe structure in an unstructured rectangular array of data. The methods seek different types of structure, although there is much overlap. Described in conventional statistical terms, factor analysis is an attempt to find a few 'independent' variables such that regression on those variables fits the observed data. Geometrically, it is an attempt to locate a linear substance that nearly fits the data. In contrast, cluster analysis is an attempt to find an analysis of variance classification of the units (a one-way or nested design) which reduces unexplained variation (Kruskal & Tanur, 1978, p. 51).

Reference to Figure 5 will show what resulted from analyzing the same collective pattern of locality-status responses through the hierarchical linkages between these responses which were arrayed across the same notional social space as when the principal factors were discussed. Using this method one can see which items are most closely related to which other items, starting with the situation on the left of the figure in which each item is on its own and proceeding by measured steps to the right where eventually all the items are considered part of the same group i.e.

localities in Malta. This sort of hierarchical cluster analysis permits the investigator to select and discuss relatively specific, tightly-related groups or more loosely associated groupings further along the process of clustering (Loether & McTavish, 1974, p. 347). The relative degrees of association or disassociation within and between clusters of locality-statuses may be observed from their points of linkage.

Figure 5. The hierarchical linkage of locality statuses (using Ward's method for calculating inter-cluster distances) as perceived by all householders in the sample.

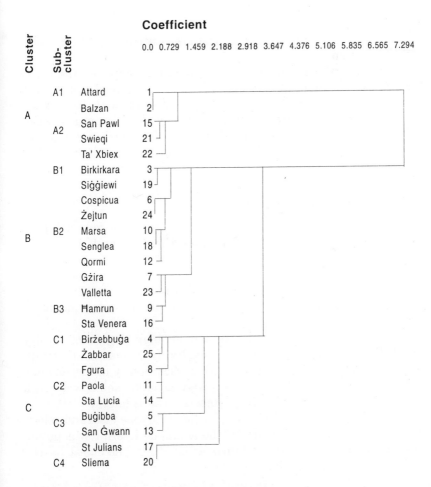

The general pattern was similar to Figure 4 but there seemed to be more regional association. Cluster A consisted of all the most prestigious old and new localities outside the main towns corresponding to loading on factors two and three. Cluster C linked St. Julians and Sliema with the expanding suburbs and holiday resorts, with the older (C4) and new (C3) towns on the Sliema-side being relatively distanced from the three on the dockyard-side (C2) and the urban village and resort on that same side of the island (C1). There appeared to be two criteria for association, urban type and regional position. Given the postwar pattern of sectoral migration in different directions from the inner-harbour core and the social significance attached to residence on either side of the harbours, it appeared that the social reputations of the latter had been extended to the areas attracting their internal emigration.

Cluster B was less obviously explicable. B2 comprised the dockyard and other industrial, low-income towns. Siġġiewi stood apart again but didn't seem to have any obvious link with Birkirkara except this difference from elsewhere. B1 and B2 shared low socio-economic status and were clustered with B3 which consisted of localities sharing disputed, ambivalent or indeterminate status that needed more investigation.

Differential Desirability and Prestige

Although the responses of householders from the four sampled localities were aggregated to consider their general perception pattern, Figure 3 has indicated that they did differ in some respects, especially when asked to rate their own locality in relation to others. Responses to an open-ended question as to where householders would most, or least, like to live provided one means of investigating these differences.

From Tables 3 and 4 one can see the high degree of loyalty residents displayed to their own locality. In Sliema and Attard, of course, this was consistent with their desirability to respondents from other localities. But Sengleans were loyal to their town, which others rejected, although they rejected the adjacent Cottonera towns of Cospicua and Vittoriosa just like everyone else, and selected, as desirable, localities outside the actual dockyard towns but on the same side of the harbour, in particular Paola, the oldest nearby

The Social Prestige of Residential Areas

Table 3. Localities most liked by householders in the four sampled localities.

Householder's place of residence

Most liked locality	Senglea	%	Fgura	%	Sliema	%	Attard	%
Own locality	Senglea	15.5	Fgura	13.8	Sliema	47.0	Attard	23.0
Capital city	Valletta	1.9	Valletta	1.5	Valletta	3.0	Valletta	3.4
Inner Harbour A		(11.7)		(17.0)		(7.0)		(15.9)
	Sliema	7.9	Sliema	9.9	Gżira	3.0	Sliema	10.3
	Floriana	1.5	Floriana	1.9	Ta' Xbiex	2.0	Swieqi	2.3
	Other	2.3	Other	4.2	Other	2.0	Other	3.3
Inner Harbour B		(14.8)		(20.0)		(1.0)		(1.1)
	Paola	6.4	Paola	14.2				
	Marsa	2.3	Cospicua	2.3				
	Cospicua	2.3	Kalkara	1.9				
	Vittoriosa	1.5	Other	1.6				
	Kalkara	1.5						
	Other	0.8	Other		Other	1.0	Other	1.1
Outer Harbour A		(7.7)		(8.5)		(17.0)		(9.1)
	Ħamrun	2.3	Ħamrun	1.9	St Julians	8.0	Ħamrun	2.3
	San Ġwann	1.9	St Julians	1.9	Birkirkara	3.0	San Ġwann	2.3
	Birkirkara	1.9	Birkirkara	1.5	St Andrews	2.0	Birkirkara	2.3
					Kappara	2.0		
	Other	1.6	Other	3.2	Other	2.0	Other	2.2
Outer Harbour B		(17.9)		(16.1)		(3.0)		(1.1)
	Fgura	7.2	Żabbar	10.7				
	Sta Lucia	4.6	Sta Lucia	5.4				
	Żabbar	4.2						
	Other	1.9			Other	3.0	Other	1.1
Region 3 (SEast)		(6.9)		(6.2)		(3.0)		
	Birżebbuġa	2.3	Marsascala	2.3				
			Birżebbuġa	1.9				
	Other	4.6	Other	2.0	Other	3.0		
Region 4 (West)		(10.4)		(11.8)		(15.0)		(27.4)
	Rabat	3.0	Rabat	3.0	Balzan	4.0	Balzan	10.3
	Attard	2.3	Attard	3.0	Rabat	3.0	Rabat	6.9
	Balzan	2.3	Balzan	1.9	Attard	3.0	Lija	4.6
			Lija	1.5	Lija	3.0	Żebbuġ	2.3
	Other	2.8	Other	2.4	Other	2.0	Other	3.3
Region 5 (North)		(7.8)		(5.0)		(5.0)		(14.6)
	St Paul's Bay	2.3			Mosta	2.0	Mosta	4.6
	Mosta	1.5			Madliena	2.0	St Paul's Bay	2.3
	Other	4.0	Other	5.0	Other	1.0	Other	7.7
Gozo		0.8				1.0		1.1
Total number of Mentions		264		261		310		87

Table 4. Localities least liked by householders in the four sampled localities.

Householder's place of residence

Least liked locality	Senglea	%	Fgura	%	Sliema	%	Attard	%
Own locality	Senglea	3.5	Fgura	13.8	Sliema	—	Attard	—
Capital city	Valletta	9.5	Valletta	12.9	Valletta	20.0	Valletta	19.2
Inner Harbour A		(7.4)		(8.7)		(7.0)		(3.8)
	Sliema	3.9	Sliema	5.1	Gżira	2.0	Sliema	2.5
	Msida	1.3	Ta' Xbiex	1.2	Msida	2.0	Msida	1.3
	Gżira	1.3						
	Other	0.9	Other	2.4	Other	3.0	Other	—
Inner Harbour B		(46.4)		(51.6)		(47.0)		(43.4)
	Vittoriosa	21.7	Cospicua	18.4	Cottonera	19.0	Cottonera	32.0
	Cospicua	19.9	Cottonera	12.1	Cospicua	13.0	Vittoriosa	3.8
	Marsa	2.2	Vittoriosa	11.3	Senglea	7.0	Marsa	3.8
	Kalkara	1.7	Senglea	8.6	Vittoriosa	4.0	Senglea	2.5
	Other	0.9	Marsa	1.2	Marsa	2.0	Cospicua	1.3
			Other	—	Other	2.0	Other	—
Outer Harbour A		(4.8)		(2.9)		(5.0)		(5.1)
	Ħamrun	2.6	Ħamrun	1.0	Ħamrun	4.0	Birkirkara	3.8
	Birkirkara	1.3	Birkirkara	1.5			Ħamrun	1.3
	Other	0.9	Other	0.4	Other	1.0	Other	—
Outer Harbour B		(10.9)		(5.9)		(10.0)		(15.4)
	Paola	3.5	Qormi	2.7	Qormi	6.0	Qormi	10.3
	Qormi	3.0	Paola	1.6			Fgura	2.5
	Żabbar	2.6	Żabbar	1.6			Paola	1.3
	Other		Other				Żabbar	1.3
	Other	1.8	Other	—	Other	4.0	Other	—
Region 3 (SEast)		(7.4)		(13.4)		(9.0)		(12.9)
	Gudja	2.2	Żejtun	6.6	Żejtun	2.0	Żejtun	10.3
	Żejtun	1.7	Qrendi	1.6			Mqabba	1.3
	Mqabba	1.3	Mqabba	1.6			Safi	1.3
	Qrendi	1.3	Żurrieq	1.6				
			Gudja	1.6				
	Other	0.9	Other	0.4	Other	7.0	Other	—
Region 4 (West)		(5.7)		(1.6)		(6.0)		(—)
	Żebbuġ	2.6			Żebbuġ	2.0		
	Dingli	1.3						
	Other	1.8	Other	1.6	Other	4.0	Other	—
Region 5 (North)		(6.7)		(3.6)		(—)		(1.3)
	Mellieħa	1.3	Mellieħa	1.2			Mellieħa	1.3
	Other	5.4	Other	2.4	Other	—	Other	—
Total number of Mentions		231		256		310		78

locality with immigration. Fgura residents, by contrast, preferred or rejected their own locality in equal numbers, which seems consistent with an aspiring and mobile population. Some were glad to have got there but others were eager to get out. A substantial number preferred the adjacent Paola although they also rejected the Cottonera towns from which many of them had migrated.

There was a pattern in these variations. The responses given by the residents of the two sides of the harbour did not present mirror-images. Local loyalties did not override the general preference for higher status localities. Within each Maltese region some localities were more esteemed than others, but this differentiation was more obvious to local residents than people living further off, so that there were broad categories of ascribed status within which lesser hierarchies of desirability, or prestige, were perceived by these acquainted with these localities. There is a close parallel between residential desirability and the perception of social prestige and between these and other kinds of reference-group patterning through ethnic or occupational categorization (see Boswell, 1982, and Mitchell, 1974 and 1987).

Table 5. First canonical correlations of the responses given by householders in the four sampled localities in their assessment of the social status of localities in Malta.

	Senglea	Fgura	Sliema	Attard
Senglea	X	0.91166	0.88256	0.85613
Fgura	X	X	0.95189	0.91780
Sliema	X	X	X	0.88833
Attard	X	X	X	X

All significant at 0.000 level

In order to investigate those differences more fully, each of the four sets of hierarchically linked responses were correlated to measure the extent to which one locality's set of responses could be predicted from those of another locality. Canonical regression is a means of calculating the extent to which the results of one calculation are correlated with those of another calculation (Cattell, 1978, p. 391). From the first canonical correlation of these responses, shown in Table 5, one can infer a significant association between all four but it was highest between Fgura and Sliema and lowest between Senglea and Attard. The old dockyard town residents shared fewer perceptions with the old villagers and their affluent suburban newcomers. Attard's small sample members and dichotomous population may have influenced their relative departure from the general pattern, but even so their response was still significantly correlated with the others.[4]

Plotting the Relationship Between the Social Prestige of Localities in a Social Space

The overall distribution of the prestige accorded to localities in a social space can be represented through the use of multi-dimensional scaling programmes. Scaling models take seriously the idea that one can calculate the similarity of one sociological set of data with another set and represent them as objects in space. The more similar these objects are, the closer they lie to each other, and the final configuration is that pattern of points which most accurately represents the original information. Most sociological data is elicited from non-experimental settings and often refers to populations which are diverse and not homogeneous. So it is worth being sensitive to differences between individuals or groups and being careful not to 'wash out' these differences which the usual procedures for aggregating data tend to do. 'Unlike conventional multivariate models, assumptions about distributions rarely need to be made and the procedures in no way depend upon the particular measures of similarity. Most importantly, however, non-metric MDS solutions are 'order-invariate' that is to say that only the ordinal content of the data is made use of in obtaining a solution, so any set of data with the same ordering of similarities or dissimilarities will generate the same metric solution' (Davies & Coxon, 1985, p. 2-3).

---

[4] A fuller version of this paper is awaiting publication in Rogers & Vertovic (eds) 'Festschrift' for J. Clyde Mitchell.

The Social Prestige of Residential Areas

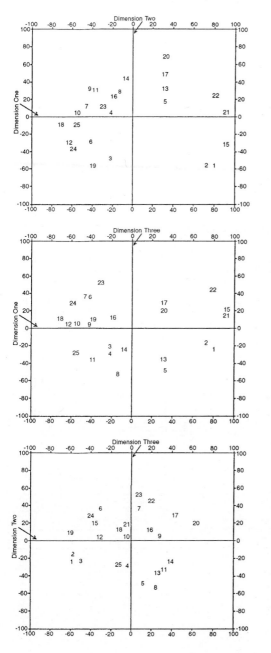

Figures 6, 7 and 8:
The relationship between the statuses of residential localities perceived by all the householders of the four sampled localities and analysed within a three-dimensional social space. (MINISSA programme included in Coxon's MDS package.)

	Dimensions		
	1	2	3
Sigma	0.7658	0.4945	0.4111

MAXMIN Clusters
Group A: 1,2,15, 21,22
Group B: 5,13,17,20
Group C:
    9,16,7,23,8,11,4,14
Group D:
    3,6,24,19,10,18,12,25

1. Attard
2. Balzan
3. Birkirkara
4. Birżebbuġa
5. Buġibba
6. Cospicua
7. Gżira
8. Fgura
9. Ħamrun
10. Marsa
11. Paola
12. Qormi
13. San Ġwann
14. Santa Lucia
15. San Pawl tat-Tarġa
16. Santa Venera
17. St Julians
18. Senglea
19. Siġġiewi
20. Sliema
21. Swieqi
22. Ta' Xbiex
23. Valletta
24. Żejtun
25. Żabbar

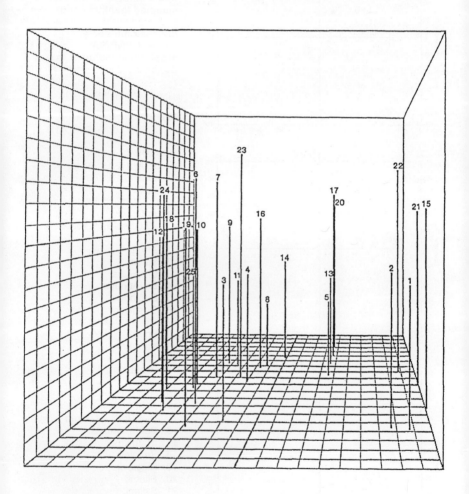

Figure 9. Three-dimensional perspective diagram of the status of localities perceived by the householders of the sampled localities (see Figures 6 - 8 for the two dimensional plots and numerical key).

Clyde Mitchell (personal communication) explains that the basic idea of multi-dimensional scaling, or least space analysis, is that if all the inter-point distances are known between any given number of points then these can be represented in space by all but one of the same number of dimensions. But the most one can appreciate is four dimensions, one of which is time. Only three dimensions can be represented spatially as in Figure 9. What one wants is some means of picking out the common features of the data collected while ignoring their idiosyncrasies.

Using mathematical procedures one can extract 'vectors' which, when multiplied matrix-wise with one another, reproduce all the exact distances between the points. The first vector (see Figure 6) accounts for most of the distance between the points, indicated by the relatively high sigma value of 0.7658. Additional vectors are extracted using definitions quite different from the first until all the distances have been accounted for. (See Figures 7 and 8) These procedures have been incorporated in computer programs[5] which have been used here and the whole perception pattern plotted within a single perspective (Figure 9) using Clyde Mitchell's program (Mitchell & Critchley, 1985). Although the dimensions are more restricted than those potentially available through factor analysis, the result confirms the impression already drawn from the modes of data-analysis which have already been presented.

What multi-dimensional scaling does is to create the smallest possible space in which the relationships between the original set of points can reasonably be represented. Having arrived at this point one can create the sort of dendrogram of linkages, using rigorous procedures such as Ward's method already discussed in relation to Figure 5, or to plot the dimensions in a spatial

---

[5] These MDS(X) programmes were originated by Roskam & Lingoes in a modification of Guttman-Lingoes's smallest space analysis and one included in Coxon's MDS package. Clyde Mitchell summarized the process as follows: Minissa Maxmin basically takes the lower triangle of the correlation matrix as its input and then finds space within which the points may be accommodated with the minimum amount of disturbance of the ordinal relationships between the original correlations (See Davies & Coxon, 1983).

representation as in Figures 6-9. These then require theoretical analysis and explanation.

Figures 6, 7 and 8 plot the relationship between locality statuses across pairs of dimensions, which are united in the perspective of Figure 9. In all cases the position of the locality code number denotes its position in the plot, the lines in Figure 9 merely indicating its place along the third dimension on the grid. Given the pattern of sub-clustering, often in pairs, and the subtly different ways in which households from different localities assessed the same set of places, there is less emphasis on one dominant dimension than was the case with the prestige accorded to occupations. But the sigma value of one dimension was much higher than the other two, 0.77 as opposed to 0.49 and 0.41, which indicates the general determinant of the whole pattern by social prestige.

The localities more loosely clustered around this were in Maxmin clusters, already discussed in previous sections, namely:

A. The oldest and newest high-cost and socially select areas of private villa building outside the main conurbation.
B. The oldest urban localities on the Sliema side of the harbour with the new resort and new town on that side of the island.
C. Most of the other localities subject to considerable urban expansion on the other, dockyard, side of the conurbation, together with adjacent localities and the resort on that side.
D. Localities of low socioeconomic status built around the dockyard and the port with outlying agricultural and industrial villages in the western and south eastern regions of Malta.

Within each cluster some localities were closely associated on all three dimensions, like Attard (1) and Balzan (2), and others were associated on some but not others, like Valletta (3) and Birżebbuġa (4). Consideration of what may be shared by localities clustered in this partial way is suggestive of the sort of criteria by which respondents may have been grading them but the examples given simply aim to open the discussion. Buġibba (5), Fgura (8), Paola (11) and Birżebbuġa (4) is an example linking two major areas of residential immigration from the Cottonera towns with rapidly growing seaside resorts on opposite sides of the island. Sliema (20) and St Julians (17) equated with San Pawl tat-Tarġa (15), Swieqi (20) and Ta' Xbiex (22) the most prestigious localities, on one dimension, but more closely associated with the socially more mixed seaside and new town developments on that side of the island, Buġibba (5) and San Ġwann (13), on other dimensions. Dimension 3 with Dimension 1 clearly separated the two sides of the harbour with only Santa Lucia, the other new town which is placed topographically between them, close to the dividing line. Birkirkara, as usual, is irregularly placed. Within the low-status sector, a quarter of the plot consists of all the towns and villages with the lowest socio-economic status, with the addition of Valletta (23) and Gżira (7), about which respondents showed divided opinions, in a marginal position.

Conclusion

Following the lead of Clyde Mitchell's (1987) use of factor and cluster analysis as well as MDS plotting, we sought to investigate the patterns, and therefore the lines of thought, through which Maltese people perceived and assessed their urban environment. The island was big enough for them to resort to broad social categorization as well as local specification, but small enough for most respondents to refer to most localities with some shared knowledge of these places or their reputations. Because Maltese people had a sense of place that was so often and so pointedly expressed, place of residence could be seen as a social characteristic like ethnicity. The survey results supported this observation.

Although there was not as much commonality in assessing the status of localities as in that of occupations, one cannot ignore the fact that the sample was stratified by locality and not occupation. There was less emphasis on one status dimension than on the clustering of localities in district groups. A broad distinction was drawn between localities either side of the social watershed that runs out of Valletta up the Ħamrun road, the distinction between 'them' and 'us' on either side of the harbours. Another type of distinction was drawn between expanding urban residential areas, usually of mixed private and public housing, and older, built-up localities within the harbour regions. Householders used these latter criteria to form clusters within the broader lines of differentiation.

Where response patterns differed between the four sampled localities these reflected not only a general loyalty to one's home town, except in Fgura, but consistency with the householders' separate evaluations of the places in which they would most, or least, like to live. But they shared a general pattern which I have discussed in relation to other information available on these localities, such as the socioeconomic evidence in the 1957 and 1967 censuses, that for 1985 coming too late to have provided a reputational guide. By asking respondents where they would most or least like to live, which streets or parts of their own locality carried highest or lowest status, and where in Malta they would be most likely to find residents like themselves, they should have been prepared to tackle the general locality prestige question from common ground. Although of course some people will have known some localities better than others, the overall pattern of responses ought not and does not appear to have been haphazard. By drawing on separate knowledge about these localities one can see the lines of reasoning behind their responses. But much of this interpretation comes from the characteristics of the respondents revealed by other sections of the survey itself, some of which have been discussed in the preambling sections.

Householders living in significantly different types of locality in the Maltese conurbation shared a general perception of the social prestige of residential areas. In some cases one locality may have acted as the model with which others were then associated, such as Sliema or the Cottonera towns as ideal types for their respective sides of the harbours. Had one wished to classify Maltese localities by urban type, one could not on the evidence then available have achieved anything more precise, nor as subtly varied, as the responses reported here. Given the fact that the 1967 census remained unpublished, it could not have predisposed the responses. One may therefore conclude that Maltese people in general have very clear perceptions not only of their own locality and its neighbours, but also of the island as a whole. These perceptions closely accord with socio-economic characteristics verifiable from other sources. They have been found in a population known to have high, but often sectorally directed levels, of association with other localities as well as a high level of participation in local festivals and a high electoral turnout. All the answers are not provided in the types of explanation and analysis of the patterns that are suggested here. They are indeed open to further local or more general sociological modes of explanation. But it is encouraging that the various methods of analysing the same data have reinforced one another. This suggests that the data is reasonably robust and the procedures capable of reliable use in other countries, or subsequent surveys in Malta. They therefore meet the important criteria for repeatability and compatibility.

References

Boissevain, J. (1965) *Saints and Fireworks: Religion and Politics in Rural Malta*, London, Athlone Press.
Boissevain, J. (1969) *Hal-Farrug: A Village in Malta*, New York, Holt, Reinhart & Winston.
Boissevain, J. (1984) 'Ritual escalation in Malta', in Wolf, E.R. (ed.) *Religion, Power and Protest in Local Communities*, Amsterdam, Mouton.
Boissevain, J. (1986) 'Residential inversion: the changing use of social space in Malta', *Hyphen*, vol. 5, 2.
Boswell, D.M. (1980) 'Patron-client relations in the Mediterranean with special reference to the changing political situation in Malta', *Mediterranean Studies*, vol. 2, 1.
Boswell, D.M. (1982) 'Patterns of occupational and residential area prestige in the Maltese conurbation', paper presented at the 10th World Congress of Sociology, Mexico City.
Bowen-Jones, H., Dewdney, J.C., & Fisher, W.B. (1961) *Malta: Background for Development*, Durham, Department of Geography.
Cattell, R.B. (1978) *The Scientific Use of Factor Analysis in Behavioural and Life Sciences*, London, Plenum Press.
Central Office of Statistics (1977) *Annual Abstract of Statistics: 1976*, Valletta, Government Press.
Central Office of Statistics (1986) *Census '85: Vol. 1. A Demographic Profile of Malta and Gozo*, Valletta, Government Press.
Central Office of Statistics (1978) *Demographic Review of the Maltese Islands for the Year 1977*, Valletta, Government Press.
Central Office of Statistics (n.d.) *1967 Census of Population, Housing and Employment*, Valletta, Government Press. Unpublished proof in University of Malta Library.
Davies, P.M. & Coxon, A.P.M., (1983) *MDS (X) user manual: the MDS (X) Series of Multidimensional Scaling Programs*, Inter-University Research Council Series Report no. 55, University of Edinburgh Program Library Unit.
Glass, D.V. (ed) (1954) *Social Mobility in Britain*, London, Routledge & Kegan Paul.
Goldthorpe, J., Lewellyn C. & Payne, C. (1980) *Social Mobility and Class Structure in Modern Britain*, Oxford, Clarendon Press.

Grech, J. (1978) *Threads of Dependence*, Malta, Malta University Press.
Hall, J. & Jones, D.C. (1950) 'Social grading of occupations', *British Journal of Sociology*, vol. 1, 1.
Harrison, A. St. B. & Hubbard, R.P.S. (1945) *Valletta: A Report to Accompany the Outline Plan for the Region of Valletta and the Three Cities*, Valletta, Malta Government.
Hope, K., & Goldthorpe, J. (1974) *The Social Grading of Occupations*, Oxford, Clarendon Press.
Hourihan, K. (1979) 'The evaluation of urban neighbourhoods', *Environment and Planning*.
Kaufman, L. & Rousseeuw, P.J. (1990) *Finding Groups in Data: An Introduction to Cluster Analysis*, New York, John Wiley & Sons.
Kruskal, W.H. & Tanur, J.M. (eds) (1978) *International Encyclopaedia of Statistics*, London, The Free Press.
Loether, H.J. & McTavish, D.G. (1974) *Descriptive Statistics for Sociologists: An Introduction*, London, Allyn & Bacon.
Malta Government (1981) *Malta: Guidelines for Progress: Development Plan 1981-85*, Valletta, Office of the Prime Minister.
Metwally, M.M. (1977) *Structure and Performance of the Maltese Economy*, Malta, A&C Aquilina & Co.
Mifsud, P.V. (1983) 'A study of the history, allocation, social composition and role of Government Housing in Malta', unpublished Ph.D. thesis.
Mitchell, J.C. (1974) 'Perceptions of ethnicity and ethnic behaviour: an empirical exploration', in Cohen, A. (ed.) *Urban Ethnicity*, London, Tavistock.
Mitchell, J.C. & Critchley, F. (1985) 'Configuration similarity in three class contexts in British society', *Sociology*, vol. 19, 1.
Mitchell, J.C. (1987) *Cities, Society and Social Perception: A Central African Perspective*, Oxford, Clarendon Press.
Richardson, M. (1961) 'Modern Malta – Population and migration' in Bowen-Jones, H. et al., op.cit.

8

Towards a Sociology of Consumption in Malta

Ronald G. Sultana

Introduction

Most Maltese, upon being asked to identify a key characteristic feature of the social formation they inhabit, would probably mention the relatively recent emphasis on the consumption of durable and non-durable goods. Of course, persons must consume in order to satisfy 'basic needs'. What is of sociological interest is first of all the way such 'needs' have been defined historically and cross-culturally, for there is very little which is natural or essential about the way in which modern persons consume goods and services which many consider they cannot do without. As Bocock (1992, p. 122) correctly argues, 'basic needs are not easy to specify in detail, and, in any case, they never arise outside a social, cultural, historical context'.

Secondly, sociological inquiry focuses on the way the overproduction of goods in modern society generates a culture of consumerism. Thirdly, this shift in culture is interrogated in order to explore the meaning that consumption has for the consumer and for groups of consumers.

All three aspects are of interest and relevance to the study of Maltese society, and each is addressed systematically in the following sections.

From Frugality to Consumerism

Given Malta's dependency status over the centuries, it is not surprising that 'frugality', 'thrift', and 'sobriety' became a characterizing virtue of the people, celebrated in many proverbs and sayings (Zammit, 1984, p. 12). Indeed, when the Labour Government was faced with the international recession of the 1970s, and was obliged to ask people to 'tighten their belts' (Boissevain, 1986a), it appealed to this traditional virtue in order to legitimize policies unpalatable to consumers. These included a wage freeze and local monopolies that limited the availability of goods as well as sharply restricted choice in brand-names for the same type of goods on the market.

On the other hand, the setting up of a welfare state and a general redistribution of wealth under the socialist government led to higher incomes which fuelled new consumer 'needs' among the working-class and lower middle-class segments of Maltese society (cf. Sant, *The Sunday Times*, 5 September 1992, p. 7). These groups now had the wherewithal to aspire for the same consumer goods and services enjoyed by the more moneyed local classes, and to follow foreign role models in terms of life styles. More women keep a job after they are married and have children, and whether this engagement in the labour market is on a full-time or part-time basis, or in the legal or underground economy, the fact remains that more money is brought into the family budget. Children too make a contribution to that 'fund' by their participation in the twilight economy (cf. Sultana, 1993).

In addition to this, one can claim that, generally speaking, the Maltese have been earning more – in 1976 the per capita income was Lm712, while in 1990 it had become Lm2,219 – and spending more – in 1983 the Maltese spent about Lm160.7 million (at constant prices), while in 1991 they spent around Lm229.7 million (Ministry of Finance, 1992).[1] Indeed, Briguglio (1988, p. 55 ff.) has documented how the average propensity to consume, or the ratio of consumption to disposable income, has undergone a pattern of upward shifts from 1973 onwards. Trade statistics for 1991, (Ministry of Finance, 1992), providing a breakdown of imports by final use, similarly show a significant increase in importation of consumer items (in Lm million, at current prices), as follows:

	1986	1987	1988	1989	1990	1991
Consumer goods	82.2	92.5	102.5	108.4	114.4	147.6

Post-war Malta has seen village and city streets transformed, architecturally, into shopping boulevards, and larger sites have been specifically constructed in order to accelerate the process by which citizens are reconstructed as consumers, who either buy or who gaze, window-shopping, symbolically consuming that which they cannot afford to own. Pedestrians are therefore engulfed in an architecture which proposes to structure their experience of life, and public space is increasingly under pressure to accommodate commercial transactions. The economic policies of the Nationalist government, elected into office in 1987, have clearly fanned the flames of a consumeristic culture. The end of the wage freeze had 'an expansionary effect (both real and psychological) on income earners and their consumer expenditures' (Scicluna, 1991, p. 4). In addition, there was now to be 'unlimited choice' through the freeing of imports. There has, indeed, been a proli-

---

[1] There is a danger here of conflating 'Maltese society' into a homogeneous unit. It is thus important to keep in mind that the trend towards higher earnings, while true for all categories of workers, is weighted differently across the different groups (cf. Tonna, 1993, p. 32).

feration of sites of consumption where imported – hitherto exotic – goods have been displayed to titillate every taste. The Department Store phenomenon, for instance, has now hit Malta and Gozo, with Standa, British Home Stores, Plaza, and the Lm2 million 'Tiġrija Palazz' complex, among others, becoming established, in the last five years, as the new meccas for the insatiable consumer. Trade Fairs, with their dual roles as markets and sites of pleasure, and customarily held once every year for the past 36 years, have proliferated in number. Fourteen fairs are planned by the Trade Fairs Corporation for 1994 (*Il-Ġens*, 25 June 1993, p. 13). From a total of 48,200 visitors to the first edition of the Fair in 1952, record attendances were registered in 1991 (160,000 visitors) and 1992 (over 170,000) (*Malta Independent*, 4 July 1993, pp. 6, 7).

Such shopping centres, the modern version of the '*suq*', become 'the busiest concourse of human activity and movement, the main focus for all those warm bodies doing things and supplying endless possibilities for observation, humour and interaction' (Willis, 1984, p. 21). The centrality of that activity has recently been emphasized in Malta by a legal notice extending shopping hours to late in the evening in certain zones (*The Times*, 28 June 1993, p. 24).

There is no doubt that the freeing of the market has proved popular. People can now find in shops what they see advertised on Italian television channels, and what they have come across in shopping malls abroad. The chances of frustration of desire and pleasure in this regard have been minimized, at least for the wealthier groups in Malta. Indeed, the Nationalist Party election posters for 1992 cashed in on the attraction of consumerism, and portrayed a supermarket trolley full of imported goods. It thus drove home the point that consumer needs would continue to be satisfied if it were re-elected into government for another term. On its part, the Labour Party recognized the drive for consumption among the Maltese middle class and affluent workers, and that aspirations and values have changed (Mifsud, 1991, p. 5; Sant, *The Sunday Times*, 5 April 1992, p. 7). Despite its traditional left-wing critique of consumerism, therefore, the Labour Party has had to come to terms with the fact that to deny citizens consumer products is tantamount to committing political suicide.

A Consumerist Culture?

But is this to say that the Maltese are consumeristic, or are they merely materialistic? Are we simply engrossed by the fundamental needs of survival, or are we increasingly becoming engrossed by consumption for its own sake? The difference is important, for, given the conditions of scarcity that have haunted the people for generations, it stands to reason that concern about the fulfilling of basic material needs should be high. The point is whether the Maltese are increasingly becoming more attracted by 'superfluous' consumer goods, whether affluence (for some groups at least) leads to the creation of new appetites and needs which then must be satisfied through expanded consumption. In this case, the

> reference point is often the 'good life', the typical American dream purveyed through television adverts and films of informal consumption, cans of coke, tight jeans, flashy cars and Hollywood glamour.[2] This is a world of pictures, images to be consumed first with the eyes and ears to make you want to really consume in order to be like that. Consume an image to make you really consume to be like the image. The image may always be elusive and illusory. Its pursuit may be never ending. But this insatiable appetite is just what commerce needs. Ever greater consumption is necessary to try to get closer to the ever retreating image. It may be crazy, but at least you're buying (Willis, 1984, p. 22).

The extent to which this kind of consumer culture has made inroads into our ways of feeling and being can be gleaned from a number of sources.[3] In the following sections I will look at the way the

---

[2] This, at least partly, explains the latest TV hit in Malta, Beverly Hills 90210.

[3] Here I only refer to a few of these sources. Further research could look into the patterns in the volume of consumption of luxury items such as automobiles, for instance. The Trade Statistics published by the COS do not, unfortunately, give details of the number of vehicles imported by type (e.g. BMW, Mercedes, Volvo, Audi and other high status vehicles). Attempts to get this information by interviewing importers proved fruitless: this researcher's letters were not even acknowledged. Another important aspect of research on consumption would be

Maltese spend their money, since expenditure is a good indicator of what people value. I will then argue that this consumer culture has taken hold of a number of areas of our lives, and that its meaning needs to be interrogated.

How Do the Maltese Spend Their Money?

The Household Budget Survey (Retail Price Index Management Board, 1993), carried out by the Central Office of Statistics over a twelve-month period between October 1988 and September 1989, is a good source of information if we wish to appraise patterns of consumption. The study focused on a sample of 1,300 households representing the households of wage/salary earners of average size and with reasonable income. This represented, therefore, a limited sample, not representative of the Maltese population in general.

The study is nevertheless particularly useful because comparisons can be made with similar studies carried out in Malta in 1971/72 and 1980/81, as well as with those reported for other nations (mainly European). The Maltese households in the 1988/89 sample, for instance, reported an average gross household income of Lm66 a week, which represents an increase of 40 per cent over that reported by a similar group of households from April 1980 to March 1981 (RPIMB, ibid., p. 7). What is of most interest in this context is the way households spend their money. Especially indicative are changes in the proportions of the total household expenditure devoted to different commodities and services. Table 1 below presents the relevant data:

---

the gathering of information related to credit purchases of the Maltese. In this way, one would be able to gauge the propensity of people to consume even though they do not immediately have the means to do so.

Table 1. Average expenditure of all households

Item of Expenditure	Weekly expenditure 1980-81*	Proportion of total expenditure 1980-81	Weekly expenditure 1988-89	Proportion of total expenditure 1988-89
	cents	%	cents	%
Food	1607.7	41.9	2060.1	36.8
Beverages and tobacco	364.5	9.5	481.8	8.6
Clothing and footwear	406.7	10.6	460.8	8.2
Housing	153.5	4.0	218.5	3.9
Fuel, light and power	119.0	3.1	158.6	2.8
Durable household goods	234.1	6.1	292.3	5.2
Transport and communication	379.9	9.9	750.6	13.4
Personal care and health	214.9	5.6	355.8	6.4
Education, entertainment and recreation	188.0	4.9	463.0	8.3
Other goods and services	168.8	4.4	360.3	6.4
TOTAL	**3837.1**	**100.0**	**5601.8**	**100.0**
Other payments	344.7	–	985.5	–

*Estimated

The table above shows clearly that total expenditure exclusive of 'other payments' has gone up by 46 per cent since 1980/81, with less funds being allocated to food (down from 42% to 37% of total expenditure), and more spent on transport and communication (from 10% to more than 13%), education, entertainment and recreation (up from 5% to 8%). The figures indicate a decline (from 59.6% to 51.7%) in the importance of household expenditure on basic necessities (food, clothing, housing, light and power), and a shift from the 'goods' component of the index to the 'services' component.

These statistics are borne out by the most recently available figures on private consumption expenditure (Central Office of Statistics, 1990, p. 13). Thus, if we compare trends in the patterns of consumers' expenditure (at 1973 prices) between 1981 and 1990, we note an increase in expenditure on food by 41%, on recreation, entertainment, education and cultural services by 49%, and on transport and communication by 62%. Total private consumption expenditure in the domestic market increased by 40% during that period.

Table 2. Average expenditure of households in various industrialized countries compared to Malta.

Item of Expenditure	Belgium	Denmark	Spain	United States	France	Italy	Japan	Germany	Great Britain	Malta
Food, beverages and tobacco	19.1	21.3	22.0	13.1	19.4	21.7	20.4	16.5	21.1	45.4
Clothing and footwear	7.5	5.5	9.0	6.6	6.5	9.6	6.4	7.7	6.2	8.2
Housing, fuel, light and power	16.7	27.4	12.6	19.3	18.8	14.3	19.2	18.4	19.5	6.7
Durable household goods	10.9	6.5	6.6	5.6	8.1	8.8	6.1	8.8	6.9	5.2
Personal care and health	11.0	1.9	3.6	15.3	9.2	6.3	10.8	14.3	1.3	6.4
Transport and communication	12.9	16.3	15.7	14.5	16.8	12.9	10.2	15.1	17.7	13.4
Education, entertainment and recreation	6.5	10.0	6.5	10.0	7.3	9.1	10.2	9.0	9.5	8.3
Other goods and services	15.4	11.1	24.0	15.6	13.9	17.3	16.7	10.2	17.8	6.4
TOTAL	*100*	100	*100*	*100*	*100*	*100*	*100*	*100*	*100*	*100*

It is instructive to compare this information with data on household expenditure for 1989 in a number of other countries:[4]

As with other developing countries, the average household in Malta spends a relatively high percentage of its budget on basic necessities such as food. But this pattern is changing and two surveys published by the Ministry for Youth and Culture (1992) confirm the trends reported in the Household Budget Survey and

---

[4] Source is Mermet (1992, p. 337). Maltese data collapsed from the Household Budgetary Survey of 1988/89 (RPIMB, 1993).

clearly show that more and more people are spending more and more money on books, magazines, leisure activities, cinema, entertainment, and so on. Businessmen are reading these as 'indications giving a clue to the way customs and habits are changing ways of life', and are proposing the systematic monitoring of the market in order that they 'can meet and satisfy our people's changing demands'. (A. Galea, President of the Malta Trade Fairs Corporation, opening address reported in *The Malta Independent*, 4 July 1993, p. 7.)

A Change in Values?

These changes in patterns of spending are significant. But does this indicate, as Galea seems to believe in the excerpt quoted above, that values have changed radically? It is after all significant that the Maltese generally tend to save a good percentage of their total income, as if their historic experience of 'feast and famine' shifts serves as a restraint on consumption, and instigates them to prepare for 'a rainy day'. It is also significant that between 1983 and 1992, savings and time deposits in Maltese banks increased at a nominal annual mean rate of 11.8% (Ministry of Finance, 1992). Abela's research into the value systems of the Maltese (1991, p. 265) suggests that, at least with reference to the early eighties, the Maltese were rather more materialistic than consumeristic. Thus, when compared with Europe, Malta did not emerge as a post-materialist society, for its inability to overcome the problem of scarcity led it to have predominantly traditional values/preoccupations dependent on material concerns rather than on such issues as the environment, for instance.

This emphasis on attending to material needs emerged clearly when we consider the efforts placed by various classes of Maltese to generate finance. Reporting on the European Value Systems Study Group carried out in Malta in 1984, Abela (1991, pp. 110-1) notes that 40% of the 467 Maltese respondents – in contrast to only 12% of other Europeans – replied that they would find extra work for the rest of the week to earn more money in answer to the question: 'How would you occupy your time if you were to receive a full week's pay and be required to work only three days a week?' Similarly, Delia (1987) has noted the high participation rates of Maltese in the underground economy, and estimates that the hidden economy could be as high as 20% of the Gross Domestic Product. The Household Budget Survey indicated that more than 10 per cent of the average gross household income came from part-time or overtime work. Elsewhere (Sultana, 1993) I have noted the extent of participation of school age children in the twilight economy, and have argued that leisure for leisure's sake is strangely missing or severely curtailed for children [and for adults] in what is, for tourists, a leisure island.

It seems to be the case, then, that the Maltese belong to a 'bicycle society' which has developed 'Cadillac tastes' and where, in a sense, they become 'puritan by day and playboy by night' (Bell, 1976). People thus take on two, three, and sometimes four jobs in order to generate the capital required to meet the demands made by the life-style aspired for. School age children with part-time jobs during term and/or holiday time, for instance, spend much of their money on food, clothes, discos and other leisure activities.[5] With these students as well as with adults, (Abela, 1991, p. 123), one notes the struggle to satisfy consumer 'needs' by sacrificing more time to work. Theft, another indicator of a consumer culture, generally indulged in by those who aspire for goods they cannot afford to buy, is also on the increase, and has become visible enough to constitute a political issue. Thus, there were 93 cases of theft reported in 1986, and this statistic rose to 117, 171, 227 and 237 in the interim years up to 1990 (COS Abstracts, 1990, p. 41).

It can be hypothesized, and there are indicators to that effect, that there has been a shift from materialism to consumerism in Malta since the early eighties. That is to say, the concern with generating finance is there, but increasingly this capital is being used for the satisfaction of increasingly sophisticated 'needs'.

That the infrastructure for the generation of these 'needs' is there, and that a consumer culture is on the increase, becomes

---

[5] The data were collected as part of a research project in trade schools in Malta. A questionnaire was distributed by the author among 680 fifteen year old students in their third year of trade schooling. (For more details regarding the Trade School Research Project, see Sultana, 1992.)

clear when we consider another 'sign of the times': sophisticated advertising. Slick image making is considered in the literature on consumption as the ultimate strategy for the generation of desire for things produced – or, in the case of places like Malta, for things imported. For, as Willis (1984, p. 22) has pointed out,

> first we must consume 'signs' – adverts, images, symbols, representations – to make us want to be something else, to create 'new' appetites and needs which then must be satisfied through expanding consumption.

Advertisements are everywhere, and have proliferated with the multiplication of media channels in Malta, as these depend on advert revenue in order to function. Most of the advertising agencies in Malta have been set up in the last decade and a half.[6]

The Meaning of Consumption

It has been argued above that the popularly held assumption that consumerism has made inroads into Maltese culture can be corroborated by a reasonably wide range of evidence. It would be important to move on from that recognition to a sociological analysis of the meaning of this shift in feeling and being, to interrogate the significance of this phenomenon in terms of such issues as the formation of taste, the pursuit of status and aspects of the experience of personal gratification.

Concern about Consumerism

Consumerism in Malta is generally regarded in a negative light by those who purport to analyze its significance. This particular viewpoint is influenced greatly by the Catholic Church, which has often expressed grave concern regarding the qualitative and

---

[6] Information obtained through a telephone interview with 15 of 26 advertising agencies/companies listed in the Business, Trade and Professions Guide (1988), and in the Yellow Pages (1993). 3 of these were set up in 1990, 5 in the 1980s, 2 in the 1970s, 3 in the 1960s, and 2 in the late 1950s.

quantitative change in the patterns of consumption of the Maltese. It has often decried the secular mentality that a culture of consumerism gives rise to, a mentality which cannot be compatible with Christianity (Segreterija Pastorali, 1993, p. 10).

The Catholic Church has, on various occasions, denounced the conspicuous consumption displayed in otherwise religious occasions, such as the celebration of holy communion, weddings, (cf. Boissevain, 1987; Abela, 1991, p. 114), and feasts (Sullivan, *The Malta Independent*, 20 June 1993). Commenting on a statement by the Gozitan bishop about wedding extravaganzas, *The Times* leader noted its agreement, saying

> Weddings have become too expensive, starting from the expensively printed invitation, to the wedding dress bought in Catania – after a special trip there, of course – and the dresses of the half dozen bridesmaids and flower girls and boys, to the rented suits and top hats, to the elaborate flower arrangements on the altar and all around, to the colour video, and photographer, to the taxis and Rolls Royce, to the country palace, and the going-away dress, and that inevitable honeymoon on the other side of the world. It has become really expensive getting married or marrying your children. It is not enough that they have to buy land and build their own house or villa and furnish it before they move in with all the latest, in equipment and taste, from the best dealers. Your son or daughter has to go one better than everybody else also at the wedding ceremony and reception (*The Times*, 30 June 1993, p. 4).

The sense of disapproval regarding extravagant consumption is sounded by the very people who have an avid interest in consuming. Thus one of the groups we have some information about, University students, while clearly enthusiastic to consume comfortable life-styles, nevertheless worry about the implications of a consumer culture. A survey on 'Consumerism and Solidarity' carried out by the University Students' Catholic Movement (Abela, 1989) shows that 97% of Maltese university students think that consumerism is increasing, and that 76% felt that the Maltese ought to be willing to accept a lowering of their standards of living for the sake of more justice in the world. The fact that most of these same students were unwilling to forego their own consumer interests in favour of solidary/communal values is highly indicative of the 'pleasures of consumption', which will be considered below.

This same pessimism is shared by the Left, which follows the Catholic Church in condemning consumerism. Their concern is captured brilliantly by Arthur Miller in his play 'The Price', (1985, Act 1, quoted in Bocock, 1992, p. 120), where one of the characters says:

> Years ago a person, he was unhappy, didn't know what to do with himself – he'd go to church, start a revolution – something. Today you're unhappy? Can't figure it out? What is the salvation? Go shopping!

The concern on the part of the Left with regards to consumerism is that increasingly, the model of commercial transactions is invading other aspects of the 'life-world' (cf. Habermas, 1987). The attractive packaging of goods and services has, for instance, been extended to the political arena. Indeed, in a key article on 'The Labour Party – Future Directions', Mifsud (1991, p. 4) argues that

> In the modern world, it is not enough to have a good product to sell. The marketing dimension is as important as the quality dimension. In trade, the packaging is as important as the product itself. The same rules apply to politics. Our opponents, while having an inferior product, have better knowledge of the marketing behavioural sciences.

The leader of the Labour Party claimed, after the loss of general elections in 1992, that, effectively, citizens had been duped by the sophisticated images projected by the Nationalist Party election campaign. He in fact maintained that the Labour Party's problem 'was that though we had substance, we lacked style; the government, on the other hand, lacked substance, but had good style; so style won over substance, in my opinion' (Sant, *The Sunday Times,* 5 April 1992, p. 7). Much of the issue was therefore couched in terms of image-making, an interesting and significant linguistic transposition from the field of consumption to the field of politics, where citizens are constructed as 'gullible consumers', who were being 'duped by false values such as those based on money' (Sant, *The Times,* 31 March 1992, p. 32).

The arch pessimists who denounced consumerism have been sociologists influenced by the Frankfurt School theorists who developed a critique of mass culture. Authors like Horkheimer and Adorno as well as Marcuse (cf. Bronner & Kellner, 1989) considered that the ever-increasing range of consumption goods and services provided by capitalist society numbed citizens' critical faculties, enveloping them in a 'bread and circuses' world where they were distracted and pacified.

As Clarke & Critcher (1985, pp. 95 ff.) have argued with reference to the consumption of leisure in contemporary Britain, a consumer culture constructs and positions citizens not as members or customers, but as consumers. The citizen-member has a commitment to the institution/social formation s/he is part of, and sees to it that the latter is run on his or her behalf, in such a way that membership grants the right to collective control. The citizen-customer interacts with the institution in such a way that mutual expectations are respected, so that a contract evolves in such a way that each partner is satisfied.

> The consumer, however, has neither the commitment of the member, nor the informal contract of the customer. His or her expectations are altogether more specific: the maximization of immediate satisfaction. If goods or services are not provided in the manner or at the price required, then the consumer will go elsewhere (Clarke & Critcher, ibid., p. 96).

For critical theorists, who were wont to see the media and the culture industry as pervasively dominant in their influence, the positioning of the citizen as a consumer involves a serious qualitative loss. In the first place, a consumer culture promises that which it cannot deliver, for the benefits that can be had by the citizen, (namely, 'free choice' from a wide range of goods), as well as the rights associated with that benefit (namely, the negative right of not to buy, or to go elsewhere) are based on the profoundly unequal distribution of wealth and income. Those with scarce material resources can ill afford to 'choose'. Secondly, the construction of the citizen as consumer gives rise to what Marcuse (1964) refers to as 'false needs', ones

> which are superimposed upon the individual by particular social interests in his [sic] repression: the needs which perpetuate toil, aggressiveness, misery and injustice... Most of the prevailing needs to relax, to have fun, to behave and consume in accordance with the advertisements, to love and hate what others love and hate, belong to this category of false needs (Marcuse, 1964, pp. 5, 9).

Life, and serious engagement in the fulfilment of humanity's vocation, freedom, are trivialized, and commodities become ends in themselves. It is in this way that advertising succeeds in attaching

> images of romance, exotica, desire, beauty, fulfilment, communality, scientific progress and the good life to mundane consumer goods such as soap, washing machines, motor cars and alcoholic drinks (Featherstone, 1990, p. 7).

In Malta, these kinds of concerns are gaining ground as image-making becomes more 'professional'. Commenting on the manipulative streak in advertising, Flores (*The Times*, 29 June 1993, p. 5) refers thus to beer adverts on the local television network:

> An unshaven young man sits under the shade at an open-air cafe...then a raving beauty trots past on interminably long legs. He ogles her, smiles at her and reaches out with a glassful of sparkling foam. She smiles back, swivels back into stride and makes it all look like a joke.

Or, as McLuhan (1951, p. 68) wittily put it,

> When producers want to know what the public wants, they graph it in curves. When they want to tell the public what to get, they say it in curves.

Alternative Views on Consumption

The domination model presented most powerfully by the critical theorists and by the likes of Ewen (1976) has been challenged, with some authors arguing that 'far from being the passive victim of commercialism's juggernaut, the consumer has progressively been recognized as having substantial and unpredictable decision-making power in the selection and use of cultural commodities' (Willis, 1990, p. 138). It is a known fact that consumers are discerning, as witnessed by the lack of success of certain products, such as digitial watches, which, while cheaper and multi-functional relative to the classical watch, failed to capture the consumer market (Mermet, 1992, p. 344). In other words, advertising alone will not necessarily dupe consumers, whose value system as well as aesthetic taste, however much socially constructed it is, does allow a margin of discrimination between products. In addition to this, the domination model is insufficient because adverts must find a responsive terrain if they are to be effective. As D.J. Boorstin (1962) noted

> The deeper problems connected with advertising come less from the unscrupulousness of out 'deceivers' than from our pleasure in being deceived, less from the desire to seduce than from the desire to be seduced (Cited in *The Penguin Thesaurus of Quotations*, 1976).

That consumers are not simple dupes can be seen by their ability to strike back and to fight for their rights. There is thus a new arena for the struggle for citizen rights, away from the sphere of the work place to that of leisure, or at least 'self-maintenance'. There is an international consumers' movement consisting of over 150 organizations in about 100 countries, which, since 1979, includes Malta (Magro, 1989, p. 13). Locally, consumer rights have been gaining in importance. A Consumer Protection Act was passed in 1981. A white paper on 'Rights for the Consumer' was tabled in 1991, a Department for Consumer Affairs, attached to the Ministry for Food, Agriculture and Fisheries, was set up in 1992, (*The Times*, 3 April 1992, p. 20), and many local newspapers, including *The Sunday Times*, *L-Orizzont* and *L-Alternattiva*, began featuring a regular customer service column. The sphere of consumption is in fact being seen by some as the locus for the exercise of concerted citizen action, (cf. Micallef, *The Times*, 5 July 1993, p. 5), at least partly against 'the most important lobby on the Maltese islands after the Catholic Church – the importers, with their Chamber of Commerce and multiple political networks within the Nationalist Party' (*Society*, 1991, p. 34).

In addition to this, studies by members of the Birmingham Centre for Contemporary Cultural Studies (CCCS) have argued that consumers actively appropriate elements of popular and youth culture generated by the media, and re-work them to generate personal satisfaction and meaningfulness. Willis (1990, p. 21) powerfully sums up the argument thus:

> human consumption does not simply repeat the relations of production – and whatever cynical motives lie behind them. Interpretation, symbolic action and creativity are part of consumption. They're involved in the whole realm of necessary symbolic work. This work is at least as important as whatever might originally be encoded in commodities and can often produce their opposites. Indeed some aspects of 'profanity' in commercial artifacts may be liberating and progressive, introducing the possibility of the new and the socially dynamic... People bring living experiences to commerce and the consumption of cultural commodities as well

as being formed there. They bring experiences, feelings, social position and social memberships to their encounter with commerce. Hence they bring a necessary creative symbolic pressure, not only to make sense of cultural commodities, but partly through them also to make sense of contradiction and structure as they experience them in school, college, production, neighbourhood, and as members of certain genders, races, classes and ages. The results of this necessary symbolic work may be quite different from anything initially coded into cultural commodities.

Indeed, as Cohen's study of East End Youth has suggested, the consumption of such fashion styles as a safety pin through the nose, a shaven head, or dressing up as 'mods', can have a powerful effect on the individual. It can be, for him or her, a source of significance, self-esteem and collective identification (Cohen, 1972).

The reworking of cultural commodities leads us very neatly into the consideration of the ways in which consumption becomes meaningful to the consumer. Such a focus entails an analysis of

> the emotional pleasures of consumption, the dreams and desires which become celebrated in consumer cultural imagery and particular sites of consumption which variously generate direct bodily excitement and aesthetic pleasures (Featherstone, 1990, p. 5).

The Pleasures of Consumption

The sense of celebration, the importance accorded to rites and rituals, the persistence of pre-industrial forms of social togetherness within the ambit of feasts, festivals, fairs, carnivals, souks, is quintessentially Mediterranean (Boissevain, 1965). While often garbed in a superficially religious dress, these occasions are, in Malta, an opportunity for the expression of popular culture, where everyday mundane reality, with its official, regulated, civilized behaviour is shed in favour of excitement, pleasure, 'excessive' consumption, and the 'direct and vulgar grotesque pleasures of fattening food, intoxicating drink and sexual promiscuity' (Featherstone, 1990, pp. 14-15, following Bakhtin, 1986; Stallybrass and White, 1986). The participation in a religious feast in Malta, not as a tourist but as a Maltese – a villager celebrating the village's feast – and who 'lets go', is in fact the partaking of a dream world that no longer exists, that harks back to a half-forgotten past (Boissevain, 1992). Clothes are new and hair has been styled for the occasion; bursts of colours and of noise link earth to the sky; the steady stream of half-familiar faces linking the past with present, the constant urge to consume: food, drink, feast specialities, refreshments offered by neighbours, friends. The brass band enveloping all the senses, marching, lifting the spirit away from a tired world to a communal unity, stealing souls from each window, from each street where it passes, with the big belly-rumbling drum calling out the most primitive and most sensual, as youths tumble about, jerking each other in a drunken frenzy of corporeal oneness. No wonder that parish priests presented a document to the Maltese prime minister, complaining that feasts had become pagan occasions where excess and not devotion ruled the day, and asking for civil intervention in the re-establishment of order (*Il-Ġens*, 18 June 1993, pp. 1, 24)!

These pleasures of consumption are reproduced, albeit moderately, in media images, rock videos, the cinema, advertisement clips, and department stores. For some theorists, such as Baudrillard (1983) and Jameson (1984), the world of modern consumption is the 'liminal space' par excellence that is left, where the everyday world is 'turned upside down and in which the tabooed and fantastic [are] possible, in which impossible dreams [can] be expressed' (Featherstone, 1990, p. 15). A consumer culture therefore

> uses images, signs and symbolic goods which summon up dreams, desires and fantasies which suggest romantic authenticity and emotional fulfilment in narcissistically pleasing oneself, instead of others (ibid., p. 19).

Consumption and the Formation of Identity

Other sociologists have focused on the sphere of consumption in terms of its function to form identities and to cultivate social bonds or distinctions. It was Simmel and Veblen who pointed out that consumption in modern, and particularly urban societies, was no longer primarily related to the satisfaction of biological needs, but rather to the construction of social identities. Simmel (1903), for instance, argued that the anonymity and indifference characterizing urban culture led individuals to

> cultivate a sham individualism through the pursuit of signs of status, fashion, or marks of individual eccentricity (quoted in Bocock, 1992, p. 126).

The person in the metropolis therefore consumes in order to transmit messages to others, whom s/he meets fleetingly and superficially, of whom s/he wishes to be taken to be. Veblen (1953) similarly argued that the self-differentiating function of consumption applies to groups as much as to individuals, so that patterns of taste are cultivated by status groups and classes in order to distinguish themselves from others. Such status groups engaged in 'conspicuous consumption' in order to display who they were, and to impress upon others their social distance.

Patterns of consumption are therefore seen as socially structured ways in which goods are used to demarcate social relationships (Featherstone, 1992, p. 8). A number of sociologists have in fact shifted their attention from the sphere of production to that of consumption, and from an economistic to a social definition of class, in order to explain how modern societies are shaped and the ways in which they operate (Bocock, 1992, p. 120). Indeed, as Zammit's research (1984, pp. 130-133) has shown, Maltese people's subjective understanding of class divisions have been influenced rather more by differential patterns of consumption than by occupation. In other words, consumption becomes a way of establishing differences between social groups rather than merely expressing such differences.

As Bourdieu (1984) has so clearly shown, anything can be used as a 'positional good', from language and clothes, to leisure activities, house furnishings, food, and manner of eating, walking and other bodily dispositions. The value of a positional good is extrinsic to itself, and an object or a style associated with high status during a particular period can easily fall out of grace and vice versa. The current popularity of Maltese farmhouses and old 'houses of character' with upper middle-class couples is a case in point. What were previously the abodes of uneducated farmers and poor villagers have become a status symbol, to the extent that Boissevain (1986b) has noted a pattern of residential inversion, with lower middle class and working class couples buying/building modern houses in government estates, and wealthier groups moving into rural enclaves. Similarly, private education is booming as a status marker in contemporary Maltese society, with an increase from 88 institutions catering for 20,230 students in 1983/84 to 119 institutions catering for 22,599 students in 1990/91 (Central Office of Statistics, 1993).

This attempt at distinguishing oneself and one's group from others takes place on shifting ground, since there is a tendency for those with lower social status to emulate the consumption patterns of those 'above them'. As Featherstone (1992, p. 5) points out, 'the satisfaction derived from goods relates to their socially structured access in a zero sum game in which satisfaction and status depends upon displaying and sustaining differences within conditions of inflation'. Status groups will attempt to exercise 'social closure' through a variety of ways. They privilege their life-style as a 'referent', and restrict access to the limited circle. It is in this way that people use goods in order to create social bonds and distinctions.

On the other hand, the excluded fall prey to what Young and Wilmott (1975) refer to as a 'psychological disposition' to want what those above them in the social structure already have. Even if we quarrel with this notion of a biologically determined 'disposition' and argue along with Clarke & Critcher (1985, p. 28) that 'emulation is not a universal human characteristic but a set of attitudes and behaviours necessary to a high consumption economy, continuously induced by powerful instruments of persuasion', the fact remains that the life-styles of 'the rich and famous' are imitated. In addition, there does tend to be 'stratified diffusion' whereby, due to the mass production of goods and services, groups who could not afford consumer good 'A' at point $t1$ are likely to be able to afford it at point $t2$, by which time the wealthier groups are enjoying consumer good 'B' (Young & Wilmott, 1975, p. 19).

The urge to emulate, whether natural or constructed, takes place in a situation where

> an ever-changing flow of commodities make[s] the problem of reading the status or rank of the bearer or the commodities more complex. It is in this context that taste, the discriminatory judgement, the knowledge or cultural capital, which enables particular groups or categories of people to understand and classify new goods appropriately and how to use them, becomes important (Featherstone, 1990, p. 9).

This need to learn – how to dress, speak, move, use and edit one's body, and so on – leads to the rise of 'cultural intermediaries' (Bourdieu, 1984) and culture magazines which instruct the new middle class, the new working class and the new rich how to value, use and display new goods. It is therefore not coincidental that these kinds of products of the new cultural intermediaries – magazines, radio and television programmes, newspapers – are produced and consumed in increasing numbers in the Maltese market.[7]

Conclusion

This chapter has argued that the study of the volume, patterns and meaning of consumption in the Maltese islands – in other words, the analysis of the ways in which Maltese people consume goods, services and symbols they produce and/or import – is crucial to the sociological understanding of the local social formation. While consumerism and conspicuous consumption have attracted the attention of the media and other figures in the public sphere, they have not been the subject of systematic sociological analysis and interpretation. The theoretical and empirical interrogation of such issues in the present paper outlines the general contours of the field, suggesting foci for future investigation.

References

Abela, A.M. (1989) 'Il-ġustizzja soċjali fl-Ewropa', *Problemi ta' Llum*.
Abela, A.M. (1991) *Transmitting Values in European Malta*, Malta, Jesuit Publications and Rome, Editrice Pontificia Università Gregoriana.
Abela, A.M. (1992) *Changing Youth Culture in Malta*, Malta, Jesuit Publications.
Anon. (1991) Review of 'Rights for the Consumer', *Society*, 12.

---

[7] It has proved very difficult to obtain hard data on this aspect of consumption. Telephone interviews with three publishers/importers of such magazines suggested that the last decade has seen an increase in the variety of fashion and life-style magazines. Some of the more popular ones, such as *Images*, and *Weddings*, are produced locally. A survey conducted by MISCO for the Ministry of Youth and Culture (1992a, p. 29) shows that the most popular types of magazines bought in Malta were 'women's magazines' (16.3% of all respondents, 44.5% of magazine readers), followed by 'magazines regarding well-known people' (6.8% of all respondents, 18.5% of all magazine readers).

Bakhtin, M. (1986) *Rabelais and his World*, Cambridge, MA, MIT Press.
Baudrillard, J. (1983) *Simulations*, New York, Semiotext(e).
Bell, D. (1976) *The Cultural Contradictions of Capitalism*, London, Heinemann.
Bocock, R. (1992) 'Consumption and life-styles'. In Bocock, R. & Thompson, K. (eds) *Social and Cultural Forms of Modernity*, Cambridge, Polity Press.
Boissevain, J. (1965) *Saints and Fireworks: Religion and Politics in Rural Malta*, London, London School of Economics Monographs on Social Anthropology, 30.
Boissevain, J. (1986a) 'Rhetoric as resource: Malta's Dom Mintoff'. In van Bakel, M.A. et al. (eds) *A Multi-Disciplinary Approach to Big-Man Systems*, Leiden, Brill.
Boissevain, J. (1986b) 'Residential inversion: the changing use of social space in Malta', *Hyphen*, vol. 5, 2.
Boissevain, J. (1987) 'Changing bethrothal and marriage ceremonies in Malta: 1960-1986', Paper presented at the International Society for Ethnology and Folklore Conference, University of Zurich.
Boissevain, J. (ed.) (1992) *Revitalizing European Rituals*, London, Routledge.
Bourdieu, P. (1984) *Distinction: A Social Critique of the Judgement of Taste*, Harvard, Harvard University Press.
Briguglio, L. (1988) *The Maltese Economy: A Macroeconomic Analysis*, Malta, David Moore Publications.
Bronner, S.E. & Kellner, D.M. (1989) *Critical Theory and Society: A Reader*, New York, Routledge.
Central Office of Statistics (1990) *Trade Statistics*, Malta, Government Press.
Central Office of Statistics (1993) *Education Statistics 1990-1991*, Malta, Government Press.
Clarke, J. & Critcher, C. (1985) *The Devil Makes Work: Leisure in Capitalist Britain*, Houndmills, Macmillan.
Cohen, P. (1972) 'Sub-cultural conflict and working class community'. *Working Papers in Cultural Studies*, 2, University of Birmingham, Centre for Contemporary Cultural Studies.
Delia, E.P. (1987) *The Task Ahead – Dimensions, Ideologies and Policies: A Study on the State of the Maltese Economy*, Malta, Confederation of Private Enterprise.
Ewen, S. (1976) *Captains of Consciousness: Advertising and the Social Roots of the Consumer Culture*, New York, McGraw-Hill.
Featherstone, M. (1990) 'Perspectives on consumer culture', *Sociology*, vol. 24, 1.
Habermas, J. (1987) *The Theory of Communicative Action, Vol. 2: Lifeworld and System: A Critique of Functionalist Reason*, Boston, Beacon Press.
Jameson, F. (1984) 'Postmodernism: Or the cultural logic of late capitalism', *New Left Review*, 146.
Magro, J. (1989) 'The agenda for consumers: what next?', *Society*, 1.
Marcuse, H. (1964) *One Dimensional Man*, London, Routledge.
Mermet, G. (1992) *Francoscopie*, Paris, Larousse.
McLuhan, M. (1951) *The Mechanical Bride*, New York, Vanguard Press.
Mifsud, A. (1991) 'The Labour Party – Future directions', *Society*, 9.
Ministry of Finance (1992) *Economic Survey*, Malta, Government Press.
Ministry of Youth and Culture (1992a) *A Cultural Assessment of the Nation*, Malta, MISCO.

Ministry of Youth and Culture (1992b) *Participation in Sports*, Malta, MISCO.
Retail Price Index Management Board (1993) *The Household Budgetary Survey*, Malta, Government Press.
Segreterija Pastorali (1993) *Lejn Knisja Adulta: Pass Decisiv lejn Pjan Pastorali*, Blata I-Bajda, Media Centre Print.
Scicluna, E. (1991) *The Outlook for the Maltese Economy in 1992 and Beyond: A Sober Assessment*, Malta, Malta Federation of Industry.
Simmel, G. (1903) 'The metropolis and mental life'. In Levine, D. (ed.) (1971) *On Individuality and Social Form*, Chicago, IL, University of Chicago Press.
Stallybrass, P. & White, A. (1986) *The Practice and Politics of Transgression*, London, Routledge.
Sultana, R.G. (1992) *Education and National Development: Historical and Critical Perspectives in Vocational Schooling in Malta*, Msida, Malta, Mireva Publications.
Sultana, R.G. (1993) 'Practices and policies in child labour: lessons from Malta, *British Journal of Education and Work*, vol. 6, 3.
Tonna, B. (1993) *Malta Trends*, Blata I-Bajda, Media Centre Print.
Veblen, T. (1953) *The Theory of the Leisure Class*, New York, Mentor.
Willis, P. (1984) 'Youth unemployment: thinking the unthinkable', *Youth & Policy*, vol. 2, 4.
Willis, P. (1990) *Common Culture*, Buckingham, Open University Press.
Young, M. & Wilmott, P. (1975) *The Symmetrical Family*, Harmondsworth, Penguin.
Zammit, E.L. (1984) *A Colonial Inheritance: Maltese Perceptions of Work, Power and Class Structure with reference to the Labour Movement*, Msida, Malta, Malta University Press.

9

Cancer in Malta:
Trends in Mortality and Incidence Rates of Lung and Breast Cancer

Yana Mintoff Bland

Introduction

In Malta, at the turn of this century, ten times as many people were dying of enteritis and more than twice as many people were dying of tuberculosis than were dying of cancer. Diagnosed cancer accounted for only two per cent of all deaths. But by the end of the second world war, cancer deaths accounted for nearly eight per cent of all deaths, and were being specified by site.

By 1991, close to 22 per cent of deaths in the Maltese islands, or 637 out of 2,875 deaths, were caused by cancer (Health Information Systems Unit, Department of Health, 1992). This rate is close to that of highly industrialized countries. Cancer is now the second leading cause of death after heart disease, and the only major killer whose incidence is on the increase.[1]

To some extent, the increase in cancer mortality reflects the increased longevity of the population (Epstein, 1979, p. 12). However, as in most industrialized countries, the greater risk of death from cancer in the Maltese Islands is an attribute of each age group. The risk, for instance, that a four year old girl or a forty year old man will die of cancer is, in both cases, far greater today than it was in 1950.

Standardized cancer death rate data, adjusted for numerical changes in each age group, show a rise in the period from 1960 to 1980. While many victims of cancer still die in later life, a growing percentage are in their fifties, forties, or even younger.

Each Demographic Review of the Maltese Islands highlights the disproportionate number of years of life lost due to cancer. People are dying earlier in life from cancer rather than from heart disease. What the statistics fail to show is the chronic morbidity – the long years of physical suffering and emotional anguish – that precedes death.

Methodological Issues

In this attempt to analyse the trends in cancer incidence and mortality in the Maltese Islands, a number of epidemiological problems were encountered. Obviously, the validity and completeness of the analysis depends on the availability of relevant data from doctors and statisticians. Analysis was made more difficult by changes in diagnostic trends, skills and classification of diseases. Contrary to expectations, the recent computerization of data has not improved the quality and depth of analysis. For the 1980s, cancer data by occupation was not available. Registration for cancer was introduced in 1957, but reliable records of cancer cases have been kept only since 1968, and notification has not been constant. A manual search was made through the register of deaths,

---

[1] The death rate from diseases of the circulatory system is now on the decline. The death rate from diseases of the respiratory system is the only one that shows a rise between 1968-86.

for deaths ascribed to lung and breast cancer for the years 1960 to 1989. However, a study of mesothelioma (cancer of the lining of the lung) trends was not possible, as incidence and mortality data were not recorded separately from that of lung cancer.

Mortality rates from malignant neoplasms are obtained from death certificates, and therefore rely upon the diagnostic accuracy of the hospital physicians or general practitioners who were responsible for registering the cause of death. Where multiple illness occurred, and the neoplasm was not coded as the underlying cause of death, incidence rates will probably be underestimated. Such underestimation is likely to be more prevalent in older age groups.

Recorded morbidity rates of breast and lung cancer depend on whether the cases are brought to the notice of a doctor, as well as the skill of the doctor's diagnosis and her/his willingness to contribute to official records. Over the period studied, the number of people with cancerous symptoms who decided to confide in a doctor may well have increased.

Determining the aetiology of cancer is also made more difficult by the long latency period between exposure to carcinogens and the eventual appearance of cancer. The upward trend may also have been exaggerated by the 1977 change-over to a more comprehensive government-run free health service. Since fewer cases were dealt with privately, registration was more likely. A local cancer surgeon, Dr Swain, estimated that one third of all cancer cases were seen privately in 1977, while only five per cent were dealt with privately in 1983. An unspecified number of people, usually in the upper classes, go abroad for diagnosis and treatment.

Political animosity may also have affected data compilation. The protracted industrial action by medical doctors initiated in the mid-1970s appears to have significantly reduced the notification of cancer incidence.

Trends

Cancer and circulatory diseases were responsible for 18 per cent of all deaths in the decade 1921-31, 48 per cent in 1957-67 and 75 per cent in 1980-86. In the 1921-31 period an increased frequency of cancer was observed, but, according to the 1929 Report on Health Conditions in Malta, 'our mortality compares favourably with that of other countries and rates are at below one half of that recorded in England and Wales.'

An analysis of the post war period from 1948 to 1970 shows how the incidence and severity of cancer and heart disease remained much higher in the British Isles than the Maltese Islands. However, evidence does not support R.G. Milne's conclusion that the 'unfavourable factors found in Britain were absent in Malta' (Milne, 1972, p. 73).

Table 1. Total cases of deaths from malignant neoplasms — Malta 1960-87.

YEAR	CASES	DEATHS	RATE PER 1000 POPULATION	
			CASE	DEATH
1960		321		0.98
1961		356		1.08
1962		333		1.01
1963		345		1.05
1964		348		1.08
1965		369		1.16
1966		372		1.17
1967		380		1.19
1968	421	361	1.32	1.13
1969	458	368	1.42	1.14
1970	534	398	1.64	1.22
1971	518	403	1.59	1.24
1972	516	362	1.62	1.13
1973	508	347	1.62	1.11
1974	392	382	1.21	1.18
1975	368	387	1.12	1.18
1976	366	407	1.11	1.24
1977	300	379	0.90	1.14
1978	462	461	1.74	1.36
1979	512	437	1.48	1.26
1980	523	488	1.44	1.34
1981		495		1.51
1982		548		1.65
1983		511		1.53
1984		528		1.56
1985		521		1.53
1986		506		1.47
1987		536		1.55

Sources: *1960-80 data from Health Department Statistician. 1981-87 data from Demographic Reviews of the Maltese Islands.*

A superficial look at the mortality rate from cancer per thousand civilian population might suggest only a slight change in cancer incidence.

But in reality, the standardized ratio, number, and proportion of cancer deaths have risen significantly. Moreover, there has also been an important change in the location of most malignant neoplasms.

Additionally, at face value, it seems that there is a lower mortality rate from cancer in Malta when compared to Britain. However, this could be expected because Malta has, thus far, a lower percentage of old age people. In making international comparisons of trends in cancer mortality rates one clearly has to standardize for age. In 1960, cancer killed 114 per thousand of those who died; in 1979, 142.6 per thousand, being second only to ischaemic heart disease as a major killer. The absolute number of deaths from cancer rose by a half, while total population increased by only ten per cent during this period. Figure 1 shows that cancer

Figure 1. Trends in cancer mortality rates in Malta 1960-68.

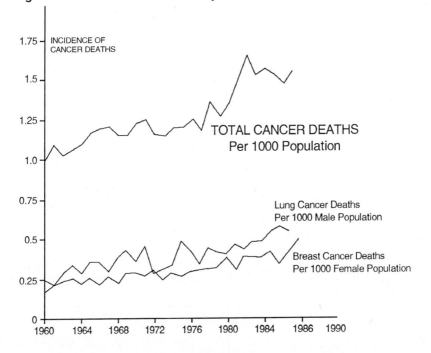

deaths per thousand of the population have risen from a rate of 0.98 in 1960, to 1.22 in 1970, and increased further to 1.34 in 1980 and 1.55 in 1987. This represents a rise of over one third in the cancer death rate in only two decades!

Table 2. Total cases and deaths from malignant neoplasms by sex — Malta 1960-87.

YEAR	CASES		DEATHS	
	MALE	FEMALE	MALE	FEMALE
1960			184	137
1961			175	181
1962			170	163
1963			185	160
1964			198	150
1965			212	168
1966			201	171
1967			212	168
1968	229	185	200	161
1969	232	226	185	183
1970	288	246	226	172
1971	289	229	225	178
1972	276	240	200	162
1973	226	242	191	156
1974	199	193	204	178
1975	202	166	229	158
1976	197	160	231	176
1977	154	146	209	170
1978	216	246	248	213
1979	226	279	239	191
1980	262	255	268	218
1981			287	208
1982			274	274
1983			286	225
1984			270	258
1985			293	228
1986			280	226
1987			310	226

Sources: 1960-80 data from Health Department Statistician. 1981-87 data from Demographic Reviews of the Maltese Islands.

The cancer mortality rate for men is still higher than that for women, so that in 1987 for instance, the male cancer mortality rate was 1.82 per thousand males, compared to 1.29 per thousand females. However, the number of deaths has risen faster among women than men (Table 2). This phenomenon is largely due to a tremendous increase in breast cancer incidence over the period. Indeed a recent WHO report observes that Malta now has the highest female breast cancer mortality rate in the world. The incidence of 35 per 100,000 per year is twice the rate of breast cancer found in Greece, for instance (*Cancer Journal for Clinicians*, 1989).

Cancer by Site.

Details of the fluctuating rise in breast and lung cancer death rates have been presented in Figure 1 above. Over the twenty year period from 1960 to 1980, female breast cancer deaths per thousand in the female population increased roughly one-and-a-half times, while during the shorter period from 1968 to 1980, the number more than doubled. (Health Department Statistics and Demographic Reviews of the Maltese Islands, from 1960 to 1987).

Male lung cancer incidence rates officially showed no substantial rise over this latter period (1968-80). But the lung cancer death rate rose by two-thirds between 1968 and 1980, with an enormous seventy per cent increase between 1968 and 1980. The cancer death rate rose by nearly a third from 1980 and 1988.

Site Changes

In 1946, cancer of the digestive organs and peritoneum accounted for nearly half of all cancer deaths, and death from cancer of the uterus was nearly double that of breast cancer. But by 1986, only five per cent of cancer deaths were due to neoplasms of the digestive organs and peritoneum and just over five per cent due to cancers of the uterus and cervix. Lung and breast cancer deaths accounted for one third of all cancer deaths, becoming far more important both in incidence and mortality than other cancers (Sultana, 1970; Safraz & Borg, 1984; Bugeja, 1987). Unfortunately, no local studies have been carried out on lung or breast cancer since 1970.

Cancer affects men and women very differently. The lungs and bronchial passages are the main sites for fatal cancers in men, killing nearly three victims out of ten (Table 3). The breast is the principal site for women, again killing about three out of ten female cancer victims. Interestingly, a higher percentage of all female cancer deaths are now of breast cancer in the Maltese Republic; while in England and Wales, for instance, only one fifth of all female cancer victims died of breast cancer in 1977 (HMSO, 1978).

Table 3. Cases of and Deaths from Carcinoma of Breast/Lung by Sex — 1960-88. (Rate per 1,000 of the Sex Specific Population.)

YEAR	FEMALE BREAST		MALE LUNG		BREAST CANCER RATE		LUNG CANCER RATE	
	C	D	C	D	C	D	C	D
1960		27		38		0.16		0.24
1961		38		35		0.22		0.22
1962		42		45		0.24		0.29
1963		42		54		0.25		0.34
1964		38		43		0.22		0.28
1965		41		57		0.25		0.37
1966		37		54		0.22		0.36
1967		43		45		0.26		0.29
1968	49	37	40	58	0.30	0.22	0.26	0.38
1969	54	47	56	66	0.32	0.28	0.36	0.43
1970	82	48	58	56	0.48	0.28	0.37	0.36
1971	86	46	61	70	0.51	0.27	0.39	0.45
1972	91	50	54	42	0.55	0.30	0.35	0.27
1973	97	41	40	47	0.58	0.24	0.26	0.31
1974	77	47	37	52	0.45	0.28	0.24	0.34
1975	59	44	60	76	0.34	0.26	0.38	0.49
1976	64	49	52	66	0.37	0.29	0.33	0.42
1977	46	52	29	53	0.26	0.30	0.18	0.33
1978	96	57	44	71	0.54	0.32	0.27	0.44
1979	113	59	33	68	0.62	0.33	0.20	0.41
1980	116	70	46	72	0.63	0.38	0.26	0.40
1981		53		74		0.32		0.46
1982		65		71		0.39		0.44
1983		64		77		0.38		0.47
1984		65		79		0.38		0.48
1985		73		93		0.42		0.55
1986		57		97		0.33		0.57
1987		70		93		0.40		0.55
1988		89				0.50		

Note: C–cases per thousand   D–deaths per thousand
Sources: Health Department Statistician and Demographic Reviews of the Maltese Islands.

In both men and women, the second most important fatal site is the stomach, killing about one victim in ten (cf. Table 6). Mortality rates from stomach cancer in Malta from 1969 to 1981 were lower than in some European countries (such as England, Wales, Italy and Sweden) but there was a slow downward trend in mortality in these countries whereas in Malta there was a slow upward trend. Here, as in the case of lung cancer, the lining of the stomach will have developed carcinomas. For both lung and stomach cancer, the greater the exposure to pollutants such as asbestos fibres, the greater the rate of cancer incidence.

A phenomenal increase in skin cancer deaths occurred in the 1960s in Malta (Table 4). Some of this increase could be due to improved diagnostics, but exposure to increasing levels of environmental and industrial carcinogens – such as chemical pesticides and petroleum products – is definitely a contributory factor (British Society for Social Responsibility in Science, 1975; Le Serve et al., 1980). The overall trend from 1952 to 1976 in skin cancer mortality rates shows a slow increase, though it remains lower than in England and Wales.

Table 4. Site specific Cancer mortality, Malta — 1952-76.

PERIOD/ DIAGNOSIS	TRACHEA BRONCHUS LUNG	AVERAGE ANNUAL NUMBER OF DEATHS		
		FEMALE BREAST	STOMACH	SKIN
1952-56	33.0	25.8	59.4	2.6
1957-61	36.0	36.4	55.0	4.6
1962-66(a)	53.6	40.0	36.2	27.4
1967-71	65.2	44.2	44.0	47.2
1972-76	60.2	46.2	39.8	31.6
1977-81(b)	73.4	58.2	45.4	n.a.
1982-86	94.2	64.8	56.4	n.a.

Note: (a) From 1962-1986, the data for male and female trachea, bronchus and lung cancer deaths and for female breasts cancer deaths is taken from death certificates at the Health Information Service Unit, previously the Health Statistics Department.
(b) Note there was a change in the classification of breast and skin cancer in 1979 agglomerating 'malignant neoplasms of bone, connective tissues, skin and breast'.
Sources: relevant Demographic Reviews of the Maltese Islands.

As with other cancers, there are signs of under-reporting in the 1974-77 period, and trend analysis is confounded by the classification changes of 1979. Future research over a longer period of time is needed.

Breast and Lung Cancer Trends

While, in Malta, total deaths from cancer increased by fifty percent between 1960 and 1980, female deaths from malignant breast cancer rose by some 100 per cent. After taking population growth into account, we find that total cancer deaths per thousand population increased by forty per cent, female breast cancer rose by 150%, and male lung cancer rose by some 66% over the two decades (Source: Health Department Statistician and Demographic Reviews of the Maltese Islands).

A graphic account of these trends is given in Figure 1, highlighting the upward trend in female deaths from breast cancer in recent years. Comparing female breast cancer mortality rates in England and Wales, we find an increase in Britain of just over four per cent between 1971 and 1977 (Doyal & Epstein, 1983), while in Malta there was an eleven per cent increase.

Age Incidence

Data on the age incidence of breast and lung cancer was collected from 1970 to 1980. The same qualifications on the validity of the data (mentioned earlier) must be considered. In addition, although ten year averages were calculated, the small size of the sample could result in differences due to random error.

Breast Cancer Age Incidence

There were no reported cases of breast cancer in women younger than 20 in the years 1970-1980. The incidence rate gradually rises from this age group to a peak of 11.6 cases per thousand in the 45-49 year olds (Figure 2). It drops slightly for women aged 50-54 but rises more steeply than ever to a peak of 23.24 cases per thousand females in the 60-64 age group. There is a slight drop, then another rise to a peak of 24.56 cases per thousand in females aged between 70 and 74.

The highest incidence rate occurs in women who are over 85

years old where on average 38.2 per thousand are affected. The usual figure is a bimodal incidence rate, peaking at 45-49 years and 60-64 years. Malta appears to be at variance with the international average in having more than two peaks in the incidence of female breast cancer.

Figure 2. Female breast cancer, Malta — 1970-80

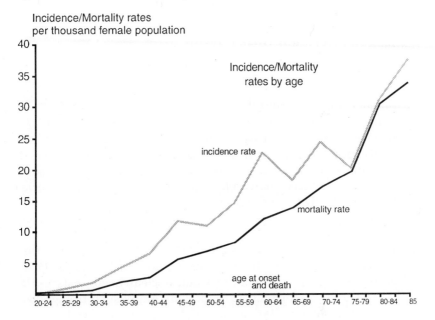

The mortality rate is lower than the morbidity rate for every age group, reflecting perhaps the medical successes in delaying death from breast cancer. There is not the same degree of fluctuation in mortality rate by age as in morbidity rate, and no tri-modal curve is exhibited in this period. Instead, there is a gradual increase from no deaths before 20-24 years of age to nearly 35 deaths per thousand females in the 85 plus age group (cf. Figure 2 above).

Analysis of trends in female breast cancer cases by age-group from 1969-1980 shows that the age-specific incidence rate increases in all age groups, especially in the 35-44 year-old female population.

Interpretation

The experience of growing older involves a cumulative exposure to carcinogens and cannot be separated from environmental effects. For women, ageing also involves changes in hormonal balance that are affected particularly by fertility rates, menopause, drugs, alcohol, stress and diet.

The extraordinary increase in female mortality from breast cancer suggests a cumulative exposure to carcinogens, such as daily exposure to the virtually unregulated use of industrial and agricultural pollutants (Bland, 1990).

A recent study carried out in the USA (*Time*, 1993, p. 24) discovered that the pesticide DDT, which is soluble in fat, can linger for decades in human tissue. The study, published by the National Cancer Institute, suggests that these residual effects may be deadly. In fact, the greater the exposure to DDT, the higher the risk of breast cancer for women. In this study it was reported that women recently diagnosed as having breast cancer were found to have an average of thirty-five percent more residue in their blood than women with similar medical histories but no cancer. This finding becomes even more significant for Malta when one considers that DDT and many other carcinogens have been banned in the USA since 1972.

In certain areas around the globe, there is also the possibility of cataclysmic exposure to carcinogens, such as through downwind exposure to French above-ground nuclear bomb tests in the Sahara in 1960-61 (Bertell, 1975, p. 200). Many such tremendous releases of nuclear radiation have either gone unnoticed or have been deliberately kept secret.

The tri-modal age incidence rates of female breast cancer suggest that three distinct ancillary experiences should be taken into account in interpreting this data. The particularly high number of cases in the 70-74 age group indicates that these women may have been more acutely vulnerable when they were forty-five to fifty-five years old in the decade 1945-55. It may also suggest an association with unhealthy postwar diets of high fat and sugar intake. Additionally, the use of pesticides such as DDT became ubiquitous during that period in Malta.

Lung Cancer Age Incidence

The recorded morbidity and mortality rates of male lung cancer begin at older ages than those of breast cancer. During the decade from 1970-1980, there were only two fatalities recorded in the under-35 age group. The incidence of mortality of lung cancer really begins to bite after men reach 35 years of age.

Mortality rates are always above recorded incidence rates (Figure 3). Multiple reasons for this would include failure to bring lung cancer to the notice of doctors, failure of doctors in diagnosis, and failure in curing the illness or delaying death.

Figure 3. Male lung cancer, Malta — 1970-80

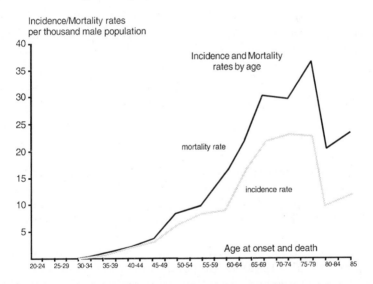

Lung cancer mortality rates rose steeply among men over 54 years of age to a peak of 29.1 deaths per thousand in the 64 to 69 age group, and a further peak of 37.2 deaths per thousand males aged 75-79. The rate then declines, leaving a clear bimodal curve in the male lung cancer mortality rate.

Likewise, morbidity rates rose steeply between the ages of 54 to 69, and continue to rise to their highest rate in the 70-74 age group, just before the highest mortality rates. As with mortality, the morbidity rates decline after the age of 79. The interpretation of rates in these older age groups is complicated by the incidence of multiple diagnoses and relative inaccuracy of available population data.

Interpretation

Lung cancer and industrialization have been historically linked, both through increased exposure to factors of production such as asbestos, nickel and chromium, and through factors of consumption such as tobacco. The bi-modal curve in the male lung cancer rates in each age group may be related to cohort differences in smoking or to cohort differences in exposure to carcinogens. For instance, an occupational study of shipyard workers and quarry workers would be necessary to determine whether work conditions are significant in causing lung cancer mortality in Malta. The following study of locality and class incidence suggests that a relationship does exist, as has been shown in other countries, between work and lung cancer.

Locality Incidence of Lung and Breast Cancer

Breast and lung cancer morbidity rates by locality of residence were available only for the period from 1970 to 1980, but mortality rates by locality were not available. For the later period from 1981 to 1988, the problem was reversed. Locality morbidity data was totally unreliable and only mortality by village of residence was collated (cf. Table 5). Problems of interpreting the data arising from internal migration are minimized by going for a time-series analysis, averaging the data over ten and then seven year periods (cf. Tables 5, 6, 7). The attempts of others (Mason et al., 1970; Gardner et al., 1982) to pinpoint high risk communities and possible socio-economic conditions causing the epidemic in cancer were of great benefit to this initial Maltese study.

To identify high risk communities, the incidence of the specific cancer per thousand of the specific sex in that locality was estimated. Data on sex-specific population by locality is not available before 1973. Therefore, the total number of female breast and male lung cancer cases identified between 1970 and 1980 in each village was divided by the average number of women and men in each village from 1973 to 1980. As with the axes in previous

Table 5. Incidence of deaths attributed to cancer per thousand civilian population, Malta — 1957-86.

AGE	1957	1967	1970	1986
15-44 years	0.23	0.25	0.18	0.17
45-64 years	2.53	2.60	2.41	2.54

Sources: Demographic Review of the Maltese Islands 1986, pp. 3 & 27; Milne, R.G. (1972, p. 67).

Table 6. Deaths from cancer in Malta and Gozo by sex and site 1979.

MALE			FEMALE		
Type	Number	Cancer deaths %	Type	Number	Cancer deaths %
lung, bronchus, trachea	68	28.1	breast	59	30.3
stomach	26	10.8	stomach	14	7.2
prostate	18	7.4	colon	14	7.2
bladder	13	5.3	ovary, etc.	13	6.7
other	115	47.0	other	94	48.5
Total	242	100	Total	195	100

Sources: Report on the Health Conditions of the Maltese Islands 1980.

figures, the denominator is the Maltese population, whereas the numerator includes cases diagnosed in foreigners living in Malta. This would tend to make incidence rates slightly above estimates in localities such as Sliema, where a relatively larger number of foreigners reside.

There were 868 reported cases of female breast cancer and 488 reported cases of male lung cancer between 1970 and 1980. The only places were the incidence of lung cancer equalled or exceeded that of breast cancer were the three dock towns of Senglea, Cospicua and Vittoriosa; the quarry area of Qrendi; and the outer towns of Mosta, Għargħur and San Ġwann.

A relatively high proportion of male employees living in Qrendi and Mqabba work in the nearby quarries, and the data contained in Tables 6 and 7 is a clear indication that the high levels of dust inhaled during this work is a health hazard. Respiratory problems are also related to the proximity of the main rubbish dump. Contrast the high male lung cancer mortality rate in Mqabba to the low female breast cancer rate there: 7.08 compared to 0.9. Similarly, the figures for Qrendi are 8.2 compared to 1.8.

Table 7. Cancer incidence, 1970-80; cancer mortality 1981-88.

Inner Harbour Region	CANCER INCIDENCE 1970-80		CANCER MORTALITY 1981-88	
	Female Breast	Male Lung	Female Breast	Male Lung
Valletta	65	31	24	30
Floriana	13	12	11	12
Sliema	86	34	44	43
Gżira	25	12	16	15
Msida	33	31	26	23
Ħamrun	53	24	26	30
Marsa	24	19	12	20
Paola	44	24	23	19
Cospicua	13	18	12	21
Senglea	9	13	12	8
Vittoriosa	12	12	5	7
Kalkara	3	2	5	4
Total	*380*	*232*	*216*	*232*
% of specific cancer	44	37.5	41	38

Taking a closer look at the highly urbanized and working-class Inner Harbour Region (Table 7), we find that one half of all male lung cancer cases occurred in this region, despite the fact that less than forty per cent of the Maltese male population was concentrated in the area. Analysis of this interesting phenomenon was inconclusive because annual data on population by age, sex and locality was not available. Access to such data is vital to future epidemiological research.

The incidence of breast cancer was also high in this densely populated, highly industrialized region. Over the 1970-1980 period, 44 per cent of all female breast cancer patients were reported to be living in the Inner Harbour Region, even though fewer than 38 per cent of the total female Maltese population resided there.

The high mortality and morbidity rates of breast and lung cancer recorded in Floriana may be exaggerated by patients of Sir Boffa Hospital, which houses the terminal cancer ward. However, the hazards of living in the inner harbour region cannot be thus discounted. Seven out of the ten highest lung cancer mortality rates occurred in the inner harbour region: Valletta, Sliema, Floriana, Cospicua, Marsa, Msida / Pieta / Gwardmangia and Hamrun.

High rates also occurred in adjacent outer harbour towns like Birkirkara and St Julians. In contrast, none of the lowest lung cancer mortality rates occurred over the period 1981-88 in the Inner Harbour Region, and only two in the Outer Harbour Region, at Santa Venera and San Ġwann.

Taking the Inner and Outer Harbour Regions together, we find that 68 per cent of all male lung cancers and 67 per cent of all female breast cancers were concentrated in these areas over the 1970 to 1980 decade. Meanwhile, less than two-thirds of the population was concentrated here. Although the ageing population of three urban areas – Sliema, Floriana and Valletta – may have some upward bias, the overall picture is that industrial and traffic pollution must be taken very seriously in the aetiology of cancer in the Maltese Islands.

Locality Incidence Rates of Breast Cancer

In the Inner Harbour Region, the female breast cancer incidence rate averaged nearly 6 per thousand women. The highest rates occurred in Valletta (8.8 per thousand) and Sliema (8.1 per thousand) (cf. Table 7). There were also high mortality to incidence ratios of breast cancer in working class areas of Cospicua, Senglea and Kalkara.

It was the Western Region that had the highest overall average, at 7.5 cases of breast cancer per thousand of the female population. This region includes Attard, Rabat, Dingli, Mdina and Balzan – areas with some of the highest incidence rates of female breast cancer in 1979-80. Still, it was Marsascala on the

South-Eastern coast that had the highest incident rate, while Għargħur in the Northern Region had the third highest rate. (cf. Table 8)

Table 8. The ten highest cancer morbidity rates by locality, Malta — 1970-80.

Ca Breast per 1,000 Females		Ca Lung 1,000 per Males	
Marsascala	11.10	Għargħur	9.10
Attard	10.40	Marsascala	8.85
Għargħur	9.30	Qrendi	6.20
Dingli	9.00	Vittoriosa	6.00
Valletta	8.80	Attard	5.70
Sliema	8.10	Senglea	5.60
Rabat	7.70	Għaxaq	5.50
Balzan	7.70	Msida	5.40
Mdina	7.50	Paola	5.30
Ħamrun	7.50	Floriana	5.10

The striking locality deviation in breast cancer incidence rates might indicate specific conditions and population characteristics in these villages which have little to do with the region in which they are located. Future researchers might find it fruitful to compare two neighbouring villages, such as Żejtun and Żabbar, which have similar population density, class composition and male lung cancer incidence, but markedly dissimilar female breast cancer rates.

It would be useful to look more closely at variations in environmental conditions such as air and water pollution, dietary habits, variations of incidence rates among married and unmarried women, and individual case histories. Gudja and Għaxaq are two neighbouring villages which show marked differences in incidence rates of both female breast and male lung cancer from 1970 to 1980; the people of Gudja being relatively fortunate on both counts. A longer period of study and age-specific data would vastly improve the quality of analysis.

Locality Incidence Rates of Lung Cancer

As expected, the highest average incidence rates of male lung cancer were found in the Inner Harbour Region, where there were

4.3 recorded cases per thousand male inhabitants. Some of the highest rates occurred in towns situated right by the shipyards: Vittoriosa 6.0 cases and Senglea 5.6 cases per thousand male inhabitants. (cf. Table 8)

The highest village-specific incidence rates occurred in Għargħur and Marsascala. These two villages also had peak female breast cancer incidence rates. The lowest male cancer rates occurred in villages such as Safi, Mġarr, Gudja, Fgura, Mellieħa and Kalkara, where the lowest rates of female cancer were also found. (cf. Table 9)

Table 9. The ten lowest cancer morbidity rates by locality, Malta — 1970-80.

Ca Breast per 1,000 Females		Ca Lung 1,000 per Males	
Safi	0.00	Safi	0.00
Mġarr	0.98	Gudja	0.00
Cospicua	2.80	Mġarr	0.00
San Ġwann	2.90	Fgura	0.50
Kalkara	3.10	Mellieħa	1.05
Żurrieq	3.20	Marsaxlokk	1.30
Kirkop	3.20	Balzan	1.90
Fgura	3.50	Santa Venera	2.00
Gudja	3.55	Mqabba	2.04
Mellieħa	3.80	Żurrieq	2.20
Senglea	3.80	Kalkara	2.20

Again it would be useful to compare the different environmental conditions between the villages with the lowest and highest cancer incidence rates and then analyse individual case histories, especially occupational profiles. The occupational and environmental hazards experienced by workers and residents of the inner harbour area could possibly be a major cause of the rising lung cancer mortality rate.

Class Incidence of Specific Cancers

Analysis of the class and occupational incidence of breast, lung and cervix-uteri cancer was severely limited by insufficient data.

For instance, the vast majority of women are placed in 'Category XI', defined as 'Others including those of no gainful occupations'.[2]

Male lung cancer is particularly high among skilled workers: more than one in five lung cancer cases occurred in skilled workers over the decade 1970-80. Unskilled workers and shopkeepers, shop assistants, and clerical workers were runner up risk groups. But, as in the case of classification of females noted above, a disproportionate number of cancer victims were classified indiscriminately in 'Category XI'.

There is a substantial need for more specific occupational data, standardized mortality rates over at least a 20 year period, and/or a retrospective cohort study. However, one can conclude both from locality and class data that people belonging to the working class – including skilled workers, unskilled workers, farmers, fishermen and agricultural workers, and others – are more likely to die from lung cancer than their counterparts in the middle or upper class of occupations.

Summary

Health and responsible national development are interlinked, as are ill-health and irresponsible social, economic, and political policies. Cancer has recently become a major cause of illness and death. A significant increase in lung cancer mortality and the world's highest incidence of breast cancer are problems that must be faced and dealt with in Malta. Locational studies show a higher incidence of lung cancer in the Inner Harbour Region where the docks, shipbuilding, textiles, other industries – and most significantly, the coal-fired power station – are located, and where the working class is concentrated.

The dearth of government controls on known carcinogens indicates an urgent need to control and eliminate local and regional carcinogenic hazards.

---

[2] 'Others' includes housewives, homeworkers, students, those seeking work and retired persons.

This paper is a first step in the epidemiology of breast and lung cancer over the last thirty years. It provides raw material and suggestive correlation for further research and immediate preventive action. Data on tobacco consumption (collected for the first time in the 1985 Census), if broken down by sex, age and locality and then correlated to lung cancer rates, might strengthen the anti-smoking lobby and lead to stricter controls on cigarette smoking (Lockhart, 1989).

The enormous rise in breast cancer incidence and mortality has been discussed in detail. Many factors, such as changes in diet, the reckless prescription of dangerous medicines, changes in reproductive activity, and rapidly increasing environmental pollution, have been linked to the rise in breast cancer incidence in industrialized countries.

Dietary and reproductive changes may well have had multiplicative effects. In the 1950s, Maltese women went through a revolutionary change in fertility rates and in their nurturing roles. In the sixties and seventies their environment and workplaces became increasingly industrialized, stressful and contaminated. The intake of hormones, both in medicine and food, increased, as did the consumption of sugar, meat, cholesterol and food additives (Fenech, 1977).

There is also recent evidence that carcinogens are more potent in certain climatic conditions, such as bright sunlight and heavy rain. Many people react to cancer with a fatalistic shrug. Prevention seems absolutely impossible. We are all playing a lethal game of Russian roulette with the myriad of carcinogens contaminating our air, food, and water. A shipyard worker, for instance, must expose himself to many hazards during the course of a day. Doctors prescribe hormonal tablets to women every day without a word of warning. Ill-informed farmers liberally spray pesticides while Government spokesmen even broadcast recommendations to poison crops. So many people are addicted to smoking, eat fat-laden or pesticide-laced food, and breathe air polluted with leaded petrol and other contaminants.

But consider the revolution that was required in our grandparents' time, for example, just to eliminate cholera. Who would have dreamt, during the last century, that there would be running water and drainage systems in every home?

Such a revolution in lifestyles and values, in production techniques and worker-employer relationships, in health care and restoration of a healthy environment, is necessary if we are to curb the escalating epidemic of cancer in the Maltese Islands.

References

Benjamin, B. & Pollard, J. (1980) *The Analysis of Mortality and Other Actuarial Statistics*, London, Heinemann.
Bertell, R. (1975) *No Immediate Danger: Prognosis for a Radioactive Earth*, London, The Women's Press.
Bland, (Mintoff), Y. (1990) 'The Economics of imperialism and health: Malta's experience', unpublished Ph.D. thesis, London.
Bland (Mintoff), Y. (1990) 'Cancer in Malta', *Economic & Social Studies Journal*, Malta, vol. 5.
British Society for Social Responsibility in Science (1975) *Oil: A Workers' Guide To Health Hazards and How to Fight Them*, London, BSSRS.
Bugeja, M. (1987) 'Malignant melanoma of the gastro-intenstinal tract', *Mediscope*, 11.
Cancer Journal for Clinicians (1989), vol. 39, 1, Jan./Feb.
Central Office of Statistics (1986) *Malta Census 85: Vol. 1: A Demographic Review of the Maltese Islands*, Malta, Government Press.
Central Office of Statistics (1987) *Demographic Review of the Maltese Islands 1986*, Malta, Government Press.
Doyal, L. & Epstein, S. (1983) *Cancer in Britain*, London, Pluto Press.
Epstein S., (1979), *The Politics of Cancer*, Doubleday, New York, Anchor Press.
Fenech, F., (1977) 'Changes in the epidemiological pattern of disease in the Maltese Islands', *Journal of Faculty of Arts*, VI, 4.
Gardner, M.J., (1982) 'Variations in cancer mortality among local authority areas in England and Wales: Relations with environmental factors and searches for causes', *British Medical Journal*, vol. 284, 3.
Health Information Systems Unit (1992) *Statistics*, Malta, Department of Health.
HMSO (1978) *Mortality Statistics, Office of Population Census Survey*, London, HMSO.
Le Serve, Vase, Wigley, Bennet, (1980) *Chemicals, Work and Cancer*, Surrey, Thomas Nelson & Sons Ltd.
Lockhart D.G., (1989) 'Socio-economic aspects of cigarette smoking in Malta and Gozo', *Maltese Medical Journal*, 45, vol. 1, 3.
Mason, T. et al., (1970) *Atlas of Cancer Mortality for US Counties, 1950-1969*, DHEW Publication, USA, National Institute of Health.
Milne, R.G. (1972) 'The contribution of public expenditure to social development: a case study of Malta 1945-1967', unpublished M.Phil. dissertation in Economics, University of London, Department of Economics.

Ministry of Health & Environment: *Memorandum on the Dispute with the Medical Association of Malta*, Department of Information, August (1977); *Addenda* December (1977) and *Volume 3* December (1978).
Report of the Health Conditions of the Maltese Islands, 1929
Safraz, A. & Borg, R. (1984) 'Malignant Lymphomas', *Mediscope*, 6.
Sultana, H.M. (1970) 'Incidence & treatment of cancer of the lip in Malta', *Saint Luke's Hospital Gazzette*, vol. 5, 1.

10

The Maltese Community in Metro Toronto: Invisible Identity/ies

Carmel Borg & Peter Mayo

In this article, we focus on the Maltese community in Toronto which, we argue, is suffering from a particular kind of oppression that is given little or no consideration in the existing literature. We name this oppression as that of small nation identity. We feel that it is important to deal with this oppression in a sustained way, given that emigration has historically been an important aspect of life relating to the Maltese islands.[1] Also, our constant

---

1
   Literature on Maltese emigration is considerable, even though we discover little relating specifically to the situation of the Maltese in Toronto. An important study on the latter is Sciriha (1989-90), a work which will be referred to throughout this paper. Much of the literature centres around Australia (see, for

meetings with first generation Maltese emigrants in Toronto have driven home the fact that they rely heavily on their Maltese identity to affirm their roots, and therefore difference, in a cosmopolitan society. One may argue, noticing the great pains they take to affirm this identity, that they are probably more 'Maltese' than those, like ourselves, who live in the country of origin. And given that there are more Maltese living abroad than in Malta itself, a review of different sociological issues confronting Maltese society/ies would, in our view, be incomplete without some focus on Maltese emigrants.

---

example, Yorke, 1986), which is quite understandable, given that this continent has the largest number of Maltese living abroad – over 91,000 Maltese born people in 1986 (Lever-Tracy, 1988, p. 70). There are works relating to Maltese emigrants in other countries/cities, notably Dench (1975). A lot of literature deals with the costs and benefits of migration, a debate which, as Delia (1984, p. 16) points out, dates back to the early part of the previous century. The key source for an analysis of nineteenth century Maltese emigration is, of course, Price (1954). Migration became an important matter of public policy in the post-war years, having been regarded, by the Maltese governments of the period, as an effective way of 'combating structural unemployment and economic stagnation in Malta' (Delia, 1984, p. 17). In fact, governments went so far as to subsidize, through the Emigrants' Passage Assistance Schemes (introduced in 1948), some of the transportation costs incurred by Maltese emigrants (Delia, 1984, p. 20; 1981, p. 1). Needless to say, the literature on Maltese migration of this period, is considerable (see, for instance, Cirillo, 1959; Delia, 1981; King, 1979) as is also that on the issue of 'return migration' (see, for instance, King, 1979; King & Strachan, 1980; Delia, 1981; Lever-Tracy, 1988) which has been relatively high since 1974 (Delia, 1981, p. 8). Of course, one cannot deal with the subject of emigration and its effects on the individuals involved without considering the issue of identity. This is what we set out to do in this paper. A recent discussion on this issue is provided by Frendo (1989) who, drawing on his own first hand experience of life in Australia, examines the topic within the context of a larger discussion dealing with the Maltese as a whole, that is to say, Maltese people in both the country of origin and that of foreign settlement. What we would like to bring into the discussion on emigration, is the issue of drawing on one's cultural roots in order to affirm one's voice. One struggle for the affirmation of voice/s by people coming from a small nation state like ours is, we shall argue, a struggle against a particular form of oppression.

When one lives abroad, the idea that the country of origin is part and parcel of one's identity is somewhat reinforced (cf. Frendo, 1989, p. 17). As such, we feel, as people coming from a small nation state, that the particular kind of oppression we are dealing with in this paper is more likely to be felt when one lives outside the country of origin. The trivialization of such countries in the minds of ethnocentric individuals, and institutions/organizations, has a strong bearing on the subjectivity of immigrants from these places of origin. We felt that we have also shared in the oppression of having had our experience as Maltese trivialized since we have operated largely during this period within the ethnocentric walls of western academic institutions.

By highlighting aspects of everyday life experienced by members of the Maltese community,[2] the voice of a subordinate group is reclaimed, providing visibility to a community which has hitherto been invisible, its voice having been immersed in the 'culture of silence'. Furthermore, by unveiling the contradictory discourses that characterize the community, this exercise will provide us/readers with a possibility for interrogation.

It should be made clear from the outset that we have no intention of romanticizing the people with whom we, two Maltese males, strongly identify ourselves. The elements of our subjectivities, which contribute to the creation and perpetuation of structures of oppression, are also to be found in this community. We have no intention of romanticizing not only this sector of the Maltese Diaspora but we Maltese in general. Our country's long history of colonization could easily mislead us into projecting ourselves

---

[2] One of the characteristics of the postmodern movement is its affirmation of the existence of what Laclau & Mouffe (1985), echoing Bakhtin, would regard as a 'polyphony of voices', the recognition of 'the multiple forms of otherness as they emerge from differences in subjectivity, gender and sexuality, race and class, temporal (configurations of sensibility) and spatial geographic locations and dislocations' (Huyssens, 1984). In contrast with the metanarratives of modernism, where binary oppositions limit the discourse of oppression, and eurocentric transcendental subjects occupy the centres of power and become the historical agents (Giroux, 1992), postmodernism underlines the multiplicity of oppressions in existence within and across societies.

solely as victims of oppression, without recognizing our complicity, as a White, predominantly Catholic and Mediterranean race, in perpetuating processes of White, Western, European domination worldwide. We also recognize the way we are positioned in relation to the Maltese community in Metro-Toronto. In the first place, we must acknowledge our privilege, as graduate students on a scholarship, which certainly has a debilitating effect on any working class roots that we may have, thereby undermining our identification with the predominantly working class Maltese community in metro Toronto. Furthermore, our stay in Toronto is a short one and, therefore, there is always the danger that this renders our analysis of the Maltese community an anthropological mission.

Nevertheless, it is our strong identification with and ethical commitment to this community, however undermined this may be by the factors outlined above, that have led us into writing this article. Small nation identity is an issue which we feel, should matter in an age when different oppressions are being named and difference is affirmed. This is not to say that in terms of degree of oppression, it is on a par with the oppression of being, for instance, a black person or a person of colour within an ocean of whiteness, a woman within a patriarchal system, a gay/lesbian in a society characterized by the heterosexual hegemony or a disabled person in a world which prizes ablebodiedness. But it is a form of oppression nevertheless, one which, we feel, needs to be accounted for in the literature. It stands to reason that anybody who suffers from any of the various forms of oppression referred to above and who comes from a small nation is therefore doubly or multiply burdened.

As students in foreign institutions, we find it extremely difficult to avail ourselves of a dialogical process by referring to our first hand educational and cultural experiences in our home country. The hidden message we obtain is that it is one thing to talk about Britain, Latin America, the US, Germany or Africa, albeit for different motives, but it is another to talk about what is perceived as an insignificant, far off 'out of the way island'.[3]

---

[3] This phrase was used by an anonymous reviewer for *Curriculum Inquiry* when

'Whose way?' we are inclined to ask. Perhaps, it could be for the purposes of survival and obtaining recognition that we cling to our knowledge of some leading social theorists and constantly refer to their work and ideas. We feel that academia is, after all, very discriminatory in the knowledge and voices it values. Knowledge of certain authors can, in a specific period, be very 'marketable'. The invisibility of the Maltese is underlined in a variety of symbolic ways. Quite recently, for example, in a conference held at the Ontario Institute for Studies in Education (OISE), and ironically entitled 'Power within Diversity', a map of the world, excluding Malta, was put on display in the area where the participants socialized. Such an omission is also to be found at the Royal Ontario Museum where a map of the 'Mediterranean World' between 6,000 BC and AD 600, in the Mediterranean section, fails to include Malta. This omission is also academically surprising, considering that the islands forming the Maltese archipelago are, for example, well known for their remnants of the temple period (4,100 BC – 2,500 BC). We assume that the same applies to other small nations and their peoples, who constantly feel the pain of being excluded from what is, after all, an ethnocentric discourse which is accorded the seal of universal legitimacy.

The marginalization of the Maltese experience is institutionalized. The Council of Europe, for instance, classifies Malta as a 'peripheral' country. The obvious connotation, given that the notion of periphery implies the existence of a centre, is that the fulcrum of mainstream European activity would be a Brussels, a Strasburg or a Berlin. The notion of periphery is re-echoed in the physical location of what has come to be regarded as the hub of the Maltese community in Metro Toronto.[4] The Maltese community had originally settled close to the St Patrick's/Dundas's area (Downtown). Being largely working class, it could not cope with

---

commenting on a paper dealing with Malta and its educational system (private correspondence).

[4] Bonavia (1988), cited in Sciriha (1989-90, p. 34), states that over 8,000, of the estimated 10,000 Canadians of Maltese origin, are concentrated around The Junction.

the rising cost of housing there. It therefore opted for, and was granted, a parish church, by the Archbishop of Toronto, in what was, in 1930, and for several more years, the city's periphery or junction. In fact, the area is still referred to as The Junction. In Maltese villages and towns, the parish church characteristically constitutes the hub of social life. This is also reflected in the vernacular village/townscape, where the more important local institutions (cafes, police station, band clubs, soccer clubs, political clubs, etc.) were grouped near the centre of the town, close to the parish church. The Maltese community in Toronto, as equally fanatically religious as the Maltese in Malta and Gozo, moved from the Downtown area to settle around the new parish at what was then the periphery of the city. The marginalization of the community was therefore underlined, in physical terms, by the movement from 'centre' to 'periphery'.

Marginalization is intensified in a context where people are imbued with a sense of powerlessness. The colonial experience had immersed the Maltese into what Parkin refers to as a 'subordinate value system' (quoted in Zammit, 1984, p. 16), a mentality of adaptation rather than confrontation. The predominantly working class immigrants, who came to Toronto in the 1950s and 1960s, had been socialized in this 'value system'. Without minimizing the value of covert resistance, we argue that this mentality, transported to Canada as part of the Maltese complex, contributed heavily to the marginalization of the Maltese voice.

The notion of marginalization is, of course, strengthened by the attitudes exhibited by members of the second or third generations of Maltese immigrants in Canada. The Maltese parish priest cum community/cultural worker – Raymond Falzon – indicated, in a taped interview, that these people see themselves as Canadian and refer only to their parents and grandparents as being Maltese. The sense of Maltese identity, therefore, gets progressively lost within the family across generations. Furthermore, he also emphasized the fact that those who 'make it', including those who take up a profession, tend to leave the community and move to the suburbs. And research by Sciriha (1989-90) seems to indicate that intergenerational upward mobility seems to be high in Maltese-Canadian families where 30% of the third generation, dealt with in her survey involving twenty, 'three generation' families, are university students (ibid. pp. 35, 36). The tendency to leave the community is also manifested by members of the Maltese middle class who have emigrated to Toronto. While keeping their distance from what is perceived as the Maltese zone, they are quick in renouncing Maltese mannerisms and use their grip on the English language and their British-style education to make a quick entry into Torontonian life – buying into the 'WASP' (White, Anglo-Saxon, Protestant) hegemony. There are cases of Maltese persons who changed their last name or gave it an Anglo touch, or who kept their ethnic identity a secret. While we cannot deny the class factor involved here, it would not be amiss to state that these people consider 'being Maltese' as a ticket to nowhere and, consequently, perpetuate the community's marginalization.

The third generation of Maltese immigrants, with few exceptions, negates the importance of what could easily have been their heritage language.[5] They are generally conversant only in the dominant English language. This situation is reinforced by the fact that the Maltese parents either speak to them solely in English, given that they would normally have a smattering of the language prior to coming to Canada (this was ensured by a British colonial state educational system and a series of adult literacy classes, involving the teaching of the English language for prospective Maltese emigrants), or else continue to speak the vernacular while receiving responses in English.[6] The misconception that the learning of the heritage language may interfere with the children's progress in English, leading to their eventual relegation to an ESL (English as a Second Language) class, still looms large in parents' minds, and was often used by parent-interviewees to justify their complacency. Current research has shown that learning more than one language does not lead to

---

[5] This emerges from in-depth interviews with key informants in the community around the Junction Area. It confirms Sciriha's findings in her survey. Only 10% of third generation informants speak and read Maltese (Sciriha, 1989-90, p. 39). She also adds that, at the time of the survey, only 130 students attended the Maltese heritage programme at James Culnam School, a very low percentage of Maltese-Canadians indeed! (ibid., pp. 38, 39).

[6] Taped interviews with members of the Maltese community in the Junction area.

interference, but rather leads to an acceleration in the acquisition of a new language (Okuno, 1993).[7] A political reading of the language situation in Maltese homes leads us to suggest that complete denial of the Maltese language in a number of Maltese homes can be taken as an indication of how we Maltese are often complicit in our own oppression. The notion that we are 'small' and of 'negligible importance' is something that we internalize and, therefore, it is easy for us to dessiccate our own roots. On the other hand, the use of different languages within the same home creates a conflicting juncture of discourse. The rather ghettoized world view (*Weltanschauung*) of the parents is juxtaposed against the more expansive one resulting from the children's cultural assimilation. We can speak, here, in terms of a conflict between remaining within sharply delineated boundaries and crossing them to the point of negating them.

From interviews we have carried out among members of the Maltese community in Metro Toronto, it is clear that the community experiences very few moments of empowering pedagogy. Unfortunately, there are very few organized processes of community-based education intended to affirm the identity of the community members and to empower them to reclaim their voice. Interviewees often singled out lack of leadership as a major hurdle in generating creative energy. A few connected with the parish church, which is projected by the parish priest as a cultural centre, have been encouraged to and indeed did undergo a programme of leadership skills.[8] This programme was offered outside the community. Other than this, there seems to be little evidence of work carried out in the area of organized, community-based education.[9]

It would be foolish to regard oppression as something being

---

[7] See Ashworth (1988); Cummins (1979; 1981); Cummins and Mulcahy (1978); Cummins, Pamos & Lopes (1989); and Gulustan (1976) for further discussion of this issue.

[8] Taped interview with Fr. Raymond Falzon.

[9] A proposal for a community education programme among the Maltese in Metro Toronto has been formulated. See Borg, Camilleri & Mayo (1993).

perpetrated solely from without. The 'oppressor consciousness' inside us leads us to collude in oppressive structures. In order to be counted, we Maltese totally identify ourselves with the concept of being European, rather than with being Southern European or Mediterranean. This 'Europeanness' reveals its most unsavoury aspects in our racism and the concomitant tendency to construct anybody who does not fit the 'European image' as being 'other'. This is one reason why, for example, the Libyan community in Malta has never been accepted by the rest of the population, despite the existence of historical and economic ties between Maltese and Arabs. Even if interviewees responded negatively to our question regarding racial tension between Maltese and other ethnic groups living within the Maltese-designated area, there are strong indications that these racist attitudes are perpetuated within the Maltese Metro-Toronto community. While considering the dearth of intermarriages with non-European people as an indication,[10] in our informal conversations with some members of the community, we have been exposed to incredibly racist arguments. Members of particular races are constructed as 'other' and are perceived as sources of danger to the Maltese and their property, if not to the future of Canada![11] And one can possibly construe the Maltese traditional alignment, in Metro-Toronto, with Southern Italians, as a means of emphasising this 'Europeanness' and therefore a larger and more internationally affirmed identity. This should not, however, obscure the other more obvious reason, namely that there exists a traditional affinity with Southern Italian people with whom they share geographical, cultural and economic ties.

We also encounter overt forms of patriarchy in the very processes intended to keep alive the Maltese identity. Those social clubs which have been constructed for the purpose of promoting this identity and strengthening the development of the Maltese

---

[10] Interviewees were asked whether they have relatives or know any Maltese who have married a non-European person.

[11] We gathered this from informal discussions with members of the community held within different social meeting places in the Junction area.

community are very exclusionary, even with respect to Maltese persons. Both male and female interviewees considered these centres as 'male' territory. On each occasion that we have visited one of the most popular clubs in the area, we have rarely seen women around, except for the one or two women who serve behind the counter or in the kitchen. This replicates the machismo to be found in our towns and villages in Malta where it is common for Maltese men to spend their evenings away from the family drinking beer and playing billiards/darts or cards in the *każin*. In addition to serving as sites for patriarchal affirmation, these clubs further exacerbate marginalization by refusing to act as a common front. The Maltese strongly identify themselves with their respective clubs. Consequently, there is very little transfusion between these clubs.

The presence of racism and patriarchy does not define small nation identity, and we would concur with this view. These situations, notably the existence of predominantly men's clubs, are to be found in several other districts inhabited by people of Southern European origin. One has only to enter some of the Italian and Portuguese bars on College or St Clair to confirm this view. These are Southern European manifestations of that kind of oppression which is after all universal. We emphasize, however, this aspect of the Maltese community (one prominent way in which patriarchy manifests itself in this community), to indicate the multiplicity of subjectivities involved in processes of structural and systemic oppression.

With regard to oppression, we would like to stress two important things about this particular community. There are attempts to assert aspects of Maltese cultures. Shops specializing in Maltese bakery products can be found on the section of Dundas Street West, where many Maltese live. The feasts of patron saints, celebrated nationally or in particular Maltese parishes, are replicated in Toronto. One thing which strikes us though is that, quite often, the sense of Maltese cultures being projected is a stagnant one, which hardly reflects the organic nature of Maltese cultures in the country of origin. In this respect, Frendo's (1989) image of 'clocks at a standstill' (*bħal arloġġi wieqfa*), used to describe this situation, seems to be very apt (p. 18). Lacking in cultural transfusion, the view of Maltese cultures projected within the community in Metro Toronto is often one which dates back to the period when the Maltese immigrants left their country of origin for Canada. A perfect illustration of this is provided by the traditional Maltese bakery product *ravjul* which is still being produced, at least in a prominent Maltese bakery shop in the Junction, in a size which is almost double that currently served in homes and restaurants in the country of origin. The size still being preferred, in the bakery shop, is one which recalls the way it was cooked, in Malta, in bygone days.

We feel that, once we have named a new kind of oppression which, together with other oppressions (e.g. class location), constitutes part of the Maltese immigrants' subjectivity, it is pertinent, at this point, to echo Foucault (1980) in saying 'Where there is power, there is resistance...' (p. 95). Resistance is manifest in the way some members of the older generation have entrenched themselves within a static version of what they affirm as Maltese cultures. It is, as we have stressed, cultures as they knew them before leaving Malta for Canada. This entrenchment can be construed as a form of resistance to the sort of situation that they feared, and presumably still fear, namely that of assimilation, which fear is confirmed given, as we have stated earlier, the attitude towards 'being Maltese' shown by members of the second and third generations. Yet Foucault (1980, p. 95) elaborates on the above statement by reminding us that 'and yet, or rather consequently, this resistance is never in a position of exteriority in relation to power'. This is true of the situation regarding cultural entrenchment. In their entrenchment, members of the Maltese community in Metro Toronto are preventing borders from being crossed. These 'border crossings' (cf. Giroux, 1992), provided that they consist of a way of working across difference, could revitalize the expatriate Maltese cultures themselves. In remaining entrenched, one is feeding into the power structure of what has been constructed as a 'multicultural society'.[12]

An inorganic sense of Maltese cultures is what feeds into the present hegemony in which a dominant group is presented as the invisible norm presupposed by the existence of the 'insular'

---

[12] We are indebted to Toni Xerri for helping us develop this point.

other. As Hazel Carby (1989) states, with regard to the construction of blackness in relation to a normative whiteness, 'the process of marginalization itself is central to the formation of the dominant culture' (quoted in Giroux, 1992, p. 127).

References

Ashworth, M. (1988) *Blessed with Bilingual Brains: Education of Immigrant Children with English as a Second Language*, Vancouver, Pacific Educational Press.

Bonavia, G. (1988) *Maltese Directory*, Ottawa, Malta Service Bureau.

Borg, C., Camilleri, J. & Mayo, P. (1993) 'Invisible identity/ies – a proposal for the provision of a community-based adult education programme among the Maltese in Metro Toronto' in *Proceedings of the 12th Annual Conference of the Canadian Association for the Study of Adult Education*, Ottawa, June.

Carby, H.V. (1989) 'The canon: civil war and reconstruction', *Michigan Quarterly Review*, vol. 28, 1.

Cirillo, R. (1959) *Social Aspects of Maltese Migration*, Malta, Royal University of Malta Press.

Cummins, J. (1979) 'Linguistic interdependence and the educational development of bilingual children', *Review of Educational Research*, vol. 49.

Cummins, J. (1981) *Effects of Kindergarten Experience on Academic Process in French Immersion Programmes*, Toronto, Ontario Ministry of Education.

Cummins, J. & Mulcahy, R. (1978) 'Orientation to language in Ukranian-English bilingual children', *Child Development*, vol. 49.

Cummins, J., Pamos, J., & Lopes, J. (1989) 'The transition from home to school: A bilingual study of Portuguese speaking children', unpublished research report, Toronto, Ontario Institute for Studies in Education.

Delia, E.P. (1981) 'Return migration to the Maltese Islands in the postwar years,' *Hyphen*, vol. 11, 1.

Delia, E.P. (1984) 'Some considerations on postwar migration from the Maltese islands', in Azzopardi, E. & Scerri, L.J. (eds) *Issues: Aspects of an Island Economy*, Malta, The Economics Society.

Dench, C. (1975) *Maltese in London*, London, Routledge & Kegan Paul.

Foucault, M. (1980) *The History of Sexuality*, vol. 1, New York, Vintage Books.

Frendo, H. (1989) 'Storja u għarfien – Il-Maltin min huma?', Cortis, T. (ed.) *L-Identità Kulturali Ta' Malta*, Malta, Department of Information.

Giroux, H. (1992) *Border Crossings: Cultural Workers and the Politics of Education*, New York, Routledge.

Gulustan, M. (1976) 'Third language learning', *Canadian Modern Language Review*, vol. 32, 3.

Huyssens, A. (1984) 'Mapping the post-modern', *New German Critique*, vol. 33.

King, R. (1979) 'Post war migration policies in Malta, with special reference to return migration', *Demographic Information Bulletin*, vol. 10, 3.

King, R. & Strachan, A.J. (1980) 'The effects of return migration on a Gozitan village', *Human Organisation*, vol. 39, 2.

Laclau, E. & Mouffe, C. (1985) *Hegemony and Socialist Strategy: Towards a Radical Democratic Politics*, New York, Verso.
Lever-Tracy, C. (1988) 'Boomerangs on a small island: Maltese who returned from Australia', *Economic and Social Studies*, vol. 4.
Okuno, A. (1993) 'Ethnic identity and language maintenance: A case study of third generation Japanese-Canadians in Toronto', unpublished M.A. dissertation, Toronto, Ontario Institute for Studies in Education.
Price, C. (1954) *Malta and the Maltese: A Study in Nineteenth Century Migration*, Melbourne, Georgian House.
Sciriha, L. (1989-1990) 'Language maintenance and language shift of the Maltese migrants in Canada', *Journal of Maltese Studies*, vol. XIX-XX.
Yorke, B. (1986) *The Maltese in Australia*, Melbourne, AE Press.
Zammit, E.L. (1984) *A Colonial Inheritance: Maltese Perceptions of Work, Power and Class Structure with Reference to the Labour Movement*, Msida, Malta University Press.

part 3

continuity and change

When, for economic, geographical and historical reasons, people come together, they tend to develop structures and institutions to regulate their transactions. This social regulation tends to stabilize human relations over time, so that in the active production and reproduction of itself, society – which must never be seen to be a 'thing' but rather an achieved 'social formation' – transmits its vision of itself, as well of its know-how, to new generations. This transmission is never mechanical or assured, however, and sociological analysis sets out to address not only stasis, but also change, be this gradual or sudden.

One of the key socialization institutions in modern societies is the family. Tabone focuses on this smallest of social units in order to explore the way in which its traditional fundamental values have been affected by the many socio-economic changes that have marked post-war Malta. Abela, and again Tabone, address the same theme of continuity in the midst of change when they interrogate the modification and transformation of values, and hence the vision of Maltese society for itself. While Abela looks at a number of issues which include the environment, tradition, tolerance, solidarity and materialist and post-materialist values, Tabone singles out the phenomenon of secularization, to explore the extent to which the catholic church and traditional religious practice still have the same high profile in the institutional and cultural life of the islands. That high profile of the church is addressed, in different ways, by Boissevain and Mifsud. The former explores the way in which the key cultural/religious manifestation of village life, feasts, provide a space for the meeting of groups of people identified by a similar social class background. They also constitute resources for status attainment and mobility. On his part, Mifsud unravels the way secondary socialization agencies such as schools – and in this case, a private catholic church school – encapsulate the young in a life-world. Mifsud focuses on the symbolic and cultural material present in schools in order to show how individuals are positioned in that social world, and to argue that the transmission of values and meanings from one generation to the next, while powerfully achieved, can be as powerfully contested.

The transmission of meaning and values of a society can be the subject of challenge from factors arising from outside that particular social formation. This is especially true of peripheral and open societies like Malta, where a sharp difference can exist between traditions developed indigenously, and cultural and economic forms prevailing in metropole centres. Lauri and Inguanez raise this issue, the former by exploring the negotiation of meaning on the part of Maltese viewers of foreign-made television soap-operas, the latter by interrogating the effect of mass tourism on the islands. Both authors, in their different ways, suggest that people tend to create meanings by confronting and processing new phenomena in terms of their own past experiences. Because of this, the impact of new, 'imported' social phenomena does not depend solely on the strength of that phenomenon's impetus but also on the terrain which receives it.

The Maltese Family in the Context of Social Change

Carmel Tabone

The great economic changes that the Maltese society is passing through are leaving their imprint on the family. Being alert to such social realities requires thorough research and analysis. This paper focuses on the relationship between the Maltese family and its changing socio-economic environment. It identifies the key values which characterize the family on one hand, and the main constituents of socio-economic contemporary change on the other, concluding with a set of family typologies which represent the diverse options of coming to terms with the challenge of change.

Progress and the Family

The family must keep pace with social change, adapt itself and develop accordingly, otherwise it could become obsolete. Resisting change could be detrimental not only to the family but to society in general because a cultural lag would be created so that a social institution like the family would not be able to respond adequately to new social exigencies. Protection of the family should not be based merely on conservation. That is to say, we should not try to preserve it the way it was in former times by using the linked antithesis argument that the past was much better than the present and that today everything is being destroyed so we need to return to that former idealized state (Lee & Newby, 1987, p. 43). That can never be. The preservation of the family has to be undertaken through development, continuous development that allows it to adjust adequately to the times and to respond to the needs of the times.

On the other hand, to say that the family needs to fit within the framework of contemporary society does not imply the shedding or the negation of those traditional values that are fundamental and universalistic, for the adoption of less important or particularistic values often promoted by post-industrial society. Otherwise the family would be changing but not developing. And such a change would be detrimental to this social reality. In this case, we cannot certainly call it development. We might call it modernization, or better still modernism and that is all there is to it since we cannot even call it progress. For in the development of the family, fundamental values must remain intact. It is the way these values are applied that must be modified in order to keep up with social change. This is the new aspect that the family must continuously assume in order that it may be consistent with the signs of the times. Let us take an example.

Unity as Exemplary

Unity is a fundamental value in the Maltese family because it is one of the constituent elements of this social institution (Tabone, 1987, p. 107). Besides, from a cultural point of view, unity is a characteristic element of the traditional Maltese family. The development of the Maltese family does not, by any means, intimate change without safeguarding the unity of the family. That is, it does not intimate change at the expense of losing the unity of the family. But the development of the Maltese family entails modifications in the manner in which such unity is practised according to the needs of contemporary society. Even more than that, a pattern must be found to foster this strong value and to maintain it as a cultural characteristic.

Up to 40 years ago, a united family was one that centred around the home. Its members used to spend a lot of time together at home. The fact that the demands of contemporary society are forcing family members to spend less time together at home does not necessarily indicate that they are not united. The few moments they have together can be so intensive as to confirm relationships. They can still be interested in each other's work and co-operate among themselves thus sharing their family life. There can be other ways of promoting unity. Nowadays, it is easy to find various members of the family involved in social, sporting, and cultural activities[1] that are out-of-doors.

These activities may actually serve to strengthen family ties, because when one of the members is involved in an activity the other members may provide encouragement by their presence or support. Family celebrations in way of birthdays, wedding anniversaries, and special occasions like mother's day and father's day – events that had very little importance in the past since there was no pressing need for them – also contribute to the unity of the family. These celebrations may indeed be indicative of fashion and consumerism, but it all depends upon the way one looks at them and makes use of them.

For the family to be really developing, its modifications must fit the rapid pace of social change. It must adopt a new look to suit the signs of the times but still safeguard fundamental values, principal elements and cultural characteristics that make it what it is.

With all this in mind I would like to:
a. Consider the main features of the Maltese family and its fundamental traditional values;
b. Document current socio-economic changes and the manner in which these are affecting or may affect the Maltese family;
c. Describe and discuss the various ways in which the Maltese

---

[1] The words social and cultural are here being used in a general sense and not in a strict sociological sense.

family today responds to the pressures of social change. In particular the concern is to determine the adequacy of the family's response to contemporary social needs and at the same time its compatibility with fundamental values and cultural characteristics.

The Traditional Maltese Family

Fundamental Values

I shall construct an ideal type in the Weberian sense (Weber, 1949, pp. 90-2) to describe the traditional Maltese family in terms of values. This involves studying the structure and the common features, selecting those values which Maltese families used to uphold one way or the other, and assembling them together as if every single family used to uphold those same values. In that way we would be assembling a picture of the 'ideal' traditional Maltese family. In reality, there can never be a Maltese family that fits this theoretical description perfectly. But such a description allows us to understand what to expect from the traditional Maltese family. This could then be compared to what the Maltese family is passing through nowadays.

In the process of this construction, the following key values are identified and reviewed in turn below: unity and respect; marriage and fidelity; religion; children; identity and loyalty.

Unity and Respect

Traditionally the Maltese family is depicted as the modified extended type. Unity is a major feature of the traditional Maltese family. This unity is so strong that although the members of the family in its extended form (i.e. parents and their married children with their own families) do not live under the same roof, their family ties are identical with those of the extended family. Because of the smallness of our island those children and brothers and sisters who go to live in another village can still visit each other – as in fact they often do, so that they can still exert an influence on each other (Tabone, 1987, p. 118).

Unity was generally fostered through physical propinquity and proximity. Members of the Maltese family congregated at home. A good exemplary parent was one who had a good sense of domestic management and kept the family united. The family that loses its unity and has problems with family relationships is traditionally considered to have fallen in disgrace. This is the reason why, during a family row, members often insist on not letting the neighbours hear them.

The concept of respect is closely linked to that of the unity of the family. It was a feature that recognized and safeguarded the relationships and unity of the family. One can actually find a series of norms that regulate the reciprocal respect among relatives even within the extended family. Members of the same family are expected to help each other, intervene on behalf of each other and share their joys and sorrows with each other. These norms vary in their intensity according to the scale of kinship; the same applies to the sanctions they impose upon each other. On the occasion of a wedding, for instance, the couple and their parents feel obliged to invite all the family members and the latter expect to be invited. Trouble follows if someone, even inadvertently, is left out from the guest list: it is considered to be a disgrace if you are ignored as a family member. Likewise, in sickness or in death, relatives feel they have to make their presence felt.

Marriage and Fidelity

If safeguarding relationships in the extended family is important, it is even more important to safeguard the most intimate relationships within the nuclear family. Fidelity is a prestigious value whereas infidelity remains a social stigma both for the offender and the victim. It is a major issue in separation cases.

A significant value of the Maltese family is based on the respect that a married couple show to each other, the respect that children show to their parents, and the respect that children show among themselves. Maltese people believe that the ties of family relationships are real – at least in principle as the Maltese proverb that *Id-demm qatt ma jsir semm* (i.e. Blood is thicker than water) suggests. In a quarrel with a non-family member one normally resents offensive remarks about family members, even with those members with whom relationships have been broken.

Such a strong family relationship finds its basis in marriage and, traditionally, in that advocated by the Catholic Church which has its basis in the principle of indissolubility. The marriage rate and the percentage of married people in the population were relatively always high, although recently a decrease is noted (Table 1). The decline in the marriage rate may be due to the fact that people are getting married at a more mature age than previously. In a marriage one always expected success. And whether a marriage was successful or not, a married couple always remained together living under the same roof for the simple reason that culturally, religiously and legally they were conscious of being united for the rest of their lives 'for better or for worse'. Besides it would be a social disgrace if your marriage failed.

Table 1. Crude Marriage Rate

Year	Crude Marriage Rate
1983	8.3
1984	7.8
1985	7.5
1986	7.6
1987	7.1
1988	7.3
1989	7.1
1990	7.0
1991	7.1
1992	6.5

Source: C.O.S. Demographic Review, various issues.

Religion

Although today ecclesiastical marriage is not the only form of legal marriage, in Malta the majority of Maltese still contract marriage in the Catholic Church. In 1992 the number of civil marriages reached a figure of 10.4% of all marriages contracted that year (*Demographic Review*) although one should bear in mind that a good number of these civil marriages are later blessed by the church. If one contracts a civil marriage only, one is considered as not being 'normal' in the sense that one would have broken a social norm and that one's marriage is not founded on solid ground. The reason behind this is that religion is one of the values upheld by the family. To be a healthy family, one that enjoys unity and peace, entails being close to God. A family that does not have God's blessing because it is too remote from Him can never aspire to live in happiness. People used to say: 'Although you've got to go supperless, if you have God's blessings you'd be happy'. Others used to comment on those who do not practise religion: 'How can they pretend to be happy at home when they are keeping away from the sacraments?' Traditionally, a good family is a Christian one.

Children

Religion was a major factor which contributed towards making the Maltese family one boasting a large number of children. In 1948 one family out of every four had more than ten children (Dench, 1975, p. 15). At that time Malta was among those countries with the largest proportion of citizens under fifteen years of age (Bowen Jones et al., 1962, p. 146). In the 1963 enquiry on the average size of the Maltese family it was noted that a third of the families still included more than six children (C.O.S., 1963, p. xxxix). In 1983, the average family was estimated to consist in two to three children (Tabone, 1987, pp. 88-9).

A large family is one of the traditional characteristics, and the Maltese were proud of it. Children were considered to be God's blessing. On the other hand birth control was generally thought immoral. Children thus were considered another value in themselves. A large family used to create financial problems, and many families lived in poverty. Yet, despite the low standard of living, parents used to do anything for their children. It was a social norm for parents to deprive themselves in order that their children would not be worse off than those of others. Everyone wanted one's children to be better than those of significant others and even better than oneself. Parents often calculated their own success on the basis of their children's achievements, and similarly their children's failure was seen as their own failure.

With the development of institutional education in our islands, Maltese parents recognized the opportunities that education had to offer to their children. Education became the key to success in life so parents invested in it. Thus, the pursuit of formal education is valued by the Maltese family because it is seen as a means by which parents could socially demonstrate their success through their own children's educational achievements.

Family Identity and Loyalty

Because of the strong unity of the Maltese family, and because of the size of our islands which (as we have already said) is a contributing factor to family unity, the individual is identified with his\her family of origin. One carries the name and honour of one's family, both of which depend on the members' behaviour. A person coming from a good family enjoys great esteem, whereas one who comes from an ill-credited family does not. On the other hand, ill-conduct from one of the members is enough to spoil the reputation of the entire family. That is why family identity and loyalty are considered as values pertaining to this social institution. When a young man and a young woman start off a relationship which could lead to marriage, it becomes important that each learns about the other's family. An integral part of the couple's relationship involves inquiring about one's partner's family background. This generates loyalty towards the family of origin and one often feels one has to defend the family honour when it is under fire. On its part the family exercises great social control on its members for the same reason.

Social Conscience

Because of the strength of the Maltese family and its pivotal place in Maltese social life, a sort of 'familism' may be created to the detriment of the social conscience.

Familism occurs when an individual feels so much attached to the nuclear family, placing so much esteem and value on it, that its interests and prosperity come before anything else, at times even before personal success and definitely before public welfare and the common good. The nuclear family becomes an exclusive social group that relates with another family only if it believes that there is something to be gained for itself from such a relationship (Banfield, 1958). It is an attitude that keeps friends at arm's length and trusts them only if that trust can be somehow reciprocated. The fact that the Maltese are meticulous in cleaning their house but quite reckless in matters concerning public cleanliness is symptomatic of such an attitude. And if they do clean in front of their doorways it is only because they do not want the dirt to enter inside. This does not occur in cleanliness only but also in various other aspects of social life.

Familism concerns the nuclear family, that is that family nucleus which is immediate to the individual. At first the individual is concerned with the nuclear family of origin and then after marriage with the nuclear family of procreation. This explains, for instance, why brothers and sisters sometimes become the greatest of enemies on matters of inheritance.

Economic Development

The main characteristic of environmental change impacting on the Maltese family over recent years has been the remarkable steady and sustained growth in the quality of life of the average Maltese people. This can be documented by resorting to a variety of measuring tools. These include increases in national output and the social indicators of development.

The Gross National Product (GNP) is one indicator of economic growth. In 1981, the Maltese GNP at constant prices per capita was Lm 892; in 1989 it reached Lm 1,075. This means that during this period there was an increase of 20.7%, that is an average of 2.3% a year (M.E.A., 1990).

The GNP alone is not enough however to indicate economic development. To have a clear idea of this development we need to consider other socio-economic indicators that include: quality of life, indicators like the increase in TV and radio licences, telephones and motor vehicle licences, education, electricity consumption, and social security. All these indicators registered a steady increase over these last ten years (M.E.A., 1990).

Malta on the International Scene

According to the categories adopted by the World Bank, Malta falls between the upper middle income countries and the high income countries (see Table 2). For this reason, and in spite of a long history of colonialism, Malta has been described as an intermediately developed country (Briguglio, 1988, p. 171).

It has to be observed, however, that although Malta does not fall under the category of a developed country, or according to the World Bank's classification of a high income economy, the expectations of the Maltese are so high that they reach those of the developed countries. Many aspects of the standard of living and of the way of life of some Maltese are a carbon copy of those found in a high income economy. Sometimes the following words, uttered by the Prime Minister of tiny Montserrat (a British colony in the Caribbean) in the sixties, may be applied to Malta as well: "We live in a bicycle society with Cadillac tastes" (Thorndike, 1985, p. 8).

Table 2. Socio-economic indicators of development (1988) for country groupings and for Malta

	Population (millions)	GNP per capita (US$)	GNP per capita average annual growth rate	Life expectancy at birth (years)	Adult illiteracy Female %	Adult illiteracy Male %
Low-income economies	2884.0t	320w	3.1w	60	58	44
Lower-middle-income	741.7t	1380w	2.6w	65	32	27
Upper-middle-income	326.3t	3240w	2.3w	65	31	24
High-income-economies	784.2t	17080w	2.3w	76		
Malta	0.348t	5190	7.4	73	18	16

w = weighted average; t = total   Source: World Bank (1990)

Social Effects of Economic Development

Economic development brings with it social change at various levels. With a higher standard of living, a consumer mentality that leads to relativization of fundamental issues may easily evolve. This consumer mentality can also be one of the effects of secularization.[2]

---

[2] Secularization is a socio-cultural process which allows the autonomy of earthly realities with reference to intrinsic values and laws. One can distinguish between

A Consumer Mentality

In such a consumption-driven society, a person will be evaluated on what s/he has rather than on who s/he is. Possessions become status symbols and no longer function as needs. In Malta many own a large house not because they really need it (families are rarely numerous nowadays) but because of the social image it generates. The same can be said for clothes, cars, neighbourhood, and the use of mobile phones. A recent fad is the investment in a cabin cruiser or a yacht that spends more time tied to the pier than actually sailing.

Consumer values which are naturally particularistic may gradually replace fundamental and universalistic values. The result of this disequilibrium between values gives rise to anomalies like: large and luxurious houses for small families; the physical construction of a house and the demolition of the family; families with everything that is needed but always unsatisfied with what they have and always craving for more; an attitude of doing what one wants, even abortion or adultery, if one has the means.

Rationalization

Rationalization evolves together with a consumer mentality, and people start looking for plausible reasons for their intentions. Whatever they do they need to know exactly why they are doing it and what they are going to derive from it. Very often their yardstick is an economic one, especially in an affluent society. If something cannot be exchanged for money or some other material gain it loses most of its value. The individual no longer accepts traditional social norms and values blindly. They are accepted only if, after applying reason, they seem to make sense. The end result

---

two aspects that can be considered as two successive stages in this process: namely, desacralization and cultural differentiation. Desacralization is the gradual replacement of myth or religion from earthly realities for more rational explanations. Cultural differentiation is the fragmentation of the value system, with the result that secondary or particularistic values often replace fundamental or universalistic values.

of this can be anomie, but it can also be a process of awareness. Anomie is that social condition in which an individual does not feel tied to anyone or anything; a feeling that there are no social standards to control one's behaviour and which one can follow (Haralambos, 1988, pp. 238-9; 413-4).

In this process, however, the individual may become more aware of the surrounding reality and one's own conduct in society. People do not do things simply because they always did them in the past and because everyone else does them, but they start seeing and understanding the merits of their actions. This means that such change can have positive results since it can also lead to a process of conscientization or awareness and internalization.

Individuality and Individualism

A more conscious individual is in fact more of an individual, in the sense that a person who uses one's own brains, not somebody else's, is really living and not simply existing. This person knows exactly what is being done and is not simply being directed by external forces. This personal development is only possible if a person really manages to steer one's own course in life and does not become anomic or lets oneself get carried away by the currents of fashion and convenience.

However, if the individual manages to get through this process of rationalization, one comes to realize that to live alone is absurd, and that life has to be planned in relation to others in the society which one inhabits. The process of rationalization prevents relationships from being arbitrary, and makes them significant, bearing meaning.

On the other hand, all this can lead to individualism: the individual seeks only one's own interests and is prepared to enter a relationship with others only if it leaves some personal gain.

The Effects of Economic Development on the Family

A Scattered and / or United Family

One of the effects of socio-economic development on the Maltese family was the creation of many opportunities for family members to go out and spend long hours away from home. As has already been mentioned, both work and non-work activities are involving family members in different times of the day, so that the time allotted to family gatherings is diminishing. These changes are also actually effecting the mother, who traditionally was the one who spent most of the time at home, and who therefore is considered as the major anchor for family unity.

Married Women Employed outside the Family

A great change has occurred in the number of married women gainfully employed outside the family. It is to be remembered here that the idea of a married woman who seeks employment outside the family is incompatible with the definition of the traditional Maltese family. In the past ten years there has been a global increase of 4.3% in the number of gainfully employed married females. In 1980, out of a total of 30,917 gainfully employed women 4,122 were married, that is 13.3% (C.O.S., 1981). In 1989 there were 17.6% of females gainfully employed who were married: 5,553 married women from a total of 31,497 of females gainfully employed (C.O.S., 1990). But this figure does not show the proportion of married women gainfully employed.

Official statistics shed no light on the number of married women employed outside the family. So I have tried to establish my own estimates based on data from the 1985 Census. In 1985 the number of gainfully occupied married women was 4,833. It has been estimated that the total number of married women who formed part of the active population in that same year reached 61,435.[3] Therefore it has been estimated that during this year 7.9% of married women were gainfully employed outside the

---

[3] This number has been reached by deducting the number of married females over 60 years of age who do not form part of the active population (amounting to 18,479) from the total number of married females (amounting to 79,914). The number of non-active married females has been estimated to amount 18,479, as the population of females over 60 years of age amounted to 26,937 and from these there were 68.6% who were married. This calculation can be made if we assume that the same proportion between married and unmarried women existed in all ages. This assumption is based on the fact that normally those who get married do so before 60.

family. It should be observed, however, that this figure does not include the number of female part-timers (official or otherwise) or those that carry out odd jobs outside the family, or those who resort to piece-work even at home. If we were to include these numbers, the percentage would increase by a considerable amount.

Married women are seeking employment for various reasons ranging from financial advancement to personal development. The contemporary female has a lot more free time than before. Housework has decreased because the family has become smaller (although in most cases the house has become larger) and because appliances that facilitate housework are readily available. There seems to be an increase in the number of married women who are becoming gainfully occupied outside the family. We can easily have a situation (similar to that in other countries) where the exception would be the married woman who does not seek employment, and not the one who is gainfully employed as was traditionally in the Maltese family. In Europe the number of employed married women reaches an average figure of 61% of the female labour force (Council of Europe, 1989, p. 15).

The subject of married working women has become an issue for discussion and for debating its effect on family unity – this unity is one of the basic values and marked characteristic of the Maltese family. Some maintain that married women who seek employment outside their home have less time to dedicate to the family. Others believe that even if they work outside their home they still have ample time for the family. Several married women who are not gainfully employed outside their family often spend their time at coffee mornings, tombola parties or other similar activities. Besides, others would argue, domestic chores may be divided among all the members of the family and not left solely for the mother, thus family unity would be reinforced through co-operation. In our country this tendency is on the increase. A considerable number of males are lending a hand in domestic work (Tabone, 1987, p. 110).

The woman who proceeds in her career and seeks to develop her personal self can contribute to the personal development of her family members. Social change can alter the family's bearing and from a totally institutional form with a strict division of roles and functions which defined the husband as the breadwinner and the woman as the housewife, it assumes an aspect of companionship based on absolute co-operation rather than on the strict division of roles and functions (Burgess et al., 1963). Structural change does not necessarily imply loss of fundamental values and traditional characteristics. But this could happen if the woman goes out to work for reasons that are purely consumerist as sometimes happens in our society. The mania for large and luxurious houses and an exaggerated enthusiasm for designer clothes and holidays abroad are in some cases the reasons for which women go out to work.

Individuation

The individualism created in an affluent society can easily penetrate the family sphere. Despite the fact that the Maltese family is still united even in its extended form, there is a tendency, mostly among the younger generation, to ignore the norms that regulate relationships among kinship. Young people today base their relations mostly on friendship. They maintain relations with those they believe are their friends and not with those who are simply relatives. So the nuclear family today finds less time to meet and stay together because of contemporary social needs, and this makes it even more difficult for maintaining family relationships in the extended family. Generally these relationships are reserved for special occasions like weddings and funerals. It is, however, a fact that as long as one of the parents is alive the children continue meeting, so these relationships are maintained within the family of origin. Beyond this, kinship relationships are becoming increasingly difficult due to the fact also that the new families (those for procreation) are dispersing depending on their place of residence. For these reasons, we can only affirm that family unity is being maintained in its extension up to the family of origin. Beyond this point, unity is becoming increasingly more difficult to persist.

Consumerism and Fidelity in Marriage

As a principle, fidelity is still a fundamental value. Unfaithfulness still carries a stigma. In practice, however, contemporary society could be leading such a value to a critical end. A mentality that considers this value in relative terms may be gradually fostered so that infidelity is no longer branded as a social disgrace. This is borne out by the increase in the number of separations and annulments which very often are the direct consequence of marriage infidelity (Tables 3 and 4).

Table 3. Cases of Separations in Maltese Civil Courts

Year	No. of Marriages	Cases Lodged
1990	2498	104
1991	2541	122
1992	2377	136
1993*	865	53

*Refers to January-May
Source: Parliamentary Question.

Among the causes that lead to separation and marriage annulment, one can mention the following: married couples have less time for each other; many are the occasions when they meet with friends of the opposite sex both at work and in their social life; social constraints are not as rigid as before; and the effect of the mass media, most particularly television. But the greatest effect on this value is that left by a consumer mentality which often leaves the individual unsatisfied with life, never pleased with what one has and always demanding more.

Furthermore, this same consumer society is affecting religion which is a major family value and which involves marriage directly since in the majority of cases marriages are contracted in accordance with the rites of the Catholic Church. So an absence of religion may have certain repercussions on family life, even on loyalty. The mature practice of religion within a Church that ascribes great importance to the family on the basis of the indissolubility of the marriage bond and the primacy of fidelity, serves to safeguard family life. The crisis of the religious factor on the personal and social level, in such a case, cannot fail to affect the family.

Table 4. Marriage cases in front of the Ecclesiastical Tribunal

Year	Cases Presented	Nullitas	Rato Non Consumm.	Rogatories
Aug-Dec 1975	18	7	4	7
1976	36	20	3	13
1977	29	18	1	9
1978	37	22	4	11
1979	37	24	5	8
1980	31	21	1	9
1981	14	8	2	4
1982	30	23	4	3
1983	33	21	3	9
1984	64	49	1	14
1985	85	68	/	17
1986	64	54	/	10
1987	58	43	2	13
1988	79	68	3	8
1989	78	52	1	15
1990	68	53	1	14
1991	83	67	1	15
1992	94	81	1	12

Source: Ecclesiastical Tribunal.

Smaller Families, Better Children?

Similar considerations may be made on the effect of these changes on family size. The number of children in a family has decreased substantially. Various factors may have led to this change:
a. affluence in modern society that does not encourage a large number of children if certain standards are to be maintained (Segalen, 1986, p. 159 et seq.);
b. the change in mentality that includes the theological developments of the Catholic Church after Vatican Council II (cf. the idea of responsible parenthood);
c. the reduction of the Church's influence on people and the reduction of religious practice, these being aspects of secularization.

The change in family size seems to have had very little effect upon the 'children' as a family value. Children are still considered the fulcrum of the family. Maltese parents still invest a great deal in their children; at times in excess, so much so that some tend to spoil them, exposing them to a risky situation in the sense that life is so easy for these children that they never learn to face life properly. Parents may create in their children greater expectations which are not always within reach both on a personal and social level because of the limitations of our economy. The limitation on the number of children is undertaken with this aim in mind: to raise them in such a way so as not to deprive them of anything, and this includes a proper education. But sometimes this measure has adverse effects on the welfare of children, as pointed out above.

Social Mobility

The bond between the individual and the family of origin is still very strong in terms of interdependence, and it is not easy to loosen it because of the smallness of our country and because of the place occupied by the family in social life. Nevertheless, contemporary Maltese society offers the individual some freedom in social mobility. The developments in family life, an effect of socio-economic global development, are contributing to this. The parents' investment in the education of their children, and the new expectations created in the young are factors that favour this social mobility. This phenomenon is, however, not affecting all the levels of our society. There are some socially deprived areas with a lack of educational culture that makes social mobility still more difficult.[4]

---

[4] Socially deprived areas are those identifiable geographic areas where the inhabitants do not have the same economic and social opportunities enjoyed by the majority of the members of that society. They generally have poorer homes and less hygiene, conditions conducive to poor health. They fall in the lower-income bracket, the rate of unemployment is higher among them, and their educational standards are rather low. These features are often interdependent and this makes it difficult for those living in these conditions to detach themselves from such an environment (Sills, 1972).

The Traditional Family and Types of Maltese Families

As we can expect, the whole economic development is not having a comprehensive and global effect upon the Maltese society. Although it is one whole society yet it is composed of various types, categories, situations, and circumstances which are different and therefore affected in different ways. And this is what is happening to the family. This development is working on the Maltese family in a number of different ways according to the type and category of the family and the circumstances the Maltese family finds itself in. These categories depend on such factors as age, different generations, standards of living, educational standards, and religion. Whereas circumstances range from those that are geographical to those that are social: towns and villages, towns with a high rate of tourist contacts, and socially deprived areas.

Within the sphere of economic development types of families are evolving according to the way they are influenced by this development or according to the way they react to it. So there are families that still operate on traditional lines and others that manifest variations of difference. In general terms we can say there are at least five types of families.

The Traditional Family

There are a number of families which are run on traditional lines and which approximate the ideal Maltese family. These families cherish fundamental values and their behaviour patterns are similar to those of the traditional family. They are always ready to resist the currents of contemporary society and they view any change as a threat to stability. They are generally traditionalist and do not accept any other type of family except the one they are used to. They often revert to the past, mentioning their parents and their own childhood to show how the family should be. These are mainly families living rather remotely from the effects of development, like those families in closed community villages. In the process of development traditionalists create a cultural lag because behavioural patterns often clash with the needs of contemporary society. An indication of such an incompatibility are the conflicts (sometimes large) between parents and children.

The Conventional Family

There is also the evolution of another family type that in principle accepts traditional values but in practice follows a way of life that is incompatible with those values. The family members allow themselves to be influenced by the currents of modernism and this includes consumerism. They tend in practice to give more relevance to secondary or particularistic values than to fundamental or universalistic ones, although they are likely to claim otherwise if questioned on the values guiding their behaviour. For instance, they seek status symbols and are frequently anxious about appearances. This family type frequents an affluent environment and places which are popular with tourists, both of which project high, but artificial, standards of living.

The Modern Family

The next family type is the one that both in theory and in practice adopts a system of values completely different from that of the traditional Maltese family. There are some who are positively rejecting the behaviour patterns of the 'ideal' Maltese family with its characteristics and values. They feel undeveloped if they adhere to the model. And sometimes they do almost anything to prove that they are different. They want to be modern. They are very conscious of change and they want it just for the sake of change believing it to be the only way to enjoy progress. But at the same time they allow themselves to be carried by modernistic currents at any cost. This family type is generally found in those areas with a very high standard of living that approaches affluence.

The Deprived Family

This family type is utterly different from the traditional family, and is likely to be found within socially deprived areas. Frustration or a lack of satisfaction in life usually engenders such a development, though in this case it would be more apt to describe this as a case of modernization. Members of the deprived family realize they are not attaining and can never attain the projected standard of living. In this condition they are forced to adopt a different value system from that of the traditional family. In other words, to reach the required levels they become ready to try/do anything, even reversing values. Such areas, although limited in size, are found mostly in the oldest Maltese towns and villages.

The Progressive Family

Another family type is the one that feels the effects of social change as the result of economic development, and actually feels the need for this change, but at the same time is fully aware of the importance of traditional basic values for the protection of the Maltese family. Members of the progressive family try to follow the trends of development but still preserve the basic characteristics of the Maltese family. They choose between what is really development and what is simply modernism, they do not accept blindly all that contemporary society has to offer. Such families often manage to incorporate basic traditional values in their behaviour patterns that evolve with their economic development, and are always keen to discover new ways to preserve values. I have already mentioned examples of this type in connection with family unity in contemporary Maltese society. As a category, this family type is to be found mostly among the younger generation. On the local scene, members of the progressive family are probably religiously mature people who have managed to pass from sheer religious practice to religious conviction and commitment.

Conclusion

The Maltese family is not what it used to be. It has changed considerably, not to say radically in relation to global social change. It is hard at present to speak of 'the Maltese family' at large since families in Malta seem to be taking various forms, adopting various modes of behaviour depending on how they are influenced by social change. However there seems to be a general tendency towards the emergence of the symmetrical type of family, where the couple equitably shares roles and functions and family responsibilities. This process is taking its natural course in such a way as to avoid the stigma that the new implies retrogression and loss, while the old and past is golden. It can also easily be regarded as a healthy change safeguarding the basic values and characteristics of the Maltese family.

These observations seem to be complemented even by a radical Marxian perspective to the subject. The latter departs from a conception of the family as a social unit in the sense of a functional agent to an overriding economic principle, and therefore a social component which is being adapted by, rather than adapting to, global social change. Nevertheless, even with this more structuralist and deterministic viewpoint, there seems to be a promising outcome to the current so called 'crisis'. This is due to a reduction, if not outright elimination, of a gendered division of labour within the family, which institutionalized the dominant role of the male as head, breadwinner and economically active actor on the one hand; and the subordinate, domestic and submissive female on the other. Current local developments, including a new Family Law, suggest a movement towards a new relationship characterized by partnership and similarity rather than patriarchy and difference. Is not this a more faithful representation of the unity and oneness of marriage, and of a new found rationale of stability for the family?

References

Banfield, E. (1958) *The Moral Basis of a Backward Society*, Glencoe, IL, The Free Press.
Bowen Jones, H, Dewdney, J.C. & Fisher, W.B. (1962) *Malta Background for Development*, Newcastle-Upon-Tyne, Durham College.
Briguglio, L. (1988) *The Maltese Economy: A Macroeconomic Analysis*, Malta, David Moore Publications.
Burgess, E.W., Locke, H.J., & Thomas, M.M. (1963) *The Family from Institution to Companionship*, Cincinnati, American Book Co.
Central Office of Statistics (1963) *An Enquiry into Family Size in Malta and Gozo*, Malta, Government Press.
Central Office of Statistics (1986) *Census '85, Vol. 1, A Demographic Profile of Malta and Gozo*, Malta, Government Press.
Central Office of Statistics (various years) *Demographic Review*, Malta, Government Press.
Council of Europe (1989) *The Employment of Women*, 4th Conference of European Ministers of Labour, Copenhagen, 25-27 October.
Dench, G. (1975) *Maltese in London. A Case Study in the Erosion of Ethnic Consciousness*, London, Routledge and Kegan Paul.

Haralambos, M. (1988) *Sociology: Themes and Perspectives*, London, Unwin Hyman.
Lee, D. & Newby, H. (1987) *The Problems of Sociology*, London, Hutchinson.
Ministry for Economic Affairs (M.E.A.) (1990) *Economic Survey January-September 1990*, Malta, Government Press.
Segalen, M. (1986) *Historical Anthropology of the Family*, Cambridge, Cambridge University Press.
Sills, D.L. (ed.) (1972) *International Encyclopedia of the Social Sciences*, New York, Free Press.
Tabone, C. (1987) *The Secularisation of the Family in Changing Malta*, Malta, Dominican Publications.
Tabone, C. (1991) 'Il-familja Maltija fil-proċess ta' l-iżvilupp ekonomiku soċjali', in Kummissjoni Ġustizzja u Paċi, *Malta Llum... U Forsi Għada*, Malta, Veritas Press.
Thorndike, T. (1985) *Grenada: Politics, Economy and Society*, London, Frances Pinter.
Weber, M. (1949) *The Methodology of the Social Sciences*, New York, Free Press.
World Bank (1990) *World Development Report*, Oxford, Oxford University Press.

12

Values for Malta's Future: Social Change, Values and Social Policy

Anthony M. Abela

Social Change

Over the past few years Europe has seen a socio-political and cultural shift. The rapid events that took place at the end of the eighties brought about a radical change of mentality with great consequences on the economic, political and social structures of entire peoples. The sudden change from a closed totalitarian system to an open liberal democracy in a number of Eastern and Central European countries was a real revolution even if initially there was no bloodshed. Such an occurrence had both the aspect of a reform and a revolution. In a book addressed to a Polish friend of his, Ralph Dahrendorf (1990) makes use of the new word 'refolution' – as previously coined by Timothy Garton Ash – to explain the situation. He warns that this radical social change, which marks the end of an oppressive ideology and opens an new era of freedom is still in its infancy. We still have to face its consequences and pay the price for freedom. The high aspirations for an open and a just society have still to be worked out in the diverse local situations.

The former materialist ideology and the centralization of power in Eastern and Central Europe have fallen. Instead we are witnessing the rise of the freedom of expression, coupled, as it were, with the liberalization of the economy, the reconstruction of political and social life. This rapid process of change, however, is not devoid of its problems. The post-communist countries have serious economic crises, they lack skilled leadership in all fields, they are going through political instability and continuous change. They are divided by ethnic wars. New refugees move to the West motivated by economic interests. In Western Europe, too, well-established traditional political parties of Christian democratic origin can no longer escape the popular demands for more transparency. A silent political revolution is taking place all over Europe.

With regards to change in culture, the sociologist Ronald Inglehart (1990) has observed that the advanced industrial countries of the world – often referred to as post-industrial societies – are undergoing a culture-shift, from the predominantly materialist values of the generations born after the Second World War to the post-materialist values of later generations. In these countries, he finds that there is less concern with the accumulation of wealth or the control and possession of resources, so called the consumerism and materialism of the West. Instead, there is an emerging concern for the freedom of expression, the protection of the environment and a better quality of life. The comparative study of values in the eighties and in the nineties strengthens Inglehart's contention that a post-materialist culture is on the increase amongst the upcoming generation. This is so partly because the higher-educated new generations now have all that is necessary to ascertain a comfortable life. On a platform that can guarantee the basic material needs in the advanced industrial societies, we can observe the emergence of a post-materialist culture.

But, we might ask, to what extent does this apply to Malta? Where does Malta stand in the nineties? Which values have a priority in the nineties? Was there any significant change in people's values from the eighties to the nineties? In order to suggest answers to these pertinent questions, we shall refer to survey data derived from research on social values in Malta and Western Europe (Abela, 1991, 1994). A comparative analysis of Maltese (1983, 1991) and Western European Values (EVSSG 1981, 1990) at two points in time makes possible the identification of the salient change in people's values that has occurred in the intervening years between the two surveys. On this basis we shall posit a number of considerations in the shaping of an agenda for the future of our country.

Research and Social Policy

The formulation of a political agenda is problematic for a sociologist. Sociological research and policy making may be construed as two worlds apart. Generally, the social scientist may prefer to limit his or her terrain to the theoretical, statistical and perhaps interpretative domain, keeping consciously aloof from the policy sphere to preserve objectivity and detachment which may however translate into social impotence. On the other hand, historically, policy makers have often shown diffidence and suspicion of academe in general, pouring scorn on 'ivory tower' attitudes but then capitalizing on academic theorization and survey research which corroborates and therefore serves to legitimize a particular political agenda. In my particular case, I consider it pertinent to locate myself within this argument by acknowledging a normative framework, a sense of mission which drives my sociological imagination. Christian values provide a useful and necessary perspective to address a policy outcome to academic pursuits.

Christian Principles

When Michael Campbell-Johnston, leader of the Society of Jesus in Britain, was invited to address the British Conservative Party he posed the question: 'Can a Conservative be a Christian?'. The obvious answer was 'yes', because any politician can be a Christian. In this way, the crucial question was changed into the following: 'How can a politician become a better Christian?' On that occasion my colleague recalled a number of principles for any Christian who is committed to politics (Campbell-Johnston 1988, pp. 996-1000). As these principles are useful for the social activity of any citizen, we shall posit them for the attention of the reader.

First, politics, and, we might add, any social activity of the citizen, should not be dissociated from the values of religion and social ethics. A Christian politician or social administrator should seek to promote justice in society. Such a person should not be motivated by personal ambitions and self-interest, nor seek material gain or personal advantage. Second, the promotion of the social dimension of the Christian faith requires that the freedom and responsibility of the individual should never become absolute values, but should always be subordinated to the common good. The State is duty bound to regulate society for the benefit of all its citizens. Third, an authentic Christian faith demands a preferential option for the poor. In political decisions and the day-to-day running of social policy there should be a preferential consideration of the least and the weakest in society, the emarginated and those who are suffering from any form of discrimination. These are the value parameters infusing the policy recommendations which will follow the statistical discussion.

Values Study

A Maltese version of the European Values questionnaire was re-administered in Malta in the nineties by Gallup in association with the European Value Systems Study Group (EVSSG). The first EVSSG study was conducted in 1981 in ten European countries (Belgium, Denmark, France, Great Britain, Holland, Italy, Northern Ireland, Republic of Ireland, Spain and West Germany). In 1990 the Values Study was repeated with Denmark being replaced by Portugal. In 1990, as in 1981, a total of around 15,500 randomly selected interviews was carried out.

The Maltese Values survey, conducted for the first time in 1983 amongst a nationally representative sample of 467 respondents in Malta and Gozo (Abela, 1991, pp. 1-2), was repeated in June 1991 amongst a similar sample of 393 respondents. Interviews of approximately one hour each were carried out in the home of respondents by specially trained Gallup interviewers (Heald, 1992).

In this paper we shall outline a number of preliminary observations on the basis of the available percentages from the 1991 Maltese Values survey.[1] In order to compare and contrast Malta with Europe, we also report the average percentages for ten Western European countries from the 1990 European Values survey (de Moor & Kerkhofs, 1991; Ashford & Timms, 1992). The main areas under consideration include religion and morality, traditionality, the family, gender relations, tolerance and solidarity, enterprise culture and government intervention, levels of well-being, options for social change, issues of the environment and the European Community, materialist and post-materialist values.

Briefly, in the beginning of the nineties, Maltese society, when compared to other European societies, was found to have retained its traditionality and religiosity, to be situated on the right of the political spectrum and to enjoy a way of life where people expressed higher levels of happiness than in the eighties (Heald, 1992). However, we observe a certain number of ambivalent positions or unresolved inconsistencies as outlined in the following ten points.

Family, Religion and Morality

The initial results from the Values studies in the nineties show that the Maltese have retained their traditional value system. Just as in the eighties they still cherish marriage and the family, the Church and religion. In fact, more than in the eighties, in 1991 the vast majority of our Maltese respondents (90% in 1991, 84% in 1983) do not agree with the statement that 'marriage is an outdated institution'. As in the eighties the values they find important for a happy marriage are faithfulness (93%), mutual respect and appreciation (90%), agreement and tolerance (84%). Less importance, however, is attached to having children (79% in 1983, 65% in 1991) and shared religious faith (70% in 1983, 60%

---

[1] The author is indebted to the Maltese Government for making available the Gallup tables for consultation.

in 1991). Still less importance is given to sexual relations for a happy marriage (74% in 1983, 56% in 1991). In the same way there has been a slight decrease in the opinion favouring sexual promiscuity (9% in 1983; 6% in 1991).

In Malta, children are still expected to show respect towards their parents even if for some reason or other their parents are undeserving (88%). There is a widespread belief that for a happy upbringing children require to live in a family where both parents are living together (91%).

In the nineties and just as strong as in the eighties, and sometimes even stronger, our Maltese respondents find it highly important to educate their children in the traditional values of religion (from 43% in 1983 to 55% in 1991), thrift, saving money and things (from 32% to 40%), obedience (from 24% to 56%), hard work (from 32% to 58%) and good manners (from 70% to 79%). At the same time, however, there has been a marked increase in the need for an education in new post-traditional values such as a sense of independence (from 8% to 32%), responsibility (from 38% to 57%), tolerance and respect for others (from 24% to 40%) and unselfishness (from 18% to 41%). Generally, in the nineties Europeans attach greater importance to a sense of responsibility (73%), tolerance, respect for others (74%) and independence (41%) than to obedience (37%) thrift, saving money and things (32%), hard work (31%), unselfishness (28%) or religious faith (25%).

The Maltese have retained a very strict morality even if on some issues they have become slightly more liberal than they were in the eighties. Thus, in the nineties, there is more tolerance of abortion (the average on a 10-point scale, where 1 stands for never justified and 10 always justified: from 1.17 in 1983 to 1.6 in 1991), prostitution (from 1.17 to 1.3), homosexuality (from 1.33 to 1.8), euthanasia (from 1.34 to 1.8) and divorce (from 1.75 to 2.2).

A considerable number of our Maltese respondents consider certain reasons to be sufficient for the breaking-up of a marriage. Notably, 68% in the case of consistent unfaithfulness and 65% when either partner is violent. Again, 48% of Maltese respondents would justify abortion when a pregnancy puts the health of the mother at risk. The majority of our Maltese respondents, however, and much higher than the European average still hold that the Church should speak on the values of the family, for example, to protect people from abortion (91%; 52% in Europe), divorce (87%) and extra-marital affairs (87%; 41% in Europe).

Inconsistencies between moral strictness or tolerance and individuals' actual behaviour are not lacking. Sometimes there is an over-preoccupation with sexuality and a morality dealing with the family and a total forgetfulness of social morality such as an insufficient concern with justice, theft, crime, the protection of the environment and corruption in politics. Thus, for example, although the vast majority of our respondents favour Church intervention on issues of family life and sexuality, they do not want any intervention by the Church on Government policy (63%). This is the only position which the Maltese share with the European average (70%).

Gender Relations

In Malta there is an overall resistance to the changing roles of men and women as currently taking place in the advanced industrial societies of the world. Generally, the Maltese uphold traditional views on gender relations but there are latent social and economic forces pressing for reforms.

In sharp contrast to the average Western European (33%), most Maltese (68%) are of the opinion that when jobs are scarce men have more right to a job than women. Generally, the majority of Western Europeans (56%) but not the Maltese (20%) are against gender discrimination on the labour market. At the same time, however, the Maltese (76%) are slightly more willing than their European (64%) counterparts to give support to women's movements, possibly conducive to the advancement of women in society.

Again, the Maltese are more cautious than the average European in their support for women's paid employment outside the home. Much fewer Maltese (30%) than Europeans (67%) think that having a job is the best way for a woman to be independent. A higher percentage of Maltese (69%) than Europeans (52%) are of the opinion that what most women really want is a home with children. They are more likely to hold that being a housewife is just as fulfilling as working for pay (74% in Malta, 53% in Europe). Unlike Europeans (64%) few

Maltese (39%) believe that a working mother can establish as warm and secure a relationship with her children as one who does not work. Above all they think that a pre-school child is likely to suffer if his or her mother works (85% in Malta, 62% in Europe). Still, the Maltese (63%) share the European (69%) conviction that both husband and wife should contribute to household income. Such an ambivalent position between traditional views and the demands of the modern world sets the ground for change in gender relations.

Traditional Values and Change

Our respondents showed a propensity for change. When asked about their attitudes to change most of our respondents expressed their willingness to act boldly, experience new ideas and situations. Many were of the opinion that a person will never achieve much unless he or she acts boldly (47%) and only a few held the opposite view that one should be cautious about making major decisions in life (21%). They also welcome the possibility of something new happening (41%) instead of worrying about the difficulties that such changes may cause (19%).

Again, more are inclined to think that 'new ideas are generally better than old ones' (36%) rather than that 'ideas that have stood the test of time are generally the best' (19%). On a ten-point scale our respondents claimed to have great courage in the face of change (6.6) and that they would prefer new ideas to old ones (6.3).

Family and Society

On the one hand, 94% of our respondents have complete trust in the members of their family. On the other hand, only 8% have similar trust in the Maltese people in general. Whereas other Europeans generally assign their top priority in life to their family (81%) and then to their having friends (43%), the Maltese similarly assign their top priority to their family (94%) but considerably lower priority to having friends (29%). The Maltese order of priorities shows that, second to the family stand work (80%), religion (70%), free time (47%), friends (29%) and least of all politics (12%).

Values for Malta's Future

The highest level of trust resides in the Church (54%); least of all in the press (11%), the civil service (12%), trade unions (13%), political parties (13%) and parliament (14%).

Tolerance and Solidarity

In the intervening years between the two surveys there has been a significant lowering of intolerance in political matters. However, there still remains a measure of social intolerance and a lack of trust in others. In contrast to the eighties (20%), in the nineties only 11% of our respondents claim to dislike very much being with others who hold different ideas, values and beliefs from their own. The number of Maltese who do not dislike being with others with different values from their own has gone up by 10% (from 44% in 1983 to 54% in 1991). In the same way, those who do not want left- or right-wing political extremists as neighbours went down by over 20% (from 43% in 1983 to 22% in 1991). This compares very well with Western Europe, where the average European tends to be more diffident of left-wing (34%) and right-wing (36%) political extremists possibly because, over the past few years, there has been an upsurge of political violence in Europe. By contrast, in Malta, the implementation of a policy of national reconciliation in the late eighties ushered in a much calmer political environment.

At the same time, however, the number of those who do not want as their neighbours people with a criminal record (78%), heavy drinkers (62%), people with AIDS (66%), drug addicts (66%), homosexuals (45%), the emotionally unstable (35%), members of minority religious sects or cults (17%), large families (17%) and unmarried mothers (15%) amongst others, remains extremely high by European standards. Overall, fewer Western Europeans are intolerant of people with a criminal record (37%), heavy drinkers (50%), people with AIDS (47%), drug addicts (59%), homosexuals (31%), the emotionally unstable (28%) or large families (9%). The average European level of prejudice against people of a different race (11%), Jews (10%), Hindus (12%), Muslims (17%), immigrants and foreign workers (13%) is just as pronounced as that of the Maltese, and in some countries it is even higher.

The vast majority of our respondents still think that one cannot be too careful in dealing with people (73%), though there has been a considerable increase of our respondents who think that others can be trusted (from 9% in 1983 to 23% in 1991). In the same way, there has been an increase in the belief that people are much less ready to help each other (from 49% to 53%). While 21 percent find people to be equally disposed to help, only 17 percent think that people are much more disposed to help each other (11% less than in 1983).

Again, and in sharp contrast to Europe, a considerable number of Maltese people believe that people live in need more out of laziness and lack of will (58%; Europe 23%) than because of injustice in our society (12%; Europe 36%) or because they are unlucky (13%; Europe 19%). A few others think that poverty is an inevitable part of progress (7%, Europe 16%). Such a situation might reflect the low rate of unemployment in Malta, in contrast to a high rate in continental Europe.

Unavoidably, the observed widespread intolerance of people with social problems and the inability of the Maltese to perceive the social causes of poverty and inequality creates obstacles in the building of a caring society. An adequate strategy of social policy would have to reconcile these ambivalent positions in order to achieve a greater solidarity.

Enterprise culture and social welfare

Just like other Western Europeans, most of our Maltese respondents would prefer an increase in private (48%) instead of Government (15%) ownership of business and industry. They are more likely to see competition as something beneficial to be encouraged rather than something bad to be avoided. In their view, competition stimulates people to work hard and develop ideas (53%) and it does not necessarily bring out the worst in people (9%). Far from thinking that incomes should be made more equal, the Maltese are much more inclined to hold that there should be more incentives for individual effort (7.9 on a 10-point scale), much higher than any other country in Europe (an average of 5.76 on a 10-point scale).

Fewer Maltese (5%) than Europeans (15%) think that people can only accumulate wealth at the expense of others. Most are of the opinion that wealth can grow such that there is enough for everyone (48%), though quite a few do not know what to think about the issue (23%). Most of our respondents are of the opinion that wealth can continue to grow (7.8 on a 10-point scale) and is not something limited that needs to be shared with others.

Most significantly, however, although the Maltese generally favour private initiative and enterprise, not a few are of the opinion that the State should take more responsibility to ensure that everyone is provided for (31%), a higher percent than the European average (23%).

A consciousness for workers' rights is not lacking. For example, a considerable number of our respondents (34%) hold that the unemployed should have the right to refuse a job they do not want. When it comes to assess the social services provided by the State, 73% of our respondents claim to be happy with the medical services and 72% with the social security. There are inconsistencies with regards to the rights for social security. In a situation where jobs are scarce, the Maltese tend to discriminate between the sexes and nationalities. On the one hand, on a par with Europe most of our Maltese respondents are ready to give equal rights for a job to the handicapped and the non-handicapped (67%). On the other hand, however, and generally in contrast to other Europeans, they are more likely to give priority for work to men over women (68%; the average in Europe is 33%), to Maltese workers over emigrants (87%; Europe 63%) or to foreigners married to Maltese citizens (59%), as well as to Maltese residents over returned Maltese migrants (55%).

Well-being and Social Change

In the nineties our respondents expressed higher levels of happiness than in the eighties, possibly because there has been a perceived improvement in the socio-political and economic situation of the country. In 1991, 39% declared to be very happy with their lives (in comparison to 13% in 1983), 44% to be quite happy and 11% not so happy (17% in 1983). In fact, they are much happier than the average European where 27% are very happy, 59% quite happy and 11% not very happy. The Maltese (8.3 on a 10-point scale) also have the highest level of satisfaction with life than the average European (7.36). In the intervening years, however, there has been a considerable increase (from 1 to 12%) in the number of our respondents who hold that 'the entire way our society is organized must be radically changed by revolutionary action'. By contrast only 4% in Europe are for revolutionary action, the rest either think that their society must be gradually improved by reforms (in Europe 70%, Malta 56%), or valiantly defended against subversive forces (in Europe 16%; Malta 17%).

Materialism

In contrast to Western Europe where it has been reported that the upcoming generations are increasingly adopting post-materialist values (de Moor & Kerkhofs, 1991), the Maltese prove to have retained their strong materialist orientation. They show an ability, however, to combine materialist options with post-materialist concerns. Just as in the eighties, they remain on middle ground between materialist and post-materialist values.

In 1991, in their agenda for the future of the country, the Maltese assign top priority to the upkeep of economic growth (51%), they allocate second importance to post-material values having to do with people's participation in the workplace and their community (32%) and a commitment to beautify their cities and countryside (27%). [Table 1]

TABLE 1

"There is a lot of talk these days about what the aims of Malta should be for the next ten years. Listed below are some of the goals which different people would give top priority to:
1. *Would you please say which of these you, yourself, consider the most important? and*
2. *which would be the next most important?"* *

	Priority option	1°	2°	1+2
M	Maintain high economic growth	51	14	65
M	Ensure strong defence forces	5	8	13
P	More say in jobs and communities	27	32	59
P	Beautify cities and countryside	9	27	36
	Total M = 78; Total P = 95; P minus M = 17			

* This question was administered only in 1991.
M = Materialist; P = Postmaterialist values.

In the same way, on a second battery of questions that was administered for the first time in the nineties, the first priority is given to the materialist values dealing with the stability of the economy (40%) and the fight against crime (35%). The latter reflects the increase in theft and other criminal activity over the past few years. Second priority is assigned to the post-material option for the promotion of a less impersonal and a more humane society (13%) where ideas count more than money (15%).

Just as in the eighties, the Maltese retain the upkeep of social order (46%) and the control of prices (26%) as their top priorities. Next in order of preference are the protection of freedom of speech (25%) and giving people more say in important Government decisions (13%). [Table 2]

TABLE 2

"If you had to choose, which one of the following would you say is the most important?"

	Priority option		1°	2°	1+2
M	Maintain order in the nation	1983	39	25	64
		1991	46	21	67
M	Fight rising prices	1983	17	21	38
		1991	26	33	59
P	More say in government decisions	1983	14	19	33
		1991	13	13	26
P	Protect freedom of speech	1983	18	19	37
		1991	10	25	35

1983: Total M = 102; Total P = 70; P minus M = -32
1991: Total M = 126; Total P = 61; P minus M = -65
M = Materialist; P = Postmaterialist values

In the intervening years between the two surveys, the Maltese show no improvement on Inglehart's index of post-materialism. However, in their agenda for the future of the country (Inglehart's third battery of questions) the Maltese opt more for post-materialist than materialist values.

When asked to evaluate change in the way of life that might take place in the near future, Maltese respondents in the nineties expressed less concern with material interests than in the eighties. There has been a noticeable increase in the number of our respondents who would like to see less importance attached to money and material possessions in their lives (74% in 1991, 61% in 1983). There has also been a considerable increase in the number of respondents who would like to see less importance given to work in their lives (45% in 1991, 20% in 1983).

Environmental Issues

Quite a few of our Maltese respondents (41% in contrast to 74% in Europe) think that the protection of the environment and the fight against pollution is an urgent matter. A considerable number in Malta (34%; Europe 19%) are of the opinion that environmental issues are less urgent than is often suggested. This leads us to believe that the awareness of environmental problems in Malta is still in its early stages. In fact, quite a few of our Maltese respondents (25%; Europe 8%) do not know what to say about the anxiety generated by the propaganda against pollution. Only 30% of the Maltese (in contrast to 44% in Europe) are of the opinion that the talk about pollution makes people very anxious.

Similar to other Europeans (62%) but to a lesser extent, the majority of our Maltese respondents (51%) are of the opinion that the Government should reduce environmental pollution without the individual having to pay any extra money. Fifteen percent in Malta in contrast to 5% in Europe do not know what to think on the issue. Again, 41% in Malta (13% in Europe) are undecided in giving an answer to the statement, 'if we want to combat unemployment, we shall have to accept environmental problems'. It seems that most Maltese do not see any connection between keeping a high level of employment, possibly through the expansion of tourism and other industries, and an increase in the pollution of the environment.

Malta and Europe

Just as in the eighties, our respondents claim to be very proud (74%) or quite proud (17%) of their nationality. As might be expected, once people are happy in their country those identifying themselves with their native country (35%) tend to be on the increase. The few who would then identify themselves with Europe remain a minority (9%).

Nevertheless, many Maltese express some measure of trust in the European Community (42%). But there is a measure of uncertainty about the future of a United Europe. A considerable number cannot make up their mind (45%) on whether the country would gain or would have to sacrifice its identity and economic interests were it to join a United Europe. In their majority those who favour a United Europe do so because, in their view, this would better protect the national identity and the economic interests of the country (4.9 on a 7 point scale).

Inference for a Maltese Sociology

The results from the repeat Values Study in the nineties strengthen our earlier contention (Abela, 1991, 1994) that on the whole the Maltese have been successful in keeping their traditional values alive in the face of rapid socio-economic change. In the Maltese situation the traditional merges with the modern, forging a neo-traditionality. The outcome is often experienced as a period of indecision where inconsistencies need to be resolved and where ambivalent positions call for reconciliation. In the process of change many Maltese hold strong to their traditional values, yet quite a few favour change in their lives. Thus, for example, traditional gender relations remain strong, though new socio-economic developments and aspirations call for a re-negotiation of relations between married partners and their children. Traditionality is also apparent in their strong family ties. The vast majority express great trust in their immediate family but at the same time nurture a strong suspicion of Maltese people in general. Maltese people retain their predominantly materialist orientation but do not exclude post-materialist concerns.

As in other European countries there is a rise of an enterprise culture. In Malta, however, this is concomitant to an explicit need for Government intervention in the provision of social welfare. Over the past decade there has been an increase in political tolerance but social solidarity has not been improved. Most Maltese are happier in their life but not a few would like to see radical social changes. There is an emerging concern with the environment but not everyone is ready to pay for it in person. The Maltese have retained their national pride, show confidence in the European Community, but at the same time they are very uncertain about the future of a United Europe.

Such ambivalent positions suggest that a simple linear Western European convergence model of secularization or modernization is not adequate to explain change in Maltese society. Social change in Malta is not a pre-determined, uni-dimensional, irreversible or uni-directional process following general European trends. The negative side of development is often countered by people's resourcefulness and the timely implementation of an adequate strategy of social policy. As the latter is shaped in a process of collective choice, a consideration of people's values is indispensable for an understanding of the resultant national consensus on social welfare.

Social Policy

The special case of Malta, where religious and moral values remain much more diffuse than in any other European state, leads us to transform Campbell-Johnston's initial question into, 'how can Maltese citizens and their social and political leaders become more socially-concerned Christians?'. That is to say, how can religious faith be translated into greater tolerance, solidarity, transparency, care for others, non-discrimination and concern for the poor? On the basis of the above sociological investigations we shall suggest a number of considerations for social policy.

The apparata of the Government, management in the Civil and Public Service, Parliament and the political parties have a long way to go to win more trust from the people. The already established commissions for the investigation of injustices and against corruption, as well as the running of political parties, Government ministries, the police and public administration should strive towards greater transparency. Foremost, it seems that they would need:
(a) a more professional leadership on all levels in such a way as to render a better service to the people;
(b) the setting up of solid structures that would allow a greater and more effective participation at the grass-roots of society;
(c) more professional management, decisions to be taken by

competent people, work to be done by the qualified and those trained for the job;
(d) codes of ethics should set clear and just criteria for the regulation of the professions, posts in management, Government ministries, political organizations and the workplace.

There is a great need for the strengthening of an education for the responsible use of resources. Concrete measures need to be taken in order to cut short a consumer and wasteful mentality, not uncommon amongst certain sections of the upcoming generation in Malta. This mentality is manifest in an increasing tendency for immediate and easy money without a serious commitment. Young people in Malta need to find adequate channels, guidance and support to translate their rich human, religious and social capital into greater service and participation in the community.

The Structure Plan regulating land development and the environment needs to be enforced. Essential public services have to be upgraded and other services need to be introduced. In their absence people are being encouraged to look for alternatives in the private and commercial sectors.

The emerging enterprise culture, encouraging personal initiative and promoting private property, needs to be regulated by an intervention of the State and the commitment of other social groups that are constituted for the protection of the weakest in society. For these purposes non-governmental, Church or other private non-profit organisations, should receive an adequate financial assistance from the Government.

Social policy should have as its objective the elimination of all kinds of discrimination, sexual, political, social, inter-generational or other. Measures need be taken for the advancement of women in society, the gradual implementation of the principle of equality between the sexes with due attention to the upkeep of the unity and well-being of the family. A family focus in social policy should strive to reach the most vulnerable individuals in society. Adequate care is to be immediately provided to the individual at the level of the family, community and society.

In the shaping of a social policy for the near future, Maltese citizens and their leaders could find the following three principles as appropriate. First, the needs of the poor have a priority over the demands of the rich. Second, the freedom of the weak has a priority over the freedom of the powerful. Third, the participation of emarginated groups in society comes prior to the upkeep of a social order that excludes them.

References

Abela, A.M. (1991) *Transmitting Values in European Malta: A Study in the Contemporary Values of Modern Society*, Malta, Jesuit Publications & Rome, Editrice Pontificia Università Gregoriana.
Abela, A.M. (1993) 'European values study in Malta', in *Malta Year Book 1993*, Malta, De La Salle Brothers Publications.
Abela, A.M. (1994) *Shifting Family Values in Malta*, Malta, DISCERN.
Ashford, S. & Timms, N. (1992) *What Europe Thinks: A Study of Western European Values*, England, Dartmouth.
Campbell-Johnston, M. (1988) 'Can a conservative be a Christian?' *The Month*, London, December.
Dahrendorf, R. (1990) 'Reflections on the revolution in Europe', In *A Letter Intended to Have Been Sent to a Gentleman in Warsaw*, London, Chatto & Windus.
De Moor, R.A. & Kerkhofs, J. (1991) 'Value patterns in Western Europe, the United States and Canada', (A press conference held in Belgium, reporting the main findings of the Values Study in the 1990s, September 16th).
Heald, G. (1992) 'Malta is the most satisfied nation in Western Europe but also one of the most suspicious', Malta, Gallup Press Release, 6 February.
Inglehart, R. (1990) *Culture Shift in Advanced Industrial Society*, New Jersey, Princeton University Press.
Values Survey – Malta 1991 (1992), Report prepared for the Office of the Prime Minister, Valletta, Malta, Gallup (Malta) Limited.

13

Festa Partiti:
Parish Competition and Conflict

Jeremy Boissevain

My fascination with Maltese *festa partiti* is of long standing. Why so many Maltese villages have two bands and often celebrate two feasts was one of the central questions of my research in 1960-61. In the course of my research I concluded that one of the most pronounced characteristics of Maltese culture is intense factional competition for honour and status. This is nowhere more clearly illustrated than in the development of parish *festa partiti*.

The Festa Before 1850

By all accounts *festa* celebrations in the late eighteenth and early nineteenth centuries were very modest events, at least by today's standards. Although while one foreign observer of Maltese holiday customs in 1835 noted 'that the principal recreation of the Maltese have in general some connection with their religious ceremonies' (Badger, 1838, p. 98), he and the other two leading recorders of Maltese customs of the period (de Boisgelin, 1804; Miège, 1840) ignored the parish *festa*. The reason for this lack of attention to what today are among the most striking events of popular culture is quite simply that 'the Maltese *festa* in its present form emerged in the course of the nineteenth century' (Cassar-Pullicino, 1976, p. 35).

During much of the eighteenth century, *festa* celebrations were limited to some minor illumination, often a bonfire, and the occasional firing of small mortars. The chief events were the internal liturgical celebrations. Of course, the fact that the *festa* was a day of rest from the normal heavy daily labour, was an event in its own right.

In time, strolling musicians playing pipes and tambourines gradually appeared, as did processions. But the custom of including the statue of the patron saint in procession on the day of the *festa* was a late development, e.g. at Luqa in 1781 and Tarxien in 1829 (*ibid.*, p. 36). In Gozo this did not occur until 1840, when at Rabat the statue of St George was the first to be taken around in the procession on his feast day (Bezzina, 1985, p. 136).

By this time, other parishes apparently started celebrating other saints with almost equal pomp. For example, during 1846 and 1847 at Cospicua the feasts of Santa Kruċ, St Theresa and St Agatha, as well as that of the Immaculate Conception – the patron of the parish – were all celebrated with music, illumination and fireworks. Various confraternities took part by walking in procession behind the statue of the saint (*Giahan*, 1846-47). From the comments in *Giahan*, the satirical newspaper of the day, it is also clear that something called a *banda* had joined, or replaced, the fife and tambourine players during the *festa* of St Theresa at Cospicua in May 1847. Thus by the middle of the nineteenth century, all the *festa* ingredients with which we are familiar had come into existence. The only exception was the band club.

Band Clubs

Castagna records that the first band club was established in Żebbuġ in 1860 by Indri Borg (Castagna, 1890, pp. 248-9). Six months later he helped found Malta's second band club at Rabat and a third one, also established in Żebbuġ. After that, band clubs multi-

Festa Partiti: Parish Competition and Conflict

plied rapidly. By 1890 two military bands and 34 civilian bands had been established in 22 towns and villages in Malta and Gozo. It is significant that, in spite of the British presence, only two of the 34 bands Castagna lists have 'imperial' names. These are the 'Prince of Wales' of Valletta (which had started life in 1874 as 'La Stella' and later would become the 'King's Own' Band) and the 'Duke of Edinburgh' at Vittoriosa. (See Table 1)

It is clear that rivalry between bands was present almost from the beginning. The two Żebbuġ bands were established within six months of each other, as were those in Valletta in 1874. By 1890, 12 of the 22 villages and towns in which band clubs were established were divided by rival bands. Most of this rivalry is related to the cult of saints. This is because most divided villages celebrate two saints, the titular or patron, and a secondary saint who has come to assume almost equal social importance. Each saint is celebrated by a faction or *partit*. At the heart of this faction is the band club which forms its social and political centre. *Festa partiti* compete over almost every aspect of the feast, including the decoration of the streets, the adornment of the statue, the number of communicants, the number of lights on the facade of the church, the size and number of candles, the number of guest bands and, above all, the quantity and quality of its fireworks. Rival band clubs were both the product of and a contributing factor to this competition.

By the 1920s this rivalry had escalated to such an extraordinary degree that the celebration of many secondary saints eclipsed that of their titular rivals. In 1935, the church, long alarmed by the extreme forms that this rivalry had assumed, took steps to reduce the celebration of secondary saints. It promulgated a series of regulations designed to reduce the scale on which secondary feasts could be celebrated. These stipulated that for secondary feasts there was to be no Translation of Holy Relics on the eve of the feast, that only the church and the area immediately adjacent to it could be illuminated and that only one band on the eve and one on the day of the feast would be allowed. The regulations also placed limits on the variety, quantity and the duration of firework displays. Finally, they drew attention to existing regulations that church decorations and new works of art introduced for secondary saints and feasts should be less costly and beautiful than those for titular saints (Concilium, 1936, p. 91).

Table 1. Maltese Bands 1890

Locality	#	Band – Director
Valletta	1	Royal Malta Artillery – Dir. Eman. Bartoli
	2	Royal Malta Militia – Dir. Fil. Galea
	3	Prince of Wales Band – Dir. Alf. P. Hare
	4	La Vallette – Dir. Cav. V. Carabot
Floriana	5	Vilhena Band – Dir. Gius. Borg
Senglea	6	La Vincitrice – Dir. Gius. Portelli
	7	La Croce di Malta – Dir. Bern. Costa
Cospicua	8	San Giorgio – Dir. Carmelo Abela
Vittoriosa	9	Duke of Edinburgh – Dir. Gaet. Grech
	10	La Vittoriosa – Dir. Gius. Micallef
Sliema	11	Cavalieri di Malta – Dir. Ferd. Camilleri
Notabile	12	L'Isle Adam – Dir. Carm. Camilleri
	13	Conte Ruggiero – Dir. Fran. Xuereb
Luqa	14	Sant'Andrea – Dir. Salv. Spiteri
	15	L'Unione – Dir. Gaet. Grech
Żabbar	16	Santa Maria – Dir. Gius. Micallef
	17	San Michele – Dir. C. Abela Scolaro
Żejtun	18	Beland – Dir. Ang. Mifsud
	19	Santa Caterina – Dir. P. Caruana Dingli
Żebbuġ	20	San Filippo – Dir. Gioac. Galea
	21	Rohan – Dir. Lor. Gatt
Birkirkara	22	La Stella – Dir. Gavino Camilleri
	23	L'Alleanza – Dir. Constant. Fenech
Qormi	24	Pinto – Dir. Ant. Agius
	25	San Giorgio – Dir. Gius. Portelli
Żurrieq	26	Il Cavaliere – Dir. Carm. Zammit
Hamrun	27	Giuseppe – Dir. Carm. Doneo
	28	San Gaetano – Dir. Edwardo Farina
Naxxar	29	La Pace – Dir. Gav. Camilleri
Siġġiewi	30	La Nicolina – Dir. Ruggiero Carabott
Tarxien	31	San Giuseppe – Dir. P. Caruana Dingli
Mosta	32	Nicolo Isouard – Dir. Eman. Camilleri
Kirkop	33	L'Unione – Dir. Ignazio Catania
Victoria	34	Il Leone – Dir. Cav. V. Carabott
Nadur	35	La Stella – Dir. Ant. Agius
	36	Calypso – Dir. Fran. Decesare

Source: Castagna (1890)

Parish priests insisted on the observance of the 1935 regulations. In this they were supported by the police, who refused the necessary permissions and licenses for street decorations, band marches and firework displays that were not approved of by the parish priest. A number of very popular secondary feasts were consequently reduced to minor celebrations (St Valentine in Balzan; St Joseph in Għargħur, Mosta, and Siġġiewi; St Aloysius in Lija; Our Lady of the Rosary in Safi). Moreover, the rivalry between *partiti* in Żabbar and Qrendi had become so violent that the secondary feasts there, namely those of St Michael and Our Lady of Lourdes respectively, were suppressed completely. Not surprisingly, intense rivalry persisted between the bands in these villages in spite of the church's measures.

During the Second World War (1939-45), band clubs and *festa* rivalry was dormant. It flared up again in the postwar years, but then abated. Massive emigration during the 1950s and just before independence in 1964, together with the vicious political confrontation between the Church and the Malta Labour Party during the 1960s, drained off manpower required to keep the *festa* rivalry at high pitch (Boissevain, 1965, pp. 149 ff.).

By 1961, on the eve of Malta's independence, there were 56 band clubs located in some 37 towns and villages, 19 of which housed pairs of competing band clubs. Twelve band clubs owed their rivalry to existing *festa partiti* (Għaxaq, Gudja, Kirkop, Luqa, Mqabba, Qrendi, Rabat, Vittoriosa, Żebbuġ, and Żurrieq) or past rivalry (Ħamrun, Żabbar). Four were tied to rival parishes in the same town (Qormi, Victoria, Sliema and Valletta). In only three towns was the band club rivalry apparently unrelated to *festa partiti* (Birkirkara, Mellieħa and Żejtun) (*ibid.*, p. 2; also pp. 78, 79, 149 ff.). Band club rivalry during the period of British Malta was in virtually every case clearly linked to rivalry between *festa partiti*.

The rivalry began to flare up again in independent Malta in the early 1970s, and especially after 1975. That year, probably as part of the run-up to the 1976 elections, the socialist government instructed police to cease consulting parish priests before issuing or denying permits for festa street decorations, band marches and fireworks. This effectively removed the church's control over the external celebration of secondary feasts. Needless to say, the measure was popular among supporters of secondary saints as most of these secondary feasts are celebrated in the southern electoral districts, which were also very heavily Labour. With the removal of the church's lid on the celebration of secondary feasts, rivalry flourished. The result was a tremendous escalation of *festa* celebrations in the divided villages. This enthusiasm rapidly spilt over into undivided villages (Boissevain, 1984, pp. 164-184). Today (1993) the Maltese *festa* is booming as never before and violent rivalry has kept pace.

Why Festa Partiti After 1850?

Two important questions must now be answered.

> What reasons prompted people to join one *partit* rather than its rival? and
> Why did *festa partiti* arise in the fifty or so years following 1850?

As we have seen, chronologically *festa* factionalism developed at the same time as *festa* celebrations were expanding and band clubs were being established. Obviously the territorial cleavage between parishes in the same town (such as at Rabat, Valletta, Victoria, and later, Qormi) formed a natural basis for rivalry. But besides these divisions, I have found no clearcut preexisting cleavages onto which rivalry between *festa partiti* was grafted. This is an area which needs further research. The establishment of formal band clubs was a logical outgrowth of the growing scale of the external celebration of saints and consequent demand for band music.

The interest in band music was no doubt stimulated by the presence in Malta of British military bands. The two Maltese military bands, the 'Royal Malta Artillery' band and the 'Royal Malta Militia', trained bandsmen and generated enthusiasm. More important, however, was the close cultural link which Malta enjoyed with Sicily at the time. Sicilian influences were furthered by refugees from the Italian Risorgimento, who began to stream into Malta after 1850. They promoted Italian and Sicilian culture, especially in the urban areas. It had long been a custom in Sicily to celebrate saints with brass-bands. In fact many of the Sicilian villages in the province of Syracuse, the province nearest Malta, were divided by factions supporting rival saints (Pitrè, pp. xlviii ff., 273 ff.). Verga has given a dramatic description of this rivalry in his famous short story *'Guerra di Santi'*. Much of the vocabulary associated with the Maltese *festa* is of Italian origin (*banda, mortaletti, kaxxa infernali, trikki-trakki*), if not Sicilian (*bradella, vara*).

Band clubs were also a manifestation of a conception of social organization new to Malta. They helped promote the idea of voluntary associations for laymen, and in particular, social clubs for 'gentlemen' – an idea which was gaining currency. Following the establishment of the exclusive British Union Club in 1826, clubs of various kinds began to spring up throughout the islands. They multiplied so rapidly that Castagna could write in 1890, 'Today you don't find a village without one or two nor a city without three or five' (Castagna, 1890, p. 128).

The second half of the nineteenth century was also a period of relative prosperity for Malta. This was a consequence of increased military and naval activity following the outbreak of the Crimean War (1853-56); the expansion of government public work projects from 1859-65; and the renewed demand for Maltese cotton to meet the cotton shortage caused by the American civil war (1861-65) (Price, 1954, pp. 105 ff.). This prosperity facilitated the not inconsiderable expenses involved in the expansion of *festa* celebrations (decorations, illuminations, fireworks), and the cost of equipping a band and furnishing a club-house. The economic boom also increased the demand for wage labour from the villages and this in turn helped to disseminate urban Italianate ideas. At about this time, too, city-born school teachers began moving into the rural communities to staff the newly established government schools. In doing so, they helped to spread further these Italianate ideas. In Ghaxaq, for example, I found that it was a Valletta born teacher who introduced the custom of decorating streets for the *festa*. There were thus a number of factors which facilitated and contributed to the establishment of band clubs after 1850.

Various reasons, however, have been recorded to explain why particular clubs, once founded, divided. The most frequent reasons point to arguments over *festa* celebrations. For example, Robert

Mifsud Bonnici suggests that *festa partiti* developed out of a dispute between persons who wanted to play sacred music composed by Vincenzo Bugeja (1806-60) and those who preferred the music of his rival, Paolo Nani (1814-1904) (Mifsud Bonnici, 1956, pp. 38 ff.). As far as I was able to determine, however, the only *partiti* which arose directly out of this dispute were those in Żebbuġ.

It is worth noting, however, that many *partiti*, once established, played either the music of Bugeja or that of Nani exclusively during their feasts. The former took a star as their symbol, the latter an eagle. The symbols of the star and the eagle seem to have acquired considerable significance. Bands in three towns (Birkirkara, Valletta, Victoria) were officially named 'La Stella' (Star) when they were established. This seems to lend further support to Mifsud Bonnici's thesis. The composers, their music and their respective symbols thus became banners of faction. Today many *partiti* are still nicknamed either *ta' l-istilla* (star) or *ta' l-ajkla* (eagle), reflecting this once important division.

Sometimes persons, often priests, vigorously promoting the devotion of a secondary saint, provoked a schism in the parish and this eventually led to the establishment of *partiti*. At Kirkop, for example, the secondary *partit* of St Joseph was the result of the efforts of a new parish priest, Reverend Joseph Barbara, from Għaxaq, to establish the cult to his personal patron. In 1877, a year after his arrival, he founded a confraternity dedicated to St Joseph. In October 1878 the new confraternity celebrated its first feast. Although the new secondary feast at first was a simple affair, it grew rapidly, as did the feast of St Leonard, the titular. The members of the new confraternity also increased, and in 1880 it established an altar in the church dedicated to its patron. By 1886 the inhabitants of this poor rural village were beginning to grumble about having to contribute to two feasts. In 1888 an encounter between those who organized the St Leonard feast and the parish priest brought matters to a head. Several persons complained to the archbishop that Dun Ġużepp was buying street decorations for the feast of St Joseph with funds collected for other purposes and, moreover, that he was raising the rents of local parish property for the same purpose. Following an investigation, the archbishop sided with the parish priest's accusers, and took away the administration of the church property from him. From that day onward, I was told, Dun Ġużepp threw his full support openly behind the feast of St Joseph. This divided the village into opposing factions. The village's 'Unione' band club divided and new clubs arose. The *'St* Leonard' club played the music of Bugeja and adopted the star symbol. Its rival, of course, favoured Nani and the eagle. Both clubs still exist and are very active. The rivalry between the *partiti* today appears as vigorous as ever (Boissevain, 1965, pp. 75-96; 1974, pp. 192-94, 210-12; 1980, pp. 82-86).

Disputes over details of the celebration of the *festa* and the related cult of saints thus loom large in the explanation of why clubs split and *festa partiti* arose. But there are also other ingredients that enter into the factional mixture.

The latter half of the last century, which saw the establishment of most of the band clubs and *festa partiti*, was also a period of intense political ferment. With the guarantee of Crown Colony status and the introduction of limited franchise for the election of the Legislative Council in 1849, the way was open for the emergence of national political parties. The run-up to council elections was hotly contested. In 1878 riots took place to protest new tax measures proposed to raise revenue. 1879 saw the first mass rally in Floriana where people gathered to protest government plans to force through an ill-conceived drainage scheme for the Three Cities. Political polarization became more pronounced following the introduction in 1880 of the Keenan Report aimed at the rapid anglicization of Maltese education. This was a radical proposal, when one considers that Italian had until then been the language of church, courts, university and government. Consequently, the period 1880 to 1888 saw the rise of Maltese nationalism and the polarization of Maltese politics into pro-Italian and pro-English factions (Frendo, 1979, pp. 15 ff.).

This division at the national level provided new symbols for band club and *festa partit* factional allegiance. The 'La Vallette' band club in Valletta became a national focal point for pro-Italian supporters. Its rival, quite naturally, performed a similar function for the pro-English faction, and consequently changed its name from 'La Stella' to 'Prince of Wales' and then to 'King's Own'. Other bands followed suit. In 1903, Senglea's 'La Vincitrice' became the 'Queen's Own' band (*ibid.*, p. 125). In Vittoriosa, 'La

Vittoriosa' became the 'Prince of Wales' band. In 1899 the 'St Elena' band of Birkirkara was granted permission to call itself the 'Duke of Connaught's Own Band' (Vella, 1935, pp. 498 ff.). The *festa partit* of Our Lady of Mount Carmel in Żurrieq, nicknamed *del Cavaliere*, in 1908 bought the uniforms and the name of the 'Queen Victoria' band of Sliema (Mifsud Bonnici, 1956, p. 79). In 1910 the 'Santa Maria' social club of Mqabba's titular *partit* changed its name to 'King George V' to commemorate his coronation (*ibid.*, p. 197).

It is therefore evident that the introduction of English 'imperial' names occurred after clubs and *partiti* were already well established. The change reflected a mixture of pro-English sentiment and the competition for markers to signal excellence to rival clubs. National politics thus became one of the issues on which established *partiti* and clubs took up positions after 1888, just as the preceding generation had done regarding the sacred music of Bugeja and Nani. There is, however, no evidence that national political issues played a role in the establishment of band clubs. There is only one exception: the 'Imperial Band' club in Mellieħa was founded in the 1920s to promote Strickland's interests. It appears that local issues and sentiments related to the celebration of parish feasts and rituals were at the root of the foundation of band clubs and *partiti*.

This principle was again illustrated recently. In 1985 a second band club was established in Mosta, the 'Santa Maria Philharmonic Society'. This was the first new rival band club to be founded since the Mellieħa 'Imperial Club' was established more than half a century earlier. It was founded by ex-members of the 'Nicolo Isouard' band club, who got together after having disagreed with the club committee. Even though Malta at the time was fiercely divided politically and caught up in the frenetic run-up to the 1987 elections, the disagreement was not about politics. The divisive issue concerned a new demonstrative band march which was to be held on the morning of the feast of The Assumption of Our Lady, the patron saint of the parish. The march took place at the same time as the festive high mass was being celebrated and was organized by some members who had gone against the wishes of the archpriest. When the band club committee, not wishing to alienate the archpriest, refused to sponsor the march, the march activists hived off and, together with others, established a new, rival band club.[1]

A year later, young Naxxar *festa* enthusiasts who had also clashed with the archpriest and the committee of the Peace band club, established a second band club (Boissevain, 1991). As at the turn of the century, parochial rather than national political issues brought about factional conflict that led to the division of existing clubs, and the establishment of rival organizations.

Partiti and Class

It is altogether more difficult to establish the personal motives that prompted people to join one particular *festa partit* rather that another at the time they were founded. One possible clue is the present day correlation between occupational class and *partit* affiliation. In general, the supporters of the titular saint, in parish political terms 'the establishment' *partit*, have (or at least had in 1960) more prestigious occupations than their rivals in the secondary, or 'opposition', *partit*. The latter tend to be less well-educated, more solidly working class and generally support the Labour Party (Boissevain, 1965, p. 83). In Kirkop, for example, I found in 1960 that 83 per cent of the village's professional and white collar workers belonged to the *partit* of 'St Leonard', the parish's titular saint. The corresponding figure for '*St* Joseph' members was 17 per cent. Conversely, of the village's farmers, 62 per cent supported '*St* Joseph' and 38 per cent '*St* Leonard' (*ibid.*, pp. 84, 94).

In view of the way that membership in a *partit* is inherited rather than chosen, (*ibid.*, pp. 82 ff.), the position the founding generation occupied in the village's class structure in some way influenced the choice of *partit* of the next generation. Frequent marriages to outsiders, emigration, and the changing employment structure of the country during the past century have blurred this picture. But the underlying pattern is pronounced, and is repeated in almost every town divided by this type of rivalry.

---

[1] My thanks to J. Agius for providing valuable introductions.

In Kirkop I was also told that many young people joined the secondary *partit* when it was founded. The new secondary *partiti* must have appealed more to those who, for whatever reason, held no offices in the older confraternities or band clubs and/or did not form part of the circle who surrounded the parish priest and organized village affairs. Through the new cult and band club they could gain office and perform organizational activities which gave them greater prominence and thus higher status. In short, the secondary *partiti* appealed to the poor, the marginal, the young, and those seeking higher status. (The recent establishment of rival band clubs in Mosta and Naxxar mentioned above also reflected this pattern.)

I believe these *partiti* were a form of opposition to established authority, an expression of protest centered against the monopoly of power by the establishment cliques. The second half of the nineteenth century was a period of great social upheaval. In Malta, as elsewhere in Europe, there was a surge of nationalism. There was also an active, though diffuse, working-class movement that propagated an egalitarian ideology of the brotherhood of all men. This new ideology questioned established authority. It reached the Maltese urban area first. It seeped into the villages via the industrial areas around the Grand Harbour, where ex-agriculturists worked together as wage labourers with workers from the Three Cities. It was expressed at the national level by means of the support that the working classes gave to the pro-English language reforms. These reforms were opposed by their rivals, in class terms – the ecclesiastical, legal and university establishment that supported the Italian language (Frendo, 1979, *passim*). The radical teaching of Emmanuel Dimech (1860-1921) was another expression of this stirring of the working classes (Frendo, 1972).

I suggest that there is a third manifestation of the same movement that can be found in the establishment of secondary *partiti*. I think that besides the class-biased composition of the secondary *partiti* and their occasional political alignment, there is further evidence for my contention that these clubs reflected a pro-working class sentiment. I have already noted that a number of the *partiti* were dedicated to St Joseph. He is the patron saint of the working classes, and was declared patron of the Catholic Church in 1870. There are many signs which show that the devotion to the saint was very strong in 19th century Malta. There were many new confraternities dedicated to him after 1850 (among others in Għargħur, Kirkop, Naxxar and Xagħra) and he was chosen as patron of the new parishes of Kalkara, Msida and Qala, all towns located on or near harbours. Moreover, four parishes have secondary feasts dedicated to him (Għaxaq, Kirkop, Rabat and Żebbuġ). Besides these, Għargħur, Mosta and Siġġiewi also had St Joseph *partiti* which succumbed to the 1935 church regulations.

Conclusion

To sum up my argument then, *festa partiti* arose as part of the expansion of *festa* activities and the establishment of Italianate band clubs during the second half of the last century. Intense participation in *festa* activities stimulated factional division over details of the celebration of various saints. These divisions largely reflected class fault lines already present in the communities.

Festas provide a stormy arena which nourishes and creates an occasion for the presentation of divisive sentiments, as individuals, categories and groups compete for honour, status and power. Maltese society, like all societies, is riven with competition. Because of the country's small size and its stable, intensely inter-related population, competition easily escalates, as protagonists recruit support through ramifying networks of kin, patrons and clients. The result is intense factionalism, reflected in family disputes, parish ritual activities, sports (especially football) and national politics.

Factional conflict by its nature is corrosive, for its chief characteristics are its black and white polarization, the bitterness it engenders among rivals, the absurd lengths members go to in order to score points off each other, and the shame they feel for such pettiness in the presence of outsiders (Silverman and Salisbury, 1978). Factionalism is one of the dominant cultural themes of Maltese society and, judging by its persistent intensity, it does not seem to be mitigated by either rising prosperity or education.

References

Badger, G.P. (1838) *Description of Malta and Gozo*, Malta, M. Weiss.
Bezzina, J. (1985) *Religion and Politics in a Crown Colony. The Gozo-Malta Story 1798-1864*, Valletta, Bugelli Publications.

Boisgelin de Kerdu, P.M.L. de (1804) *Ancient and Modern Malta*, 2 vols., London, Richard Phillips.
Boissevain, J. (1974) *Friends of Friends: Networks, Manipulators and Coalitions*, Oxford, Basil Blackwell.
Boissevain, J. (1980) *A Village in Malta, Fieldwork Edition*, New York, Holt, Rinehart & Winston.
Boissevain, J. (1991) 'Ritual, play, and identity: changing patterns of celebration in Maltese villages', *Journal of Mediterranean Studies*, Malta, vol.1. The University of Malta.
Boissevain, J. (1993) *Saints and Fireworks: Religion and Politics in Rural Malta*, 3e, Valletta, Progress Press.
Cassar-Pullicino, J. (1976) *Studies in Maltese Folklore*, Malta, University of Malta Press.
Castagna, P.P. (1985) *Lis Storia ta' Malta bil-Gzejjer Tahha*, (1e 1890) 2e, Malta, Facsimile Edition, Midsea Books Ltd., Part III.
Concilium Regionale Melitense (1935), (1936) *Decreta*, Malta, Empire Press.
Frendo, H. (1972) *Birth Pangs of a Nation: Manwel Dimech's Malta 1860-1921*, Malta, Mediterranean Publications.
Frendo, H. (1979) *Party Politics in a Fortress Colony: The Malta Experience*, Malta, Midsea Books Ltd.
Miege, M. (1840) *Histoire de Malte*, 3 vols., Paris.
Mifsud Bonnici, R. (1956) *Ġrajja ta' Baned f'Malta u Għawdex*, Malta, G. Muscat, 2 vols.
Pitrè, G. (1900) *Feste Patronali in Sicilia*, vol. XXI of Biblioteca delle Tradizioni Populari Siciliane, Torino.
Price, C.A. (1954) *Malta and the Maltese. A Study in Nineteenth Century Migration*, Melbourne, Georgian House.
Silverman, M. & Salisbury, R.F. (eds) (1978) *A House Divided? Anthropological Studies of Factionalism*, Canada, Memorial University of Newfoundland.
Vella, E.B. (1935) *Storja Ta' Birkirkara Bil-Kolleġġata Tagħha*, Malta, Empire Press.

Secularization

Carmel Tabone

Secularization is a prominent theme in social thought, often used to summarize and characterize a wide variety of transformations taking place in the modern world.[1] Secularization is a term of manifold meaning which has undergone an evolution in the course of its history. Commonly speaking, secularization refers to a change in either the content of the beliefs of people or in its mode of expression, or both (Bruce, 1992, p. 8.). However the term underwent a

---

[1] Etymologically speaking secularization is derived from the Latin word *saeculum* meaning world in the sense of time, age, history, translating the Greek word *aion*. *Saeculum* differs from *mundus* which also means world, but in the sense of space, translating the Greek word *cosmos* (Cox, 1956, p. 19).

notable semantic extension during the nineteenth century and it is no longer limited to denote changes mainly in the religious sphere, but rather has connotations today of global social change. For this reason it is necessary to examine the meaning and usage of the term so as to determine the scientific notion of secularization which would serve best in any analysis of social change.

The mentioned semantic extension took place in two fields, first in the historic-political and then in the ethical-sociological one. The term secularization most probably finds its origin in the peace treaty of Westphalia to indicate the expropriation of the Church's property in favour of the National Reformed Churches (Marramao, 1983, p. xvii).[2] Weber pioneered the usage of secularization as both a descriptive and analytical term (Weber, 1978, Vol. I, p. 446; Vol. II, pp. 36 and 131). For him, and Tönnies (1955, p. 295), secularization indicates the transit of modernity from *gemeinschaft* to *gesellschaft*, from the age of community to the age of society: from a type of bond founded on obligation to a type founded on contract. On these same lines Berger argues that secularization can be understood not only with reference to what has happened to social institutions, but also as applying to processes inside the human mind. He calls this the secularization of consciousness (Berger, 1970, pp. 3-4).

In studying the history of the term's usage Larry Shiner (1967, pp. 52-59) attempts a typology distinguishing five concepts of secularization. However, his notion of secularization is limited strictly to religion, as if global social change is simply the result of decline or transformation in religious belief and practice. The relationship may be postulated the other way round, in such a way that the changes in religious belief and practice are them-

---

[2] The concept of secularization had initially a neutral value. It did not indicate solely an act of expropriation, but also acts of secularization accomplished voluntarily by the ecclesiastical institution itself, as for example the foundation of universities or the suppression of convents (Marramao, 1983, p. xvii). The concept took on the meaning of a suppression of the religious institutions and the expropriation of the Church's property by the state, during the *kulturkampf* (1872-87). Gradually people began to understand the positive aspects of secularization, particularly because it led toward the liberation from many forces impeding real religious functions (Nijk, 1968, p. 39).

selves understood as the result of global social change and only one of its various effects.

Surprisingly, in a recent publication, the so called 'Secularization Thesis' is described in terms of a decline in religious belief and practice.

> The core of what we mean when we talk about this society being more secular than that, is that the lives of fewer people in the former than in the latter are influenced by religious beliefs (Bruce, 1992, p. 6.)

I insist that what these authors are calling secularization might be only one aspect of this phenomenon of social change. One of the effects of secularization may be decline in religion. However this is only one of the effects. Secularization, as a process of social change, can also lead to a rebirth or renewal of religion. I propose to illustrate this dynamic by referring to the Church in Malta and a case study focussing on religion and Maltese youth.

Three Principles

On these lines, secularization is best defined in relation to Weber's concept based on three fundamental principles (Marramao, 1983, pp. xx-xxi), namely:
a. legitimation or the meaning which is given to one's action;
b. elicit action (internally driven), or, in other words, the principle of the individual's auto decision and determination; and
c. differentiation and progressive specialization, including roles, statuses and institutions.

In view of on these three principles, I have arrived at this definition of secularization:

> The progressive emergence of the individual's self-consciousness and self-determination and the free adoption of any selective criteria as the basis for legitimation.

Emergent from this definition, the secularization process thus implies individualization and differentiation.

Individualization

Individualization is the increasing autonomy of both the personality system and role patterns in relation to the prescriptions of a normative order. Social life is possible when the elements composing it share common principles and norms, a moral order. The moral order is made up of two dimensions. On the one hand there is the dimension moral, the vertical or normative dimension. On the other hand there is the dimension order, the horizontal or relational dimension. An action is said to be moral, and thus contributing to maintain order, when it is directed by or oriented to a symbolic system or a universe of values.

The values or the symbolic system by which action is directed to be moral are the so called 'moral standards'. Moral standards are patterns of behaviour including mutual rights and obligations which make social relationships possible. Although moral standards are not exclusively social in reference, it is not possible to conceive social action without them (Parsons, 1964, p. 14).

It is within the social that action seeks to integrate the ideal with the real and to integrate actors with one another in a system of shared values and norms (Parsons, 1966, pp. 28-29). It should be noted, however, that the *telos* (end) to which action is oriented is ultimately the idealized state of affairs (the value-orientation) envisaged by the actors. The ultimate end of action is that in which the actors embody their notion of the ultimate (Parsons, 1968, p. 427; 1964, pp. 24-26). Actors' notion of the ultimate may be religiously based, as human beings are in search of objects worthy of their passionate devotion (Weber, 1958, p. 135). The emphasis on this aspect of social action, self-determination and internalization, constitutes individualization, which does not exclude being religiously based. With individualization arises the problem of legitimation. The traditional sanction *we do not do that* is not sufficient for legitimation, even if it is religiously based.

Differentiation

Differentiation implies that the various units of the social system vary both in regard to the level of responsibility for implementing a general value pattern, and in the commitment to the kind of implementation throughout the social system. In other words, differentiation means that legitimation varies both in degree and in kind. Variation of legitimation in kind can be called qualitative differentiation which militates against the total implementation of the general value system.

The result of qualitative differentiation in the social system is threefold: the development of sub-values in contrast to the general value system, the increment of reference groups and the freedom from moral absolutism (Parsons, 1966, pp. 147-151).

In the first place differentiation gives rise to the creation of sub-systems each with its value system, which are often given priority in relation to the general value system. An example of this is an academic whose commitment is to cognitive reasoning in the general value system. However s/he can be found to be giving priority to economic reasoning as a sub-value in relation to the value orientation of his/her sub-system.

Second, it is evident that this may easily result in the growth of reference groups with the attendant fragmentation of the individual's loyalties. An example of this can be the case of the Church in contemporary society which seeks as a social unit total mobilization of commitment on the part of its members, when in fact it has to share the commitments with a variety of other social institutions and reference groups. It is worth noting that some of these commitments may be in conflict with one another. Working in a catering establishment and observing the Sunday rest is one such example.

Third, in a differentiated social structure, situational and other exigencies acquire increased significance in decision making when any particular set of values is being implemented. In such a social reality there is more freedom, more space for free choice, where it is possible to make choices free from moral absolutism. In this way a free choice would be that which is compatible with both the most generalized values of the social system and with the prescriptions of any reference group, as well as with the demands of a particular situation.

In this perspective, the autonomy which is necessarily given to sub-systems, in a differentiated social reality, jeopardizes the implementation of the general value system.[3]

---

[3] Thomas Luckmann (1967, Chapters 5-7) presents a similar analysis of the process of secularization in modern society. The process of differentiation, according to Luckmann, has increasingly undermined the incompatibility between the official world-view with its patterns of values, and the individual's

As a result it may also happen that less general (particularist) values take precedence over the more general (universalist) values in the social system. When this happens, the implied plurality and freedom of differentiation defeats its own purpose, causing restrictions to the choices of the individual (Parsons, 1966, pp. 146, 151, 154; Luckmann, 1967, pp. 50-53).

To summarize we can say that secularization in the sense of differentiation means that in a society there is a high degree of incongruence and diversity within structures, within cultural artefacts as well as between these two levels of the social system.

On the level of the social structure, determination of goals by individual or collective actors is increasingly related to individual natural tendencies and situational exigencies. These situational and subjective considerations tend to become more influential than officially sanctioned and institutional normative systems in the process of internalizing systems of ultimate significance.

Consequently, instead of a single universal religious basis to the moral order of society, as in primitive societies, there is a plurality of systems of ultimate significance competing for influence. These systems may be sources of ideological conflict in a contemporary society characterized by secularization. Such a result can follow since there is an institutionalized plurality of terrains of behaviour (such as work, leisure, sport, tourism, apart from religion). Each of these spheres of action and significance can come to appropriate a particular value system and hierarchy. However, this tendency towards conflict may be mitigated by the multiple associational membership of individual actors, who thus bridge the condition of structural plurality (Fenn, 1970, pp. 134-135; Luckmann, 1967, p. 91).

---

effective priorities. In this process, economic, political, legal and other institutions are characterized by a relative autonomy in the norms that govern each domain. The individual is characterized by a series of discrete, discontinuous role-performances, rather than by acts that are coherent in terms of superordinate 'value-orientation'. One's actions are in fact governed by norms of separate institutional domains, norms which are primarily those of functional rationality.

Desacralization

In a social reality where religion was traditionally a dominant factor and the moral order was religiously based, in such a way that there existed a universe of values synonymous with Religion, secularization might imply desacralization as well as dissacration. Legitimation, in a secular society, would not be solely and entirely religiously based and it might also be wholly religiously free, a legitimation which operates entirely without religion. Desacralization, as we shall see does not imply necessarily the loss of religion. It can even result in a religion with a different modality which can also be more mature. On the other hand however, one has to acknowledge that secularization can lead to decline and even loss of religion, which I have termed dissacration (or secularism). Desacralization is the gradual deprivation of the world's sacral character; when the human being and nature become objects of both scientific accounts and haphazard phenomena. The historian Eric Kahler (1943) interprets secularization on these lines of desacralization and describes it as the independence of the person from religion as s/he lives rationally in relation to nature understood in its physical and objective sense (Shiner, 1967, p. 56).

It is evident that this process is an effect of individualization in the main, as well as differentiation encompassing the rationalization of the world and of man's consciousness. According to Max Weber, rationalization is the *entzauberung* (disenchantment) of the world where the latter loses its sacral connotation. The world is no longer conceived solely as something sacred or divine, but as something natural having its proper laws. Such rationalization, according to Weber (1919, p. 33), is a 'historical irreversible destiny', although it does not necessarily lead *tout court* to a deideologized or desacralized world.

Therefore, this disenchantment of the world, though historically irreversible, does not necessarily lead to a concept of the world deprived of any relationship with a religious or ideological concept. The *entzauberung* shatters the totalitarian or closed interpretation of the world as religious, to make way for a rationalized interpretation. But there could still be a place for religious or ideological interpretation along with the rationalized one.

Desacralization can be defined as the progressive reduction of the sacral modality of the concept of the world. Consequently, there is a parallel rise in a rationalized modality. In this way, there emerges a more secular concept which can be also called the secular modality.

The sacral modality can be described as the tendency to conceive the presence of the divine quid in the world in an immanent sense. Consequently the humane and the natural tend to lose their autonomy as they are almost absorbed by the Divine. The Divine here is imagined as an exhaustive explanation of all phenomena. The immanent conception of the presence of the divine can generate the belief that one can manipulate the divine according to one's own needs. This may lead to a magical, superstitious, utilitarian and exploitative type of religion. Moreover, in a community with a religiosity of this kind, a sacred character is also attributed to the conception of authority. The religious institution here is also considered as a *societas perfecta* (Milanesi, 1979, pp. 98-99).

The rationalized modality, on the other hand, is the tendency to conceive the presence of the divine *quid* in a transcendent sense, a relationship which implies distinction without separation. Here the humane and the natural tend to gain significance and acquire their own autonomy. The conception of the world and reality is free from an exhaustive sacral explanation. This freedom, however does not mean total separation from any sacral or religious implication. It is only freedom from the comprehensiveness of such implication. It can also lead to a more mature type of religion free from magical, superstitious, utilitarian and exploitative connotations.

The passage from the sacral to the rationalized modality, desacralization, implies that the human sciences progressively assume the task of explaining the issues and problems of everyday life in a rationalized way using their own instruments of knowledge. Even on the level of individual and collective experience there is the tendency to look within for self legitimation on the basis of the principles emanating from the human sciences. This makes human experience more and more autonomous. The hypothesis of the *ganz andere* (wholly other) – the utilization of an external being or referent to ascribe meaning to human action and existence – constitutes only the point of departure and the point of arrival of autonomous human experience. The relationship with the Divine is one of inner freedom, and this explains why there is no room for a magical, superstitious, utilitarian and exploitative type of religion. The action of the individual, or the collectivity, is characterized by two dimensions, one vertical and the other horizontal. The horizontal dimension which makes sense in itself becomes the basis for the vertical dimension, the relationship with the divine (Milanesi, 1979, pp. 99-100).

Desacralization can operate on various levels, namely: the institutional, the social and the individual level. On the institutional level, desacralization effects the decline in power, influence, range of prestige and control of the religious institution. Such desacralization can take various forms: the loosening of the power and the influence of the religious institution in the State apparatus and the emergence of a secular legitimation of society (Martin, 1969, pp. 48-50).

On the social level, desacralization can take the form of a decline in the traditionally socio-religious conditions which formerly sustained the sense of belonging and the consequent conduct in ethics, family life, politics and education. Traditionally there was the possibility of people going to Church not out of religious belief and conviction, but because of social control and constraint. Through desacralization there is less place for this externalism in religious practice.

On the individual level, desacralization can result in the decline of traditionally religious and devotional practices, customs and rituals when these are merely the effect of a magical, superstitious, utilitarian and exploitative mentality. This can be seen empirically in the reduction in the frequency, number and intensity of such practices, including decline in attendance at church services.

In this way, desacralization can easily be interpreted as a decline in religion, but it is not necessarily so. Desacralization implies a decline, not in religion, but in a type of religiosity, the sacral modality. In the process of secularization, including this aspect of desacralization, religion can still be the *weltanschauung* of one's experience, that which constitutes the basic meaning of one's own life, forming thus the value system of the individual. It is only in the context of dissacration that religion is totally excluded from one's construction of meanings (Martin, 1969, pp. 50-51).

In Malta, as will be argued below, we can report a decline as well as a revival of religion. Hence the so called 'secularization thesis', in terms of exclusive decline in religion, is not applicable in the Maltese context. However this analysis suggests the lesson which may be found to be repeated in other environments. For example the revival of Islam in its Fundamentalistic expression could be interpreted as revival of that particular religion; in other words an expression and consequence of global social change. Faced with the threat and possibility of loss of religion, individuals react by, for example, going to the very roots of their religion. Hence the loss of religion, dissacration or secularism, is only one, and not an automatic and inevitable product of secularization.

The Malta Case

In a country like Malta, traditionally characterized by religious hegemony where universal values and religious values used to be considered as synonymous, the analysis of the social reality under the perspective of secularization would present a valid case study.

Religion and the Church

The Church occupied a predominant position in the Maltese social structure. This remained till some time after the second world war. At this time the Church alone had universal presence which operated effectively at all levels of social life (Vassallo, 1979, p. 23). One can say that it was the Church to give Malta its identity and construct much of its culture, such that the religious defined the social in a practically social manner. Religion is a strong traditional feeling pivotal to Maltese social life, in such a way that, at this time, between the social and the religious there was little separation, if any. This is manifested in the celebration of the town or village *festa* where the religious and the social are intertwined, in such a way that one cannot be celebrated without the other, and where it is difficult to distinguish where one finishes and where the other starts.

Today, though one can no longer speak of this predominance of the Catholic Church in Malta, it still has a major influence on the lives of the people, and religion is still relatively widely practised. The secular calendar is to this date overridden by numerous religious signposts which continuously chart and rechart the individual's social life.

This long history of religious tradition on the Island may have led to traditionalism and externalism, manifested in a particular type of religiosity which in our terminology can be called 'sacral'. Religiosity is incorporated in the common sense of culture, but it leaves little space for internalization and critical assimilation (Tabone, 1987, pp. 149-156).

However, notwithstanding traditionalism and institutionalism, the Church still succeeds in instilling a religious imprint in the individual. Almost each and every individual is baptized, attends catechism classes, makes his first Holy Communion, receives the sacrament of Confirmation, and is generally married in Church, and this irrespective of whether the person is a believer or not.

Whether one likes it or not, the individual is somehow involved in religious manifestations which are rudimental in the social life cycle. It is very hard for a Maltese brought up in such a religiously imbued culture not to bear a minimum of religious imprint. Even swearing is a manifestation of religious influence albeit as a case of inverted imagery. For this reason, there is little or no space for atheism in Malta, but only for antitheism or religious indifference.

Unfortunately this imprint may emerge as an archaic one, not bearing relevance to contemporary youth culture and society at large. It resorts to symbols including language, liturgy, status difference, ritual and dress language which are hollow, appertaining to a bygone age.

As an example of this, one can mention that in 1967 Church attendance at Sunday Mass amounted to 83.4%. The latest information available (Tonna, 1993, pp. 56-58) shows that by 1982 it had dropped to 72.7%. However, despite this obvious decline, it does not necessarily mean that Malta is moving towards secularism or religious indifference. It may be a crisis of religious symbols which are not adequate to the current culture. This crisis could be overcome and could lead to a more mature type of religion reflecting internal conviction. In fact, one can even report a religious revival among youth on the Island. This can be seen from the various new and active religious movements such as the Charismatics, Focolarini, Neo-Cathecumen and the Christian Life Communities. In more scientific terms, the religious decline, in a situation like that of Malta, may be only a stage in the secularization process, incorporating desacralization. In this sense, this decline, may be reflecting a change from a type of religiosity which is 'sacral' to one which is more 'secular'. It is the passage from a religion which emerges in the individual from the outside, deductively, as a result of a predominant and highly institutionalized Church, to a religion emerging from the individual's internal feelings and convictions. In the latter the individual does not resort to stereotyped symbols to manifest his/her religion, but strives to create one's own, reflecting more sincerely one's innermost feelings and personal convictions. Even when one borrows stereotyped symbols, as are candles, water, bread and the like from the Church liturgy, one strives to give them a personal touch.

When, in this process of desacralization, the religious person does not manage to find a convincing manifestation of one's innermost religious feelings, one may gradually put aside one's religion and even lose it. In other words, if the individual in this secularization process does not succeed, for some reason or other, to embrace a secular religion, the outcome may easily turn out to be a resort to secularism. A secular religion is one attuned to the present in such a way that it manifests itself as a relevant response to the fundamental needs and exigencies, concerns and ideals of the individual in contemporary society. In this case, religious decline becomes the result of failure in the secularization process. When this process is successful, the result is a rebirth of religion.

Case Material

The empirical evidence which I would like to bring in this regard is the outcome of participant observation among a youth group of university students.

As a start it is worth clarifying that although there is both status and age difference I managed to be accepted in the group and become one of them as much as possible. They did not show any inhibitions to speak openly in my presence. On my part I made an effort to lay aside my professional status in order to gain acceptance within the group. It is known that a totally objective and value free approach is impossible to achieve in practice, and I am fully aware that this applies also to my case study. The value of this character sketch, if I may add, is mainly a sociological one, in the sense that it constitutes one manifestation, perhaps even a prototype of secularization. This prescinds from any validity the material may have for pastoral work.

This group started from the friendship of three youths Adrian, Bert and Conrad (the names have been changed to preserve anonymity). To remember them I used to call them A. B. C. I had met them after a session of Lenten sermons. It came to my knowledge later that they had come to the sermons as a last resort; they were finding religious practice meaningless and religious ideals conflicting with theirs.

Here are some of the queries which they put forward to me at the beginning and which reflected their religious crisis.

> How is it we get bored during Mass? It takes only about 40 minutes. We were taught that it is the most sublime act of worship towards our God, and we do not question that, yet we still have to make a special effort to go, and once there to stay till the end.

> The Church presents itself as a perfect institution, where more or less its members live in harmony, and then we notice that there is a net separation between clergy and laity. Some priests look down upon us as inferiors and at times as ignorant, just because we beg to differ.

> We are in full bloom of our sexual life ready for every kind of adventure, and as Church members we feel restrained by religious precepts 'you should not do this' and 'you should not do that', because it is a sin. We cannot see founded reasons for such restrictions. We are taught that sexuality is God's gift, yet it seems that it is given to us to keep it intact according to our religion.

I didn't answer these questions there and then, but solutions possibly emerged as we went along together searching and longing for the religious experience that was lacking. I have noticed that although these youths were brought up as Catholics, as are the majority of Maltese, they knew nothing about the religious experience. The religious experience is the individual's personal meeting with the Divine, that which in theological terms is called the leap of faith. We carried out this search in enhancing our friendship in the light of the Bible which we periodically read together. Subsequently we shared our reflections.

After four years in this experience they all claim now that they feel that God is very near as a personal friend, and not somebody at a distance beyond, of whom one is afraid and always frightened not to offend. This is reflected in their religion.

> For me Religion is the utmost expression of what is good within myself, whether it manifests itself as love or friendship. Nonetheless, I no longer consider religion as being a restrictive force restraining my natural human behaviour. On the contrary, it helps me to accept my limitations and start afresh, with no useless phases of depression. It is, in other words, an intimate relationship with 'a Being' whom I love, trust and respect, and whose trust, love and care for me are unlimited. (Adrian)

When we celebrate Mass together it usually takes from two to three hours, and neither of us even notices the duration. Perhaps this happens because it is celebrated in a way where one can experience personal and direct participation, while following the prescribed rite. We sit around a table laid up as an altar and everyone is free to express oneself at any time sharing one's feelings with the others.

> Now I feel proud to be Christian, and I know what it means; to have a personal relationship with God through Jesus Christ expressed in a sincere relationship of love and unity with my friends. This does not mean that I feel continuously this close to my God. There are instances when I experience some void. However when we meet to read the Bible and to celebrate Mass together in our small group I feel my religion revived and renewed. (Bert)

Since in the group we experience sincere unity, we came to understand that this is a realization of the Church, as our unity is in the name of Christ, and it matured in living the Gospel. In this light we can easily understand the shortcomings of the Church on the institutional level. Those defects in the Church which used to confuse us, do not trouble us anymore. In this atmosphere the members of the group claim that they have come to understand the objective human meaning of their sexuality. Though sexuality should not be restrained, it has to be controlled and guided to reach its aim and serve for personal fulfillment.

> I was feeling far away from God and his Church as I could not live according to some of the Church's principles. For example, it was hard for me to understand why I had to refrain from experiencing sex before marriage, and why an unsuccessful marriage cannot be dissolved. Such thoughts made me feel a hypocrite when attending Church services, as I was not living according to the principles of the Church and did not want to. In the meantime, in the love and unity which I shared with my friends I started to experience a new type of religion, more broad-minded than that in which I have been brought up. I realized that a son can

still love and respect his mother though differing in some ideas. With this in mind I committed myself to live my religion, without feeling a hypocrite now. Gradually I came to understand that sex as passion is not the most exciting experience I can make in life, and that the Christian principles are objectively right, especially when one understands the full meaning of Christian marriage and how much it is fulfilling. (Conrad)

Now the group is bigger, yet all the members of the group witness that they have experienced a shift from an archaic type of religion, which was becoming more and more meaningless, to one which is more personalized and at the same time more communal and for this reason meaningful and fulfilling.

This is one empirical proof of how the secularization process does not necessarily imply decline in religion but on the other hand a rebirth or renewal of religion.

Conclusion

Richard Niebuhr has suggested that there lies an iron law of regeneration at work in institutions whereby a monolithic and hollow religious establishment naturally spawned offshoots which eventually lead to new, perhaps informal but charismatic religious movements (Niebuhr, 1929). A similar dynamic process might be conceived within the parameters of social change. Our predicament is that we are living on the crest of a rising wave of transformation which from the paradigmatic perspective can only appear to be negative, and this determines our perception and evaluation of the situation.

Secularization may be more profitably conceived as a neutral, value-free term, with possibilities for both religious renewal, as well as degeneration. Perhaps it is this packaging of the religious product – its discourse, attire, liturgy, ritual, social involvement, and community – which is ultimately responsible for determining this crucial outcome.

Bibliography

Berger, P. L. (1970) *A Rumour of Angels: Modern Society and the Rediscovery of the Supernatural*, New York, Anchor Books, Doubleday & Co.

Bruce, S. (ed.) (1992) *Religion and Modernization*, Oxford, Clarendon Press.

Cox, H. (1956) *The Secular City: Secularization and Urbanization in a Theological Perspective*, New York, Macmillan.

Fenn, R.E. (1970) 'The process of secularization: a post-Parsonian view, *Journal for the Scientific Study of Religion*, vol. 9, 1.
Kahler, E. (1943) *Man the Measure*, New York, Macmillan.
Luckmann, T. (1967) *The Invisible Religion*, New York, Macmillan.
Marramao, G. (1983) *Potere e Secolarizzazione*, Roma, Ed. Riuniti.
Martin, D. (1969) *The Religious and the Secular*, New York, Schoeken Books.
Milanesi, G. (1979) *Sociologia della Religione*, Torino, Elle Di Ci.
Niebuhr, H.R. (1929) *The Social Sources of Denominationalism*, New York, Holt, Rinehart & Winston.
Nijk, A. J. (1968) *Secularisatie*, Rotterdam, Lemniscat, Italian trans. (1973) *Secolarizzazzione*, Brescia, Ed. Queriniana.
Parsons, T. (1964) *The Social System*, Glencoe, IL, The Free Press.
Parsons, T. (1966) *Societies: Evolutionary and Comparative Perspectives*, Englewood Cliffs, NJ, Prentice Hall.
Parsons, T. (1968) *The Structure of Social Action*, Glencoe, IL, The Free Press.
Shiner, L. (1967) 'The meaning of secularization', *The International Yearbook for Sociology of Religion*, vol. 3.
Tabone, C. (1987) *The Secularization of the Family in Changing Malta*, Malta, Dominican Publications.
Tonna, B. (1993) *Malta Trends*, Malta, Media Centre Publications.
Tönnies, F. (1926) *Gemeinschaft und Gesellschaft. Grundbegriffe der reinen Soziologie*, Berlin. English trans. (1955) *Community and Association*, London, Routledge & Kegan Paul.
Vassallo, M. (1979) *From Lordship to Stewardship: Religion and Social Change in Malta*, The Hague, Mouton.
Weber, M. (1919) *Geistige Arbeit als Beruf. Vier Vortyrage vor dem Freistudentischen Bund*, Munchen, Italian trans. (1966) *Il Lavoro Intellettuale Come Professione*, Torino, NUE.
Weber, M. (1956) *Wirtschaft und Gesellschaft*, Tubingen. English trans. (1978) *Economy and Society: An Outline of Interpretative Sociology*, 2 vols, Berkeley, CA, University of California Press.
Weber, M. (1958) 'Science as a vocation'. In Girth, H.H. & Mills, C.W. (eds) *From Max Weber: Essays in Sociology*, Oxford, Oxford University Press.

15

Television and its Viewers: The Case of Soap Opera

Mary Anne Lauri

Introduction

The mass media have permeated our daily lives. They provide a rich source of complex, social stimuli to which people from all strata of society are exposed. It is therefore not surprising that social scientists have found the mass media to be a fertile area of exploration. Television, the medium which, most of all, has invaded our lives dramatically, has become a prime target for such study. It offers social scientists a wide area of research in which a number of questions are asked, for example:

What are the effects of television?
Why do people watch or enjoy television?
Do they take on the values portrayed in the programmes?
Do children distinguish between fact and television fiction?

Soap opera is one particular genre where the relationship between television and audience has been studied. Their popularity in Britain, United States, Peru, Columbia, Angola, India, Australia and many other countries all over the world is interesting not only from the point of view of media studies but also from a sociological and a psychological perspective. Malta is no exception. The many television stations which can be watched by the Maltese viewer offer between them an extensive selection of soap operas and telenovelas each week. Most series are scheduled to broadcast five episodes per week. Such a multitude of daily soap opera programmes followed assiduously by people from various age groups and socio-economic classes is a social phenomenon worthy of deeper investigation.

This paper focuses on one particular question namely: Why do people watch soap operas? This question will be discussed from a social psychological perspective. We shall first review some of the theories which have been put forward primarily as a result of studies which investigate reasons which viewers themselves give for watching soaps, and how these studies throw light on people's patterns of involvement with the genre. We shall then describe the results of this type of empirical research carried out with Maltese audiences.

What is Soap Opera?

The soap opera is a serial, characterized by a permanent cast of actors, numerous story-lines interwoven in a complicated manner, with an emphasis on dialogue instead of action. The skeleton of soap opera is made up of the personal relationships of people in a small community such as a neighbourhood, a hospital, a hotel or a business organization. In the case of the Latin American telenovelas, they also feature historical and political content. The genre's slow pace and the daily scheduling of long series of programmes enables the viewer to follow the characters' vicissitudes almost in 'real time', facilitating involvement by the audience.

One can distinguish between a number of major types of soap opera. There are the American soaps such as 'Beautiful' which feature the world of the rich, with power struggles, business deals, glamorous people and beautiful houses; then there are the

English and Australian soaps such as 'Neighbours' which feature everyday characters, plots and language with which the viewer is more familiar. The Latin American 'telenovelas' fall somewhere in between this scale. Of course there are exceptions to these broad generalizations.

Liebes and Katz (1988) have compared soap operas to Claude Levi-Strauss's concept of myth. Just as myths are about basic human experiences like birth, death, love and hate, so are soap operas. Interwoven with these basic human experiences are contemporary issues. Very often the themes chosen reflect the current social issues in a particular country. The British soap opera 'EastEnders' deals with problems such as integration of racial or national minorities, and the German serial 'Lindenstrasse' with ecological problems. Several Latin American countries produced telenovelas focusing on adult literacy, family planning, child rearing and female equality. If themes are inappropriately chosen the popularity of the particular soap opera diminishes. The Indian serial 'Hum Log', for example, had family planning as one of its initial themes. It was not very popular and it was only when the direct approach to family planning was de-emphasized in favour of themes which are closely related to family planning – such as the status of women and family welfare – did the serial acquire its outstanding popularity.

The Soap Opera and the Viewer

For many years, television was looked upon as a powerful medium influencing a passive audience. The failure of many important studies to demonstrate the effects of television led researchers to investigate this relationship from other perspectives. One such perspective was the Uses and Gratifications approach. According to this theory, the viewers are not totally passive in that they are selective and decide what to watch according to their needs, thus using the media to satisfy their own desires (Blumler & Katz, 1974). This approach does are not study what the media do to people, but what the people do with the media.

Another important development was the applications of semiotics to television. While traditional mass communication theorists strongly debated whether power lay with the media or the audience, a new approach began to gain ground. Known as critical mass communications, this approach emphasized the power of the text and the meanings inherent in the aesthetic construction of the message which a particular programme is conveying.

Recent interdisciplinary research is showing that we can neither view television as the powerful medium nor the audience as the powerful determinants of the message. There is an interplay between the two and this relationship is influenced by the culture of the audience, their past experiences and their psychological make-up.

For example, Allen (1985), who upholds the semiotic approach, believes that, in order to understand why people enjoy watching soap operas, one must study not only the formal properties of the soap such as the use of close-ups and two-shots, lighting, music, and the use of time and space, but also the mechanisms by which readers of soap operas construct meaning on the basis of these properties.

Another theory put forward by Ang (1985) is that a text can be read at various levels. The first level is the literal, denotative level which concerns the manifest content of the narrative. This level may not be regarded as realistic and there may be very little resemblance between the fictional world portrayed on screen and the real world. However the soap opera text can be read on another level – the connotative level. This level relates to the associative meanings which can be attributed to the text. Ang notes that it is primarily at this level that the programme is judged by the viewers to be realistic. It is striking, says Ang, that the same things, people, relations and situations which are regarded at the denotative level as unrealistic and unreal are, at the connotative level, apparently not seen at all as unreal, but in fact as 'recognizable'.

Allen (1985) also suggests that soap opera texts open up multiple levels of meanings, making possible different readings and different interpretations. These various readings are facilitated by the 'gaps' within the text. The reader inserts himself or herself into the text through these gaps, filling them in part according to his or her own frames of reference. Allen explains it thus:

> What the text leaves unsaid is, nevertheless, made to signify within the imagination of the reader (Allen, 1985, p. 78).

Because of this phenomenon the same story or theme is understood differently by different people (Liebes & Katz, 1988).

Not all viewers of soap opera become involved in the story to the same degree. Katz and Liebes (1986) argue that viewers may either 'involve' themselves in or 'distance' themselves from the story. In the former the audiences accept the soap opera world as real and hence become involved with the characters. The second mode of viewing, on the other hand, involves the ability to stand back at a distance and evaluate the programme.

Schroder (1988), however points out that the experience of the viewer cannot be confined to just one of the two categories for, he explains

> every viewer moves back and forth, commutes, between these two polar opposites. On one hand there are those viewers who sustain a general involvement in the programme, interspersed with moments of critical distance to some fictional features. On the other hand, there are those whose basically distanced experience is interspersed with moments of fictional involvement (Schroder, 1988, p. 68).

Schroder points out that those who are critical of soap operas still enjoy watching them. They attain pleasure through feeling self-confident and superior to those people who become very involved with the characters and the story. For the critical viewers, watching soap operas is

> a weekly reconstruction of self-confidence – a pleasurable experience of feeling superior.

Women as Consumers of Soap Opera

The fact that women are the most frequent viewers of soap opera has attracted the attention of a number of researchers who have investigated the viewing motivations of the soap opera audience from a feminist point of view. The daytime soap opera had its origins in American radio in the 1930s. These programmes were often sponsored by major soap manufacturers and they were originally used as advertising vehicles to attract housewives. Hence they were dubbed as a female genre. The words 'soap opera' binds them to a sphere which is held to be socially unimportant – the sphere of housework. Furthermore, they are held to reflect a sentimental, escapist and hysterical sensibility and it is typically assumed that their audience consists of those whose lives are so deprived as to need spurious enrichment (Glaessner, 1990). Because of this, some viewers do not like to admit that they enjoy soap operas.

Feminist writers are divided on the issue of soaps. Some criticize soap opera for portraying stereotyped, anti-emancipatory and role-conforming images of women. These writers claim that soaps reinforce the status quo. Others on the other hand see them in a different light. They claim that soap operas offer the possibility of different interpretations of the 'text'. This absence of closure of soap opera narratives makes ideological consensus impossible to achieve and hence they are uniquely 'open' to feminist readings.

Modleski (1992) tries to discover what, in soap operas, attracts the female audience. She believes that because soap operas are based on dialogue and a slow-paced narrative movement, they are more open to female ways of seeking pleasure. It is preferred to the classic film narrative where there is the minimum of dialogue and a lot of fast action. She also points out that the visual style of the soap opera, with its numerous close-ups, is preferred by women because it signifies intimacy. Close-ups also invite and encourage the female audience to become involved in the lives of the characters. This is further facilitated by the slow movement of the soap opera plot which allows the audience to dwell on it and to be totally engrossed in it.

Feuer (1984) argues that the slow-moving pace of soap operas and what Fiske (1987) calls 'the hyperbolic excess', – that is the constant repetitions – open up 'a textual space' which may be read in more than one way. She also argues that soaps consists of two 'texts'. The main text usually moves in line with the dominant ideology and is the obvious, superficial reading. The second text subverts the dominant ideology. Because the structure of soap operas do not allow for clear-cut ideological positions and constructions

> every ideological position may be countered by its opposite. Thus the family dynasty sagas may be read either as critical of the dominant ideology of capitalism or as belonging to it, depending upon the position from which the reader comes at it (Feuer, 1984, p. 15).

Soap operas are pleasurable because they make it possible for the viewers to work out for themselves what is happening and why.

Brown (1990) says that soap operas are more connected to the oral tradition as opposed to the literary genre. Contrary to the established tradition of linking soap operas to the novel, Brown suggests that soap operas are more related to gossip. She points out that although men look upon gossip with disdain, at the same time they feel threatened by it. Consequently, she argues, female gossip can be subversive of the patriarchal system and a source of female power. She suggests that the soap opera, as a source and object of female gossip, can play a positive role in female empowerment.

Why do Maltese Viewers Watch Soap Operas?

This section of the paper will try to investigate the viewing motivations of Maltese viewers and to discuss them in the light of theories and research carried out in other countries. This investigation is patterned on that of Livingstone (1988). Other authors who carried out similar research are Rubin (1985), Carveth and Alexander (1985), Perse (1986), and Dohnalik (1989). It is mainly exploratory, aimed at obtaining first indications of regular Maltese viewers' own explanations of why they watch soap operas, and the findings could serve as a basis of comparison with the motivations found by researchers in other countries.

Method

Sample
The sample was made up of seventy-one viewers. These viewers applied to participate in the research by answering an advertisement in the weekly magazine *Il-Gwida*. Ages ranged between 12 and 74 years; twenty-seven of the respondents were housewives and thirty were students. Another twelve were in gainful employment – three were in the professional-managerial category, seven had clerical jobs whilst two were manual workers. Two respondents were unemployed. The subjects came from twenty-four different towns and villages. Only five respondents were male. All the subjects were regular viewers of soap operas. Because the sample was self-selected, it is not represen-

tative of the population of all Maltese soap opera viewers and hence it cannot be used to infer firm quantitative conclusions about the overall population.

Questionnaire

Each subject was sent a questionnaire with two questions. These were
  i. Which are the soap operas you watch regularly?
  ii. Why do you watch soap operas?

The second question was open ended so as not to lead the respondent into any preconceived answers and to allow the viewers to mention any reason which they considered to be relevant. The respondents were also asked their age, sex, occupation and village or town they came from.

Coding

All soap opera titles mentioned in reply to the first question were coded and the number of respondents mentioning each title was recorded. The answers to the second question were analysed, coded according to the explanations given, and put into categories. An explanation could be made up of one word, a sentence or even a whole paragraph. A random sample of twenty questionnaires was chosen and a coding scheme was set up on the basis of the explanations given in these questionnaires. To test the reliability of this coding scheme another twenty questionnaires were chosen and coded independently by two individuals. The coding reliability scores varied between 76 and 90 per cent.

The 71 respondents produced 184 explanations which were grouped into seven categories. When a respondent used the same explanation twice, these duplicates were eliminated. The number of explanations in each category therefore corresponds to the number of respondents who mentioned that particular reason as an explanation.

A Note on Methodology

The issue of qualitative or quantitative methods is worth mentioning, if only briefly, because it is at the heart of a wider debate amongst researchers. This debate centres around the two main paradigms prevailing in mass media research: the social science paradigm, rooted in empirical research based on quantitative techniques; and the critical paradigm, whose main methodological tools are qualitative, derived from literary or linguistic/semiotic theories. The present trend is to bring the two paradigms together and the methodology used in this paper is based on that approach. (For a detailed discussion of this issue, see Schroder, 1987.) In the present study, although the material gathered from the soap viewers who answered the questionnaire is qualitative, it is subjected to quantitative content analysis. This way the relative importance of different viewers' motivations can be more clearly brought out and the results can be more easily confronted with similar work done in other countries. On the other hand, categorizing open-ended responses can be restricting. It can lose detail and can ultimately have a reductionist effect. Therefore, in work of this type, the discussion of results should take into account both quantitative considerations and textual analysis of responses.

The categories of reasons for watching soaps which emerge from this study could serve as a basis for a deeper investigation, for example by means of focus groups or by using a larger sample more representative of the socio-economic and demographic profile of the general soap opera audience in Malta.

Results

Over thirty different soap operas were mentioned. The most popular in order of mention were 'Beautiful' and 'Celeste' (both watched by 35% of the respondents), 'Grecia' (27%) and 'Sentieri' and 'Renzo e Lucia' (both 24%).

The major categories of reasons for watching were, in order of mention, entertainment (suggested by 69% of the respondents), emotional experience (38%), reality exploration (35%), ritual (23%), modelling (13%), critical response (10%), and escapism (10%).

Reasons for Watching Soap Operas and Telenovelas

	Number of Respondents	Age 10-19	20-49	50+
ENTERTAINMENT	49	26	12	11
Entertaining & enjoyable	23	15	7	1
To fill free time	17	8	5	4
Relaxing	15	4	4	7
Prefer to other genres	4	2	0	2
Interesting	4	3	1	0
Easy to follow	3	2	1	0
Nothing else to watch	3	2	0	0
EMOTIONAL EXPERIENCE	27	19	4	4
Suspense	16	13	2	1
I like the actors	12	11	0	1
Happy ending	6	5	0	1
Keep me company	3	0	2	1
REALITY EXPLORATION	25	12	7	6
Educational	9	3	4	2
Familiar situations; true to life	8	4	1	3
Learn how other people live	5	3	1	1
How others solve problems	3	2	1	0
To see other countries	2	0	2	0
RITUAL	16	9	5	2
Watch with family members	8	7	1	0
Structures time, personal space	6	2	2	2
Addiction	4	2	2	0
Watch with friends	2	1	1	0
MODELLING	7	2	4	3
Clothes, hair styles	9	2	4	3
Home decor	6	1	2	3
CRITICAL RESPONSE	7	4	1	2
Far-fetched but enjoyable	4	3	1	0
Silly but enjoyable	3	1	0	2
Enjoy being critical	2	2	0	0
ESCAPISM	7	3	3	1
To forget worries	3	1	2	0
Distraction from tedious life affairs	3	1	1	1
To forget work I have to do	2	1	1	0
TOTAL NUMBER OF RESPONDENTS	71	35	21	15

Discussion

Although all respondents watched soap opera regularly, some were more assiduous viewers than others. The average number of soaps watched by the respondents was three. However two respondents watched as much as ten soaps regularly, another two watched nine while two others watched eight. Out of these six subjects, five were students between twelve and thirteen years of age. This, coupled with the fact that 42% of the respondents who sent for the questionnaire were students, might be an indication that soap operas are very popular with the younger age group.

Some soap operas such as 'Marilena' were mentioned more frequently by the under twenties while others, such as 'Renzo e Lucia' were more popular with the over fifty's. Some, like 'Beautiful' and 'Celeste' were popular with all age groups. It might be interesting to investigate possible reasons for such preferences. No pattern of preferences based on socio-economic status emerged.

It is interesting to note that whilst the respondents mentioned over thirty different soap operas, only one of these is broadcast on Malta Television. According to a 1993 survey carried out by MISCO fo the Broadcasting Authority, the number of people who watch 'Neighbours' regularly is about 6,000. On some days this number goes up to 18,000. Considering that 'Neighbours' is not a favourite (only 11% of the respondents mentioned it) and considering the awkward time of its scheduling, this number is substantial.

Another interesting thing to note is the names of the soap operas. Many of them are first names such as 'Micaela', 'Grecia', 'Maria', 'Marilena' and 'Renzo e Lucia'. These titles, together with others such as, 'Febbre d'Amore', 'Quando Si Ama' and 'Anche I Ricchi Piangono' suggest intimacy. This seems to fit in well with the genre's characteristic of inviting involvement, familiarity and identification from the audience.

We shall now discuss in some more detail the seven main categories of reasons for watching soap opera which were mentioned by the respondents.

1. Entertainment

The most common reason for watching soaps is, as expected, that the viewers find them enjoyable. They prefer them to other genres for various reasons: there is no physical violence, they have a happy ending, they are about love, and they are true to life. Some viewers watch soaps to kill time. They find them relaxing to follow. For example Respondent 41 said:

> I watch soap operas simply as a means of relaxation. They are normally pleasant and not violent and hence I find them enjoyable.

If for some reason they fail to see a particular episode they can easily pick up the story in the following one. Respondent 61 said:

> Even if I miss some episodes I can make up the story.

The unconscious choice of words by this respondent seems to confirm what Allen (1985) claims about the audience filling in the 'gaps' with their own version of parts of the story.

Other viewers go to greater lengths in order to avoid missing their favourite soap opera programmes. They make it a point to record episodes when they coincide with their work shift. These recordings are then exchanged amongst friends at the same place of work. A similar finding was found by Gray (1990). In her study Gray found that women often get together during the day and watch films they like. They also record soaps for each other so that those who have to go out to work do not miss any episodes. According to Gray, these popular texts form part of an almost separate female culture which viewers share within the constraints of being wives and mothers.

2. *Emotional Experience*

The second most common reason for watching soap opera is because viewers become involved emotionally. The emotions experienced can be of various types. They can be sexual in nature where the viewers feel physically and sexually attracted to one or more of the characters/actors in the soap opera. These respondents were mostly teenagers. For example Respondent 44 said:

> I watch telenovelas, because the actors who take part in them are always good-looking and fascinating.*[1]

---

[1] Asterisked excerpts are transliterated from the Maltese original.

Sometimes the viewers identify with the characters and situations portrayed. When this happens the viewer puts himself or herself so deeply into the story that he or she can feel the same emotions and experience the same events as the character in the story. Respondent 63 explained it thus:

> I become very emotional while watching telenovelas or soap operas and sometimes I feel like crying with them.*

Sometimes, viewers, especially those who have been watching a particular series for many years, become so involved with the characters that they come to interact with them as if they are real people. They become an extension of their social networks, part of their everyday lives, almost part of the family. Noble (1975) suggests that sometimes viewers recognize in a character someone they know in real life, and henceforth interact with him or her as if they are interacting with the person the character reminds them of. This is one of the factors that gives rise to divergence in reading and in making sense of the text.

Another type of emotion could be suspense. Often episodes end in dangerous situations, leaving the audience on edge until the next episode. This device is known as the 'cliffhanger'. In television and radio soap operas this term came to refer to situations of unresolved emotional tension rather than to physically dangerous situations. Respondent 75 said:

> ...more often than not it is curiosity to watch the final episodes that makes me follow them.

Zillman (1980) tried to investigate the issue of suspense and pleasure. Soap operas offer many situations where characters are in some type of danger. Zillman claims that although the viewer knows that somehow or other the danger will be overcome, this fact does not reduce the pleasure that he or she experiences when the dangerous situation is resolved. On the contrary, the audience has learned to expect that this distress is generally followed by a favourable turn of events and this triggers a pleasurable reaction.

3. Reality Exploration

Although the problems presented in soap operas, especially the American ones, may be somewhat far removed from the problems which a typical viewer may be experiencing in life, yet there seems to be a level at which the audience can identify with these characters and with their problems. To go back to Ang's terminology: the same story is unrealistic on the denotative level but realistic on the connotative one. Involved viewers watch from this latter position. Respondent 9 echoed what several viewers said:

> I like true stories because telenovelas happen just like what happens in a person's life.*

Soap operas focus on contemporary social issues. Very often they are designed to present a certain number of contemporary social problems, such as AIDS, abortion, divorce and adultery in a realistic way. Because soap operas are problem oriented and perceived as very close to reality they provide an opportunity for the viewers to think through their own problems vicariously. They present the viewers with models of problem solving and coping strategies. As Respondent 1 said:

> I like them mostly because the stories are about things we confront in everyday life and they have great educational value.*

One of the major criticisms leveled at soaps is that they promulgate values which are different from the values held in mainstream society. However, contrary to the claim made by non-viewers that soap operas encourage promiscuity and portray a decadent life-style, viewers seem to see them from a completely different angle. Respondent 47 claimed that:

> In my opinion, they teach you to be careful of men and not to sell your body.*

And Respondent 22 said:

> I love watching telenovelas because very often they are events from everyday life, my husband says that they give a bad example, but I always say that I look at the end of the telenovela, because then the lesson definitely comes out.*

4. Ritual

Some viewers watch soap operas because they become a habit, a regular thing to do at a particular time of the day. Respondent 62 said:

> ...they offer a break between study periods, where I can remove all thoughts from my mind. The time is convenient (7.15); just the time when I need a break.

For some this habit means much more than simply doing something at a particular time. For example, Respondent 10 said:

> Today, I have become so used to them that these series mean to me what the daily mass means to some people.*

Such a comment leads one to question some claims that television has little, if any, influence on the audience.

Some viewers described how, once they get hooked on the story, they rearrange housework and other work to fit the schedule. Sometimes soap operas are used by housewives to structure their working day. They arrange their housework around their favourite soap opera. Watching soap operas can therefore mark an interval of leisure for the housewife. Respondent 20 said:

> I feel I relax, I stop doing housework and other routine house chores.*

This is somewhat similar to what Radway (1985) found about the reading of popular novels. The time allotted by the housewife to read these novels is a legitimate way of releasing her temporarily from her duties and of replenishing the energy used up in performing them. It provides her with much needed personal space and time.

This, however, is not the case for all housewives. Those housewives who do their work in a less structured way often do not manage actually to sit down and watch, and their viewing becomes what Modleski (1982) describes as the 'decentred viewing-experience'. She says that the soap opera text becomes reduced to what can be heard while working in different parts of the house.

In a study among urban families in Peru, Alfaro Moreno (1988) found that the activity of watching soap operas is firmly tied in with the ritual and habits of work and leisure of families. She found that the soaps which were on air in the afternoons were mainly watched by women and, especially in poorer families, it was often a public occasion when neighbours visited each other's houses and watched television together. In the evening, watching soaps was more of a family activity, one in which the whole family, the mother, the father and the children, participated. In these families, soap operas became an interaction medium between the individual members. This phenomenon, although probably less common, occurs with Maltese viewers as well. Respondent 6 said:

I was brought up in a family where everybody watches soaps, from the oldest to the youngest. It could be a habit, however, although they can be long and farfetched, I think there is always something to learn.*

5. Modelling

One particular reason, mentioned in this research, for viewing soap operas is that the viewer is able to see how other women decorate their houses, what clothes they wear and their hairstyles. Respondent 18 said:

> The reason I watch (Beautiful) is one, so as to get ideas on clothes and also how to make the house beautiful.*

Many respondents said that they copy ideas when sewing their own clothes and when decorating their houses. This reason is particular to the Maltese audience. In other research (for example Rubin, 1985; Livingstone, 1988; Dohnalik, 1989) respondents do not mention that they watch soaps specifically to copy ideas of fashion and home decor but as a form of escapism, of wishful thinking, of imagining themselves living in magnificent houses and wearing beautiful clothes.

6. Critical Response

Some viewers pointed out shortcomings in soap operas but admitted that they enjoyed watching the programmes in spite of these shortcomings. Others even watched soaps because they enjoyed criticizing the genre. Some respondents commented that although at times they find the soaps farfetched, they still enjoy watching them. Respondent 5 described them as

> just plain silly but enjoyable

while Respondent 3 said that while enjoying them, at times, they become too unrealistic. Respondent 3 said:

> I hate those kind of soppy, crying, hysterical woman so when it gets a bit farfetched I just do not watch for a week or two...

Respondent 54 said that since she is a teacher she watches at least one soap opera to give her an inkling of what students watch.

7. Escapism

This viewing motive includes a number of elements such as to put aside everyday worries, to prevent boredom, to postpone doing one's work and to be transported in fantasy into another world. In the case of American soap operas this world is usually rich and glamorous and while watching it the viewers put themselves in the actors' roles and imagine their dreams and fantasies coming true. Though the British soaps are usually considered to be more down to earth, they still provide a source of escapism. They provide the viewer with a different world, with different problems to think about. In becoming involved in the problems of others, the viewer can escape and, for a short while, forget his or her own problems and worries. Respondent 52 explained it thus:

> While I am watching them, I immerse myself in the story and forget my housework and my children's work, and the more intrigues there are the better, although sometimes, once the programme is over, I worry about what happened. I don't know what I would do without them.*

Comparison with British Viewers

Livingstone (1988), has conducted a study in which she analysed the explanations which British viewers give for watching soap opera. The question put forward to the subjects was 'Why is soap opera so popular?'. The major categories of the viewing explanations were, in order of mention, escapism (mentioned by 92% of respondents), realism (89%), relationship with characters (62%), critical response (52%), problem-solving (42%), role in viewer's life (40%), emotional experience (37%) and entertainment (35%).

Since Livingstone's question did not ask specifically why the respondents themselves watched soap opera but why it is so popular with people, we cannot make strict comparisons. It does however provide us with a base with which we can compare the viewing motivations of the Maltese viewers. One difference that comes out is the category of 'Escapism'. While this reason was mentioned by 92% of the respondents in Livingstone's study, it was mentioned by only 10% of the Maltese subjects. This could either mean that they are not aware that they use soap opera as a form of escapism even if they do, or else that they take soap opera more seriously. It also seems that Maltese viewers are less critical of soap opera. Only

10% compared to the 51% of British viewers made statements which indicated that they kept a certain critical distance or detachment while viewing soaps. Could this be an indication that the Maltese viewers take soaps more seriously?

Another difference worth mentioning is the explanation related to the modelling of clothes and home decor as seen on these programmes. This viewing motive seems to be particular to the Maltese viewers and somehow it fits in with the tendency of the Maltese to imitate rather than create. Another possible explanation for this difference could be that in Malta there is still a large percentage of women who make their own clothes. This in turn may be a result of the fact that the proportion of women who have a full-time job in Malta is smaller than in England. Hence Maltese women would have less money and more free time making it easier and economically more desirable for them to make their own clothes.

Conclusion

Soap operas have traditionally been considered the Cinderella of television programming. Yet few other genres, if any, can boast of uninterrupted series running for more than thirty years and consistently enjoying high levels of popularity. The great popularity of soaps has spread to several countries and amongst widely differing cultures. This phenomenon cannot be ignored or simply attributed to programmers' or viewers' unsophisticated tastes. Audience research has been trying to analyse more deeply why the genre is so popular and how viewers make sense of its content.

That people watch soap opera because they enjoy it is clear. Why they enjoy it is more complex to answer. Some find it educational, others relaxing. For some it provides a topic of conversation, for others it makes life bearable. The various studies carried out in different countries seem to converge towards a number of reasons. Some of these reasons now need further investigation.

It seems that one important reason for finding these soaps entertaining is precisely because viewers find them realistic. One third of the viewers involved in this study said that they watch soap operas because they see situations and people that are true to life. As discussed earlier, both the themes and the aesthetics of soaps are used in perfecting the illusion of 'reality' of the narrative. This involvement in soaps is therefore intentional and engineered. Identification is made easier and the borderline between reality and fiction becomes blurred. It is precisely this that worries many people who see soap opera in a bad light. They claim that viewers see role models in soap opera characters and hence they identify with them and imitate their behaviour. They also claim that they take up their values and life-styles.

From the answers given in the questionnaires it seems that viewers are influenced by what they see and they do imitate certain behaviour but certainly not in the blind manner which some people seem to believe. The relationship between the audience and television is still a grey area in mass media research. It is still not clear whether television has the tremendous influence on viewers which some researchers claim or whether viewers are weighing out and analysing what they see.

Although many involved viewers described the programmes as very real and true to life, a few others did keep a critical distance and described soaps as far-fetched and silly. It is easy to ascribe such differences in involvement to the sex, intellectual abilities or even social class of the viewer, but research shows that such assumptions are incorrect. Again this is one other area which needs to be investigated more deeply.

The fact that a large percentage of viewers finds this genre realistic and becomes so involved with its content has many implications for the social scientist. Soap operas are providing viewers with a source of information. They have become a socializing agent, an appropriate forum for social and moral education. It is now time to study 'how' this is being achieved.

> How does the audience make sense of the different levels of messages put forward?
> Are the processes involved the same as in interpersonal communication?
> Are mass communication and interpersonal communication converging?

Investigation of these questions could help us understand better the important role which the mass media have come to play in our lives.

References

Abelson, R.P. (1981) 'The psychological status of the script concept', *American Psychologist*, vol. 36, 6.

Alfaro Moreno, R.M. (1988) 'Los usos sociales populares de las telenovelas in el Mundo Urbano', *Estudios Sobre Las Culturas Contemporaneas*, vols. 4/5.

Allen, R.C. (1985) *Speaking of Soap Operas*, Chapel Hill, University of North Carolina Press.

Allen, R.C. (1987) *Channels of Discourse*, Chapel Hill, University of North Carolina Press.

Ang, I. (1985) *Watching Dallas: Soap Opera and the Melodramatic Imagination*, New York, Methuen.

Blumler, J.G., & Katz, E. (ed.), (1974) *The Uses of Mass Communications: Current Perspectives on Gratifications Research*, Beverly Hills, CA, Sage.

Brown, M.E. (ed.), (1990) *Television and Women's Culture: The Politics of the Popular*, London, Sage.

Carveth, R. & Alexander, A. (1985) 'Soap opera viewing motivations and the cultivation process', *Journal of Broadcasting and Electronic Media*, vol. 29, 3.

Cassata, M. & Skill, T. (ed.), (1983) *Life on Daytime Television: Tuning-In American Serial Drama*, Norwood, NJ, Ablex.

Communications Research Trends (1990) vol. 10, 1 & 2.

Compesi, R.J. (1980) 'Gratifications of daytime television serial viewers', *Journalism Quarterly*, vol. 57, 1.

Dohnalik, J. (1989) 'Uses and gratifications of "Return to Eden" for Polish viewers', *European Journal of Communication*, vol. 4, 2.

Feuer, J. (1984) 'Melodrama, serial form and television today', *Screen*, vol. 25, 1.

Fiske, J. (1987) *Television Culture*, London, Methuen.

Glaessner, V. (1990) 'Gendered fictions', in: Goodwin, A. & Whannel, G. (eds), *Understanding Television*, London, Routledge.

Gray, A. (1990) 'Household culture: Women, television and video in the home', unpublished Ph.D. thesis, University of York.

Horton, D. & Wohl, R. (1956) 'Mass communication and parasocial interaction', *Psychiatry*, vol. 19.

Kaplan, E. A. (1983) *Regarding Television: Critical Approaches – An Anthology*, Los Angeles, CA, American Film Institute.

Katz, E. & Liebes, T. (1984) 'Decoding "Dallas" overseas', *Intermedia*, vol. 5, 1.

Katz, E. & Liebes, T. (1986) 'Patterns of involvement in television fiction: A comparative analysis', *European Journal of Communication*, vol. 1, 1.

Liebes, T. & Katz, E. (1988) 'Primordiality and seriality in popular culture', in Carey, J. (ed.), *Media, Myths and Narratives: Television and the Press*, London, Sage.

Livingstone, S.M. (1988) 'Why people watch soap opera: An analysis of the explanations of British viewers', *European Journal of Communication*, vol. 3, 1.

Livingstone, S. M. (1990) *Making Sense of Television: The Psychology of Audience Interpretation*, Oxford, Pergamon.

McQuail, D., Blumler, J. & Brown, J.R. (1972) 'The television audience: A revised perspective', in McQuail, D. (ed.) *Sociology of Mass Communication*, Harmondsworth, Penguin.

Modleski, T. (1982) 'The search for tomorrow in today's soap opera', in Modleski, T. *Loving with a Vengeance: Mass Produced Fantasies for Women*, Hamden, CT, Archon Books.

Mulvey, L. (1981) 'Visual pleasure and narrative cinema', in Bennett, T. (ed.), *Popular Television and Film*, London, British Film Institute.

Noble, G. (1975) *Children in Front of the Small Screen*, London, Sage.

Perse, E.M. (1986) 'Soap opera viewing patterns of college students and cultivation', *Journal of Broadcasting and Electronic Media*, vol. 30, 2.

Radway, J. (1985) 'Interpretive communities and variable literacies: The functions of romance reading', in Gurevitch, M. & Levy, M.R. (eds), *Mass Communications Review Yearbook*, vol. 5, Beverly Hills, CA, Sage.

Rubin, A. (1985) 'Uses of daytime television soap operas by college students', in *Journal of Broadcasting and Electronic Media*, vol. 29, 3.

Schroder, K.C. (1988) 'The pleasure of DYNASTY: The weekly reconstruction of self-confidence', in Drummond, P. & Peterson, R. (eds), *Television and its Audience: International Research Perspectives*, London, British Film Institute.

Zillman, D. (1980) 'Anatomy of suspense', in Tannenbaum, P.H. (ed.) *The Entertainment Functions of Television*. Hillside, NJ, LEA.

16

Schooling and Socialization: Rituals, Symbols and Hidden Messages in a Private School

Emmanuel Mifsud

Introduction

Sociological studies of education carried out by Apple (1979, 1982), Giroux (1983) and McLaren (1986, 1989) among others have pointed out that schooling is a political process which is far from being neutral, and that everyday experiences at school are pregnant with hidden messages. Schools have in fact come to be seen as social sites with a dual curriculum – one overt and formal, the other hidden. The informal, or hidden curriculum, is constituted by norms and values which are unstated but which successfully transmit world views to students through the kinds of relationships developed in classrooms and also through other activities which make up everyday routine.

This paper sets out to report data collected through observation of one of Malta's élite Church schools, here referred to as 'St David's College'.[1] It will be argued that the symbolic and cultural material presented in this school positions participants in a powerful social world, and is a crucial, though often unexamined, factor in the transmission of values and meanings. The following sections focus on only a few features of the socialization processes taking place in the school in question. These are:
a. the social construction of distinction through hierarchical relationships;
b. the formation of a specific and distinctive school identity through sports events and rituals;
c. the politicization of students through moral/religious messages.

The paper concludes with a study of students' resistance to this socialization process, in order to argue that schools do not merely do things to people, but that students are active beings, capable of restructuring what is presented to them in order to express their needs and concerns. Further insights into these four processes can be gleaned from a longer account of the present study in Mifsud (1991).

Methodology of Research

Studies focusing on the hidden and political activities and rituals taking place in a social institution are generally carried out through qualitative means (Willis, 1977; McLaren, 1986; Aggleton, 1987; Darmanin, 1989; Sultana, 1992). Such 'interactive methods of research' (LeCompte & Goetz, 1984) enable one to give a clearer and more detailed picture of the field of study, since they operate

---

[1] The issue of Maltese private schools is rather a complex one since not all private schools have the same standing. Darmanin (1989) and Sultana (1991b) note that private schools cannot, as a matter of fact, be clustered in one group since there are evident differences in the clientele different private schools attract. History and old students' occupations generally dictate which private schools are at the top. 'St. David' – which is, of course, a pseudonym – is commonly considered to be one of the top private schools for boys.

in an unorchestrated environment and, perhaps more importantly, record changes and reactions to such changes on the participants' side. Qualitative research includes participant observation. This serves 'to elicit from subjects their definitions of reality and the organizing constructs of their world' (LeCompte & Goetz 1984, p. 41). Not only do qualitative studies give the participants' perceptions of how things stand (McNeil, 1988); they also expose features which were previously seen through unquestioning eyes (Hargreaves, 1984). Such an exercise helps to make the familiar strange.

There are, of course, difficulties specific to ethnographic research, but the contribution that qualitative data makes to the experiential understanding of what takes place in the social field has been substantial and convincing. To help lessen the shortcomings of ethnographic research, I put down, in as detailed a way as possible, all decisions, choices, biases, expectations and so on that I recognize as having influenced my action in the field. In this way, the reliability and validity of data and analyses can be critically evaluated by the reader.

The research reported in this context draws on a data base which I collected between April and December of 1989. Close to a hundred and fifty hours were spent observing different school sites (including staff rooms, assembly gatherings, recreation rooms, classrooms, library, chapel) and interviewing students, teachers and administrators. An important aspect of the research was the focus on Forms 4A and 4E, promoted to 5A and 5E respectively in October 1989, with the A students being the most achieving, and the E the least. Another aspect of my research involved the careful perusal of the College publications and year books in order to elicit ideological messages within the texts.

Distinction

A key element in the formation of the school's identity was the constant emphasis made by administrators and teaching staff, on the fact that St David's College was the best private school, and therefore the best school on the island. Students – especially those who were succeeding academically – generally accepted this message, with many expressing genuine pride at belonging to the school.

Locke: I'm very proud to have attended St David's. It's the best there is [...] It's known world wide. The order is found all over the world. And I have had the opportunity to go to a school like that!²

The message that St David's was 'the best' was transmitted both overtly as well as covertly through the rituals and symbolism that permeated school life. Many students reported teachers in interviews as saying that St David's was a 'high class' school. Yet it was through the rituals and symbols that the message got across most effectively, and my observations corroborate Kertzer's (1988, p. 30) point when he noted that 'the transmission of messages through ritual dramatization is much more powerful than communication through verbal declaration'. The following excerpts from my fieldnotes (26/4/89) are illustrative of such processes. The occasion here is the official opening of an athletics meeting:

> Before the events started there was a ceremony: the children were given a stencilled colour programme each indicating events and players taking part. Children were seated on the steps on one side of the race track. Then all athletes jogged in twos around the pitch led by their sport masters. Each house sported a banner. During this jog the sports anthem of the Seoul Olympics was played. After the athletes had taken their places a student carrying a torch ran around the ground and then lit a stand portraying the College emblem. The national anthem followed and then the events began.

This opening mirrored professional athletic meetings, and by using the same symbols and rituals, the College expressed not only its high esteem for sport, but more importantly its association with the best that high culture could provide. For the elite deserved only the best!

The message of belonging to the best was also transmitted to the students whenever the College won some inter-school competition. For instance Small, an A student, won a speech contest for

---

² Ethnographic excerpts are in English because that was the most widely used language at the College.

secondary school boys. The next day the headmaster addressed the assembly, saying:

> When we congratulate the few we congratulate everyone for many of you can do just as well since all of you attend this school. It is a tribute to you, the teachers and the families; it is a tribute to the College. (Everybody applauds).

Authority: The Head

The social construction and reproduction of distinction in this particular school, and hence the political socialization of students into a world where people inhabited differentiated social (and physical) spaces, was sustained in the hierarchical arrangement and divisions between different members of the school community. St David College's administrative machine was rigidly hierarchical. This apparently common-sense observation is of great sociological interest, and many sociologists have written extensively about this issue. MacDonald (1977) holds that the way in which private schools are run is characterized by rigid hierarchies of authority, privilege, rank and prestige. Fox (1985, p. 3) comments that the private schools' 'very existence symbolizes the principle of hierarchy as opposed to egality'.

Everybody knew his and her place in the hierarchical set-up at St David's. First came the headmaster, followed by the Year Teachers (who took care of all the classes in one particular form, made reports and made sure that the students and teachers got along well), form teachers (who assumed responsibility for one particular class), teachers, prefects (whose uniform varied slightly from that of other students, since they wore a different tie) and students. The higher a place one occupied, the more privileges s/he enjoyed.

In the case of the headmaster, for instance, I noted that a key symbol of his superior status was the amount and quality of space he occupied in the College, namely a large office which had all the trappings of esteem, signalled by paintings, fitted carpets, a sofa, desks and other office accessories. The office also had a verandah overlooking the main yard where the senior students' assemblies were held. Although the headmaster only rarely conducted the assemblies himself, he generally followed the proceedings from the top of the stairs joining the verandah to the yard. He thus adopted a high profile which could easily be interpreted by the students as a physical reproduction of his status at the helm of the school.

The Head also distinguished himself by wearing the traditional habit of the Order. As teachers and students themselves noted, the distinctive apparel became a symbol of power:

Mewey: The head must wear it (the habit) for he's the Friar.
Manuel: Yes, but aren't the others friars as well?
Mewey: But he's greater than the rest for he's the Head of School.

When a change in headship took place, the new headmaster made sure of keeping certain characteristics of his predecessor while changing others. Kertzer (1988) notes that leaders themselves become important symbols of authority and power, and organizational unity. Thus, the removal of such leaders may jeopardize this unity and therefore one possible solution is to sustain the symbolism related to that leader (Kertzer, 1988, p. 18). The new headmaster thus wore the habit during school hours, wrote the foreword to all the College publications as his predecessors had done and used the same office.

The Teachers

Teachers joined the head in the continuous use of rituals and symbols in order to exert their authority over students. Indeed, Haywood Metz (1978, p. 55) has noted that teachers generally 'tend to pay special attention to the structuring devices which spell out the school's goals and procedure in tangible terms'. Thus they attach prime importance not only to curriculum and textbooks, but also to the school rules. Teachers envisage themselves as, to use Haywood Metz's term, 'impersonal conduits' for the set of rules established by the school.

Teachers at St David often referred to this world of rules. They generally took it for granted that students knew all the rules. They simply had to be reminded of them.

E class – Italian

Mrs. Green asks questions and everyone shouts out answers. She bangs her ruler on the desk.

Mrs. Green: Don't you know the rules? You have to put up your hand.

Different teachers used different tones to express the students' duty to obey. At times, teachers spoke of rules in a rather aggressive manner. At other times a serious threat followed.

E class – Religion
Don Petrus: You have to obey the rules of the school, whether you like it or not. If you don't, leave, go to another school.

Similar threats were recorded by McLaren in his study of St Ryan Catholic school in Canada, where he noted that 'Offenders and culprits became 'polluters' of the sacred workplace. Sometimes they were 'excommunicated' and transferred to a different school entirely' (McLaren, 1986, p. 132).

It follows, then, that no discussion was possible in the issue of obeying rules. As a letter sent to the newly-appointed school prefects declared: 'Many a time you have to do things simply because they have to be done – regardless of whether you feel like it or not.'

Teachers were conscious that the rules, together with often irksome school work, could lead to overt resistance on the part of the students. To avoid this, teachers often disguised their 'command-authority' into a 'belief authority'. McKercher (1989, pp. 233, 235) distinguishes between these two types of authority in the following manner: Command authority is exhibited 'in the type of authority relation where the source of the command, order, or directive issues the command with the expectation that he or she will be obeyed [...] or else bring sanctions, in the form of unpleasant consequences to bear'. Belief authority, on the other hand is a 'legitimate influence which exists when the person being influenced sees fit to behave in a manner in which he or she otherwise would not have adopted'.

Teachers often legitimate their exercise of authority by implying that rules are beneficial for the students' future welfare. As a letter to the new prefects pointed out:

Students may think that sticking to a system is irritating. They thus rebel to look 'cool'. On the other hand a person who sticks to any system shows his capability of controlling himself [...] The College, universities, employers and friends are all after people with a good formation.

Since authority was legitimate and unassailable, it 'naturally' followed that non-conformists deserved to be punished. And most students considered this organization of social relations in the school as natural and appropriate. As we shall see in another section of this paper, however, not all students accepted this state of affairs, and actively or passively contested the legitimacy of the hierarchy established by the school.

Hierarchy Between Students

Hierarchy and distinction were also classificatory principles regulating the relationship between students, with age and ability being the key categories used for discrimination. Older students clearly had more privileges than younger ones, with sixth formers enjoying the prerogative to shed blazer and tie in favour of casual sweaters, to skip assemblies, to jump queues at the tuck shop, and to leave school premises during free periods.

But age was not the only justification for differential treatment. Much more insidious was the 'hidden' streaming of students according to 'ability' levels and academic attainment, despite the insistence on the part of the College that there was no streaming between classes at St David's. Careful and detailed observation of classroom pedagogy in the A and E streams revealed that which many educational sociologists have been pointing out for some time, namely that teachers use different control strategies and teaching styles with groups of different ability (cf. Anyon, 1980; 1981; Apple, 1982; Connell et al., 1982; Hallinan, 1987; Mifsud & Mallia, 1991). At St David's, while students in the A stream were often challenged with difficult questions, those in the E were asked simple factual ones. While in the A class emphasis was put on originality and individual effort, lessons in the E were teacher-centred and stressed collectivity, such as collective answering and classroom correction.

A class – Maths

In one particular case a boy has a different solution to a problem in similarity of triangles.

Mrs. Barnacle: In your opinion, how do you want to do it ... very good.

E class – Maths

Collective correction. Mrs. Barnacle writes answers on the board. Then she tells the students to call out the next answer.

Mrs. Barnacle: Together and no shouting.
Pino asks her a question.
Mrs. Barnacle: Now I'll tell you afterwards.

A class – English Literature

Mrs. Weaver gives an oral synopsis of Act 3 Scene 3 of *Macbeth*. She gives an interpretation of the scene.

Mrs. Weaver: I tend to disagree with the critics. You might agree after reading the scene but I don't.

E class – English Literature

Mrs. Weaver gives an oral synopsis of Act 3 Scene 3 of *Macbeth*. Then she dictates some notes which she intends to explain 'later on'. Then she reads the excerpt and explains the difficult words. She asks various questions like: Who was Banquo? What was his son's name? What did Macbeth want to do to Banquo and his son? Often the children have no answer and she answers the questions herself.

These two examples illustrate the type of differences in teaching practices in the two classes. Teachers tended to be more dogmatic with the E's and more demanding with the A's. The upper-stream boys were invited to participate more actively in their learning activities. In other words, students were being socialized differently, for teachers were encouraging the development of different sets of cognitive and attitudinal characteristics.

Control techniques too varied across the streams. Teachers thought that the most troublesome of all streams were the boys in the E class. The preferred control strategy used with the E's was domination, i.e. strict authoritarianism, sarcasm and aggressive management of classroom situations. The wielding of power for its own sake was also frequently observed in the E class.

E class – Accounts

Long opens the windows.

Miss Smil:	How come you open the windows without asking? Close them.
Long:	Come on, miss.
Miss Smil:	Close them, you have to ask.
Long:	All right! (*Closes the windows.*)
Miss Smil:	Now ask.
Long:	Now let them be.
Miss Smil:	Ask or get out.
Long:	Come on, miss.
Miss Smil:	I said ask or get out!
Long:	May I open the windows?
Miss Smil:	Please?
Long:	Please?
Miss Smil:	Yes you may.

Another method of keeping order and discipline in the E class was what McNeil (1986) terms as 'defensive instructional strategies', i.e. simplifying content so as to diminish the demands on the students in order to maintain classroom order.

Mrs. Green:	Usually I give them these leaflets to read, or else they write something on the leaflets themselves. These aren't hard to work; otherwise they get fidgety. The best thing to do is to keep them quiet.

These and other differentiated ways of interacting with diverse groups in the school constitute important messages about the place of students in the particular universe that is the school, and in the place they are considered fit – or likely – to occupy in the world outside the school. The ideological construction of such worlds is, of course, intensely political inasmuch as it organizes groups within a previously-structured social space.

Sports, Symbols and Hidden Messages

Distinction between students at St David's, and between Davidians and other students in other secondary schools on the Island, was fostered through sports activities. The latter, as in many public schools in Britain, were accorded an important place at the College, and fulfilled a number of functions. One of these was announced clearly in the College annual publication:

> The emphasis on participation and sportsmanship is geared towards meeting the physical and recreational needs of students through participation in a wide variety of physical activities that will lead to the development of coordination of skills, strength and endurance. Physical activities have continuing lifetime values. They maintain physical, social, emotional and mental health.

The College believed that through sports it could, or perhaps should, communicate to the students certain 'continuing lifetime values'. Indeed various rituals pregnant with hidden references to the future careers of the students were engaged in during sport activities. Next to academic achievement, sport was central to life at St David's. It is small wonder, then, that next to the Headmaster's office stood a large showcase exhibiting trophies and shields which the college teams had won through the years. This practice prevails in a number of private schools in Malta and imitates similar displays in British boarding schools (Darmanin, 1989, p. 518).

Sport activities generally mirrored the competitive world of work. Sports entailed competition, either on an intraschool basis or, more importantly, between different private schools. The strong feeling of rivalry led to the development of other aspects of the school ethos, including an emphasis on team spirit, a sense of belonging and a celebration of 'heroism'. Competitions, therefore, urged and motivated the students to work hard for the glory of the College.

Locke: No one tells you 'be competitive', but the words they put make you feel that way, especially Mr. Robson when it comes to sports.

Some students were well aware of the similarity between the sport competitions organized by the College and the competitive world of work.

Locke: Mr. Robson motivates unity between us and at the same time makes us competitive ... we support our school to win. The same thing goes here – we encourage workers to unify so that the company goes ahead of other companies.

Team spirit was insisted upon by the staff since it created a strong school identity and students were urged to support the school's competitors whenever a sport event took place. The college organized its own competitions through the house system. There were four such Houses, and each student belonged to one House or other. Houses however meant much more than mere groupings. Every student was held responsible for the success of his particular house. The intraschool competitions culminated in the annual athletic meeting. On the eve of the 1989 meeting the headmaster addressed the morning assembly in the following manner:

Headmaster: Tomorrow we're having the annual athletic meeting. I expect everyone to attend in full uniform and cheer his house players.

Heroism was another characteristic to be developed from participation in sport competitions. College publications displayed many photographs celebrating winning teams, and individual students in action or wearing medals or showing off trophies. The fact that the College organized a wide range of sports events is significant. Students were not only involved in playing football and basketball matches, but in more exclusive activities such as tennis, squash and diving. Studies on leisure such as those by Parker (1976), Clarke & Critcher (1985) and Sultana (1993) refer to the relationship between social class and the variety of leisure activities. In providing such a wide range of sports, then, the College was taking a social stand. The hidden messages imparted through sports not only referred to work, but also aimed at creating a school culture which was clearly (upper) middle class. The College took care not only to channel students towards high status jobs but also to initiate them in the leisure activities which would go along with their jobs.

Morals, Religion and Politics

Assemblies, streaming, sport events, and ceremonies were by no means the only occasions where political and ideological messages were transmitted to students. Religion lessons and activities played a very important part in putting across ideological messages. Given that the College is a private Catholic church school, it is interesting to focus on how religion and morality intersected with a conservative political ideology which stressed the reproduction of the status quo.

This interplay can be clearly seen in the way the school, through its religion programme, transmitted its image of the 'ideal man'. Studies on private and church schools generally point out to a dualistic approach on the part of the particular religious order towards its role (religious) and objectives (as an educational institution). Tapper & Salter (1985) note, for instance, how private schools impart the 'essential cultural style', i.e. the formation of the Christian gentleman. Church schools are generally considered to be engaged in giving students enough academic education to guarantee a top job and, simultaneously, moulding them into ideal, Christian social beings. This was Archbishop Mercieca's very message of what a Catholic school should do, as reported in a publication commemorating an anniversary of the College. It is worth noting the significance of the intertwining of 'morality' and 'religion', in that the meaning conveyed to students was that becoming good men implied becoming good Catholics.

The ethos of the College revolved around these two important paradigms: making white collar workers and making Catholics. Although some studies have shown that what actually takes place in such schools gives more weight to the former (Kapferer, 1989; Walford, 1986), others refer to the coupling of secular and Catholic values (McLaren, 1986, pp. 183-4).

A class – Religion

Don Fonius speaks about Christian values. As an example to simplify his argument he takes traffic in Malta.

Don Fonius: We Maltese are very good at breaking the law. We have an eleventh commandment: 'Thou shalt not get caught.' [*Laughter*]

During the sermon of the weekly mass:

Don Petrus: Sometimes you see people in church sitting cross-legged, or with their hands in their pockets. That's lack of respect, isn't it? Even if we're not in Church we should never speak to anyone with our hands in our pockets.

Here we have two instances of the coupling of secular and Catholic values. There are secular values or referents (transgression of traffic laws and of rules of etiquette) which are transposed to a Catholic/religious context (the Commandments, the Church).

This collapsing together of the secular and religious worlds was used to great effect in order to exercise and legitimate the school's authority in defining the world. For instance, it is grave enough to have an adult criticizing you publicly for your behaviour; but being told off by a priest in sacred clothing in a chapel full of people is quite an overwhelming experience, and difficult to contest or resist!

Even secular subjects, such as lifeskills and literature, were encapsulated in a Catholic vision of the world. With regards to the former subject, newly introduced into the curriculum in order to provide space for students to communicate their concerns on their own terms (cf. Sultana, 1992a), this was taught by a seminarian. The political themes addressed by the literature syllabus were similarly hinged to a religious framework.

E class – Maltese Literature

> Mr. Bird gives a general introduction to the novel *Leli ta' Ħaż-Żgħir*. In his introduction, Mr Bird explains that the main character is an anti-hero and a social reformer. But the notion of a 'social reformer' seems to challenge the idea of the status quo. To avoid this discrepancy Mr. Bird switches to religion.

Mr. Bird: The best example of a social reformer remains Christ.

In this way, the teacher apparently achieved an ideological compromise between politics and religion. Any challenge to the social status quo had to somehow conform to the larger picture presented by the school. In this case there was only one possible construction of reality, and hence only one social reformer to follow: Jesus Christ, of whom the Davidian friars were faithful disciples.

The construction of this very particular world was achieved not only through material and ideological practices, but also through symbolic and cultural ones. Thus, religious symbols, such as pictures, crucifixes and statues, played their part as well. In every classroom there was a crucifix and a picture of St David next to it. Pictures of the patron saint, in fact, could be found almost everywhere, including the tuck shop. The corridor joining the junior to the senior school was lined with six different images of St David. Children from the junior school had to walk along this corridor at least once a week to go to the chapel where other portraits of Davidian saints looked on fixedly. Another statue, near the trophies showcase, depicted St David with a book in his hand looking at a child near him. These symbols, therefore, served as constant reminders of the community's authority, not only in the regulation of school life, but also in the regulation of civic life and its relationship to the universe of values. The political connotations of these insignia were very effective. For instance, when I asked Mewey what all those pictures represented he gave a straightforward answer identifying the saint with political figures.

Mewey: Well, he's the founder so he's sort of a leader. It's like when you go to some government building – you see the photos of the president or the minister.

Control and Resistance

Thus far I have stressed what school does to children, identifying some of the processes through which individuals and groups are socialized into accepting the school's definition of the world as legitimate, as the only referent. But students are neither structural nor cultural dopes, and they actively appropriate messages and symbols in order to subvert mainstream ideological representations so as to voice their own concerns and experiences.

This was especially true of the E class, who, feeling treated by the school as second class citizens, hit back at the system. Resistance itself was exercised symbolically through various rituals. Resistance, then, can be considered a counter-ritual aiming at desecrating and violating the rituals of the dominant order. Furthermore these rituals were observed taking two forms. The active form of resistance constituted the conscious effort of the student to attack authority. Passive resistance, on the other hand was 'less overt and less demonstrative' (McLaren, 1986, p. 81). Thus the minutest action, or non-action, could very often prove to be a naive yet intrinsically valuable form of resistance.

In the case of the boys in the E class, the classroom became the site where resistant acts were most frequently acted out. The reasons for this are obvious. First the classroom was the place where direct oppression was generally perpetrated. Secondly, the classroom gathered a large group of students in one place, and resistance was most effective when performed with or in the presence of the whole class. Thirdly, the sharing of the same experiences gave a feeling of security to those performing resistant acts.

Favourite modes of resistance on the part of the E class included making fun of teachers, passing satirical comments, selecting a teacher's particular habits or characteristics and mimicking them or commenting on them, copying homework exercises, writing love letters during religion classes, making funny faces behind the teacher's back, and so on. The boys engaged in passive resistance when a particular teacher was strict. They stared out of windows, and sometimes even dozed off. One student always had the latest issue of *Amateur Photography* open under his desk. Other resistant acts had a symbolic value. Nikos bit his textbooks as soon as his teachers looked in a different direction, for instance. Once the E's took what eventually become considered to be a 'legendary' decision: they whitewashed their classroom. That in itself was a symbolic act signifying their dislike of their room and their disapproval of the authority's mismanagement. It also gave the boys a feeling that they had some say (however limited) and that they could stand up for their own interests without anybody's help.

Resistance to the school was manifest in places other than the classroom, and spilled into the corridors, recreation field, and even chapel. The E class, for instance, did not mix with other students from other classes. Rather they split into two groups or gangs, spending the breaks either hanging around (hence resisting the sportsmanship ethos of the college) or playing it tough, like bullying some junior pupil or stalking a female sixth former. Away from their 'dungeon' (as they referred to their classroom) the E's sought ways and means to resist the power structure of the College, often to the disgust of the other students and, naturally, the administration. In so doing, the E's were 'dismissed' from the Davidian Family. On their part they did not share the sense of belonging which the authorities attempted to foster in the College.

These 'outcasts' and outsiders' therefore ended up rejecting the school as much as it rejected them. They ridiculed those ceremonies where the College body was unified into one mass ritual dictated by the dominant structure of the College as in the case of the opening of the annual athletic meeting quoted above. Those few who attended made fun of the whole performance, and booed and laughed most of the time. When the Headmaster congratulated Small for his success in the speech contest all students applauded except the E's who 'dared' ridicule the 'holy' occasion by blowing raspberries, jeering and over-clapping. They were thus attacking the ritual symbolically, for they did not feel that the glory to which the headmaster was referring, applied to them, and so disassociated themselves by counter-acting. In this way the E class challenged the dominant culture of the College by adopting opposing cultural traits. Thus they rolled up their sleeves; Spotts let his hair grow and had to be called to get it cut, they sprayed deodorant after Physical Education lessons, spoke foul language and seldom received Holy Communion at Friday masses. Dress offered ample opportunities for symbolic resistance. For instance they wore plastic bangles in spite of Mrs. Weaver's threat of confiscating 'those things', and they also had a particular way of wearing the tie.

Resistance in or out of the classroom was triggered off by the whole process of schooling which created a lack of sense of belonging in the lowest stream students. Thus while resistance in the classroom aimed at attacking the teacher and classroom practice, resistance outside the classroom challenged the whole structure of the College. The former took the form of a 'private' combat, enclosed within the four walls of the room. The 'public' combat set out to ridicule every single aspect of the College: religion, culture, school heroes, and, indeed the whole ethos of the College.

Conclusion

In this article I have attempted to show how one of the more elite private (church) schools in Malta socializes students into a particular form of life. The elements I emphasised in this description include the construction of distinction as a key principle in the organization of social relations within and outside of the school. This manifested itself through both the overt and the hidden curriculum, and especially through the hierarchical structure which rigidly regulated interaction between administrators, teachers, and students. Emphasis was also placed on the way rituals, symbols, and everyday interaction construct the particular ethos of the school in such a way that students become enveloped in a miasma of almost subliminal messages which take on a common-sense, 'natural' quality that is difficult to contest. It has been argued that this social construction of reality within schools entails a political positioning of students within the social world, and that students with different abilities are positioned differentially within that world. This positioning is not final or uncontested, and has to be continuously achieved through all the means – physical, structural, cultural and symbolic – that the school can muster. On their part, students actively accept, contest, resist, and/or modify the socialization processes they are exposed to, striving to voice concerns, needs, frustrations, and so on. The description and critical analysis of such processes in this and other schools in Malta is crucial if we are to understand the production and reproduction of elites and outcasts in the local social formation.

References

Aggleton, P. (1987) *Rebels Without a Cause? Middle Class Youth and the Transition from School to Work*, Lewes, Falmer Press.
Apple, M.W. (1979) *Ideology and Curriculum*, London, Routledge & Kegan Paul.
Apple, M.W. (1982) *Education and Power*, London, Routledge & Kegan Paul.
Clarke, J. & Critcher, C. (1985) *The Devil Makes Work: Leisure in Capitalist Britain*, London, Macmillan.
Connell, R.W., Ashendon, D.S., Kessler, S. & Dowsett, G.W. (1982) *Making the Difference: Schools, Families and Social Division*, North Sydney, George Allen & Unwin.
Darmanin, M. (1989) 'Sociological perspectives on schooling in Malta', unpublished doctoral thesis, Cardiff, University College of Wales.
Firestone, W.A. & Herriott, R.E. (1984) 'Multisite qualitative policy research'. In Fetterman, D.M. (ed.) *Ethnography in Educational Evaluation*, Beverly Hills, CA, Sage.
Fox, I. (1985) *Private Schools and Public Issues*, London, Macmillan.
Giroux, H.A. (1983) *Theory and Resistance in Education*, South Hedley, MA, Bergin & Harvey.
Hallinan, M.T. (1987) *The Social Organization of Schools*, New York, Plenum Press.

Hargreaves, A. & Woods, P. (eds) (1984) *Classrooms and Staffrooms*, Milton Keynes, Open University Press.
Haywood Metz, M. (1978) *Classrooms and Corridors: The Crisis in Desegregated Secondary Schools*, Berkeley, CA, University of California Press.
Kapferer, J.L. (1989) 'Schools for the state'. In Walker, S. & Barton, L. (eds) *Politics and the Process of Schooling*, Milton Keynes, Open University Press.
Kertzer, D. (1988) *Ritual, Politics, and Power*, New Haven/London, Yale University Press.
LeCompte, M.D. & Goetz, J.P. (1984) 'Ethnographic data collection in evaluation research'. In Fetterman, D. (ed.) *Ethnography in Educational Evaluation*, Beverly Hills, CA, Sage.
MacDonald, M. (1977) 'The education of élites', Unit 29 of 73 *Educational Studies Course: Schooling and Society*, Milton Keynes, Open University Press.
McKercher, W.R. (1989) *Freedom and Authority*, Montreal/New York, Black Rose Books.
McLaren, P. (1986) *Schooling as a Ritual Performance*, London, Routledge & Kegan Paul.
McLaren, P. (1989) *Life in Schools*, New York, Longman.
McNeil, L. (1988) *Contradictions of Control*, London, Routledge.
Mifsud, E. (1991) 'Power and politics in a private school in Malta', unpublished B.Ed.(Hons.) dissertation, University of Malta, Faculty of Education.
Mifsud, J. & Mallia, M. (1991) 'Bells and punch clocks: The ideology of work in four Maltese schools', unpublished B.Ed.(Hons.) dissertation, University of Malta, Faculty of Education.
Parker, S. (1976) *The Sociology of Leisure*, London, Allen & Unwin.
Sultana, R.G. (1991a) 'Research in teaching and teacher education: qualitative methods and grounded theory methodology', *South Pacific Journal of Teacher Education*, vol. 19, 1.
Sultana, R.G. (1991b) 'Social class and educational achievement in Malta'. In Sultana, R.G. (ed.) *Themes in Education: A Maltese Reader*, Msida, Malta, Mireva Publications.
Sultana, R.G. (1992) 'Personal and social education: Curriculum innovation and school bureaucracies in Malta', *British Journal of Guidance and Counselling*, vol. 20, 2.
Sultana, R.G. (1993) 'Practices and policies in child labour: Lessons from Malta', *British Journal of Education and Work*, vol. 6, 3.
Tapper, T. & Salter, B. (1985) *Power and Policy in Education: The Case of Independent Schooling*, Lewes, Falmer Press.
Walford, G. (1986) *Life in Public Schools*, London, Methuen.
Willis, P. (1977) *Learning to Labour: How Working Class Kids Get Working Class Jobs*, Farnborough, Saxon House.
Woods, P. (1977) 'Teaching for survival'. In Woods, P. & Hammersley, M. (eds) *School Experience*, London, Croom Helm.

17

The Impact of Tourism in Malta: Cultural Rupture or Continuity?

Joe Inguanez

For most of us, tourism is just fun! This is the impression one gets when one meets people who, after having 'toured' for a brief spell some exotic tourist destination, narrate their experience. As far as they are concerned, this may be quite a fair comment. However there is much more to the tourist phenomenon than meets the eye. It requires a deeper and more complex analysis.

Let me start with some facts and figures. Tourism is the world's largest single industry; more than 360 million tourists cross international borders every year. It is estimated that by the end of the coming decade this figure would be doubled. It is also one of the largest single sources of employment: the tourist industry is responsible for about 112 million jobs, thus providing employment for one-fifteenth of the world's workforce. From the financial point of view, its dimensions are similarly colossal: it generates an annual revenue of 2.5 trillion dollars. In terms of production, tourism is responsible for five and a half per cent of the world's Gross National Product.

I am referring to these figures to indicate the enormity and exigencies of the tourist industry and its enormous effect on the lives of many people right across the globe, including tourists themselves. As a result of this, many policy-makers believe that the effects of tourism are so wide ranging that the techniques to foster, control, or contain it are too complex to be left to individual host communities and much less to individuals.

The Impact of Tourism

Within the considerable amount of literature on tourism impact, the step or stage models have been quite widespread. Smith (1978) analysed the development of tourism in terms of distinct waves of tourist types. She has elaborated a tourist typology made up of seven categories in order of expanding impact on the host community. Doxey (1975) proposed a four-step scale called 'irridex' or irritation index to assess the interactions and relationships between locals and tourists as they develop over a time.

Others have analysed tourism by exploring the different target groups where its impact was felt to be mostly critical. Pearce, Moscardo & Ross (1991) refer to this as the segmentation approach. Such a perspective is readily adopted by the tourist industry. In his study of the effects of tourism on the Balearic island of Ibiza, Cooper (1974) refers to an Ibizan saying that if tourists were to stop going to Ibiza, there would not be enough pine trees on Sa Talaia for the people to hang themselves from. When I was carrying fieldwork in 1983 in the Maltese tourist resort of St Paul's Bay, I discovered a similar attitude: As far as tourism was concerned, the major preoccupation of my informants was the slump in tourist arrivals. When asked what they liked least about tourists, one informant succinctly replied, 'their absence'![1]

---

[1] This same attitude is portrayed in the concluding paragraph of Nicholas Monsarrat's novel *The Kappillan of Malta*:
... Malta is in the way of people, so they want to take it. We've tried to say No,

In the mid-nineteen-sixties, several small economies turned to tourism as a new, and very often much needed, source of employment. Similarly, larger underdeveloped countries which lagged behind in traditional, industrial development transformed their unspoilt environment – previously considered as a sign of 'backwardness' – into an economic asset by promoting a tourist industry.

When Britain decided to dismantle her naval potential in Malta, the island's economy had to face the enormous challenge of diversifying its economic structure. During the British colonial period, most of Malta's wealth accrued from the manifold services it rendered to the British navy. The first five-year economic development plan (Department of Information, 1959, p. 3) prefixed amongst it objectives the exploitation of

> the climatic, scenic and historical assets of Malta by mounting a concerted and swift drive to build up a tourist industry.[2]

It is clear that the major reason for developing tourism in Malta and elsewhere was an economic one. The focus of this paper is rather more on another aspect of tourism, namely its social and cultural impact. At the conceptual level, it is possible to circumscribe the different types of impacts – economic, social, cultural, environmental and so on. The practice, however, is not quite as neat. The impact on one sphere readily, though perhaps unwittingly, spills over onto others.

---

time after time. Now we want to say no for always.
–On your own?
–If we can.
–So you don't want any outsiders?
–We want tourists... Just like rich America and London. But we don't want soldiers or sailors.

[2] It is worth noting that, in the immediate post-war period, Sir Wilfred Woods (1946), in his report on the finance of the Government of Malta, gave little weight to such a strategy: 'It seems improbable that Malta can derive much wealth from this activity [tourism]...'.

Social and Cultural Impact Studies

Since the late seventies, extensive studies of the social and cultural impact of tourism have been carried out by various scholars (Pizam, 1978, 1982; De Kadt, 1979; Belisle & Hoy, 1980; Ladewig & McCann, 1980; Cooke, 1982). These studies have concentrated primarily on the various ways locals reacted to tourists, and the latter's impact on community life. These reactions were analysed along a wide range of variables, including number of tourists, length of stay, socio-demographic characteristics of both locals and tourists, size of the resort and the size of the local community.

A wide range of impacts has been identified. Such facts as crowding, congestion, noise, litter, uncontrolled development, environmental degradation were indicated as having a negative impact on the locals, whose reactions ranged from a diminished sense of hospitality to open hostility. It was found that a general resentment towards tourists was created by the ostentatious living of wealthy tourists. Belisle & Hoy (1980) concluded that a positive attitude among locals was dependent on the stage and extent of tourist development in the area.

Tourism in Malta

In the nineteen-twenties, the Maltese Government indicated that it was in favour of exploiting Malta's scenic and historical assets to attract tourists to the islands. This notwithstanding, tourism in Malta never developed into an industry. It seems that several governments, both colonial and local, have opted to take the line of least resistance and leave the island to rely heavily on income generated from its fortress economy. As I have noted earlier, it was only when the British Government unilaterally decided to withdraw its forces from the island that tourism started to be seen as an alternative worth developing into a fully-fledged industry in its own right.

This development occurred at a time when tourism, spurred by the development of safer and larger aeroplanes, charter tours, and economic affluence in European and North American countries, was becoming a major economic activity in several countries. These included several developing countries which had only few resources other than their benign climate, beautiful beaches and unfamiliar and fascinating cultures.

The start was very unassuming. This is indicated by the fact that between 1955 and 1959, the expenditure of the Malta Tourist Bureau[3] amounted to a meagre Lm76,122. The number of hotels in 1959 amounted to 25, providing 1,218 beds and employing 505 workers. Tourist arrivals stood at 12,583, from whom gross income amounted to Lm765,000. Working on the assumption that tourism would benefit from other infrastructural developments and private investment, the 1959-1964 Development Plan only earmarked half a million pounds for tourism. However, notwithstanding various vicissitudes, the tourist industry kept advancing and in 1992 the one millionth tourist arrival was reached for the first time. According to available data, 1992 has seen a 12% increase in tourist arrivals and income from tourism stood at Lm180.5 million as compared to Lm175.3 million in 1991. It was however estimated that the per capita earnings from tourism had gone down by 8% in 1992 (Central Bank of Malta Quarterly Review, 1993, p. 13), indicating that the spending capacity of tourists had fallen considerably.

The Maltese tourist industry has traditionally relied heavily on the United Kingdom tourist market. However, successive governments have felt the need to diversify the market away from this single source. Thus in 1992, only 52.2% of tourists visiting the island of Malta came from the United Kingdom. German tourists came next, making up 18.1% of the total number of visitors.

Hotel ownership is divided among local and foreign entrepreneurs. The largest number of tourists are brought over to Malta by foreign tour operators. This results in heavy dependence not only on tourist fads but also on the goodwill of these operators.

The Phenomenology of the Impact of Tourism

One cannot understand an impact without delving deeply into its origin. This is one of the reasons why explanations of tourist impact are very often generic explanations.

---

[3] In the mid-nineteen-fifties this Bureau formed part of the Government Public Relations Office. It was only in 1955 that it was developed into an independent office.

Tourism is about people: people who are in search of something new or at least different. They might be looking for new sights or new sites. According to Urry (1990, p. 1), tourism is

> about pleasure, about holidays... about how and why for short periods people leave their normal place of work and residence... about consuming goods and services which are in some sense unnecessary.

Urry, (ibid.) says that part of this experience is to gaze upon or view a set of different scenes and landscapes or townscapes which are out of the ordinary, at least one's own ordinary. This gaze implies an encounter which is similar to that of a doctor on his patient. Thus tourism involves also a variety of social practices. These practices are characterized by some form and level of reciprocity and reciprocal effect. This is what is normally subsumed under the concept of tourist impact.

The nineteen-sixties saw the global euphoric acclamation of universal tourist growth. It was seen as the boon of the century. More and more countries, especially those lacking in conventional industrial development, viewed the tourist industry as the great occasion to acquire a share of foreign currency through the activities of the 'golden hordes' in their own country. It was looked at as one of the few open possibilities for economic development free from colonial strings. The economic benefits accruing from tourism were so attractive that they blurred the vision of anything else.

This euphoria was bound to end. Indeed it did. And it was followed by disenchantment. It was becoming evident that the tourist industry had a price-tag attached to it. The most obvious and polemic issue which became the subject of hot debates was environmental degradation. Osborne (1978, p. 19) described London as a tourist slum and *The Evening Standard* gave open vent to his strong feelings:

> Tourists, whether they be Americans, Germans (especially), Japanese (perhaps most of all), even the biggest nation of geniuses in the world – the Italians, all are human garbage...

The issue was soon widened to include a fundamental economic perspective besides an environmental one. Tourism clearly has an international character, not only in terms of the diverse origins of the tourists themselves, but also in terms of the international investments it represents. The question therefore can be raised as to whether tourism has led to development or to a new more subtle form of dependence on core capitalist countries and their transnational corporations.[4]

Comparatively recently, the argument spread to the domain which merited earlier attention, namely the social and cultural effects of tourism. There are now worldwide discussions focussing not only on the economic cost and benefits of tourism, but also on the social and cultural costs. Besides this, the discussion is not limited to a restricted academic circle interested in the way people live. People are becoming aware that tourism's fast growth rate, as well as changes in both the social structure and social consciousness, have led to new problems. These preoccupations cannot be easily dismissed, and lead us to the central question addressed in this paper: is tourism leading to cultural rupture or continuity?

Rupture or Continuity?

The answer, or better answers, to this question vary according to both temporal and spatial variables. The crisis of the grand theories makes this stance obvious. In my view, the popular saying that what is sauce for the goose is sauce for the gander fails the test of logic because it fails the cultural test. Sociological and anthropological studies have shown how difficult it is to premise a sociological hypothesis with the statement 'all things being equal', because many agree that this premise is more exceptional than rare.

The impact of tourism has an element of continuity which is both positive and negative. If one analyses the international tourist industry, one can detect that this industry fits into the logic of international capitalism just as much as conventional industries do. What we can refer to as the 'software' of the industry, namely finance, marketing and management, is found in core capitalist

---

[4] This view is contested by, for example, Richter (1989) who holds that the strident critique of multinational firms in the travel industry is misplaced. These firms are not the villains for promoting a type of tourism that provides the criteria by which tourism policies are currently evaluated – numbers of arrivals and amount of revenue achieved.

countries. The 'hardware', namely the service labour is found in underdeveloped countries, or transported through a migratory process from third world countries to tourist destinations in core capitalist countries. This division could be said to represent a continuity of the exploitative relationship between core and periphery, which had its historical antecedent in colonialism.

One aspect of that exploitation relates to the ways in which tourism generates activity in the black economy. The latter sector employs workers on a part-time basis, and offers very little in terms of security and conditions of work, even though there is the 'advantage' that such workers do not pay any taxes on their salaries. Even though the pay they get is not necessarily low compared to that of full-time workers, the position of workers in the black economy renders them accomplices in a system of exploitation which often works against their interests.

This axis of continuity also has a positive side to it. Newly emergent states, or emergent communities within such states, have, thanks to tourism, acquired a sense of self-awareness, self-confidence, and identity. The 'we' and 'them' discourse has had the positive effect of isolating local and national interests, discriminating domestic talents and heritage from those of the foreigner. Although the tourist industry may have placed the receiving state and community on a specific level in the international division of labour, the members of that state or community have come to understand that serving the tourists does not necessarily imply subservience to them. This was more so when a language divided the 'hosts' from the 'guests' very often to the advantage of the 'hosts'.

Besides this, tourism very often encourages the maintenance or revitalization of the indigenous culture in its varied expressions. Music, dance, crafts, painting, sculpture and other artistic forms which the locals had taken for granted and consequently did not consider worthy of preservation, became estimable because the tourists enjoyed seeing them or wanted to buy them.

The film *High Season*[5] gives a very good portrayal of one effect

---

[5] Written by Mark Peploe and Clare Peploe, directed by Clare Peploe and produced by Clare Downs.

which tourism can have on a community. Jani, a young Greek 'entrepreneur', substitutes the Greek name of his father's shop by the name of the English poet 'Lord Byron'. Change of values is also illustrated by Jani's reaction to his mother's claim that his father merited a monument for his involvement in the revolution: this sparks off his imagination and he decides to build a monument dedicated to the 'Unknown Tourist'! Although this is fiction, it nevertheless conveys a lot of truth. It depicts a cultural and social rupture between generations. Traditional values may become irrelevant to the younger generation.

However, one cannot easily generalize about the elements of continuity and rupture with the past because the past itself, in terms of both biography and history, always serves as a buffer to possible impacts by exogenous factors which include tourism.

Malta's traditional contacts with foreigners during its long history of dependent existence has engendered in the Maltese culture a strong element of brokerage skills even in the social and culture spheres. These skills, and consequent attitudes, have served as a shield against a massive culture shock.

Another important element which has to be considered is the environment in which the tourist industry is implanted. In communities where tourism is the only agent of change, then it is relatively easy to infer a correlation between tourism and the continuity and/or rupture which one detects. This is what happens in isolated tourist resorts whose economic mainstay prior to the arrival of tourists was poor pre-industrial agriculture and where 'distances' have isolated such communities from metropolitan cultures. However this is not the case with Malta. Malta's livelihood depended on international 'exchanges' rather than 'isolation'. Years before Malta experienced the growth in the number of tourist arrivals, the Maltese had already been exposed to foreign presence, which during the second World War took the form of a massive military machine. The presence of foreigners is also reflected in the most varied spectrum of surnames of different nationalities existing on the island. Besides this, the Maltese have long been exposed to foreign mass media. In fact one can, in my view, even speak of 'media colonialism'.

Having said that, in my view, the future of tourist impact is more problematic now than the past. Familiarity with tourists is likely to provoke contempt just as much as it can generate liking. The consequences of this on social cohesion can be quite significant.

References

Belisle, F.J. & Hoy, D.R. (1980) 'The perceived impact of tourism by residents: a case study of Santa Marta, Columbia', *Annals of Tourism Research*, vol. 7.

Cooke, K. (1982) 'Guide-line for socially appropriate tourism development in British Columbia', *Journal of Travel Research*, vol. 21.

Cooper, R.J. (1974) 'An analysis of some aspects of social change and adaptation to tourism in Ibiza', unpublished PhD dissertation, University of Oxford.

De Kadt, E. (ed.)(1979) *Tourism: Passport to Development?*, Oxford, Oxford University Press.

Department of Information (1959) *Development Plan for Malta: 1959-1964*, Malta, Government Press.

Doxey, G.V. (1975) 'A causation theory of visitor resident irritants, methodology, and research inferences'. *Sixth Annual Conference Proceedings of the Travel Research Association*, San Diego, CA, Tourism and Travel Association.

Ladewig, H. & McCann, G.C. (1980) 'Community satisfaction: theory and measurement', *Rural Sociology*, vol. 45.

Osborne, J. (1978) 'Insult them and they may go away', *Evening Standard*, 28 July.

Pearce, P.L., Moscardo, G. & Ross, O.F. (1991) 'Tourism impact and community perception: an equity-social representation perspective', *Australian Psychologist*, vol. 26, 3.

Pizam, A. (1978) 'Tourism's impacts: The social costs to the destination community as perceived by its residents', *Journal of Travel Research*, vol. 16.

Pizam. A. (1982) 'Tourism and crime: Is there a relationship?', *Journal of Travel Research*, vol. 20.

Richter, L.K. (1989) *The Politics of Tourism in Asia*, Honolulu, University of Hawaii Press.

Smith, V. (ed.) (1978) *Hosts and Guests*, Oxford, Blackwell.

Urry, J. (1990) *The Tourist Gaze. Leisure and Travel in Contemporary Society*, London, Sage.

Woods, W. (1946) *Report on the Finance of the Government of Malta*, London, HMSO.

part 4

control and resistance

One characteristic of every society, where power is by definition unequal, is the active positioning of its members in such a way as to encourage them to uphold philosophies and partake in behaviour patterns which meet the designs of the powerful. In the Maltese circumstance, we come across institutionalized and informal, individual and amorphous agents engaged in such a construction of submission, deference and consent. These agents resort to a variety of cultural symbols, appealing ideologies and preferably covert control techniques to ensure compliance and agreement to preset goals.

Political parties deploy their agendas by personal, oratorical charisma and information technology, as evidenced from the respective articles of Boissevain and Saviour Chircop in this section. The attractive but possibly deceptive rhetoric of privatization sets out to reformulate the relationship between state and civil society as Darmanin elaborates. While O'Reilly Mizzi grapples with the non-technological but possibly more powerful socializing effect of peers and of the gossip information market.

Concurrently, there exists some appreciation by the power holders that no battle plan survives contact with the enemy: There exists an interplay across the unequal power relationship, intimating the importance of cultural affinity, ideological assimilation and consent for the positioning exercise to succeed as intended by its instigators. Otherwise, recipients can produce their own alternative, normative and rational behaviour patterns, devising their own script in disassociation with the promulgated designs of the stage managers. Bell and Denise Chircop illustrate this in the respective spheres of rock music and trade school attendance.

18

As We Sit Together, Should We Use the Phone? A Research Agenda for the Study of Media in Malta

Saviour Chircop

It is interesting that a country measuring 316 square kilometres with a population of 360,000; where *'in-nies taf lin-nies'*[1] and *'l-ajru għandu għajnu u l-ħajt għandu widintu'*[2] should develop its communications media so rapidly and with such vehemence! Given the intricate social and communication networks on the

---

[1] A common proverb loosely translated as 'everybody knows everybody else'.

[2] Another common proverb saying that the ambiance around you has watching eyes while the walls have listening ears.

Island, within which detailed gossip travels like a tornado, one could question the need of the mass media in Malta. Truly, one might discount such an argument by referring to the role that the media plays in connecting Malta to the outside world and in providing entertainment. But this justification is not enough to explain the current existence of the media in Malta. A very small proportion of media resources are used to connect Malta to its global counterparts. Other explanations have to be sought.

The media – in conjunction with other social institutions – simultaneously shape society and are themselves a symptomatic manifestation of the society they create. The former assertion proposes a study of the media infrastructure as a creator of social institutions, networks and behaviours; the latter seeks to identify how the infrastructure created is just another artifact of society – managed by the dominant interests – that is highly indicative of the type of society currently prevailing in the country. Thus, for example, Fagen (1966) shows how certain media structures and programme contents are complementary to specific political viewpoints. In the latter case, the media could also become the object of psychoanalytical analysis which discerns the characteristics/traits of this nation.

The current fragmentary nature of media research in Malta offers a number of challenges for an insightful reading and construction of a rich history of media that is still in the making. Obviously the first attempts at a research agenda are directed towards a historical perspective. This agenda would point out the milestones in media development, in terms of practical methods and procedures, hardware, and key players in the process. Yet such an approach, albeit important and inclusive of some interpretation of facts, deprives the reader of an assessment of the sociopolitical forces behind the presence of the media.

Similar comments can be levied at the 'media influence' or 'media effects' perspectives, largely imported from American studies, to the local situation. This type of approach has been used, at times simplistically, by social institutions to defend a nostalgic understanding of traditional values that are being eroded due to media effects.[3]

---

[3] The Catholic Bishops' Pastoral letter for Lent 1993 (24 February, 1993).

However, industry and media itself are gradually awakening to the use of scientific rigour in determining authentic media influence. Such quantitative studies, only recently introduced on the local scene, are beneficial for market research and advertising purposes. Yet these studies do not question the presence of the media in our society. One hopes that in the coming years such studies will move beyond their current descriptive nature.

This short article discusses an outline for alternative questions in the area of media research as related to culture, social structures, power and equity. This research agenda attempts to explain why an island with such scarce resources, overwhelming professional and financial overseas competition and abundant local social networks, has managed to sustain more than two centuries of journalism, and in a short span of time initiate and support a cable audio system, a TV station, a cable TV system, a TV in every household, and recently ten radio stations.

The Past

If one conceives 'mass media' as over-arching symbolic/language systems that provide communication, information, education and entertainment, then the study of Maltese history could provide intriguing examples of such systems that kept alive the Island's identity as separate from the ruling interests through several millennia of imperial or colonial occupations. These 'mass media' were a mixture of language, oral traditions, interpersonal networks and social institutions changing their appearance over the years.

These 'mass media' allowed the Maltese to develop systems of communication in support of their unique characteristic in history: being hospitable brokers among (and to) different parties.[4] This

---

[4] The Island survived thousands of years of upheavals. The Maltese managed to make a living with the Phoenicians, the Romans, and the Greeks. In spite of a Catholic tradition, Malta survived the Arab presence and managed to integrate features from their culture into its own. In the span of half a century, Malta survived the fall of the Knights of St John, entertained the French – from whom Malta gained a civil code – and worked with the British.

characteristic, carried even unto modern times, is a position that many fail to understand.

The medieval socio-religious-political institutional structures, often brought together by the territorial-social structure of 'the parish' are but one example of such mass media. Through a socio-religious-political system information was exchanged and education was imparted as subjects were entertained. In the process they assumed an identity distinguishing them from other 'parishes'. On a national level, these same communication patterns provided the 'Mdina defence syndrome'[5] whereby any foreign power would be baffled by intricate communication systems masquerading as simplicity itself. Thus the Maltese, over many generations of imperial and colonial domination, were able to sustain a mass communication system to serve their interests, within a larger communication system designed to serve whoever happened to represent the predominating interest in Malta. Indeed, some of these microcosm characteristics are still prevalent in the writings of Jeremy Boissevain (Boissevain, 1964) when describing a Maltese 'parish' in the 1960s. Given the presence of these deeply embedded traditional mass media, the advent of modern media of mass communication becomes more intriguing.

The geographic position of the Island as well as the political undercurrents which impacted it, especially during the last two centuries, contributed to the development of modern mass communication media. Besides local needs for information dissemination, the interplay of two factors – close proximity to Italy and the British domination during the last 200 years – played a key role in the development of our media. Italian printers found safe havens in British Malta during the struggle for the unification of Italy in the second half of the 1800s. The British, in turn, trying to counteract the Italian influence on the Island promoted the advent of the press (Grima, 1991) in the

---

[5] Mdina, the old citadel, is depicted as a seductive, simple, silent medieval city. Yet for the 'visitor' it is always a microcosm of deceiving narrow streets – with apparently indistinguishable features – that could allure the foreigner into the helplessness of being lost.

hope that this would give them a share in the pie of public influence. Mass media were used to balance the 'Italian party' and the 'British party' in Malta.

The same interplay of forces brought about the installation of a cable audio system, run by the Broadcast Relay Service (Malta) later known as Rediffusion (Malta) Limited since November 1935. The system provided a means of dissemination through public address speakers set up in the *pjazza* of towns or villages and in private homes. Although one cannot doubt the inestimable service given by the system especially during the war, further research is required to explore the extent to which such a medium favoured British political interests and colonial policy.

By 1957, the Maltese population was getting access to the Italian television networks through a relay antenna in Sicily. This seems to have made it easier to justify the installation of a television station in Malta. A series of events starting in 1958 led to the first Maltese transmissions on 29 September, 1962 (Vigar, 1993). It was a night to be remembered. By that time the estimated number of TV sets in Malta was over 20,000.[6]

Once established, the broadcasting media services became an object of contention. The different opinions as to the political content of programming which arose in the few years after the introduction of TV service were a foretaste of an uncomfortable relationship between power and the media in Malta.

The media situation remained largely sluggish until a change of Government occurred in 1971. Soon after the June elections, Government was hinting that it was not satisfied with the current arrangement. February 1975 brought about drastic changes: the broadcasting mass media services were taken over by the Maltese, following a sit-in strike (Kester, 1980). Those days of turmoil and the events leading to them are still an open challenge for scholarly research. In hindsight, studies of these events might lead a scholar to conclude that one is dealing with a historical landmark whose

---

[6] By December 1971 there were 65,000 TV sets in Malta. This amounted to 208 sets per 1,000 persons, already one of the highest rates in the world (Malta Television Services, 1972).

impact on political development was on a scale similar to that of the *Sette Giugno* affair. The transition was not an easy one: it took time to develop the local expertise, technical and managerial, to manage the operations of local broadcasting.

Moreover, this was a period of local history when two major theories of media were constantly clashing. One theory, seemingly adhered to by government, contended that Malta could not afford multiple broadcasting channels and this justified the fact that what was available should be devoted to the development of the national identity as perceived by the dominant interests purposely excluding all other dissenting interests. A second theory, adhered to by the opposition, sustained the belief that the media were to serve as a national forum where national issues are debated. In short, the people had the right to be informed and to make their own judgements. Both sides of the argument have scholarly support as can be evidenced in the MacBride Report published by UNESCO (MacBride, 1980).

The escalation of hostilities between the two sides following the 1981 general elections created a boycott of the broadcasting media by the Nationalist Party and a counter action by the Labour Party, who in turn, boycotted the Leader of the Opposition. This was a case where interpersonal communication was used to counter the media. This and similar instances (e.g. Iran in the time of the Shah) become for the media researcher a golden opportunity to study the extent to which the approach which views the media as 'all powerful' is in fact correct. And yet the media became key symbols in the struggle that ensued. The Nationalist Party set up its broadcasting facilities overseas, while the Labour Party was accused of having used *Xandir Malta* as its mouthpiece.

This clash of ideologies affected the Malta Broadcasting Authority, the Government-controlled broadcasting media and the print media in Malta.[7] A content analysis of the main speeches

---

[7] The reader is invited to consult the annual reports of the Broadcasting Authority, and the controversies about the media as evidenced in the political party newspapers. The laws regulating the print medium were further 'clarified' by the Seditious Propaganda (Prohibition) Act of 1981.

by the different key players in this period of Maltese history could uncover further insights into the intricate relationships between the media and power structures. It offers the reader a reconstruction of a neo-colonial model, only this time it was one faction of the Maltese population over another. Both before and after independence, the broadcasting media were channeled to serve a dominating political interest and although the persons holding the dominating political interest changed, the model of operation, by and large, remained consistent. It would be interesting to ask whether the changes effected in the local media structures in the first 25 years after the islands' independence were merely cosmetic changes or even a 'change of tyrannies'.

The issue of foreign military presence on the Island is an appropriate topic around which one can reconstruct the emergence of Malta as a maturing nation in the seventies. In the eighties the defence issue was replaced by the media issue. An in-depth study of these events, would attest how political agents, having acquired the power to determine the future of this nation from 'foreigners', were now engaged in a struggle to shape the identity of this emerging nation in their own image. Within this approach the development of local media offers fertile ground for the study of how a small nation came to terms with its newly acquired power and consequent management problems.

The Present

The 1990s ushered other drastic changes and challenges. Government relinquished its monopoly on audio and TV broadcasting media. Radio frequencies, national and regional, were offered to commercial enterprises (Broadcasting Authority (Malta), 1992). The three dominant structures of power on the Island, who incidentally were the first to get a radio frequency – the Nationalist Party, the Malta Labour Party, and the Catholic Church – created commercial partnerships to manage their respective frequencies.

But now the Maltese middle class, through business enterprises, became another structure of power which gained access to the control of local media. This is another milestone in the social development of the Maltese Islands: the business community, a newly emerging dominant interest, is being acknowledged as a fourth partner in the previously closed triangle.

By early 1993, the Broadcasting Authority had already allotted eleven national radio frequencies. Furthermore, the major political parties have agreed to allow TV broadcasting frequencies to operate in competition with the national station.

With the introduction of TV frequencies the argument for a strong tie between political structures and the development of media might be further clarified. While the Maltese authorities had eleven different radio frequencies available for distribution, there are only two other frequencies for TV broadcasting. Could not the allocation of one of these to the Malta Labour Party be seen as problematic?

The argument is constantly brought up that more broadcast frequencies mean a greater democracy for the country. But this is not an automated process. Truly enough, more frequencies on the air potentially allow for more voices to be heard. But the Maltese experience may be pointing to other indications. It is often the case, for instance, that the same people express their opinions in different phone-in programmes. Diversity here gives more air time to the same few, rather than to the many. Furthermore, it is not uncommon for the same personalities to be heard on different stations, at a few days' interval, discussing the same topic. Thus the multiplication of frequencies seems to be generating parallel discourses without much of a convergence. It is interesting to note however that, according to a recent survey, the radio station with the highest listenership is dedicated, almost exclusively, to music (MISCO, 1993).

To highlight the democratic aspect and increase listeners' attention, radio stations have emphasised audience participation — through phone-ins, for example. Yet it is not an uncommon occurrence for a listener to phone in and state an opinion which may be totally unrelated to the subject being discussed. An indepth study of the type of people who regularly phone radio stations to air their problems provides an interesting challenge. So would a content analysis of the types of problems being presented.

Currently there is scepticism as to whether the Island's advertising revenue can even sustain ten radio stations. This type of question would be valid if the media (print and broadcast) were to be simply a business proposition. If, however, the media as implemented on the Island, are akin to ideological billboards, then their existence will continue beyond financial feasibility. This was the case of political party newspapers, the General Workers' Union's paper and also the Church-run newspaper *Il-Ḥajja*.

One can ask whether the recent developments in the broadcasting media indicate that our politicians have come to a tacit understanding: resigned to the fact that since each party is a large force to reckon with (whether as a party in government or opposition), then it is better for each party to have its own broadcasting opportunities. This is a step further than the Italian experience where each of the three national networks has been leaning to a specific political viewpoint, without each network being effectively managed by the political interest. It is still too early to say how the Maltese experiment will work out. Truly, each dominant interest is guaranteed its multimedia public address system. However will this arrangement reinforce the existing polarization of the population?[8]

Journalists are also trying to rise to new challenges. Given the demand for more personnel in the field, their ranks have swelled and many are in a position to ask for better working conditions. In recent years great efforts were made by the Press Club (Malta) and the Institute of Broadcasters to promote journalism as a profession. Towards this aim they have jointly published a code of ethics to be adhered to by their respective members. But it is still doubtful whether the code can be effectively enforced. Given that the major newspapers often become political notice boards, one can see how the journalist has to compromise between her/his profession and the political structure, which is the employer. This subtle interference starts at the very moment of recruitment.

The Broadcasting Authority has to redefine its role because of these new developments. Up till the '90s the Broadcasting Authority, following the pattern of the Independent Broadcasting Authority (IBA) in the United Kingdom, held the post of referee among

---

[8] It is interesting how in Malta there is no provision for a common emergency service among radio stations. In the US, for example, stations that are designated as part of this emergency system fulfil certain requirements and run appropriate tests to ascertain that in case of a national emergency vital information could be transmitted to the whole population from one co-ordinated centre of operations.

players. However, following the broadcasting changes of the '90s, the Authority accepted to be responsible for a community channel. The Broadcasting Authority will eventually have its own studios and its own programming. Thus, besides being a referee, the Authority becomes also a player. It is very likely that at some point the situation will lead to a conflict of interest.

When there was only one TV channel and cable radio in Malta, it was relatively easy for the Broadcasting Authority to exercise its regulatory function through the monitoring of all programmes. Will the Authority now continue to operate its regulatory function in the same way, but on a larger scale?

The Future

Positive signs for the development of local media are evident. The recent discussions about a telecommunications infrastructure that would make the Island a hub in the Mediterranean could become a significant sign of the future. It is a return to the Maltese tradition of brokerage, a strategy which thrives in volatile environments. If previous experience has any predictive value, then one could talk about a number of eventual possibilities in this area.

New information and communication technologies are being very rapidly integrated into the Maltese environment. The use of video recorders, telephones and mobile telephones, faxes, modems, computers, satellite antennas and telecommunications are rapidly becoming a transparent technology. Malta is becoming part of a global network of communications as evidenced by the number of tourist arrivals, the number of Maltese visiting foreign countries and the amount of pulses on the international telephone exchange.[9] While offering more opportunities to individuals, such services are also gnawing at the strength of the traditional dominant power interests. One will have to ask whether this is just a phase of our history or an indicator of things to come. It is still possible to

---

[9] By 1990 the use of international telephone had already surpassed 13.5 million minutes per year (TeleMalta Corporation, 1991).

invest in a longitudinal study of the impact of such technologies on the political, social and cultural life of the Island.

The slow tentative separation between media and power could eventually follow the steps of the emerging separation between Church and State. This could eventually lead to a discrimination between national and party interests: politicians and people will understand that what benefits a particular power structure (in government, opposition or otherwise) need not be in the best interest of a country. This might eventually translate itself into a parliamentary voting system that goes beyond party lines.

With the advent of communication technologies, political structures are being challenged to create innovative mechanisms whereby the opinions and concerns of the population at large could reach the decision-making bodies of government and opposition parties. The use of such technologies for the democratization of political management and structures could provide another research possibility.

The rise of investigative journalism must be taken seriously. It has the potential of becoming the backbone of journalism acting as a conscience for society. This is not easily achieved when each major newspaper is the notice board for a structure of power. Furthermore, an over-zealous journalism might willingly indulge in a popular trial without safeguarding the viewpoint or the innocence of the victim until proven otherwise. Legislation will have to attend to such a peril.

Further research will have to be devoted to the gender issue. The media is still a male-dominated industry. Although we now witness a number of females engaged in the media industry, great gender discrepancies exist when one studies the decision-making bodies of local media enterprises. All in all, the local environment offers a challenging microcosm where different forms of power are constantly shaping and being shaped by the media. This paper has sought to chart this interplay by unfolding its historical evolution and suggesting potential research pursuits where pertinent. As an emerging nation, Malta is still coming to grips with a negotiated co-existence of the media and power structures. Once this issue is settled, one could then anticipate a shift of interest from the mass media to the personalized media as is currently happening in the industrialized countries.

References

Boissevain, J. (1964) 'Factions, parties and politics in a Maltese village', *American Anthropologist*, vol. 66, 6.

Fagen, R.R. (1966) *Politics and Communication: An Analytic Study*, Boston, MA, Little, Brown and Co.

Grima, J. F. (1991) *Printing and Censorship in Malta 1642-1839: A General Survey*, Valletta, Malta, Valletta Publishing Co.

Kester, G. (1980) *Transition to Workers' Self-Management: Its Dynamics in the Decolonizing Economy of Malta*, The Hague, Institute of Social Studies.

MacBride, S. (1980) *Many Voices, One World: Towards a New, More Just and More Efficient World Information and Communication Order*, Paris, UNESCO.

Malta Broadcasting Authority (1993) *Annual Report 1992, Broadcasting Authority, Malta*, Blata I-Bajda, Malta, Broadcasting Authority.

Malta Television Services 1962-1972 Reprint from *Il-Gwida* of 22 September, 1972, Valletta, Malta, Union Press.

TeleMalta Corporation (1991) *TeleMalta Corporation Annual Report*, Gwardamangia, Malta, TeleMalta Corporation.

Vigar, M. (1993) 'TV in Malta: The history of television in Malta with particular attention to how it was affected by the political institution', unpublished B.A. (Hons). dissertation, University of Malta, Faculty of Arts.

19

Gossip:
A Means of Social Control

Sibyl O'Reilly Mizzi

Gossip is a phenomenon found throughout the world in all cultures and climes. In its most ubiquitous form, it can be defined as a private conversation that is intended to collect or divulge information about people and their activities (Paine, 1967). But it can also be understood as a covert attack on one's rivals (Gluckman, 1963). Gossip fills a very special and important niche within society. It is one of the most widespread and effective means of social control within local Maltese communities. The reason why it operates so successfully is because of other social and environmental conditions that are peculiar to Malta. These include:
    the existence of a code of honour and shame,
    the central position of the Catholic Church in Maltese society,
    the concept of the sacredness of women as an underlying construct in Maltese culture,

the small size of the island with the concomitant face-to-face nature of social interaction,
the physical layout and architectural style of Maltese communities, and,
the strong division of social role by gender which is common among many Mediterranean cultures.

All of these social and environmental conditions acting together in traditional communities allow gossip to operate in a very special and critically effective manner. In order to understand the importance and the impact that gossip has, and the way in which it operates, it is necessary to understand each of these social and environmental factors and conditions.

Research Methods

This paper is based on research conducted in Malta from 1972 to 1976, and again from 1992 to 1993. The research was initiated in 1972, while I was studying the status of women in Senglea through participant observation. Basic information was gathered over several months each year for four consecutive years. This information came from 158 in-depth interviews with women in Senglea, from fifteen to 75 years of age. Each interview is representative of several hours, often spread out in a few sessions, in the person's own home. These personal interviews described their kinship, attitudes, daily life-style and activities. I was able to determine the nature of household composition and family types by canvassing fifty per cent of the households of the entire community. Key informants, including priests, doctors, teachers and other community leaders, in both formal and informal discussions provided data and insights into issues of importance to women in society. These informants are both within the Senglea community and from outside, in the larger community. This research includes a description of gossip as a means of social control (Mizzi, 1981).

From 1977 to 1991 I visited Malta regularly every one or two years. In 1992 I moved to Malta on a permanent basis and began to work in Senglea again. This research was to determine what changes had occurred in the lives of urban, working class women in the twenty years since the initial findings.

In 1992-93, another 150 interviews with women living in Senglea, some of whom had been part of the original 1972-76 study, were conducted. At the same time, discussions with women throughout the island on the subject of gossip and how it impinged on their lives today were held, along with further interviews with key informants.

Although this paper is based mainly on research in the traditional urban working class community of Senglea over a period of twenty years, I submit that the model of gossip as a means of social control developed here is valid in many other traditional communities and sub-communities still extant throughout Malta today. Currently, as much of Malta moves toward post-traditional communities (Abela, 1991), social and environmental parameters are changing and gossip is becoming less effective as a means of social control. However, it remains a potent force within the larger society.

Honour and Shame

Malta, by virtue of its central location in the Mediterranean Region, participates in a cultural phenomenon known as the code of honour and shame (Schneider, 1971). This code is found to exist in one form or another in all the countries of this area and has become one of the key indicators of Mediterranean culture.

The concept of honour found in traditional Maltese society is the value of a person in his/her own eyes as well as in the eyes of the community. It is a matter of having a good name and being of good repute. Honour accrues to those who comply with traditional patterns of behaviour like goodness and virtue, industriousness, uprightness and other, similar, valued traits. It is a sense of the collective consciousness of the community brought about through the evaluation of the congruence of belief and observed behaviour in the life of an individual person.

Shame, the reciprocal of honour, is the state of being in disgrace, showing no decency, or modesty; losing, or lacking the respect of one's fellows. It is the painful feeling of having done something one shouldn't have; of embarrassment caused by improper or inadequate behaviour. The conditions leading to honour, or shame are mostly positive for men, but mostly passive or negative for women (Peristiany, 1966).

According to the code, a man's honour is determined to a great extent by the behaviour of the women of his family, especially their sexual behaviour. The virginity of unmarried daughters and the chastity of women after marriage are of utmost importance to the men of the family. Women are taught both by admonition and by example, from their earliest childhood, how they should behave in relationship to men. Young women who flirt with boys too much or have too many boy friends are talked about within the community and their opportunity for a good marriage to a local youth is threatened. There is a Maltese proverb: *'Baqra tajba tinbiegħ f'pajjiżha'* or 'A good cow is sold at home'. This emphasizes the fact that Maltese prefer to marry within their own community, and that a young woman who damages her reputation through careless behaviour, may also damage her chances for marriage. A married woman who shirks her household responsibilities, is overly familiar with non-related men especially in public, or transgresses other cultural rules is openly discussed by other members of the community and develops a bad reputation which reflects poorly on her husband and family. Thus, most women try to follow the social and legal rules of the society as closely as they can.

For example, a married woman, an acquaintance, working in Malta, had some experience with this concept. This winter, a male family friend of many years' standing, met her at an academic reception. She tried to discuss some details of family management with him in the presence of several other academics. He was very curt and left her in the middle of the discussion. At a later date she inquired why he had seemed so displeased with the attempted conversation. He explained that the discussion was very inappropriate and that he really had been protecting her reputation as well as that of her husband.

The honour of a man or a woman implies completely different modes of conduct. A woman is dishonoured by the tainting of her sexual behaviour while a man is not (Pitt Rivers, 1966). A woman's honour depends on the reputation the community is willing to concede, not upon the evidence of facts; therefore she protects her honour most effectively by conforming in every outward aspect of her behaviour. If a woman's honour is soiled, she marks by her dishonour or shame, all those who are close to her through kinship or marriage (Campbell, 1964).

Importance of the Church

According to tradition, Malta was converted to Christianity in AD 60 by St. Paul. While on his way to Rome to stand trial, he was shipwrecked in Malta and stayed there for several months, preaching to the people. The Maltese take great pride in this tradition. The Catholic Church has been established for over nineteen hundred years and is firmly rooted in the life of the community. For a great part of this time, the parish priest was the leader of his people in his community, in all matters, civil and ecclesiastical. There are hundreds of churches and chapels, large and small, scattered throughout the island (*Malta Yearbook*, 1993). The parish church, with a square in front of it, is usually at the very centre of towns and villages, and has been the hub of local, social and cultural life as well as its religious spirit. Over 90% of the population is Roman Catholic. Practicing one's religion, from regular attendance at mass to participating in preparations for the village *festa*, or assisting in cathecetical instructions is a central activity of many people's lives (Vassallo, 1977). The social and cultural rules in Malta, especially those concerning sexual behaviour, have been formulated by the Catholic Church and are widely preached throughout the community. Because of the unanimity of religious belief, and the important economic and political role played by the church through time in Malta, the models for proper Catholic behaviour are extremely well defined and promulgated in every corner of society through the local clergy. Everyone knows the rules of the church and of the culture, and feels capable of privately judging another person's level of conformity.

Sacredness of Women

A more subtle influence on women in Malta is the underlying idea that women are sacred in some way. Historically there is evidence for this idea in Malta. Archeologists believe that during neolithic times, Malta was a holy island, a centre of religious practice in the Mediterranean (Trump, 1980). Four giant temples, at *Hagar Qim, Hal Saflieni,* The Hypogeum (Tarxien) and *Ġgantija*, have been excavated in the Maltese Islands. The remains of these imposing structures tend to substantiate the theory. Statues of obese women, thought to be fertility goddesses, have been found in the excavations. There is also evidence of the worship of Astarte, probably by Phoenicians, at a later date. Her temple has been identified at Fort St. Angelo in Vittoriosa. Thus the myth of the sacredness of women had fertile soil in which to flourish.

Women, because of their reproductive powers, as well as their periodic bleeding, have often been viewed as something apart, something sacred. As Douglas (1966) says

> The sacred needs to be continuously hedged with prohibitions. The sacred must always be treated as contagious because relations with it are bound to be expressed by rituals of separation and demarcation by beliefs in the danger of crossing forbidden boundaries.

Certainly Maltese women are hedged in with numerous restrictions, especially with respect to sexual activities. Maltese men seem to place women on a par with religion. Support for this attitude was demonstrated when several key informants told me that they feel that the British were successful and accepted in Malta because they kept away from Maltese religion and Maltese women. In men's minds these two institutions appear to be linked as sacred institutions and their linkage is of critical importance. This 'acceptable British attitude' may be traced back to the 1812 Royal Commission of enquiry which recommended that the crown must bear in mind that the objective is to provide for the tranquility of a people

> whose habits, customs, religion ...are in... opposition of our own (Blouet, 1967).

Thus, Maltese women are bound by the convergence of three ideas: the role model for women set by the Catholic church, the code of honour and shame, and the myth of the sacred woman. These ideas interact to reinforce one another and to place women at the same time in a position of importance and influence, as well as a position of subservience and subordination.

Women's behaviour is monitored by the men, whose reputations they uphold and by the church which threatens eternal damnation. Gossip plays an important part in enforcing normative behaviour. The women of the community watch for any breach of the code of honour and shame, or the rules of the church, or the sacredness of women and quickly inform others as to the extent and type of deviance. Thus they uphold the status quo and reinforce the role models.

Small Size of Island, Physical Environment

The Maltese Archipelago consists of three small inhabited islands, Malta, Gozo and Comino, and two uninhabited islets. The total area is 316 square kilometres. Several Maltese communities have the highest population density in all of Europe. The largest island is Malta, at 246 square kilometres, with a population of 345,000 according to the 1985 census. It is the cultural, administrative, industrial and commercial centre of the island group. The next bigger island is Gozo, with a population of 30,000 on 67 square kilometres. The longest distance in Malta, northeast to southwest is about twenty-seven kilometres, and the greatest width is not quite fifteen kilometres, in an east west direction. It is of major importance to note that the population is not evenly distributed throughout the island but is mainly concentrated along the east coast especially surrounding the capital city of Valletta. Even the villages are built in what may be considered an urban land use pattern. Streets are lined with terraced or attached houses surrounding a central square in which the main church is located.

In such a small country, everyone tends to know everyone else (Boissevain, 1974). It is commonly said that if one knows five families, one would have a connection to everyone in the island! Thus there is no sense of anonymity. It is virtually impossible to get away from a situation in Malta because of its small size and interconnected networks. If your behaviour deviates from the norm, you cannot move to another part of the community and start again. Your reputation will follow and catch up with you very quickly.

The physical layout of most Maltese communities, combined with the Maltese architectural styles, facilitate opportunities for observing one another's daily activities and the generation and dissemination of gossip. Streets are often narrow and houses are generally set closely to each another. Many houses have a closed balcony, an ideal observation post for the street below and the activities of passers-by, without one's self being observed. Many older women, and some men, sit just inside their doorway, with the door left ajar and while away the hours watching the world go by. Towns and villages are densely populated, so that there is almost always someone passing, some activity to interest a watcher. It is a perfect arrangement for neighbours to watch each other surreptitiously. It enables them to become familiar with the daily routine of everyone in the neighbourhood. Any deviation from routine, even a minor one, is immediately noticed. It is in just such an environment that gossip can be most effective.

Division of Social Roles by Gender

Gossip has no respect for age or gender. Both men and women of all ages participate in gossip, but about different things. Men talk mainly about sports, news, and whatever project they may be involved in. Women talk about themselves, how they feel and about their own and others' private lives. Men have their individual friendships, often outside the kin network, while women spend most of their time and energy within the home and the kinship network.

Maltese men occupy a separate world outside the home, a world which is closed to women. It consists of job, friends and male associations. They spend only short periods of time inside the home, and have little or nothing to do with the daily activities and routines of managing the household. The pressure of school or work allows boys and men to separate and excuse themselves from household chores and responsibilities. They spend their spare time with male friends, at football clubs, band clubs or local bars. One can often see groups of men talking at the local hunting/fishing supply store, or gathered around an old man sunning himself on his own doorway, exchanging current news and gossip.

Men within the kinship system do not unite with one another in the same way women do. The emotional relationship between fathers and sons is close, but the structural organization of the society tends to pull each man into a separate orbit, the orbit of the woman to whom he is married. Fathers help to train their sons in a more concrete way than they do their daughters, but as the boy grows, his leisure time is more and more devoted to his girl friend and her family until finally, he is incorporated into their network. The feeling of independence and of competition form part of the relationship between father and son. More important is competition for the time and attention of the mother (Mizzi, 1977a). Later, competition for prestige and honour within the community becomes a concern. In an urban, working-class community, boys do not work with their fathers in the same way that they frequently do in an agricultural or upper class community. In effect, all men are in competition with all other men in the community for access to jobs that are in limited supply. The spectre of emigration hung heavily over young men who, in the past, were often forced, against their will, to leave their homeland because of the lack of employment (Price, 1954; Vassallo, 1977).

A woman's home is her domain and she administers it with care and attention. Women do all of the food shopping, preparation, cooking and cleaning up. Men attend to household physical repairs, and women hold themselves entirely responsible for the management of the household. Child care is primarily a woman's job, but men do spend some of their free time minding the children especially on Sundays. Traditionally, women do not encourage their husbands to help in the house for there is a strong feeling that the home and household is their responsibility; that this responsibility is their chief *raison d'être* and that any encroachment would lessen their worth to the family. Thus they do much more than is asked for or even necessary. The Maltese proverb: *Ma jsir xejn mingħajri* – (Nothing gets done without me) expresses the indispensability of the housewife.

Women, on the other hand participate in kin centered female networks (Yanagisako, 1977). The unity of sisters and of mothers and daughters, is very strong in Malta. Unlike the men, they are not divided by differences in education, occupation, income and life style. Sisters, mothers and daughters can be relied upon for emotional support and services and they form the core of a kin oriented female network (Mizzi, 1977b). Added to this core group are sisters-in-law, their mothers and aunts and female cousins forming an interlocking group of consanguines and affines living within the community or in neighbouring communities. On the periphery of this group are included close neighbours who can be enlisted for assistance as needed.

These kin-centred female networks are the basis for the generation and flow of gossip within the community. Gathering places are scattered throughout the neighbourhood, on the church steps, inside the baker's, the neighbourhood grocery store, the TV/VCR tape centre and outside the local school where one brings and collects young children, to name a few. All of these locations feature in the everyday lives of most women as they carry on their daily activities.

Role of Gossip

Myth tells us that gossip has always been a concern among Maltese people. The story of St. Paul and the viper is well known as it is narrated in the bible. However variants of the story have become part of Maltese folklore. One variant relates that when he was shipwrecked on the island, he reached for a piece of wood to add to the fire and was stung by a viper. He flung his arm so that the venom landed in the mouth of a woman who was nearby, explaining and underscoring the predisposition toward gossip of Maltese women. Gossip is a way of life. Everyone participates in it to some extent. It is not good, however, to have the reputation of being a 'gossip', and women are careful of their behaviour so that others will not have cause to think of them as such. But most women meet and chat during the course of the day, after church, in the shops, while taking the children to school, or while taking a *'passiġġata'* (stroll) in the evening. There is very little home visiting except among family members, but it would be considered impolite to keep totally to oneself while performing daily chores.

One subject of gossip is any deviation from the acknowledged proper pattern, no matter how small or insignificant. Changes in behaviour patterns become noted, and others seek to find the reason. If it is obvious and understood, the new pattern is accepted and no more thought is given to the matter. But if something is being hidden or seems out of the normal order of things, the neighbours make their own decision as to its value and acceptability and act accordingly. If over a period of time there are many deviations from the norm and they tend to be unacceptable to the rest of the community, social pressure is brought to bear on the family in many subtle ways. Children are not allowed to play near the house of the 'deviate', or with the children living in the house. Mutterings or other noises or signs are made when passing the house. People decide not to 'recognize' the individual on the street. A man may find his friends reticent and uncommunicative. These are all means of social control and tend to regulate the behaviour and keep it close to the prescribed rules. As Bailey (1971) observes, in a discussion on gossip:

> The small politics of everyone's everyday life is about reputations; about what it means to have a good name; about being socially bankrupted; about gossip and insult and about 'one-

upmanship'; in short about the rules of how to play the social game and how to win it.

Particularly important is the power of gossip over a Maltese woman's reputation for sexual purity. Women are expected to be virgins at the time of marriage and wives must be chaste and dutiful, according to the ideal model that is in the minds of the people. A man is ranked among his peers by the chastity and fidelity of his wife and the purity of his daughters. Therefore a woman's reputation is of significance to all his family, father, mother, daughters and sons.

And yet, in fact, this reputation monitored by women of the community who watch each others' behaviour and comment upon it in. Gossip then becomes an important weapon in the hands of women. They can make or break reputation and influence another's position in the community. Time and again I have been told that the reason that women didn't have friends outside the family was because they feared being talked about and they worried about gossip (Mizzi, 1981). There was general agreement that if they greeted everyone in a friendly way and yet refrained from becoming intimate with anyone, that they were then safe from adverse comment. This fear of gossip has a significant effect on the social structure of the community, and is in contrast to other sexually segregated societies, such as Turkey, where although women gossip, they did not develop inhibitions against building a friendship with non-kin women (Starr, 1979).

There are many ways to control other people's reputation. An excellent example is that of a young, fourteen year old girl who had been keeping steady company with a local youth for several months. They had a falling out and the girl found herself another boy friend with whom she also broke off. This happened several times. In almost any other culture, these events would have been known by, and possibly of consequence to, just her family and very close friends. However in her community – one of the traditional ones of Malta – it became cause for adverse comments by the local watchers and she was perceived as a flirt and an unstable young woman. She became subject to unflattering and possibly dangerous attacks on her reputation.

In another case, an older married woman, whose husband was taken suddenly ill and hospitalized, was being taken by car to see him by an outside male friend of the family's. The friend came from another community and therefore was not known locally. She felt obliged to stop at the house of her husband's best friend to tell him of the news of the illness, but more importantly, to make sure that there would be no gossip about her 'driving around' with another man. Had she had the time, she would have been safer and more comfortable if she had been able to arrange for a third party, preferably another female, to accompany her, so that she would not have to be alone with a strange man.

Even such inconsequential factors as manner of dress, lack of neatness, being always *'pulita'* (neat as a pin) or maintaining the front of the house, including not only the sidewalk, but also the gutter *'nadif tazza'* (as clean and shiny as a drinking glass) are subject matters for comment by local women. Thus if you leave your home looking anything but well turned out, neat and clean, or if debris accumulates in the gutter in front of your house, you are in danger of being talked about in a negative way.

This type of close scrutiny leads women to be very conscious of the persona they present to the world, especially in their demeanour and behaviour, and to seek avidly to conform to the agreed upon norms as closely as possible. Individuals who either refuse or are unable to conform suffer from community scorn and ill repute, and are without honour.

Conclusion

In summary, it becomes clear that, particularly in traditional Maltese communities, gossip as a means of social control is enhanced by an unusual and unique set of circumstances peculiar to a certain time and place. However, gossip fills several other functions in society. It establishes a sense of intimacy between people that is important in the development of friendship (Tanner, 1990). Small talk is crucial to maintain a sense of camaraderie. For many women, getting together and talking about their feelings and what is happening in their lives is at the heart of friendship. Telling secrets is not without risks since someone who knows your secrets has power over you. Maltese women avoid having close friendships with outsiders because of this risk of giving them power. Instead, they keep close female friendships within the family organization. Jill Dubisch (1989), an anthropologist, writing about Greek culture suggests that talking about family matters to non-family members is taboo because it destroys a sacred boundary between inside and outside, taking outside the home what properly belongs inside. This could also apply in Malta.

Gossip fulfils a further function in society – that of reinforcing shared values. It plants in us an image of what a good, or a bad person is and does. Hearing people criticized for being stingy, disloyal or sloppy, we get the idea that these things are not good things to be. On the other hand, hearing people praised for being generous, self effacing and industrious we get the idea that these are good things to be (Tanner, 1990). People often measure their behaviour against the potential for gossip, hearing in their minds how others might talk about them. This function of reinforcing shared values works best in a homogeneous society with a single ethic such as Malta. Finally it appears that talking about someone who is not present is a way of establishing rapport with someone who is. By agreeing about their evaluation of someone else, people reinforce their shared values and world views (Eckert, 1990).

Gossip, therefore, is a very important social activity operating within local communities. It can foster social cohesion, uphold agreed upon values and world views. It may be used to monitor and enforce an internalized model of behaviour in society. Although often viewed negatively, seen merely as an attack on one's rival and a weapon in the battle of reputations, it can also be viewed as an activity that helps to build solidarity, friendship, and a sense of community.

References

Abela, Anthony M. (1991) *Transmitting Values in European Malta*, Malta, Jesuit Publications, & Rome, Editrice Pontificia Università Gregoriana.
Bailey, F.G. (ed.) (1971) *Gifts and Poison: The Politics of Reputation*, New York, Shocken Books.
Blouet, B. (1967) *The Story of Malta*, London, Faber & Faber.
Boissevain, J. (1974) *Friends of Friends: Networks, Manipulators and Coalitions,* Oxford, Basil Blackwell.
Campbell, J.K. (1964) *Honour, Family and Patronage*, New York, Oxford University Press.
Douglas, M. (1966) *Purity and Danger*, London, Routledge & Kegan Paul.
Dubisch, J. (1986) 'Culture enters through the kitchen; women, goods and social boundaries in rural Greece', in Dubisch, J. (ed.) *Gender and Power in Rural Greece*, Princeton, NJ, Princeton University Press.

Eckert, P. (1990) *Jocks and Burnouts*, New York, Teachers College Press.
Gluckman, M. (1963) 'Gossip and scandal', *Current Anthropology*, vol. 4, 3.
Hilary, B. (ed.) (1973) *Malta Year Book*, Valletta, Malta, De La Salle Brothers Publications.
Mizzi, S.O. (1977a) 'The changing position of urban working class women in Malta', *Anthropology*, vol. 1.
Mizzi, S.O. (1977b) 'The changing status of women in Malta', in Vassallo, M. (ed.) *Contributions To Mediterranean Studies*, Malta, Malta University Press.
Mizzi, S.O. (1981) 'Women in Senglea: The changing role of urban working class women in Malta', unpublished dissertation, University of Malta, Faculty of Arts.
Paine, R. (1967) 'What is gossip about? An alternative hypothesis', *Man* (ns) vol. 11, 2.
Peristiany, J.G. (ed.) (1966) *Honour and Shame: The Values of Mediterranean Society*, London, Weidenfeld & Nicholson.
Pitt Rivers, J.H. (1966) 'Honour and social status', in Peristiany, J.G. (ed.) *Honour and Shame*, London, Weidenfeld & Nicholson.
Price, C.A. (1954) *Malta and the Maltese,* Melbourne, Georgian House.
Schneider, J. (1971) 'Of vigilance and virgins: Honour, shame and access to resources in Mediterranean society', *Ethnology*, vol. 10.
Starr, J. (1979) 'On hearsay, gossip and method in the anthropology of law', *The Middle East Journal*, vol. 33, 3.
Tanner, D. (1990) *You Just Don't Understand: Women and Men in Conversation*, New York, Ballantine Books.
Trump, D.H. (1980) *The Prehistory of the Mediterranean*, London, Penguin.
Vassallo, M. (1977) 'Religious symbolism in a changing Malta' in Vassallo, M. (ed.) *Contributions to Mediterranean Studies*, Malta, Malta University Press.
Vassallo, M. (1979) *From Lordship to Stewardship: Religion and Social Change in Malta*, The Hague, Mouton.
Yanagisako, S.J. (1977) 'Women centered kin networks in urban, bilateral kinships', *The American Ethnologist*, vol. 4, 2.

20

Absenteeism: Deviance, Resistance and Contestation

Denise Chircop

Introduction

There is a body of research to suggest that working class students do not achieve at school.[1] This failure also manifests itself through high rates of truancy and absenteeism, especially in trade schools, which cater for a student population which comes mainly from a working-class background (Sultana, 1992). Common sense explanations to account for both school failure and for absenteeism construct students as deviant and puts the blame either on the absentees

---

[1] For an overview, see Sultana, (1991a).

themselves, or on some deficiency in their background. This paper sets out to show how a number of absentees in a girls' trade-school contest this notion, constructing a different understanding. Absenteeism to them is but one form of resistance towards an institution that has not only abandoned them to failure but proves to be irrelevant and restrictive.

The fact that this paper reports data collected from one school means that one cannot generalize the findings to account for the whole gamut of reasons which lead students to absent themselves from school. As in the case of other social phenomena there are a multitude of elements which impinge on the individual or group of individuals and which encourage them to absent. My ethnography does, however, provide an in-depth exploration of the definition of reality of fifteen absentees, and of their reasons for resisting and contesting school. While no definite attempt is made at generalization, it is argued that the insights developed in this study could possibly apply to other school sites and situations as well.

Research Methodology

In seeking an answer to the question 'Why do students stay away from school?' I looked into the experiences of fifteen habitual absentees 'attending' a three year course at *It-Torri*, a Girls' Trade School in an urban area in the southern part of Malta. Qualitative methodology was preferred to quantitative techniques as it was felt that the latter would not really reflect the cultural experiences of the subjects in the study. As a tool the questionnaire seemed too rigid. Positivist criteria of reliability and validity do not apply to qualitative methodology in the same manner as they do in the quantitative tradition. Rigour is assured by the researcher being aware of his own dispositions and declaring them in order to ward off, as much as possible, any potential threat to the credibility of the emerging theory. Using Grounded Theory methodology developed by Glaser & Strauss (1967; cf. Sultana, 1991b) I started my research project by first outlining clearly what I thought might become key issues in my research project.[2]

---

[2] For further details refer to Fenech (1991).

Data was collected through participant observation at school and at the homes of key informants. From time to time, I accompanied these girls to their places of work and leisure in order to become more familiar with their culture. Other data were collected through the use of semi-structured or unstructured interviews with habitual absentees, teachers and persons in key positions who were connected with my field of interest. These interview schedules were based on categories that emerged from the initial experiences in the field. Hypotheses were formulated and refined, through a process of constant comparative analysis.

Sixty-seven hours were spent in participant observation at the school, seventeen hours outside the school, eighteen hours were spent in interviewing teachers, other key persons as well as in attending fora on the topic, and eleven hours were dedicated to interviewing absentees. This totals to one hundred and thirteen hours spent in the field. Excerpts quoted from the data generated by the field research are to be considered typical of others, and not anecdotal information.

Explanations for Absenteeism

Defining Absenteeism

Before proceeding with the causes for absenteeism, it would be important to refine the definition of this key term as used in this paper. The group of absentees I observed during my study resorted to different forms of absenteeism. The most obvious type, the one that initially attracted my interest, involved staying away from school for reasons not justified by the law. Students however absented in other less overt ways, thus participating in what Willis (1977) calls 'informal mobility'. This included leaving the class on impulse, not going in for lessons, being in the wrong class, or even staying in class but not following the lesson and doing other things instead. As Willis (1981) has shown, students enliven their school experience by creating their own informal timetable and attempting to gain control over the class by misbehaving.

| *Cynthia* | Allavolja aħna nagħmlu ta' dik l-iskola! Għax li rridu nagħmlu... | Even though we belonged to that school, we used to push the limits. For we used to do as we pleased... |

Author	Meta tgħid "konna nagħmlulhom" x'tip ta' affarijiet kontu tagħmlulhom jiġifieri?	When you say "we pushed the limits" what kinds of things did you actually do?
Cynthia	Jew ma niktbux, jew noqogħdu nitkellmu. Skond il-burdati.	We either didn't write, or we used to chat, depending on the mood.
Veronica	Għax di' l-iskola naraha għalxejn jien. Ma jitgħallmux. Kulħadd imur biex jidħaq. Meta konna mmorru 'qas kont naf x'kienet it-'timetable'. La pitazzi, iġifieri...	For I think that this school is useless. They don't learn. Everybody goes for a laugh. When we used to attend I didn't even know the timetable. No copybooks, that is...*

In practice, therefore, though students go to school, they still absent themselves from schooling. They do not accept to engage in the 'serious business' and investment of self that the school requires, but rather redefine the situation as an opportunity for socializing and having a laugh. By being present physically in the school, students avoid a confrontation with the power of the state invested in the law, and contend instead with the power of the school and more often, with that of a specific teacher.

Author	Qed ikollkom xejn tfal li ma jiġux?	Are there many girls who are not attending?
Doris	Le, iktar f'ta' Giselle. Dawk minn eighteen, sitta biss qed jiġu. (...) U jien x'noqgħod infalli l-iskola! Tiltaqa' ma' sħabek, toqgħod tidħaq. Ommok mhux ħa toqgħod tidħaq hux?	No, mostly in Giselle's (year). Out of the eighteen in her year, only six attend. (...) What's the point in absenting! You meet your friends, you have a laugh. Your mum won't give you a laugh, will she?

.
 * Maltese ethnographic data has been transliterated into English to maintain the "strangeness" of the text.

Explaining Absenteeism

The reasons for absenteeism are complex, and any attempt at generating causal explanations needs to take into account the fact that this particular ethnographic study concentrates on girls, coming from a working class background who were attending a trade school. Each of these three factors poses particular structural pressures and constraints for the absentees, ultimately influencing their decisions and actions.

Three main theories emerged from the data to explain student absenteeism. The first two theories involve a pathological explanation and were mainly provided by teachers and other official representatives of the school. These considered students to be either not intelligent or emotionally not stable enough to cope with the educational experience and challenge they were being provided. These deficits led to disaffection with schooling, and hence to absenteeism. Thus, a chief welfare officer accounted for the higher rate of absenteeism in trade schools in the following manner:

Chief Welfare Officer	Issa tispikka fit-trade schools għax, bħalma taf int, jimmotivaw, dawk it-trade schools mhux l-iktar li jkollu, eh, l-iktar li jkun motivat lejn xi sengħa imma aktarx dawk illi jiddejqu, jew għax m' humiex kapaċi jew għax ma jridux l-iskola.	Now it is more apparent in trade schools because, as you know, they do not attract those who have eh, those who are most motivated for a trade but most probably those who are fed up either because they are not capable or because they don't want schooling.

Closely linked to this is a second approach, whereby the deficit is identified in the student's family rather than in the student herself. This view is particularly well underscored in the following excerpt taken from a local newspaper (*Sunday Times*, 25 June 1989):

> Most children of school age are interested in the work adults do.(...) Some parents take advantage of this trait in their children to obtain gainful employment for them while they are still below school-leaving age.(...) Many secondary schools face a high percentage of absenteeism for both boys and girls as a result of this clandestine employment...

The data suggest a third factor to explain absenteeism, namely that rather than the students or their families, it is the school which is to blame. Thus, students stay away to shelter themselves from what they consider to be an unpleasant experience (cf. Corrigan, 1979), to challenge the value of schooling itself (cf. Willis, 1976), and/or to respond to pressures arising from their particular situation as classed and gendered beings and to which the school is insensitive (cf. Reid, 1985). In this particular paper, I will focus on the third explanation, which is that given by students. It is a definition of a situation put forth by social actors – 'deviants' – whose voice is often neither acknowledged or even heard. This means that the finger is pointed at the school system, rather than at the absenting student.

Blaming the Victim or the Institution?

Many of the absentees I interviewed found schooling an unpleasant experience and most of them attributed their non-attendance to this fact:

Author	Int kuntenta li qed terġa' tiġi l-iskola?	Are you happy that you have returned to school?
Angela	Insomma, għax jien taf x'idejjaqni hawn hi, għax it-teachers peress li jarawni ngħajjat, kull ħaġa li tiġri jwaħħlu fija. Diġà fallejt ta... kemm ili niġi.	Not really. Do you know what bothers me here? Since I speak loudly, the teachers blame everything that happens on me. I've already absented myself, you know... since I've returned.
Author	Minn dejjem kont tfalli?	Did you always absent yourself?
Angela	Le minn mindu bdejt niġi din l-iskola. Qabel qatt ma kont fallejt.	No only since I started attending this school. Before that I never used to absent myself.
Author	Fejn kont tmur skola?	Which school did you used to attend?
Angela	Santa Bernarda.	St. Bernarda.
Author	Kont għal qalbek hemm?	Were you happy there?
Angela	Uħħ!	Yes! Quite!

Absenteeism: Deviance, Resistance and Contestation

Author	Għalfejn?	Why?
Angela	Jien naf, kont nieħu gost f'dik l-iskola.	I don't know, I used to enjoy it at that school.
Author	Imbagħad għalfejn ġejt hawn mela?	Then why did you come here?
Angela	Għax jibagħtuk hux.	Because I got sent.

Both interactionist and structuralist functionalist perspectives throw insights on how and why students become disaffected with schooling. Data collected suggest very strongly that absentees are deeply affected by the labelling processes that prevail in Maltese schools, and that they generally consider themselves to be failures and inadequate. Such feelings naturally lead students to feel uncomfortable in schools and classrooms, and absenteeism and truancy are the strategies they employ to escape from such a situation. This leads teachers to further emphasise the label which streaming bestows informally on students. As a result the latter enter into a vicious circle where attempts to escape from negative feelings and self-images end up reinforcing those very same experiences. In addition, labelling theory shows us how students end up accepting the powerful labels used by teachers and think of themselves as ignorant and incompetent.

Ms Sammut	Huma, huma meta ġġegħelhom dik il-ħaġa ta' bilfors, poġġi bil-qegħda u ikteb ta' bilfors, ma jistgħux għaliha, u l-'concentration span' hija żgħira ħafna, f'lesson' ta' 'forty-five minutes' jekk jirnexxilek ikollok 'their full attention for six minutes', hekk 'its the maximum' jiġifieri. 'It's very difficult' eh u biex ikollok tifla bil-qegħda u taqbżilha ma trid xejn.	When you make them do something, sit down and write, it's a must, they can't stand it, and their concentration span is too short, in a lesson of forty-five minutes you might get their full attention for six minutes, that's the maximum. It's very difficult, eh, and it isn't unusual to have a girl sitting quietly and then suddenly she loses her temper.
Carmen	Il-mapep ma nifhimhomx... Gieli kont nifhem u ġieli ma kont	I don't understand maps... Sometimes I used to understand and

nifhem xejn (...) Ġieli kont ngħidilha "ħa mmur it-'toilet'", noqgħod hemm niskanta.	sometimes not at all.(...) Sometimes I used to tell her "Can I go to the toilet?", and I used to stay there staring.

Labelling by significant and powerful others demobilizes and demotivates the best-intentioned of students. But this is not all. There are structural reasons which account for the fact that groups of students must fail at school, besides the reasons which become apparent after an analysis of the ways teachers interact with students. I am here referring to the fact that the Maltese educational system operates on the premise that a number of students must fail, for how else would the labour market, for instance, cope with a very high percentage of successful young people? In order to understand the causes of absenteeism, therefore, we must move away from individualistic to systemic explanations. Thus, if as Sultana (1991, 1992) has argued, the Maltese educational system encourages intra- and inter-school selection and streaming, and trade schools have the important function of channelling students into industry, then selection becomes an important function of schooling. 'Failures', in this context, become inevitable, since they are 'required' by the system.

Symbolic Violence

As most teachers attribute failure to some deficiency on the part of students or their home background, they are not required to question their pedagogy, or the roles they play up at school or in society. The teachers at *It-Torri* in fact adopted a kind of missionary discourse (Da Silva, 1988), constructing a stereotypical image of their students whom they see as suffering from an array of problems caused by their cultural deprivation and home background.

Madam	Veru u taf x'kultura għandhom hux, kultura ta' sess, kliem ħażin u taħwid. Dik hi l-kultura tagħhom. U ma nafx kemm quddiem Alla dawn huma ħatja għax dawn 'they	That's true and do you know what culture they have? A culture of sex, foul language and muddles. That is their culture. And I don't know how guilty they are in God's eyes because they know no better,

know no better' ħi. Huma hekk trabbew. Jien in-nies tal-grupp hekk ngħidilhom, dawn in-nies ma tistax tiġġudikahom għax ma nafx kemm jafu aħjar.	dear. That is how they are brought up. That's what I tell the people in the [prayer] group, you can't judge these people since they know no better.

This not only provided school staff with an explanation for student resistance and absenteeism but gave them a vision of the school as a shelter for students. In this way teachers were consoled by the fact that they were providing some respite to their otherwise troubled students, and at the same time felt justified for having lowered their expectations of academic standards. It also gave them licence to attempt to engrain moral values which were considered to be wanting in the students' homes. Such a simple view of schooling causes teachers to commit on students what Bourdieu (1973) describes as symbolic violence, even if they do so unintentionally. For teachers impose their understanding of the situation, of what counts as culture and what counts as knowledge, without taking into account the definitions which the students themselves might have. In this way, young people in schools are condemned as 'deviant', 'ignorant', 'un-motivated' when in fact they are 'resisting' a system which does not recognize their 'cultural capital', a process which leads them to become 'demotivated'. But often students are not able to articulate these experiences, and the definitions of the powerful lead them to concede to failure and to leave schools with an impaired self-image. They conclude that indeed, they are not intelligent and give up on the project of education.

The very low standards that are achieved within the school convince students of lack of academic ability.

Author	Hemm tfajliet li ma jafux jaqraw?	Are there many girls who can't read?
Doris	Uħħ!	A lot!
Giselle	Jane hi l-ewwel waħda. Dik ma tafx taqra xejn u bl-Ingliż iktar mill-Malti. Dik hi biex taqra bil-Malti tagħmel hekk [*imitates*	Jane, to begin with. She can't read a word in English especially. This is what she does to read in Maltese (...) And

	Jane as she does some very slow phonic sounding sotto voce] (...) U bl-Ingliz xejn. X'inhu xejn? Xejn. (...)	in English nothing. What is nothing? nothing. (...)
Author	Imma Jane mhux xi ħmar.	But Jane isn't stupid.
Giselle	Le brava! Ma twas-salx ħi! Taf kemm hemm hekk, ġdur!	No she's intelligent! She simply hasn't got it! There are so many like her, turnips!

What few teachers seem to realize is that failure does not reside within the students but is located within our institutional structures and mediated through culture (McLaren, 1989). As McLaren explains, the difference of achievement between working class and middle class children comes from the fact that they occupy different positions in what he calls 'decision-fields' which include the family, peers, and work place. These involve particular class and gender relationships. Trade school girls are unwilling to take up the 'cultural capital' which is particularly middle class in its emphasis of the school values related to femininity and work. Instead they draw from working class values which emphasize toughness, sexuality, and a subversive attitude towards authority.

Christine	Shirley ara Ivan! [*On seeing him Shirley sat up and arranged her skirt. She had an embarrassed but pleased smile on her face. She fidgeted with her fluorescent bangles and short cropped hair as she continued to chew on the bubble gum. She looked at the boy and smiled at him though she seemed quite hesitant about the situation. Ivan tried to communicate something but fell back*].	Shirley, there's Ivan.
Jane	Hii madonna! Hemm it-teacher qed tara	Hii Our Lady! The teacher is seeing

	kollox. [*The girls tried to draw Shirley's attention to the presence of the teacher, who was sitting on the steps a few metres away from us. The boy popped up again, waved and went away. A little later the teacher stood up and walked towards us*].	everything.
Christine	Issa mur peċlaq mal-madam ja gażżejja!	Now go and tell the head-mistress, you tell-tale!
Ms. Cortis	Min jien immur ngħid lill-madam?	Who, me, go and tell the headteacher?
Jane	Mela jien.	It won't be me, surely.

Irrelevant Knowledge, Alienating Curricula

The practices of selecting, stratifying, and labelling students represent only a few of the school processes that lead to alienation and absenteeism on the part of specific groups of students. Another feature of schooling which has a similar effect is the rigid distinction between different subjects in the formal curriculum of schools. The strict compartmentalization of knowledge reflects the division of labour in our society, preparing students to accept the fragmentary reality of work (Scott, 1988). This, compounded with a pedagogy that is solely concerned with the transmission of 'knowledge', decontextualizes learning making it completely alien to students' reality (Tripp, 1986). The situation is made worse by virtue of the fact that teachers are given the status of sole experts in the class and students are treated as empty vessels that need to be filled. This means that valuable knowledge is held almost exclusively by the teacher. Students at *It-Torri* often complained about the lack of relationship between what they were obliged to do at school, and the concerns they had in their lives and in the communities where they lived. Such complaints were seldom given any weight and were simply considered as a sign of their unwillingness to 'co-operate' or of their inability to learn.

Sharon	Jien qatt ma smajt b'ħajjata li tagħmel il-'patterns' hekk!	I have never heard of a dressmaker who makes patterns like these!
Ms. Galea	Imma skond x'ħajjata hi. Il-ħajjatin tajbin kollha hekk jagħmluh il-'pattern'.	But it depends on what kind of dressmaker she is. The good ones always make such a pattern.
Nathalie	Eh mela mhux veru ta' għax hija magħruf kemm hu ħajjat tajjeb u fuq id-drapp mill-ewwel ifassal.	That's not true, because my brother is renowned as a tailor and he cuts patterns straight out of the cloth.
Sharon	U mela daqs kemm iddum biex tpingih 'pattern'.	Of course! it takes such a long time to make a pattern.
Ms. Galea	Imm' intom min ikun tal-prattika f'ħames minuti joħorġu dak. Il-ħajjatin li ma jkunux bl-iskola ma jagħmlux hekk.	But you, those who are experienced do this in five minutes. It is those that don't have the theory that skip the pattern.
Nathalie	Eh, jien hija l-iskola tgħallimha l-ħjata.	Eh, my brother learnt tailoring at school!
Claudine	Qed tara l-iskola tgħallimha l-ħjata u veru kulħadd jafu li hu ħajjat tajjeb.	See, he learnt tailoring at school! And it's true he is renowned as a tailor.
Marcona	U mela dawn haw' ma nafx x'qed nagħmlu 'qas biss qed nagħrfu l-'pattern'.	What's the use of this, I don't even know what we're doing. I can't even recognize the pattern.
Ms. Galea	U issa tagħrfuh ħa npinġihulkom bil-ġips tal-kulur. Intom tpinġux bil-kulur għalissa ħa nara x'ħawwadtu. Ara dil-biċċa tiġi 'two', din haw' 'three', qed taraw haw' kif tinqata'.	Now you'll recognize it, I'll draw the outline in coloured chalk. Don't colour yours just yet I want to check what you've muddled. Look this part is two, this here is three, can you see how it will be cut here.
Marcona	Imma miss x'hemm għalfejn?	But Miss what's the use?
Ms. Galea	Ara hi mhux ħa tipperswaduni. Dan il-ħajjatin jagħmluh f'ħames minuti u anke	Look here you are not going to persuade me. Dressmakers do this in five minutes, and so

| intom imiskom, li ma kontux injoranti. Imma intom biex tmeru biss tinqalgħu. | should you if you weren't ignorant, you should be able to do it in five minutes. But you are only capable of contestation. |

There were a few teachers who did not take this stand and instead encouraged the emergence of the students' point of view in their class. Such a pedagogy was successful with students during a Personal Care lesson. Here, students who had, during other lessons, been defined as deviant and unruly, co-operated with the teacher, paid attention, and invested a lot of energy into what they were asked to do. There were not more than fifteen girls in the class seated in a wide U shape facing the teacher. The lesson was on pregnancy. The girls seemed very interested, and the teacher was answering the girls' questions; students often referred to what they had heard especially if this did not confirm what the teacher had just said. This developed into an interesting discussion towards which both teacher and students contributed. Eventually the teacher took out a typed note, in a plastic folder from her file and read it out to them. Two girls went out of their seat to the dressers. They took a pile of attractively covered files and distributed them. In the meantime, the teacher distributed copies of the hand-out she had just read. They too were in plastic folders. The girls shared them, found the appropriate page and copied the note and some drawings. This continued till the end of the lesson and though there was some noise the girls seemed to be taking the task quite seriously. It is significant that one absentee had said she liked this subject because it was adult.

A Waste of Time

A schooling which does not connect with the everyday realities of life can hardly be expected to provide students with motivation. When I visited the school as the students were doing their finals, the atmosphere was very calm. Most students finished very early, especially if the paper was of an academic nature. There were a number of conversations going on in the classes but this did not disturb the teachers as they knew there was little they could copy from each other. They only checked students' behaviour when the head was in sight. For the exam session 1989-90, none of the students was awarded a final certificate because not one of the students passed in all the subjects. Schooling is made even more vulnerable when students decide they do not need the extrinsic rewards (grades or certificates) on offer. The emphasis on extraneous compensation not only affects students' attendance but also has other long-term implications. As Bowles & Gintis (1976) have argued, students are socialized to expect little intrinsic gratification from work. The lowering of standards, so that there was only a semblance of work, combined with students' resistance and informal mobility meant that school was essentially a waste of time and so was easily dropped once other, more serious demands were made upon the students.

Author	Kif sibt taħdem?	How did you find work?
Giselle	Jien? Din konna morna darba, kont iddejjaqt l-iskola, u kien bagħat għalija u ma ridtx immur naħdem. Umbagħad mort.	Me? We went once, I was fed up with school, and he sent for me and I didn't want to go to work. And then I went.
Author	Għax kont tgħidli ma ridtx taħdem ġo fabbrika.	Because you used to say you didn't want to work in a factory.
Giselle	Imma qegħda għal qalbi. Għax qegħdin għoxrin biss.	But I'm happy. Because we're only twenty.

Students who did not engage in the same kind of resistant behaviour as their friends were even more reluctant to go to school, given that school not only failed to provide an opportunity to learn, but was not even a form of social diversion.

Author	It-tfajliet f'liema sens idejquk?	Why did the other students bother you?
Veronica	Għax, hekk, jagħmlu ħafna storbju. 'Qas tkun tista' tagħmel xejn. Il-ħin kollu jtellfu. Għalxejn uħ tmur l-iskola.(...)	Because, well, they are very rowdy. You can't do anything. They are always disturbing. It was useless going to school.

Culture Clash

Schools of course do make efforts to make their curricula responsive to the needs and interests of their students. In the case of girls' trade schools, the curriculum reflects the presumed interest girls have in the preparation for their unquestioned future role as wives and mothers. But the understanding of these roles differs between teachers and students because of the latter's different class location. Thus, the facts and skills related to these two roles that were taught at school often came into conflict with practices at home. As McRobbie (1978) points out, here lies one of the major contradictions of the dynamics of schooling. On one hand, school is perpetuating the cultural role set for women by preparing these students for the traditional adult role; on the other hand it is placed against the family of these students in that the norms which it promotes pertain to the middle class perception of the family. According to Bourdieu (1973), each social class arrives at a particular world view resulting from a correlation of factors such as value systems, perceptions and meanings which are embedded in the social location of that class. Therefore each social class has its own habitus, but in promoting the middle-class perception of family, and other norms, as the only or best ones in society, the school is alienating its students and at the same time committing the kind of symbolic violence I have referred to earlier.

| Ms. Camenzuli | (...) ikollna ħafna 'barriers' għax aħna s-suġġett kif inhu, 'strictly speaking very directly' mal-'home life'. Allura meta qed ngħidilhom 'manners and habits' ta' per eżempju, "You shouldn't smoke' fil-kċina", ta' 'hygiene' u hekk, tiskanta kemm joħroġ il-'family background'. | (...) we face many barriers in this subject as it is, strictly speaking, very directly related to home life. So when we speak about manners and habits of, say, "You shouldn't smoke in the kitchen", of hygiene and that kind of thing, it's amazing how their family background comes out. |

Second, the predominant language used in text books, hand-outs, and charts is English. Edwards (1980) correctly notes that use of the second language could serve to alienate students who are not confident in the language. Such an unquestioned use of a second language can be seen as an extension of the cultural imposition I have just described.

Turning to the Community

Given this state of affairs, girls find that school does not help them acquire the feminine identity that they require. The home therefore remains the more important 'informal agency of education' (McRobbie, 1978) for these girls. It is here that students learn about their future role as there is no basic contestation of values related to social class. The girls actively make provisions for their future. They seek to form lasting relationships with boys with a view to marriage from a very tender age and they participate in household chores, sometimes assuming roles of major responsibility.

Author	U kemm ilek miegħu? Sentejn?	And how long have you been dating him? Two years?
Nathalie:	Eh, mela erba' snin.	No, four years.
Author	Ill! Kellek tnax-il sena meta bdejt toħroġ miegħu?	So were you twelve years old when you started going out with him?
Nathalie:	Ħdax! Imma mbagħad wara ftit kont għalaqt tnax-il sena.	Eleven! But I soon turned twelve.
Author	Issa fadlilkom biex tiżżewwġu?	Will you be getting married soon?
Nathalie:	Boqq.	Dunno.
Author	Imma bdejtu taħsbu għal xi ħaġa?	But do you have any plans?
Nathalie:	Eħe, krejna 'flat', haw' Ħal Niedu stess, ta' nannuh.	Yes, we have rented a flat, here in Ħal Niedu from his grandfather.

In turn, mothers tend to treat their daughters as adults, allowing them the responsibility of choice over such matters as school attendance. In part this is probably because mothers do not see school as providing any worthwhile experiences for their daughters.

Absenteeism: Deviance, Resistance and Contestation

Diane's mum	Ma nafx qisha, qisha, sugu ta' xejn, għax ank' hi kienet qed tgħidli mhix qegħda għal qalbha... Mhux bħal meta kienet Pinto, ifhimni (...) ma' l-imħarbtin. Griefex wisq dik l-iskola naraha jien.	I don't know, there does not seem anything worthwhile, because even she used to tell me she was not happy... Not like when she was at Pinto (...) they're too troublesome. I think that school is far too disorderly.

On the other hand, Willis (1977) commented that in working-class family relations adolescents are considered to be independent. Absentees sometimes have to act as substitutes for their mothers who work – given that responsibility for housework falls exclusively on females and state-funded support systems, such as daycare centres, are non-existent. Such a state of affairs is quite typical of patriarchal societies where, as McRobbie (1981) shows, men expect to be serviced within the family and this expectation is met by the women. Furthermore, these absentees identify with their adult role and, for the time being, pride themselves in their responsibilities. Very much like Willis's lads, (1977) the girls are eager to take up such roles.

Susan	Hi [oħtha] għandha tnejn [tfal], dejjem miegħi u mbagħad hemm ħija. Iġennuni ta! Għandi ħija mqareb ma nafx kif raqad illum, mhux is-soltu jmur jorqod imma kont qed innaddaf u ntefa' fuq is-sodda u raqad.	She [her sister] has two [children], they are always with me and then there is my brother. They drive me mad! My brother is really mischievous I don't know how he slept today. He doesn't usually go to sleep but I was cleaning and he slumped on the bed and fell asleep.
Author	Jiġifieri qisu kulħadd għadu jdur qisu inti għadek il-'mummy' tal-familja.	So everyone depends on you as though you were the mother.
Susan	Qisni jiena! Kollox jien. Issa għadni kif ħsilt 'il-[?] missieri. Qalli "Aħsilli l-ħwejjeġ". Issa għadni kif ħsilt is-Sibt imma m'n Alla tkun il-'washing	It's as if I were. I do everything. I have just washed the [?] of my father. He told me "Wash my clothes". I had just done the washing on Saturday, thank God for

	machine'. Għax ħsilt ħasla ħwejjeġ! L-aħħar darba għedtlu "laqqas li lukanda hawnhekk, kollkom imbarazz".	the washing machine. Because I had a load! Last time I told him "This is worse than being in a hotel".

Similarly they are eager to start work because, though on the whole they do not seem to expect fulfilment at their jobs, at least there are financial returns.

Author	Mela qed terġa' tiġi?	Are you attending again?
Nathalie	X'taghmel?	What can I do?
Author	X'kien?	How come?
Nathalie	Għax qed jibagħtuli ċ-ċitazzjonijiet hu.	Because they sent the summons.
Author	Aħjar haw' imma?	Is it better here, though?
Nathalie	Eh, aħjar taħdem ħa taqla' l-flus.	It's better at work, it earns you money.

Attending school therefore is not valued by some girls as they realize that school qualifications are not indispensable. Whereas preparation for marriage is catered for in the home, work is easily found even before the school course is finished. So they reject what the school has to offer as matters are complicated with what they consider unnecessary and irrelevant knowledge.

Author	(...) apparti x-xogħol jiġifieri, taħsbu li hi utli l-iskola jew taħsbu li ma kontu titgħallmu xejn li hu utli?	(...) apart from work, that is, do you think that education is useful or did you feel that it was a waste of time?
Cynthia	Le, edukazzjoni jekk trid taf iġġibha waħdek. Għax jekk ħa titkellem ma wieħed pulit, ħa titkellem bħalu bil-pulit. Jekk titkellem ma wieħed annimal, t'annimal ħa titkellem bħalu. Jiġifieri ma' min tiltaqa' trid tagħmilha.	No, you can educate yourself if you want to. Because if you speak to someone who is polite, you speak to him in the same way. If you speak to someone who is an animal, then you are going to speak roughly, like him. So you have to adjust your behaviour to the person.

Absenteeism: Deviance, Resistance and Contestation

Certainly, as one mother pointed out, absentees did not seem to have much difficulty in finding a job in the underground economy but school was not found to have been particularly an asset in acquiring a job.

	[*The mother was showing me the family album*]	
Gabbie's mum	Dan ara t-tifel. Hemm-hekk qiegħed jaħdem [?] kok qiegħed. Kok tajjeb hu!	Look this here is my son. He is working with [?] as a chef. It's a good job eh!
Author	U żgur ħafna.	Of course.
Gabbie	U jiġifieri ma kienx jaf skola dak.	And he didn't know any school.
Gabbie's mum	U mbierek Alla jagħ-laq fej huwa fis-sbatax ta' Novembru jagħlaq erbatax, eh erba' snin hemmhekk fej' qiegħed. Qatt ma ħabbatni għax-xogħol 'qas xejn. Da' ilu jaħdem xi disa' snin. [*Previously I was told he was just twenty years old.*](...) Jesmond ma ħabbatnix għax-xogħol, u di' la ġrejt magħha u dan, Giselle qaltli "is-sinjur għidtlu 'il-ħabiba', qalli 'ġibha'", ħadtha. Qalli "nhar it-tnejn tibda x-xogħol".	And bless God, on the seventeenth of November it will be his fourteenth, eh fourth year there, on his job. He never gave me any trouble as far as work is concerned. He has been working for the past nine years. (...) Jesmond posed no problems with work and this one, I didn't even have to go around with her, Giselle told me, "I mentioned my friend to the boss, and he told me, 'Bring her along'". I took her. He told me, "She will start work on Monday".

Willis (1981) contends that this suspicion of formal learning is shared throughout the working class, as there is some intuition that it is used by the middle class not simply to inform their practice but also as a means of legitimizing their social position. Others, however, acknowledge the value of qualifications as they might help them gain access to better jobs. In such instances the girls go for private lessons to learn what is not available to them at school.

Ritienne	...irid ikollok xi ħaġa biex tidħol is-'sixth form'?	...what do you need to go to sixth form?

Author	'Six 'O' levels'.	Six 'O' levels.
Ritienne	Mit-trade-school ma tidħolx is-'sixth form' għax ma tagħmel xejn.	You can't go to sixth form from the trade school because you don't do anything.
Author	Imm' int qed tagħmel is-'City & Guilds'.	But you are sitting for the City & Guilds.
Ritienne	Imm' għax mort l-'evening classes'. Nispera li ngħaddi għax inkun ħlejt sena.	Only because I go to evening classes. I hope I will pass otherwise I will have wasted a year.
Author	X'ser tagħmel wara li titlaq?	What do you intend to do after you leave?
Ritienne	'Qas naf.	I don't know.

Power and Resistance

Earlier on in the paper I referred to the fact that pedagogical practices have important implications on the power relations within a school. Bowles & Gintis (1976) point out that the organization and the relationships in schools reflect economic needs in as much as they reproduce the same hierarchical paradigm rather than a more participative mode of relating. The relationships within *It-Torri* are very hierarchical leaving students with no formal control over their educational experience.

Ms Busuttil	Kieku kellek karta tat-transfer kienet taċċettak, imma int kif qbadt u ġejt haw' mingħajr il-karta tat-transfer?	If you had the transfer permit she would have accepted you, but why did you just come here without a transfer permit?
Ms Bellizzi	Għax haw' oħtha al-lura ġiet hi ukoll.	Because her sister is here so she came too.
Ms Busuttil	Imm' int ġejt 'trans-ferred' haw'?	But were you transferred here?
Student	Le ġejt jien.	No I just came here.
Ms Busuttil	Eh, hekk sew kieku, insib xi dar u mmur fiha, u ngħidilhom "haw' ġejt jien!"	Oh, that would be fine, I would find a house and go inside and I'd tell them [the owners] "I just came here!"

Absenteeism: Deviance, Resistance and Contestation

Ms Bellizzi	Irid ikollok transfer ħija biex tiġi haw'. Mel' aħna hekk, naqbdu u nagħmlu li jfettlilna. Smajtha x'qaltlek hu? Trid tobdi. Int m'intx 'trouble' bħal oħtok hu?	You need the transfer permit to be able to come here. We can't just do as we please? You heard what she told you. You have to obey. You wouldn't be a trouble maker like your sister, would you?

Classroom practices are equally hierarchical as teachers assume the role of experts and students are expected to follow their teachers' instructions. Students are given few opportunities to take their own initiative and sometimes when students try to do something on their own their attempts are met with criticism.

Stephanie	Miss, jien ġibt dan.	Miss I brought this.
Sharlene	Hi, jien lestejtu d-dar ġie ikrah bil-ħotba f'rasu.	Oh, I finished mine at home, it's really ugly, it has a hump on its head.
Ms Grech	Imma dak għax għamiltu waħdek; dawk li għamluh fil-klassi ma ġihomx bil-ħotba.	But that's because you sewed it up on your own, those who did it in class don't have a hump.
Christine	Eh tiegħi ukoll bil-ħotba, ġie ikrah.	Well mine too has a hump, it's really ugly.
Sharlene	Iss, mhux inti m'għamiltulix!	It's not fair, you didn't want to make it up for me.
Ms Grech	Ijwa Sharlene ħi kif nista' nagħmel disgħin teddy bear jien! [*The teacher took out a set of books from a locked cupboard and sent one of the girls to fetch a pile of copybooks from the staff room. The girls were given a book and a copy-book each and made to copy a note on hems. As they did so the girls chatted, roamed about the class and even into the corridor unless the head*	Well Sharlene, dear how could I make up ninety teddy-bears myself!

*was in sight. Some
girls from another
class came in and
formed discussion
groups with the girls
in the class. In the
meantime the teacher
was kept busy trying
to supervise the girls
and sewing the teddy
bear till the end of
the lesson*].

This type of exchange can be likened to Jean Anyon's (1980) description of a working class school, whose hidden curriculum (that is the messages given explicitly by the rituals, symbols and social interaction organized by the school) is important for the way it prepared students for working class jobs. Within the educational system, hierarchical relationships are not justified on economic grounds but rather on an educational rationale. Paul Willis (1981) indicates that our concept of teaching is based on an exchange: knowledge for the respect of authority. This exchange occurs within a framework which places the teacher in a position of superiority. The framework is established by the school ethos. The distribution of space at *It-Torri* is, for instance, a very clear indication of this framework. The head has her own office and a private toilet, the teachers share a staff-room and a toilet. The students have no private space of their own except for the toilets and these too are regulated by the key in the headmistress' office. Manifestations of this hierarchy in relationships are evident in almost every other aspect of school life, the positions taken up during assembly, the continuous control over student behaviour from which staff is free, and the ratio of time spent in self expression by teachers and students during a lesson all help in establishing and maintaining this framework. Ideally the framework is justified on the basis of the exchange which, as Willis points out, can be examined for its fairness. But at *It-Torri* students have, to a large extent, refused school knowledge and so come to challenge authority in very direct ways.

Given that many students feel that they gain nothing or very little which is relevant to them from school they resent even more being subjected to this type of regime. It is not surprising therefore that they should rebel to the extent that they refuse to go to school especially since they have greater freedom of choice at home.

Carmen	Jien, ngħid għalija, aħjar noqgħod hawn ġewwa milli l-iskola.	As far as I'm concerned, I'm better off here than at school.
Author	Għaliex?	Why?
Carmen	L-iskola qisha ħabs għalija. Ara ġewwa, jekk tiddejjaq ġewwa tista' toħroġ barra.	School is like a prison to me. At home, if you are fed up with staying inside you can go out.

As Furlong and Bird (1981) point out students have little opportunity of expressing their dislike of school and if they want to protest they can only do so either by being disruptive or else by staying away. Corrigan (1979) claims that schooling was made compulsory precisely to curb such an action. Students in turn respond with masked truancy, that is, by staying away from specific lessons or by being disruptive.

Students at *It-Torri* did not find the present educational welfare service set up to solve the problem of absenteeism as fair.

Author	...Jiġifieri, intom kontu tagħmlu ċ-ċertifikati u tibagħtuhom l-iskola. U qatt ġiet dik tal-'welfare'?	And you used to send medical certificates to school. Were you ever visited by the welfare officer?
Cynthia	Għandi qatt ma ġiet. Imma bagħat għalija it-tabib ta' l-iskola. Qalli "għax qed tagħmel dawn iċ-ċertifikati?" Qalli "l-iskola trid tmur bil-fors!" Għidtlu "bil-fors għalfejn?" Għidtlu "jien ma rridx immur skola". Għidtlu "jaqbadni attakk nervuż". Qalli "x'iġifieri" qalli. "Trid tmur". Beda jgħajjat miegħi. Għidtlu "toqgħodx tgħajjat għax jien m' inix it-tifla tiegħek".	She never came for me. But the school doctor sent for me. He told me, "Why are you sending these certificates?" He said, "School attendance is compulsory!" I told him, "Why compulsory?" I told him "I don't want to go to school". I told him, "I get nervous attacks". He said, "What do you mean". He said, "You must go". He started yelling at me. I told him, "Don't yell, I'm not your daughter".

Għidtlu "l-iskola jien m'inix sejra". Qalli "mela agħmel li trid". Qalli "u issa jekk jibagħtulek iċ-ċitazzjonijiet, affarik", qalli. Imbagħad għamilt xahar immur strejt, wara reġgħu waslu l-eżamijiet u erġajt qbadt ma mortx.

I told him, "I'm not returning to school". He said, "Do as you please". He said "and now if they fine you it's your business", he said. Then I attended for a whole month, then there were the exams and I didn't go any more.

Students 'attending' *It-Torri* are much more assertive in the way they expressed their disaffection with school than are the adolescent girls described by Sara Delamont in her overview of research carried out in England (Delamont, 1980). One reason could be that *It-Torri* is an all girls' school whereas educational provision in England is mainly co-educational. Feminist writers have expressed a preoccupation with co-education as, among other things, girls seem to receive further pressure from their male counterparts to conform with their gender stereotype by outwardly complying more to school rules, leaving deviant behaviour to boys, who end up gaining more attention. The behaviour of students in *It-Torri* in fact, could be likened much more with that of Willis lads.

(...) tidgħi u titpastaż iktar turi kemm inti brava. Dak li trid biex tkun intelliġenti illum, mhux skola tkun taf titkellem ħazin u titpastaż. Mhux veru. Xejn dat-tfajliet m' hemm x'tagħmel magħhom.

(...) swear and be vulgar, that's the way to show how smart you are. That's what you need to show you're intelligent these days, not schooling, but to know how to use foul language and be vulgar. Isn't that true. There's nothing to be done with these girls.

This deviant behaviour has a two-fold effect. First, the girls have made it very difficult for educational authorities to ignore their problems – though the response was simply to further buttress the system by introducing a welfare officer who must somehow cope with what is, for the time being, a hopeless situation. Secondly, as McRobbie (1978) points out, through their own resistance, paradoxically, the girls are willingly taking up the role towards which all institutions, including the school, are leading them. As students turn to their developing gender identities to add resonance to their resistance, (modifying uniforms to make them more feminine, doing housework instead of going to school) they are preparing themselves to do what their mothers have done before them. The process is very similar to the one described by Willis (1977) who argues that this happens as students only partially penetrate through the ideology of schooling, refusing intellectual work, along with the reality of school, which could be employed to improve their situation. One must not forget however that students at *It-Torri* are being actively channelled by the curriculum into low paid jobs and housewifery and an active participation in learning would not have changed their future prospects.

Conclusion

Students at *It-Torri* absented themselves because formal education failed to engage them. Through such processes as selection, they were made to see themselves as failures and, in this way, symbolic violence is committed against them. Curricular content and its organization, along with pedagogical practices, alienate students further so that school attendance is robbed of its educational worth. It is within this context that the hierarchy in power relations is contested and students put up their resistance. In practice, students who attend do so mainly for social diversion and so stop attending as soon as more important demands are made on them. Students that did not fit in with their peers' resistance, absented themselves as disruptions made it impossible for them to learn.

Whereas common sense opinion labels absenteeism as deviant, from the absentees' point of view, it is the 'logical' way to act in the given situation. Policies very much depend on whose view is accepted and here lies the danger in the unquestioned acceptance of labels.

References

Anyon, J. (1980) 'Social class and the hidden curriculum of work', *Journal of Education*, vol. 162, 1.

Bennett, T. et al. (1981) *'Antonio Gramsci'* in *Culture, Ideology and Social Process*, London, Oxford University Press.

Bourdieu, P. (1973) 'Cultural reproduction and social reproduction', in Brown, R. (ed.) *Knowledge, Education and Social Change*, London, Tavistock.

Bowles, S., & Gintis, H. (1976) *Schooling in Capitalist America*, London, Routledge & Kegan Paul.
Corrigan, P. (1979) *Schooling the Smash Street Kids*, London, Macmillan.
Da Silva, T.T. (1988) 'Distribution of school knowledge and social reproduction in a Brazilian urban setting', *British Journal of Sociology of Education*, vol. 9, 1.
Delamont, S. (1980) *The Sociology of Women*, London, Allen & Unwin.
Edwards, A.D. (1980) 'Perspectives on classroom language', *Educational Analysis*, vol. 2, 2.
Felsenstein, D. (1987) *Strategies for Improving School Attendance in Combating School Absenteeism*, London, Hodder & Stoughton.
Fenech, D. (1991) 'Phantoms of the classrooms: Why students stay away', unpublished B.Ed.(Hons.) dissertation, University of Malta, Faculty of Education.
Furlong, J. & Bird, C. (1981) 'How can we cope with Karen', *New Society*, 2 April.
Glaser, B.G. & Strauss, A.L. (1967) *The Discovery of Grounded Theory: Strategies for Qualitative Research*, Chicago, Aldine.
Guidance and Counselling Unit (1988) *Report on the Prevalence of Absenteeism in Twelve Trade Schools in Malta and Gozo* (mimeo), Malta, Department of Education.
McLaren, P. (1989) *Life in Schools*, New York, Longman.
McRobbie, A. (1978) 'Working class girls and the culture of femininity', in *Women's Study Group, Women Take Issue: Aspects of Women's Subordination*, Birmingham, Centre for Comparative Cultural Studies.
McRobbie, A. (1981) 'Settling accounts with subcultures: a feminist critique', in Bennet, T. (ed.) *Culture, Ideology and Social Process*, London, Oxford University Press.
Reid, K. (1985) *Truancy and School Absenteeism*, London, Hodder & Stoughton.
Scott, M. (1988) 'Teach her a lesson: Sexist curriculum in patriarchal education', in Spenser, D. & Sarah, E. (eds) *Learning to Lose*, London, The Women's Press.
Shor, I., & Freire, P. (1987) *A Pedagogy for Liberation*, London, Macmillan.
Sultana, R.G. (1991a) 'Social class and educational achievement in Malta', in Sultana, R.G. (ed.) *Themes in Education – A Reader*, Msida, Malta, Mireva Publications.
Sultana, R.G. (1991b) 'Educational inquiry: qualitative research and grounded theory methodology', *South Pacific Journal of Teacher Education*, vol. 19, 1.
Sultana, R.G. (1992) *Education and National Development: Historical and Critical Perspectives on Vocational Schooling in Malta*, Msida, Malta, Mireva Publications.
Tripp, D.H. (1986) 'Greenfield: a case study of schooling, alienation and employment', in Fensham, P. (ed.) *Alienation from Schooling*, London, Routledge & Kegan Paul.
Willis, P.E. (1977) *Learning to Labour: How Working Class Kids Get Working Class Jobs*, Farnborough, Saxon House.
Willis, P.E. (1981) 'Class and institutional form of counter-school culture', in Bennet, T. (ed.) *Culture, Ideology and Social Process*, London, Oxford University Press.

21

A Politician and His Audience: Malta's Dom Mintoff

Jeremy Boissevain

Every successful 'Big-Man' must occasionally speak in public, whether to plead his own cause or to defend those of his followers. His object is to persuade and influence his audience. He often does this by showing that his message is merely a common sense extension of already accepted truths. This is certainly true of Dom Mintoff, Malta's erstwhile peppery and persuasive socialist prime minister, who has been a major figure on the island's political scene for more than forty years. I attempt to analyze his very successful rhetorical techniques by examining one of the public speeches he delivered when he was still prime minister.

This analysis serves a number of sociological purposes. To begin with, it shows how systems of power are inhabited by real people who have their own personalities, idiosyncrasies and understandings of situations. Secondly it indicates the 'character' of the people that rallied to hear them.

Too much emphasis is generally placed by certain brands of sociological writing on structures and occasionally on roles – without adequate attention being given to the social actors involved (Boissevain, 1974, pp. 1-23). These actors may author their own scripts as they stride through history. Like Mintoff in this particular case study, they make considered, if occasionally instinctive, choices as they select from alternative possibilities of action in order to position their audience in particular ways. It is in such particular positioning that power relations are built, extended and approved.

In this particular episode, Mintoff draws ably on cultural resources he shares with his audience, where linguistic register, humour and folk wisdom are combined to construct a special event. What stands out most from these cultural artifacts is perhaps the notion of *għaqal*, a basic Maltese virtue: a combination of reason, soundness, respect for money, and the ability to make the best of any situation.

This discussion is introduced with a brief sketch of Dom Mintoff – the man and his charisma – as well as with highlights of the 1976 social context in which the speech at hand was delivered. Only extracts from the speech are herewith reproduced, due to space limitations.

Dom Mintoff

Dominic Mintoff was born in Cospicua, the industrial heart of the Grand Harbour area, in 1916. His parents were comfortably-off working-class people, his father serving as a cook in the Royal Navy. Mintoff was briefly a student at the Archbishop's Seminary and completed his education at the Government Lyceum and the Royal University of Malta. He obtained his B.Sc. in 1937, and a degree in engineering and architecture in 1939. He then received a Rhodes scholarship and earned a MA in engineering at Oxford in 1941. After working as a civil engineer in Britain from 1941-1943, he returned to Malta and was appointed General Secretary of the Malta Labour Party in 1944. In 1945 he was elected as a Member of the Council of Government which prepared the way for the reintroduction of the

Maltese Parliament, to which he was elected in 1947. That year he also married Moyra de Vere Bentinck, the daughter of a prominent British fabian socialist. He took over the leadership of the MLP in 1949 after a bitter internal faction dispute. He held on to this post until 1983, when he relinquished it voluntarily.

Upon assuming the leadership, he set about moulding the party into a sound organization based on village-level clubs. Between 1955 and 1958, he was the Prime Minister of Malta, and afterwards leader of the opposition until the MLP was re-elected to power in 1971. Under his leadership the organization of the MLP was strengthened. He became the party's chief symbol, its undisputed leader. His tactical skill, knowledge of the local political scene, his eloquence and energy all combined to endow him with unprecedented power.

Mintoff's Charisma

Dom Mintoff unquestionably had, and still has, charisma. As leader of the Malta Labour Movement, he was hard driving, energetic and tough. After 450 years of foreign rule designed to produce docile subjects and gentle Christians, such qualities were obviously as admired by the people as they were scarce. At the helm of government, Mintoff worked long hours, expecting others to do likewise. He could be harsh, even cruel, verbally lashing and battering, punishing where he encountered opposition or incompetence. He was respected and feared. Subordinates consequently passed all major decisions up to him, thereby increasing his already considerable power. Above all he was firm, rarely admitting error, consulting with few. Yet, if the occasion demanded, he could be immensely charming and hospitable. He radiated an aura of confidence, of knowing exactly what he wanted and what he was doing. He behaved, in short, like the traditional Maltese father – aloof, manly, harsh and looked after his own (Boissevain, 1979). This authoritarian figure was familiar to all Maltese. Most of them had grown up in and formed part of families dominated by such fathers.

Mintoff also had a reputation for being physically tough. Even when over sixty, he kept up his daily swim all through the year, water skied, rode horseback and bowled, all with great vigour. His physical toughness was epitomized for many by his 1974 accident. He was allegedly kicked unconscious by his horse, hospitalized and required thirty-five stitches. The impact of a horseshoe was clearly visible when he appeared on television shortly afterwards. Many people do not get up after being kicked in the head by a stallion. Yet Mintoff's survival was no more than most people expected. Such was his image of toughness.

This toughness and his willingness to strike hard and swiftly have stood him in good stead in negotiating. He ordered followers to cut down cable radio poles all over the island when the British governor refused to recall a message barring Maltese fishing boats from a bay during the 1956 Suez crisis. Fifteen years later he 'drove' the British off the island because they would not meet his new terms for their use of the island as a military base.

When he threatened action he did not bluff. This firmness won him much admiration from working-class Maltese. For them, Mintoff is a man's man. He has become something of a cult object. Though he has now given up smoking, during the '50s and '60s his pipe became his personal symbol. Bowling (*boċċi*) and horseback riding became popular sports in Malta after Mintoff took them up. Even his style of dress was copied. Many devotees took to wearing large belt-buckles in imitation of the giant buckle he wore when dressing casually, as he normally did. But if he wore a tie, all his associates put on one, even in hot weather. If he appeared without one, they removed theirs.

Keeping people off balance was one of his techniques of ruling. Would he wear a tie or come with an open collar? Uncertainty generally prevailed. Visitors were summoned suddenly, often late at night, to discuss weighty matters. Dignitaries invited to his country hideaway, *L-Għarix*, for Sunday lunch were often disconcerted by his working class table guests, or completely confused when he disappeared into the kitchen with cronies for the duration of the visit. What would Mintoff do next?

His person, his style, even his idiosyncrasies became Labour Party symbols. Up till 1983, many a Labour supporter was a *mintoffjan*, (mintoffian), and some still are nowadays. These mintoffians were devoted and obeyed him unquestioningly. This provided him with a comfortable base of support, which could, if necessary, be formed into a fist. He was an undisputed leader – like the traditional Maltese father.

Mintoff's Rhetoric

It is generally acknowledged both by Mintoff's supporters and his enemies that, for a considerable period of time, he was the island's first orator. He applied his rhetorical skills in both private and public spheres. As already mentioned, his private confrontations with the party officials, ministers and senior civil servants who surrounded him were often harsh. His public appearances, however, fell into a number of distinct categories, each of which was characterized by its own rhetorical style. There were the semi-public annual party conferences, during which he was normally at his persuasive best. Then there were the parliamentary debates in which he could be both persuasive and eloquent, if the occasion demanded, but often also harsh, sarcastic and crude. In parliament, he was as prime minister masterly at finding a small chink in his opponents' defence, often picking on a minor issue and exploiting it to the full. In the ensuing debate the main issue would be ignored, with his opponents being kept off balance by his ferocious heckling. Nationalist members of parliament and leading lawyers have told me that they considered themselves fortunate that Mintoff was not a lawyer as he would have deprived them of their choicest cases. In addition, Mintoff made periodic appearances on television and at specially arranged outdoor meetings. His television appearances were usually serious, benign and statesman-like. He then dressed conservatively. He announced new targets or economic measures, or reported some achievement. Armed with detailed statistics, he could be very persuasive. As a critical columnist noted,

> The Prime Minister must be the only person in the whole wide world who can make a sizeable increase in the price of gas and electricity sound as if it were a sizeable decrease (*Sunday Times of Malta* 24 February 1974).

Mintoff at a mass political rally

Mintoff's outdoor speeches provided both information and entertainment. Let us imagine ourselves to be present at such a meeting. Among several speakers slated to appear, he is usually the last. He arrives towards the end of the preceding speech, which is interrupted by cheers and whistles as Mintoff takes his place on the podium. This serves to emphasize to all and sundry

– including the speaker – that he is number one. When he rises to speak, the audience breaks into a deafening din of whistles and firecrackers. He holds up his hand for silence. When he finally lowers it, he smiles and greets them with *'Ħbieb!'* ('Friends!') or *'Merħba!'* ('Welcome!').

He begins slowly in a friendly, paternal tone. This is always refreshing, following, as it does, the frenzied demagoguery and ranting styles of the earlier speakers. He is at his best attacking his opponents. His style is slow, direct and clear, and his messages are repeated several times. His speeches are good entertainment. He delights in amusing his audience by telling stories that ridicule the Nationalists or reminding them of some simple aspect of the poverty of the past in the *Tal-Bastjun* area of Cospicua. He is vague about just how far in the past, thus telescoping time, and building a bridge between then and now, between them and him. He does this by saying: 'I remember when I was young ...' and goes on to describe how, before the war, vendors used to sell *'gaxinn'* (left-overs) collected from naval kitchens, how people used to eat pieces of bread 'as big as pillows', how fishermen shuffled down to their boats in the early morning. These reminiscences are told in an amusing fashion. Mintoff telegraphs the humour by his chuckles and the tone of his voice.

The experiences are accurately described, and so shared with the poorer members of his audience. They create a direct bond between him and the predominantly working-class audience: he and they have known poverty. Mintoff then goes on to build his argument on this experience.

Mintoff frequently used direct simple similes and crude humour. A dilapidated army barracks can be converted to a holiday camp in the same way as a dash of lipstick converts a tired woman into a tart. The nationalization of foreign firms is no more complicated than getting cows at bargain prices and milking them. These were direct and simple comparisons, but chosen because many also had sexual overtones.

Passing on unpleasant news is one of the more challenging tasks faced by any leader. Normally, Mintoff did this swiftly, seizing a sudden crisis as a lever to implement a long planned but unpopular measure. Thus the oil crisis in 1974 was used to increase government revenue from petrol; a crisis threatening two local banks resulted in their nationalization 'to protect the people's savings'; student unrest in 1977, generated by failure to open the medical school on time (because staff had been sacked as part of Mintoff's confrontation with doctors over planned national health measures), provided the occasion to introduce a long contemplated reorganization of tertiary education. In short he converted crises into opportunities with the aid of his rhetorical skills.

Mintoff also faced unpleasant crises directly. One of the best known local crisis which he met head on occurred in 1973 when he faced the dockyard workers, the hard core of his support in his own constituency. The government-owned dockyard, Malta's largest industry, was rapidly losing money. The metal workers were the most militant section of the pro-Labour General Workers' Union. They rejected all proposals to rationalize the yard's wasteful, permissive setup, a legacy of Royal Navy over-staffing and union muscle. Union officials could not budge them. Furious, Mintoff decided to speak directly to the workers. He called a meeting to take place in the square just outside the dockyard's entrance. Contrary to his usual casual dress at public meetings, he faced them in a dark suit, white shirt and tie, emphasizing his distance from them and the seriousness of his message.

A large audience had gathered from all over Malta. The dockyard workers that attended formed a minority group at the far end of the square. He accused them of laziness, dishonesty and irresponsibility. He then jarred his audience by accusing them, the dockyard workers, of having no balls. A crude, powerful message to Mediterranean men. They were furious and booed him. He then gave them three choices. He would resign (a threat he often made in negotiating with his supporters); he would declare the yard bankrupt; or they would do exactly as he said. He required them to give an immediate answer. He was in a hurry. They had of course little choice, for the entire situation was stage-managed. He asked those who did not want him to remain to raise their hand. No one did. He then asked who wanted to declare the yard bankrupt. Again no one raised a hand. He then stated that the vote on the third choice was not necessary. This was rhetoric on a grand scale. The dockyard's work setup was rationalized, and for a short time reported a profit.

Usually Mintoff's public speeches were much more pleasant occasions. They consisted mainly of a sustained attack on the Nationalists, a report on the Labour Party's progress and, sometimes, plans for the future. He adjusted his rhetoric to his particular audience. His public speech at St. George's Square, Qormi on Saturday, March 27th, 1976 was a typical example.

The Speech at Qormi

Qormi then was a town with a population of some 15,000 farmers, industrial labourers, small businessmen, rural entrepreneurs and bakers. The town had a reputation for being populated by extremely hard-working, shrewd, money-minded people of peasant or working-class backgrounds, who were moving up the economic ladder through their own efforts. There were many poor people in the town, but there were also many rough-and-ready entrepreneurs who had become wealthy in one or two generations.

It was a well-attended mass meeting. Supporters had come by cars and hired buses from all over Malta. As is usual, most local Labour sympathizers, except hard-core *mintoffjani*, stayed in the background. They listened from doorways, half-closed windows and side streets. In a village it never pays to be too obvious about anything.

Mintoff came late, looking fit and energetic. He was dressed in a leather jacket and open shirt, the Labour torch on his huge belt buckle reflecting the cold March light. The speech can be roughly divided into three parts: the first is a rebuttal of the Nationalists' criticism that his government is miserly and has built no hotels; the second part demonstrates the working of state capitalism: government not only saves but also makes money. The final section is an exhortation to vote socialist in the forthcoming general election.

Mintoff begins with a resounding attack on the Nationalists and their earlier government under the premiership of George Borg Olivier. At issue is Nationalist criticism that the Labour government failed to provide a suitable climate for investment by not offering incentives to investors: it had refused to provide grants to hotels, causing hotel building to come to a halt. Mintoff seizes this issue. He easily demonstrates that many hotels had been opened during the Labour period in office. Tourist arrivals had doubled. In the process of elaborating this point, he scores other points off his rivals, and sidesteps the underlying issue: government policy on industrial investment. He ridicules his opponents for having wasted money when they were in power with their grants for hotels. Imagine giving huge presents of the people's money to rich people to help to make them even richer! Here he stresses the already widely-held disapproval of the Nationalist subsidy scheme.

Mintoff does not stop there. To emphasize his point, he provides other examples of the wastefulness of his rivals. He ridicules their high-living junketing. He leaves much unsaid that is common knowledge as he has been over this ground with them many times before. He chuckles over the fact that his rivals have taken a substantial drop in income since they left government, and alludes to kick-backs and so on. Many are unable to leave, he suggests, because there may be other impediments to departure besides poverty, such as involvement in *sub judice* law cases. He skilfully relates a third example of waste through subservience to Britain: the Nationalists squandered public funds on a hotel-sized kitchen that was used only for the Queen's visit.

Next he converts the charge of government 'miserliness' into a compliment. He is 'honoured' to be considered miserly with the people's money. He goes on to show that the policy of not subsidizing hotel building actually benefits the people since the slow-down in hotel building provides tourist tenants for their empty houses. In a final thrust he states that everyone inevitably was tarred by the brush of bribery during the Nationalist period of easy money.

Well away now, he launches into the main section of his speech: the new enterprises his government has created for the people of Malta. He is in fact setting out how state capitalism works. At the same time he gives a lesson in *għaqal*, making the best of every situation. He begins by showing how something profitable can be created out of a wreck. An abandoned military camp is transformed into a holiday camp. Here he gives off a few sexual allusions that greatly amuse his audience. Fixing up an old barrack is like making up a woman; implicit in this is that if an old woman paints herself up to make money, she is a prostitute. He is on to a very good thing, and the crowd is delighted.

He slides over to another sexual metaphor:

> Instead of the people paying taxes to have schools ... we get a military camp – *and now whenever we find a cow, we will milk it.*

Here the sexual innuendo is clearer, for the Maltese word for cow is slang for prostitute. To milk a cow thus also means to live off a prostitute's earnings. Milking is also sexual exploitation, as when a man 'milks' his wife of strength by giving her too many children. The audience roundly applauds his verbal sleight of tongue.

In building up to his metaphor, Mintoff gets in a dig at the British, which is aimed at boosting local pride. He is able to furnish the Holiday Village free of charge. This is because when he threw the British out in 1971, they fled so hurriedly that they left behind them their bombs and furnishings. Left unsaid, because it is self-evident to his audience, is: 'Look how we made our former masters jump!' The Maltese sense of humour is often at someone else's expense.

Having found his splendid milking metaphor, Mintoff now works it for all it is worth. Various fat 'cows' such as banks, the airline, shipping and the dockyard are turned over to the Minister of Finance, Ġużè Abela, who is standing for re-election in the constituency of which Qormi forms part. Ġużè Abela is told over and over to milk them, to drain them, to exploit them. *'Aħleb, Ġuż! Aħleb!'*

In the process Mintoff milks his audience for applause. The crowd loves it. It appreciates not only the crude innuendo, but also the way he plays with it: cows' milk buys milk for children. The public likes being told Malta is getting something for nothing. Moreover, he continues, Air Malta and Sea Malta have freed the Maltese from dependence upon outside carriers – an autonomy that is vital for a small-island economy. Mintoff is proud of having achieved this, and so are most Maltese.

Discussing the dockyard, Mintoff points again to the supposed subservience of the Nationalists to Britain. A wealthy titled Englishman is paid LM 150,000 a year for running the dockyard. He evokes a Nationalist conspiracy of politics and big business by referring to their prime minister as *Capo*, mafia boss. (This is a standard Labour rhetorical cue for the crowd to boo the Nationalists for their alleged corruption.)

The Church is another of Mintoff's regular targets. Members of the Labour Party at all levels still carry with them wounds inflicted by the Church in the 1960s (Boissevain, 1965). Mintoff needs only brush the keys to evoke sympathetic chords from his followers.

Next, Mintoff slowly begins to build up his final 'vote socialist' exhortation. In his lifetime the gap between rich and poor has been reduced considerably, and it would continue to shrink as the Maltese State became more socialist. He appeals directly to the people, reminiscing about a childhood neighbour, a fisherman. He evokes neighbourhood patriotism from his constituents, stressing that he too was brought up in a popular quarter in Bormla. He suggests shared poverty in the past by his detailed description of the fisherman's humble fare. In setting out the poverty and danger fishermen are exposed to, he manages to carry forward the sexual theme begun earlier, for the little fishes which are caught, *għarajjes*, (red sea-bream) is also Maltese for brides. Laughing, he explains that he did not mean the ones you marry off. There was a good bit of ribaldry exchanged at that point, to the public's great delight.

After setting out further steps that he is taking to attain greater self-sufficiency in food production, he winds up by castigating the Nationalists again for squandering the people's money through corruption and bad investments. Reaching the climactic final section, he urges his audience to vote socialist. His final point is a rhetorical question about the future. He has reached his climax, and ends, as he always does, by shouting, '*Malta l-ewwel u qabel kollox!*' ('Malta first and foremost!'). The crowd roars its support.

Discussion

It is evident that Mintoff was able to make his political messages acceptable because he used a simple clear style of presentation and started from a shared experience in poverty. His economic measures made sense to the peasants and the working class. The central themes of the MLP record – those of protecting people's money and state capitalism – are, in the case described above, aptly chosen for his audience of farmers, rural entrepreneurs, labourers, bakers and small businessmen. Past poverty was not God's will, as the Church had argued, and the gap between rich and poor was now closing. Mintoff not only provided an afternoon's entertainment; he also reduced complex national economic affairs to the sort of everyday financial issues his audience is used to dealing with. Rhetorically, national finance becomes no more complex than farming or trading: he set his Minister of Finance to milk the rich cows he has so shrewdly obtained for Malta at bargain rates. State capitalism is a common sense extension of peasant *għaqal*.

His simple, basic and often crude humour was also perfectly attuned to his audience's taste and level of education. His rivals, even colleagues from his own party, lacked this touch. Their public speeches were full of facts and figures, attack and parry, but with little or no humour. But Mintoff's were occasions for the faithful to hear their leader, to see him, to laugh with him at the expense of the opposition. A Mintoff speech strengthened bonds of solidarity, as people physically became part of a movement of thousands. Isolated voters felt united into a group. The transcendental verities he preached were self-determination, pride in self, patriotism, and care for the people's money.

His rhetorical skill was, for him, a major political resource.

References

Boissevain, J., (1965) *Saints and Fireworks: Religion and Politics in Rural Malta*, London, Athlone Press.
Boissevain, J., (1974) *Friends of Friends: Networks, Manipulators and Coalitions*, Oxford, Basil Blackwell.
Boissevain, J., (1979) 'Mintoff en Malta: een heerser met haast', *Symposion*, vol. 1.

22

Rock Music and Counter-Culturalism in Malta

Albert Bell

Introduction

To the untrained eye, Maltese society might appear to be a homogeneous, uniform entity deprived of the cultural pluralism inherent to more complex, industrial societies. Hopefully, this paper will serve to reveal that Malta is also imbued with the existence of a myriad of subordinate, counter-cultures striving to legitimize their own values and life-styles within the prevalent social environment. Confronted by the inertia of the established culture, a counter-culture promulgates a social reality that signals discontent, protest and rebellion against the mainstream forces of social control.

Counter-culturalism, therefore, is the expression of the dissatisfied, structurally marginated youth; it is the epitome of youth resistance and the 'barometer of social change' (Brake, 1985). Counter-cultural formations often flourish beyond the boundaries of conventional art. Indeed they create or adhere to culturally-subversive genres. This is the case with rock music. The rise of rock music to the pinnacle of youth leisure consumption patterns throughout recent decades has spearheaded rock to the forefront of counter-culturalism and youth subcultural association. Through its widespread appeal and international popularization, rock has developed into the embodiment of youth demands for freedom and authenticity and the articulation of value transition. It is the established stereotype of cries for rebellion and self-expression; a 'rebel yell' that cuts across generational, gender, status and even territorial boundaries.

Malta has not been left isolated from this counter-cultural 'rock invasion'. Television, cinema, vinyl outlets, imported music press journals and the tourist in our streets, introduced the local adolescent to the bohemian traditions of generational, adolescent Western rock 'cult' heroes and their stylistic and ritualistic preferences. Ever since the sounds of Bill Haley and the Comets, Elvis, Kay Starr and other trailblazing rockers of the 50's were first heard on the Island, rock 'n' roll and the multitude of its subsequent, hybrid derivations, have influenced affiliation to a legacy of subcultures, imbued with particularistic life-styles, rituals and values. These subcultures have all advocated, in one way or another, a new order of social relations; an order free from the routine and conservatism of traditional Maltese society.

Methodological Concerns

However, despite its evident sociological significance, this phenomenon has rarely captured the interest of local researchers. The scarcity of preceding research in the field makes the objective analysis of Maltese rock configurations and their impact on youth counter-culture quite an arduous task. This article, in attempting to remedy the void in such a fertile ground, could not bank on reference to previous studies on Maltese counter-cultures. Moreover, theories on the evolution, structure and ideology of domestic subordinate youth groupings could only be substantiated by data collected from in-depth interviews conducted with local rock personalities, from Maltese music publications or articles, and from the lyrical contributions of those bands that personify the 'cultural rebel' concept in Malta. This author's involvement and firsthand experience in the field – extending to a decade of participation in various Maltese 'underground' bands – has also yielded further insight into the ideological, stylistic and structural constructs of domestic rock subcultural configurations.

Besides these methodological constraints, the predicament of any study analyzing the relationship between counter-culturalism and rock music in Malta is also accentuated with problems of location. Can rock music and counter-culturalism in Malta be unequivocally considered as indigenous phenomena? After all, could not the studded wristband, long hair or the bullet belt be understood as symbols of adolescent insecurity and icons of passing trends or isolated fads imported from alien Western youth contexts? It is true that association to youth subcultural groupings may be generally interpreted as solutions to problems of status adjustment. However, to dismiss rock movements – prevalent in any social context – as ephemeral trends without any tangible impact on societal arrangement would be to miss the point entirely.

Admittedly, the behavioural and stylistic standards of local rock cohorts are often set by their Western counterparts. Rarely has Malta been able to produce its own distinct forms of rock sub-cultural association. The movements that have come to fruition on Maltese shores often make their appearance long before in foreign social contexts. Yet, the maxim to be followed here is not whether local rock subcultures have enough non-imported, home-grown facets to merit consideration in the analysis of Maltese contemporary society. Rather, what should be of primary concern to such a study is whether these movements have their roots in anti-social ideology and whether they can be envisaged as effective carriers of indigenous counter-cultural change. It is the hypothesis of this paper that – unlike other homespun subcultural formations which are restrained by regional, class and status rigidity – Maltese rock subcultures are instilled with the ability to transcend the boundaries of social differentiation. Hence they enjoy a better position to permeate counter-cultural ideology beyond the rigid echelons of stratified society.

Thus, for example, the 'Punk Rock' movement that erupted in Malta and abroad in the late seventies, (and inspired the more recent 'Hardcore', 'Crossover', and 'Grunge' rages)[1] has encapsu-

---

[1] The genres identified here can all be considered endemic to the post-punk,

lated affiliation from both working-class and middle-class environments. The abrasiveness of this style of music and the anarchic utopia it enunciates, have made Punk appeal to a whole plethora of youth – the intelligentsia, the artistically rebellious and the politically militant.

A Socio-historical Analysis

This reference to punk rock to exemplify counter-cultural movements in Malta might perhaps give the wrong impression that rock subcultural association in Maltese society is a more contemporary phenomenon. Yet close scrutiny of the socio-historical development of Maltese rock subcultures would reveal that these groupings had already flowered in Malta by the mid-fifties.

Towards the end of the 1950's, Malta's first counter-cultural, rock 'n' roll 'folk-devils' the 'Teddy Boys' appeared at the forefront of Malta's cultural configurations. 'Teds' began to appear in London as early as 1954, adorned in drape jacket, thick crepe soled shoes and an over-abundance of Brylcreem (hair-dressing cream). By 1958 the 'Teddy' boy image was also common-place in Maltese urbanized localities, particularly Ħamrun, Valletta and Paola and in the profusely working-class, inner harbour regions. The fact that Maltese 'Teds' pertained to largely working-class backgrounds is not a consideration to be ignored. They were the first rebellious youth, left out of the upward social strata and unable to gain entrance into white-collar work. As with their US and British counterparts, their 'slick' image manifested their own solution to

---

1980's music wave. Whilst the 'Hardcore' movement largely consists of those modern, conservative punk bands that remained more faithful to the original anarchic ideology and abrasive artistic expression of 70's punk rock, the fusion of musical genres typical in Grunge and the Crossover styles highlight the tendency of the post-punk movement to experiment with alternative forms of music and stylistic options. Crossover, for example, can be defined as the concoction of Rap, Funk, Punk, Pop, Hardcore, Metal, Industrial and Thrash elements: a combination of genres that is symptomatic of contemporary rock's endeavors to supersede traditional music barriers.

their 'status frustration' resulting from the deprivation of entrance into upper-class circles:

> Thus the 'Teddy Boy' expropriation of an upper-class style of dress 'covers' the gap between largely manual, unskilled near-lumpen real careers and life chances, and the 'all-dressed-up-and-nowhere-to-go' experience of Saturday evening (Hall & Jefferson, 1976, p. 48).

The Maltese 'Teddy boy' subculture (short living a revival in the early eighties) shrivelled out with the arrival of 'Beatlemania' and the beat generation, around 1964. However, this subcultural fad was to have long-lasting effect on the nature of subsequent rock subcultures that were to develop in the local social context in later years. 'Teds' everywhere set high standards of stylistic behaviour that served as a measuring rod for the dress styles of future non-conformist subcultures.

The Ħamrun and Valletta 'Teds' who rock 'n' rolled every Saturday night to the sounds of Bill Haley and the Comets, Chuck Berry or Little Richard at the Phoenicia, set the pace for an alternative form of culture and life-style to that imposed by the 'straight' adult world. It added new dimensions to a youth culture that until then was considered to stop at the ping-pong tables of the local village MUSEUM (cathecism) centre.

As the popularity of the pioneering rock 'n' rollers swayed in favour of the upcoming Beat bands, circa 1963, the youth subcultural patterns in Malta underwent considerable change. The shaggy 'Beatle' hairstyle replaced the former 'Teddy Boy' image. The mass popularization of beat music and its idols saw popular music transcending class differences. Beatles and Rolling Stones records became the defining symbol of an identifiable youth culture, rather than of a particular youth class. Music now served a 'missionary purpose'. An ideological commitment to change became fundamental to the new youth culture. Organized mixed youth clubs, ardent against sexual segregation and promoting innovative youth leisure pursuits, started to flourish throughout the Island:

> Mixed youth clubs in Malta are spinning up like mushrooms, despite the 'organized opposition' which exists especially in the villages. The now long campaign, to discourage the new initiative of establishing such modern clubs for youths in our Island home, shall have to end. The growth of mixed youth clubs in

> Malta is now at its height... in Paola we now find the Black Kits, and Cupids; in Hamrun we find the Malteen and the Sparteens; in Cospicua we find the Kiksters and the Mixed teen clan; in Birkirkara we find the Saints and the Diamonds; in Sliema we find the Gayteens and Teensville; and in Qormi, the Pinsters (Agius, J. in *The Malteen*, January 1965, p. 14).

In Malta, the mid-sixties were essentially marked with a unified youth culture, which strived to combat the traditional hierarchies that objected to the internalization of modern values. The Maltese youth of the 60's was preoccupied with achieving his/her right to self-expression and sought to dispense with the attitude that 'youth hates dictatorship but needs it' (*The Malteen*, January 1965, p. 16).

Unlike any era before, the sixties in Malta were characterized by a growth of a multitude of 'Beat' bands including The Phantoms, the Twilights, the Savages, the Graduates, the Boys, the Vipers, the Fireflies, the Addicts and the Meteors (Pace & Xuereb, 1965). Influenced by the 'Mersey Beat' generation, these bands communicated to Maltese youth the values dominant in the Western pop music of the post-fifties. They helped facilitate the passage from traditional life-experience to non-conventional life-styles and aspirations.

Yet, the advent of counter-culturalism in Malta and abroad can be associated with the emergence of utopian radicalism of the 'Hippy' movement towards the end of the sixties. The 'Hippies' fused radical and bohemian traditions and developed their own forms of liberationalism in an effort to reach alternative dimensions of consciousness and self-expression. Theirs was a quest for a deeper existentialist reason than that explicated by the conformist society. This drive for intellectual existentialism saw youths world-wide – including Malta – attacking conventional systems which, to them, were choking with passivity and stagnant 'respectability'. It was then that rock music, in Malta and abroad, shed its traces of 'teeny-bopper', commercialism and provided the counter-culture with ideologically subversive, 'underground' foundations.

The record-buying public in Malta welcomed the likes of the Grateful Dead, Jefferson Airplane and Arthur Brown. The polished melodic sounds of the sixties Maltese 'Beat' bands became replaced by the raw, uncompromising overtures of local rock bands such as Ocean 4 and Slug. Passionate cries for lost love had now been replaced with concern for mysticism, Zen Buddhism, the overthrow of rigid political institutions and aesthetic dimensions of the counter-culture.

The psychedelic, progressive rockers and folk revivalists of the late sixties and early seventies, articulating their strong opposition to dominant values and institutions, ensured an overt political response to the constraints of the control culture. As elsewhere, the impact of the 'Hippy' movement on Maltese society fragmented into different directions, with on one hand, the retreatist, drug, utopian culture, purveying 'life-style revolution' through narcotics and spiritualist practices, and on the other, the more politically-militant groups, pursuing protest ideology through artistic output and political involvement. It was the latter that were to have considerable influence over the process of social change in our societal context. The protest 'Hippy' subculture created an awareness on new issues. 'Hippy' ideology became the voice for the social, non-economic aspect of political decisions, environmental policy and community empowerment – ideological constructs that are inbred in the social nature of the modern political system, Malta's political setup notwithstanding.

Counter-culturalism in Malta received further impetus with the impact of Punk Rock on Maltese shores toward the end of the seventies. By the early eighties, identification of Maltese youths with the 'Punk' ideal escalated to unprecedented heights. For most local cohorts, the 'Punk' subculture with its strong anti-social sentiments, acted as an attractive 'solution' to the bleak prospects generated through the ambiguities of the domestic political arena at the time. As elsewhere, the marginalized status endured by the 'Punk' subculture in Malta gave rise to an overwhelmingly nihilistic 'Punk' ideology, one that could not foresee the restoration of social order, until that order itself is overthrown. As the seminal Maltese 'Punk' band The Rifffs contended:

> Driving down the road in the middle of the night
> Never knowing what could happen
> Never knowing what's in sight
> Fighting, rioting, happens everywhere,
> Depressed by the memory, unemployment everywhere
> 1981's, hit a limit, its begun
> The law is reinforced by the big tommy-gun
> Tear gas acting flash, the big boy in blue
> No one really knows what the hell to do, to do.
>   The Rifffs 'Dance Music for the 80's
>   Depression', (1981).

Moreover, for Malta, the 'Punk' explosion also instigated the diffusion of non-conformist youth culture. Whilst the 'Teddy Boys' and 'Hippies' before enjoyed near-exclusivity as counter-cultural formations, 'Punk Rockers' encountered strong competition for their 'cultural space' from other subcultural genres, (particularly 'Heavy Rockers' and 'Rock-a-Billies'), also existent at the time. Maltese counter-culturalism was now rigidly divided in different and often violently conflicting subcultures, with each group struggling for 'subcultural territorial' domination and the affirmation of their own 'focal concerns'.[2]

This brief socio-historical analysis of rock subcultural movements in Malta is essential for one's understanding of the prevalent contemporary counter-cultures. Some, such as the rave 'Heavy Metal' movement, have enjoyed consistency over the last two decades, gathering momentum with the gradual demise of other counter-cultural trends. Subcultures cannot be considered as mere contemporary phenomena. Their development is not extemporaneous, but is, rather an evolutionary process. The survival of subcultural movements appears to depend on their ability to transform and adapt their ideology to new societal conditions. This adaptability appears to be the common element of the subcultural movements which this article considers to be representative of counter-culturalism in present-day Malta. However, these subordinate configurations still embrace a number of differentiating characteristics which make the separate analysis of each subculture necessary.

Malta's Headbangers: Renaissance or Metamorphosis?

The 'Heavy Metal' or 'Headbanger' subculture has been perhaps the most long-standing youth subcultural configuration throughout Malta's subordinate culture history. Ever since the sounds of

---

[2] The term 'focal concerns' encompasses the differentiated needs, expectations, aspirations, and the stylistic/ritualistic options of subcultural movements. Miller (1958, p. 6) introduced this term in the analysis of subcultures to define those 'areas and issues which command widespread and persistent attention and a high degree of personal involvement'.

Black Sabbath, Deep Purple, Led Zeppelin, Blue Oyster Cult and Uriah Heep hit the local radio airwaves and vinyl outlets in the early seventies, local youth have been 'converted' in their hundreds to the uncompromising rhythmic beats of 'Heavy Metal'. However, 'Metal' reached its popularity in Malta with the explosion of the New Wave of Heavy Metal towards the end of the 1970's. The sheer energy displayed on such albums as Saxon's 'The Eagle has landed' (1982) and the Motorhead 'live' classic, 'No Sleep 'til Hammersmith' (1981), attracted a loyal army of Maltese fans to the worldwide renaissance of this genre, marked by admiration to fret-board antics, escapist lyrics, shock theatrics and frenzied stage shows.

From the 1980's onwards, local 'Metal' cohorts started proudly parading themselves in the streets of Valletta, sporting long-hair styles, jeans, leather jackets and the essential Ozzy Osbourne, Iron Maiden and ACDC T-shirts. The demigod status of 'Metal' superstars still serves as a catalyst for potential 'Metal' fans today. 'Metal' mega-stars act as role models, filling the void left by the youth's disaffiliation to conformist standards. To the prospective member, his/her integration to the 'Metal' subculture means going against what significant others expect of him/her. Once relinquishing these pre-determined expectations, the individual's self-identity will be formed through the internalization of 'Metal' subcultural values and stylistic imagery. When interviewed by local music magazine 'Far Out!' regarding the mass appeal of 'Metal' for several youths in Malta, Karl Fiorini, frontman/vocalist with the now defunct Maltese 'Metal' band, Kremation, articulated thus the spell-binding effect Metal may have on its followers:

> I think Heavy Metal has a power, an image, a look, a certain appeal that attracts a lot of people, The showmanship and stage-acts as well as the songs themselves appeal to a lot who want to be like them (in *Far Out!*, No. 17, 1987, p. 6).

In a discussion of the impact subcultures have on individual behaviour patterns, Glaser (1966), asserts that association to cultural sub-groups is effected through 'differential identification' processes whereby members de-construct their previous identity and take on imaginary or realistic subcultural attitudes, and values. Glaser's observations are indeed relevant to the explanation of the strong hold the 'Metal' establishment world-wide appears to relish over its members. Affiliation to this subculture is rationalized as a reaction to what youth conceive – often justifiably – as persecution by mainstream forces. The arcane concerns of 'Heavy Metal' lyrics, for example, have provoked vehement condemnation and censorship from purveyors of the traditional order. 'Metal' Lp's are constantly censored. Bands, in the USA particularly, have had to cope with accusations of encouraging violence, and even suicide, through the 'back-masked' messages of their lyrics. Heavy Metal's response to this 'persecution' has been through calls for the assembling of a united metal fraternity that will withstand and finally overcome the incursions of mainstream forces:

> They wanna keep us down
> but they can't last
> When we get up we're gonna kick your ass
> Gonna keep on burning
> We always will
> Other bands play Manowar kill.
> Manowar 'Kings of Metal', (1988)

These lyrics give 'Metallers' the right to their own life-styles and values. This contention for the legitimization of collective expression is also reflected in the ritualistic practices inherent in the local metal subcultural formation. A sense of unity abounds on the local metal scene when it is ripe for the metal community to display a show of force. 'Heavy metal' concerts or 'gigs', exemplify the manifestation of anti-social sentiment. Here, studded, leather-jacketed, 'Metal disciples' indulge in the obligatory headbanging ritual, where the audience members 'bang' their heads in unison and in appreciation of the 'riffs' on ensemble. Entract, the now defunct, Tarxien-based, glam/hard-rock/metal band, in 'Rock Through the Night' (1988), clearly highlight the feelings of coalescence inherent in 'Heavy Metal':

> We rock through the night
> Don't care what you say
> Together we stand,
> The whole night away
> No weak shall survive
> This hot, crazy life.

Such values of 'belonging' take on a semblance of institutional arrangement founded on a socialization process whereby subcultural values are internalized to long-lasting effect. Close circumspection of the local 'Metal' movement also reveals a quasi-hierarchical rank order. High status positions are left for long-standing members. They act as a source of reference for discussions on new albums and promising new bands, as well as for nostalgic recollections of the bands of yesteryear. New converts to the 'Metal cause', on the other hand, undergo an informal process of initiation by being subjected to 'interrogation' by connoisseurs. A failure to show an adept knowledge of the ideology, stylistic options and ritualism of the 'Metal' subculture could reduce a newly-bred 'head-banger' to the derogatory 'poser' status – a status which, used in this subculture, refers to an undeserving member.

Gender and Intergenerational Considerations

A superficial examination of the local 'Metal' fraternity might lead one to think that female members are ostracized from the high-ranking strata of the 'Metal' hierarchy. Such an observation is not peculiar to the analysis of Maltese counter-cultural movements. For decades, researchers have relegated rock music to a celebration of masculinity where females are regarded only as 'back-stage' conquests:

> Rock is a pedestal sport, as in being a monarch – whenever a boy inherits the throne – females are not thought to be the stuff worship/idols are made for/of. Girls are expected to grovel in the mezzanine while the stud struts his stuff up there, while a girl with the audacity to go on stage is always jeered, sneered and leered up to – rock and roll is very missionary, very religious, very repressive (Burchill & Parsons, 1978, p. 86).

However, whilst these observations might objectively describe the sexist attitudes prevalent in the cock-rock 70's glitter genre and the more recent US glam/sleaze revival, it would be misleading to hold that such a discriminatory temperament is inbred in the whole plethora of rock genres and subcultures. One major characteristic of the 80's 'Metal' renaissance was precisely the surge of talented and relatively successful all-female bands. The dexterous technicality of Girlschool, Rock Goddess, Phantom Blue and Lita Ford usurped the male-centred ideal of the 'Metal god'. In Malta, feminine participation in 'Metal' bands also contributed to a commensurate gender representation within the local 'Metal' subculture. Overdose, Ivory Cross, Talisman and Jungle Mania are all compatriot 'Metal' bands that have included women throughout their line-up itineraries. The stage success of such female band members showed that anyone can reach the echelons of the 'Metal' hierarchy, irrespective of ascribed status.

It is thus a 'status passage' process (Glaser & Strauss, 1971),[3] rather than gender division that determines the level of attachment and identification to the local 'Metal' subculture. The investment female or male 'Metallers' devote to asserting their status as fully-fledged and 'deserving' members of the group creates a deep, enduring bond to 'Heavy Metal', and in turn enhances the resilience of this subcultural genre. Few members would be expeditious to forsake their hard-earned subcultural standing, even when confronted with the pressures of occupational, and parental status. Committed association to the 'Heavy Metal' subculture, thus persists, despite the perennial pulls towards social conformity.

The longevity of the 'Heavy Metal' subculture in Malta also defies the logic of generational analysis. Affiliation to this subculture is not exclusive to narrowly-defined age cohorts or generational units and thus not susceptible to the time factor. The 'Heavy Metal' subculture, rather, has survived in the local context as it gratifies its members' basic need for belonging and identification. This is its *raison d'être*. It has refrained from aligning itself to political stances or social comment conducive to particularistic issues. The 'Hippy' protest movement lost its impact after it compromised its ideological foundations with political subjectivity. Through its lack of social commentary and despite 'taming' attempts by conventional social forces, 'Metal' launched a barrier against mass culturalization, thereby preventing the fragmentation of the movement.

'Rock' concerts organized by Malta's preponderant political parties and other mainstream organizations may be considered

---

[3] Glaser & Strauss (1971) apply the notion of 'status passage' to refer to the chronological development of a youth's career as s/he goes up the echelons in the subculture's hierarchical structure. They argue that the different stages of subcultural association pose particular contingencies and problems to the actor (Brake, 1985).

as definite examples of direct/indirect attempts at 'taming' local counter-cultural groupings. Whether these attempts have been successful at rallying subcultural cohorts behind one ideology or another is a fact to be questioned. Whilst local rockers usually attend such festivities in their hordes, it is more probable that their participation emanates from the possibility of indulging in the celebration of particularistic subcultural styles/rituals whilst supporting the bands on stage, rather than from commitment to the ideology of the organizers:

> What can I say about Rock Ambjent? ... The people enjoyed every minute of it. But it was doubtful if many of them, especially the rockers and head bangers up front, knew that the main idea was part of drive to stress the need of safeguarding nature. Indeed, I would say that three-fourths of those who attended did not know the agenda at all. But then again, rockers usually care little about this. So long as the sound is good and the beer is plenty, let the show go on. (Tanti, J. 'Rock-Pop-Jazz' in *The Times*, 9 February, 1990.)

Once it becomes part of the mass culture, any counter-culture loses its uniqueness and consequently its appeal to marginalized youth.

'Thrashers' in Malta – From Escapism to Social Awareness

The roots of the 'Thrash Metal' movement in Malta date back to the tape-trading boom of the mid-eighties. At that time the more extreme factions of our metal population came across early 'Metallica' and 'Slayer' recordings, amongst the first North American bands to announce the advent of 'Thrash' in the international rock market. The sounds of 'Ride The Lightning' (Metallica, 1984) and 'Hell Awaits' (Slayer, 1985) led many a 'Headbanger' to deviate from the now comparatively melodic chords of 'Heavy Metal' to the unrivalled disharmonious brutality of Thrash. Musically, Thrash Metal's uniqueness lies in the fact that it combines, often to an extreme, the best moments of 'Punk Rock', 'Heavy Metal' and even sixties' Psychedelia. It started out with the British barrage of Venom and Motorhead, but took on a more distinct shape with the onslaught of a multitude of American, San Francisco Bay Area bands, such as the aforementioned Metallica, and with a non-compromising, Teutonic, 'Thrash' blitz, fronted by the likes of Kreator, Destruction, Sodom, Tankard and Accuser.

Sociologically, the relevance of the 'Thrash' subculture lies in its encapsulation of individual expressionism and politically committed ideology. Rather than speaking in terms of a united community against the conventional enmity, 'Thrash' ideology allows space for the assertion and expression of individual concerns. Leo Stivala, main spokesman for Maltese 'Doom' merchants Forsaken, clearly expounds this point in an interviewing session with long standing local rock journalist Eric Montfort:

> In no way do we want to glorify death or gore but we try to look at its unconscious aspect albeit in a pessimistic manner. We try to show how the individual views death and what effects does it have on him. (in 'Weekend Pop', *The Times*, 31 January, 1992).

Unlike other movements it does not entail rigid role-behaviour patterns. Female members, for example, are not ascribed with the 'gig-groping' status that is common-place in other more sexist Rock genres. It offers an 'individual' rather than a 'collective' solution to the restraints of symbolic universalism. 'Thrash' is not bound to strict stylistic restrictions. Boxer-shorts, baseball caps, denim and leather waist-jackets, long, short and even dreadlocked, 'reggae' styled hair are all compatible with the 'Thrasher' image.

There is also no apparent hierarchical or organized structure to the movement. Unlike Metal or Hard Rock gigs, 'Thrash' concerts are characterized by constant active participation from members. There are no psychological 'idolization' boundaries between the band and its audience, with the latter living out their own stage fantasies by 'air-guitar' playing. Ritualism in 'Thrash' concerts rather sees audience members sharing the same space as the band on stage, 'diving' off the podium at different intervals to allow other audience members the same possibility. The 'moshpit' below the stage also acts as a channel for the acting out of individual aggression and frustration. 'Moshing', a derivative of the punk 'po-go' dance that obliges the audience members to bump frenziedly into each other, also denotes appreciation for the local bands on stage, that in turn do not hold back from forwarding anti-conformist sentiments and ideology through lyrical values:

> Maintaining of Habitual Sabbaths
> Excessive devoid of the brain
> Committing yourself to communion
> Subjected to holy defects

> Approval of forced contribution
> A symbol of merciful faith
> Misleading you to plunge into darkness
> Assumption of heaven decays.
> Vandals 'Condemned Legacy' (1990).

From a Denouncement of Conformity...

This excerpt from the lyrical repertoire of veteran Maltese underground band 'Vandals', belies the skeptic persuasions of the authors and questions the rationality behind traditional ritualism and shared symbolic meanings. Antagonism towards mainstream attitudes is, as we have seen, archetypical of counter-culturalism. Yet, close scrutiny of 'Thrash' ideology reveals something deeper than mere anti-conformism. Rather, it forwards critical social comment and a strong commitment for a 'new world order'. In the late aeons of 'Punk Rock' and 'Hippy' psychedelia, such ideological concerns were common-place. However, in the contemporary age of fabricated, 'Techno-pop' – which is oblivious to any lyrical content, and to iconoclastic, ideological stances – Thrash Metal's lyrical exposition of the Machiavellian nature of extant social arrangements, indeed, merits special consideration.

The forerunners of the international 'Thrash invasion' have all invariably denounced the disparity of the 'democratic order'. New York 'Moshers', Anthrax, for example, locate racial discrimination and ethnic disaffiliation as indigenous to the US structural system:

> Acting out of pure cold hatred
> Cause of what another's race is
> Cause of what another's face is
> Different, and your own frustrations
> Taking on a violent nature
> Full of hate, so full of hate
> You'd kill a man, is that your fate?
> Your street becomes a police state
> Why the hell do you hate?
> Anthrax 'All in the Family' (1990).

Metallica in '... And Justice for all' (1988), condemn what they perceive to be the bureaucratized and corrupt setup of democratic justice systems:

> Rolls of tape seal your lips
> Now you're done in
> Their money tips her scales again
> Just make your deal

> Just what is the truth?
> I cannot tell
> I cannot feel.

Testament's 'Souls of Black' (1990) attacks the 'political lies' and 'corporate decisions' of modern political structures and Megadeth call for the diffusion of power and the right of the average citizen to be fully active in the decision making process:

> What do you mean I couldn't be president
> of the United States of America
> Tell me something, it's still 'we the people', right?
> Megadeth 'Peace Sells' (1986).

The ideological constructs of such lyrics are also central to Malta's own 'Thrash' subculture. Ray Savage, for example, veteran guitarist with Maltese thrash/death metal band Vandals claims:

> I do not accept that people are not interested in politics ...you have to participate to change things, otherwise your beliefs and interests will remain unrepresented and our political elites will remain in power only to represent the interests of conventional society (in Bell, 1990, p. 102).

...to an Articulation of Political Alternatives

The reference made above to participation in the mainstream setup must not be misinterpreted as passive conformity to prevalent systems. On the other hand it refers to a commitment to change, to create a social reality where different interests are represented and where the pursuit of individual expression is respected. The domestic Thrashers' calls for justice and equity are not restricted to Maltese society. Rather they override conditions of their immediate environment. Manslaughter, in 'No End to the Killing' , and Extremity in 'They Call It Justice' for example, repudiate the universality of human oppression. Extremity's 'They Call it Justice', denounces warfare as symptomatic of humanity's betrayal to the shared goals of liberty, freedom and human dignity:

> Invading a nation without any reason
> Searching for justice you find a war
> They call it power, I call it treason
> Filling the emptiness, without any choice.

Similarly, Manslaughter's 'No End to the Killing' expounds on the futility of wasting human life, irrespective of colour, creed, race or religion:

> Red skies rollin' thunder
> Into the atmosphere
> Stop this endless pain before
> It kills you and me
> Holocaust lays on death
> Environment to forget
> Lay the papers down and sign
> It's the killing of time.

Subcultural studies often minimize the ideology of subordinate youth groupings to statements of reactionary statements of anti-authority as if they have no real base of ideological conviction. Parkin (1971), for example, holds that 'subordinate value systems' reflect the subculture's most immediate concerns of establishing the right for the expression of its life-styles and attitudes. Whilst this may be consonant with 'Heavy Metal' ideology with its incessant celebration of non-conformist life-style, it is clear that the ideology of the 'Thrash' subculture worldwide rises beyond the assertion of particularistic 'focal concerns'. The lyrical excerpts quoted above implore notions of justice, human dignity, self-worth and equity – values that are crucial to the cultural blueprint of mainstream society. The articulated political statement of 'Thrash' ideology condones the widespread and just application of the dominant value system. What 'Thrash' ideology opposes and condemns is the distortion of mainstream values through the 'anomic' structures of the modern social system.

The structure, ritualistic practices and ideology of the 'Thrash' subculture clearly denote that the rudiments of this movement are not essentially an escape from personality, the acting out of a male-centred ego-fantasy typical of the 70's cock-rock, sexist fetishism or the dismemberment of conventional values. The epitome of contemporary counter-culturalism in Malta, 'Thrash' metal has discarded fantasy for the documentation of ostensible solutions to the paradoxes of social reality.

Conclusion

This study has been concerned with identifying indigenous rock subcultures as a manifestation of counter-culturalism in Malta. It has shown that the Maltese society is not a uniform entity as many would think it is.

As a final comment, however, it must be accentuated that rock subcultures do not essentially enjoy a monopoly on counter-culturalism and, hence, social change. Subordinate groupings in any society, irrespective of their differentiated relationships to the dominant, parent culture, all explore and experience new dimensions of social reality. What amplifies the potentiality of rock subcultures for social change in Malta is their ability to communicate and personify the spirit of the counter-culture. Rock embodies the expression of youth rebellion – the source of ideological and cultural innovation. For the unconvinced reader, such claims might appear to be mundane, sweeping statements. Yet the crux of the matter is that rock culture is an entirely different explanation of social reality – one that has to be lived to be experienced:

> Rock culture is not confined to ceremonial occasions but enters people's lives without aura, taking on a meaning there independent of the intentions of its original creators. The rock audience is not a passive mass, consuming records like cornflakes, but an active community, making music into a symbol of solidarity and an inspiration for action (Frith, 1978, p. 198).

References

Agius, J. (1965) 'Youth clubs', in Xuereb, V.C. (ed.) *Malteen*, Malta, G. Muscat & Co.
Bell, A. (1990) *Rebel Yell: Rock Music as an Expression of Youth Culture*, Malta, University of Malta.
Brake, M. (1985) *Comparative Youth Culture*, London, Routledge & Kegan Paul.
Burchill, J. & Parsons, T. (1978) *The Boy Looked at Johnny; The Obituary of Rock and Roll*, London, Pluto Press.
Frith, S. (1978) *The Sociology of Rock*, London, Constable.
Glaser, B.G. & Strauss, A. (1971) *Status Passage – Formal Theory*, London, Routledge & Kegan Paul.
Glaser, D. (1966) 'Criminality theories and behavioural images', *American Journal of Sociology*, 61.
Hall, S. & Jefferson, T. (eds) (1975) *Resistance Through Rituals*, London, Hutchinson. Originally published as *Working Papers in Cultural Studies 7/8*, University of Birmingham, England, Centre for Contemporary Cultural Studies.
Miller, W.B. (1958) 'Lower class culture as a generating milieu of gang delinquency', *Journal of Social Issues*, 14, 1.
Pace, G.E. & Xuereb, C. (eds) (1965) 'Stop, look and...' in *Bond*, August, Malta, G. Muscat & Co.

Parkin, F. (1971) *Class Inequality and Political Order*, London, MacGibbon & Kee.
Pisani, V. (ed.) (1987) *Far Out*, 17, Malta, Printwell Ltd.
Xuereb, V.C. (ed.) (1965) 'Youth in the family seminar' in *Malteen*, January, Malta, G. Muscat & Sons.

Discography

Anthrax, 'All In the Family', Lyrics: Anthrax, Publ.: Anthrax Music, 1990.
Entract, 'Rock Through the Night', Lyrics: Entract, 1988.
Extremity, 'They Call It Justice', Lyrics: Extremity, 1991.
Manowar, 'Kings of Metal', Lyrics: J.De Maio/Ross the Boss, Publ.: Inan Music, 1988.
Manslaughter, 'No End to The Killing', Lyrics: Manslaughter, 1991.
Megadeth, 'Peace Sells', Lyrics: D. Mustaine, Publ.: Mustaine Music/Theory Music, 1986.
Metallica, 'Ride the Lightning', Publ.: Music For Nations, Ltd., 1984.
Metallica, '...And Justice For All', Lyrics: J.Hetfield, Publ.: Creeping Death Music, 1988.
Motorhead, 'No Sleep 'Til Hammersmith', Publ.: Bronze Records Ltd., 1981.
Rifffs, The, 'Dance Music For The 80's Depression', Lyrics: The Rifffs, Publ.: Alternative Music, 1981.
Saxon, 'The Eagle Has Landed', Publ.: Carlin Music Corp. Carrere, 1982.
Slayer, 'Hell Awaits', Publ.: Roadrunner Productions B.V., 1985.
Testament, 'Souls of Black', Lyrics: Chuck Billy, Publ.: Cotlod Music, 1990.
Vandals, 'Condemned Legacy', Lyrics: Vandals, 1990.

23

Privatization: Policy and Politics

Mary Darmanin

Introduction

Privatization is a complex social issue. Within the realm of political economy it is considered to have mainly economic effects but since privatization is a result of public policy and therefore of intended political decision making it is not surprising that it has pertinent effects on all aspects of social life. For this reason it is necessary to move beyond political economy to a sociological understanding of privatization, in particular of its place in the coordination of social life.

This paper starts with a brief introduction to privatization and its various modes, placing it in a broader discussion of the relationship between government and market and of the neo-liberal philosophies and politics which underpin it. A typology of different types of privatization in the market will be proposed and described. Reference will then be made to recent moves towards privatization in the Maltese economy.

Having established that this trend now exists in this country, it will be useful, to examine the effects this has on both the market and public policy making. Elsewhere (Darmanin, 1993) I have outlined some of the consequences that privatization *as a social policy* has on government provision of public goods such as education. The commodification of public goods is an extension of the neo-liberal principles which have generated privatization policies in modern democracies. Whilst there may be a strong case in favour of a number of privatization policies in the market, the same should not be argued for the commodification of public goods (Darmanin, 1994).

Definition

It is not argued here that there is a causal relationship between economic ideas and economic policy, or between political ideologies and policy (Mullard, 1992, p. 289). However our understanding of privatization is greatly enhanced by understanding some of the philosophies which have given it credence. In this paper I shall show that privatization is to be understood as distinct from private enterprise. It implies a conscious orientation of government to policies which commit the State to the promotion of market practices. This could be done through

a. divestiture or denationalization whereby the state releases ownership of public sector investments;
b. legislation which encourages free market mechanisms and which allows previous public monopolies such as waste disposal, energy and water production to operate in a competitive environment (liberalization of interest rates, deregulation);
c. other mechanisms whereby the State retains ultimate responsibility for the supply of certain services but contracts out for parts of it, as with road digging and hospital meals (Cook & Kirkpatrick, 1988). The commodification of public goods (for example the promotion of parental choice in education) should also be included here.
d. the substitution of customer fees for tax finances. This means that consumers can use the monies retained from tax reductions to purchase services outside the State sector as is the case of the National Health Service in

England. The state sector will then be able to reduce its role in the provision of services in general (Ascher, 1987).

The existence of a private sector is thus not synonymous with privatization. Privatization is premised primarily on a shift in State policy regarding the public sector itself.

Philosophical Foundations: the Legacy of Hayek

Perhaps the most useful way of understanding the distinction between private enterprise and privatization is to turn to the philosophical premises of the separation that has been made in neo-liberal discourse between freedom and coercion and between government and market. The most influential proponent of this distinction has been the Austrian economist/philosopher F. A. Hayek. His arguments are premised on what Hindess (1987) has called a negative concept of freedom for it imputes a freedom *from* rather than a freedom *to*. Writing on the constitution of liberty, Hayek (Hindess, 1987, p. 128) defines freedom as the state in which a man (sic) is not subject to the arbitrary will of others. He sees coercion as arising mainly in the context of the relation between the State and its citizens. Only with the withdrawal of the coercive role of the State and the working of a spontaneous order of the market (Hayek, 1991) can true liberty be achieved. For Hayek therefore (1986, p. 146) prices are signals which tell people what to do. He holds that the market has a moral imperative.

> You must allow prices to be determined so as to tell people where they can make the best contribution to the rest of society – and unfortunately the capacity of making good contributions to one's fellows is not distributed according to any principle of justice.

Individual effort is directed towards achieving the means (working for a wage with which to purchase commodities) by which to enter into what is seen to be free and unfettered exchange. As Levitas (1986, p. 91) puts it, in this view 'economic freedom is the essence of personal freedom'. The neo-liberal argument therefore is that markets are beneficial and governments harmful. Gamble (1986, p. 30) finds that this leads to a belief that the best ordered economy is 'one in which scope for individual choice is greatest and scope from government responsibility smallest'.

A Critique of 'Freedom'

In the critique of this negative concept of freedom (Hindess, 1987) we are concerned with how individuals may acquire the freedom to participate in the market, once they have the freedom from the supposedly coercive mechanisms of the State. As Hindess (1987) has reminded us, some forms of planning by government may involve restrictions but these cannot be interpreted as a threat to liberty in general. Perhaps the most biting critique against this simplistic belief in the morality of the market, in which exchange is seen to be just and efficient, is that made by Beetham (1991).

> If you possess some commodity that is highly valued on the market, for whatever reason, you will receive a lot in exchange; if you have nothing that is so valued, or insufficiently, you will receive little or nothing in return. In extreme cases you may starve. If so, it is a death penalty that is executed, as it were automatically and impersonally, not by personal decree or conscious human agency.

Mocking the crassness of Hayek's market views of freedom and of their exclusion of any concept of needs and rights, Belsey (1986, p. 186) comments thus, 'to be in a disadvantaged position in a market society is not a limitation of freedom, so long as the disadvantage is the product of spontaneous order'.

Markets: For and Against

Not all free marketeers necessarily share the same unquestioning belief that the market is the most natural and therefore the best mechanism for achieving liberty. At the same time, critics of state intervention and in favour of markets raise a number of valid points. Brietenbach et al. (1991, p. 50) summarize them thus: markets create incentives for producers, force firms to develop new products, coordinate without conscious human intervention millions of individual decisions and allow individuals greater freedom of choice as producers and consumers.

On the other hand, the mainly Marxist case against markets (Brietenbach et al. 1991, p. 50) included the understanding that markets can intensify inequality and add to the number of poor. There are unavoidable economic cycles of expansion and contraction. Markets do not ensure that producers respond to human needs but, as pointed out earlier, only to the needs of those who have necessary purchasing power. Finally the point is also made that markets are insensitive to externalities, for example to the effect of industry on environmental pollution.

Some of the assertions of these seemingly irreconcilable positions will be examined in relation to the empirical research later on in this paper. What interests us at this stage is to understand how the argument in favour of market coordination of social life leads to an interest in privatization as a major social policy option. Privatization not only rolls back the State because it rids the State of its ownership of large companies, but is accompanied by legislation which favours private provision of goods, including welfare goods and it supposedly allows the natural mechanisms of the market (such as prices, supply and demand) to operate. Politically, it appears that the State now has a minimal role in coordinating social life and this may have useful legitimating functions in that the State can no longer be held responsible for inefficiencies and injustices.

Global Competition, Less Developed Countries and Privatization Options

The renewed interest in privatization does not arise solely from the political dominance of neo-liberal regimes. As Drache and Gertler (1991) have pointed out, historical economic processes have led Western democracies away from macro-policy frameworks. These were themselves a response to chronic structural weaknesses of competitive capitalism. In these earlier policies the role of the State was seen to be pivotal. Global market 'stagflation' (stagnation and inflation) has led to a reevaluation of these strategies. There is now a world-wide interest in reducing the role of the state in national economies, which in the case of the developing countries has been accelerated by the exigencies of aid agencies such as the World Bank (Commander & Killick, 1988). Privatization embraces both the ideological desire for smaller government and a belief in the superior economic performance of the private sector (Cook & Kirkpatrick, 1988, p. 3).

The case for privatization in less developed countries centred around the argument that the result of planning was disappointing, public sector investment projects performed badly and import substitution was inefficient (Cook & Kirkpatrick, 1988). However, despite the supposed gains, the data now suggest that the claims of success for privatization are greatly exaggerated, and this applies to developed as well as less developed countries (Ascher, 1987; Bishop & Kay, 1988; Cook & Kirkpatrick, 1988; Millward, 1988). For example divestiture is supposed to benefit the consumer by low cost production, since public enterprises usually have larger work forces with higher wages. It therefore follows that divestiture reduces employment and lowers real wages. Apart from the effect that this may have on employees, we must also ask along with Commander & Killick (1988) whether the benefits of lower costs are passed onto consumers or retained by new private owners. Moreover the same authors suggest that the private concern will often retain monopoly power so that though there is a change in ownership there is no change in the competitive environment.

This is now the case in Malta where proposals to denationalize the energy industries have been criticized on the grounds that they would still retain a monopoly.[1] The Labour opposition has also argued (*The Times*, 1 February 1992) that

> It is a contradiction that the quarters most vociferous in favour of democratic values are probably the same who would favour narrow private sector control over these strategic sectors outside the ultimate check of the electorate.

Moreover it has been noted that (*The Sunday Times*, 19 September 1992; *The Times*, 27 March 1993) limited liability companies such as the Management Systems Unit now has a monopoly on the provision of information technology and systems management for government agencies.

There is the fear that there will not be a reduction in the skewness of wealth ownership[2] despite the desire expressed by the Minister

---

[1] *The Sunday Times*, 20 September, 1992, 'General Workers Union agains energy privatization.' *Il-Helsien*, 5 June, 1992, 'Is-settur pubbliku bilfors inefficjenti?' In another article in *The Times*, 21 June, 1992, John Cachia has argued that the 'takeover by private companies of government functions such as the issue of car licences and the testing of road transport... will not work because [there will be] no change in the competitive environment'.

[2] *Society*, 14. April-June Dossier. 'Privatization, Anti-privatization or expediency?' 'It goes against our democratic values to see the benefits of such monopoly or oligopoly being enjoyed by narrow private sector segments...'

of Economic Services for a 'nation of shareholders' (*The Sunday Times*, 8 March 1992). A form of 'crony capitalism' might develop in which, in Commander and Killick's (1988) words, 'relatives, friends and supporters of members of the government are the chief beneficiaries'. Whilst the issue of *tangenti* in Italy and charges of corruption in Malta itself indicate that the public sector has been prone to allegations of bribery and corruption, privatization can also lead to this scenario. That it can privilege dominant in-groups in the 'crony capitalist' mode is evident in our own case as with the granting of leases for the development of Fort Chambray (*The Times*, 15 January 1993).

It has also to be understood that privatization cannot eliminate the role of the state. Often it is private enterprise itself that asks for state legislation to protect it from 'unfair' market competition. The Federation of Industry has found that accelerated liberalization and deregulation has dealt a harsh blow to indigenous manufacturing enterprises in Malta.[3] It is pointed out that larger countries with solid economies and home markets have, for many decades, nursed their infant industries by subsidies and other protective measures. More recently the Chamber of Commerce has proposed the setting up of an Office of Fair Trading (*The Times*, 18 May 1993), and the government has earmarked legislation on this issue in the 1993 Budget speech. Calls have also been made on the State to liberalize interest rates and to set up new banking procedures for venture capital. Often however, rather than less regulation, there has only been a change in the means of regulation in several industries. Vickers (1991, p. 166) has called this re-regulation. For example the new Industrial Development Bill (*The Times*, 10 March 1993) which regulates which firms or types of firms are allowed to engage in which activities (structure regulation) can be seen to re-regulate the economy. Within re-regulation, conduct regulation introduces measures which control how firms behave in their chosen activities. Arguments in favour of 'civic virtue' or the move towards Fair Trading are also

---

[3] *The Sunday Times Industry Supplement*, 8 April 1990. 'Tales of free Trade: An excuse to bury indigenous manufacturing enterprise in Malta?

part of this re-regulation. Thus it is clear that the separation of regulation from deregulation is not as simple as it might seem. Indeed Gramsci (1976) argued over forty years ago that

> The ideas of the free trade movement are based on a theoretical error... it is asserted that economic activity belongs to civil society, and the State must not interfere to regulate it. But since in actual reality civil society and the State are one and the same, it must be made clear that laissez-faire too is a form of State 'regulation' introduced and maintained by legislative and coercive means.

Privatization and the Maltese State

In Malta it has been the Nationalist Party which has most vociferously argued in favour of the rolling back of the State whilst in opposition and of privatization whilst in government (since 1987). The neo-liberal discourse is tempered by neo-conservative thought. This is captured in the slogan of solidarity. Solidarity is seen as a relation between individuals rather than as a social relationship between groups or institutions. The main social relationships that are encouraged, as with the attitude to private education, are those based on property rights rather than person rights (Apple, 1989).[4] The clearest declaration of this philosophy is found in a pre-election Nationalist publication *Basic Principles*, the third premise being

> III. MAN (sic) DOES NOT LIVE BY POLITICS ALONE The Christian idea of the dignity of man (sic) is the basis of all the Nationalist Party's policies. Human dignity is rooted in man's relationship with God and with his fellow men within the family and other voluntary associations, which the State is obliged to assist and promote.

---

[4] Apple's (1989, p. 8) definition is useful here. A property right vests in individuals the power to enter into social relationships on the basis and extent of their property. This may include economic rights of unrestricted use, free contract, voluntary exchange; political rights of participation and influence and cultural rights of access to the social means for the transmission of knowledge and the reproduction and transmission of consciousness. A person right vests in the individual the power to enter into these social relationships on the basis of simple membership in the social collectivity. Thus, person rights involve equal treatment of citizens.

This principle is explored in further detail in the Party's 1987 electoral programme (Progress Press, 1987, p. II). In translation, the text reads thus:

> The N.P. as a Demochristian Party, believes that the government should not intervene into every sphere. There are certain areas of life which the government should keep out of as much as possible.

The ideology of solidarity is turned into market or efficiency principle. This is captured in the Prime Minister's reply to the Leader of the Opposition in the 1992 Budget Debate.

> The whole had to be considered against the government's commitment to solidarity... Efficiency, Dr Fenech Adami [PM] said, was the example of solidarity in that every individual would make a greater contribution to the common good. In the case of the Civil Service, solidarity would mean a better service to the public, increased productivity and greater job satisfaction.[5]

Another example which demonstrates how close the Prime Minister is to the Hayekian concept of individual freedom is to be found in the following exchange between him and the Leader of the Opposition. During an ecological summit on the question of vacant houses and development, the Leader of the Opposition commented to the effect that in a free market, personal choice only existed insofar as one could satisfy one's own personal desire for land and property. If one did not have the means for this or if one was excluded by the crowding of others, then choice did not exist. The Prime Minister answered that (*The Times*, 19 October 1992) 'he did not agree on a free market as an absolute principle, but, on the one hand, if it was to be seen as part of **individual liberties** [my emphasis], it had been found to give the best results'.

Model Reform or a Model for Reform?

The reform of the public service should be seen as the first indicator of the present Government's intentions to introduce market systems in the State apparata. A direct consequence has been the dismantling of previous structures and the creation of new

---

[5] *The Times*, 3 December 1992, pp. 7, 40.

sites of power outside the direct control of the State.[6] In a special supplement in *The Sunday Times* (19 September 1992) an account is given of the setting up of the Management Systems Unit [MSU] which appears to be the model for neo-liberal practices in the public sector. According to this and following the Operations Review in 1987, the MSU was set up as a government owned agency 'to facilitate public reform'. In the 1992 Budget debate, Leader of the Opposition Dr Alfred Sant, made the following critiques, which point to the problems resulting from new configurations of the State. He held that MSU was supposed to operate as a company but was taking over civil service planning, and favoured the employment of foreigners with higher salaries and perks including training which was formerly available to other civil servants. Champions of privatization have linked civil service reform with the creation of a cadre of civil servants who can easily transfer expertise to the private sector.

In the Market

In the market it has been argued (*Society*, no. 14) that 'the sale of shares in banks was more conditioned by the need to augment the Government's revenue sources (selling the family silver) rather than by any stubborn belief in privatization'. By 1991, due to fiscal crisis and massive public sector debts, 40 % of the assets of Mid-Med Bank[7] were floated on the market. This was followed by the argument at a time when both commercial banks were registering handsome profits that 'financial market deregulation [was] best prior to EC membership' (*The Times*, 10 December 1991). More recently (Parliamentary Debates, *The Times*, 27 January 1993) it has been pointed out that Government borrowing has

---

[6] *The Times*, 31 March 1993, p. 5. The Chairperson of MSU writes about the objectives of the company which include amongst others a major change in the public service, the preparation for the launching of local councils, the establishment of multi-year business and financial planning for ministries.

[7] Called in *It-Torċa* 9 June 1991 'il-qliegh tal-poplu' (the wealth of the nation) for by the end of the year Mid-Med had recorded a Lm7 million pre-tax profit.

shot up to 28.1 % of GDP compared to 12.3 % in 1986. The Minister of Economic Services has also called for the privatization of banks so that government can sell its majority shareholding. Ironically at the same time that this supposed divestiture is being promoted, the government depends on the control of interest rates so as to be able to structure its borrowing. In the proposals in favour of deregulation (*The Times*, 11 May 1993), the government's position as Malta's leading borrower may be seen to be one of the 'main setbacks' for a hasty resolution of present problems. In the meantime fixed interest bonds in government utility companies such as Telemalta and Enemalta have been floated on a new Stock Exchange. It is worth noting that many of the companies that have been privatized or hinted as candidates for privatization have either recently received substantial government investment to be put on their feet (as with MP Clothing-Gozo, and the San Antnin Waste Recycling Plant in which government has recently invested Lm10 million) or are currently performing well as with Air Malta.[8] The government therefore forfeit substantial future income. In a talk given in his capacity as President of the Chamber of Commerce, the Chairperson of Air Malta argued against the monopoly power of public corporations and also called for a reduction in government competition 'at an unfair commercial advantage' (*The Times*, 18 May 1993). A conflict of interest here which seems to favour the privatization of successful public corporations.

The danger of 'crony capitalism' should lead us to ask who would be the beneficiaries here? As Commander and Killick (1988, p. 100) point out this may include international investors. In a recent Finance and Insurance supplement of *The Sunday Times*, (16 June 1993), it has been pointed out that public utility company Enemalta has borrowed US $100 million from a foreign consortium and that the Freeport is to follow suit. The commentator, Labour ex-Minister

---

[8] *The Times*, 20 June 1992. MP Clothing Workers buy 33 % of shares. *The Times*, 21 June 1992 "Having successfully nurtured this previous loss-maker back to health, MIMCOL last Friday sold this increasingly successful enterprise to its Management and employees. *The Times*, 17 September 1992, p. 19. Private sector offered chance to run waste recycling plant. *The Sunday Times*, 11 October 1992 on Air Malta's record profit.

of Finance, Lino Spiteri, implies that government has turned to foreign funds to benefit from lower loan rates and to reserve Maltese banking funds for future public sector borrowing. Another agenda could be that government is preparing for the privatization of these natural monopolies. Maltese critics of these policies emphasise the monopoly power which these companies muster (*The Times*, 21 June 1992). Subsequently there is no real change in the competitive environment. Moreover the privatization of profit and the socialization of costs is blatantly upheld by statements such as that made by a prominent exponent (*The Times*, 21 June 1992) of local private enterprise

> the private shareholder will feel comforted that Government is there to underpin the **privatized enterprise** [my emphasis] in the event of financial difficulty.

The ideological manoeuvres in favour of privatization continue to draw on common sense or populist arguments such as 'trade unions destroy jobs' or that if Malta does not privatize it will lose the respect of the EC (*The Sunday Times*, 11 October 1992). These arguments cash in on fears that Malta will not make it into the third wave of economic development. Whilst there have been new openings in the private labour market, jobs have been lost in the divesting of public sector companies by MIMCOL, the public company set up specifically to close down 'loss making' or 'defunct' firms.

According to a report (*The Times*, 15 March 1993) over 80 such firms have been 'hived off', though it is held that the privatization process could be accelerated. Ironically at the same time that sources, such as the *Commercial Courier*, argue against over-manning (sic) because it raises the wages bill, distorts the work ethic of a large number of employees and renders them afraid of competition, government contracting out has left a number of public employees grossly underemployed. In large infrastructural projects, parastatal companies have had to sub-contract. Public corporations are losing tenders to private companies because of the Treasury turnkey policy (awarding contracts to large companies only). On receipt of the tender these then sub-contract to smaller private companies (*It-Torċa* 18 October 1992). Clearly therefore reconfiguration of the market has implications for all aspects of economic life and, despite the desire of government to withdraw from intervention, this is not as simple or as straightforward as it may seem to free marketeers. As has been shown above, it is often these same proponents of markets who ask for state regulation in the shape of fair trading or other mechanisms.

Moreover since these groups depend on government planning of other sectors of the economy, government remains obliged to direct its own investments in a way that can both guarantee capital accumulation and legitimate its policy decisions. In doing so it is often seen as a competitor to private industry.

Government and Market: Straight or Simple?

In the discussion above I have allowed the heuristic and political division between government and markets to direct the argument against and in favour of privatization. It is necessary for the sociologist to regard both government and markets with critical suspicion. But it is perhaps also important to consider that there exist options which do not make such a rigid distinction between government and markets. It will not be possible to explore all these options here but it is sufficient to note that a number of sociologists (Le Grand & Estrin, 1989) have made a strong case for what they call market socialism. Though socialists would want to ensure specific ends and satisfaction of basic needs, the means through which these can be achieved need not be restricted to state planning. Recognizing many of the advantages of the market, Estrin & Le Grand (1989) argue that there is nothing intrinsic in markets that prevents them from being used to achieve these ends. Hindess (1987) has likewise provided a compelling case against the essentialism of both planners and marketeers to suggest that we should move from this position to consider the benefits both can give to social life. In his words 'it makes no sense to analyse societies as governed by one or more organizing principle' (Hindess, 1987).

Public Goods and Private Bads?

Having argued that there are advantages in both planning and markets, it still needs to be demonstrated that as currently advocated in Western democracies including Malta, markets, and privatization in particular, are dislocating a number of social and political objectives especially as regards the allocation of welfare goods. It is not possible here to account for the growth of the welfare state in our democracies nor to enter in detail into the debate surrounding the objectives of social policy formulation. However it should be acknowledged that there is considerable debate in social philosophy regarding the identification of needs and wants and the obligations that arise form the social recognition of these needs (Plant, Lesser & Taylor-Gooby, 1980).

For our purposes here it is useful to note that there is a variety of different approaches to the question of social needs which have been dichotomized into two main camps. These correspond to that of the free marketeers who argue against a moral basis of welfare provision (Hayek, 1960 and Nozick, 1974 are most commonly cited here) and more left-leaning social philosophers such as Rawls (1972) who argues in favour of social and distributive justice. Hayek (1976, p. 64 cited in Plant et al., 1980, p. 59) claims that the market is the most beneficial allocative system, adding that

> to demand justice from such a process is clearly absurd, and to single out some people in such a society as entitled to a particular share evidently unjust.

Rawls (1972, cited in Plant et al., 1980, p. 61) on the other hand, has made a strong and sustained case for state welfare as a corrective to natural (sic) facts of distribution. He argues that

> The natural distribution is neither just nor unjust, nor is it unjust that men (sic) are born into society at some particular position. These are simply natural facts. What is just and unjust is the way that institutions deal with these facts. The social system is not an unchangeable order beyond human control but a pattern of human action.

In their discussion of this position, Plant et al. (1980) have found that particular material conceptions of justice are contestable. This has not prevented them from trying to provide an account of the recognition of need as a means to socially approved ends which give rise to strict obligations on the part of those with resources. Since public (or welfare) goods are defined and distributed on normative criteria of social justice, it is unlikely that market mechanisms would be suitable for their allocation.

Conclusion

Elsewhere (Darmanin, 1994), I have used the case-study method to demonstrate that privatization policies in the arena of public goods such as education have benefit neither for those who parti- cipate in an education market nor for those who are excluded from participation. Following Jonathan (1989, 1990), I have argued that education, by virtue of its positional function, must not become a commodity. The commodification of what have normatively been understood as public goods cannot be acceptable in democratic societies for it erodes the basis of justice on which many of these societies have purported to be based. Moreover there are a number of arguments which show that just as markets themselves can never function successfully without some form of state regulation, this proviso is even more applicable when it comes to public goods such as health, education and housing.

It has not been possible to enter into this aspect of the argument here. However, it is hoped that the complexity of the issue will be understood. Privatization is a specific political and economic policy orientation which has repercussions on all levels of social life. The distribution of wealth, power, employment, property, education and others are all affected by these policies. Privatization should involve an examination of the role of the state in our societies and of the way a reconfiguration of the state is likely to affect both powerful and less powerful groups. It is not a neutral issue and can only be understood in the context of a concrete conjuncture, as has been attempted here.

References

Apple, M. (1989) 'How equality has been redefined in the conservative restoration', in Secada, W.G. (ed.) *Equity in Education*, Basingstoke, Falmer Press.

Ascher, K. (1987) *The Politics of Privatisation: Contracting Out Public Services*, Basingstoke, Macmillan.

Beetham, D. (1991) 'Models of bureaucracy', in Thompson, G. et al. (eds) *Markets, Hierarchies and Networks: The Coordination of Social Life*, London, Sage.

Belsey, A. (1986) 'The new right, social order and civil liberties', in Levitas, R. (ed.) *The Ideology of the New Right*, Cambridge, Polity Press.

Bishop, M. & Kay, J. (1988) *Does Privatization Work? Lessons from the UK*, London, Centre for Business Strategy.

Brietenbach, H., Burden, T. & Coates, D. (1991) 'Socialism, planning and the market', in Thompson, G. et al. (eds) *Markets, Hierarchies and Networks: The Coordination of Social Life*, London, Sage.

Commander, S. & Killick, T. (1988) 'Privatisation in developing countries: A survey of the issues', in Cook, P. & Kirkpatrick, C. (eds) *Privatisation in Less Developed Countries*, New York, Harvester Wheatsheaf.

Cook, P. & Kirkpatrick, C. (eds) *Privatisation in Less Developed Countries*, New York, Harvester Wheatsheaf.

Darmanin, M., (1993) 'More things in heaven and earth: Contradiction and co-optation in education policy', *International Studies in Sociology of Education*, vol. 3, 2.

Darmanin, M. (1994) 'Sufficient for the day: privatization in Maltese education policy', in *Discourse*.

Drache, D. & Gertler, M.S. (1991) 'The world economy and the nation-state: The new international order', in Drache, D. & Gertler, M. (eds) *The New Era of Global Competition: State Policy and Market Power*, Montreal, McGill-Queen's University Press.

Estrin, S. & Le Grand, J. (1989) 'Market socialism', in Le Grand, J. & Estrin, S. (eds) *Market Socialism*, Oxford, Clarendon Press.

Gamble, E.A. (1986) 'The political economy of freedom', in Levitas, R. (ed.) *The Ideology of the New Right*, Cambridge, Polity Press.

Gramsci, A. (1976) *The Prison Notebooks*, Hoare, Q. & Nowell-Smith, G. (eds) London, Lawrence & Wishart.

Hayek, F.A. (1960) *The Constitution of Liberty*, London, Routledge & Kegan Paul.

Hayek, F.A. (1976) *Law, Legislation and Liberty – Vol. II: The Misuse of Social Justice*, London, Routledge & Kegan Paul.

Hayek, F.A. (1986) 'The moral imperative of the market', in Anderson, M.J. (ed.) *The Unfinshed Agenda: Essays on the Political Economy of Government Policy in Honour of A. Seldon*, London, Institute of Economic Affairs.

Hayek, F.A. (1991) 'Spontaneous ('grown') order and organized ('made') order', in Thompson, G. et al. (eds) *Markets, Hierarchies and Networks: The Coordination of Social Life*, London, Sage.

Hindess, B. (1987) *Freedom, Equality, and the Market: Arguments on Social Policy*, London, Tavistock.

Hindess, B. (1990) 'Liberty and equality', in Hindess, B. (ed.) *Reactions to the Right*, London, Routledge.

Jonathan, R. (1989) 'Choice and control in education: Parental rights, individual liberties and social justice', *British Journal of Educational Studies*, vol. 37, 4.

Jonathan, R. (1990) 'State education service or prisoner's dilemma: The 'hidden hand' as source of education policy', *Educational Philosophy and Theory*, vol. 22, 1.

Levitas, R. (1986) 'Ideology and the new right', in Levitas, R. (ed.) *The Ideology of the New Right*, Cambridge, Polity Press.

Millward, R. (1988) 'Measured sources of inefficiency in the performance of private and public enterprise in LDC', in Cook, P. & Kirkpatrick, C., (eds) *Privatisation in Less Developed Countries*, New York, Harvester Wheatsheaf.

Mullard, M. (1992) *Understanding Economic Policy*, London, Routledge.

Nozick, R. (1974) *Anarchy, State and Utopia*, Oxford, Blackwell.

Plant, R., Lesser, H. & Taylor-Gooby, P. (1980) *Political Philosophy and Social Welfare: Essays on the Normative Basis of Welfare Provision*, London, Routledge & Kegan Paul.

Progress Press, (1987) *Is-Sisien Għall-Ġejjieni*, Valletta, Malta, Progress Press.

Rawls, J.A. (1972) *Theory of Justice*, Oxford, Clarendon Press.

Vickers, J. (1991) 'New directions for industrial policy in the area of regulatory Reform', in Thompson, G., Frances, J., Levacic, R. & Mitchell, J. (eds) *Markets, Hierarchies and Networks: The Coordination of Social Life*, London, Sage.

part 5

work and production relations

Understanding the social and technical relations into which people enter in the process of production is bound to generate a penetrating analysis of a particular societal configuration. More so when, as in the Maltese case, labour is hailed as the only available natural resource. This section of readings purports to problematize the diverse aspects of the Maltese working environment. It illustrates the overbearing presence of the state as employer, legislator, arbiter of labour relations and a pervasive actor – with its own political agenda – in economic affairs. The operations of the local economic plant are understood better by their contextualization in the local sphere of work habits and the supra-national circuit of global capitalism and market forces. The accounts also identify the impact and interests of workers (male and female, young and old), of their trade union representatives and of professional management in negotiating their way across the contested arena of work. Consideration is also given to departures from traditional wage labour relations, ranging from rather widespread narratives of participatory workplace democracy to more marginal episodes of cooperative entrepreneurship.

Two enterprise case studies, one of an industrial dispute in a luxury foreign owned hotel (by Grixti) and an account of less dramatic, more routine, contestation of market and technological labour control in a clothing firm (by Borg Bonello) document the dependent status of the Maltese private, open economy. Within the latter, there is also an articulation between formal, core and stable employment on one hand and the part-time, seasonal and sporadic work often taking place in the semi-official, 'twilight' economy, as illustrated by Sultana in his focus on child labour practices. The overview by Delia strengthens the case for the adoption of such a bi-modal perspective to an appraisal of local labour market segmentation, adding also a consideration of the strategic combination of public sector and private sector wage or entrepreneurial activity. The relationship between a peculiar kind of collective effort, market efficiency and state interference is documented by Baldacchino with respect to cooperative pursuits by the Maltese. Finally, the issues of worker participation and of normative orientations to work are identified as major future challenges for local labour relations: Zammit organizes the major perceptions of work in Maltese society, describing a corresponding work ethic which is argued to be in transition; while Baldacchino engages with the varied experiences of workplace democratization and its ambiguous purposes at the mercy of competing interests.

24

A Labour Market in Transition

E.P. Delia

Introduction

An understanding of the forces which condition the demand and supply of labour in Malta is a prerequisite for a proper analysis of the performance of the Maltese economy. Yet studies on the labour market are few and far between. One outcome of this dearth of information is that policies on trade, education and labour pursued in recent decades leave much to be desired, and they fail to provide co-ordination and complementarity in helping Malta to attain its foremost socio-economic objective. This is the creation of an open, competitive, market-oriented economy which generates profitable employment at wages which enable a life of reasonable comfort. Such an objective demands efficient capital and labour markets which provide a continuous flow of funds and skills at competitive prices.

This paper reflects on several issues related to the labour market in Malta. Some labour market characteristics are examined first. In turn, labour market models for Malta are reviewed highlighting the critical role of the heavy post-war emigration movement and the need for reliable data bases. The aptitudes of Maltese workers are considered next, basing the impressions on two recent manpower surveys. The paper concludes by identifying implications for the Maltese economy over the next three decades arising from the demographic shifts identified.

Labour Market Characteristics and Policies: Then and Now

In the mid-seventies, Koziara (1975, p. 2) observed that the labour market in Malta was characterized by a

> high rate of emigration, high unemployment, low wages, increasing labour force participation by women and a high geographic mobility.

A somewhat different scenario prevails at present. Emigration has practically stopped; fewer than two hundred Maltese emigrated annually in recent years. Instead, labour immigration, in part clandestine, is now recorded. At the same time, the registered unemployed represent about 4.2% of the labour supply, a statistic which may not be duly worrying, socially and politically, given the sizable underground economy in Malta. Furthermore, a marked improvement has been registered on the income side: the average earnings per employee were valued at Lm55 (US$ 171) in 1991, while the national minimum wage was Lm39 (US$ 121) if bonuses are included. These statistics compare favourably with a national minimum wage of Lm12 (US$ 30) in 1975 even when account is taken of price increases. When eliminating the effects of inflation, real earnings per employee are estimated to have been Lm50 (US$ 155) in 1991 (Economic Planning Division, 1991, p. 36). Similar gains are recorded in the real Gross National Product per capita which grew from Lm544 (US$ 1,348) in 1975 to Lm1,200 (US$ 3,720) in 1991, at constant 1973 prices. The former statistic includes income from facilities rented to, and employment generated by, the British Defence Establishments in Malta; in contrast, the latter figure excludes any such incomes. Finally, the female activity rate now approaches 30% of the gainfully occupied population, a relatively historical high for Malta, but still comparatively low by European levels.

Although the present labour market environment may appear strikingly contrasting with that of two decades ago, yet in some respects there are close similarities. Paramount among these is the aspiration by the majority of employees for employment security coupled with the prospects of improving living standards. During the hey-day of the fortress economy, when material fortunes depended on the cycles of war and peace concerning the British Empire, security of employment was accorded priority by the Maltese labour force, then also experiencing high rates of population growth. At the time, unemployment was rife and synonymous with emigration to distant Australia or Canada. Employment with the British Defence Establishments was correlated in the minds of many with stable jobs, rising wages, and a pensionable retirement. From the national economy's view point, it represented an inflow of foreign exchange in the form of wages and salaries and transfers for pensions, apart from rent. However, the rapid rundown of the UK military sector – from the engagement of 26% of gainful employment in 1957 to zero in 1979 – brought to an end this sheltered labour market niche for many who had to emigrate, be absorbed in the Maltese public sector, or seek employment in the emerging profit-motivated activities in manufacturing and the services sector, primarily tourism. It was the public sector which replaced, to a great extent, the UK Defence Establishments as the focus of attraction for employment security by the Maltese.

This attraction was further reinforced during the seventies when, as a matter of policy, the Maltese government switched its economic role. Previously it had supported an economy based primarily on private initiative promoting economic diversification and growth. It then started upholding a mixed economy policy, that is, an economy where the State was a key actor in production and trade. Indeed, the State was envisaged as the catalyst of economic growth (Economic Division, OPM, 1981, pp. 64-65). In addition to assuming the responsibility for the development of infrastructure and personnel, the State acquired assets in manufacturing, construction, services and agriculture. Gradually, the search for job-security extended over larger segments of the labour market.

The emigration programme faltered in 1975, when Australia, Canada and the United Kingdom introduced more selective immigration policies to meet the changed labour market condition in their economies (Delia, 1981, 1982a, 1985). Since then, the drive for employment with the public sector became even more urgent. Job tenure was sought in sectors where the profit motive was either absent or ambiguous, for example in public corporations meant to provide services and at the same time absorb as much manpower as political decision makers determined. This time, however, such decisions were not backed up by foreign currency earnings as used to be the case of employment enrolment in the UK Defence Establishment. This factor has a great economic significance for a small, island economy where imports represent around eighty percent of the Gross National Product!

The past two decades have seen an ongoing debate on the optimal way of creating wealth, generating income and reducing excessive income disparities in Malta. This discussion reflects, in general, the economic and psychological insecurity of Maltese workers in an economy which gradually dismantled a centuries-old foreign military base and replaced it by a widening range of economic activities in manufacturing and services. It has been a time when the goal of productive efficiency came in direct conflict with the urgent need to create jobs and with the workers' desire for job security and improved working conditions.

Such a socio-economic conflict is a variant of the more general and problematic relationship between Production and Distribution, in which labour market policies, legislation, regulation, and action have to be devised and implemented (Delia, 1991). On the one hand, there is the necessity to examine how a quantity of commodities should be produced. This would imply making best use of the country's resources (both human and material) as well as shifting resources from one sector to another. It would also involve drawing up incentives geared primarily to production with the aim of inducing the highest obtainable output. On the other hand, it is necessary to examine how distribution could be organized to exert the greatest influence on production without causing hardship. That is, how to redistribute a nation's growing wealth among those who are active in production but also among those who, for valid reasons, e.g. age or infirmity, are unable to participate in the productive process. Viewed thus, distribution becomes an incentive or a brake to economic growth.

Policies directed to enhancing a country's productive capacity – those on infrastructure, direct foreign investment, training schemes and general education, financial and legal institutions – as well as policies aimed at fulfilling an individual's aspirations and needs in a caring society – such as, welfare programmes and their funding – could be integrated in some respects when their social and economic implications are involved. This amalgamation of dual social and economic objectives can be clearly manifested through a study of industrial and labour market policies.

Since the late fifties, Maltese economic policy makers have repeatedly emphasised export-led economic growth. In a way, this reflected a 'natural' sequel to the export of services to the UK Defence Establishments which were being phased out. The policy mix of fiscal incentives, emigration, and labour training programmes were meant to achieve a triple objective: first, to ease the pressure on the labour supply caused by new entrants to the job market, second to attract foreign capital and know-how crucial to encourage and spur investment, and third, to match the envisaged demand for adaptable labour in industries with skills that could be imparted within short time periods. Such policies provided a stimulus for the training and, hence, the upgrading of manpower and exposed a wider segment of the labour force to international trade competition.

A totally different set of policy instruments encourages domestic production in order to reduce importation. Such an import-substitution strategy generally gains short term employment and generates windfall profits. But it fails to earn foreign exchange to pay for necessary imports, such as fuel, food and clothing. More important perhaps, such a policy fails to build up an inherent mechanism in the economy whereby there is continuous upgrading of skills and communications. The development of an extensive domestically-oriented manufacturing sector behind a strong protective wall of tariff barriers, eliminates the spur of competition and creates a false sense of job security based on product mediocrity at the expense of the consumer.

Again, the use of cash handouts and other transfer payments as a policy tool produces both a social and an economic effect: it increases a household's income, thus combating destitution, and at the same time it generates the demand for domestic goods and services, driving up employment in the process. However, income transfers generally do very little, by themselves, in attaining the long-term goal of economic diversification and growth. There is still the need to link together financial assistance to training schemes. By doing so, it would be possible to increase the pool of technical expertise, thus rendering feasible the matching of new demand for labour skills. In addition there is the need for a short-term discouragement of activity in the underground economy, and the compilation of reliable statistics on the unemployed. The unemployed will be turned from numbers into individuals and their skills.

In Malta's case, the fairly rapid shifting of policies regarding the role of the State and the primacy of the objective of export-led economic growth in the past decade or so could be expected to lead to uncertainty in the labour market, inducing, as a consequence, a resistance to change. The absorption of labour in the public sector and Government-owned industry has created an artificial economic structure which has to be dismantled relatively rapidly if Malta is to join the European Union, as it applied to do in June 1990. In addition, those workers who embarked on personal financial commitments on the implicit understanding that protective tariffs were here to stay could find themselves in financial difficulties unless their incomes could somehow, be 'guaranteed'. One undesirable offshoot of the fairly rapid change in the industrial and employment policies over the past twenty years could be the inability of the education and training support systems to upgrade labour in time, in order to entice investment in goods and services on a scale large enough to absorb the replaced labour.

About 43% of the gainfully occupied are still safeguarded under Government's financial 'protection' – roughly the same share that obtained in the mid-50's under the combined Malta Government Sector and the UK Defence Establishments! Surely, it cannot be expected that such an employment composition will be conducive to the officially acclaimed, efficiency-driven, export-oriented search for suitable niches where Malta can create a comparative trade advantage for herself. But that is precisely what the government, employers, trade unions and business interests – the social partners, as they are collectively termed – are striving to achieve within a reasonably short time frame. Success demands a clarity of vision and consistency of policy in all markets, in particular the labour market where a resistance to change could be expected to lie deep.

Labour Market Models and Data Bases

Research on labour market relationships in Malta, both on an aggregate and on a sectoral level, has been very sparse. One example is Inguanez and Briguglio (1986). So are manpower surveys which evaluate the skill composition of the labour force and the demand for skills (Education-Industry Unit, 1987; Delia, 1990) and studies on workers' needs and enterprise facilities (WPDC, 1992). Surely, there is scope for a more systematic analysis of the rapidly changing demand for labour skills, and their supply, especially in the coming years.

Inguanez & Briguglio (1986) attempt to quantify the relative strength of the parameters which 'conditioned' labour force performance in Malta since 1960. Specifically, these parameters are the size of the labour force, the size of the working age population, the average real wage rate and the unemployment rate. The authors, however, omit entirely considerations of the massive migration movement which characterized the period. Emigration influences directly three of the parameters – the size of the working age population and its composition; the size of the labour force and its composition, and the unemployment rate; indirectly, it influences also the nominal wage rate, and, hence, the average real wage rate. Any study which claims to assessing the performance of the labour supply in Malta, including participation rates, and omits migration, which conditions both the size and composition of the population and the labour force, apart from labour propensity to work and expectations for the future, is bound to be restricted in nature (Delia, 1982b, p. 149).

a. Emigration and Immigration

About 155,000 Maltese emigrated between 1946 and 1990. Of these about one fourth, or 39,000, are estimated to have returned to Malta (Delia, 1981, Lever-Tracy, 1987). About 115,000 Maltese settled permanently abroad. Surely, the impact of such a massive outflow of persons on the socio-economic development of a colony, or ex-colony after 1964, cannot be ignored. There were instances when net yearly migration exceeded five thousand, with net annual outflows in excess of a thousand becoming a regular feature. Apart from the creation of jobs required, in part following the running down of the British Establishments after 1962 at a time of comparatively high rates of natural increase in population, the amount of social capital allocated for the provision of education and housing would have been enormous had these 115,000 Maltese opted not to leave (Delia, 1982b).

Indeed, the extension of public sector employment in Malta during the late seventies arose partly as a direct result of the blockage of the emigration flow after 1975. The targets laid down for net emigration in the 1973-80 Development Plan were not met, thus increasing the labour supply, pushing up temporary employment in the labour corps set up for the purpose. Eventually, these labour corps were absorbed by public sector jobs (Delia, 1983a). Witness, also, the so-called 'illegal recruitment' in public sector posts immediately before the 1987 general election (Economic Planning and Management, OPM, 1987, p. 26).

More recently, migration is producing an opposite effect on labour supply from that it traditionally had. In the past, migration was associated with reductions in labour supply. At present, immigration, legal and illegal, is increasing the supply of skills. About 1,000 foreigners work in Malta, legally. Between 1,000 and 2,000 other immigrants could be working without a permit on seasonal assignments, in the tourist industry, for example, or even on a regular basis, in construction and manufacturing. The presence of illegal immigrants distorts the labour supply statistics, both in their aggregate and in their sectoral composition. In addition, such workers could artificially create labour supply shortages by enabling the Maltese to be selective in their choices for jobs. These would thus either move up the social job ladder, or, probably, exert pressure on public sector recruitment. Surely, clandestine labour reflects an active underground economic activity which in a small economy would render more difficult the formulation of economic and social policies.

b. Reliable Statistics

The compilation of reliable statistical information may be considered a relatively easy task in a small country. Yet, surprisingly, the number of the gainfully occupied population and unemployed and, hence, the size of the labour supply have been a subject of quasi-permanent controversy in Malta. The size of the Maltese population itself was also a topic for debate lately. Discrepancies in population statistics were first noted in Delia (1982c) in a study on the elderly, but these were rectified by the 1985 Census when the population data was topped up by around 11,000. At the same time, doubts were raised on the reliability of the gainfully occupied population; it was suggested that official statistics overestimated this parameter (Delia, 1983b). Indeed, the Central Office of Statistics revised downwards the gainfully occupied population by 2,100 in 1987, and could be revising them downwards again in the near future. In the Census of Agriculture held in 1991, the recorded number of full-time farmers was given as 1,471. Given 1,333 full-time and part-time fishermen, the employment complement in the sector of Agriculture and Fisheries becomes 2,804, compared to the official datum of 3,231 (FAO, 1992). The gainfully occupied population and the labour supply would thus have to be reduced by at least 427.

These statistical shifts in population and employment bear directly on labour participation ratios; they imply that estimates of activity rates before these data adjustments had been overestimated. Another downward revision of the gainfully active would reduce the present participation rates, unless these reductions are compensated by unrecorded employment which is not captured through shortcomings in data compilation, as in the case with underground economic activity.

Curiosa in labour statistics at times remain unexplained. Thus, the 1985 census recorded 105,293 Maltese in employment. This number fell short of the official 113,070 gainfully occupied by 7,777 jobs. The census commented on this discrepancy by observing (Central Office of Statistics, Malta, 1986) that

> it is partly attributable to the reluctance of some persons to disclose whether they and other members of the households were gainfully occupied as well as the fact that most of the apprentices and trainees, pupil workers and student workers were classified as still attending school but not in gainful employment.

This explanation was considered weak (Delia, 1987). Indeed, the fact that the Central Office of Statistics later revised downwards by 2,100 the number of full-time fishermen and farmers shows that part of the discrepancy could be explained simply through inflated employment statistics. However, there remains a gap between 2,100 and the 7,777 recorded in the census which is not accounted for. A satisfactory explanation has not been forthcoming from official quarters! But what is imperative at present, of course, is accuracy in today's labour statistics upon which future policy projections may be carried out with confidence.

c. Profit-Driven Economic Behaviour and Beyond

Analyses of labour markets in Malta may assume different degrees of complexity. However, even at relatively simple levels, analyses could be fruitfully undertaken if the labour market is segmented in terms of activities which are profit-driven and activities which are not. On the supply of labour, it is essential to consider the role of part-time employment, whereby an employee turns himself/herself into a self-employed person and carries out work during one's supposed leisure time. In this way, account could be taken of underground activity by linking together both the formal and the informal sector through labour's supply of effort. Indeed, the proposals to introduce fiscal incentives to encourage workers to disclose part-time employment for income tax purposes (announced by the Minister of Finance in the Budget Speech for 1993 for consideration by the social partners) reflects such labour behaviour. Apart from revenue purposes, such information on part-time employment would enable the planning of training schemes to upgrade labour skills.

Official statistics do not provide the wealth of information which a researcher would deem necessary for a comprehensive analysis. However the data available may be considered sufficient to enable the identification of the main forces at work in delineating the labour market performance over selected time periods. Data refer to the sectoral distribution of employment, output and wages in the different sectors of economic activity (Central Office of Statistics, *Annual Abstract of Statistics*; *Census of Industrial Production*). On a more aggregated form, information is made available by general sectors, private and public, the latter referring to the Civil Service, the Armed Forces, and companies in which the Government is the sole or majority shareholder (Central Office of Statistics, *Economic Trends*). An example of such data is given in the table below (cf. Table 1).

Table 1. Employment Performance 1980-1993

		Dec 1980	May 1987	Sep 1993
1	Population	325700	345600	365600
2	Labour Supply Total Male Female	120737 89236 31501	125402 94623 30779	139868 102803 37065
3	Gainfully Occupied Male Female	116698 85781 30917	120531 90783 29748	134052 97856 36196
4	Private Direct Production[1]	42954	35686	37633
5	Private Market Services[2]	33049	29409	38856
6	Public Sector[3]	37506	46534	51053
7	Temporary Employment[4]	3189	8902	6510
8	Registered Unemployment % of Labour Supply	4039 3.30	4871 3.90	5816 4.20
9	Self-Employed % of Gainfully Occupied	15735 13.50	15513 12.90	16307 12.20
10	Private Sector Share of Employment %	65.13	54.01	57.05
11	Public Sector Share of Employment %	32.14	38.61	38.08
12	Temporary Employment Share %	2.73	7.39	4.85
13	Total Public Sector Share % (11+12)	34.87	45.99	42.93
14	Labour Supply as a % of the Population	37.10	36.30	38.30

Source: *Economic Survey, January-September 1993, Malta, Economic Planning Division, Ministry of Finance*, p. 49.

[1] *Manufacturing, agriculture and fisheries, quarrying, construction, and oil drilling.*
[2] *Wholesale and retail trade, insurance and real estate, transport, storage and communications, hotels and catering establishments.*
[3] *Government departments, armed forces, independent statutory bodies and companies with government/Malta Development Corporation majority shareholding.*
[4] *Temporary Employees stand for workers who were engaged in public corps on a temporary basis; the latest of such corps, The Auxiliary Workers Training Scheme, was wound up in 1992. Also included under such a heading were university students engaged under the worker-student scheme, who used to be guaranteed employment, generally in the Public Sector, on the successful completion of their course. This scheme has also been terminated.*

The main features of labour market performance since 1980 are summarized in Table 1. The year 1987 represents a breaking point, and reflects a change in general policy pronouncements regarding the extent of State intervention in the Maltese economy. The highlights may be summarized as follows:

i. the overall activity rate fell from 37.1% in 1980 to 36.3% in 1987, thereafter rising again to 38.3% by September 1993;

ii. the supply of male labour increased by 13,500 while that of female workers declined during the first half of the eighties but increased by 6,300 in the last quinquennium;

iii. gainful employment grew by 17,350 posts, of which 13,500, or 78%, took place in the last five years;

iv. the share of Private Sector Employment fell from 65% to 54% between 1980 and 1987, but edged upwards to 57% in the following years. Conversely, the share of Public Sector Employment increased from 32% to 39%, respectively, and remained at about that level after 1987.

v. However, the share of Temporary Employment almost trebled, from 2.7% to 7.4%, falling again to 4.9% in 1993. As a result of these shifts, the relative share of Total Public Sector Employment increased from 35% in 1980 to 46% in 1987, falling thereafter to 43% in 1993.

vi. The share of the self-employed declined from 13.5% to 12.2% over the twelve year period.

The main criteria which distinguish Private Sector Economic Activity from Public Sector activity are profits and competition. Closely correlated with these two parameters are the roles of labour productivity and remuneration, investment in both physical and human capital, and managerial organization geared to produce goods and services efficiently and profitably. Hence it is essential to consider the labour market in Malta as being segmented in relation to the main criteria which condition the demand for labour.

In a simplified labour market model for Malta, the demand for labour function, D_l, could be expressed as being made up of four components, namely, two components of demand in the Private Sector, D_p, represented by the demand for the services of employees, D_m, and those of the self-employed, S_e; and two components of demand in the widely-defined Public Sector, D_g, made up of demand for employees by Government Administration at the national and local council levels, C_s, and demand for employees by public corporations and enterprises in which the Government is the majority shareholder or the main financial backer, D_c. Thus:

$$D_l = D_p + D_g \quad (1)$$
$$\text{and} \quad D_p = D_m + S_e \quad (2)$$
$$D_g = D_c + C_s \quad (3)$$

The factors which condition the demand for labour in the four main sub-markets above are bound to differ. One cannot simply assume a straightforward relationship between the demand for labour, labour productivity and wages in order to deduce an aggregate demand for labour relationships. Other parameters, such as the electoral cycle, bilateral financial aid, and investment promotion campaigns, would also have to be considered. In addition, the role of immigrant labour could be assessed in terms of a domestic labour supply shortage, at least in the short to medium term.

A look at the labour demand function as segmented above would enable the identification of the various forces at work in conditioning employment and costs. It would bring out in stronger light the interplay of economic, political, demographic and social forces and their respective contributions to employment generation at particular time periods.

On the labour supply side, one must distinguish between those workers who rely for their income solely on selling their labour services to others and those who undertake two or more jobs on a part-time basis in addition to their basic work. One has to carefully assess the roles of public sector employment, and the system of registration for work when unemployed, in facilitating the undertaking of full time employment parallel with a public sector job, or with jobs running on a shift system.

A 'total' labour supply function for individual j (S^j_1) would, therefore, take the general form:

$$S^j_1 = S(w/p) + S_e \qquad (4)$$
$$\text{or} \quad S^j_1 = S(w/p)^1 + S(w/p)^2 \qquad (5)$$

that is, j's supply of effort reflects the real wage earned (W/P) on a 'basic' job and the possibility of carrying out further work as a self-employed, (equation 4), or in terms of income earned from hired employment in two activities of which one could be full-time (equation 5).

If the supply of effort in the basic job leads to a wage which surpasses the effort put into the activity – as is the case in departments where overmanning is great – then part of the wage could be considered as a transfer payment.

Such considerations enable a researcher to distinguish among various labour market conditions and then assess better both the role of technology and a re-organization of tasks in inducing a rise in labour productivity. When applied to the whole economy, these considerations could also be used to generate an understanding of the complex relationship between government expenditure in Malta and private sector activity, with the aim of encouraging a wider use of effective resource management. Similar models have been applied elsewhere to test for Adolph Wagner's 'Law of Increasing Government Expenditure' (Baumol, 1967).

Part-time employment is generally assumed to fall within the informal economy. It is sometimes claimed that part-time employment is inevitable for Malta if living standards are to keep on rising. Case studies on the informal sector are almost non-existent. However, lately, one area, child labour in Malta and Gozo, has been the subject of research (Sultana, 1993; Cremona, 1989). The two studies suggest that the resort to child labour could be relatively extensive. Apart from the quantification of this phenomenon, these studies are important for policy orientation. They identify young people's attitudes towards training, their propensity to work, and their expectations for better living. They also reflect the complexity of labour markets in Malta, and to some extent, the degree of effectiveness of labour market supervision by state officials!

Labour Skill Bottlenecks

Young people's attitudes towards work and training are partly the outcome of the educational system. The educational standards of the Maltese are quite high for a Mediterranean country but considerably below the Central European level, both with regard to levels of secondary vocational training and university or equivalent training. The main problems facing potential labour supply of skilled personnel are: the high drop-out rate after the age of 16, the low proportion of students following technical and vocational courses, the low proportion of university students following engineering and science subjects, and the general lack of interest in apprenticeship schemes by employers and students alike (Coopers & Lybrand Europe, 1991, p. 95; Sultana, 1992).

These propensities have resulted in skill bottlenecks which have been attributed to the absence of an industrial tradition and culture in Malta. Skill shortages are considered the single most important obstacle in the transition of Malta's economy in general – and industry in particular – towards higher productivity levels and local wealth generation. Although efforts have been recently made, with success, to entice more students to continue their education after the obligatory school leaving age of 16, yet it is essential to identify continuously the extent of the skill supplies problem and plan to remedy it effectively.

A manpower survey on Skill and Training Needs in Maltese industry carried out in 1987, (Education Industry Unit, 1987), highlighted a shortage of workers

> who can read and follow simple instruction, convey messages accurately, understand simple diagnosis and perform basic calculations.

In addition there was a need for a general improvement of managerial and supervisory skills. Similar shortages were observed in the Tourist Accommodation Sector in a manpower survey in 1990 (Delia, 1990). Staff bottlenecks were visible in all departments. It was then envisaged that as hotels and complexes diversified their operations and offered a wider range of facilities, apart from accommodation, the demand for leisure management would become widespread and the inadequacy of personnel more evident.

Surely, an economy's diversification and growth should not be sacrificed because of a gross misjudgment of labour expectations and training. Workers feel more comfortable in a life-tenured employment, sheltered from international competition. But, unfortunately, such aspirations cannot be met in a small, independent state like Malta. Economic survival could come about only if the country were to decide on one crucial issue: either be happy with a relatively low income per head and less skill-intensive types of production, or a higher income per head but using higher technology, thereby implying higher training and improved organization systems all along.

A country that is less productive than its trading partners across the board will be forced to compete on the basis of low wages rather than productivity. It will export those goods in which its productivity disadvantage is smallest. A country will always find a range of goods in which it has a comparative advantage even if there are no goods in which it has an absolute advantage. However, it is always beneficial for a country to manoeuvre itself into a position where it can exploit its strategic assets, and create a trade advantage for itself. Recent analyses of international trade are placing increasing emphasis on the role of history, accident, and government policy in producing trade patterns (Krugman, 1991).

A created niche for Malta's output surely cannot be expected to emerge from a lop-sided labour market where workers strive to move away from a competitive, profit-motivated environment to a life-tenured public sector post. Nor can it be attained through a labour force which is unprepared to compete on ever-higher quality targets and productivity, both in the manufacturing of goods and the provision of services.

The move towards an efficiency-driven labour force starts from a social awareness and acknowledgement that the universal upgrading of technical and managerial skills is a prerequisite for Malta's future economic and social development. This condition holds irrespective of the outcome of Malta's application for membership of the European Union or the search for oil. A streamlining of public sector employment coupled with successful investment promotion drives and training programmes could induce the shift in labour productivity, overall – a shift which Malta needs at present. Privatization, a more cost-effective management in public corporations, and a more selective recruitment in public administration would facilitate the drive towards labour market efficiency.

The deployment of human resources towards the production of internationally-traded goods and services would possibly improve the quality of Maltese labour. But it also implies stress and demands individual and social adaptation to change. A profit-oriented work environment and increasing female participation rates, for example, would bring about a need to reassess the traditional bread-winning role for men and housecaring roles for women. It seems that working women still have to take care of the children and carry on with the traditional household tasks, like shopping, cooking and washing clothes (WPDC, 1992). The combination of insecurity at work and a demanding family life may exert great stress on many women and it is bound to influence a worker's decision on whether to join the labour supply, particularly in the case of married women.

Demographic and Labour Supply Changes in the Near and Distant Future

Labour market behaviour in the future is bound to be conditioned in many ways by the envisaged demographic changes. The Maltese population is growing and ageing. The present 362,000 Maltese are projected to increase to 381,000 by the turn of the century and to reach 406,000 in the year 2015. During the nineties the population growth is expected to occur primarily in the age-bracket 16-59 years. The overall rise in persons eligible for work would be of one percentage point, from 61.8% in 1990 to 62.9% of the population, representing an additional 22,000 potential job seekers throughout the decade, if retirement age is retained at 60 years. The economy will be facing strong pressure for generating new job opportunities as the nineties develop.

With the turn of the century, the demographic configuration will shift towards the dependency groups, especially those over sixty years of age. The share of the sixty-plus in the population is projected to rise from 14.6% in 1990 to 16% in 2001 and to a high 21.2% in the year 2015. At the same time, the share of the 16-59 year old would fall to around 58% from the high of 63% expected to be recorded in the year 2001. In absolute terms, it is projected that there would be 237,000 Maltese of working age in 2015, compared to 220,000 in 1990 and 240,000 in the year 2001.

The challenge of the nineties lies in job creation. New jobs would have to be generated to absorb the increasing number of entrants on the labour market, to account for a higher female participation in the market sector, and to undertake a restructuring of the present distribution of the gainfully occupied population. The employment configuration would have to look very different from what it is now. If Malta is to earn her living through profitable production and sales, there will have to be more skilled workers and more employees in the private sector.

The recent resurgence of private sector activity is encouraging. Recording real growth rates of the Gross Domestic Product – that is the sum total of wealth created by all local private firms and government – in excess of 6% in the Maltese economy in recent years, in a difficult world-trade environment may be considered an impressive feat. But the pressure for the economy to keep on providing new employment outlets is bound to increase in the near future and the rate of new job generation obtained lately, though positive, would not be sufficient to enable a relatively fast restructuring of labour force distribution. Government's commitment to eventually reduce public sector employment to around 25%-30% of the gainfully occupied population from its present 43% (Budget Speech, 1993), and reliance on local labour resources rather than on immigrant labour, is bound to induce a general shake-up of the present labour demand configuration and of the factors which condition wage levels and work performance.

If the State is 'to be rolled back', private sector employment has to absorb an ever-rising share of new employment in the coming years. The challenge presently facing private enterprises and government agencies attracting foreign investment is great.

In September 1992, the Private Sector accounted for 58% of gainful employment. On the assumptions of a labour force growth of 1% annually, and an unemployment rate of 4%, (Budget Speech, 1993), the labour supply will be 143,400 in 1997. The Private Sector will have to generate a net, additional 4,000 jobs if it is to maintain its present labour market share. If its share is to rise, the number of productive outlets it generates must obviously exceed 4,000 (Delia, 1993).

Success in creating employment and national wealth would not only lead to social stability but it would also enable the government to plan for the heavier expenditure on welfare programmes to meet the demands of an ageing society. Finally, national wealth will help the government provide the assistance and services which a society under work stress may demand in the form of support or leisure.

Summary

The end result of inconsistency in the pursuit of an export-oriented economic growth has led to a consolidation of the sheltered-type mentality in the labour market in Malta. With an ever-increasing competition, as more countries turn to exports to finance their economic growth, it becomes necessary to undertake a close look at labour mentality regarding job tenure, wage increases and productivity. A change in such an outlook is probably called for. Such a change cannot be successfully attained unless labour is trained to compete through technical and managerial skills which are presently in short supply.

Labour Market analyses could profitably be carried out in terms of a detailed segmented studies of a number of sector-specific labour markets. The coming years are meant to witness a drift towards profit-oriented economic activity, away from public sector employment where the profit motive was totally absent or uneasily married to employment generation. While emigration is at a standstill at present, yet labour market studies which omit emigration during the period 1946-1980 are bound to understate by a wide margin the relative influences of demographic and labour supply factors.

No analysis can be carried out in the absence of reliable data. To date, labour market statistics have been an object of dispute. This situation should not be allowed to continue, particularly in such a small country. Furthermore, there is a need for field surveys assessing the expectations and skills of the labour force, and the labour requirements by entrepreneurs. A continuous flow of information would enable the drawing up of suitable training programmes, thereby contributing to higher economic growth rates and to lower social tension.

References

Baumol, W.J. (1967) 'Macroeconomics of unbalanced growth: The anatomy of urban crisis', *American Economic Review*, vol. 77, 6.

Central Office of Statistics (1986) *Malta Census 1985 – Volume 1: A Demographic Profile of Malta and Gozo*, Malta, Government Press.

Cremona, J. (1989) 'The underground economy in Gozo', unpublished dissertation, University of Malta, BA (Hons) Public Administration.

Coopers & Lybrand Europe (1991) *The Effect of EC Membership on Industry in Malta*, Malta, Federation of Industries.

Delia, E.P. (1981) 'Return migration to the Maltese islands in the postwar years', *Hyphen*, vol. 3, 1.

Delia, E.P. (1982a) 'The determinants of modern Maltese emigration', *International Migration*, vol. 20, 1 & 2.

Delia, E.P. (1982b) 'Modern emigration from Malta: a liability?', *Hyphen*, vol. 3, 4.

Delia, E.P. (1982c) 'The characteristics and life style of the aged in the Maltese Islands' in Centre for Social Research, *Malta, A Study on the Aged*, Malta, Social Action Movement.

Delia, E.P. (1983a) *Unemployment: Internal and External Factors*, Malta, Chamber of Commerce.

Delia, E.P. (1983b) *The Outcome of Fiscal Policy*, Malta, Chamber of Commerce.

Delia, E.P. (1985) 'Maltese migration: A critique of two views', *Economic and Social Studies, (New Series)*, vol. 2.

Delia, E.P. (1987) *The Task Ahead: Dimensions, Ideologies and Policies*, Malta, Confederation of Private Enterprise.

Delia, E.P. (1990) *Tourism Manpower Survey: The Accommodation Sector*, Malta, Secretariat for Tourism.

Delia, E.P. (1991) 'The Maltese economy and the external challenges: Some considerations', *Central Bank of Malta, Quarterly Review*, vol. 24, 2.

Delia, E.P. (1993) *The Maltese Economy: Policy Outline for 1993 and Beyond*, Malta, Chamber of Commerce.

Economic Division, Office of the Prime Minister (1981) *Malta: Guidelines for Progress – Development Plan 1981-1985*, Malta, Government Press.

Economic Planning and Management, Office of the Prime Minister (1987) *Economic Survey, January-September*, Malta, Government Press.

Economic Planning Division, Ministry for Economic Affairs (1991) *Economic Survey, January-September*, Malta, Government Press.

Education – Industry Unit (1987) *Skill and Training Needs Survey Report*, Malta, mimeo.

Food and Agriculture Organisation (1992) *Malta Agriculture Policy and the EC Membership: Challenges and Opportunities*, Rome, FAO.

Inguanez, C. & Briguglio, P.L. (1986) 'Factors affecting the size of the Maltese labour force', *Economic and Social Studies* (New Series), vol. 3.

Koziara, E.C. (1975) *The Labour Market and Wage Determination in Malta*, Malta, The Royal University of Malta, Department of Economics.

Krugman, P.R. (1991) 'Economic competitiveness: myths and realities', *Science*, vol. 254, 5033.

Lever-Tracy, C. (1987) 'Boomerangs on a small Island: Maltese who returned from Australia', *Economic and Social Studies (New Series)*, vol. 4.

Sultana, R.G. (1992) *Education and National Development: Historical and Critical Perspectives on Vocational Schooling in Malta*, Msida, Malta, Mireva Publications.

Sultana, R.G. (1993) 'Practices and policies in child labour: Lessons from Malta', *British Journal of Education and Work*, vol. 6, 3.

Workers' Participation Development Centre (1992) *Women Workers in Industrial Estates: A Survey of their Needs and Facilities*, Malta, WPDC for the Commission for the Advancement of Women.

25

Maltese Orientations to Work

Edward L. Zammit

Introduction

Social behaviour is characterised by the ideas, values and norms which people attach to it. Each of these characteristics adds a specific dimension to social behaviour and provides an important direction and justification for future action. A certain pattern of social behaviour is more likely to be followed if the reasons for it are well understood by the actors, it is perceived as normal and considered worthwhile under specific circumstances. Such valuations of social behaviour tend to be assigned by individual actors on the basis of their present and past experiences and future aspirations. They are also usually embodied within a particular cultural tradition.

In this essay, the term 'orientation' refers to a generalised concept of social perceptions, pre-dispositions, meanings, values, aspirations and norms which surround work activity in Malta. The term includes both the socially endorsed attitudes and the interpretations by individuals of their own life experiences. It incorporates the view of work as having both an 'intrinsic' (or terminal) value, in terms of its contribution to the personal development of the worker as a human being and an 'extrinsic' (or instrumental) value in terms of its outcomes such as income, power and social rewards for the worker. Of course, the two sets of values need not be viewed as mutually exclusive and have, in fact, sometimes been presented as forming part of a hierarchy of human 'needs', whereby more extrinsic and materialistic 'lower order' values need to be satisfied before an individual can aspire to 'higher order', intrinsic needs (Maslow, 1954).

In other words, 'orientation' encapsulates a synthesis made by individuals and groups in a given society between the traditional cultural influences on work, their assessments of it, based on their own experiences, and their normative aspirations about it.[1]

The Maltese orientations to work are explored in this essay by looking at some of the data which has been uncovered through a series of empirical investigations on work in Malta, in the context of the traditional culture.

It is often assumed a priori that in many respects, Maltese orientations are simply a reflection of those which prevail in other, nearby European countries. However, just as it soon becomes evident to any foreign visitor that Malta has its own particular landscape and cultural identity, it is also reasonable to expect that there are some characteristic features in the Maltese orientations to work and that these may contribute towards a complete picture of this society with its distinctive and common features.

---

[1] The term 'orientation to work' gained sociological currency following the pioneering research of the 'affluent worker' studies of the late 1960s (see Goldthorpe et al., 1968, 1969). Normative aspirations may be about the substantive or the procedural aspects of work, that is about the content of one's job or about the rules and regulations governing the conditions of one's work. Refer also to Fox (1971).

The orientation to work held by individuals within a particular society usually stems from various sources. A person's orientation to work does not merely reflect actual work experiences but also commonly held ideas and values within a sub-culture. Nevertheless, the experience of work provides a necessary though partial explanation of popular orientations to work and thus deserves attention in its own right.

For this reason, it is relevant to find out how these orientations vary among the different worker categories. For instance, it is important to know whether any variations in orientations may be detected between the manual and non-manual categories of workers. Such categories are obviously very broad as each groups together a variety of occupations. Nevertheless, there are sociological studies which have established that the demarcation between manual and non-manual workers is an important dividing line in workers' orientations (Runciman 1972, Mackenzie 1975).

The Occupational Background

The Maltese employment situation has for generations been subjected to severe fluctuations. Throughout the nineteenth and most of the twentieth century, the Maltese economy – particularly its varying employment levels – was heavily dependent upon the strategic value which was placed from time to time upon the Island by the colonial policy makers (Busuttil 1973; Zammit 1984). During this period, Malta's economy underwent successive periods of economic booms and depressions which were locally unpredictable and uncontrollable, being dictated by the changing needs of an imperial strategy with worldwide commitments. Naturally, the needs of the Maltese workers were hardly taken into account in these decisions.

Most Maltese workers thus came to regard periodic unemployment as an inevitable, though unpalatable, part of their life-cycle. Such an experience was bound to have repercussions on the type of social orientations towards work which emerged in Malta. This is quite evident in the proverbs and other expressions of conventional wisdom prevalent among Maltese workers. Unemployment generates insecurity and fatalism about one's future which may be expressed in popular sayings like 'Save for a rainy day' (*Erfa' u sorr għal meta tiġi bżonn*). Likewise, the traditional virtues among Maltese workers include *'l-għaqal'* (combining a quiet, cautious submissiveness with sensibility, self-restraint and thriftiness) and *'il-bżulija'* (a natural inclination for working hard). Hard and 'honest' work brings 'honour' to a person and his/her family and saves them from the humiliations of dependence on others or from disreputable activities which are considered even worse. As a practical rule, Maltese workers when young are taught to follow the working example of the ant, a common insect in Maltese homes, which is seen busily hoarding its food throughout the endless summer months in preparation for the coming winter. These traditional virtues ('honour', *'għaqal'* and *'bżulija'*) are here seen as inter-related. Combined together, they form the concept of the Maltese Work Ethic.

The Maltese preoccupation with security in employment is particularly manifested in the traditional popular search for secure government jobs, sometimes even in preference to better paid jobs elsewhere – though admittedly, these were not often available on the market.

There are in Malta approximately 64.4% of the total labour force in manual occupations and 35.6% in non-manual ones.[2] The latter include professional, administrative, executive, technical, clerical and supervisory grades whereas the former include all skilled, semi-skilled and unskilled workers and tradesmen.

The occupational distribution in Malta manifests some unique features by comparison with other developed or developing countries. According to the latest officially published statistics on the labour force (C.O.S., 1993), out of a total labour supply of almost 138,000, the registered unemployment rate is only of approximately 4%. Among the gainfully occupied, there are no fewer than 42% employed in the public sector. There are also 28.7% employed in directly productive activities including a small but vibrant private manufacturing sector. The rest are occupied in providing a wide range of services (29.3%), notably

---

[2] See C.O.S. (1986). A survey carried out by the author during 1977-78 (Z/2) found that 68% of the Maltese labour force could be classified as manual and 32% as non-manual workers.

those connected with tourism. Clearly there is also a rampant 'black' or 'informal' economic activity – though no reliable estimates of it have yet been published. Nevertheless, it is well known that many workers opt for the security of state employment, where the wages and salaries are relatively low, partly because of the attraction of an undeclared, additional income through part-time work elsewhere. This enables many individuals to raise their living standards and help the economy cope with more than one million tourist arrivals annually in recent years. However, in addition to severe strains on the environment of a small island, this situation is also fomenting feelings of relative deprivation among the wage earners who, for various reasons, depend exclusively on their regular income. Such feelings may escalate and prove socially divisive, as well as threatening to supplant some of the traditional values of 'The Maltese Work Ethic' which are deeply embedded in Maltese culture.[3]

As a result, some tangible changes in traditional orientations to work among contemporary Maltese workers might be expected to emerge.

The empirical evidence on which the arguments presented in this essay are based is drawn from the following sociological explorations carried out over the past two decades:

1. A survey of Maltese migrant workers in London: Zammit (1974), hereafter referred to as Z/1.
2. A survey of certain categories of Maltese workers' perceptions of work, carried out in 1979: Zammit (1984, pp.69-97), hereafter referred to as Z/2.
3. A survey of shop stewards at Malta Drydocks carried out as a supplement to (2) above: Zammit (1984), hereafter referred to as Z/3.
4. A survey of the opinions of workers at Malta Drydocks carried out in 1982: Baldacchino (1984), hereafter referred to as B/4.

---

[3] The traditional cultural influences relating to work in Malta are described in detail in Zammit (1984, pp. 31-41).

5. A hitherto unpublished comparative study on the interplay between worker participation, technology and production in two of Malta's leading enterprises: Zammit & Mintoff Bland (1992), hereafter referred to as ZM/5.
6. A study on changing values about a wide range of issues carried out by Gallup in Malta as part of the European Value Systems Studies: Abela (1991), hereafter referred to as A/6.

Work Expectations and Experiences

Work expectations and job selection are normally restricted to the options available on the local labour market and dictated by the exigencies of one's position in this labour market. The reasons for which a person 'selects' a particular job may, of course, be very different from those for which s/he stays in it or moves to another one. Work orientation, therefore, is partly the result of the cumulative impact of changing circumstances, personal experiences, actual decisions and adjustments which are made throughout one's career. Such common experiences in time become incorporated into the worker sub-culture. Hence individual work experiences provide a useful starting point for analyzing work orientation.

The respondents in the Z/2 survey who were under 40 years of age tended to have more 'desirable' jobs (i.e. non-manual or skilled) as against those which are unskilled or manual. This reflects higher educational standards and increased opportunities for these types of work, which may not have been available for the previous generation. Less than half of the respondents (43.8%) had worked at their jobs for more than ten years, while one third (32.8%) had worked there for a period of less than five years. In fact, only 4.5% had not left their first job. However, 61.8% had been constrained to find alternative employment due to redundancy or dismissal; while only 33.7% had the opportunity to move to better jobs. Most respondents regarded the temptation to leave their jobs in exchange for better jobs elsewhere as a rare and risky luxury. This attitude was epitomised in two often repeated proverbs: *Aħjar għasfur f'idek milli mija fl-ajru* (A bird in hand is worth two in the bush) and *Għal kull għadma hawn mitt kelb* (There are a hundred dogs for every bone). In this way, respondents described the security of a government job as an important asset, not to be dismissed lightly.

When asked to indicate how they had landed on their first jobs, few respondents suggested that this was the result of a systematic exploration and a weighing of their prospects through a thorough search of opportunities in the labour market. Most manual workers had found their jobs through recommendations from influential persons or from friends, priests, teachers and the like. On the other hand, many of the professionals, skilled tradesmen and self-employed workers had followed on their father's footsteps, often with their parents' material assistance. Even in the case of the highly prized government jobs, which were usually obtained through public examinations, parents, friends, teachers or other trusted persons also played an important part.

Almost all respondents in the Z/3 survey who were over 30 years of age recalled a large scarcity of job opportunities at the time they had started their apprenticeship. Clearly, among the job alternatives available at a given time, few could compete with government employment in terms of security and wages. However, work at the Drydocks was in most cases also placed in the same category. It was obtained as a result of an aspiration and a pre-disposition. In the words of one respondent: 'It was considered as something special to work at the Dockyard'.

Many respondents had joined the Drydocks because they had planned to do so. Family pressures and, more frequently, family links played an important part in the choice of those who had opted specifically for the Drydocks. It is clear, from the responses of the Z/2 national sample, that the importance of family and friendship networks in obtaining jobs in Malta cannot be minimised.

Other influences that apparently played a major role in job selection were the desire for security and a good pay. They stated: 'The Dockyard has always been unsurpassable with respect to wages'. Both of these factors will be discussed later on in this essay.

Some workers from the Z/2 national sample stated that they had been indifferent with regards to choice of particular employers or types of work. Work for these had simply served as an opportunity for leaving school. They preferred 'working for money' and having come into contact with friends who had already been earning money, reinforced this feeling.

The question of job selection leads to the related question of job changes or that of labour turnover.

Maltese workers who manage to obtain a 'secure' job are not generally keen on changing jobs. At the Drydocks, for instance, it was found that 86.3% of the sample (in the B/4 study) had been working there for more than 5 years. But this cannot be said of all Maltese workers. In the Z/2 national sample, about half (50.4%) preferred to stay on working in the same job; but among non-Government employees, the percentage of would be movers is much higher (83.4%). This suggests that many Maltese workers are actually prepared to swap jobs if better conditions, (such as pay and security) were offered to them.

Even among Drydocks' shop stewards (Z/3) there were as many as 61% who had at some time actually considered leaving their jobs. Apparently the main reason was because of the physical dangers and hardships that their present job entailed. Nevertheless, it became quite clear that these respondents were very strongly attached to their work after all. Admittedly, their first contact with the 'grim industrial environment' of the Drydocks had been a tough experience for them and it triggered off a wish to run away. Nevertheless, only three of them had actually sat for Government examinations in an unsuccessful attempt to change their jobs.

The situation in private enterprise can, however, be quite different. It was reported in the ZM/5 study that in one of Malta's leading manufacturing industries, there is a high labour turnover – particularly among the highly skilled layer of engineers. About one in three engineers left their job in 1991. It was reported that pressure of high output targets and long hours of work, together with a lack of opportunities for skill development, job enrichment and job discretion were cited as the main reasons. Relatively low pay and the lack of uniform employment conditions among university graduates also explain some of the phenomenal turnover.

Similarly among the shop floor workers where a turnover of 17% was recorded in 1990, a low level of workplace satisfaction was monitored. This was manifested in long working hours, constraining overall working conditions, inadequate communication, and poor management-worker relations. These may not surface at all at the formal, industrial relations level. It was argued that 'all indicate a high degree of alienation at work' (Zammit & Mintoff Bland, 1992).

It is hardly surprising, therefore that when the respondents of the Z/2 survey were asked hypothetically to state whether they preferred a Government job or one with a private employer, only 10.4% opted for the latter even if it were better paid. The vast majority (89.6%) preferred a Government job mainly because of its 'conditions' and the 'security' it offers. It will be shown later on that among the unofficial 'conditions' of a Government job there is the possibility of a second job.

Additionally, the reluctance to change jobs manifests a psychological dependence issuing from a paternalist tradition (Zammit, 1984). As was stated by a young engine fitter

> I would like to leave but it is too risky, because I have a great deal of security here...the Drydocks has become a second home and a way of life for me.

Meaning and Value

Among the ingredients which contribute towards the development of work orientation are the various meanings and values attached to work activity. These convey the reasons for which work is performed, for which one job may be preferred to another and may instil a sense of obligation to it in terms of its worth. These meanings and values are embedded in culture and transferred through various socializing agents – including the work experience itself. The following are the main work values and meanings which emerged from the various empirical investigations cited above.

a. Economic and Material Considerations

— to meet one's own means of survival (financial needs) and those of one's family.
— to be self-reliant: not to become dependent on others.
— for security: guaranteed employment.
— for good working conditions.

b. Social and Psychological Considerations

— to possess the traditional virtues of honour, *'għaqal'* and *'bżulija'* – hereafter referred to as the 'Maltese Work Ethic'.

— to mix with people and to socialize.
— for personal identification with a job as 'my life'.
— for self-development: to acquire new skills, meet challenges, perform interesting activities.

Work is predominantly presented as being linked to meeting economic needs and aspirations. This fact was confirmed by respondents in all the investigations cited, with an overall average of 65.5%. The respondents' inclusion of their families among their 'financial needs' was usually meant to dispel any impression of greed and egoism on their part. The Maltese traditional workers' accent on work as a means of subsistence and self-reliance contrasts with the reported, instrumental orientation which motivates contemporary 'affluent workers' in other countries (Goldthorpe et al., 1968, 1969). Evidently the value of work as a means of survival is given top priority when that aspect seems under threat. Once that is secured, however, other aspects may assume greater importance though this will not necessarily happen. In this sense, the respondents' spontaneous answers indicate their order of priorities, although the instrumental value of work tends to be predominant among all categories of workers, the 'economic self-reliance' aspect is relatively more pronounced among manual workers while the values embodied in the Maltese work ethic are more evident among respondents with non-manual work experience. This does not suggest that non-manual workers are not interested in the financial rewards from work but rather that they are likely to take subsistence for granted.

The non-manual workers include the better educated persons, those with higher incomes and the regular church-goers. These still focus on the financial aspects of work as a main value; but they also tend to appreciate the other values of work. This suggests that among these categories of persons there are more who identify with the central value system of Maltese society. It is likely that such respondents, because of their education, training and work situation can express themselves better in the established, middle-class terminology. They are more likely to appreciate the social and psychological aspects of work.

Further probing into work values revealed that when the financial value was controlled in the Z/2 survey the traditional values of the 'Maltese Work Ethic' were highly rated – after economic self-reliance. After this, the personal values of 'learning new skills', 'gaining new experiences' and 'developing one's talents' were given significant rating – particularly among the non-manual and skilled respondents. The other social values mentioned were those of 'meeting other people', 'sharing experiences with them' and 'helping each other to solve common problems'.

Similar probing in the Drydocks' survey (B/4) further revealed the importance of non-financial personal and 'intrinsic' values like that of 'doing one's duty' and 'living up to one's human dignity' (45.0%).

These results may be interpreted in the light of sociological studies on job orientation conducted elsewhere. The emphasis on the extrinsic values of income and satisfying social relationships reflects the impact of various socializing agencies – and of the work experience particularly in large organisations. Nevertheless, contrary to the arguments proposed by Dubin and others, the Malta evidence supports the view that such 'extrinsic values' are complemented by latent aspirations and values of a different kind; even if these may appear low in the workers' order of priorities.[4] In other words, even among workers who fail to perceive any other positive value in work apart from the financial one, they may also have latent aspirations for personal, 'intrinsic' and traditional values. In fact, there were no fewer than 54.1% of the Z/2 sample who, in addition to financial values, expressed an appreciation of such values.

In addition, as a result of the efforts in recent decades by trade union and political leaders promoting industrial democracy, there was a demand for participation by workers in managerial decisions or for participative industrial relations as a new work value among some worker categories – notably among Drydocks workers (Zammit 1984; Kester 1980). These agree with the principle of worker participation and/or want to improve the participative system (88%: B/4). They also associate participation with

---

[4] Dubin et al. (1956) had argued that deprivations in work may be compensated by satisfactions in non-work life which are rendered possible through the income derived from work.

improved industrial relations and see it as contributing to most aspects of work activity such as productivity, flexibility, work conditions, cooperation and morale (B/4).

Nevertheless, work is often merely accepted as a necessary fact of life, which is indicative of an attitude of resignation rather than happiness. Some respondents (Z/2) have expressed a view of work as a moral duty or an obligation towards one's family. This concern with the family as the ultimate end for work may 'spill over' to the activity of work itself (Z/2). This confers on work an added, intrinsic meaning which may transcend the actual tasks performed. As a result, work may even be considered as a 'blessing' for which one should be thankful to God.

A minority of respondents (15%: Z/2) further viewed work as an opportunity for moral-personal development. This is linked to a condemnation of laziness, expressed in statements 'an idle person would go mad', 'work gives the human being an aim in life', 'a man who does not work is no man at all' and occasionally, 'the country cannot afford to support idlers'.

As a result many workers expressed a sense of accomplishment and overall satisfaction at the end of the day, and took pride in a job well done. In the words of one respondent

> At home, I often say to myself, 'I succeeded in that task, and it was not so bad after all'. (Z/3)

Job Satisfaction

The question of job satisfaction is closely related to that of orientation – in fact both are based on work expectations, aspirations and values in terms of which the actual experiences of work are assessed. However, job satisfaction is a complicated matter to explore because work has many facets. If a particular aspect of work is valued highly, satisfaction or dissatisfaction is measured according to the extent to which the work experience satisfies this value or need.

For such reasons, Fox and others have pointed out that one cannot gain much useful information about the workers' real levels of work satisfaction from general 'sponge' questions. Workers may be satisfied with, for instance, pay, security and status but dissatisfied with workmates, work activities, superiors and future prospects. Nevertheless, such general questions do provide some rough indication for comparative purposes of the varying extent of subjective assessments of different work experiences.

In answer to a general question: 'Are you satisfied with your work?' the following positive responses were given in the various surveys: 91.2% (Z/2); 82.0% (Z/3); 74.8% (B/4).

The reported high level of general job satisfaction in Malta compares well with studies conducted in various other countries. Even employees engaged in unrewarding tasks and receiving minimal extrinsic rewards often express such levels of satisfaction. Significantly, those occupying superior positions within the occupational structure tend to express somewhat higher satisfaction levels than the rest. Nevertheless the overall results in various countries for all categories of workers are impressively positive, similar to the trends as observable in Malta. The respondents' statements emphasizing the positive worth of their work are interpreted as an indirect expression of self-respect. Undoubtedly, work is a manifestation of the individual's identity or self-image. As such, admitting dissatisfaction with work for whatever reason is tantamount to a lowering of one's self-esteem.

Perhaps a more realistic assessment of the individual's state of satisfaction or dissatisfaction with work can be obtained through some hypothetical questions such as the following: What job would you select if you were to start life again with new opportunities? What job would you like your son or daughter to take? What work would you do if you won the National Lottery?

In answer to such questions most respondents clearly state that they would undertake something else other than their present jobs. The vast majority would like their children to do something 'better' than themselves (83% : Z/3). And, given the chance, the majority would likewise opt to do something 'better' than their present occupations – if possible, not having to 'work for money at all' (74% : Z/3). Such statements betray an indirect verdict on their own actual work experience. There is also a clear preference for upward occupational mobility among all the categories of Maltese workers.

It appears that although most workers are satisfied with the work actually available to them, this positive disposition does not extend to the general desirability of their actual work as opposed to other possible types of work.

The apparent ambiguity between the two types of answers may

be explained in terms of cognitive dissonance theory (Fox, 1976). Workers, when declaring themselves satisfied, have in mind only a very limited view of the extent and type of rewards which work can offer them in practice. They have therefore learned to be satisfied with their lot. Logical enough, these same 'satisfied' workers assert that they would ideally not prefer to get into the same job again (Argyris, 1964).

Sources of Job Satisfaction

An even more meaningful statement about the sources of job satisfaction or dissatisfaction may be given by respondents when asked to specify 'those aspects of their work which they like and/or detest most'. The following categories reflect the aspects which they mention.

a. Personal Identity

As stated above, work conveys a deep sense of personal and social identification with one's trade and ability. As Gouldner has pointed out, it is not simply important to keep oneself occupied – but to be usefully occupied. This contrasts with a sense of shame, dependence and uselessness which accompanies unemployment (Gouldner, 1969). Respondents often expressed this feeling through statements like: 'My work is my life' (Hajti ħidmieti); or 'It's my bread – my trade. I've got used to it' (Dak il-ħobz tiegħi, is-sengħa tiegħi; hekk jien imdorri).

All workers, especially those in the manual categories, express a great awareness of the social identity and general usefulness which their work bestows on them. Non-manual workers moreover exhibit a comparable tendency to rate their actual tasks highly. It seems that the latter tend to take extrinsic satisfaction for granted and aspire to 'higher order needs'. The high personal identification with their work roles and tasks expressed by both white collar and skilled manual workers (80% and 82.2% respectively : Z/2) contrasts with the lower level expressed by unskilled manual workers (56.1%). Moreover, there is a much higher proportion of manual workers who could not point to any particular work which they liked (76% : A/6; 62% : B/4).

b. Physical Conditions

As manual workers are more likely to work under unpleasant, dangerous, dirty and physically demanding conditions than the non-manual, they – particularly the unskilled – tend to be more concerned with their physical working environment and hours of work than the non-manual. They also resent their long working hours (61.6%: Z/2; 42.9%: B/4; 63%: A/6). These concerns, along with wages, are usually reflected in union-management negotiations and in collective agreements.

c. Social Environment

Many workers tend to appreciate the importance of working in pleasant company and of getting along well with superiors (40%: B/4; 38.4%: Z/2; 64%: A/6).

Social relationships are an important source of satisfaction at work. The pattern of responses indicate that work is associated with a considerable degree of companionship and fellow-feeling. At the Drydocks, most workers are on their own or working in small groups of two or three. They often report almost unlimited freedom in chatting and joking with their workmates, and describe one or two as 'close friends'. They (74%: Z/3) perceived a high degree of cooperation among their workmates which was expressed as follows:

> We help each other a great deal at work, and this is particularly evident when an accident occurs;

and

> If one completes one's task in less time, one will help one's mate;

and again

> The workers are very united. When you need assistance everyone is ready to help you. They will immediately forget that they might have quarrelled with you only a short time before.

Cooperation is very important for these workers, and conflict can be highly disruptive. Some workers reported having had to leave their previous jobs because relations with work-mates had became unbearable. Many stated that:

Life would be very difficult here if there was no cooperation among us.

This does not mean that competition, manipulation, rivalry, jealousy and conflict are absent at the Drydocks. That would be unrealistic. This is rather an expression of the predominant values within the workers' subculture and an idealised perception of social relations within it. In general, workers are brought together through constant physical proximity and through the sharing of a common way of life, even though they may be divided in a subdued struggle for prized, limited resources.

This contrasts very markedly with the attitudes of non-industrial workers, who, because of their job situation, training and social background, are more likely to be pre-occupied with relativities, status, seniority, promotion prospects and the like. Hence they more often find themselves in open conflict and experience direct competition, rivalry and hostility with their colleagues. In this sense, they find their social environment more problematic and develop attitudes which militate against the emergence of a powerful, disciplined trade union organisation in contrast to industrial workers.

d. Meaning and Purpose

The work activity may be appreciated both for its ultimate meaning or purpose – which may extend beyond the activity itself – and for its immediate and obvious relevance to the finished product. This was an important source of job satisfaction among Drydocks' workers (Z/3; B/4) for ship-repair is not an ordinary kind of job. It is an activity which necessarily carries with it a certain amount of pride and almost personal concern. The product is a huge grand and impressive object in its shape, movement and dimensions.

Inevitably, repairing the engine or even painting the name on to a 100,000-ton oil tanker is a unique kind of productive activity which does not bear comparison to the standardised products of an assembly line; in the latter case, the division of labour prevents the line operator from seeing the link between one's work and the end-product.

Thus, Drydocks workers are very conscious of the skill, precision, importance and responsibility of their particular tasks. Only a few unskilled workers stated that they experienced monotony at work due to the kind of task they had to perform. One of these, a ship-painter, even stressed the need 'to implement one's ideas at work'. Drydocks workers generally recognize the need for freedom in decision-making: 'One has to put to good use both one's imagination and one's experience – this is not learnt from books, for every ship has a different design', said a skill-conscious gearcutter.

With reference to this and various other aspects of work, most Drydocks workers stated (B/4) that through the participative system they are better informed (60.5%), feel more dignified (71/6%) and are in a better position to influence events at their enterprise (62.1%). Most Drydocks workers demand even more of these 'participative rights'.

The vast majority of Drydocks respondents (91%: Z/3) saw their work as important. 'If it weren't for my kind of work, the Yard would not be able to function'. There were only slight differences between skilled and unskilled workers on this point.

A final aspect of the meaning of work is the responsibility perceived by the individual for the tasks under one's discretion. Only a few respondents at the Drydocks (22% Z/3) stated that they did not feel enough responsibility at work. Those who answered negatively were mainly unskilled workers. A common reaction among this minority was that there are other people who assume responsibility; 'so why should I bother?'

Clearly the prevailing atmosphere among Drydocks workers was one of considerable pride in one's work, particularly among tradesmen. They were conscious of the fact that they worked in the largest enterprise of the island, and one which attracts constant public attention. They were also aware of their political muscle within the General Workers' Union. Characteristically, therefore, most workers (74%: Z/3) replied in the affirmative to the question 'Are you proud of your work?'

Apart from the Drydocks, however, Maltese workers generally have little direct experience of worker participation and their understanding of the different meanings of work tend to be limited. Nevertheless, an overall appreciation of the 'intrinsic' aspects of work has been recorded (51.2% : A/6).

e. Job Dependence

The traditional importance attached to security has already been mentioned above. Most of the Drydocks respondents (96%: Z/3) described their job as one of the most stable in Malta. For

> Malta can never allow the Drydocks to close down

because

> Government would be burdened with the responsibility of finding alternative employment for all those people who would otherwise go on the dole.

Thus, for Drydocks workers, security is not really a problem and many of them see their job security further guaranteed through the participative system. (66%: B/4)

Likewise, in Malta generally, it appears that the problem of job security is not as acute as it once was (57%: A/6). However, this does not exclude the possibility of a high level of employment dependence.

The question for many workers is: How far do the existing rewards for work, including the less tangible 'intrinsic' ones, tie the workers to their present employment? For instance, are Drydocks workers dependent upon their employer or can they find an equally attractive, alternative employment elsewhere? Since, as already stated, unrivalled opportunities exist for skilled workers at the Drydocks, offering both 'extrinsic' and some 'intrinsic' rewards. Hence, many workers are reluctant to leave and thus remain attached to their jobs.

The younger workers tend to be attached to their wages and other fringe benefits. The older workers are not merely attached to their formal benefits and welfare schemes, though these are certainly appreciated. For them, employment also means a 'way of life'. Thus among all workers – young and old – the element of job attachment, dependence and security has retained some importance even if it no longer seems to occupy top priority (26.8%: B/4; 57%: A/6).

Conclusion

In this essay, an attempt was made to look at the contemporary orientations towards work which prevail in Malta and to detect whether any significant shifts are taking place from the traditional orientations. It has to be acknowledged, of course, that such observations can only be meaningful at a generalised level of social behaviour. They tend to overlook minor trends and undercurrents among specific groups and categories of people. Following Alan Fox (1971), the concept of 'orientation' here refers

> in a general way to a central organising principle which underlines people's attempts to make sense of their lives.

In this way, social orientations form an integral part of a people's culture (or sub-culture) as much as attitudes are integrated into an individual personality. As such, social orientations may be explored through enquiries into people's experiences, expectations, meanings, perceptions, aspirations, values and norms which govern their behaviour. Such investigations should also leave room for broad structural, traditional and organisational factors which may leave their mark on orientations in particular historical circumstances (Gallie, 1978). Accordingly in this essay, the data which has emerged from a series of empirical investigations among Maltese workers on certain aspects of work have been explored with the aim of constructing a composite picture of social orientations to work. These investigations were aimed at finding out people's responses to questions on various extrinsic and intrinsic aspects of work. It is generally recognised that while, over time, certain shifts in emphasis among the different aspects of work may take place, such shifts may not necessarily signify progress from one level to a higher one (Maslow, 1954).

In fact, some shifts have clearly taken place in Malta, as in other countries, with respect to the financial rewards for work. The higher incomes available for work nowadays when compared with those of the past have not shifted attention to other aspects of work but simply raised expectations for a higher and higher standard of living and thus for more incomes. Ironically, respondents may still claim to be working in order 'to earn bread for their families'. Simultaneously some other aspects may also be added on board so that the emerging orientation would incorporate a variety of traditional and modern values, possibly in a re-shuffled order of priorities. Thus, for instance, while the contemporary Maltese worker needs no longer be so consciously preoccupied with the 'security' aspect of a job, nowadays this aspect may be taken for granted. It was argued, for instance, that while a 'job with the government' may provide a guarantee of security, more importantly, it also offers the possibility of taking on a second job in the 'informal economy'.

In the meantime, the traditional aspects embodied in the 'Maltese work ethic' (honour, *'għaqal'*, *'bżulija'*) are given a lower priority and mainly restricted to certain categories of workers.

The corresponding differences between the 'traditional' and 'contemporary' Maltese orientations to work are summarised below in order of priority:

Traditional Orientation	*Contemporary Orientation*
Survival ('earn one's living').	A 'high' financial reward.
Security ('a job for life').	A regular income, combined with opportunities for additional, undeclared income.
'Maltese Work ethic' (honour *'għaqal'*, *'bżulija'*).	Divergent standards and values among different worker categories.
Personal identification with work ('My trade is my life'); acquire new skills.	Greater emphasis on: physical conditions of work (hardship, danger, hours) among manual workers.
'Personal' values: doing one's duty, responsibility, moral obligation; particularly among self-employed, non-manual and professional persons.	Work which is interesting, challenging, varied particularly among professional, non-manual and young workers.
Social solidarity with fellow workers (community, companionship).	Social status (be respected; opportunities for promotion).
Paternalist – compliance relations between employers and	Perceptions of conflict in industrial relations ('us and them');

management – particularly in small enterprises.	extrinsic goals pursued through militant trade union action particularly among industrial workers in large enterprises.
	Participative and corporatist industrial relations: trend towards negotiated settlements of trade disputes.

The reasons for the above shifts in orientation, merit serious investgation. In one view, they merely reflect changes in work orientations which have already taken place in other, more industrialized countries and are imported into Malta. Once introduced, many new customs and ideas are rapidly assimilated and spread to the remotest parts of the island, producing an impression of a modern, flexible society characterized by a remarkable uniformity in artistic tastes, living standards and social aspirations (Zammit, 1984).

The influence of political, industrial and trade union leaders on popular work orientations can also be detected.

More importantly, changes in work orientations may be explained with reference to the constant developments taking place in the whole Maltese economy and society. The reasons for some of these changes may be also indigenous. Perhaps nowhere else are the effects of such developments better felt than in Malta's largest, traditional industry, the Drydocks. A more recent study carried out at that enterprise has concluded that:

> As the Maltese economy has recently been going through a period of expansion, fuelled by touristic, public and consumer spending, working at the Drydocks is becoming increasingly uncompetitive and unattractive to prospective workers in Malta's contemporary labour market. It is proving difficult to recruit and keep apprentices at the Drydocks with all its associated dangers, hardship and uncompetitive wages (Zammit & Mintoff Bland, 1992).

This also suggests that in the still-changing, contemporary economic climate, some of the survey findings cited above are already being superseded.

Just as the shifts in orientation to work are a reflection of the profound changes which are taking place in society at large, so their impact is bound to reverberate on work-related issues such as human resource management, unionisation and industrial relations. It is for such compelling reasons, that the state of popular orientations to work and its root causes merit constant empirical investigation.

References

Abela, A.M. (1991) *Transmitting Values in European Malta*, Rome & Malta, Pontificia Università Gregoriana & Malta Jesuit Publications.

Argyris, C. (1964) *Integrating the Individual and the Organisation*, New York, John Wiley & Sons.

Baldacchino, G. (1984) *Il-Parteċipazzjoni fit-Tarzna: Kif Jaħsibha l-Ħaddiem*, University of Malta, Workers' Participation Development Centre.

Busuttil, S. (1973) *Malta's Economy in the Nineteenth Century*, Malta, Malta University Press.

C.O.S. (Central Office of Statistics) (1986) *Malta Census 1985: Volume 1, A Demographic Profile of Malta and Gozo*, Malta, Government Press.

C.O.S. (Central Office of Statistics) (1993) *Economic Trends*, June, Malta, Government Press.

Dubin R. (1956) 'Industrial workers' worlds: A study of life interests of industrial workers', *Social Problems*, vol. 3, 1.

Fox, A. (1971) *A Sociology of Work in Industry*, London, Collier-Macmillan.

Fox, A. (1976) 'The meaning of work' in *Occupational Categories and Cultures*, Milton Keynes, Open University Press.

Gallie, D. (1978) *In Search of the New Working Class*, Cambridge, Cambridge University Press.

Goldthorpe, J.H., Lockwood, D., Bechhofer, F & Platt, J. (1968, 1969) *The Affluent Worker in the Class Structure* (3 vols) Cambridge, Cambridge University Press.

Gouldner, A. (1969) 'The unemployed self' in Fraser, R. (ed.), *Work: Twenty Personal Accounts*, Harmondsworth, Penguin.

Kester, G. (1980) *Transition to Workers' Self-Management: Its Dynamics in the Decolonizing Economy of Malta*, The Hague, Institute of Social Studies.

Mackenzie, G. (1975) 'World images and the world of work' in Esland, G. (ed.), *People and Work*, London, Holmes McDougall.

Maslow, A.H. (1954) *Motivation and Personality*, New York, Harper & Row.

Runciman, W.G. (1972) *Relative Deprivation and Social Justice*, Harmondsworth, Penguin.

Zammit, E.L. (1974) 'The economic orientations of Maltese migrants in London: Work, money and social status', *Economic and Social Studies*, vol. 3.

Zammit, E.L. (1984) *A Colonial Inheritance: Maltese Perceptions of Work, Power and Class Structure with Reference to the Labour Movement*, Malta, Malta University Press.

Zammit, E.L. & Mintoff Bland, Y. (1992) 'Participation, technology and production', paper presented to the International Industrial Relations Association (IIRA), Study Group 4.

26

Worker Cooperatives in Malta: Between Self-Help and Subsidy

Godfrey Baldacchino

Preamble

It is imperative that the Maltese people understand a grave, practical truth: We must help ourselves. We cannot sit idle, waiting for the Government to send manna from heaven...

To conclude, this is my plea: The Maltese worker is shrewd, patient, capable, not disposed towards communism, righteous, intelligent, learns fast and is motivated to improve performance. What is lacking is one thing only: The courage to associate with others; a cooperative spirit.

[1]

Dr. Amabile Gulia – Valletta, Malta, 11 August 1891.

---

[1] Translation of a letter addressed to Dr. Enrico Zammit, official of the Società Maltese di Pesca – apparently a fishing cooperative in formation. Published in

The date is not a misprint. The concerns expressed in the above excerpts from a letter, now over a century old, strike the reader by their freshness and contemporary relevance. It evokes, on one hand, a sense of purpose and mobilization by nineteenth century Maltese intelligentsia towards solidary rather than solitary production; on the other, an inkling of a certain resignation, perhaps even fatalism resulting from an (already ingrained?) disposition to ascribe to the state full responsibility for its citizens' welfare.

Bridging the Great Divide

The worker, or producer, cooperative is an association of self-employed producers. It is a productive organization which is owned and controlled by its own workers. Capital and labour are embodied in one and the same person. Ideally, they are thus truly reconciled. An elegant solution to the fundamental divide between who owns and who does not which, albeit historically and culturally marginal, appears worthy of serious consideration.

The Argument

This paper will introduce the attractions of worker cooperation, tempered however by the regrettable manner in which worker cooperative practices have not matched the promises. The Maltese cooperative sector is critically reviewed next, with a description of the few registered worker cooperative initiatives. The ensuing discussion, grounded in the concepts emergent from the review of theory and practice, Maltese experiences and from my own exposure in the field, highlights the peculiar nature of worker cooperative initiatives in Malta. Such characteristics serve as illustrative material on the Maltese social formation: the wary disposition of the Maltese towards cooperative ventures; a predilection for benevolent paternalist leadership and a deliberate ploy to tap the resources of an omnipresent and well disposed state apparatus. What is past is prologue, indeed.

Gazzetta di Malta – Corriere Mercantile Maltese, 21 August 1891.

Making A Case

On paper, the case for worker cooperatives appears formidable (Baldacchino, 1987). Democratic control and management can avoid the dichotomy of interests between managers and managed and the normative conflict which ensues (Fox, 1971). This is costly in terms of reduced motivation and in keeping untapped a vast resource: the workers' own initiative, creative skills and decision-making acumen, nurtured by the direct ongoing experience of work (Blumberg, 1968). Worker cooperatives can also be seen as schools of democracy. The institutionalized practice of democratic participation at the workplace is in itself an educational, self-supporting and self-generating process. The act of participating improves the quality of participation; while the cooperative context in which this occurs is a positive-sum one where self-gain is also collective gain and not fellow workers' loss – as would otherwise result from an unequal distribution of organizational power. Thus, participation encourages individuals to be free via socially responsible action, and so provides for the political and economic liberation of men and women (Vanek, 1975). Worker Cooperatives offer the promise of self-control, in stark contrast to widespread social encounters. Workers thus elevate themselves from being disinterested consuming objects who relinquish substantial responsibility into the hands of the few (Sik, 1984, pp. 261-2).

The democratization and humanization of work and workplace relations suggested by worker cooperation vindicate the centrality of work to most people's lives, not simply as a prerequisite for survival, but as a potential avenue for self-actualization, self-identity and integral human resource development (Goulet, 1989). Worker cooperatives also permit the winning combination of, on one hand, economies of scale whereby unit costs are reduced (and therefore profitability is enhanced) by deploying a higher volume of investment, human resources and sales; this is a condition typically enjoyed by large scale enterprises. On the other hand, there is the preservation of the pride of skill, craft and discretion – often associated with small-scale, self-employment (Baldacchino, 1990, p. 15). Their economic performance indicates a higher marginal productivity of labour with respect to capital which therefore incentivizes the resort to higher employment quotas than would otherwise obtain in conventionally run firms (Cable & Fitzroy, 1980). The internal cohesiveness and camaraderie generated by cooperation augurs to produce a greater responsiveness to market conditions (Jackall & Levin, 1984).

The equitable distribution of control and of profits are other notable characteristics of worker cooperatives. The partial allocation of any surplus may also be guided by social objectives as are cheaper products and services, participation in civic initiatives, investment in socially useful projects, or the establishment of new worker cooperative ventures. These initiatives are recognized in various countries as contributing to economic justice and societal development, justifying some modicum of support by governments towards cooperative promotion.

The Many Faces of Failure

Yet, in spite of this promising assemblage, the performance of worker cooperatives has been consistently reported as disappointing.

First of all, most worker cooperatives have failed to survive. Failure may result from a number of factors, namely

a. the consequences of small size and small scale (under financing; enthusiasm without skill or experience; operation in high risk and harshly competitive product domains);
b. a denigration of managerial skills (a failure to recognize the need for skilled professional managerial expertise); and
c. internal dissension (the absence of conventional authority figures and disciplinary structures which could lead to frequent cases of insubordination, abusive practices, a vacuum of accountability and responsibility).

Secondly, where worker cooperatives have managed to weather the above storms, they may have nevertheless fallen victim to their own favourable accomplishments: large size – an almost inevitable consequence of economic success – causes bureaucratization and a resort to representative (indirect) in lieu of participatory (direct) democracy (Pateman, 1970). Economic prosperity may lead to 'founding member egoism' because it increases the incentive to limit membership and to employ cheap, second class labour (typically part-timers or workers debarred from shareholding), or else to liquidate/sell the concern and recoup the market value of their shares (Baldacchino, 1990, p. 28).

The Maltese Cooperative Sector

At this point, let me shift my focus from abstract, generalized considerations to the specific and actual case of Malta. In this way, it will be possible to appreciate the extent to which the bland idealism needs to be tempered by the bitter pill of reality.

What have traditionally been called cooperatives almost totally consist in agricultural and fishery service cooperatives. Established since 1947, these provide centralized services – such as veterinary advice, bulk fertilizer and seed imports, marketing of agricultural produce – to their farmer and fisherman/woman members (Rizzo, 1985). The cooperative qualifier reflects their one member, one-vote system, irrespective of capital contribution – probably the only way to entice large numbers of small, traditionally suspicious, homogenous producers to join forces rather than to succumb to market forces which would see them savagely in competition with one another as well as at the mercy of powerful middlemen, the *pitkali*.[2] Otherwise, these organizations share no similarity with worker cooperatives because they employ labour just like any other conventional firm. Most owe their origin to government initiative. They thrive on the basis of the state's concern to provide all the benefits necessary to ensure a decent livelihood to the precariously dwindling local agricultural and fishing community (OPTIMA, 1985a). Indeed, those financially strongest enjoy a monopoly position in their respective market, with the state's blessing.

> ...the Maltese cooperative movement was ushered in specifically as a cost-saving, profit enhancing mechanism to boost agricultural efficiency and productivity. It involved no commitment to cooperative values and it was not inspired by a cooperative ideology. (Baldacchino, 1990, p. 90).

---

[2] These middlemen typically charge commission rates of over 8% and manipulated the principles of supply and demand to their own benefit. (Letter from Romeo A. Formosa, dated 22 June 1993). Zammit (1973) claims that animal breeders got only 50-65% of the final price, the difference being shared between the middleman and the retailer. The gender bias here is intentional.

The cooperative saga in Malta does not appear to warrant much celebration. Barbuto (1992) paints a dismal, yet factual, picture: 47 coops have been registered since the 'cooperative movement' dawned in 1947. Of these, 27 have been wound up; another 8 exist on paper but are not functioning. Of the remaining 12, 5 have been registered for less than ten years and may fail to survive their 'teething troubles'. (See Table 1)

Table 1. Position of the Cooperative Movement in Malta (1993)

Name	Nature	Date of Registration	Membership	No of Employees
Żabbar Farmers' Coop Soc. ~	service	15.01.47	66	nil
St. Paul's Bay Farmers' Coop. Soc. ~	service	17.01.47	83	nil
Żebbuġ Farmers' Coop. Soc. ~	service	21.01.47	50	nil
Siġġiewi Farmers' Coop. Soc. ~	service	24.01.47	93	nil
Rabat Farmers' Coop. Soc. ~	service	03.02.47	292	1ft, 1pt
Farmers' Central Coop. Soc. *	service	08.02.47	*	24ft, 2pt
Dingli Farmers' Coop. Soc. ~	service	06.06.47	123	nil
Qormi Farmers' Coop. Soc. ~	service	11.06.47	23	nil
Mġarr Farmers' Coop. Soc. ~	service	24.07.48	94	1pt
Koperattiva Produtturi tal-Ħalib.	service	16.05.58	220	50ft
Moviment Azzjoni Soċjali (MAS) Coop.	consumer	21.06.58	28	nil
Gozo Milk & Agric. Producers Coop.	service	23.02.59	772	3ft
Farmers' Wine Coop. Soc.	service	27.08.60	74	3ft, 1pt, 2ol
Koperattiva tas-Sajd.	service	29.12.64	94	1pt wr
Agricoop.	consumer	18.06.65	882	16ft
Koperattiva ta' Min Irabbi l-Majjal.	service	18.04.83	196	2ft
The Catering Cooperative Society.	worker	07.12.84	12	10pt+
Koperattiva tal-Burdnara (1987).	worker	21.08.87	45	2ft+
Għaqda tal-Mini Buses Coop. Soc.	worker	28.07.89	270	1ft, 1pt+
Għaqda Kop. Nazzjonali tas-Sajd.	service	19.04.91	281	nil
Koperattiva Snajja' tal-Bini.	worker	14.01.93	7	nil+
University Coop. Bookshop Soc.	consumer	21.01.93	210	nil
Motor Towing Coop. Soc.	worker	15.09.93	8	nil+
Spotless Maintenance & Cleaning Coop. Soc.	worker	15.09.93	7	nil+
Total			3929	117 ft 18 other

A Litany of Woes

Case studies of various agricultural service coops, carried out mainly by University students over recent years, consistently identify a litany of woes. Farmer-members refuse to consider the cooperative's long-term interests in favour of maximizing their own, short-term gains. There is a dearth of business acumen, as well as of the recognition for its need; hence there is often only a token investment in managerial skills. There is also an intermittent invasion of the spheres of competence of professional management by the farmer-members elected on the committee of management, which strains the organizational set-up and blurs respective responsibilities. In many cases, there seems to be a precipitous vicious spiral pointing menacingly towards dissolution. (Baldacchino, 1990; Camilleri, 1984; Grech, 1992; Stafrace, 1985; Villegas, 1990).

Worker Cooperation in Malta

The documented experiences of formal worker cooperation in Malta are much fewer. The first registered initiative was a stevedores' cooperative set up following the initiative of the General Workers' Union (GWU) in 1974. The cooperative's attempt to operate as a practical monopoly in cargo handling was not successful. The decision was taken to dispose of the equipment and, eventually, to liquidate the coop. The 15 members, contrary to

Source: Secretary, Board of Cooperatives, letter dated 27th May 1993; updated December 1993.

* The FCCS is a secondary-level coop; set up by the eight agricultural service primary cooperatives marked ~ above.
+ this statistic excludes the worker members in the case of worker cooperatives

   ft = full-time;
   pt = part-time;
   ol = on loan;
   wr = without remuneration

normal procedures, dissolved the coop and made off with all outstanding assets.[3]

Instigated by the GWU and the Malta Labour Party (MLP), then in government, two clothing cooperatives were set up in 1983. These were the First Clothing Coop (21 worker members) and the Kordin Clothing Coop (26 worker members). The coops were twin 'rescue' companies, providing employment particularly to female workers made redundant from the recession hit textile industry. The coops operated on a 'cut, make and trim' basis, usually handling small orders on subcontracting terms. Unfortunately, the coops lacked marketing expertise; they remained completely dependent on sporadic subcontracting and given pattern designs; efficiency levels remained low because of constant shifts in garment specification; and the machinery they operated was obsolete. After five years of operation, the two coops were liquidated. They remain to date the only registered cases of worker cooperatives within the local manufacturing sector (OPTIMA 1985b).

Cooperative Maintenance Services, with 10 registered worker members, was set up in 1983, pooling the skills of unemployed youths who offered plumbing, electrical installation and pest control services. The coop worker members benefited from loans, free office premises and a stream of orders through the Government's Board of Cooperatives. Centrifugal tendencies however escalated. Members persisted in non-cooperative, individual odd jobs and failed to set up and consolidate an organizational fabric. The cooperative was liquidated in 1988.

The Catering Cooperative was set up with 23 workers in 1983. A private firm, bent on cutting down its number of operating catering outlets because of escalating losses, offered three 'surplus' outlets lock, stock and barrel to its redundant employees, in lieu of terminal benefits. With the backing of the General Workers' Union, in which the workers were (and still are) unionized, the redundant employees took over the three outlets and have been

---

[3] I am grateful to Romeo A. Formosa, Secretary to the Board of Cooperatives, for providing me with this and other factual information otherwise not available in print.

operating them since on a worker cooperative basis. The coop, down to 12 worker members and a number of part-timers, is now at a critical watershed, having sold one of its three outlets and hoping to employ this new liquidity to undertake desperately needed major refurbishment (Baldacchino et al., 1993; Bonett, 1989).

Still in operation is a second stevedore cooperative, established in 1987 with 47 worker-members. This is in part a refoundation of the previous stevedores coop, since the motivation was practically identical: to dominate the sea merchandise handling market and to be able to apply and win state contracts in this sector. Indeed, it is not excluded that various members of this coop were also members of the 1974 setup. Perhaps the major difference was a realignment of the cooperative's leadership to reflect the realignment of political power with the change of Government in the May 1987 general elections.

There is also a Mini-Buses Cooperative, set up in 1989, with close to 200 worker-members. In this case again, the main spur towards collective registration was the necessity to cast a single, corporate identity enabling the various individual mini-bus owners to register for, and obtain, substantial state contracts without depressing prices via suicidal cost-cutting competition.

On reading through the above narrative, can one fail to raise a pertinent question: are these real worker cooperatives? What about the noble ideals of solidarity, job satisfaction, democratization and humanization of work which are allegedly part and parcel of the cooperative unit? Is the cooperative label an expedient? Is the cooperative spirit a myth?

Recent cooperative developments have occurred under the aegis of the University of Malta (Baldacchino, 1994). The principal idea is to offer work contracts to workers on a competitive basis, on condition that they band together as a worker cooperative unit rather than – as is more conventional – either employing extra staff on the University's payroll or contracting out the work to a private company. The University has thus been serving as a catalyst for such forms of cooperation, providing also financial, managerial, organizational, legal and technical advice mainly via the University's Precincts Officer and the Workers' Participation Development Centre. The Employment & Training Corporation has also been instrumental in identifying potential worker members from among the registered unemployed. To date, and since December 1991, one building trades worker coop – Koperattiva Snajja' tal-Bini (7 worker members) and a Maintenance and Cleaning worker coop (7 worker members) have been registered; a University Bookshop was also registered as a consumer coop, membership being open to staff and students; and a second building trades worker coop in formation was aborted.

An appraisal of the last venture sheds some very interesting light on the issues surrounding worker cooperation in Malta. I was fortunate in having closely monitored the events leading to this failure by virtue of conducting a series of semi-structured interviews with these proto-cooperators, in conjunction with the University Precincts Officer, during July 1992.

The Coop Which Never Was

The proto-coop consisted initially in four brothers who were however obliged to increase the team to the minimum number of seven stipulated by law to qualify as a coop and, consequently, to undertake masonry works required by the University. As it turned out, however, the three latecomers remained in an unequal power relationship in contrast to the brothers. Apart from enjoying an unassailable block vote situation, the Four owned all the working capital and equipment with which the coop carried out its work. One of the newcomers had actually worked with the brothers before as their employee. In spite of working together for a number of months, the would-be cooperators did not take steps to remedy this uneven situation by, for instance, establishing a common bank account and issuing share capital in which each member would contribute equally. The workers preferred cash in their pockets rather than investing even a token percentage of their earnings for the sake of the collective. The cooperative setup was an obligation, permitting them to make hay while the sun shines. And as far as the three latecomers were concerned, they were still employees, uninterested in responsibility and management but then adamant in the importance of job security, work guarantees and wage stability.

The elaborate hoax may have persisted had not the profitability of the work being undertaken suddenly dropped to a low ebb. Wage-labour perceptions then became ascendant, and there was no organizational fabric or collective identity to hold the would-be cooperators together. The proto-coop disbanded at the first inkling of crisis (source: personal interview notes).

Critical Discussion

Interestingly, the stevedores, motor towing and mini-buses cooperative ventures were/are also characterized by centrifugal tendencies – the worker members remain essentially individual, self-employed, responsible for their own livelihood in splendid isolation. Capital (in these cases transport equipment and machinery) is not pooled but remains individual, private property. The cooperative structure is nevertheless handy because of a centralized depot to receive and transmit messages and service requests; a convenient format for registration purposes; plus a structure to articulate interests effectively if, and only if, the need arises – much like (in more senses than one) a trade union for the self-employed.

One critical reflection based on this experience is the extent to which worker cooperatives, or any cooperative for that matter, would have been registered in Malta were it not for active support by government, political party, trade union organizations and, of late, the University. Among these, pragmatic policy considerations and ideological commitment have provided a sensibility towards cooperative promotion. Thus, top-down initiatives, or none at all, have been the order of the day; and such may be, to a considerable degree, inevitable given that (and I will hazard being bold here) the Maltese are largely an individualistic people, competitive and wary of taking risks, more likely to resort to individual manipulation and deferential behaviour than to collective or cooperative action to improve their social position and advance their interests.

Witness the typically quite predictable civic reactions to problems which are recognizably of a collective nature (such as consumer protection, upkeep of public spaces; provision of water, electricity and other (especially scarce) services; employment opportunities). These reactions include (and not necessarily in this order): outward grumbling; vocal outcries against the government of the day which is held fully responsible and which is harangued to do something about the issue; a resort to discreet individual solutions, often in competition with other, fellow (*sic*) citizens. Grass-roots, bottom-up, collective mobilization is a rarity indeed.

Spurs for cooperative formation in Malta have included economic factors (a large number of small producers, each of whom has no influence on the terms of trade of his/her product or service; a common external threat or competitor); but these *per se* have not constituted the 'structural bind' to catalyze organization (Young, 1970; Baldacchino, 1990, p. 91). The exemption of cooperative organizations from company tax (equivalent to a saving of 30% tax on registered profits when compared to conventional firms) legislated in 1990 has not led to anything remotely resembling an avalanche of applications for registration. There has had to be a reliance on a trustworthy, charismatic figure to prod the ever-suspicious potential members into concerted action; and the co-operative organization has often been looked at (by members and political agents) as an efficient channel for political lobbying.

The Maltese are thus doubly blessed when it comes to cooperative membership. Paternalistic leadership figures with near-divine attributes control the cooperative structure, typically with the members' full blessing – leadership figures no doubt having been ascribed with such a towering stature by the general membership itself. This relationship, even in the small worker cooperatives where (on paper) equitable participation is most likely to flourish, ensures the cooperative's survival in economic terms but hardly in democratic ones. Meanwhile, the economic circumstance is always prone to the infusions and supports of the policy maker, who may have a political (apart from ideological) interest in the existence and expansion of the cooperative sector. With pressures from within and without, even the worker coops can degenerate into another, culturally comfortable, variant of benevolent paternalism which the cooperative member may easily be tempted to expect, maintain and demand.

In many other countries (Bangladesh, Costa Rica, India, Jamaica, Mexico, Spain, USA...), cooperatives emerged as self-help organizations in the context of a political vacuum. Ideological and visionary promoters were still often essential to catalyze the coops into formation. But these were themselves driven into action because of a marginalization of the would-be cooperators from policy considerations.

But in Malta, the notion of a political vacuum is practically inconceivable. It seems more valid to argue that local cooperatives have emerged to plug better into the all-pervasive and bountiful circuitry of Big Government, capitalizing on its positive disposition towards the cooperative cause.

A *Different Perspective?*

Such an evaluation of worker cooperation in Malta is annoying, to say the least. But perhaps it is the population of worker cooperatives I have been considering which is problematic. Policy initiatives for, and academic research on, these organizations is obviously based on identifiable cooperative units – typically firms registered as cooperatives with some state agency or registrar. There is much more than what official statistics suggest. Hence, one could argue that this population is only the tip of the iceberg and will tend to prejudice any observations and conclusions forthcoming from the analysis of cooperative performance.

One must remember that the unstable condition of the fortress economy, with the unpredictable cyclical fluctuations of boom and depression, of prosperity and poverty, also fostered a sense of entrepreneurship among the Maltese. Low-risk, labour-intensive self-employment, family enterprise and cooperative work efforts have been and remain widespread. They embody one natural reaction to unstable formal employment. These are also opportunities which generate extra income, preferably without this being declared for taxation purposes. Fishing (particularly in the *lampuki* season) and construction are such activities, involving small sized work teams typically practising non-hierarchical power relations, job flexibility and informality (Baldacchino, 1990, p. 98).

Cooperative work efforts may also be envisaged expressly as project specific exercises with a clear time horizon. One of the few such experiences which has been documented (though not registered as a cooperative affair) was the Solidary Building Scheme, initiated by the Social Action Movement: the venture, which lasted a couple of years, involved the collective construction of seven houses at Santa Lucia by their seven eventual occupiers (S.A.M., 1971).

Without the precondition of registration, it is also possible to appraise cooperative efforts dating earlier than 1947 when cooperative legislation was first introduced and activated in Malta. Such efforts include other forms of formalistic, collective organizations such as trade unions, mutual help associations, benevolent and friendly societies. Among these is the impressive story – again, still largely unresearched – of the Società Operaia Cattolica which, in August 1919, started operating a consumer cooperative. Within a year, this could boast over 400 members and was running a large retail outlet at 200-2, Victory Street, Senglea, employing in the process more than 30 employees.[4]

On an equally dramatic scale, the Xewkija parish church in Gozo, bearing the fourth largest dome in the world, is also an expression of a worker cooperative effort of sorts. In this case, the worker members consisted, as a church brochure declares, in the entire village community.

Implications

In reformulating the parameters of the population, worker cooperation in Malta remains a marginal, but more widespread, affair. Looked at in this new light, the economic rationality and democratic attraction of the cooperative form are more clearly understood as subservient to wider considerations. The preference for anonymity, informality and tax evasion are explanations for the reluctance of the Maltese to form officially registered cooperatives; a deliberate short-term orientation is another.

A third crucial factor is the experiential effect: once bitten, twice shy. If the Maltese are, at a generalized level, a wary and individualistic people, this may also be a rational reaction to nasty collective experiences. After all, in a number of village cooperatives in Malta and Gozo, retail outlets were profitably operated for poultry, goat and pig breeders besides selling seed potatoes, fertilizers and other agricultural material. Herdsmen and wine-growers grouped together and forked out 60% of the cost of bringing a feedmill and a winery into operation. The practice of cooperation may have generated its own set of misgivings about the cooperative cause. These second thoughts

---

[4] *Malta: Organo del Partito Nazionale*, Tuesday, 19 October 1920, No. 11,137.

result from mismanagement, misappropriations of finance, despotic leadership and market failure. No wonder that initial enthusiasm may have turned sour.

The arguments above therefore suggest explanations for the reluctance to entertain cooperative forms of organizing production, especially of the official kind, in Malta. This is likely to persist unless there is a clear demonstration effect, whereby a number of Maltese cooperatives become models of market efficiency and democratic participation. The short-cut to this would be to provide financial benefits, as are the tax incentives currently in place. The catch here is that worker and other cooperative organizations could be formed explicitly to exploit such benefits, as has happened elsewhere (Schneider & Schneider, 1976; Zwerdling, 1980).

References:

Baldacchino, G. (1987) 'Education and worker cooperatives: Obstacles and opportunities', *Education, Journal of the Faculty of Education*, University of Malta, vol. 3, 1.
Baldacchino, G. (1990) 'Worker cooperatives with particular reference to Malta: An educationist's theory and practice', *Occasional Paper No. 107*, The Hague, Institute of Social Studies.
Baldacchino, G. (1991) 'Labour education in the Information Age', *Education, Journal of the Faculty of Education*, vol. 4, 1.
Baldacchino, G. (1994) 'Cooperative developments on campus', *The Qroqqery*, Malta, University of Malta Publication, 2.
Baldacchino, G., Baldacchino, P.J., Grima, J. & Mifsud, J. (1993) 'A consultancy report on the catering cooperative', unpublished document, Malta, Board of Cooperatives.
Barbuto, J. (1992) 'Failure of cooperatives in Malta', unpublished document, Effective Cooperative Management Course, University of Malta, Malta University Services & Workers' Participation Development Centre.
Blumberg, P. (1968) *Industrial Democracy: The Sociology of Participation*, New York, Schoken Books.
Bonett, S. (1989) 'A financial performance of the catering cooperative', unpublished B.A. (Hons.) dissertation, University of Malta, Department of Accountancy.
Cable, J. & Fitzroy, F. (1980) 'Cooperation and productivity: Some evidence from the West German experience', *Economic Analysis and Workers' Management*, vol. 14, 1.
Camilleri, P. (1984) 'A study of the management of agricultural cooperatives: The case of the Farmers' Central Cooperative Society', unpublished B.A. (Hons.) dissertation, University of Malta, Department of Management Studies.
Fox, A. (1971) *A Sociology of Work in Industry*, London, Collier Macmillan.
Goulet, D. (1989) 'The search for authentic development' in Baum, G. & Ellsberg, R. (eds) *The Logic of Solidarity*, New York, Orbis.

Grech, S. (1992) 'A cooperative in search of a future: A case study of Gozo Milk & Agricultural Producers' Coop', unpublished B.A. (Hons.) dissertation, University of Malta, Department of Management Studies.

Jackall, R. & Levin, H.M. (eds) (1984) *Worker Cooperatives in America*, Berkeley CA, University of California Press.

Optimal Performance Through Internal Management Action (OPTIMA) (1985a) 'The cooperative movement in Malta', unpublished case study, 4, Ljubljana, Yugoslavia, International Centre for Public Enterprises.

OPTIMA (1985b) 'First clothing cooperative', unpublished case study, 1, Ljubljana, Yugoslavia, International Centre for Public Enterprises.

Pateman, C. (1970) *Participation and Democratic Theory*, Cambridge, Cambridge University Press.

Rizzo, S. (1985) *Koperattivi*, Malta, Workers' Participation Development Centre and Central Cooperatives Board, Ministry of Agriculture and Fisheries.

Social Action Movement (S.A.M.) (1971) *This is the Social Action Movement*, Malta, Lux Press.

Schneider, J. & Schneider, P. (1976) 'Economic dependency and the failure of cooperativism in western Sicily' in Nash, J., Dandler, J. & Hopkins, N.S. (eds) *Popular Participation in Social Change: Cooperatives, Collectives and Nationalised Industry*, The Hague, Mouton.

Sik, O. (1984) 'The process of democratizing the economy' in Wilpert, B. & Sorge, A. (eds) *International Yearbook of Organisational Democracy*, vol. 2, New York, John Wiley.

Stafrace, P. (1985) 'A case study of the Farmers' Wine Cooperative', unpublished dissertation, University of Malta, Department of Management Studies.

Vanek, J. ed. (1975) *Self-Management: Economic Liberation of Man*, Harmondsworth, Penguin.

Villegas, R.V. (1990) 'The situation of the Gozo Milk & Agricultural Cooperative and suggestions for its revival', unpublished report, Germany, Akademie Klausenhof.

Young, F.W. (1970) 'Reactive Subsystems', *American Journal of Sociology*, vol. 35, 2.

Zammit, J. (1973) 'Report on the reorganisation of the purchasing, processing and marketing of pork and beef by the cooperatives', unpublished document, Hamrun, Malta, Milk Marketing Undertaking.

Zwerdling, D. (1980) *Workplace Democracy*, New York, Harper & Row.

27

School Children in Malta's Twilight Economy

Ronald G. Sultana

Introduction

Malta's economy is characterised by a very active 'underground' sector that produces between ten to twenty per cent of the country's GDP (Delia, 1987). This article reports on an aspect which has received little attention from researchers or from policy makers: the activity of under-age ('child') workers who labour in what Finn (1984) has called the 'twilight economy'.[1]

---

[1] Readers interested in situating the data within a more elaborate theoretical context and in exploring the implications of the study for the development of social policy in Malta are referred to Sultana (1993).

In order to draw up any statistics regarding the extent to which child labour is present in a country, one must first define the words 'child' and 'labour'. According to Convention No. 138 of the International Labour Organisation, 'child' refers to persons below fifteen years of age.[2] The same convention (Article 2) also states that the basic minimum age for employment or work shall not be less than the age of completion of compulsory schooling and in any case not less than 15 years. It is important to note that Recommendation No. 146 (Paragraph 7) states that the objective of ILO Members should be to raise this minimum age to 16.

The same Convention attaches great importance to the term 'employment or work'. Swepston (1982) notes that this definition of labour ensures that all economic activity done by children is taken into consideration, regardless of their formal employment status. He notes that in many countries

> many young persons who do not work under a contract of employment simply are not covered by the legislation. They therefore have no protection in regard to the minimum wage at which they may work, nor in such basic matters as wages, hours of work and social security benefits (Swepston, 1982).

This is further complicated by the fact that

> measuring the productivity of children's economic activities is very difficult, since their contribution is so often indirect, and their activity may not be considered as work (Schildkrout, 1980).

It is important to point out that the ILO Convention does not impose a blanket prohibition on 'child labour'. What it does set out to do is to regulate the conditions under which these young people may be allowed to work. It prohibits the imposition on

---

[2] See the 67th Session of the International Labour Conference (Convention No. 138, 1973 – ratified by Malta in 1988). The Convention takes into account the fact that there are large differences between countries when it comes to economic development as well as to the availability of compulsory mass schooling. The Convention therefore allows the minimum age to be set at 14 initially. Malta has the necessary educational infrastructure to provide schooling up to and beyond that age, and indeed compulsory schooling was extended to 16 in 1974.

children of labour which calls for greater physical and mental resources than they normally possess or which interferes with their education and development.

If we take into consideration the above clarification regarding the meaning of 'child labour', and if we look at the results of statistical surveys carried out by a number of international organisations, it becomes immediately clear that the incidence of children's involvement in industrial and non-industrial work is very high indeed. ILO statistics (Swepston, 1982, p.591) estimate the number of working children under 15 to be 55 million for the world as a whole.

However, as Schildkrout (1980, p.379) points out, such figures are often based on census reports which take only the formal wage sector into account. In fact, a United Nations study (Economic and Social Council, 1981) considers that the figure of 145 million children is much closer to the mark.

While the problem is clearly more prevalent in developing countries such as India, Colombia and a number of African nations, it is also present in economically developed countries such as the United Kingdom (MacLennan, 1980), New Zealand (Sultana, 1990), and the United States (Bingham, 1990), to mention only three.

Child Labour in Malta

The problem of child labour within the terms outlined above prevails in Malta, and indeed it has surfaced as a public issue of some importance over the past few years. Evidence of this is the fact that the Minister for Social Policy pointed out in Parliament that measures were being taken to intensify inspections to check child labour practice. So far, however, only 7 children were reported to have been working in 1984, another 7 in 1985, 11 in 1986, 12 in 1987, and 16 in 1988 (*It-Torċa*, 12th August, 1990, p.16). Thirty cases were reported in 1989 (*Il-Ġens*, 24th August, 1990, p.4). It would appear therefore that there is no cause of alarm regarding 'child labour' in Malta.

However, the figures quoted above fail to reflect the real situation. The data which I shall present in this essay will show:

The possible number of young people who hold jobs;
The kinds of jobs they do;
The reason why young people seek to work;

The age at which they commence work;
The number of hours they put in and the wages they receive;
The working conditions and experiences.

Two empirical studies have been carried out regarding the extent of child labour practice in the Maltese islands. Both research projects are of a statistical nature and further research needs to be done to explore, through qualitative means, the phenomenological significance of this work for minors (Sultana, 1992).

The first study was carried out by the present author in 1989. It focuses on participation in paid employment on the part of all third year Trade School[3] students (age = 15 years) in Malta. The data are drawn from The Trade School Project, intended to focus on building a complex profile of trade school students.

For this study, a questionnaire form was distributed among all the third year trade school students found in their classrooms during the survey period between October and December of 1989. According to official lists of trade school population supplied by the Department of Education for the year 1989/1990, 1182 students should have been present. In actual fact only 680 students (male = 486; female = 194) were present to answer the questionnaire.

A second study, that carried out by Cremona (1989), focuses on all secondary level students in their last three years of compulsory schooling (ages = 13 to 17 years) on the smaller island of Gozo.

The questionnaire set out to collect data on the socio-economic background of these students, their educational and occupational experiences and aspirations, as well as information on their leisure activities. Part III of the questionnaire focused specifically on the part-time and full-time work these students had experienced during term and/or holiday time.

Cremona (1989) reports on questionnaire data collected from 905 Gozitan students (male = 434; female = 471) attending the last three years of academic and technical secondary schools.

---

[3] Trade Schools were set up in Malta in 1972, and in 1989 were catering for 2,868 boys and 1,509 girls, or about 17.5% of all secondary school students attending government schools (Central Office of Statistics, 1990).

While Cremona's research offers less details than that provided by the Trade School Research Project, it is useful in that it shows that similar patterns of child labour exist in Gozo as in Malta. It also shows that participation in paid employment on the part of minors differs depending on whether they are in academic or technical schools. Cremona's findings also help to highlight similarities and differences in child labour in Malta and Gozo.

Number of Young People Holding Jobs

Starting first with data which emerged from the Trade School Project, 378 students – or over 55% of those who answered the questionnaire – said that they had worked for money at some stage or other in their life. Of these 330 were male students. In other words, almost 70% of the respondents from boys' trade schools had found some sort of paid job.

Only 48 female students, or close to 25% of the total number of girls sampled, admitted to having worked either in term time or during the holiday seasons. Of the total 378 students who worked, 203 did so before and/or after school hours, and on weekends in term time. 341 students worked during the holiday season, and 166 students worked both during term time and during holidays.

Cremona (1989) reports similar patterns for his study of young people in Gozo. Thus, 46.8% of Gozitan boys and 16.4% of Gozitan girls were engaged in some form of waged employment. The lower percentages in Cremona's study are probably due to the fact that his sample included students attending both trade and technical schools as well as modern secondary and junior lyceum schools. In the latter, more academic-oriented institutions, students were found to be less involved in paid employment, and this reduced the global percentage of working children.

It needs to be pointed out that the above statistics are conservative ones. This is due to a number of reasons. In the first place and with reference to both studies, it was clear that some students preferred to withhold information out of fear of being caught out by the authorities. They were quite aware that they were not entitled to work without a work book and the permission of the Minister of Education.

A second reason which suggests that the statistics/percentages should in fact be higher is that both questionnaires measured only 'paid employment'. In another section of the Trade School questionnaire it became clear that girls, for instance, were often involved in carrying out domestic chores – such as taking care of younger children and doing housework – which were either remunerated by 'pocket money' allowances, or not at all. It will be argued that such activity has an economic function as it often releases adults so that these can work, or reduces the need for such adults to employ domestic help.

Finally, and again with reference to my research, 42.4% of trade school students were missing from their classroom during the survey months. A study by Scicluna Calleja et al. (1988) found that, on average, girls attending trade schools absented themselves for 50.5 out of 148 days, an absence rate of 33%. The frequency for boys stood at 35 days out of 148, yielding an absence rate of 24%. For the academic year 1987-88, the Department of Education had approved 861 requests for permission to leave school before students had reached the age of 16 (cf. It-Torċa, 12th August, 1990).

The high rates of early school-leaving and of absenteeism are a clear indication of the students' readiness to start working, if possible with a work permit (as in the case of early school-leavers), but not necessarily so.

It is instructive to compare the Maltese and Gozitan data with those emerging from other studies carried out in parts of England and Scotland. MacLennan (1980) for instance found that 20 to 30% of all 14 to 16-year-olds were in part-time employment in the United Kingdom. Finn (1984) reports that 75 of his sample of 150 boys and girls in their last year of compulsory schooling in 3 Coventry and 1 Rugby school had had some involvement in the juvenile labour market. Griffin (1985) found that 50% of her Birmingham girls had experienced some form of part-time employment prior to leaving school. Howieson (1990) reports that 45% of a sample of school-leavers in Scotland had done part-time work during term time. The first three studies mentioned above confirm the patterns of child employment that have been found locally. In other words, more of the 'non-academic' students tend to be working than 'academic' ones, and more boys than girls tend to be in paid employment.

Type of Work

The range of jobs reported in the Trade Schools Project questionnaire was very wide. However, most were involved in work in the informal sector, which afforded them little educational experience and practically no useful training for adult work roles other than 'conditioning' to form part of an unskilled, uneducated proletariat. Among the most common jobs done by the 203 students who worked during term time are: shop assistants (n = 32), and helpers in a variety of small-sized trade enterprises such as carpenters (n = 17), mechanics (n = 12), and electricians (n = 7). A substantial number were employed as farm-hands (n = 13). Before and after school hours as well as during weekends students cleaned wood, helped builders and butchers, acted as salespersons, polished wood, sprayed wood and cars, worked in kitchens, painted houses, and sold produce. If we had to group these different jobs into larger categories, the top three work categories for term time jobs would be as follows: Trades (n = 64); Catering (n = 42) and Shop Attending (n = 32).

Similar patterns can be found in the jobs done by students during holiday time. Some of the more popular jobs were, again, helping out in small trade establishments such as carpentry (n = 32), auto mechanical work (n = 13), panel beating (n = 8), and electrical installation (n = 11). Student summer work also consisted in street vending (n = 6), tile laying (n = 3), painting houses (n = 10), shop assisting (n = 26), and working in hotels and other catering establishments as waiters or waitresses (n = 27), barmen or barmaids (n = 17), pool attendants (n = 9), beach attendants (n = 5), take-away operators (n = 9), kitchen hands (n = 7), cleaners and maids (n = 20), and confectioners (n = 3). If we again grouped the jobs into categories, summer time work would have the following profile: Catering (n = 130); Trades (n = 100) and Shop Attending (n = 26). It is indicative that during holiday time, 17 students were involved in some form of factory work.

Gozitan students were employed in similar kinds of work, and Cremona (1989) reports a concentration of children in the catering sector -- which employs 29% of all male children who work – and in work related to shops. Fewer Gozitan than Maltese children and young persons were found working in the agricultural sector. It is interesting to note that 30% of Cremona's female sample were involved in knitting work for the textile industry. This form of home-based labour was not reported in the Maltese data.

Another point worth noting is that trade school students, for instance, were involved in work which has been specifically designated as dangerous by ILO Convention No. 138, and which could not be excluded from the Convention's application. If we take into account all student work done during term and holiday time, these included quarrying (n = 2), electrical works (n = 18), construction (n = 22) and transport and storage (n = 5). Convention No. 138 also identifies manufacturing as a form of dangerous employment which could not be excluded from its application. Eight students worked in a factory during term time, while 17 did so during the holiday season. A number of ILO Conventions regarding work done by minors have been careful to specify that certain forms of employment – such as work in restaurants and in bars – present particular problems for the moral safety of young persons. It is therefore relevant to point out the large numbers of students employed as barmen/barmaids, and as waiters/waitresses. The reason why so many students are absorbed in the catering industry reflects not only the importance of the tourist service sector in the overall economy of Malta but also, the nature of this sector characterised as it is by the 'need' for cheap labour that can be easily employed and easily shed.

A general point that can be made about the kind of jobs done by these young workers is its reflection of the different destinies in the sexual division of labour. Hence, in both the Maltese and Gozitan studies, girls tended to be found in what are locally considered to be traditionally female jobs such as cleaning, tailoring, hairdressing and baby-sitting. Another fact that needs to be highlighted is the large number of students employed by their adult family members. Of the 196 trade school students who replied to the question regarding details about employers, 62 – or 31.6% – answered that employment was provided by a family member. Cremona (1989) found a similar pattern for his sample in Gozo, and reports that 104 children work for their parents, while 30 were employed by somebody related to the family. As in many other areas in the world, children often work in familial contexts (Bequele & Boyden, 1988).

Reasons for Seeking Work

It is commonly believed in Malta that trade school students seek to work in the trade they are following at school. My research however does not bear this out to any large extent. Of the 341 students who worked during the holiday season, only 43 – or 12.6% – were employed in a sector where they could practise the trade skills they were learning at school. With regards to the group of 203 students who worked during term time only 49 students – or 24.1% – were involved in work which could help them make progress in the skills they were studying at school. In another question, students were asked to identify what they liked about the work they did. Only 28 said that learning a trade was a positive aspect of their experience in paid employment.

The major reason for working was undoubtedly related to financial remuneration. Thirty-eight students explicitly stated that what they liked about the work they did during term or holiday time had to do with 'money' and 'pay'. Cremona (1989, p.60) notes that 35% of the boys and 32% of the girls in his sample of Gozitan students had remuneration in mind when they decided to work. 44% of the girls and 25% of the boys said that they were pushed to work for 'family reasons', which Cremona interprets as helping out in family business or in augmenting the family budget.

Child labour, both within the house and outside it, and whether it is formally remunerated or not, should therefore be considered as an economic contribution to the household economy rather than an educational experience. This economic contribution is made in both direct and indirect forms. In the first instance, the Trade School questionnaire revealed that 145 out of the 378 students – or 38.3% – who worked throughout the year gave a percentage of the money they earned to their parents. Secondly, the fact that these young people were earning money meant that parents were not obliged to provide allowances to support expenses on clothes, travel, food, and entertainment and leisure activities. Some of these young people were therefore financing most if not all of their own leisure activities, besides helping out their parents.

It has been noted in a number of countries that economic recession and high rates of unemployment have put even greater pressure on young people to contribute to the family budget (see Finn, 1984; Howieson, 1990; Sultana, 1990). While Malta has not gone through the same kind of economic problems experienced in other countries, and while Malta enjoys a highly developed social service system, it is nonetheless postulated that high taxation levels, relatively low wages, and the current increases in the cost-of-living have very much the same effect. It is held that parents actually encourage their children to find some form of paid employment. This proposition is borne out by the fact that 41% of the students who replied to the Trade School questionnaire admitted that they had found their jobs with the help of parents, older siblings, or uncles and aunts.

Finally, it should be noted that work provided students with the possibility of socialising. Twenty-six trade-school students mentioned this factor as a pleasant thing about their work experience. Meeting tourists or members of the opposite sex and making friends with adult workers provided them with positive experiences. It became clear from my study that many students were working in jobs which allowed mixing with older workers. While 79 students claimed they worked with persons of their own age, 248 said that they did not. Work during term and holiday time also encouraged, to some extent, the mixing of genders. Despite the fact that boys and girls were involved in work roles which generally revealed the sexual division of labour in Malta, 181 students worked in a mixed sex environment, while 148 were in a single-gender workplace. Working alongside adults of the same or different gender can have both positive and negative effects on young students. One such negative effect is the tendency of full-time, non-seasonal adult workers to impute a lower status on younger, casual labourers (cf. Clark, 1986). Sexual harassment is also often reported when adult males work alongside younger females (Sultana, 1990).

Age at Which Students Commence Work

The Trade School questionnaire reveals that 'working' students had taken up a job before their fifteenth birthday. Indeed, 20 admitted that they had entered into paid employment at the age of ten or at a younger age, while 10 had started working at the age of eleven and 33 students had begun at the age of twelve. Seventy-six students had started working when they were thirteen years of age, and 130 when they were fourteen. Only 79 students admitted to having had their first work experience at the age of fifteen and over.

A similar pattern emerges if we examine the data presented by Cremona for his sample of Gozitan students. In this case, while there were a few who began work at 6 or 7 years of age, the majority entered into some form of paid employment at the age of 12 (15.7%), 13 (17.2%), or 14 years of age (21.6%).

Hours of Work and Wages

In this section it is useful to distinguish between term and holiday jobs. An analysis of the Trade School questionnaire data shows that on average, both male and female students holding term jobs were involved in 4.7 hours' work per day. This they did before, during and/or after school on school days and weekends. There was very little difference in the number of hours of work between male and female students. Male students worked a mean 4.72 hours per day, while female students worked a mean of 4.59 hours daily. It needs to be pointed out however that these averages conceal a skewed distribution: 16 students reported working for six hours, 12 did 7 hours work or more per day, 18 laboured between 8 and 11 hours daily. Cremona (1989, p.54) reports that most of the Gozitan male and female students worked less than 10 hours per week during term time.

The average number of hours of work for students involved in holiday work was almost twice that for term time jobs. Male and female students worked a mean of 8.42 hours per day, with males clocking up 8.6 hours and females 7.01 hours daily. Again, such averages conceal the fact that 47 students claimed to have worked for 9 hours daily, 33 for 10 hours, 16 for 11 hours, another 16 for 12 hours, 3 for 14 hours, and 5 for 15 hours per day. Similar data was reported by Cremona (1989, p.53) with regards to Gozitan students: 22.1% of his sample of boys who worked during the holiday season laboured between 31 and 40 hours per week, while 16.7% worked between 41 and 50 hours. 23.3% of the girls worked 10 hours or less per week, while 19% of them worked between 41 and 50 hours per week. Fewer girls than boys worked more than 70 hours per week during the holiday season.

The Trade School questionnaire data permit the calculation of the average hourly and weekly wages that these students received, although it does not permit the identification of cases where there was a combination of cash and kind as remuneration. There is an important degree of difference between the average hourly rate of pay for term and for holiday jobs. During term time, the average was Lm1.18c per hour, with a difference of five cents between the average hourly pay for males and for females, in favour of the former.

The average conceals the fact that 83 students who worked during term time did not know their hourly rate of pay. This, it will be argued later, enhances the employers' possibility of exploitation of young workers. It is possible that rather than not knowing the hourly rate, students were unwilling to declare how much money they made out of fear of getting into trouble with the authorities. This is the reason which Cremona (1989, p.55) advances in order to explain the non-response rate for this question. It could also be postulated, however, that flexible hourly rates of pay is a characteristic feature of the informal sector in which most of the students laboured.

The average hourly rates received by trade school students also hide the fact that some students were getting far below the Lm1.18c mentioned earlier. Eighteen were getting only between 25c and 50c per hour; 26 were earning between 55c and 80c an hour. Other students were earning more than the average: 15 were earning between Lm2 and Lm2.50c an hour, 3 were earning Lm4 and 2 were earning as much as Lm5 per hour. On average, the weekly earning for males who worked during term time was Lm23.20c while for females the figure was Lm18.[4]

Holiday work earned students less money – below the 86c per hour which constitutes the official minimum wage in Malta. On average, an hour's work gave trade school students between 67c9 – if they worked five days a week – or 56c6 – if they worked for six days a week. This meant that most students were earning between Lm30 and Lm50 a week (n = 122), while a minority were earning between Lm55 and Lm70 a week (n = 14). Five students were earning Lm100 per week in the holiday season. It needs to be noted that while the average weekly earnings for holiday work are higher than those for term time, students were working for much longer hours.

Cremona provides similar information, although it seems that Gozitan students are even more underpaid than Maltese students.

---

[4] The minimum wage for a forty hour week was Lm34.37c at the time the study was carried out. One Maltese lira was then equivalent to around 2.5 ECUs (or 3.35 USD).

Cremona (1989, p.55) notes that 52.5% of his respondents were earning between 51c and Lm1 per hour, while 27% were earning less than 50c per hour.

The Experience of Work

One needs to look beyond wages to have a better understanding of the exploitative conditions under which child labour is usually carried out. With regards to remuneration, both Cremona's study and mine indicate quite clearly that young persons are satisfied with very little: Cremona (1989, pp. 56-57) notes that only 25% of the girls and 12% of the boys claimed that their wages were low for the type of work they performed; 47% of the girls and 63% of the boys claimed that the remuneration was good while 19.5% of the boys and 19.2% of the girls claimed that their wages were very good. In my survey, 38 students identified money as the main thing they liked about work; only 4 complained about the low pay!

Trade schools students were clearly more alert to exploitative work conditions. Thirty students complained about the physical suffering that their job entailed, such as the long hours of standing on their feet, and the heavy loads they had to carry. Twenty-three students found fault with the hierarchical relationship with their boss or supervisor. Another 20 lamented about the work environment, such as dirt, foul smells, and exposure to extreme weather conditions. When responding to a question asking them whether they would like to do the same kind of job after they left school, 157 of the 267 who answered the question (or 58.8%) said that they would not. The major reasons they gave were that this work caused too much suffering (n = 46), was monotonous (n = 6), had low pay (n = 15), and offered very bad conditions of work (n = 15).

Despite the generally exploitative conditions in which these trade school children laboured, it is worrying that as many as a 110 out of 267 or (41.2%) who responded to the same question felt ready to continue with the same work they were doing after they left school. 50 students said that they felt that they were 'happy' and were 'good' at what they were doing. Nineteen were keen to remain in the trade they were practising, while another 19 believed that they were making enough money in that job as to warrant their staying on. Nine felt that their job offered them opportunities to socialise, and they felt accepted and respected at work, while 4 mentioned that their particular job did not cause them any physical stress, and therefore they found no reason to leave it on reaching compulsory school-leaving age.

Whatever the reason, it is significant that so many students did not desire – possibly not even foresee the possibility of – a better working future with improved conditions of work, better salaries, and enjoying more rights and/or responsibilities.

Cremona's data is limited when it comes to providing information on the Gozitan students' experience of work. The latter were simply asked to state whether they thought their conditions of work were good or bad. They were not asked to actually provide any indication of the specific conditions in question. In his sample (Cremona, 1989, p.58), 62% of the boys and 49% of the girls claimed that their conditions at work were good; 30% of the boys and 39% of the girls said the conditions were fair, while 4% of the boys and 5% of the girls admitted that the conditions were bad. Again, it becomes apparent that these students were basically satisfied with their work experience, and were largely unaware of the exploitative conditions they were labouring under.

Conclusion

The data presented above show the urgency with which the problem of child labour should be treated in Malta. One important step forward would be the formulation of a strong social policy which ensures that the rights of the child for education and from material constraints are guaranteed. Such a policy would also ensure that children will no longer need to labour – at least not in situations which permit exploitation. A strong and effective policy with regards to child labour is necessary because, in Malta as elsewhere:

- children are involved in doing repetitive, alienating and fragmented tasks, having little or no control over the work process, and learning and using few skills. These unskilled and often simple jobs offer little opportunity to move on to other, better paid, safer or more interesting occupations. Children are therefore often trapped in fluctuating or unstable labour markets characterised by low pay and insecurity of employment.

- These working children have few rights, and the few they do have are not clearly stipulated. They are thus more subject to the whims of their employers.

- Their vulnerability is emphasised by the fact that they have no collective representation and thus little protection from exploitation or harassment. The fact that they are voluntarily working illegally means that they will be even more hesitant to complain to authorities as this would mean admitting to having broken the law. They have few alternatives for employment, and this fact renders them even more dependent on their employers.

- Children are often expected to do adult work for a wage far below that normally given to adults, even when they are involved in doing the same tasks. There are offered no fringe benefits, no insurance or social security and are thus cheaper to employ than are adults. Their low wages give employers an advantage in national – and in some cases, international – markets. In addition, these employers can often avoid the obligation of complying with national employment requirements.

- Employers do not generally take into account that most work-places, work tasks as well as tools and machinery were designed with adults in mind. Hence, when children perform the same work they are more likely 'to suffer occupational injuries due to inattention, fatigue, poor judgement or insufficient knowledge of work processes' (Bequele & Boyden, 1988, p. 154).

- These children are involved in long hours of work, especially if we consider school to be work. Many labour on through the weekends, attracted by the added incentive of special rates of pay.

- It is moreover not often pointed out that child labour seems to initiate students into capitalist work relations and conditions, enveloping young people in a world of hard facts. Youngsters are made to assume the 'what is' as common-sense and are divorced from the alternative and humane vision of the 'what could' and the 'what should be'. Experience in the twilight economy therefore seems to mould young persons into the future workers who will find naive joy in the 'improved' conditions of their full time work. Such an experience produces ideas, feelings, desires and forms of consciousness which lead to an adaptive mentality rather than to one which yearns – and struggles – for alternative arrangements in the social formation/structure.

References

Bequele, A. & Boyden, J. (1988) 'Working children: Current trends and policy responses', *International Labour Review*, vol. 127, 2.

Bingham, C. (1990) 'The child-labour sting', *Newsweek*, 26 March.

Central Office of Statistics (1990) *Education Statistics: 1988-89*, Valletta, Malta, Government Press.

Clark, A. (1986) *Part-time Work in New Zealand*, Wellington, New Zealand Planning Council.

Cremona, J. (1989) 'The underground economy in Gozo: The case of child workers', unpublished dissertation, B.A.(Hons.) Public Administration, University of Malta.

Delia, E.P. (1987) *The Task Ahead – Dimensions, Ideologies and Policies: A Study on the State of the Maltese Economy*, Malta, Confederation of Private Enterprise.

Federation of Industry [Malta] (1988) 'ILO Conventions ratified by Malta', *Industry Today*, August.

Finn, D. (1984) 'Leaving school and growing up: work experience in the juvenile labour market', in Bates, I. et al., *Schooling for the Dole: The New Vocationalism*, London, Macmillan.

Ġens, Il- (1990) 'Tfal li jaħdmu', 24 August.

Griffin, C. (1985) *Typical Girls? Young Women from the School to the Job Market*, London, Routledge & Kegan Paul.

Howieson, C. (1990) 'Beyond the gate: Work experience and part-time work among secondary school pupils in Scotland', *British Journal of Education and Work*, vol. 3, 3.

MacLennan, E. (1980) *Working Children*. Pamphlet No.15, London, Low Pay Unit.

Scicluna-Calleya, S., Sultana, R. & Zammit, R. (1988) 'Absenteeism in Trade Schools', unpublished report (mimeo), Malta, Department of Education.

Schildkrout, E. (1980) 'Children's work reconsidered', *International Social Science Journal* (UNESCO), vol. 32, 3.

Sultana, R.G. (1990) 'Breaking them in? School kids in the twilight economy', *New Zealand Journal of Industrial Relations*, vol. 15.

Sultana, R.G., (1992) *Education and National Development: Historical and Critical Perspectives on Vocational Schooling in Malta*, Msida, Malta, Mireva Publications.

Sultana, R.G. (1993) 'Practices and policies on child labour: Lessons from Malta', *British Journal of Education and Work*, vol. 6, 3.

Swepston, L. (1982) 'Child labour: Its regulation by ILO standards and national legislation', *International Labour Review*, vol. 121, 5.

Torċa, It-, (1990) 'Il-ħaddiema tfal qed jiżdiedu!' 12 August.

28

The Locus and Distribution of Power: The Phoenicia Hotel Dispute

Alfred Grixti

Introduction

A critical appraisal of the manner in which industrial relations dynamics are played out in practice can have very powerful explanatory value in the context of the negotiation and relative distribution of power in a particular social setting. At the macro level, powerful and not so powerful institutions, of national and international character, bring to bear different and differential leverage in influencing particular courses of events and in conscribing or positioning the choice of action available to other concerned parties and individuals in specific episodes. An understanding of this political environment can therefore provide vital insights towards an understanding of why certain industrial relations issues emerge; how they unfold the way they do; how they shape, to some extent, the ensuing gains and losses experienced by concerned parties.

This paper takes the 1989-90 dispute at the Hotel Phoenicia in Malta as its point of departure in an attempt to examine the power balances in Maltese industrial relations.[1] Nonetheless, the research offers sufficient information for an examination into the way 'power' in Maltese industrial relations is wielded by the state, owners/management and the trade unions.

In order to achieve this, the paper is divided into three sections. Section I briefly outlines the Phoenicia Hotel dispute. Section II then sets out the theoretical framework dealing with 'power' in industrial relations. Section III points out conclusions which can be made first by relating the theory to the empirical discussion and then by extrapolating the evidence from the Phoenicia dispute to discuss 'power' in Maltese industrial relations in general. The structures and relationships between the different levels of management of the hotel in question, the trade union which represented the employees in the dispute and the Maltese government, are singled out for detailed analysis.

Brief Outline of the Dispute

The Nationalist Government elected at the Maltese General Elections in May 1987 pledged to liberalize imports and end the wage and price freeze policy adopted by the outgoing Labour Government during the mid-1980s. Consequently, the new Government announced changes to this effect in its Budget for 1988. One effect of these liberalization policies was a rise in the cost of living. Government, therefore, announced a marginal cost of living increase of Lm1.00 a week in the Budget for 1989, and a more substantial increase of Lm3.00 per week in the subsequent Budget of 1990. It added in the latter, however, that in those cases where there was a collective

---

[1] I had conducted a descriptive/critical case study into this dispute in 1991 in connection with postgraduate studies (Grixti, 1991). Relevant research was carried out by a systematic analysis of media pronouncements relating to the dispute and a series of in-depth interviews with the main protagonists of the episode.

agreement, employers would only be bound to grant the difference between the rise in the collective agreement and the Lm3.00 to make up the Lm3.00. (National Standard Order – Legal Notice 169 of 1989.)

In its reaction to the Budget the General Workers' Union (GWU) declared that it did not agree with this proposal and that it expected employers and managements to grant the Lm3.00 as a cost of living adjustment apart from any other rises in existing collective agreements. The union also announced that it would support this claim by industrial action.

The management of the Phoenicia Hotel was one of those which declared that it would not give its employees any rise other than that stipulated by the Government. Consequently, the GWU took industrial action. This first consisted of two all out stoppages, after which the kitchen staff were put on an indefinite sit-in strike. The Phoenicia Hotel Company Limited referred the dispute to arbitration by the Industrial Tribunal. The union, however, declared that it would not be attending the tribunal hearings because it had no confidence in its chairman and in the employers' side representative; apparently, the latter had also been a member of the National Labour Board which had issued the National Standard Order (Industrial Tribunal Secretariat proceedings case No. 507). During the tribunal proceedings, the GWU informed the management that it was to take action over its unilateral decision to grant a wage increase to certain staff thus breaching the collective agreement. This 'safety-valve' action consisted in the continued sit-in strike by the kitchen staff immediately after the Tribunal's decision in favour of the management was announced on 11 January 1990 (See GWU-Phoenicia correspondence 5 January 1990 and 11 January 1990). In the meantime, the Government had not intervened in the dispute. On Friday, 9 February, 1990, however, the GWU was in tripartite talks with the Prime Minister. At the end of these talks, Anġlu Fenech, the GWU's General Secretary asked the PM to have a word with him and it was then that the union directly asked the Government to intervene. The PM replied that he would see what he could do. This was at about 9.30 at night. When the General Secretary arrived home after the meeting at about 10.00 p.m. he received a phone call informing him that the owners had decided to close the hotel and, therefore, all workers on duty had been told to vacate the premises.

The next day the management informed the employees that they were all being discharged. The Hotel was closed and guarded by a private security firm. The GWU had since claimed that the closure was animated by the owners' plans to refurbish the hotel during which they preferred not to carry the burden of labour costs. Indeed no refurbishment was carried out between 10 February, 1990 and 25 September, 1991 when an agreement was finally reached between Forte PLC, the hotel's owners, and the GWU. While the Phoenicia was closed the sacked workers appealed to the Industrial Tribunal to declare that they were unfairly dismissed. This action has since been dropped due to the provisions of the final agreement. Surprisingly, this agreement came about after mediation by the then Minister for Social Policy, Dr. Louis Galea.

The agreement basically satisfied the wishes of both sides. The Phoenicia was to reopen within approximately 20 months from 25 September, 1991, the day the agreement was signed. Forte PLC were to upgrade the Phoenicia to their 'Grand Hotel' category. They also bound themselves to interview all former Phoenicia employees to assess whether they were capable of working in the upgraded Phoenicia. The Government gave the union a commitment that it would re-employ all

> workers who, either because of age, health reasons or 'incapabilities', or because they have found new employment are not re-employed with the hotel...(*The Times*, 26 September, 1991).

Forte PLC also agreed to pay these employees

> ... an ex-gratia payment, which Mr. Fenech described as substantial (*The Times*, 26 September, 1991).

Furthermore wages for those re-employed

> ...would not be less than those established in the last collective agreement plus cost of living increases (*The Times*, 26 September, 1991).

The Minister pointed out that the mediation process was started after:

> ... it had been realized – because of the involvement of the Industrial Tribunal and through court cases – that the problem would take long to be solved (*The Times*, 26 September, 1991).

The Minister first held discussions with the GWU and the Company in Malta. After this he is reported to have met Alfonso Giannuzzi, Forte PLC's Deputy Managing Director in Rome in October 1990. Mr. Gianuzzi came to Malta in January 1991 while the Minister was mediating between Forte PLC and the GWU (*The Times*, 26 September, 1991). Still no agreement could be reached probably because of the GWU's insistence that all former employees should be re-employed. Eventually, it is reported that:

> Dr. Galea met Mr. Rocco Forte, Chief Executive of the Hotel Group, in London recently. This, Dr. Galea said, had been a breakthrough in discussions and had led to the first direct meetings between the Forte Group and the GWU, held earlier this month, which in turn resulted in yesterday's agreement (*The Times*, 26 September, 1991).

In a press conference, Mr. Fenech said that five sessions of talks were held directly between him and Mr. Giannuzzi. Forte's Maltese Legal Representative, Dr. Victor Ragonesi, did not take part in these negotiations. Mr. Fenech maintained that, therefore, the GWU obtained the first goal it had consistently sought, that of direct negotiations with Forte PLC. He added that if these had taken place earlier, an agreement would then have been reached without the need for the workers to bear so many sacrifices. The agreement was therefore honourable to the GWU and to the workers, since it provided for the re-employment and alternative employment of all the employees (*L-Orizzont*, 26 September, 1991).

The Theory of 'Power' in Industrial Relations

Any discussion of 'power' in industrial relations must begin from the approach one takes in studying the subject area. Broadly speaking there are four approaches to industrial relations. These are:

a. The labour process approach which is Marxist inspired and mostly connected with the French *syndicats*. It takes the view that employers 'hire' the labour power potential of the workers but not the workers themselves. This distinction between labour and labour power invests the worker with more autonomy.

b. The frames of reference approach developed by Alan Fox in the UK, which studies industrial relations by examining management style broadly classifying it into two categories namely

(i) the unitary principle – where management regards all issues as its own prerogative and maintains that the objectives of employees must be the same as its own; or

(ii) the pluralist principle – where management does not treat all issues as its own prerogative and accepts that the workers' objectives may be different from those of the firm.

c. The institutional approach, sometimes referred to as the Oxford School, having been developed in the 1960s by Oxford Scholars Hugh Clegg, Alan Flanders and Bill McCarthy. This studies industrial relations by examining the institutions connected with it namely trade unions, employers associations and bargaining structures. This approach thus lays emphasis on examining industrial relations simply as it is expressed through the institutions which make it up, describing what its problems are and why they exist.

d. The systems approach, developed in the late 50s by John Thomas Dunlop in the USA. His approach embodies a theoretical framework which considers industrial relations to be a game which is fundamentally played within a set-up agreed upon by the different players. The systems approach thus looks at industrial relations in context and regards it as a sub-system of the wider social system within which it exists. Consequently, the systems approach lays great emphasis on the larger environment which is seen as deterministic and causal in that it fashions both the behaviour of the actors and the rules they create to make the industrial relations system work.

While all these approaches implicitly touch on the issue of 'power' it is Dunlop who discusses it at length and in detail. Dunlop also emphasises that industrial relations is a cross road of various disciplines, considering it to be set in the context of the larger society. I find it, therefore, appropriate to resort to Dunlop's theoretical framework for illuminating and analyzing research in the field of industrial relations. It is, therefore, worthwhile to give an overview, albeit briefly, of Dunlop's systems theory of industrial relations.

Dunlop's Industrial Relations System

Primarily Dunlop sees industrial relations as an 'analytical subsystem of an industrial society' (Dunlop, 1958). He sees the industrial relations system as being made up of actors, contexts, an ideology binding the system together, and a body of rules. There are three groups of actors namely the managerial hierarchy; the employees and their representative hierarchy; and government and its agencies (Dunlop, 1958, p. 7). These actors interact in a context determined by the larger society of which the industrial relations system is a sub-system. Importantly for Dunlop this context is deterministic:

> these features of the environment of an industrial relations system are determined by the larger society and its other subsystems. These contexts, however, are decisive in shaping the rules established by the actors in an industrial relations system (Dunlop, 1958).

Dunlop then identifies three constraints on the industrial relations system. These are:

a. the technological characteristics of the workplace which influence management style, employee organizations and the degree of public regulation of work methods and patterns

b. the market and budgetary constraints which directly affect management decisions while impinging on all the actors in industrial relations (Dunlop, 1958).

c. the locus and distribution of power in the larger society. Dunlop maintains that:

> The relative distribution of power among the actors in the larger society tends to a degree to be reflected within the industrial relations system; their prestige, position, and access to the ultimates of authority within the larger society shapes and constrains an industrial relations system... [yet]... The distribution of power in the larger society does not directly determine the interaction of the actors in the industrial relations system. Rather it is a context which helps to structure the industrial relations system itself (Dunlop, 1958).

Having outlined the contextual constraints which simultaneously constitute and determine the industrial relations system, Dunlop then describes what the structure of the system consists of. Interestingly his approach here is very similar to that of the institutionalists, since for Dunlop also the structure of industrial relations is based on rule-making and the observance of these same rules:

> ...rules for the workplace and work community, including those governing the contacts among the actors in an industrial relations system. This network or web of rules consists of procedures for establishing the rules, the substantive rules, and the procedures for deciding their application to particular situations. The establishment of these procedures and rules – the procedures are themselves rules – is the centre of attention in an industrial relations system (Dunlop, 1958).

In fact, these rules create experts within the industrial relations system who then bring stability to it. This is explained by Dunlop's observation that the ultimate contextual constraint – the ideology informing the larger society – makes all the actors in the industrial relations subsystem understand clearly what their place and role in the same system is in relation to the place and role of the other actors. The existence of a common ideology is very important for Dunlop as it enables practitioners and researchers to distinguish between disputes that occur either:

— ...over the organization of an industrial relations system or disputes that arise from basic inconsistencies in the system...
or
— ...disputes within an agreed and accepted framework.

Dunlop, thus, concludes that the actors, while having their own ideology must have some common overlap if they are to tolerate a minimum co-existence for each other. The relevance of Dunlop's systems approach both to the dispute in question and to the issue of power in Maltese industrial relations, therefore, lies in the fact that, although separated by time and space, it appears, at face value at least, that it is applicable mainly for two reasons.

Relevance of Dunlop's Approach to the Maltese Case

Firstly, with regard to the 'market and budgetary' constraints, Dunlop pointed out that these may be local, national or international. This is very true in the Phoenicia Hotel Dispute. The hotel, long considered the flagship of the Maltese tourist industry, is owned by Trust House Forte (THF) PLC, subsequently Forte PLC. The 'market and budgetary' constraints influencing managerial decisions were thus not only the result of the fluctuations of the international tourist market but also connected to the performance objectives of a foreign owner – a leading multinational company (MNC) in the hospitality industry with a chain of over 850 hotels world wide. Naturally this had an effect on the operation of the hotel in the host country, especially since the Phoenicia's local general manager, in spite of his being Maltese, had worked abroad with Forte PLC for over 20 years.

MNCs present difficulties to unions in host countries in that the latter have no direct access to the ultimate holders of power on the management side (Bean, 1985). Unions seem to come up against a brick wall. They are led to believe that in dealing with local management they would be dealing with the relevant actors in a local/national context. However, local managers have clearly defined parameters, set by the MNC head office, within which they have to operate. This has been called the 'illusion of decentralization' (Kinnie, 1987).

This influences the so called 'nationalization of management' which depends ultimately on '...the degree of corporate decentralization of decisions' since 'the higher the proportion of expatriate control, the greater the risk of ethnocentric practices' (Rosow, 1974).

This is all highly relevant to the Maltese context. In the particular case of the Hotel Phoenicia it appeared all along that the GWU did not seem to be aware of this kind of management policy. In interviews with the union's leadership, these always maintained that as far as they were concerned, all the management's decisions were influenced by the company's Maltese legal advisor Dr. Victor Ragonesi. Yet, as has already been observed in the outline of the dispute, the union wanted to have direct talks with Forte PLC in order to bypass Dr. Ragonesi not realizing that, as Dr. Ragonesi told me, all decisions were being taken by corporate headquarters. It is perfectly understandable, then that the company would not accept to have direct talks with the union even if for no apparent reason other than to preserve the illusion of decentralization. More importantly, however, as will be shown, it suited the company better to take the strategic decision of playing the game within the parameters of Maltese Law – the macro 'agreed and accepted framework' while the union unsuccessfully tried to persuade the Government to do something or to talk directly to the corporate management.

Secondly, the issue of rule-making, as explained by Dunlop, shows the applicability of the systems approach in the Maltese industrial relations context.

Rules are the result of negotiations. The outcome of the negotiations naturally depends on the actual power of the actors in the industrial relations system. Thus, while there was only one formal meeting between the managerial and union hierarchies in the Phoenicia Hotel dispute, it is relevant to consider all their actions in the light of negotiation theory since what the actors were trying to do all along was to attempt to renegotiate the terms of their co-existence. Indeed, Walton and McKersie (1965), in their negotiation model,

> ...conceive of labour negotiations as an example of social negotiations, by which we mean the deliberate interaction of two or more complex social units which are attempting to define or redefine the terms of their interdependence.

The authors then distinguish four sub-processes within the labour negotiation process, namely:

a. distributive bargaining – the 'winner take all' approach to negotiations;
b. integrative bargaining – the common-ground approach;
c. attitudinal structuring – the attempt to change the other party's point of view;
d. intraorganizational bargaining – the consensus approach (Walton & McKersie, 1965).

In the Phoenicia Hotel Dispute, it appears that the 'negotiation' model adopted by the two sides was the 'distributive' one. Consequently, the outcome could only depend on the parties' relative position of power. This will be understood more clearly in the next section of this paper which draws conclusions from the case study itself and then seeks to shed light on its relevance to the general question of power in Maltese industrial relations.

Conclusions

Through its descriptive and explanatory nature this single case study has critically tested Dunlop's 'systems theory' of industrial

Table 1. Strike statistics in Malta 1970-1992

Year	No. of Stoppages	Workers Involved	Working Days Lost
1970	35	23979	148499
1971	23	2103	24070
1972	42	11999	14677
1973	60	12513	42300
1974	36	8573	15069
1975	30	5262	14136
1976	17	3724	6971
1977	62	10980	75984
1978	15	6715	28401
1979	19	3619	50412
1980	12	764	5818
1981	14	1594	1340
1982	12	2415	6421
1983	17	651	1371
1984	14	6352	53287
1985	6	975	873
1986	7	1575	10033
1987	2	322	714
1988	7	685	280
1989	91	13565	6598
1990	25	3601	4485
1991	3	N/A	N/A
1992	4	99	68*

Source: *Industrial Tribunal Secretariat, Department of Labour, Valletta, Malta (August, 1991).*
* Source: *Economic Survey Jan-Sept. 1992, p. 225, Economic Planning Division, Ministry of Finance, Malta.*

relations along with the theories of multinational management style and labour negotiations which resulted from it. The study has, therefore, sought to adopt an 'explanation – building analysis' to answer the 'how' and 'why' questions of the dispute.

Given this methodological and theoretical framework it is possible to draw the following conclusions.

Firstly, Dunlop's theory considering industrial relations as 'an analytical sub-system of an industrial society' where the

...features of the environment of an industrial relations system are determined by the larger society and its other sub-systems

is argued to be valid and relevant to this case. It has been seen that Maltese industrial relations are a subsystem of Maltese society being, as they are, regulated by legal provisions (cf. Attard, 1984). Furthermore, Maltese industrial relations are determined by the 'contextual constraints' created by this Maltese society. Indeed, it is clear that Maltese industrial relations are ultimately determined by the 'locus and distribution of power' in Maltese society, particularly where wage determination is concerned since the Labour Board created by the 1952 CERA (Conditions of Employment Regulations Act) practically carries out Government policy.

The foregoing, means that it can also be generally concluded that at the micro-level, the Phoenicia dispute was also a direct result of the macro-influence of the 1989 National Standard Order, the 'market and budgetary constraint' of the 'larger society' which impinged on Maltese industrial relations in general and those at the Phoenicia Hotel in particular.

The strike at the Phoenicia was one of a series which the GWU had ordered in what can be described as its attempt to 'organize' Maltese industrial relations. This needed setting right owing to the 'basic inconsistency' created in the system by the manner in which Government had implemented the Lm3.00 wage increase. The GWU did not agree that this was a minimum increase 'to continue to improve the standard of living' but considered the Lm3.00 to be a cost of living increase to be given over and above any wage increases contemplated in existing collective agreements.

In order to achieve this the GWU was constrained to adopt the win-lose strategy associated with distributive bargaining as explained by Walton and McKersie. This was because the gain the GWU was seeking to achieve for its members and other workers could only be made at the expense of employers. This strategy seems to have had both micro and macro aims. At the micro level the union wanted to make employers accept its claim and at the same time hoped to achieve a macro-level change of policy which would thus also ensure success at those workplaces where employers had not accepted the union's claim. It is here that the GWU's strategy was not completely successful. While there was almost complete success at the micro-level the GWU was powerless to change Government policy at the macro-level specifically, and especially, when the Labour Board practically rubber stamped Government's policy.

This meant that at the micro-level any employers wanting to reject the GWU's claim could do so while remaining 'within the agreed and accepted framework'.

This is what happened in the Phoenicia dispute where Forte PLC, following an inflexible, home country directed 'ethnocentric management policy' (Rosow, 1974, p. 154), decided that all it had to do to win the dispute was to go to arbitration. The GWU also acted within the agreed framework by presenting an injunction against the Arbitration Tribunal. However, the union took what may have been a critical step further. It adopted an even more hardline position by refusing to go to arbitration. This hard-line reaction strengthened Forte's position since it could now retaliate in the same manner, also acting outside the agreed and accepted framework. This strategy becomes even more lucrative if one considers that the company had plans to close the Hotel for refurbishment. Ironically, therefore, the GWU seems to have further strengthened THF's position when the union, again in breach of the legal industrial relations framework, commenced its second dispute, the 'safety-valve action', in spite of the ruling by the Arbitration Tribunal. The Company did not accept the GWU's thesis that it had given a pay rise to certain workers in breach of the existing collective agreement while Government considered this as an excuse by the union not to respect the rule of law. One should here take particular note of the fact that a sit-in strike constitutes an acute form of industrial action because it interferes directly with the respect for private property.

The Government may thus have contemplated using the dispute for a 'demonstration effect' so as to show it would not tolerate disrespect for the rule of law. Consequently, when the THF closed the Hotel, it beat the union by its own strategy of acting outside 'the agreed and accepted framework'.

Sadly, for the 158 Phoenicia employees, the GWU's strategy did not achieve the positive result it achieved at other work places. In this case the contextual determinants and power balances of the larger society were totally stacked against the workers.

At a macro-level it therefore appears that 'power' in Maltese industrial relations is to a great extent directly determined by the relative position of the actors within the industrial relations system. It appears primarily that the extent of influence of the state, as represented by the government, is wide-ranging and crucial. It is ultimately the government who decides how to apply the laws governing industrial relations and it is the government which decides if, when, how and why, it should 'intervene' in a dispute between the other two actors. The law, as applied by the arbitration tribunal – an agency of the government – also influences the relative strength of the actors. Indeed, the Phoenicia dispute amply shows that the actor respecting the rule of law – that is, the management – was in a stronger position than the actor which took the dispute outside the 'agreed and accepted framework', that is, the union.

It also appears that those actors who have access to the government as the ultimate centre of power in Maltese industrial relations, thereby also increase their power. This can be seen, albeit somewhat generically and superficially, if the situation of the last 20 years is taken into account. Indeed it can be seen that under the Labour administrations of the 70s and 80s when the role of the state was largely interventionist, the position of employers/management was weakened as those governments were generally 'hostile' to them. On the union side, conversely, it could be seen that these had more power vis-à-vis employers/management simply because the government was ideologically 'friendlier' to the workers.

Even here, however, there is a typical Maltese caveat. The union movement, not being united but divided between the GWU (at that time statutorily tied to the MLP) and the CMTU (Confederation of Malta Trade Unions) umbrella, which wanted to keep their distance and remain independent of political parties, did not enjoy an equal access to power. Generally speaking, it was the GWU, with its close links to the Labour government, who had access to the ultimate power centres of the state in the years under Labour administrations. The opposite generally held for the unions under the CMTU umbrella whose dealings with the Labour government were mostly adversarial since they dealt with it almost entirely as an employer as they represented most white-collar workers in the public sector.

The change of government in 1987 meant a change in the balance of power. Generally, the more christian democratic inspired Nationalist administration was less antagonistic towards employers and management and much less interventionist in enterprise industrial relations. What this meant is that the post-1987 government has sought to adopt a more conciliatory role between employers/management and the unions. It has not enacted any anti-union legislation. Ironically, it may have been helped in this by the GWU which steadily distanced itself from the MLP, to the extent that even the statutory link has now been severed. Indeed, the GWU can hardly be accused of whipping up industrial unrest since, as official statistics show, the only year of increased stoppages was in 1989 and this was in reaction to the Lm3.00 increase that triggered the 2-month long Phoenicia dispute.

Thus, while the structure of the Maltese industrial relations system has remained largely the same, it appears that it has not been entirely deterministic. The membership strength of the unions, especially of the GWU (the largest union with consistently more than 50% of total union membership) means that any government has to take the potential power of the unions into consideration. Under Labour administrations this was achieved by the agency of the traditional close links between the Labour Party and the GWU. Presently the strategy has been to achieve consensus in industrial relations by creating a new feature in the industrial relations system's structure. This has been achieved via the creation of the Malta Council for Economic Development, a tripartite body which in 1990 spawned an incomes policy agreed to by the three social partners and which expired its first 3-year term on 10 December, 1993. The incomes policy primarily aims to take the centrally decided statutory cost-of-living increase out of the area of contention by the introduction of a wage indexation system based on the retail price index. Thereby, all actors are bound to a mechanism to which they have agreed voluntarily.

This mechanism has changed Maltese industrial relations as it has placed them more in the sphere of economic reality thereby making them more respondent to this downstream of the larger society than the former model which was based more on the old balances of power.

The fact that this new incomes policy mechanism was negotiated and came into effect in the aftermath of the Phoenicia dispute and the related industrial unrest shows that these events may have been a watershed in the way in which the locus and distribution of power influences Maltese industrial relations.

References

Attard, J. (1984) *Industrial Relations in Malta*, Marsa, Malta, PEG.

Bean, R. (1985) *Comparative Industrial Relations: An Introduction to Cross-National Perspectives*, London, Croom Helm.

Dunlop, J.T. (1958) *Industrial Relations Systems*, New York, Holt-Dryden.

Grixti, A. (1991) 'The Phoenicia Hotel dispute (Malta): A case study', unpublished M.Sc. dissertation, University of Oxford, October.

Kinnie, N. (1987) 'Bargaining with the enterprise; Centralised or decentralised?', *Journal of Management Studies*, vol. 24, 3.

L-Orizzont – Union Press, Workers' Memorial Building, South Street, Valletta (various issues).

Rosow, J. M. (1974) 'Industrial relations and the multinational corporation: The management approach' in Flanagan, R.J. & Weber, A.R. (eds) *Bargaining Without Boundaries*, Chicago, University of Chicago Press.

The Times – Progress Press, St. Paul's Street, Valletta. (various issues).

Walton, R.E. & McKersie, R.B. (1965) *A Behavioural Theory of Labour Negotiations*, New York, McGraw Hill.

29

Threads For Survival: Workplace Relations in a Clothing Firm

Benny Borg Bonello

Introduction

> If you don't succeed in finishing a bundle by the first two hours, you won't make it that day.

This is one expression of the general philosophy of life embraced by so many factory girls who toil in our clothing industry. It is one manifestation of a manufacturing culture which appears ready and able to condone an inhuman production process for the sake of short-term financial rewards; a negotiated cooperation to maximize output, with the promise of materialist indulgence in return. Hence, this is a philosophy of life which unites the realms of work and non-work, as the factory girls commute from the universe of production to that of consumption.

This paper seeks to describe such a reality of contemporary Maltese society. It identifies how workplace culture is constructed by social agents and how this is in turn moulded and made subservient to the overarching logic of the capitalist system. To qualify this interplay, particular emphasis will be placed on the relationship between the worker and her work, other workers and enterprise authority figures. Such an analysis of the sociology of Maltese work relations in the clothing industry will be placed in the context of an open economy condition, the whims and changes of which must perforce be addressed by the enterprise's corporate strategy in its struggle to survive.

The Economic Context

Local economic statistics clearly demonstrate the development patterns of the clothing sub-sector within Malta's export-oriented manufacturing industry. By far the largest constituent of local export-manufacturing for many years, this sub-sector also offered the first serious chance for Maltese women to enter the economically active population. Employment in clothing establishments, mostly foreign subsidiaries, reached its peak in 1978 when 9,591 workers were employed. By the beginning of 1993, this had fallen to 5,984 (C.O.S., 1991). Clothing exports to the EU, which is one of our main export markets, decreased by about a quarter between the years 1983 and 1987, (*The Economist Intelligence Unit*, 1989). This is an indication that the activity is emerging a net loser as it is now in fierce competition with developing countries of North Africa, South East Asia and even post-cold war Eastern Europe. Investment in such countries is proving to be more cost effective.

Malta followed the example of many developing countries by initiating its industrialization process with an emphasis on 'light' clothing industry, given that this is labour intensive and absorbs a good part of the labour force. Besides, the work done requires essentially very little skill. The operations carried out are usually of a short repetitive cycle and comparatively easy to learn. In spite of this set of attractions, it remains nevertheless a volatile industry. Economies must be prepared to watch their clothing industry collapse as they hopefully move from the initial stages of industrialization to more sophisticated 'niche' products and services.

The composition of the clothing sector in Malta is varied. Out of the 130 establishments operant in 1988, only 35 employed more than 70 workers. These establishments accounted for 93% of the total output and 89% of the employment in this sector (C.O.S., 1992). The small establishments produce mainly for the local market. Their output per head is about half that obtaining in the larger firms and this is reflected in the basic wages which hover very near the minimum wage. (C.O.S., 1992) In contrast, wages in large manufacturing firms are about 1.4 times the minimum wage.

Foreign owned companies employ more than three quarters of the workers and account for about 90% of the island's total textile and clothing exports. The relationship between the local clothing subsidiaries and their mother company is one of dependence. The Maltese company relies on the mother company for markets, technology, research, design and product development. This dependence reflects Malta's peripheral position within the international economic system. The prospects of our clothing industry have been aptly described to be 'dependent on multinational sourcing policies' (*The Economist Intelligence Unit*, 1989).

This is understandable as most of the foreign-owned firms operate on a CMT (cut, make and trim) basis. Thus, the local firms receive the cloth, design, trimmings and the instructions. The cloth is cut to specifications, the completed garment then being sent back to the mother company. Local management is generally only involved in the production stage.

Methodology

This paper is based on research conducted by the author in one such clothing firm. This is a relatively large subsidiary with 300 odd full-time employees. The firm has been operating in Malta for the last 25 years and which has, within this period, changed multinational ownership. Most of the critical interpretations which follow are based on first hand observations derived from site visits. These visits were further substantiated by casual semi-structured encounters held in Spring 1993 with line employees at the factory. A few longer discussions were also carried out with managerial and trade union representatives and other worker activists with some of whom the author enjoys a long standing relationship.

The main objective of this research endeavour was to witness the concrete outcomes of the negotiation of discipline and alignment to enterprise goals by employees who are both agents and victims of social circumstance.

As is typical of textile manufacturing in Malta and elsewhere in the developing world, most of the employees are young females. The names of all employees referred to are fictitious, to preserve anonymity. The pseudonym which I have chosen for this ongoing concern is the Maltese word for cloth, *drapp*. Hence Drapp Ltd.

Managerial Discretion

The efficiency and productivity of the Maltese worker in this firm has surpassed those reached by other workers in the other subsidiaries of the firm elsewhere. Still, it has been reported that the local company management used to receive its instructions on a daily basis. Local management was allowed to take certain decisions only if they were of an immediate and relatively unimportant nature. The absence of any room for initiative and discretion by local management was starkly highlighted when the mother company decided to curtail its operations in Malta. The only union allowed then, a house union, did not survive the change-over, having proved to be embarrassingly powerless in influencing the issue. When the mother company was taken over by the present multinational, there were changes in the local management. The latter was granted more leeway and the mother company was successfully convinced to tolerate the recognition of general trade unions with a strong membership outside the company.

Such a strategy is, however, only a symbolic expression of local managerial discretion. Enterprise strategy is primarily dictated by the need to develop an effective market response.

Corporate Strategy

> Presently, the aim of the mother company is to become the leader in the jeans market within a year or two.

The market which Drapp Ltd. faces, is very stable and growing. These factors set the parameters within which the local management operates. The corporate strategy depends on what is described as the extension of the reach of the Market Response System.

The rationale behind this strategy is that, given that competitor firms can match both quality and price, then the company must beat this competition by developing its flow replenishment capability. The target is for retail customers of the company to have their stocks replenished within as little as five days.

To attain these very bold targets, local management has sought to reduce the production cycle time. It knows that if it tries to achieve this at the expense of its workers by for instance, more stringent supervision or longer working hours, the strategy could easily backfire. One alternative is to use overtime; but too much resort to this will increase costs prohibitively. The alternative is to opt for sub-contracting, which is very common in the local set-up. It is estimated that about 30% of Drapp Ltd.'s production is attained in this way.

The manager described the situation thus:

> The advantages are obvious. Our targets of price, quality and time are being met. In the meantime, we are offering a good and stable job to our girls. And, if demand falls, we just cut the contracting out and maintain our workforce. We have learned that the workforce is the most important component of our production system. Redundancies surely won't help in maintaining the good relationship we have established with our workforce.

The union shop stewards at the company are aware of the situation. From their point of view, this is acceptable because, on one hand, the workers' interests are being safeguarded. At the same time, workers in other firms – which are mainly locally owned – and whose economic circumstances are currently much less rosy, would have the opportunity of partaking in the company's job orders. What is not stated is that this situation allows managerial discretion in determining the balance between how much work goes to 'core' and how much to 'peripheral' employees, effectively maintaining very strong control on the distribution of work. Thus, at the periphery, 'small suppliers can be played off, one against the other' (Nichols, 1980), to the advantage of those at the centre (Friedman, 1977). The unions are aware of the disadvantages faced by peripheral workers. However, as the General Secretary of one of the trade unions in which Drapp Ltd's employees are organized is reported to have said:

to attain higher production levels would mean turning the workers into human robots and squeeze blood instead of sweat from them (Micallef, 1992).

The Issue of Labour Control

But there is one crucial distinction between human operatives and robots. Production levels require strict managerial control of the production process. This is because since effort is not defined, 'the formal contract between employer and employee is incomplete in a very fundamental sense' (Baldamus, 1961). 'The problem of how to get work out of the worker still remains. At the root of this problem is the need to extract sufficient effort to ensure the eventual realization of profits' (Nolan, 1984). Consequently, employers have sought to develop systems of labour control which minimize tensions and conflict and facilitate profitable production (Burawoy, 1979; Edwards, 1979). Studies of managerial control – such as that of Friedman (1977) – tend to emphasise ideal-types. In real life situations, management pursues a mixture of control strategies (Edwards & Scullion, 1982). To understand the complexities of management-labour relations one must delve into the production process.

Drapp Ltd. produces jeans. A look at the specifications sheet of the jeans which Drapp Ltd. manufactures boggles the mind: It identifies more than 55 distinct specifications. These control the design and the material used. The production engineer at Drapp Ltd confirmed this, adding that:

> The tolerances within which we work, though not as strict as in engineering, are not that wide.

It is through these specifications that these jeans are recognized for value, quality, fit and comfort. Although the continuous-flow production process appeared first in textiles, this process never reached its fullest potential as in the car industry. It is the nature of the operations in the clothing industry which prevents the conveyor belt being used. However, a managerial representative commented:

> Through-put time is one of those engineering factors which are constantly studied as it influences the production time and hence the costs and our commitment to deliver on time.

Traction

On entering the shop floor, one is immediately struck by the sense of urgency. Girls speeding their machines to cut down operation time, while others move their finished work briskly away, allowing them to start work on a new bundle. Others shout at their supervisor over the noise, pointing out that their machine has broken down, while others watch impatiently as the engineer tries to see what is wrong with their machine. Rose, one such machine operator, complained:

> You can easily ruin a whole day's production bonus while you're waiting to have your machine repaired.

She recollected that this was the third time that week that her machine had broken down. One can feel the tension among the girls, but also among the supervisors and the production engineer. All are being pushed to achieve the task in hand in the least possible time. It is a fast, continuous cycle – girls pushing machines to their limit while they themselves get carried away with it and, in turn, push others. The experience of traction is brought to mind: 'the feeling of being pulled along by the inertia of a particular activity. The experience is pleasant and may, therefore, function as a relief from tedium' (Baldamus, 1961).

Female machine operators are conscious of this. At Drapp Ltd., workers do attempt to control the speed with which the whole assembly line moves. During a trade union meeting, there was pressure on the shop steward to bring to the attention of management that the work performed by Charmaine was causing problems further down the production line. Her speed was causing problems to the other operators. Helen blurted to the shop steward:

> We have been complaining about Charmaine for quite a long time to reduce speed and improve quality but to no avail.

Elements of Control

It is pertinent here to resort to the three dimensions of control – identified by Edwards (1979) – which go to make up the technical repertoire available to management for enforcing labour compliance to the production regime. Their discussion is applied to the Drapp Ltd. machine operators to reveal its practical dimension.

a. Machine Pacing

Machine pacing is one form of technical control. Workers are machine disciplined and the continuous-flow production establishes a work rhythm. In contrast, if left on their own, the girls would tend to work furiously for a short while and then slack off or even stop entirely to rest. Another attribute of machine pacing is that this system stops mobility while at work. Being fixed to a physical location in the production process virtually stops contact among workers.

The assembly line format has got other advantages. Task specialization and routinized operations are a natural way of achieving cost efficiency in relatively labour intensive production processes such as that of the clothing firms. The total number of stages that are required to manufacture a jeans at Drapp Ltd. are over thirty. This eliminates the need for high-wage skilled labour while achieving generous increases in labour productivity. Extensive division of labour shortens and simplifies each operation and thus reduces the skill level required. This enables the girls to perform the operations with practically thoughtless, impulsive motions. Their actions become so standardized and routinized that it enables operators to perform with the least effort of thought and hence of brain fatigue. As one of them commented:

> Will-power and brains are the two things that you don't need here. Otherwise, you get crazy or get yourself in trouble!

Even though machine operators are officially classified as unskilled workers, their work requires skill. The definition of a skill is in itself a social and political process, not merely one of ascription. Training a machine operator to a level which matches the required production level may take up to six months. Each stage of the manufacturing process may require different levels of skill. Watching Connie on her machine, one is amazed that a human being is able to perform many precise finger operations in a work cycle lasting only a few seconds for eight hours a day without any noticeable effort. Yet, it is not uncommon for her to fail to reach the required production quota. The allocation of a quota is itself a component of the strategy of control and motivation.

Management can still make a difference. There was a time when the workers were harassed. Lydia, who has been working at

Drapp Ltd. for the last fifteen years, still remembers the difference:

> Sitting for hours crouched on my machine gives me back pain. I still remember having the supervisor on my back whenever I used to stand up or go to the toilet. Now, we tend to work in a more relaxed way, though we still have to reach the production.

b. Performance Appraisal

Evaluating the workers' performance is the second managerial control element. Since the machinery is standard, the quality of every operative's output is more or less identical and thus the management's problem is reduced. This function, presently, is performed by quality controllers and is currently very strictly adhered to. Still, management is not satisfied. One manager opined:

> Soon we will introduce quality control along the line. Leaving it till the very end is not that satisfactory, as in some cases the damage will be irreparable.

In cases where the quality is not satisfactory, the operator will have to rectify mistakes out of her own time. Here managerial, especially middle management, discretion is operative. Girls complain that in such cases, the supervisor may or may not decide to send someone to help. The outcome of this decision appears to depend substantially on one's relationship with the supervisor:

> At the factory, wearing a provocative dress may help. It also helps if the girl does not object to the supervisor's passes and jokes (Mallia V., 1991).

Sexual harassment is another condition girls have to face. One union official described sexual harassment as

> the monster that many know to exist but on which rarely anyone talks about in the open and much less do anything about. (Mangion, 1991).

c. Sanctions

The third and last control element identified by Edwards (1979) is the action of disciplining and rewarding workers. The pay system here plays a very effective role. The piece-rate system means that the girls' wages partly depend on how fast they work. The wage actually embodies two distinct components – the basic wage, topped up by the piece-rate bonus. The basic wage which is always guaranteed is relatively low and, in some cases, less than the national minimum wage. Thus, the workers' attention turns to the production bonus. To be eligible for the extra pay, a worker must exceed the particular job's 'rate', or the assigned minimum level of output needed to trigger the incentive system. The worker then earns a bonus depending on how many units she produces above the rate.

The problem here is that the rates are invariably high. This is especially so for the newer and older workers. For the newer workers, the problem is temporary. After a while, they will reach their peak, but for the older workers the problem becomes worse. They are still expected to reach the set output:

> It is impossible to expect girls to produce at such high rates in such conditions, year in year out (Mallia, H., 1991).

It is not the first time that these 'older' workers will be under pressure to leave their job. 'Older' in this context means older than 25-26 years of age, which is the industry norm at present in Malta (WPDC, 1992). Piece-rates effectively punish operators who, for whatever reason, lag behind the output standard. But alongside the piece-rates stand the management's power to hire and to fire. In such a situation, having a union at the workplace helps. When the relations are good, management concedes to such a request. A union shop steward commented:

> It is not the first time that, with the girl's approval, at our request, management transfers the girl to another job – where the 'rates' are not that tough or where the job is not on the piece-rate system.

The piece-rates or the standard output are determined by management. A common complaint is that the girls feel that whenever they begin to make large premiums, the time-study engineer appears on the scene to 'restudy' the job. This causes great resentment and at times friction between management and workers. The former insists that rates setting remains its absolute prerogative. The union, in such cases, seems powerless, as piece-rates and standard output are undefined. Thus apart from submitting a typical complaint, it usually leaves the workers to deal with the problem themselves.

When the rates for a new operation are being calculated, it is usual for the management to increase the rate by about 25% as it knows that, after a short period of time the girls will match the rate. The girls, on the other hand, become very conscious of their work movements when an engineer starts 'loitering', even at a distance.

> On average, a machine operator in the clothing industry spends only about 20% of her time actually sewing. The rest of the time is spent handling the fabric (Grech, 1978).

The girls, subconsciously, know this and they tend to use it to their advantage. Rates set are achieved by reducing the time utilized to handle the material. One way of doing this is to have the bundles open and ready before production time starts. Another technique is to pick about 10 jeans at a time and leave them on one's lap. This does reduce the time of the operation considerably but at a cost. Jeans are made of heavy material and this time-cutting technique may have implications on a worker's overall health. Nevertheless, these aspects of labour strategies come to an abrupt halt as the engineers start going around. One gets the feeling that both sides know the games which the other plays. However, both are very careful not to allow bad blood to come between them.

This points to the crux of the relationship between labour and capital:

> The capitalist labour process is at one and the same time a co-operative and conflictual activity (Hyman, 1984).

Management must achieve both control and compliance if not consent. The strategies open to management are varied.

> There is no 'one best way' of managing these contradictions, only different routes to partial failure (Hyman, 1987).

Social Regulation

But, apart from the relatively straightforward technical forms of control, (Edwards, 1979), 'social forms of regulation', (Burawoy, 1984) also come into play. These mechanisms are not embodied in the technical, but rather in the social relations of production. One method which is becoming more popular with management today is that of resorting to generous communication flows:

> At Drapp Ltd. management is doing its best to inform the workers of our objectives, achievements and failures. We are ready to listen to any suggestion which can help our productivity.

This exercise is not a 'one-off' phenomenon. Periodically, managerial personnel meet groups of workers in a conference hall outside the factory. This exercise is not only directed at the workers but also at their leaders. The two shop stewards coming from different unions as well as the union officials are involved in this 'open-door' policy which encourages communication flow. As a union official conceded:

> These meetings are very fruitful as we feel that, through them, we are understanding each other better.

This readiness to promote dialogue is also laced with elements of traditional, benevolent paternalism. The Managing Director feels it is his duty to tour the shop floor daily in an informal way. Through his exercise, he succeeds in building up a personal relationship with most of the large workforce. One can feel the positive reaction of the girls being called by their first name: Connie's reaction sums it up: 'Somehow we feel that we matter'.

This relationship is consolidated by the fact that management typically lunches at the same canteen tables with the workers. This exercise in bridging social distance and traditional status demarcations is very important; management feels that it must be able to cultivate an enterprise ethic. This ethic erodes the conventional us-and-them divide and makes employees more disposed towards responding quickly to changes in the product market.

> Changes in the external environment of corporate activity, which in one sense narrow the range of strategic options, may compel an internal restructuring which facilitates strategy within the area of choice which remains (Hyman, 1987).

Countering Individualism

But the promotion of enterprise solidarity is apparently being sabotaged by the technological setup at Drapp Ltd. Management feels that the present assembly line approach and the individual piece-rates may have outlived their use because they generate excessive individualism. A managerial representative admitted:

These systems have made our workers individualistic in their approach to such an extent that they do not care about the girls further down the line.

Two strategies are being proposed to counter, or at least temper, this tendency. The first is the introduction of work groups and the second is the introduction of microprocessor-based machines. These changes are likely to transform the nature of the relationships on the shop floor.

a. Work Groups

The introduction of work groups is not something new at Drapp Ltd. This firm has already introduced work groups in the final stage of production – the pressing stage. At this level, each group consists of five operators. All are trained to perform all the operations. It is the group which decides which girl does what. The girls do switch from one operation to another but usually each tends to stick to the operation she prefers. Bonuses are allocated on a group basis. As Marx (1967) had observed with respect to the piece-rate system:

> [...On the one hand] it tends to develop individuality, and with it the sense of liberty, independence and self-control of the labourers; on the other, there is competition one with the other.

The reason for this type of relationship is that each factory girl can dictate the speed with which she and her machine operate. Working in a group system will change the relationship from one of independence to one of interdependence. The performance of the individual will, in the new scenario, depend on the performance of the whole group. This will tend to deviate the conflict that arises on the shop floor into a more 'lateral' expression (Burawoy, 1979).

b. New Machinery

The introduction of new machinery is likely to 'deskill' the labour force even further, robbing it of what pride of craft and skill it still manages to control. The new machines will perform complex operations on their own with little guidance from the operator. Joanna, one of the first girls to operate such machines, notes:

It is much more boring but it is easier and less tiring to handle.

These machines tend to reduce the small but delicate finger and arm movements which were previously necessary. As such, the power relationship between labour and capital will tilt more in favour of capital. New technology leaves less space for manoeuvre to labour since the latter's work is subject to stricter control. It will also render the pace of production beyond the tolerance limits of personality factors, hopefully eliminating the significance of and impetus for, any inter-employee rivalry.

Individual Resistance Beyond Work

The repertoire of actions resorted to by workers to 'beat and defy the system' are not limited to the shop floor. Such actions are generally restricted to individual actions; but there is a limit to which these actions can be taken. This is because overt conflict, without the blessing and security of organized, collective mobilization, will be punishable with serious consequences. The economic power of Labour on the open market is limited; and state institutions come into play to ensure compliance. Three common expressions of individual reaction at Drapp Ltd., as at other production sites, are sabotage, absenteeism and labour turnover.

a. Sabotage

Sabotage is very difficult to measure. Workers do not go around talking openly about it: apart from the fact that this carries immediate dismissal, it may also constitute criminal action and therefore liable to legal proceedings against the individual. Management itself, although usually aware of and concerned with the problem, has surprisingly little control over it. Because of this, it is very rare to find management admitting the practice:

> Open admission of such internal problems does not help public relations, and it may even give previously isolated individuals some sense of solidarity (Taylor & Walton, 1971).

At Drapp Ltd, as with all other firms where there is a collective agreement in force, the consequences of sabotage are crystal clear: immediate dismissal, apart from the firm's right to press for criminal charges.

b. Absenteeism

Official absenteeism also carries with it the ultimate sanction, the termination of employment. But there is another circumventing way of going about this. An employee may resort to sick leave entitlement and thus avoid incurring the consequences of absenteeism. Again, all collective agreements in this sector deal with this problem in a very clear and uncompromising manner. Operators are sent home on sick leave only if the sustained injury on work is very evident, such as a cut. When workers absent themselves because of sickness the procedure to be followed is again rigidly imposed. The relevant section from an extant collective agreement in this sector reads as follows:

> No payment shall be made for sickness which is not certified by a medical certificate. The only medical certificates recognized by the company shall be those issued by a Company Doctor, who will visit sick employees at their home, if necessary, and issue a certificate (G.W.U., 1987).

This procedure has created problems both to workers and their unions. Their main complaint is that 'sick leave is given according to the exigencies of production' (Mallia, H., 1991). One union official quoted a recent case where one of these company doctors was of the opinion that the worker could attend work and so did not issue a sickness certificate. The worker went to the local Polyclinic and, to her surprise, the doctor who was attending was the doctor who had visited her the previous morning. However, her initial surprise mellowed into amazement when the same doctor, not recognizing the girl, issued a medical certificate stating that this girl should not report for work for a whole week.

But how serious is this problem? From a survey conducted in the clothing industry, (Caruana, 1986), it was estimated that the average absentee rate is approximately 4%, a very low figure by any account. Moreover, it was found that the highest absences are registered during December and January, and at the beginning of summer, in June and July. It therefore appears valid to argue that the statistical change is correlated to flu and common colds contracted because of the change in weather conditions. But overtime could prove to be another contributing factor. When overtime becomes more frequent and is worked for lengthy periods, absenteeism increases, the probable reason being fatigue and increased stress suffered by the operators (Caruana, 1986).

If absenteeism is not such a major issue, why indeed are the factory girls, their unions and management so concerned about it? Management feels that if such control is relaxed then absenteeism might easily escalate, especially at a time when they can least afford it. The workers feel they are being pressured to attend work even when sick. Furthermore, when they fall sick, they only qualify for sickness benefit, losing out on work and productivity-related pay. On the other hand, the union's main concern is that this kind of pressure might create the conditions for serious accidents.

c. Labour Turnover

Labour turnover – i.e. 'the number of members who leave during the period divided by the average number of members during the same period', (Price, 1977) – has long been identified as another source of individual protest. In the UK, the mean rate of labour turnover associated with the clothing industry until mid-1986 was 28% per annum; the mean labour turnover in Malta was estimated as 20-21% per annum during the same period (Caruana, 1986). However, the range concealed behind this statistic extends from 17% to 50%. A high labour turnover in this industry has been a standard, characterized as it is by factors such as job dissatisfaction, the strenuous physical work environment, intrinsic aspects of the job, the supervisory style and work group dynamics (Lefkowitz, 1971). In Malta, factors which significantly condition labour turnover are marriage, pregnancy and (possibly) repetitive strain injury.

Management at Drapp Ltd. estimates that pregnancy accounts for about 50% of the labour turnover:

> During the last ten years we have seen a shift. Previously, the work cycle for factory girls ended with marriage. Today, about 50% of those who marry still carry on for a number of years. The rest resign when they get pregnant. We estimate that today's cycle has been extended to 8-10 years. Girls tend to join when they are 16-17 years old and resign when they get pregnant at about the age of 26-27 years.

This conforms to the national trend of postponing pregnancy to a later age. One of the shop stewards at Drapp Ltd. commented:

> Some girls wish to continue working after they get pregnant. There is no official policy against this. But I doubt whether this is the true situation. Recently, a pregnant girl was ready to continue in the job. Management got to know about this, and the girl was referred to the company doctor. Soon after, the girl was informed that she could not continue working as her job was detrimental to her pregnancy and the firm could not assume responsibility. Her job was terminated.

The union wanted to take up this problem, but the girl refused, to the consternation of the shop steward.

Repetitive Strain Injury (RSI) is increasingly becoming an important preoccupation of trade unions nowadays and possibly a powerful reason behind relatively high labour turnover levels. RSI is known to be caused by factors such as awkward posture, the amount of repetition, the physical force exerted in the activity and workplace stress level – all of which constitute normal fare for a factory girl.

When dealing with RSI, unions face the same problems as in sexual harassment:

> Few would believe that some of our youth are being handicapped because of their work (Mallia, H., 1991).

In fact, the trade union had a tough battle when a girl in one of the local clothing firms was declared redundant because of RSI she allegedly contracted due to her work. The Industrial Tribunal (Case No. 413) accepted that the injury was an occupational disease and thus declared that the girl had been unjustly dismissed. However, few doctors are ready to link RSI directly to their patient's job; furthermore, even after being declared permanently partially disabled, workers may ironically be sent back to their same, previous jobs.

Conclusion

The interplay of structure and agency, action and reaction is thus neatly expressed and illustrated by Maltese female factory operators in the clothing industry. The life of factory girls is neatly subsumed within the overarching cultural dimensions of individualism, tempered with a competitive drive, patriarchy, powerlessness and rampant consumerism (Tonna 1993; Zammit 1984). And each of these in turn reinforces and strengthens the other. On the one hand the individualism and competitive spirit is reinforced by the production process and the pay system. On the other hand the factory girl, tired after a day's hard work, will find herself isolated as she tries to recoup enough energy for another day's labour. The powerlessness fits the environment: working on one's own in a drone of machines each groaning monotonously at different rhythms, one is caught into the traction and becomes a robot in the process – 'everything is done automatically, the way they do things at work' (Mallia, V., 1991).

Previously, a typical factory girl's goal was to work hard for a couple of years, get

> married and as soon as she gets pregnant, she will say good-bye to work forever, and concentrate on her home and children (*Tomorrow*, 1983).

Nowadays, these aims are spiced with a sense of urgency. Freddy Mercury's lyrics 'I want it all, I want it now' is the powerful maxim of our consumer-oriented society. Presently, 'family life, collapses into rituals of mass consumption', (Crook et al., 1992), resulting in 'large and luxurious houses with very small families, families who have everything yet feel unsatisfied' (Tabone, 1991) In the process of aspiring to an idealized Western standard of living, the factory girls have unwittingly become the fodder on which the system feeds and grows. Referring to them as 'girls' is not only indicative of paternalist managerial practice but also of their relative impotency to influence the system other than to consent to its frenzied logic of maximizing output. Once having served their purpose, they may yet be left by the wayside, at times permanently disabled: Society's waste?

References

Baldamus, G. (1961) *Efficiency and Effort: An Analysis of Industrial Administration*, London, Tavistock.

Burawoy, M. (1979) *Manufacturing Consent: Changes in the Labour Process under Monopoly Capitalism*, Chicago, University of Chicago Press.

Burawoy, M. (1984) *The Contours of Production*, Berlin, IIVG Publication Series.

Caruana, J. (1986) 'Labour turnover and absenteeism in the Maltese clothing industry', unpublished dissertation, University of Malta.

Central Office of Statistics (1992) *Industrial Statistics 1988*, Malta, Government Press.

Central Office of Statistics (1994) *Annual Abstract of Statistics 1993*, Malta, Malta Government Press.
Crook, S., Pakulski, J. & Waters, M. (1992) *Postmodernization: Change in the Advanced Society*, London, Sage.
Economist Intelligence Unit (1989) 'Mediterranean textiles and clothing: competitive threat or investment opportunity?, *The Economist Intelligence Unit, Special Report no. 1121*, London, The Economist Intelligence Unit.
Edwards, P.K. & Scullion, H. (1982) *The Social Organisation of Industrial Conflict: Control and Resistance in the Workplace*, Oxford, Basil Blackwell.
Edwards, R.C. (1979) *Contested Terrain: The Transformation of the Workplace in the Twentieth Century*, London, Heinemann.
Friedman, A.L. (1977) *Industry and Labour: Class Struggle at Work and Monopoly Capitalism*, London, Macmillan.
Grech, J.C. (1978) *Threads of Dependence*, Malta, Malta University Press.
General Workers' Union (1987) *Collective Agreement between G.W.U. & Heidemann Sportswear Ltd.*, Malta.
Hyman, R. (1984) *Strikes*, London, Fontana.
Hyman, R. (1987) 'Strategy or structure? Capital, labour and control', *Work, Employment and Society*, vol. 1, 1.
Industrial Tribunal (1986) *Case No. 413, Textile, Garment & Leather Workers' Section, G.W.U. versus Bleimund Ltd.*, Malta.
Lefkowitz, J. (1971) 'Personnel turnover', *Progress in Clinical Psychology*, vol. 73.
Mallia, H. (1991) 'Kif thares il-Union lejn il-qagħda preżenti tal-mara fil-fabbriki', in Kummissjoni għall-Avvanz tal-Mara, *In-Nisa fil-Fabbriki*, Malta.
Mallia, V. (1991) 'Il-kundizzjonijiet li l-mara qed issib fil-fabbriki', in Kummissjoni għall-Avvanz tal-Mara, *In-Nisa fil-Fabbriki*, Malta.
Mangion, A. (1991) 'Id-dinjità u s-saħħa tal-ħaddiem fil-fabbriki', in Kummissjoni għall-Avvanz tal-Mara, *In-Nisa fil-Fabbriki*, Malta.
Marx, K. (1967) *Capital Vol. 1*, New York, International Publishers.
Micallef, K. (1992) 'The rise and fall of the textile industry', *Labour Post*, General Workers' Union, no. 72.
Nichols, T. (1980) *Capital and Labour – A Marxist Primer*, Glasgow, Fontana.
Nolan, P. (1984) 'The firm and labour market behaviour', in Bain, G.S. (ed.), *Industrial Relations in Britain*, Oxford, Basil Blackwell.
Price, J.L. (1977) *The Study of Turnover*, Ames, IO, Iowa State University Press.
Tabone, C. (1991) 'Il-familja Maltija fil-proċess ta' l-iżvilupp ekonomiku-soċjali', in *Kummissjoni Ġustizzja u Paċi, Malta Llum – u Forsi Għada: Analiżi tar-Realtà Soċjali Maltija*, Kummissjoni Ġustizzja u Paċi, Malta, Veritas Press.
Taylor, L. & Walton, P. (1971) 'Industrial sabotage: motives and meanings', in Cohen, S. (ed.), *Images of Deviance*, Harmondsworth, Penguin.
Tomorrow Magazine (1983) 'One day in the life of a factory girl', February.
Tonna, B. (1993) *Malta Trends 1993: Report on the Signs of the Times*, Malta, Media Centre.
Workers' Participation Development Centre (1992) *Women Workers in Industrial Estates: A Survey on their Needs and Facilities*, WPDC, University of Malta for the Commission for the Advancement of Women.
Zammit, E.L. (1984) *A Colonial Inheritance: Maltese Perceptions of Work, Power and Class Structure with reference to the Labour Movement*, Malta, Malta University Press.

30

Workers' Participation and the Control of Labour

Godfrey Baldacchino

A Peculiar Configuration

Malta's labour topography resembles that of industrialised states, with a negligible agricultural segment, and a substantial industrial and service oriented labour force. But, apart from five modest gifts of nature – sun, sea, sand, salt and stone – the archipelago is bereft of mineral or other exploitable resources. Cheated of economies of scale and limited by insufficient indigenous investment capital and lack of state-of-the-art, technological competence, the island archipelago has had to earn its keep by mainly advertising itself as an attractive base to others. Today's 'cargo' – tourists, finance, pleasure craft, merchandise – has replaced the military strategists and colonial administrators of the not so distant past. Hence was born a dependence on a different interpretation of resourcefulness: the ingenuity, flexibility, skill and productivity of the Maltese labour force for economic survival (Baldacchino, 1993a).

The other side of the coin is that this dependence requires to be complemented with an attitudinal compliance by labour to the promotional package. Prosperity and stability hinge crucially on the consent and accommodational responses of labour, both at the individual and the collective levels of organisation. Hence, there is an inbuilt concern, held by those in control of production, to reap a surplus and to maintain and increase the productivity and attraction of labour to outside sponsors.

The above is a concern universal to all systems of production; hence all economic systems can be envisaged as essentially systems of labour control (Harrod, 1986; Baldacchino, 1988a). The concept of labour control is used to refer to the construction, by no means automatic, of labour as a viable factor of production – responding positively to the demands and objectives of the economic system. Such labour control is typically engineered via a complex pattern of socialization, technology and managerial strategies, motivators and penalties.

Thus, while outwardly prosperous and stable, the enviable quality of life enjoyed by most Maltese today conceals a particular expression of labour control: A configuration between economy, politics and labour which I hold to be crucial to a proper and contextualized understanding of the practice of workers' participation and the control of labour (Zammit & Baldacchino, 1989).

Ensuring Labour Control

Obtaining the required condition of labour control is rather difficult owing to the disproportionate strength of individual and organized labour in the Maltese economy. Any Maltese policy maker has to face up to a series of hard facts: Firstly, the proportion of wage and salary dependents within the labour force is very generous: over a third of the population are wage and salary earners; secondly, the representation of such employees within labour unions is just as impressive. The implications of alienating even a fraction of this organised mass could be politically very damaging, given in particular the anxiously fine margin of votes separating partisan sympathies between the two main political parties. This would be the third hard fact. Labour, the one main readily available source of wealth creation is thus a significant lobby both at the ballot box and behind the union banner. Rampant proletarianization, innate mineral poverty, neck-to-neck bipolar democratic politics and high union densities combine to produce a formidable people/worker power machine.

The same problematic had asserted itself to some extent during the centuries of fortress economy. In that context, loyalty was engineered for and by the colonising power by virtue of it becoming the only source of gainful employment to a rapidly expanding population (Baldacchino, 1988a; Zammit, 1984). Today, the political actors have changed but the pattern has stubbornly persisted. All post-independence Maltese governments have sought, perhaps more out of necessity than desire, to control Maltese labour covertly through appeasement. The tactics have included nationalistic belt-tightening appeals, charismatic leadership, state-trade union collaboration, prices and incomes policy and widespread employment in the public and parastatal sectors. These can all be construed as important and viable policy instruments of 'high trust relations' (Fox, 1974). That is, they constitute a particular form of labour control which is durable because it is based on consent rather than coercion. Hence, it does not generate resistance, resentment and, subsequently, costly industrial action, an insecure investment climate or electoral defeat.

Proposal

I propose that the issue of worker participation in Malta be considered as another important tactic in the context of the appeasement agenda. It is a powerful form of non-coercive labour control which concurrently promises to create a more cooperative and productive labour force, and offers the opportunity of experimenting with novel, social relations of production. Such a tactic was particularly entertained when the country's political leaders were faced with a very powerful trade union organisation and a not too certain economic future (Baldacchino, 1988a; Zammit, 1984).

Non-Coercive Labour Control

Not only is Malta's unionization rate – around 53% – easily in the world's top ten league for nation states today (Baldacchino,

1991). The largest union within the local setup – the General Workers' Union (GWU) – is in all probability the largest single trade union in the world, relatively speaking, counting within its ranks 11% of the total resident local population (Walls, 1989). This situation is probably due to the fact that trade union membership and recruitment is also a function of partisan political mobilisation whilst, at the same time, trade unions have made powerful inroads in public administration, manufacturing and large private market service establishments. Corporatist arrangements of some sort have in fact been in place ever and only since the setting up of the GWU in 1943 and the immediate astronomical increase in membership of this union. Over the years, these arrangements have included the Labour Coordination Committee (1945-49); the Malta Government Joint Council (1950-68); a close affinity by the GWU with the policies, practices and ideologies espoused by the Malta Labour Party (MLP) in office (1971-87); a statutory fusion between the GWU and the MLP (1978-92); and, most recently, participation on a National Economic Development Council, set up by the Nationalist Government in office since 1987, incorporating the latest incomes policy agreement initialled in December 1990 (Baldacchino, 1993b).

No wonder therefore that the first recorded instance of worker participation in decision making in Malta had already occurred in the early 1950s, when port workers (hard core GWU members) agreed to cooperate, manage and distribute both the work load and the fees collected for their services. The arrangement was formalised by the Port Workers' Scheme of 1952 and updated by the Port Workers' Ordinance of 1962 (Baldacchino et al., 1986).

No wonder also that the most far-reaching development in worker participation in Malta occurred at Malta Drydocks, still the country's largest, if not also oldest, enterprise with 3,700 employees, 3% approximtely of the gainfully occupied population where levels of political activism and trade union consciousness reach record heights.

The introduction of worker participation at Malta Drydocks was incremental: German style co-determination (where equal numbers of directors were appointed by the GWU and Government, and where the Chairperson was acceptable to both) was introduced in 1971 soon after the MLP's electoral victory. From 1975 onwards, the Drydocks Council started being completely elected by and from the workforce with the exception of the Chairperson, introducing the first and only experience of full worker self-management in Malta. Then in 1977, the first of eighteen departmental level worker committees signalled a further progressive refinement, decentralising the decision-making machinery down to the shop floor level (Baldacchino et al., 1986; Kester, 1980). In the early 1980s, the Council Chair started being nominated from among the elected council members and no longer from outside.

Expansion...

The introduction of full blown worker participation at the Drydocks was in all probability an *ad hoc* solution to what appeared to be a vicious circle of sour industrial relations and chronic bankruptcy (Portelli & Zammit, 1983). Indeed, both industrial peace and (for a short spell) profits were dramatically restored within a few years. In much the same pragmatic spirit, various forms of participatory management were ushered in by the MLP in the 1970s and early 1980s. These top-down initiatives bear the unmistakable stamp of Dom Mintoff, former MLP leader (1949-84) and former Prime Minister (1955-58; 1971-84).

While the establishment of a socialist society remained his foremost long-term objective, such a development could not, in Mintoff's mind, take place without the achievement of national economic self-reliance through worker self-sacrifice and higher productivity. Not only did worker participation capture the essence of the socialist project; it was a pleasant departure from the confrontational and economically wasteful industrial relations practices which had plagued the country in previous years, practices which threatened its uncertain prospects after the appointment with the fateful day of destiny – the winding down once and for all of the fortress economy after 31 March 1979. It also permitted an acceptable *modus vivendi* between union and party, justifying the collaborationist policy of the GWU as a cost-effective strategy which secured gains for workers in line with national economic considerations. Inspired by the then remarkable experience of the Yugoslav self-managed economy, Mintoff signalled the go ahead for further novel arrangements, particularly in areas which were comfortably organised by the GWU (Kester, 1980; Zammit, 1984, *passim*).

A lone worker director was appointed to each of the boards of various public and parastatal corporations, usually following a nomination by the GWU. Management committees were set up within eighteen state-owned manufacturing companies, as well as within certain civil service departments. A number of producer cooperatives were also established following GWU backing, to find or preserve employment for discharged employees.

A number of worker sit-ins and take-overs in the private sector also took place, again mostly with the full backing (and, often, the outright instigation) of the GWU. In the late 1970s, these multiple initiatives across the board were being hailed as a veritable (perhaps hegemonic) transition to full worker self-management: then, almost one out of every three Maltese employees worked in an environment which had some formally constituted form of worker participation in place (Bayat, 1991; Kester, 1980).

...and Degeneration

Political and economic circumstances however precipitated starkly different results. The parastatal industries had run into financial difficulties. As a result, they were converted, fully or partly, to foreign or local private ownership. This meant the dismantling of all other than orthodox industrial relations practices. The civil service management committees were captured mainly by Confederation of Malta Trade Unions (CMTU) union activists, then engaged in a bitter and protracted struggle with the GWU. A power contest ensued between these non-GWU representatives and the responsible authorities, leading to a *de facto* winding up of these civil service participatory structures.

At Malta Drydocks, economic viability did not keep pace with innovations in democratic management. The enterprise had to fall back once again on state-guaranteed finances for its financial flows. And worker-managed enterprises in the private sector were generally temporary, stop-gap affairs: they reverted back, sooner rather than later, to private capital or were transformed into a form of public, state-owned corporation (Baldacchino, 1990, p. 101).

Thus, when the Nationalist Party assumed office in 1987, it inherited the residue of what had appeared to be, hardly a decade before, a fully fledged participatory economy in the making. The legacy included: Eight worker directors on the boards of eight separate corporations (seven of which was state-owned); a self-managed Malta Drydocks which had reverted to chronic loss making in 1982; and three producer cooperatives (two of which were in the process of liquidation).

An Assessment

A sober assessment can be made today with the powerful advantage of hindsight. The so-called transition to industrial democracy in Malta was, not unexpectedly, introduced from above with the backing and inspiration of the Maltese Labour Movement – the MLP and the GWU. Perhaps because of this all too transparent partisan packaging, it was inevitably met with suspicion and disapproval by the civil service rank and file: moves to greater democracy in action were perceived (perhaps even construed?) as a threat to established non-GWU trade union interests and power relations. The transition moreover remained subordinate to economic considerations where international investment was involved. All in all, rather than having a spillover, expansionary and transformative effect – as was espoused by enthusiastic progressive academics and as evidenced from policy rhetoric – the outcome of the participatory experience, rather than an ambitious transition, can now be more aptly described as a corporatist and integrative strategy (Stephens, 1980).

Post 1987

Worker participation initiatives have taken an altogether different cast since 1987. Malta Drydocks and its militant employees (a headache for any party in power) have been placed in suspended animation with a multi-million, 10-year package deal (D.O.I., 1989); the number of worker-directors has not increased, though all directors which still exist are now in office on the basis of a free election. The pressure for innovative work relations, threatening to control other than through ownership, appears spent, a victim of passing fashion. Enticing more foreign investment has meant a more obvious policy orientation towards a stronger integration of the Maltese economy with satellite status into the capitalist world system (e.g. Camilleri, 1990). There is no urgency to experiment with participatory schemes: although an ongoing public sector reform may be disposed to consider schemes which encourage autonomous work groups. Public employees enjoying security of tenure may also be allowed the space to self-manage specific projects awarded under competitive tendering (Parliamentary Secretariat for Human Resources, 1993). The CMTU, organising practically all workers not unionised within the GWU, has yet to press for its first worker director. The few developments to speak of, have been limited to experiences of partial employee shareholding, isolated profit sharing and the setting up of a few new producer cooperatives. These initiatives in no way threaten established power relations and in more ways than one actually consolidate the premise that only who owns, controls the predicament of work.

Nonetheless, this does not imply a regression to traditional industrial relations: Both the GWU and the CMTU have persevered, albeit with fits and starts, for three years, in an incomes policy accord with the other social partners, these being employers, Government and business interests. The inbuilt pressures towards corporatism remain; but these are today confined almost exclusively to superstructural arrangements. Their activation is far removed from the actual work environment.

Reinventing the Wheel

The retrenchment of trade unions away from the important arena of 'shop floor participation' may permit discourse on new forms of worker participation schemes, this time employer and management driven, to gain popularity. We have of late in Malta turned the spotlight on worker empowerment, job enlargement, quality circles, excellence teams and other devices intended towards the spectacular unleashing of the worker's innate potential, the human resource development of individuals and groups. The promises of effective worker participation are being reproposed and, in the process, repossessed. The discourse is now different. This 'innovative management approach' (BASE, 1993) is now advertised without the terminology which elicits threatening images of worker control, employee take overs, nationalisations and other communist chimeras now consigned to history.

We have so admirably reinvented the wheel: Workers have been rediscovered as 'partners' in the production process. Worker participation... oops! sorry; I mean employee commitment and involvement, is now a management slogan, exhorting employees to collaborate with the enterprise goals. The invasion of human capital theory into industrial relations is the new exciting issue. Labour has been upgraded almost overnight from another factor input, an energy pack, to a veritable resource, where the human factor, and all his/her assorted faculties, are now hailed as indispensable assets to organisational success (e.g. Barbara, 1990). Will this shift fuel a genuine (albeit often inadvertent) democratisation of power relations at the workplace? Or will it contribute to the 'participation strip-tease', systematically robbing workers of job security, minimum wage legislation, trade union representation and other gains which they have secured over many decades of mobilisation and collective action (Kester, 1991)?

Enter the Worker

But where is the worker in all this? Accounts of the Maltese participatory saga are too easily subsumed under the predetermined principles and objectives of econometric modelling and of powerful mass interest groups: trade unions, political parties, lay and religious pressure groups, civil bureaucracies, state, employer and business interests. All these remain important players and spokespersons within the project and they invariably dominate and mould the rampant discourse in accordance with a priori motives and ambitions. Every interest group seeks to make its voice heard; but the voices of the actors who perhaps matter most – those of the individual employees concerned – may be lost within the overall roar of confused noises.

This observation is a critique also of mainstream academic accounts of labour relations and trade union studies which do not dislodge themselves from the institutional paradigm. They remain narrow domains and avowedly technicist in orientation, failing to consider workers as other than members of collectivities: unions, social classes, party machines and other organisations (Cohen, 1991). Workers are considered as having neither an existence nor a will outside such boundaries; as if they never question the motives and declarations of the organisations within which they are enrolled.

Worker Perceptions

Some insights into the opinions and perceptions of Maltese workers on their participatory experience are at hand;, thanks to the social science survey research pioneered by Gerard Kester (Kester, 1974) and subsequently by the Workers' Participation Development Centre (WPDC) at the University of Malta. Having been closely associated with most of these research projects, I shall hereunder endeavour to encapsulate the dominant worker perceptions which have emerged to date concerning the phenomenon of worker participation in Malta. The aim is to tease out the main sociological strands to the issue, enabling an appraisal of the impact of the experiences.

a. Malta Drydocks Employees

Pride of place must definitely be assigned to Malta Drydocks employees. They remain the most intensely studied research population on this theme locally. In the most ambitious survey conducted on this topic so far in Malta, a representative sample of these employees have exposed a vision of cooperation, joint effort and internal harmony which is embodied in their working definition of participation. They envisage a scenario where Council, professional management, the GWU and the worker committees cooperate in the process of decision making when no differences of interest are at hand. The workforce appears generally satisfied with the participatory system and this overall satisfaction finds vent in positive attitudes with respect to other aspects of work. The development of 'social objectification', meaning a proper participatory culture and consciousness (Bernstein, 1976; Kester, 1980), is evidenced by strong demands for further power sharing and for a wider spread of information.

A number of exogenous factors colour the workers' perceptions of the work environment. The economic crisis infesting the ship-repair industry generates a concern for job security, increasing effort and calls for greater efficiency. Social inequalities perceived to exist in the wider Maltese society tend to generate feelings of relative deprivation among the employees in relation to privileged social groupings. Finally, partisan politics is cited as another influential variable which acts both to create in-group interpersonal bonds and out-group hostility.

Workers' Participation and the Control of Labour

But perhaps the most powerful external variable influencing the Drydocks worker's frame of mind is a cultural one. A long colonial experience has led, *inter alia*, to the emergence of irresponsible trade union and political activism. Antagonism is thus a natural perceptual framework, further supported by the often unexpressed radical notion that different social groups have fundamentally irreconcilable and conflicting interests. Drydocks workers have after all formed the vanguard to this spirit of opposition and they owe their privileged position as a local 'aristocracy of labour' partly to the benefits accruing from such a historically sustained stance (Baldacchino et al., 1986; Baldacchino, 1984).

Such a long tradition, which has paid hefty dividends, is not easily curtailed, let alone replaced. From the trade union standpoint, this antagonistic perspective persists even more strongly because collective bargaining is the incarnation of antagonism. It remains the dominant instrument for negotiating conditions of work in local private industry. This means that both the workers and their union officials are bound to feel ill at ease in adopting the requirements of full worker self-management: accepting responsibility for decisions taken, concerning themselves with the viability and profitability of the firm, developing long-term expectations and goals, possibly accompanied by short-run sacrifices. Hence one comes across, for example, an ambivalent situation with regards to wages policy: relatively high, secure and fixed wage rates in a self-managed firm operating with chronic non-profitability (Baldacchino, 1989); a belief in the advantage of reverting to state management; a professional management which appears to be an uncomfortable bedfellow with the operant participatory structures (Portelli & Baldacchino, 1988; Smole-Grobovsek, 1986); a desire for a militant shop steward; substantial pressure for an equally militant, trade unionistic worker committee, which finds its extreme form when this committee is controlled by GWU shop stewards (Kester, 1986).

A stylistically elegant way of taking stock of this situation is to argue that there are two systems of decision making in place, based on two opposing sets of principles: one participative and one traditional (e.g. Baldacchino, 1984; Kester, 1986). But a more rational explanation can perhaps be based on the notion of the existence of an ambiguous multiplicity of channels, a 'polycentric decision making structure' which can be manipulated differently by different workers (or by the same workers at different times) at will, all in the obvious pursuit of personal, interest satisfaction (Smole-Grobovsek, 1986). The condition is thus not so much one of role conflict but one of role diffusion and role confusion (ibid.). This "identity crisis" may prove convenient and indeed functional to those intent on manipulation (Baldacchino et al., 1986). The issue is not to determine whether the participatory system at the Drydocks is subsumed within the traditional us-them, capital-labour dualism, or vice versa. Rather, both of these may be subsumed and deftly assimilated within a culturally comfortable behaviour pattern which cultivates 'networks, manipulators and coalitions' (Boissevain, 1974). Within this framework, an immediate superordinate, a union steward and a worker committee member 'are equal potential candidates for patronage and social brokerage' (Baldacchino, 1994).

b. Worker Directors

Interestingly, a similar set of difficulties can be documented in a brief survey of the opinions and experiences of worker directors (Baldacchino, 1988b). The worker director owes his/her existence to a willingness, on the part of the GWU, to experiment with the appointment of representatives in this capacity in the mid-1970s (Zammit & Baldacchino, 1989). The status of the worker-director is, since 1987, based on an open franchise; but an indication of the crucial backing of the GWU is provided by the union's success in getting its nominee elected in every contest to date. The trade union support for the position may however prove to be its own undoing because it generates pressure on the candidate to behave, once in office, like a glorified shop steward. One ought to keep in mind that the electorate is primarily composed of union members and that the candidate usually already has a history of union activism. The invasion of the sanctity of the boardroom by rowdy trade union demands would naturally drive the other, non-elected board members to take corrective and defensive action, possibly isolating the worker representative still further. The latter's relative incapacity to act effectively is sealed by the absence of any adequate legal, institutional or educational machinery which somehow defines the specific terms of reference and equips him/her for the task at hand. The condition spirals precariously towards oppositional trade unionism, domesticated collaborationism or else to a 'board with a board' situation which leaves the worker director in a policy limbo; the seat of decision making being stealthily moved away from his/her influence.

c. Private Sector Employees

My third and final example of participation as experienced by the grass roots is drawn from a case study of worker perceptions in a medium sized private firm. Since the fieldwork was confidential and the company is an ongoing concern, its identity had best remain undisclosed.

The flirtation with workplace democracy was once again a top-down initiative. The recommendation was made by the company's executive director (a priest) who suggested introducing worker participation in management and profits on the agenda of a collective agreement which was being finalised. There was some enthusiasm, even concern, on the part of the workers, to start profit participation; but the eagerness cooled down dramatically when the company accounts revealed a series of regular losses.

The proposal to set up a workers' committee, eventually paving the way to worker directors on the company board, took off with good intentions. There were, however, two hitches. On the one hand, the dominant personality of the executive director proved too difficult to live with. As the founder, ideator and manager of the company, he exercises paternalistic management with employees, most of whom he knows personally and intimately; he remains the hub and fulcrum of most human interactions within the company, on business as well as private matters. On the other hand, the incumbents of the participatory structures could not (perhaps did not want to) break this 'small firm management syndrome'; this was, from the workers' point of view, convenient because it spared them the burden of responsibilities and duties they had been obliged to accept by virtue of being shop floor representatives. When in this capacity, they had felt it their duty to come up with welfarist demands – fans, air conditioners, wage increases – which were summarily dismissed as impossible by the director. The agenda was strictly trade unionistic, the elected committee effectively replacing the trade union as the mouthpiece for worker demands. Lack of progress reduced the relevance and interest in the participatory structures by all concerned. Participatory structures in session became useless, chat encounters. 'Social objectification' had not materialized. The participatory initiative was allowed to fold up after a year or so, the exasperated director refusing to continue what had become merely an institutionalised, time-consuming farce.

The Politics of Discourse

Despite a long history of armchair theorisation, and an almost equally long experience of assorted practices, we must humbly recognize that the term workers' participation is highly ambiguous (Bayat, 1991; Roca & Retour, 1981). The concept has implications for workplace humanization, social justice, equity, industrial peace, worker flexibility and dignity, social partnership, self-discipline, economic efficiency and productivity boosts. It is precisely its amenability to all shades of ideology and intent that has allowed, in different conditions, the most disparate of interest groups to jockey for pride of place as standard-bearers of participation, seeking to enslave the concept and define it rigorously with a particular slant. As with the proverbial Indian fable, we are all touching the elephant. But, blinded by ideology, tradition, culture or pure self-interest, we prefer to point our finger at different attributes: The thick skin of worker self-management; the supple proboscis of worker empowerment; the ivory tusk of employee share ownership; the hairy ear of co-determination; the dangling tail of profit sharing.

A Strategy of Avoidance?

It seems that the complimentarity and interlocking nature of roles in a participatory situation has remained just as vague in Malta. Individual actors and powerful organisations have found themselves adrift in uncharted waters as they sought to fashion an alternative industrial relations system piecemeal. Admittedly, this was carried out in a pragmatic and unassuming manner which may have nipped in the bud significant resistance from established interest groups, as well as tapping generous popular support. Still, it left participatory initiatives amiss of a consistent ideology (Kester, 1980, Chap. 9). So while the pressure to participate somehow remains, the organisations involved seem today much more disposed to do so in non-threatening, role comfortable ways: Labour control is understood in terms of union (rather than worker) participation, aloof and far removed from individual worker concerns and expectations which could get out of hand, which could rock established practices and power demarcations, which could scare foreign capital. It is as if, on the basis of local experiences, there is a definite clampdown to prevent a snowballing of exorbitant demands: participation in profits without participation in losses; participation in rights but not in duties; options for short-run concessions without long-run considerations. The absence of explicit policy measures directed towards building a direct relationship between effort and reward, along with the absence of supportive legal, educational and cultural baggage both undermine participative dynamics. These degenerate from potential mobilization and democratization to a socialization into traditional, defensive trade unionistic practices or else integrative managerial ploys. Simply put, more of the same.

The Challenge of Managerial Initiatives

But what about the challenge being posed to trade unions by employer and management initiatives in the participatory domain? If properly worked out, quality circles, excellence teams and other group-based participatory structures can be strengthened and legitimized with active trade union backing. Their agendas can be extended to incorporate other areas of competence – such as worker education, environmental protection, occupational health and safety and perhaps other issues so far viciously defended as sole managerial prerogatives (Kester & Pinaud, 1992; Baldacchino, 1993c). Such programmes appear to stand a better chance of success (whether measured by worker, labour or capital yardsticks) because they are based on a set of clearer provisos: both the trade union and professional management maintain their traditional checks and functions. Meanwhile, deterrents and joint stake-holding interests will minimise the likelihood that one of these parties will deploy the participatory organs to override or silence the other. These organs are also politically non-partisan and concern the rank and file employees. They can therefore be much closer to the experiential domain of the workers who matter than other legalistic arrangements located somewhere aloof and far away in the institutionalised labour relations architecture.

The lessons of the past, at home and abroad, suggest that participation ought not to be envisaged as in lieu of traditional trade unionism. This either erodes professional managerial authority or else questions the very legitimacy of trade unionism. A powerful organisation to represent workers at the level of the firm, and a professional team driven by market logic and enterprise loyalties are both essential prerequisites. The participatory organs need to be juxtaposed next to these, rather than replacing any one to the presumed tactical advantage of the other. Perhaps crucially, both for the trade union and the company, such worker participation schemes could mean survival in today's pragmatically driven and economically competitive world.

References

Baldacchino, G. (1984) *Il-Parteċipazzjoni fit-Tarzna: Kif Jaħsibha l-Ħaddiem*, University of Malta, Workers' Participation Development Centre.

Baldacchino, G. (1988a) 'The industrialisation of Malta: A historical analysis of the formation, control and response of labour' in Azzopardi, E. & Heywood, P.L. (eds) *Issues: Aspects of an Island Economy*, Malta, The New Economics Society.

Baldacchino, G. (1988b) 'Id-direttur ħaddiem', *Perspettivi Newsletter*, Issue No. 3, University of Malta, Workers' Participation Development Centre.

Baldacchino, G. (1989) 'Wages policy at Malta Drydocks: Analysis of an ambivalence', *Economic and Social Studies (New Series)*, vols 3-4.

Baldacchino, G. (1990) *Worker Cooperatives with Particular Reference to Malta: An Educationist's Theory & Practice*, The Hague, The Netherlands, Institute of Social Studies.

Baldacchino, G. (1991) 'A review of Maltese trade unionism', *Economic and Social Studies (New Series)*, vol. 5.

Baldacchino, G. (1993a) 'Bursting the bubble; The pseudo-development strategies of microstates', *Development and Change*, vol. 24, 1.

Baldacchino, G.(1993b) 'Il-kontribuzzjoni tal-General Workers' Union matul dawn l-aħħar ħamsin sena: Perspettiva soċjologika', paper presented at a forum organized by the Workers' Participation Development Centre and the Friedrich-Ebert Foundation, University of Malta, March. Subsequently published in Zammit, E.L. (ed.) *It-Trejdunjoniżmu f'Malta: Ħarsa Lura u 'l Quddiem*, Malta, Workers' Participation Development Centre.

Baldacchino, G. (1993c) 'Human resource developmnent: Is it a con?', *The Malta Independent*, 12 December.

Baldacchino, G.(1994) 'Peculiar human resource management practices?: A case study of a microstate hotel', *Tourism Management*, vol. 15, 1.

Baldacchino, G., Gauci, A., Portelli, J. & Zammit, E.L. (1986) 'Workers' participation at Malta Drydocks' in Vahcic, A. & Smole-Grobovsek, V. (eds), *Workers' Participation and Self-Management in Practice*, vol. 1, Ljubljana, Yugoslavia, International Center for Public Enterprises.
Barbara, A. (1990) 'Why human resource development?', *Bank of Valletta Review*, No. 1.
BASE (1993) *Journal of the Foundation For Human Resources Development*, Malta, Vol. 1, 1.
Bayat, A.(1991) *Work, Politics and Power*, New York, Monthly Review Press.
Bernstein, P. (1976) *Workplace Democratization: Its Internal Dynamics*, Kent OH, Kent State University Press.
Boissevain, J. (1974) *Friends of Friends: Networks, Manipulators & Coalitions*, New York, St. Martin's Press.
Camilleri, A. (1990) 'Malta Development Corporation', position paper in Zammit, E.L. (ed.) *Workers' Participation in Malta; Options for Future Policy*, University of Malta, Workers' Participation Development Centre and Ministry for Social Policy.
Cohen, R. (1991) 'Theorizing international labour' in *Contested Domains: Debates in International Labour Studies*, London, Zed.
D.O.I. (Department of Information) (1989) 'Ftehim għat-tarzna', supplement to *Pajjiżna*, Malta, Department of Information, July.
Fox, A. (1974) *Beyond Contract: Work, Power and Trust Relations*, London, Faber & Faber.
Harrod, J. (1986) 'Social relations of production, systems of labour control and Third World unions' in Southall, R. (ed.) *Third World Trade Unions and the Changing International Division of Labour*, London, Zed.
Kester, G. (1974) *Workers' Participation in Malta: Issues and Opinions*, Malta and The Hague, University of Malta and Institute of Social Studies.
Kester, G. (1980) *Transition to Workers' Self-Management: Its Dynamics in the Decolonizing Economy of Malta*, The Hague, Institute of Social Studies.
Kester, G. (1986) 'Workers' representatives versus workers' representatives: The struggle for effective and meaningful workers' participation in a ship-repairing industry', *Working Paper No. 31*, Malta and The Hague, Workers' Participation Development Centre, University of Malta and Institute of Social Studies.
Kester, G. (1991) 'The participation striptease', paper presented at International Conference on Return of Work, Production and Administration to Capitalism, Chemnitz, Germany, October.
Kester, G. & Pinaud, H. (eds) (1992) *Scenario 21: Trade Unions and Democratic Participation*, Paris and The Hague, Confédération Français Démocratique du Travail & Institute of Social Studies.
Panitch, L. (1977) 'The Development of corporatism in liberal democracies', *Comparative Political Studies*, vol. 10, 1.
Parliamentary Secretariat for Human Resources (1993) *Koperattivi u Kunsilli Lokali f'Malta u Għawdex*, Malta.
Portelli, J. & Baldacchino, G. (1988) 'Survey dwar is-sistema tal-parteċipazzjoni tal-ħaddiema fit-tarzna ta' Malta', unpublished mimeograph, University of Malta, Workers' Participation Development Centre.
Portelli, J. & Zammit, E.L. (1983) 'Workers' participation at Malta Drydocks', *Public Enterprise*, vol. 4, 2.

Roca, S. & Retour, D. (1981) 'Participation in enterprise management: Bogged down concepts', *Economic and Industrial Democracy*, vol. 2, 1.
Smole-Grobovsek, V. (1986) 'More or less workers participation?', *Public Enterprise*, vol. 6, 3.
Stephens, E.H. (1980) *The Politics of Workers' Participation: The Peruvian Approach in Comparative Perspective*, New York, Academic Press.
Walls, H. (1989) 'The case for a Trades Union Council', *Society*, 3.
Waterman, P. (1975) 'The labour aristocracy in Africa', *Development and Change*, vol. 6, 3.
Zammit, E.L. (1984) *A Colonial Inheritance: Maltese Perceptions of Work, Power and Class Structure with reference to the Labour Movement*, Malta, Malta University Press.
Zammit, E.L. & Baldacchino, G. (1989) 'Workers on the board: A sociological comment on recent developments in workers' participation in Malta', *Economic Analysis and Workers' Management*, vol. 23, 1.

part 6

deviance and social problems

The claiming of voice by constituent members and groups of a society or the delegitimation of such a voice constitutes a political game of exclusion and inclusion. When and if this is properly identified, it can shed much light on the unequal positioning of certain social groupings with respect to others, and on reasons for this discrimination. When summarily dismissed as social problems, the character of marginalization becomes a given rather than a focus of investigation; and this attitude effectively and intentionally disguises crucial workings and policies, the ramifications of power at work.

The sociological imagination can be a great eye-opener here, demystifying and questioning what appears to be solid, unquestionable and even logical, exposing and perhaps even embarrassing in the outcome.

The contributions to this section have opted to visit particular 'problem areas' in contemporary Maltese society: Some, like drug abuse (analysed by Abela) and the elderly (tackled by Troisi) appear to be currently basking in the public eye, the foci of current policy instruments by the state and non-governmental organizations. Others, like the environment (explored by Mallia) appear to be still struggling to make the grade, trying to justify their intrinsic significance and relevance as a social problem which merits being considered as such and therefore calling for concerned and corrective policy action. Others still, like the issue of alcohol abuse (documented by Baldacchino) and socially emarginated individuals, such as widows, unmarried mothers and handicapped citizens (issues which are engaged by Cole) persist in the zone of non-problematization, and therefore ripe candidates for a sociology of absence. Finally the terrain of official criminality is explored (by Tanti Dougall) and an attempt is made at interpreting its nature and causes.

In the process, the rationale behind classifying, or not classifying, a social group or a behaviour pattern as a problem can be profitably explored at a general, non case specific, level of discussion.

Outsiders

Maureen Cole

Introduction

This paper will consider those social groups which are marginalized in Maltese society. Three of these groups are studied in some depth, namely, gay men and lesbians, victims of family violence and children. Following this analysis, an attempt is made to examine the process through which certain groups have come to be 'outsiders' in our society. This analytical process draws upon sociological perspectives which are normally used to analyse social problems, namely the Critical Perspective, the Feminist Perspective and the Labelling Perspective. Finally, a social network analysis of four persons who are members of marginalized social groups is presented.

'Outsiders' is a term borrowed from Howard S. Becker and used in the title of his book *Outsiders: Studies in the Sociology of Deviance* which was published in 1963. This term suggests the existence of 'insiders' who have access to status, opportunity, information and resources which persons away from the mainstream of Maltese society do not have. The term also draws on the interactionist tradition in sociology, an approach which will be referred to in an attempt to understand how certain groups become marginalized in society. This tradition or perspective reflects the author's stance as it allows the possibility of looking at the world from the vantage point of persons who have been socially defined by others as deviant.

Who are the 'Outsiders' of Maltese Society?

Substance abusers; the aged; the mentally ill; persons with physical or mental disabilities; children, especially those living outside the traditional family structure; prisoners and ex-prisoners; gay men and lesbians; refugees; women; young single mothers; juvenile offenders; homeless persons; prostitutes; illiterate persons; people with AIDS... a long list which changes from time to time but despite changes, variations are minimal. A closer look at some of these groups will help us understand who these 'outsiders' are and how they have come to be so.

Gay Men and Lesbians

The oppression[1] of gay men and lesbians has taken form in most societies through religion, culture, law and social sanction. This process has also taken place in Maltese society. Where are the Maltese homosexuals? How are they spoken of? In what ways are they considered? Who are they? When considering homosexuality, in any society, it is important to keep in mind that we

---

[1] Oppression is the social act of placing severe restrictions on a group or institution. Typically, a government or political organization that is in power places these restrictions formally or covertly on oppressed groups so that they may be exploited and less able to compete with other social groups. Definition taken from Barker (1987).

are referring to a substantial number of men and women from all social groups. Estimates based on data from cross-cultural studies undertaken in the USA by Martin Weinberg and Colin Williams in 1974 (Babuscio, 1988) lead us to conclude, as Weinberg and Williams did, that 10% of the adult population is homosexual. More conservative data from the UK arrive at estimates of incidence at 5% of the adult population (Babuscio, op. cit.). Accepting this last estimate and applying it to the Maltese population, the conclusion one would reach is that about 18,000 Maltese persons are homosexual, given that the Maltese population stands at 355,910 (C.O.S., 1992). The sheer size of this group is overwhelming. And yet one would ask: Where are these people? Their numbers suggest that they must be men and women from all walks of life and coming from very different social backgrounds. It seems, therefore, as though close to 18,000 lesbians and gay men might endure lack of access to social, physical, and emotional resources and could even face discrimination and stigmatization as a result of being perceived as criminal, deviant and pathological.

During the past two decades a change occurred in Western society which many people termed a sexual revolution (Humphreys, 1972). The Gay Liberation Movement gave homosexuality a very different social meaning to what it previously had in most Western countries. Somehow, this widespread social phenomenon had little or no effect on Maltese society. Why is this so?

The reasons for the minimal effect of Gay Liberation and the social change which it heralded in other parts of Europe are possibly linked to a number of features of Maltese society. Homosexuals everywhere have to function within the context of homophobia[2] and this is true also for Malta. Our society is certainly one where everyone is assumed to be heterosexual unless proved otherwise. Gay people are thus likely to feel

---

[2] Homophobia – 'Dread of Homosexuality' as defined by Weinberg and quoted by Donadello, G. (1986).

inferior, not so much because of what they do but rather because of the threat which they represent. At the core of homophobia is the issue of power. Gay men and lesbians challenge the traditional existing relationships of male power and authority. The reaction to this challenge would be expected to be particularly strong in Malta which, compared to other European countries, scores high on traditionality (Abela, 1991). The strength of the family as a social institution gives further basis for the buttressing of traditional values and the reduced likelihood of the emergence of homosexuality as a social force. Opposition to homosexuality is closely bound up with the nature of our Judaeo-Christian heritage. The official position of the Catholic Church on homosexuality refers to it as a 'moral disorder' and that it cannot be promoted in a Christian society (Babuscio, 1988). With such a position as a backdrop it is hardly surprising that persons with a homosexual orientation are practically invisible in Maltese society.

An additional factor which has affected homosexuals in Malta as elsewhere is AIDS (Acquired Immune Deficiency Syndrome). From the mid 1980's a perceptible change of attitude has been encountered by homosexuals in most Western countries with a resulting increase in anti-gay violence and discrimination against gay men and lesbians. This has taken place in countries like the UK and USA which had previously begun to take measures to counteract discrimination. Such a backlash has undoubtedly affected Malta where this process of counter-discrimination is as invisible as the homosexuals themselves.

Victims of Family Violence: Women, Children, Young, Old.

Violence in family and primary relationships has existed throughout history but only recently has it been documented and begun to be considered a social problem. Family violence refers to physical, sexual and emotional acts of commission and omission knowingly, purposely, or recklessly committed by and on family members. The term family is here being used to refer to individuals related by blood or marriage as well as those who constitute primary associations. Family violence includes abuse, neglect and the exploitation of one family member by another resulting in harm, injury, humiliation and sometimes death (National Association of Social Workers, 1988).

The changed perception of sexual and physical abuse of children, wives and elders is a relatively new phenomenon both locally and internationally. Attention was first drawn to the problem of child abuse in America in the late 60's through the work of researchers like Kempe and Gil (Boss, 1980). In the early 70's the Women's Movement contributed to the identification of spousal abuse. Subsequently child sexual abuse emerged as a major social problem in both the USA and Europe. It was not till the late 1970's that elder abuse was given prominence in the literature on the subject. And it is only in the 1980's and 1990's that the abuse and neglect of handicapped children has been highlighted as a fairly widespread phenomenon. Likewise, ritual abuse has been acknowledged in recent times.

Prevalence studies were undertaken in the USA in the midseventies to try to estimate the extent of child and wife abuse. Data which emerged from a national survey in which family members were asked about their own experiences indicates that 12% of spouses had been in an incident of violence in the previous year and 4% of parents admitted to having used severe violence against their child in the previous year (Finkelhor, Hotaling & Yllo, 1988).

Maltese data which indicates the size of child abuse and wife abuse is not easily available and no study comparable to the prevalence study quoted above has been carried out locally. The data available is primarily help seeking data. In 1990[3], 100 women aged between 17 and 50 sought help from St Luke's Hospital because of injuries suffered as a result of violence. Of these, 51 had been battered by their husband and 49 had been involved in fights or been injured by relatives or close friends. Three women aged over 50 sought help, one of these having been injured as a result of a physical attack by her son.

This data is useful and indicative up to a point. Firstly because as with all data relating to family violence, it only sheds light on the incidence of physical violence but does little to help identify instances of emotional and sexual abuse.

---

[3] Information given by the Action Team on Violence against Women of the Secretariat for the Equal Status of Women on 19 June 1991.

Table 1. Reported incidents of wife battering to the police over the last five years (by year).

YEAR	Number of Reports
1989	152
1990	142
1991	162
1992	203
1993 (up to 28/4)	71

Source: Response to a Parliamentary question given by the Minister for Home Affairs and Social Development on 3 May 1993, Parliamentary Sitting No. 131.

Table 2. Number of persons accused of wife battering who appeared before the Law Courts over the last five years (by year).

YEAR	Number of Persons who appeared before the Courts
1989	83
1990	87
1991	98
1992	118
1993 (up to 28/4)	35

Source: Response to a Parliamentary question given by the Minister for Home Affairs and Social Development on 3 May 1993, Parliamentary Sitting No. 131.

Secondly, there is little means for calculating the numbers of those who have suffered some injury but never sought help. That the numbers may well be far greater than those indicated in Tables 1 and 2 is also suggested from research being undertaken by S. O'Reilly Mizzi on women in Senglea. More than 51% of the women interviewed in the age cohort 15-29 expressed a fear of being beaten up (*The Malta Independent*, 13 June, 1993). The very expression of this fear denotes that physical violence may well be a phenomenon not so foreign in these women's lives (Miceli, 1991). Despite limitations, data referred to above, although of little use in determining prevalence, is of great value in continuing to draw attention to the plight of these persons.

The situation is better camouflaged in cases of sexual abuse. As has happened in other countries, extreme cases have been publicized, gained prominence temporarily, only to be then discounted as rare occurrences which happened only in certain 'types of families'. Overseas research (Finkelhor et al., 1986) later demonstrated the various gradations and widespread nature of these phenomena. The fact that denial, doubt, disgust and disbelief tend to be the most common reactions to instances of family violence, make it very easy for such problems to be ignored and forgotten about. The very difficulty in finding data about these persons is a reflection of their position in Maltese society, clearly placing them outside the mainstream.

There is little mention of child abuse in Malta. The tragic cases reach the media and occupy society's collective attention briefly. Corporal punishment is still an acceptable means for disciplining children and it is not always clearly distinguishable from physical abuse. Over the past two years or so all cases of suspected non-accidental injury to children who are admitted to St. Luke's Hospital are referred to social workers at the Ċentru Ħidma Soċjali. These workers would then undertake an assessment of the child's situation and may invoke statutory machinery to protect the child if necessary. On average, referrals from the hospital stand at around 25 per annum. Social workers would also receive referrals from other sources and these would reach 16 or so per annum.[4]

Children who have been neglected may suffer a number of difficulties too. They may be withdrawn and miserable, be particularly aggressive, have nutrition problems and emotional problems that may last a long time. Sexual abuse can have very complex and lasting effects too. Children abused in this way are not easily identified and no action may ever be taken to protect or help them.

Various forms of elder abuse are identified by social workers, who encounter in their practice physical, psychological and financial abuse of elders. Although local data about this phenomenon is not systematically compiled, this does not in any way reflect its

---

[4] Estimates based on information obtained from Ċentru Ħidma Soċjali for the number of referrals received from January to June 1991.

non-existence. The relative silence of Maltese society about these victims of abuse is an indicator of the stand taken by 'mainstream' Maltese, a stand which defines them as 'outsiders'. Other factors which likewise reflect this stance are: the limited education of the public about these issues; the little attention which has been given to legislative measures which promote removal of a perpetrator from the home rather than the victims; the very rudimentary attention which has been given to providing holistic services which are intended to help all those touched by an abusive experience whether victim or perpetrator; and also the very limited emphasis which has been given to continuing education of professionals about these phenomena.

The prevalent belief in the family as essentially harmonious and conflict-free has blinded both professionals and the public at large to the many possible violations that may and do occur in families (Sayers, 1991).

Are these not ways of ensuring that these persons remain 'outsiders' in our society?

Children

Historically, children have at one time or another been considered as property. It was primarily the 19th century reformers who challenged this philosophy and pressured for legislation which protects children from undue hardship and provides for their more basic developmental needs. This can be said to be the case locally. However despite legal advances made on children's behalf all too often they may still be treated as second-class citizens. A question that one might ask about childhood is whether it is visible in Maltese society. Would childhood be more visible if children had the right to vote? As Moir (1988, p. 121) points out, 'The right to vote is a powerful force in gaining recognition of your needs'.

What follows is an attempt to analyse children's position by evaluating some of their basic rights and examining whether these are sufficiently promoted and safeguarded.

Children have a right to a positive social identity and this should include pride in family and national culture and individual differences. Such a positive identity can only be achieved if the child is free from discrimination because of social or political origins.

Can this truly be said to be the case for all Maltese children? Are resources truly distributed according to need? Is the greater need always the primary consideration in the allocation of resources?

The well-being of children is enhanced through policies which respect the child's right to be part of a family. Is this right being safeguarded for around three hundred children who are currently residing in Children's Homes? Is every effort being made to preserve the child's home and family links? Is similar effort being made to intervene to help the family before a child is sent back home, so as to ensure that the child's home return proves a positive and healthy experience (Kerslake & Cramp, 1991)? Is sufficient effort being put into implementing legislative changes such as those of guaranteeing that these children's rights are safe guarded and ensuring that their best interests are always given primary consideration (*The Rights of the Child*, United Nations, 1991)?

Are Maltese children sufficiently protected from economic exploitation and work that may interfere with their education and be harmful to their health (Sultana, 1993)? What concrete changes have accompanied Malta's ratification of the UN Convention on the Rights of the Child on the 30 September 1990? Could it be that the superficial attention which has been given to these matters is a symbol of the overall attitude towards children? Is this another way of producing outsiders in our society?

How Have They Become 'Outsiders'?

Maltese society deals differently with its members; inequalities experienced are based on differences in class, in gender, in age, in sexual orientation, in economic opportunities, in prestige, in power. As a result of these inequalities, some members have greater access to what is considered valuable by our society whereas others have lesser access. This seems like a 'natural' state of affairs in our society, a situation which ensures that these inequalities continue, that some members sit comfortably 'inside' and others continue to struggle 'outside'.

The Critical Perspective, which stems from the Marxist tradition in Sociology, is one of the perspectives used in trying to better understand society and its problems. This perspective suggests that social institutions are interrelated and exercise influence on one another. But, out of these institutions, it is the economic one which exerts the greatest influence on people, their prospects, and the manner in which they interact with one another. Though people have numerous social statuses, their position in the economic institution is viewed as the most important. Thus, as Marx and Engels argued in *The Communist Manifesto* it is the very form of social organization of capitalist societies which causes a wide range of specific social problems that are endemic in a social system based on social inequality. According to this perspective the 'haves' hold on to what they have and maintain what they have at the continued expense of the 'have-nots' (Rubington & Weinberg, 1989).

In using the Critical Perspective to understand the oppression of women, Rubington & Weinberg (op. cit.) quote Liazos who draws on Engels to explain that Capitalism has reinforced sexism as through its social structure it makes the economic and social exploitation of women a permanent necessity. The strength and usefulness of this perspective in analysing social problems is that it focuses attention on how important the economic structure is in defining people's position vis-a-vis one another in society and facilitates an understanding of social inequality.

However, although economic standing is a basic determinant of social standing, prestige does not always accompany it. Stratification based on prestige involves the distribution of respect. Some people are highly regarded simply because they are born into a certain family. Likewise prestige is frequently linked to occupation and some occupations are regarded as prestigious whereas others are not. Most individuals receive the prestige associated with the kind of work they do (Abercombie, et al., 1988; Boswell, 1982; Zammit, 1984).

The Critical Perspective also highlights the way power is wielded in a social formation. Power refers to the ability to take action which will somehow affect how other people will behave. In Maltese society power is exercised primarily by government. Government exercises power by making the laws that everyone must obey. These laws determine financial responsibilities of both individuals and companies, they define government's responsibility to support the needy. The Government sees to the enforcement of legislation and to determining penalties for breaking the law. Government plays a crucial role in creating and maintaining social inequality. The Roman

Catholic Church exercises power through its teachings which '...inform the religious beliefs, attitudes and practice of the Maltese' (Abela, 1991, p. 68). Other organizations act as pressure groups and succeed in bringing pressure to bear upon government and other political institutions to achieve ends that they favour.

A useful perspective for defining social problems – one that is closely linked to the critical tradition outlined above – is the Feminist Perspective. The latter implies a consideration of all problems in terms of their specific impact on women's welfare. Feminist work on redefining social problems has focused on identifying specific ways in which women experience their existence, drawing people's attention to the lack of resources, emotional fulfilment and opportunity which frequently hold women down (Dominelli & McLeod, 1989). A feminist analysis of domestic violence draws attention to addressing the subordinate status of women in intimate family relationships in general. A key strength of this perspective is its ability to take into account the actor's definition of the situation. In other words, the voice and analytical accounts of the subjects under study are acknowledged as important. Many other traditions of analysis submerge such accounts in favour of the analyses provided by 'experts'.

Another useful perspective which may also be drawn upon in an attempt to understand inequality is the Labelling or the Interactionist Perspective, which is known as such because it fits into the tradition of 'Symbolic Interactionism'. This perspective helps us to recognize that in some cases people respond more to labels than to the actual behaviours, and that by so doing they contribute to producing the very behaviours they condemn (Manis, 1976). The central notion of the perspective is that social problems and deviance exist in the eye of the beholder. After a person has been labelled as 'deviant' most people will expect him or her to continue violating norms of conventional behaviour. This may limit the person's life chances and lead that person to continue to behave in ways which fulfil the deviant role. An ex-convict may be unable to obtain employment in a conventional job and may return to crime to make a living. This perspective can provide powerful insights in considering a small community like Malta where the consequences of labelling may last for several generations resulting in forces which push people outside the mainstream and continue to keep them there.

The different perspectives outlined above are all useful in analysing social problems as each is more or less valuable in understanding and dealing with some types of problems more than with others. In drawing on these specific perspectives and excluding others the author's bias in favour of examining social problems in terms of social reactions, class and gender relations has emerged.

Some Personal Experiences

Although the process through which a person becomes an 'outsider' in our society is a social, political and economic one, the experience of being 'outside' is very much a personal one. Each person lives this experience in his or her own unique manner, as each interacts with specific social agents. Personal accounts of such networking highlight both the individual experience and serve as pointers for a better understanding of the collective experience as well. These personal accounts are intended to focus on the reports of those affected and draw on their experiences. They are rooted in the Feminist Perspective on social problems, described above, which has contributed substantially to validating personal experience.

Interviews were carried out with four persons who may be considered marginalized in our society. The selection of these four persons was determined by the author's wish to interview persons who are widely considered 'outsiders' by our society. Contacts with these persons were made through Caritas Malta, a Catholic Social Welfare Agency, and the choice of interviewees was not made with the aim of selecting persons who are in any manner representative of a group. Choice was primarily determined by the respondents' consent to be interviewed. The very fact that these persons were in contact with a social welfare agency may very well set them apart from society at large and contribute to a description of them as atypical.

Information was collected about the social network of a woman who is separated from her husband and who has one child, a physically disabled young woman and an elderly couple who live alone. The interviews were guided by the use of an adapted version of a social network grid, the dimensions of the grid being illustrated in Figure 1, below. (Tracy, 1990). This was translated to Maltese and utilized into structure the interviews.

Figure 1. Social Network Grid

RESPONDENT	AREA OF LIFE	CONCRETE SUPPORT	EMOTIONAL SUPPORT	INFORMATION/ ADVICE	CRITICAL	DIRECTION OF HELP	CLOSENESS	HOW OFTEN SEEN	HOW LONG KNOWN
	1. Household	1. Hardly ever	1. Hardly ever	1. Hardly ever	1. Hardly ever	1. Goes both ways	1. Not very close	0. Never	1. Less than one year
	2. Other family	2. Sometimes	2. Sometimes	2. Sometimes	2. Sometimes	2. You to them	2. Sort of close	1. Four times per year	2. From one to five years
	3. Work	3. Always always	3. Almost always	3. Almost always	3. Almost always	3. Them to you	3. Very close	2. Monthly	3. More than five years
	4. Organizations/ Church							3. Weekly	
	5. Other friends							4. Daily	
	6. Neighbours								
	7. Professionals								
	8. Other								
NAME 01									
02									
03									
04									
05									
06									

Adapted from Tracy, (1990).

Interviewees were asked about the size and composition of their social network, the extent to which network members provided various types of support and the nature of relationships. They were asked about the length of their relationships with persons they had identified and the frequency of contacts. Respondents were also asked about availability of assistance, emotional support and information/guidance from members of their social network. Besides, other qualities of the social network relationships were assessed such as closeness, criticalness (i.e. the number of network members who are perceived as critical of the respondent) and the reciprocity or otherwise of help between members of the network (Tracy, 1990). At the end of the interview the respondents were asked about how they feel in society as a whole.

Tracy argues that network size alone appears to be a poor indicator of perceived social support. Therefore the analysis needs to include who the network members are. Networks which are dominated by relatives are regarded as more obligatory then voluntary and may be perceived as a burden. When a person feels that a relationship is reciprocal, he or she is likely to feel more comfortable in the relationship, ready to both give and receive help as required. This reciprocity may be an important determinant with respect to whether the person feels that he or she is part of society's mainstream or not. Length of relationships was also queried, as it is used as an indicator of stability of the relationships.

Respondent's names have been altered in an attempt to ensure anonymity.

Marija
(A physically disabled young person who has mobility problems)

Marija named 20 people in her social network.
- 3 are family and household members.
- 3 are other family members.
- 5 are persons she has met through work.
- 3 are like her, members of a voluntary organization for disabled persons.
- 2 are neighbours.
- 3 are professionals whose services she has sought because of her disability.
- 1 is a volunteer from a religiously-affiliated organization.

Marija is in contact with:
— members of her household and work colleagues on a daily basis.
— members of the voluntary organization for disabled persons of which she is a member, on a monthly basis.

Marija has known:
— 6 of the persons in her social network for more than 5 years.
— 7 from 1 to 5 years; this group includes her work colleagues.
— 3 for less than 1 year; this group includes social network members whom she has met through the voluntary organization for disabled persons.

Marija feels very close to ten members of her network and close to the other ten. She feels very close to: her parents, her two year-old nephew, four of her work colleagues, one of the persons she encountered via the voluntary organization for disabled persons, one of the professionals who frequently helps her out with her personal problems and the volunteer from the religiously-affiliated organization.

When asked about reciprocity of network relationships with respect to the network members mentioned above, Marija perceived thirteen of her network relationships as reciprocal. Marija reported that she provides help to one person and that six persons provide help to her.

Marija feels that the network members who provide her with the greatest emotional support are two persons, who like herself are physically disabled. She also obtains emotional support from the volunteer, with whom she goes out sometimes, and from the professionals who help her out with her difficulties.

Marija perceives her main sources of concrete support to consist of her parents and sister, her supervisor at work, one of her neighbours, one of the professionals whose services she has sought and the volunteer from the religiously-affiliated organization.

Is Marija an 'Outsider' or Not?

Marija feels closest to persons who like her are disabled, to a volunteer and professionals, all of whom she has become acquainted with as a result of her disability. This factor confines her to relationships which are primarily linked to her identity as a disabled person and may marginalize her. Marija is employed in a sheltered setting which provides job training for disabled persons; thus her colleagues are mainly disabled persons like herself. Hence, despite the important contacts which work provides her with, this sector of her social network is a select one and may result in Marija's further confinement to this world of the disabled and as a result marginalize her.

When Marija was asked how she feels as a member of society, she stated that her greatest problem is mobility as she must make use of public transport wherever she wants to go. She stated that she does have the 'courage' to do so; however it is very difficult for her to use buses and besides she is also aware that her mother becomes very concerned about her when she does so. This affects her use of public transport and increases her dependence on family and friends. This restrained mobility affects Marija's social network and is one of the main reasons why network members are primarily family members, work colleagues and persons she has come to know as a result of her disability.

Although the size of Marija's network does not suggest marginalization, the composition is a very likely indicator of a life lived outside the mainstream of Maltese society, a life lived within the confines of the world of disability. Drawing on the Critical Perspective, Marija's position in the economic structure suggests a situation of social inequality, primarily because she works in a setting which is set apart for persons with a disability.

Rita
(A woman in her mid-thirties who is separated from her husband and has an eight year old son)

Rita named 39 people in her social network.
    3 including her son are family and household members.
    10 are other family members.
    11 are persons she has met through work.
    8 are like herself members of a self-help group for single-parents.
    3 are other friends.
    3 are professionals whose services she has sought.
    1 is a neighbour.
Rita is in contact with:
— members of her family who form part of the same household, that is, her son and her parents, and her work colleagues on a daily basis.

— other family members and members of the self-help group she forms part of and her neighbour on a weekly basis.
— other friends and one of the professionals on a monthly basis.

Rita has known:
— 26 of the persons in her social network for more than 5 years.
— 12 from 1 to 5 years.
— one person for less than a year.

Rita feels very close to twenty-three members of her network, close to seven and not very close to nine. She feels very close to all the members of her family of origin, to two of her colleagues at work, to three members of the group for single-parents, to two other friends and to one of the professional persons whose help she seeks on a regular basis.

When asked about reciprocity of network relationships with respect to the network members mentioned above, Rita perceived thirty-one of her network relationships as reciprocal; she provides help to five persons including her son while three others help her. This latter group is made up of the three professionals whose services she makes use of.

Rita feels that the network members who provide her with the greatest emotional support are members of her family, her parents, her son, her two sisters and their respective husbands. She also obtains emotional support from two of her colleagues at work and from six of her friends, three of whom are single-mothers like herself. Rita also feels that she receives emotional support from the three professionals whose services she has sought: a priest, a doctor and a lawyer.

She perceives her family, two of her work colleagues, her neighbour and the professionals as her main sources of concrete support.

Is Rita an 'Outsider' or Not?

Rita's good relations with her family, who provide her with both concrete support and emotional support, are important determinants which help her to participate actively in society. Work offers the opportunity for social contact, increased status and the possibility for Rita to give her share in society. It also provides her with financial independence. Although Rita has a number of friends who, like herself are single parents, they are not her only friends. Rita has the opportunity to meet with different people through work and other friends, and this helps her to perceive herself in relation to a range of persons thus helping her to avoid linking her identity to a restricted group.

Rita has a substantial number of reciprocal relationships and this suggests that her social relations reflect interdependence rather than dependence. Thus it is more likely that Rita perceives herself as a full member of society taking and receiving. When asked about how she feels as a member of society, Rita stated that she feels that her experience is very different from that of other women who are separated from their husbands and who would like to work but cannot do so as they have no one to care for their children. The author's experience as a social worker confirms this. Few are the separated women with young children who are able to take up employment and find appropriate care for their children.

Rita said that she thinks that her attitude has changed markedly over the past seven years.

> In the first job I had when I was first separated seven years ago I did not mention my status to anyone at work. I lived a lie. Now I can live my life more openly.

Rita's behaviour confirms the notion drawn from the Labelling Perspective that she felt that she was being perceived by society as 'deviant'.

Rita mentioned leisure as an area in her life which causes problems. She said that she prefers the company of other women who like herself are single mothers. However she is sorely aware of the uncomfortable feelings generated when they go to public places as a group with their children. She feels that in such a setting they stand out as 'too different'. However her greatest hurts are caused when her son is ostracized in any manner because of his family background. Then, she certainly feels they are marginalized as a family.

Ċensina and Pawlu

(An elderly couple who live alone; Pawlu has had a severe visual impairment for the past five years)

> Ċensina and Pawlu named 29 people in their social network.
> 9 are family members but not their offspring as Ċensina and Pawlu never had any children.
> 3 are members of the same local parish group for older persons.

4 are friends (a family, a couple and their two children who came to know Ċensina and Pawlu through a voluntary organization).
  5 are neighbours.
  7 are professionals, this number includes 4 priests who serve in their parish.

Ċensina and Pawlu are in contact with:
— 2 of the neighbours and with the priests who serve in their parish on a daily basis.
— the other 3 neighbours and the family whom they have befriended, on a weekly basis, though the latter make more frequent telephone contact with them.
— the family doctor, on a monthly basis.
— two social workers, four times per year.

They have no contact with any of their relatives.

Ċensina and Pawlu have known:
— 22 of the persons in their social network for more than 5 years. This includes 9 relatives with whom they now have no contact whatsoever, and hence can hardly be considered as part of the social network any longer.
— 2 from 1 to 5 years and these two are both professionals.
— 6 for less than 1 year and this group includes the young family whom they have befriended and one of the professionals whose services they have sought.

They feel very close to the family whom they have befriended, the parish priest and two priests who serve in their parish. They feel close to all their neighbours, one of the priests who serves in the parish, one of the social workers, three friends who like themselves are members of an organization for older persons and to two nephews who reside in Australia. They do not feel at all close to seven of their relatives who live in Malta and to a second social worker with whom they have contact.

When asked about reciprocity of network relationships with respect to the network members mentioned, Ċensina and Pawlu stated that they receive their emotional support from four persons and this number includes their family doctor, the priests from the parish and the young couple whom they have befriended. Their main sources of concrete support are their family doctor and the parish priest. These are followed by the neighbours, the other professionals except one, the family whom they have befriended and one of the members of the voluntary organization for older persons.

Are Ċensina and Pawlu 'Outsiders' or Not?

At the beginning of the interview with Ċensina and Pawlu, Ċensina told me 'we are alone'. This comment referred to the fact that they have no children and that their relations with their relatives are not very good. They both feel that ever since their need for help has grown, their relatives have distanced themselves from them and now their contacts with them are very seldom. This response to their increased needs has made them feel that they are a burden on others and that people are fearful of approaching them because of this.

This element may also be read into the fact that Ċensina and Pawlu feel very close to the parish priest, to two other priests and to the young family whom they have befriended. With the priests and parish priest, the relationships are ones in which Ċensina and Pawlu are on the receiving end. Being unable to reciprocate, they often think of themselves as a burden, and are therefore reluctant to make more demands. With regards to the young family whom Ċensina and Pawlu have befriended, although the relationship is now a reciprocal one it was not always that way as it was initiated by the young family who offered their help and support to Ċensina and Pawlu via a voluntary organization.

This dependence factor is also manifested through the fact that with fifteen of the network members, Ċensina and Pawlu are on the receiving end of help and support. It is only with five network members that relationships are reciprocal. When Ċensina and Pawlu were asked how they feel as members of society, they said that they spent most of their days indoors and that if they did go out it was only to attend a religious service at their local parish church or to attend activities organized by their local organization for older persons. They occasionally leave the house to see doctors or visit the hospital and are sometimes taken out by the young family whom they have befriended and who in turn have befriended them.

Ċensina and Pawlu are very fearful of the possibility that their home may be broken into and that they may be assaulted. This fear accompanies their every waking moment. They feel that elderly persons, who like themselves reside in the community, have the greatest needs. This constant fear which Ċensina and Pawlu expressed may prove very important in determining how these two older persons view themselves in relation to society. It may well be a key element in a process which results in marginalization and isolation. Ċensina and Pawlu are also extremely concerned about their economic position as for the first time in their life they have to be particularly frugal. This situation has been further aggravated by the new health-related needs which have grown and the cost of which Ċensina and Pawlu are finding very hard to meet. This situation is generating a lot of stress for both of them. Ċensina and Pawlu commented positively about people's willingness to help them get around whenever they realize that Pawlu's vision is very impaired.

Ċensina and Pawlu are slowly experiencing a process of marginalization that is both economic and social. Pawlu's decreased mobility, their decreased economic ability and growing fears all contribute to slowly pushing Pawlu and Ċensina to the periphery.

Conclusion

The 'outsiders' vantage point proves crucial in helping to redress the imbalance which may result from relying too heavily on a structural analysis of society. Yet, paradoxically, it is the continued attempt at a structural analysis of society that is likely to lead towards a better understanding of social inequality and marginalization which may result from it. The sociological perspectives on social problems cited earlier in this paper are not simply theoretical constructs to help sociologists to study social problems; they are also intended to help us solve social problems. However, both the analysis and the solution of social problems are important steps in the direction of increased social justice.

References

Abela, A.M. (1991) *Transmitting Values in European Malta: A Study in the Contemporary Values of Modern Society*, Malta & Rome, Jesuit Publications; Editrice Pontificia Università Gregoriana.
Abercrombie, N., Hill, S. & Turner, S. (1988) *The Penguin Dictionary of Sociology*, 2e, Harmondsworth, Penguin.

Babuscio, J. (1988) *We Speak for Ourselves: The Experiences of Gay Men and Lesbians*, 2e, London, SPCK [Society for Promoting Christian Knowledge].
Barker, R.L. (1987) *The Social Work Dictionary*, USA, National Association of Social Workers.
Boss, P. (1980) *On the Side of the Child: An Australian Perspective on Child Abuse*, Australia, Fontana/Collins.
Boswell, D.M. (1982) 'Patterns of occupational and residential area prestige in the Maltese conurbation'. Paper presented at the 10th World Congress of Sociology, Mexico.
Central Office of Statistics, (C.O.S.) (1992) *Quarterly Digest of Statistics*, Nos. 123-124, Malta, Government Press.
Cole, M. (1991) 'L-Imwarrbin'. In Kummissjoni Ġustizzja u Paċi, *Malta Llum... u Forsi Għada: Analiżi tar-Realtà Soċjali Maltija*, Malta, Veritas Press.
Dominelli, L. & McLeod, E. (1989) *Feminist Social Work*, Basingstoke, Macmillan.
Donadello, G. (1986) 'Integrating the lesbian/gay male experience in feminist practice and education'. In Van den Bergh, N. & Cooper, L.B. (eds) *Feminist Visions for Social Work*, USA, National Association of Social Workers, Inc.
Finkelhor, D. et al. (1986) *Sourcebook on Child Sexual Abuse*, Beverly Hills, CA, Sage.
Finkelhor, D., Hotaling, G.T. & Yllo, K. (1988) *Stopping Family Violence: Research Priorities for the Coming Decade*, Beverly Hills, CA, Sage.
Humphreys, L. (1972) *Out of the Closets: The Sociology of Homosexual Liberation*, New York, Prentice-Hall.
Kerslake, A. & Cramp, J. (1991) 'A new model for child care'. In Carter, P., Jeffs, T. & Smith, M.K. (eds) *Social Work and Social Welfare: Yearbook 3*, Milton Keynes, Open University Press, 1991.
Malta Independent, The (1993) 'Rebuilding broken lives', Malta, 13 June.
Manis, J.G. (1976) *Analyzing Social Problems*, New York, Praeger.
Miceli, P. (1991) *Maria-Eva: Ġrajjiet ta' Nisa Maltin*, Malta, Dipartiment tat-Tagħrif, Partit tal-Ħaddiema, Marsa Press.
Moir, C. (1988) 'A Nova Scotia perspective on children's rights'. In Hepworth, H.P. (ed.) *Canadian Seminar on Childhood Implications for Child Care Policies*, Gananoque, Ontario, Canada 29-30 June, 1988, European Centre for Social Welfare Training and Research.
National Association of Social Workers (1988) *Social Work Speaks*, NASW Policy Statements, USA, National Association of Social Workers.
Rubington, E. & Weinberg, M.S. (1989) *The Study of Social Problems: Six Perspectives*, 4e, New York, Oxford University Press.
Sayers, J. (1991) 'Blinded by family feeling? Child protection, feminism and countertransference'. In Carter, P., Jeffs, T. & Smith, M.K. (eds) *Social Work and Social Welfare: Yearbook 3*, Milton Keynes, Open University Press.
Sultana, R.G. (1993) 'Practice and policy in child labour: lessons from Malta', *British Journal of Education and Work*, vol. 6, 3.
Tracy, E.M. (1990) 'Identifying social support resources of at-risk families', *Social Work*, vol. 35, 3.
United Nations (1991) *The Rights of the Child*, Fact Sheet No.10, Geneva, Reprinted at United Nations.
Zammit, E.L. (1984) *A Colonial Inheritance: Maltese Perceptions of Work, Power and Class Structure with Reference to the Labour Movement*, Malta, Malta University Press.

32

Substance Abuse: Focus on Alcohol

Alexander M. Baldacchino

Introduction

Drug use in some form or other is virtually culturally universal. Humanity has a love-hate relationship with substances that produce a transient change of consciousness with resultant 'waking dreams'. They inspire awe, fear and even lust. Their pursuit seems not only universal but also inescapable (Siegel, 1989). Drug usage is to be found across time and various societies; in the private lives of high-ranking politicians and common citizens alike. Recent anthropological studies indicate that around 90% of human societies have implemented some form of substance use (Plant, 1987). Many societies are in search of the ideal intoxicant which would balance optimal positive effects such as stimulation or pleasure, with minimal or non-existent toxic consequences.

The use of intoxicants, whether legal or illegal, safe or risky is not, however, inherently problematic behaviour. Social scientists would argue that, since there must always be some form of acceptable drug use before people misuse it, a drug problem is really a social construction rather than a social fact. Millions of people today find tea, caffeine and alcohol acceptable, actively indulging in these while participating in several socializing rituals such as parties and coffee mornings. This global pattern of drug use falls within the ambit of sociocultural norms and must therefore be understood within a sociocultural context (De Rios & Smith, 1984).

During the 20th century, substance abuse has been widely regarded as a threat to the framework of the current social structure. Drug use – or better still misuse – becomes a social problem when it challenges current systems or institutional practices. Substance abuse is defined by the health care system as an organic illness or mental disturbance; this would hence necessitate treatment. The legal system would unequivocally state that substance abuse constitutes in itself a form of delinquent behaviour; and since drug users are purported to come frequently in contact with criminal elements, they are themselves readily dumped within the amorphous cauldron of criminality. The identification of a physical 'disease' or legal issue becomes an essential element in transforming an individual 'evil' into a 'scientifically' identified societal threat. The rapidly expanding welfare system which includes statutory social services and voluntary organisations would clearly define drug use as the expression of a problem in the management of living.

Another view that transcends the above argument is the moral perspective. Moralists still embrace the substance abuser as a hedonist, indulging in self-pleasure. The result is a condemnation of these undeserving 'junkies', accompanied by an emotional appeal for self-restraint, celibacy, return to traditional family values, and simple conventional pleasures (Strang & Stimson, 1990).

However, substance abuse does not neatly fit into any of the above-mentioned common conceptual categories. Therefore, much effort goes into arguing about what sort of problem it is, and whether it is a problem at all. From a sociological perspective, understanding the problem of substance abuse involves understanding the social context through which it is constructed as a problem, and not just a question of coming to terms with the behaviour itself. Often, the labelling of certain forms of drug use as 'deviant' behaviour is not the result of self-evident properties of that behaviour. Rather, it is the result of the way certain groups and institutions in society judge that particular behaviour, an activity whose outcome is indicative of the power of different social groups (Plant, 1987). This will be discussed later on in this chapter when the Maltese scenario is taken on board.

Theoretical Approaches

An appraisal of different theoretical approaches will enable us to dwell into the complex debate of how different social scientists have conceptualised and tried to explain the genesis of a drug user. Such an evaluation becomes all the more relevant now that even some forms of licit medicinal use are being considered as problematic; for example the use of benodiazepine tablets like diazepam and triazolam (Gabe & Bury, 1988). The progressive loss of distinction between illicit and licit drug use has highlighted the issues that equate and contrast deviance with what is considered a state of normality.

I must at this point clarify that considerable information on such deviant behaviour is generated from research carried out with typically extreme cases under study; and the interpretations emergent from such information are often a prerogative of professional incumbents. These hold privileged positions in society, a privilege which may extend to the authority to construct models of proper, or improper, human behaviour. Resorting to a different methodology, as would be, for instance, an ethnography, is likely to fuel a surprising diversity of results, with more animated interpretations (Agar, 1985).

I hope first to describe critically the different theoretical approaches to the consideration of substance abuse; these would then provide a conceptual outline to introduce and diagnose the case study at hand.

i. Functionalist Approaches

What are collectively referred to as the functionalist approaches have dominated the definition of social problems for most of the twentieth century. At the level of the social system, functionalists attribute the origins of a social problem to a breakdown in the usually dynamic equilibrium of the parts of the system due to social change. At the individual level, the origins of problematic behaviour are attributed to ineffective or inappropriate socialisation. This can also result from a disjuncture between internalised goals and the opportunity to attain them (Merton, 1968). Such a disjuncture builds up the pressure towards the breakdown of social norms; a condition of normlessness or anomie, wherby a tension exists which can precipitate a breakdown in societal regulation (Giddens, 1992, p. 127). Merton (1971) addresses this tension systematically, identifying a set of four deviant response typologies, attitudinal factors indicative of members of a social group who find themselves denied the capacity to fulfil the dominant cultural goals.

a. Innovation

One of these adaptive responses involves the condoning of illegitimate means for achieving one's goals, even though the person remains largely faithful to the cultural objective symbols in place. The person is considered as an 'innovator', acting upon a situation in fulfilment of socially acceptable values without however pursuing socially condoned techniques in the process. The high flier, successful businessmen taking amphetamine to temporarily enhance their work power and the athletes taking anabolic steroids can be viewed as substance abuse innovators in Merton's functionalist view. This framework considers the resort to heroin or other illicit drug use as an active endeavour, and not as a manifsetation of a passive submission or dejection. Likewise, where drugs are seen as an economic commodity, 'marketing' drugs is one way of keeping the local economy going even though it is 'irregular'. Drug use hence becomes a black market affair, 'providing [an] alternative opportunity structure for achievement of social goals' (Auld et al., 1986, p. 169). A similar occurrence prevails in certain impoverished third world countries like Columbia, Jamaica, Nigeria and Pakistan where people seem to indulge in this 'irregular economy', exporting illicit intoxicants to richer industrialised countries.

b. Rebellion

A second pattern of response is that which challenges the socio-cultural norms and values of a society by adopting a new set of values, one pertaining to an alternative society. In this case, the person is typically referred to as rebellious. This brings to mind the era when the hippies of the 1960's were seen as a potential political threat since they advocated a society that does not condemn drug use and campaigned for the legalisation of such intoxicants. Rebels thus constitute the germ of an alternative but workable social order; and their delegitimation by established social interests is in part an acknowledgement of their strength in referring to a different yet comprehensive, self-contained, cultural framework.

c. Ritualism

Merton's third variant of adaptation is known as ritualism. In this case, the person persists in the pursuit of legitimate symbols of success such as hard work and educational performance. In actual fact, however, such a behaviour pattern is not directed by an incorporation of societal values, but more by a hollow and dejected attitude empty of meaning and motive. The individual has here given up the values of achievement and merely goes through the motions. The drug user is not viewed as using the ritualistic form of adaptation.

d. Retreatism

Merton terms a fourth pattern of response as retreatism. It applies to 'psychotics, autistics, pariah, outcasts, vagrants, vagabonds, tramps, chronic drunkards and drug addicts' (Haralambos & Holborn, 1992, p. 589). In this case, the retreatist abandons not only the dominant cultural goals but also the institutionalised approved means of achieving these goals, without the psychological and sub-cultural refuge of an alternative as enjoyed by the rebel. The substance abuser is viewed as a failure and drifter in the eyes of society.

Sub-Cultural Focus

Another interpretation of deviance is set up in terms of the subculture of a social group. Substance abuse seen in this light is aptly illustrated in a qualitative study performed by Preble & Casey in New York's four lower class communities.

> Heroin use today by lower class ... people does not provide for them a euphoric escape from the psychological and social problems which derive from ghetto life. On the contrary it provides a motivation and rationale for the pursuit of a meaningful life, albeit a socially deviant one. The activities these individuals engage in, and the relationships they have in the course of their quest for heroin are more important than the minimal analgesic and euphoric effects of the small amount of heroin available to them. If they can be said to be addicted, it is not so much to heroin as to the entire career of a heroin user (Preble & Casey, 1967, p. 23).

This approach has been further developed and modified by interactionists like Stephens (1985).

The functionalist view has been savagely criticised for failing to take subjective definitions of social problems seriously. It emphasises normative and value consensus whilst ignoring the extent to which norms and values are bound with the material interests of distinctive social groups. Functionalism tends implicitly to encourage the maintenance of the status quo. The problem drug taker is therefore perceived as a junkie or hawker striving to survive within the existing social order; the social order itself is beyond question.

ii. The Conflict Approach

The conflict approach is usually identified with Marxism; however, it also encompasses non-Marxists interested in alienation. Both camps hold that society does not offer people equal access to wealth and to economic and political power. It is this alienation which is seen as the catalyst for the generation of social problems. Within this framework, proponents of the conflict approach view substance abuse as either a form of escape or indeed of resistance for members of subordinate social groups. Dorn (1980) follows the argument that youths use drugs as a weapon to resist current social trends. Given that such behaviour constitutes a threat to the reproduction of control over labour power, the social establishment would typically respond by imposing medical treatment or legislative restrictions. As is illustrated in Charles Chaplin's movie classic *Modern Times*, the legal and health care systems are thus seen as allies and instruments of a dominant ruling class, deployed to control its workforce, increase its efficiency and further its interests in general. To achieve this, the same control agencies need to remove, 'treat' or punish unproductive human assets (Haralambos & Holborn, 1992). This approach has its own set of limitations, particularly in its failure to address the cultural and symbolic aspects of drug use; no space is granted for an appreciation of the social processes that generate drug related problems, as would be the case when individuals take to drugs in order to belong to or identify with a sub-culture.

iii. The Interactionist and Constructionist Approaches

The interactionist and closely related constructionist approaches are, in the meantime, determined to adopt the actor's frame of reference and definition of the situation, rather than 'objective' conditions as a starting point for an analysis of substance abuse (Gabe & Bury, 1991). They are concerned with process rather than structure and meaning rather than causality.

There are, however, important differences between these two views. It is primarily a question of 'scale'. Symbolic interactionists tend to focus on small-scale settings such as neighbourhoods, schools and psychiatric wards and the interactions between individuals in these settings. They also tend to operate with a more explicit notion of reality as seen from the standpoint of the participant (e.g. Becker, 1953). On the other hand, the constructionists generally take a wider physical environment into consideration and tend to target their investigation on the behavioural processes and related perceptions which lead individuals to confer certain patterns of human interaction with the problematic label, leading to claims of deviance.

A case in point is the interpretation of the street drug addict role as developed by Stephens (1985). From this symbolic interactionist viewpoint, involvement in drug use is sustained by a commitment to this role via membership of a subculture and the practice of a particular lifestyle that increasingly establishes itself as a way of life. The drug user has a place in the structure of roles and status positions; commitment to drug use derives not simply from effects of the drugs, but also from the rewards of the subcultural way of life as a whole. It grants a sense of belonging, an identity as an addict. It provides the person with a code of conduct, dress and language. It also distinguishes one drug-taking group from another, one deviant group from another.[1] Social scientists like Pearson (1987) have also suggested that users of intoxicants offer a form of resolution of the problems of 'de-routinised time structure' which faces the unemployed. Dependence on drugs like heroin imposes a time-cycle of activities, a rhythm and a purpose to the day.

Becker (1953) is another symbolic interactionist who emphasises the importance of the subjective meanings given to experience. He sees this experience as a process, a natural history. The drug user has different reasons for experimenting with specified types of addictive substances. These reasons change with time and movement, undergoing constant refinement and impetus. He noted the growth of marijuana usage and the specific processes involved in becoming a marijuana user. The individual becomes involved in drug use through the exposure to the culture of other users; it becomes necessary to learn techniques of use, how to recognise effects of use, and to define them as pleasurable. Becoming a confirmed drug user develops through participation in the symbolic (communicative) environment of a drug-using subculture. Once such an individual becomes a member of such a drug subculture, society itself puts a label on to this member; labels like 'a deviant', 'a junkie', 'an alcoholic', which ultimately amplify the original problem. Similar studies have been performed by Young (1971) in London on the 'hippie' marijuana population

---

[1] An example, drawn on the basis of insider knowledge of the local scene, is that a Gozitan drug user is likely to consider intra-venous use of intoxicants as unhealthy, messy and disgusting; whereas users from the Cottonera area tend to start their career through the IV method because it is a certain way of getting value for money.

showing the power which labelling can have on groups in encouraging them to marginalise themselves even further and create their own exclusive niche in society.

In contrast, the constructionist approach is exemplified by Waters & Lidz (1980). They undertake a critical analysis of the manner in which emerged certain claims which alleged that there was an epidemic increase in heroin use in the United States during the 1970's. They conclude that the episode turned out to be a rather excessive declaration but alas a good excuse to repress certain political and cultural groups.

Both interactionist and constructionist views do indeed extend sympathy to the drug taker, victimised and labelled by agencies of social control: the police, judges, probation officers and the doctor. This attitude, therefore, lacks the commitment to tackle the causes of deviant behaviour. Certain constructionists have gone so far as to argue that social problems are nothing more than definitional activities or fabrications. On a more positive note the interactionist is seen as the person close enough to appreciate that drug related behaviour is the consequence of variable influences between the intoxicant, the individual personality and the social processes present. None of the component factors alone is sufficient to cause drug dependence and their relative importance is different in different circumstances (Ghodse, 1989).

In the light of the foregoing remarks, a social scientist may be tempted to take sides. There is in fact a need for a new perspective which combines the analytic strengths of the conflict and interactionist approaches with a flavour of functionalism, while trying to avoid the pitfalls. Prevalent among these dangers is the apparent disdain of the sociological community for 'medicalisation' and the evils of the disease concept. Such a disdain could cripple any attempts at developing a badly needed medical sociology critically directed at the structure, function, economics and politics of, for example, treatment systems and access to health care (Roman, 1991).

Application

The main sociological theories and perspectives try to guide us through the murky waters of deviance and conformity, culture and social interaction, structures of power and social institutions.

But the issues related to the study of substance abuse seem to be, and to have been historically, inherently controversial. I will therefore now attempt to grapple with these rather loose theoretical issues, locating them within a practical framework and a local meaning. A special reference will be made to alcohol and the relatively complacent position it enjoys within the Maltese sociocultural setting.

Alcohol Problems in the Maltese Islands

The present situation of the Maltese population with regards to alcohol is better understood by examining various sociocultural interactions. This will help us understand what the Maltese perceive as a serious alcohol problem, and the limitations of any interventions offered.

No statistics are available on the actual size of the alcohol-related problems in Malta. There are no existing figures, official or otherwise, that may indicate the incidence or prevalence of such problems (Baldacchino, 1991). Figures on alcohol production, distribution and per capita consumption have never been published because of the absence of a monitoring board to control the quality and true concentration of alcohol imports. Figures on alcohol importation showed a rough estimate of 2.5 million litres of alcoholic beverages between 1980 and 1988 (C.O.S., 1989). Although there are fourteen wine producing factories and co-operatives in the Maltese Islands, with a value output and sales of approximately 8 million Maltese Liri during 1988, the practice of producing wine at home is widespread (Ghodse, 1980). These figures can only shed light on a behaviour pattern that forms an integral part of the Maltese way of life. Malta is a country with a Latin culture where alcohol is socially and traditionally accepted. Drunkenness is generally only tolerated during the village or town festa. Beyond these festive days, people abusing alcohol become targets of malicious gossip and even overt hostility (Baldacchino, 1991).

Considering the laissez-faire attitude of the Maltese community on the issue of alcoholism, it is not surprising that local law enforcement agencies do not officially consider excess drinking as a main cause of dangerous driving or other related crime (Sciberras, 1988). Although there are close to 200,000 registered vehicles driving on 1,463 km of roads, there are no laws about drinking and driving. There is therefore no data available on drink-driving offences or alcohol-related road traffic accidents. There are also no figures available on alcoholics among the criminal and prison population.

Advertisements of alcoholic drinks are common in both media and entertainment venues. While there are restrictions by law on the type and content of tobacco advertisements, there are no such constraints as far as alcohol promotion in Malta is concerned.

In spite of this level of tolerance, there has been ample evidence from studies performed abroad that suggest a direct relationship between the level of alcohol consumption and the presence of specific physical morbidity (H.C.E.I.A., 1991; R.C.Psych., 1987a). Apart from these medical complications, the number of alcohol-related admissions to Mount Carmel Hospital (Malta's main psychiatric hospital) and the psychiatric unit in St Luke's Hospital (Malta's main general hospital) can be taken as another indicator of the extent of alcohol-related problems in the Maltese community.

The statistical evidence with regards to the mortality rate due to liver cirrhosis and other hepatic complications in Malta does in fact show an estimated incidence of 8.15 per 100,000 population (C.O.S., 1990). This is a relatively lower rate to that found in wine producing countries like Italy and France but a higher rate than that obtaining in industrialised countries like the United Kingdom. There is also a local non-controlled study that showed an indirect but significant association between the current rate of peptic ulceration and carcinoma of the upper respiratory tract in clients exhibiting a history of excessive alcohol consumption. These results have been derived from a study of a specific sample, this being those who have sought medical treatment due to their physical problems. It is therefore misleading to assume that such a sample is representative.

The number of patients referred to the psychiatric service in Malta, and ultimately admitted for treatment due to either primary diagnosis of alcoholism or mental disturbances precipitated by alcohol consumption, have shown a significant progressive increase. In fact there has been a 135% increase reported between 1971 and 1989 (Baldacchino, 1991; Sultana, 1992). In 1989, about 19% of male and 5% of female total admissions at Mount Carmel

Hospital were due to alcohol related problems (Sultana, 1992). Unfortunately these admissions were never classified according to the presence or absence of specific standardised measures to determine the severity of the patient's inebriety: The reasons for their referral were not grouped according to demographic variables.

Survey Data

All this data would prove rather vague and inconclusive if it were not compared with other studies undertaken within the Maltese community to determine the pattern of normal drinking in the population. This is only available after evaluating information and results obtained from two national surveys.

The first is the result of the 1984 MONICA project, a W.H.O. initiative whose primary aim was to determine predisposing factors in the environment which could lead to ischaemic heart disease (Cacciattolo, 1984). The interviewees were also questioned on their normal drinking patterns. This study identified a high correlation in incidence of alcoholic drinking, obesity and ischaemic heart disease, but they have not reached any conclusive remarks on the factors that encourage drinking in the first place.

The second study was performed in 1986 as part of the National Diabetes Programme (Schranz, 1986). Part of this study was concerned with the life-styles and eating habits of the sample interviewed. There were no conclusive indications on the origins or variables that could shed light on the processes which encouraged more males than females to be present in the 'moderate /severe drinking band'. It is evident that the selection criteria chosen for this study were not sensitised to cater for the Maltese drinking population but rather to a sample with potential diabetes. It is worth pointing out that all of the above mentioned studies were performed by medical personnel as part of an audit process or epidemiological study to be able to cater for a better treatment service.

It is unfortunate that there is no data available on the incidence of normal drinking following the lastest census survey carried out in 1985. Not even a glimpse is provided by the latest household budgetary exercise, carried out in 1988-9, where the relevant statistics are collapsed within the much broader category of 'beverages and tobacco' which consumed 9.5% and 8.6% of total household expenditure in 1980-1 and 1988-9 respectively (R.P.I.M.B., 1993, p. 10).

A study performed in 1992 as part of a project in partial fulfilment of a B.Sc. Pharmacy degree did indeed approach the subject of trying to understand the reasons for alcohol consumption and the attitudes of certain professionals towards this behaviour, with a more humane flavour (Sultana, 1992). Such a localised fact finding mission was well planned to evaluate and positively criticise the data obtained. The individuals taking part in this project were chosen from either a treatment setting or attenders at A.A. group meetings.

Results showed that the majority of individuals interviewed were males in the 36-45 year bracket (31%), who are residing in the inner harbour region (44%). A total of 73% out of the whole sample reside in this high-density area. Furthermore, the study showed that the majority of the participants (67%) began drinking with their friends whilst 22% started drinking with their family members. The average mean age when the respondents started drinking was 17 years of age and the mean age of the person showing signs of addictive behaviour was around 26.5 years. Other interesting results show that only 33% of the 'alcoholics' were habitual excessive drinkers. The majority of respondents preferred spirits rather than beer and wine. The main reason given was that you get better value for money with spirits than with other alcoholic beverages! It is also interesting to note that all the female respondents were married as compared to about 75% of the male group.

These figures help us build a profile of one type of Maltese alcoholic. It is the first step in trying to identify the social processes prevalent within social groups that are identifiable as heavy drinkers and who are nonetheless motivated enough to become and remain sober.

Community-wide epidemiological research geared to determine the extent, nature and quality of alcohol consumption and related problems is highly recommended, both as a sociological and as a policy instrument. This will provide a more dynamic picture of the needs, attitudes and characteristics of the individuals who are exhibiting addictive, abusive and/or dependency behaviour as a result of alcohol. In objectively defining the evidence one is able to place alcoholism in Malta in its proper perspective. It is only then that representatives of pressure groups are able to legitimize their concerns and claim-making activities in public, subsequently encouraging the mobilisation of action with the hope of forming an official plan. This plan would be then able to define priorities and establish strategies needed to tackle the problems associated with excessive alcohol consumption. It is simply not sufficient to focus on claim-making activities of various interest groups with no inclination into what these claims purport to achieve.

The location of alcohol within its proper perspective as a form of substance abuse constitutes a developmental perspective first outlined by Fuller & Myers (1971) and further refined by other sociologists and social psychologists like Blumer (1971). It highlights the dynamic nature of the history of a social problem. The developmental approach helps to foster an appreciation of the hopefully closing gap between the illicit form of substance abuse in Malta and the responses present to deal with alcohol related problems.

Alcoholism as a Non-Problem

The illicit abuse of 'drugs' is officially recognised as a national problem. Registered clients with drug-related problems are offered an extensive medical and social assistance. The Maltese government is tackling the illicit drug problem comprehensively, engaging in close collaboration with non-statutory and ecclesiastical bodies. This includes setting up of an inter-ministerial committee and an inter-departmental commission against drug abuse. These bodies have in fact identified, defined and are implementing a national policy dealing with treatment, demand and supply aspects of the Maltese drug issue. There have lately been pilot studies carried out to identify the social characteristics of the problem drug taker currently undergoing treatment (Azzopardi, 1992). There were also community studies carried out by volunteers as well as by the ecclesiatical body, CARITAS, which have obtained vital information on the sociodemographic characteristics of the young drug taker (Sciberras & Gouder, 1989; DISCERN, 1993). Other similar studies were performed in schools throughout the Maltese Islands.

In the meantime one can appreciate that there is no parallel official action with the problems related to alcoholism. A report evaluating treatment services for alcohol and drug issues commissioned by the Ministry for Home Affairs and Social Development (M.H.A.S.D., 1993) has urged the prioritization of alcohol-related services for the Maltese population. Along with recent recommendations to reform mental health provision, such issues may at last start being tackled in a more proactive manner.

This example gives us the opportunity to focus our attention on trying to explain why certain claims resonate with the general public while others fail to do so. This involves a cultural analysis so as to examine the growth and spread of general beliefs. Malta is an ideal laboratory to undertake such an investigation into the apparent inequality in commitment towards alcohol-related problems in comparison to declared, illicit forms of substance abuse. This may also provide an insight into the acceptance of social realities and allow an examination of the sociological perspectives of scapegoating.

Conclusion

Over recent years, the international community under the auspices of the World Health Organisation (WHO), has moved from listing the effects and/or legality of these and other intoxicants into a greater appreciation of a more arbitrary and value-laden definition. It is now accepted that the range from use to misuse of such 'drugs' is of an uncertain and loose nature. The term 'misuse' is now employed to define an act of 'taking a drug which harms or threatens to harm the physical or mental health or social wellbeing of an individual, of other individuals, or of society at large' (R.C.Psych., 1987b).

This new, rather more dynamic way of looking at this concept has been positively received by many health professionals involved in the substance abuse field. It corresponds to their own concerns based on the observation of clients attending drug related services. The general impression is that these clients not only had problems in stopping their heroin intake but also had problems in not substituting it with other intoxicants, namely alcohol and benzodiazepines – substances that are cheap, legal and easily available. It is also quite common to find people who are poly-substance abusers or else exhibiting different forms of severity and dependence with respect to different substances, along the time-span of a drug career. It is therefore time to remove words like drug addict and alcoholic from our working dictionary and substitute them with multidimensional, more meaningful descriptions such as substance abuse.

This paper hopes to have shaken the Maltese complacency with respect to the drug issue. Sociological analysis can be valuable in revealing how attitudes may be constructed as deviant by powerful social actors; while others may escape the 'deviant' classification when they appear to be more meritous of joining the category, at least on medical grounds. Why indeed are heavy drinkers not meted the same treatment as drug addicts? And what is the contemporary social location of smokers? It is hoped that such a line of inquiry will challenge and encourage social scientists to venture into the arena of alcohol and other substance abuse related issues. Although the problem is compounded by a dearth of relevant statistics, Malta needs to look forward and join other countries in defining its stand on the issues of abuse and addictive behaviour.

References

Agar, M. (1985) 'Folks and professionals: Different models for the interpretation of drug use', *International Journal of the Addictions*, vol. 20, 1.

Auld, J., Dorn, N. & South, N. (1986) 'Irregular work, irregular pleasures: heroin in the 1980s' in Matthews, R. & Young, J. (eds), *Confronting Crime*, London, Sage.

Azzopardi, M. (1992) 'Social characteristics of drug addicts in treatment in Malta', unpublished B.A.(Hons.) dissertation, University of Malta, Faculty of Arts.

Baldacchino, A.M. (1991) 'Alcohol and alcohol problems research 17: Malta', *British Journal of Addiction*, vol. 86, 8.

Becker, H.S. (1953) 'Becoming a marijuana user', *American Journal of Sociology*, vol. 59, November.

Blumer, H. (1971) 'Social problems as collective behaviour', *Social Problems*, vol. 18, 2.

Cacciattolo, J. (1984) *MONICA Project: Phase I*, Copenhagen, Denmark, World Health Organisation.

C.O.S. (Central Office of Statistics) (1989) *Malta Trade Statistics 1988*, Malta, Government Press.

C.O.S. (Central Office of Statistics) (1990) *Annual Abstract of Statistics 1989*, Malta, Government Press.

De Rios, M.D. & Smith, D.E. (1984) 'Drug use and abuse in cross-cultural perspective' in Mezzich, J.E. & Berganza, C.E. (eds), *Culture and Psychopathology*, Columbia, Columbia University Press.

DISCERN (1993) *Adolescent Drug Use in Malta: A Survey Conducted by CARITAS, Malta, in November, 1991 with the Technical Assistance of PRIDE International*, Malta, CARITAS.
Dorn, N. (1980) 'The conservatism of the cannabis debate', in National Deviancy Conference (ed.), *Permissiveness and Control; The Fate of the Sixties Legislation*, London, Macmillan.
Fuller, R.C. & Myers, R.R. (1971) 'The natural history of a social problem', *American Sociological Review*, vol. 6, 2.
Gabe, J. & Bury, M. (1988) 'Tranquilisers as a social problem', *The Sociological Review*, vol. 36, 3.
Gabe, J. & Bury, M. (1991) 'The analysis of substance abuse' in Glass, I. (ed.) *International Handbook of Addiction Behaviour*, London, Routledge.
Ghodse, A.H. (1980) 'Drugs and alcohol dependence in Malta', unpublished report, London.
Ghodse, A.H. (1989) *Drugs and Addictive Behaviour; A Guide to Treatment*, London, Blackwell.
Giddens, A. (1992) *Sociology*, Cambridge, Polity Press.
Haralambos, M. & Holborn, M. (1992) *Sociology: Themes and Perspectives*, 3e., London, Harper-Collins.
H.C.E.I.A. (Haute Comité d'Etude et d'Informations sur l'Alcoholisme) (1991) Report, Paris, Ministry of Social Affairs and Social Solidarity.
Merton, R.K. (1968) *Social Theory and Social Structure*, New York, Free Press.
Merton, R.K. (1971) 'Social problems and the sociological theory' in Merton, R.K. & Nisbet, R. (eds), *Contemporary Social Problems*, 3e., New York, Harcourt Brace Jovanovich.
M.H.A.S.D. (Ministry for Home Affairs and Social Development) (1993) *Rapport mill-Kumitat ta' Xogħol dwar Evalwazzjoni tas-Servizzi ta' Trattament fil-Qasam tad-Droga u Alkoħol*, Malta, Ministry for Home Affairs and Social Development, August.
Pearson, N.G.(1987) 'Social deprivation, unemployment and patterns of heroin use', in Dorn, N. & South, N. (eds), *A Land Fit for Heroin*, New York, Macmillan.
Plant, M. (ed.) (1987) *Drugs in Perspective*, London, Hodder & Stoughton.
Preble, E & Casey, J. (1967) 'Taking care of the business: The heroin user's life on the street', *International Journal of the Addictions*, vol. 4, 1.
R.C.Psych. (Royal College of Psychiatrists) (1987) *Drug Scenes. A Report by the Royal College of Psychiatrists*, London, Gaskell Publications.
Roman, M.P. (ed.) (1991) *Alcohol: The Development of Sociological Perspectives on Use and Abuse*, New Brunswick, Rutgers Center of Alcohol Studies.
R.P.I.M.B. (Retail Price Index Management Board) (1993) *Household Budgetary Survey: 1988-89*, Malta, Government Press.
Schranz, A.G. (1986) *National Diabetes Programme*, Malta, Department of Health.
Sciberras, M. & Gouder, A. (1989) Unpublished Report, Malta.
Sciberras, P. (1988) 'Inter-relationship between legislation, alcohol abuse and road traffic safety in Malta', unpublished report, Malta, Mount Carmel Hospital.
S.C.R.C.P., (Special Committee of the Royal College of Psychiatrists) (1987) *Alcohol: Our Favourite Drug*, London, Gaskell Publications.

Siegel, R. (1989) *Intoxication: Life in pursuit of Artificial Paradise*, London, Simon & Schuster.
Stephens, R. (1985) 'The socio-cultural view of heroin use: Towards a role-theoretic model', *Journal of Drug Issues*, vol. 15, 4.
Strang, J. & Stimson, G. (eds) (1990) *AIDS and Drug Abuse*, London, Routledge.
Sultana, A. (1992) 'Alcoholism in Malta: Role of pharmacists and doctors', unpublished dissertation, University of Malta, Department of Pharmacy.
Waters, A.I. & Lidz, C.W. (1980) *Heroin, Deviance and Morality*. Beverly Hills, CA, Sage.
Young, J. (1971) *The Drugtakers*, London, MacGibbon & Kee.
Young J. (1973) 'The amplification of drug use', in Cohen, S. & Young, J. (eds), *The Manufacture of News; Social Problems, Deviance and the Mass Media*, London, Constable.

33

Patterns of Crime

Michael Tanti Dougall

Definition of Crime

The eminent jurist Carrara provides us with a very important legal definition of a crime. He states that a crime is

> the violation of the law of the State promulgated for the protection of the safety of the subjects by an external act of man, whether of omission or of commission, for which the agent is morally responsible.[1]

---

[1] As quoted by Professor Anthony J. Mamo in his *Notes on Criminal Law*, University of Malta.

This means that a crime is any act or omission which in itself or in its outcome is considered to be harmful to the community as a whole. Moreover, the State deems it necessary in the interests of the public, to render the individual(s) responsible liable to some form of punishment upon criminal proceedings.

Therefore, in simplistic terms, a crime may be defined as a breach of the criminal law of a state since

> no act of man can be charged against him unless it is prohibited by the law. An act becomes a criminal offence only if and when it goes counter to the law (Mamo, p. 9).

However, given the fact that legislation is enacted by those in power, it can be argued that a criminal offence may also be any act committed in breach of the interests of those in power. Radzinowicz & King (1977) opine that this interpretation projects criminal law as 'the creature of powerful vested interests rather than the protector of the rights of all'. Indeed, many laws have been held to be oppressive and reprehensive to the moral convictions of the members of a given society and individuals have felt the obligation to disobey them. In Sophicles' Greek tragedy 'Antigone', written around 441 BC, for example, Antigone did not obey the law of King Creon which specifically prohibited persons from burying the fallen enemy's bodies.

Moreover, it must be emphasised that the concept of a criminal offence has to be understood within a given time and space. Under the Criminal Code of Malta, for example, adultery was considered as a criminal offence liable to a punishment for a term not exceeding one year imprisonment, until it was repealed. Again, what is a criminal offence in one state, may not be so in another state. Marital rape, for example, is not considered to be a criminal offence in many contemporary societies, Malta included; however, charges would certainly be brought against the husband for raping his wife in European countries like Sweden, Norway and Denmark, and in most of the states in the USA.

Whatever the interpretation given to a criminal offence, criminal behaviour is usually always condemned. Moreover, it is accepted and expected by the members of every society to sanction the perpetrator(s) of criminal offences. And in this sense, law is the most powerful means of social control, applied by every society in order to protect its very own interests against deviant behaviour.

In this paper, an attempt is made to explain and understand further the phenomenon of crime in Malta which is undoubtedly an under-researched topic. A distinction between the notions of crime and deviance is drawn and this enables the reader to appreciate the sociological analysis of crime in the Maltese islands. Such an analysis is primarily based on data provided by the Data Processing Branch of the Malta Police. The paper discusses various types of crime, their frequency and location patterns, taking into consideration the limitations one would usually encounter when using official statistics on crime.

What is Deviance?

Those who behave against the interests of a given society are labelled as deviant. Deviance may be defined as 'non-conformity to a given norm, or set of norms, which are accepted by a significant number of people' (Giddens, 1992, p. 118) within a given society. To this effect, it would be rather difficult to define 'deviance' since it 'can only be defined in relation to a particular standard and no standards are fixed or absolute' (Haralambos & Holborn, 1991). Therefore, different interpretations may be given to identical behaviour within a given space and time. In fact, sociologists tend to agree that in any society, norms evolve gradually over the years and what might have been deviant before, might not be so considered nowadays.

Deviant behaviour is an abnormal behaviour to the extent that it is considered as having disruptive effects on society. But who decides which behaviour is deviant and which is normal? According to labelling theorists, it is those who

> represent the forces of law and order, or are able to impose definitions of conventional morality upon others, [who] provide the main sources of labelling (Giddens, 1992, p. 129).

Indeed, this whole process of labelling is a social response to certain abnormal social activities and those who carry out such activities are consequently labelled as deviant. But not all deviant behaviour is criminal behaviour. In fact, some deviant behaviour is tolerated by the members of a particular society; for example, having some two dozen cats in a home is not normal behaviour, but it is still tolerated.

In this respect, sociological studies tend to focus only on that deviant behaviour which is specifically sanctioned by criminal law.

Classification of Crimes

Criminal Law is that body of laws which forbids unjustifiable and inexcusable conduct. However,

> the fact that an act is known to be forbidden by criminal law may, for many persons, be sufficient to ensure that they will not commit such an act but for others this will not be enough (Smith & Hogan, 1988, p. 4).

In fact, criminal law rarely prevents unjustifiable and inexcusable behaviour. For this reason, the need was felt for a criminal law of procedure. In this respect, therefore, any unwarranted conduct is publicly condemned and such condemnation is specifically meant to discourage those who intend carrying out similar activities.

Crimes are many and varied. Legally, they may be classified in a number of ways;[2] but by far the most important classification is that made with reference to the nature and gravity of the offence. English Law divides offences into two: indictable and non-indictable offences. The former are those offences which admit of trial by jury, whilst the latter are those which can be tried summarily without a jury. Our law also divides offences into two main categories, according to their degree of gravity. These are crimes and contraventions; the former are the more heinous offences and the punishment which is awarded in their respect reflects their gravity.

This paper limits itself to a focus on some of those offences which fall under crimes and, although limited, it still renders a sociological analysis of the patterns of crime in Malta, a most fascinating exercise. In fact, this study attempts to identify the types of crimes which have occurred most in the Maltese islands, as well as their frequency and location patterns.

The crimes chosen for this paper have been broadly classified into two main categories. The first category deals with those

---

[2] For a comprehensive classification of criminal offences, see Mamo, pp.11-16.

crimes which are manifested against property, and these include theft from all types of premises, theft of/from seacrafts and motor vehicles as well as wilful damage to such property. The second category involves crimes of violence against the person, in particular crimes which take place within the family, like child sexual abuse, incest, wife/husband battering and marital rape.

Crime in Malta

The reported crimes in the Maltese islands for the period 1982-1992 provide us with a suitable perspective on the phenomenon of crime in Malta. For example, the number of crimes reported to the police increased from 3,949 in 1982 to 6,554 in 1988 (see Table 1.1). This represents an overall increase of 65.9 per cent in the total number of crimes reported to the police over a period of seven years. However, it is to be observed that this increase in the number of crimes is not reflective of the increase in the size of the Maltese population since demographically speaking, our population is only growing at the rate of 1.04 per cent annually (Tonna, 1993, p. 3).

Table 1.1 Incidence of reported crimes.

Year	Number of Reported Crimes	%	Increase / Decrease per cent over the previous year.
1982	3949	10.2	
1983	5163	13.4	+ 3.2
1984	5472	14.2	+ 0.8
1985	5166	13.4	– 0.8
1986	5193	13.5	+ 0.1
1987	7121	18.4	+ 4.9
1988	6554	16.9	– 1.5
Total	38618	100	

Of particular significance is the number of crimes reported in 1987, with an overall increase of 37.1 per cent over the previous year. This sharp increase in the number of reported crimes in that particular year may be attributed to the fact that it was the year in which the General Elections in Malta were held and there was some degree of friction between the supporters of the two main political parties. Such partisan friction may have been responsible for the increase of 31.7 per cent in the crimes of wilful damage to property and 140.0 per cent increase in anonymous phone calls and letters over the previous year. (see Table 1.2).

Table 1.2 Types of crime pattern – Crimes reported per year (1982-1988)

Type of Crime	1982	1983	1984	1985	1986	1987	1988	*Total*	%
Urban Theft	364	1028	1238	1177	1220	1866	1776	8669	24.7
Rural Theft	279	450	503	506	445	537	544	3264	9.3
Theft of / from seacraft	63	94	87	104	96	96	104	644	1.8
Theft from unattended motor vehicles	1352	1666	1541	1427	1272	1408	1513	10179	29.0
Theft of motor vehicle	688	862	641	597	658	1093	902	5441	15.5
Pickpocketing	84	60	75	91	54	82	115	561	1.6
Snatch & Grab	20	37	48	38	26	35	93	297	0.8
Wilful Damage	257	522	692	627	764	1006	621	4489	12.8
Crimes of Violence against the Person	58	80	133	109	126	194	144	844	2.4
Fraud	1	5	0	7	7	21	8	49	0.2
Sexual Offences	13	23	15	31	29	41	27	179	0.5
Anonymous Phone-calls and letters	37	30	119	42	55	132	58	473	1.4
TOTAL								35089	100

Again, the number of certain types of crime reported to the police for the year 1984, reflects the socio-political situation in the Maltese Islands during that particular time. In fact, in summer and autumn of that year there was a protracted dispute between the Church and the Malta Government on the status of private schools, as well as a seven-week teachers' strike and lock-out. During this period, both private and state schools buildings were directly or indirectly subjected to continuous monitoring by all interested parties, as a result of which there were only 4 reported cases of theft from schools in 1984 as compared to the 47 reports of the previous year and the reported 44 thefts in the following year (see Table 1.3).

Table 1.3 Crime Target Pattern – Thefts reported to Police (1982-1989)

TARGET	1982	1983	1984	1985	1986	1987	1988	1989	Total	%
Bars	40	64	64	f83	88	132	108	111	690	6.3
Churches	5	7	12	14	3	11	17	16	85	0.8
Cinemas	5	3	4	0	1	2	2	4	21	0.2
Clubs	23	16	35	50	39	55	40	52	310	2.8
Commercial Offices	29	27	34	54	55	70	68	49	386	3.5
Factories	54	65	62	39	42	64	52	67	445	4.1
Garages	34	49	51	38	40	53	40	62	367	3.4
Hospitals	5	8	16	15	6	10	10	12	82	0.7
Hotels	43	60	80	114	98	184	227	167	973	8.9
Houses	417	435	515	444	497	832	821	741	4702	42.9
Kiosks	5	1	6	8	9	12	10	11	62	0.6
Pharmacies	6	4	5	7	1	6	5	4	38	0.3
Petrol Stations	5	5	6	3	5	1	2	4	31	0.3
Schools	27	47	4	44	43	36	39	49	289	2.6
Shops	119	114	153	108	139	244	185	257	1319	12.1
Stores	31	26	48	71	42	70	69	56	413	3.8
Others	16	95	103	85	112	84	81	153	729	6.7
Totals	864	1028	1238	1177	1220	1866	1776	1815	10942	100

It may be also pointed out that during the same period there was a certain degree of social restlessness between those supporting the stand taken by the Malta Government and those who opposed it. In fact, numerous physical threats and attacks were carried out on individuals as well as private houses. This is reflected in the increase of 32.5 per cent in the crimes of wilful damage to property and the increase of 66.3 per cent in the crimes of violence against the person as well as an increase of 296.7 per cent in anonymous phone calls and letters, over the previous year.

Trends of Crime in Malta

Although there has been an increase in the total volume of crime reported to the police, there has not, in fact been very much change in the types of crimes mostly reported. The three most reported types of crime for the period 1982-1988 remain theft from unattended motor vehicles with a total number of 10,179 reports, followed by urban theft and theft of motor vehicles with a total number of 8,669 and 5,441 reports respectively (see Table 1.2).

Grid showing Malta Police Districts and Divisions

District No.	REGION A Division	Localities
1	A B	Valletta; Floriana Water
2	C D	Qormi Żebbuġ; Siġġiewi; Lapsi
3	E F	Paola; Fgura; Albert Town; Laboratory Wharf; Għajn Dwieli; Corradino Industrial Estate Luqa; Tarxien; Santa Luċija; Marsa Industrial Estate
4	G H	Cospicua; Kalkara; Senglea; Vittoriosa Żabbar; Xgħajra; Marsascala
5	I J K	Żejtun; Gudja; Għaxaq Birżebbuġa; Marsaxlokk Żurrieq; Qrendi; Mqabba; Kirkop; Safi
	REGION B	
6	L M N	Sliema; Gżira; Kappara Msida; Pietà; Ta' Xbiex St Julians; Paceville; San Ġwann; Swieqi; St Andrews; Ta' l-Ibraġġ; High Ridge
7	P Q	Ħamrun; Marsa; Santa Venera; Gwardamangia Rabat; Dingli; Mdina; Ta' Qali (excluding Pitkali Market)
8	R S	Birkirkara; Lija; Balzan; Attard; Mrieħel (including Ta' Qali Pitkali Market) Naxxar; Għargħur; Madliena; Baħar iċ-Ċagħaq
9	T V	Mosta; Mġarr; Bidnija; Wardija; Burmarrad; Għajn Tuffieħa St Paul's Bay; Buġibba; Qawra; Mellieħa; Cirkewwa; Marfa; Manikata
10	Z	Gozo; Comino

These represent 29.0, 24.7 and 15.5 per cent of a total number of 35,089 indicated crimes. It is a known fact that the number of registered motor vehicles has been constantly increasing over the years, and with the sharp boost in tourism, the number of self-drive motor vehicles has also increased. The above-mentioned types-of-crime pattern shows that thefts from and of motor vehicles signify the principal reported crimes in the Maltese Islands. With respect to urban theft, it is interesting to observe that from the various premises in the towns and villages in Malta indicated in Table 1.3, the crime target pattern for 1982-1989 was primarily directed towards houses, with 42.9 per cent of all reported thefts, followed by shops with 12.1 per cent, and hotels with 8.9 per cent. The least earmarked for theft are cinemas with 21 reported thefts or 0.2 per cent. This is expected when we consider the ratio of the number of cinemas in relation to that of houses, shops and hotels.

Crime Location Pattern

The regional crime pattern in the Maltese islands seems to follow the same trends from one year to another. The crime location pattern being applied, follows the localities of the Police Districts as revised in 1988 (See GHQ Circular No: 63/88 issued on 26 August, 1988).

Thefts from urban premises, including bars, hotels, kiosks, and shops, seem to be mostly reported at the police stations of Police Districts 6 and 9, with 22.8 per cent and 21.9 per cent respectively for the period 1989-1992 (see Table 1.4). The same trend can be found in connection with wilful damage to premises and motor vehicles by means of acid, arson, oily substances, paint, paint remover, shots or explosions. In fact, the same Police Districts have the highest reported crimes of wilful damage, with 21.2 per cent and 13.9 per cent of the reports being lodged at the police stations of Police Districts 6 and 9 respectively (see Table 1.5).

Both districts include the prime touristic localities in Malta like Sliema, St. Julians, Paceville, St. Paul's Bay, Buġibba and Qawra, with the various hotels, bars, restaurants, and discotheques. In this respect, therefore, these localities as areas of leisure and entertainment, attract thousands of youths from all over Malta, especially during week-ends. And with moral values thought to be

Table 1.4 Crime Location Pattern – Thefts from urban premises as reported per district (1989-92)

Police District	1989	1990	1991	1992	Total	%
1	171	185	131	186	673	8.5
2	73	55	93	87	308	3.9
3	168	195	188	151	702	8.9
4	146	118	144	141	549	6.9
5	124	150	122	138	534	6.7
6	422	486	445	450	1803	22.8
7	154	169	180	187	690	8.7
8	154	166	225	211	756	9.6
9	364	487	471	411	1733	21.9
10	34	46	34	48	162	2.1
Totals	1810	2057	2033	2010	7910	100

Table 1.5 Crime Location Pattern – Wilful Damage to Property and Motor Vehicles as reported per district (1989-92)

Police District	1989	1990	1991	1992	Total	%
1	75	106	94	108	383	12.5
2	42	39	48	50	179	5.8
3	43	55	60	50	208	6.8
4	49	47	69	81	246	8.0
5	57	68	82	66	273	8.9
6	160	165	158	165	648	21.2
7	76	76	67	86	305	9.9
8	61	76	73	104	314	10.3
9	118	98	119	93	428	13.9
10	31	19	19	14	83	2.7
Totals	712	749	789	817	3067	100

in decline and permissiveness on the increase, it is a common belief that youths are the ones who are increasingly committing a good percentage of these crimes. However, as can be seen from the figures in Table 1.6 which shows the number of juveniles who are known to have committed criminal offences for the period 1983-1990, there is a slight increase in the tendency of juvenile delinquency. It may therefore be observed that it has not increased in such a way as to corroborate what is commonly believed. Indeed, contrary to what is thought to be the contemporary trend of adolescents in Malta,

> departure from traditional morality, measured in terms of greater permissiveness on personal and sexual morality, is still very low in Malta (Abela, 1992, p. 33).

Table 1.6 Offences committed by juveniles

Year	Males	Females	Total
1983	66	10	76
1984	105	10	115
1985	88	33	121
1986	46	23	69
1987	69	15	84
1988	77	11	88
1989	82	5	87
1990	124	5	129

Source: C.O.S. (1993, p. 40)

Interesting is the fact that Police District 10, which primarily consists of the islands of Gozo and Comino, has the least reported crime rate in the Maltese Islands; with 2.1 per cent of the reported thefts and 2.7 per cent of all the reported crimes of wilful damage to property and motor vehicles. Besides the number of the population being relatively smaller than that in each of the other nine Police Districts, one primary reason behind these low rates in crime within this particular district could be the fact that Gozo is a relatively closer, more tightly-knit society than the island of Malta.

Crimes Within the Family

Most married couples try their very best to live up to the marital images of harmony and romance which have been stereo-typed over the years by various social agencies, including the media and religion. However, there exists an unattractive side of married life which is indisputably leaving devastating consequences on the members of the family. In fact, over the last decade or so, feminist movements have managed to

> cast a searchlight on very dark aspects of family life: such things as child-beating, incest, wife-beating, marital rape, and women's mental illness (Worsley, 1987, p. 160)

suggesting that the family may at times be far from a haven of peace.

Child Sexual Abuse and Incest

More often than not, child sexual abuse and incest, tend to take place within the family context. Giddens (1992, p. 406) remarks that incest, and child sexual abuse more generally, are phenomena which are proving to be disturbingly common, with some incestual relations being transitory whilst others are much more extensive and may occur over a number of years. In a nation-wide study concerning reported cases of child sexual abuses in the USA, a 600 per cent increase in these types of abuse is indicated between 1976 and 1982 (Finklehor, 1984).

Child sexual abuse may be defined as any sexual act manifested by an adult with a person who is below the consenting age of eighteen years old.[3] Under Title VII of the Maltese Criminal Code, entitled 'Of crimes affecting the good order of families', it is provided that whoever carries out lewd acts with a minor of

---

[3] Under Maltese Law, a minor is a person who has not yet attained the age of eighteen years. However, minors between fourteen and eighteen years of age are deemed to be responsible for their acts, to the extent that they are awarded the same punishment as that of adults, decreased by one to two degrees, if convicted. Under Italian and English law a person under the age of sixteen is deemed to be still a minor.

either sex, would be affecting a defilement of that minor.[4] By lewd acts it is meant any act, including carnal knowledge, carried out either on the person or in the presence of the minor. The Malta Police Statistics (MPS) indicate that during the twelve-year period of 1982-1993, there was a total of 151 cases solved by the Malta Police which involved defilement of minors.

Reference to incest often brings to mind a sexual relation between two relatives. However, incest does not always involve sexual abuse. Whilst a sexual relation between an adult and a minor is an abuse, the one carried out between two consenting adults whose relationship is for example, that of a brother and a sister, is definitely incestual but not necessarily abusive.

Our law caters for incest under the same legal provision referred to previously. The same lewd acts together with certain aggravating circumstances would give rise to incestual relations. The aggravating circumstances include a relation involving any relative by consanguinity or affinity, an adoptive father or mother, as well as any person who is responsible for the care, education, or custody of a minor.[5] Giddens (1992, p. 406) opines that in most cases, incestual relations involve father-daughter or step-father-daughter relationships but 'uncle-niece, brother-sister, father-son, mother-daughter and even grandparent-grandchild relationships also occur'.

According to a study carried out by Gomes-Schwartz, Horowitz & Cardelli (1991, p. 64), 19.2 per cent of the sexual abuses on children were carried out by the natural parent, whilst 20.5 per cent by step-parents, adoptive or foster parents, as well as by parent's live-in partner. Other relatives, including uncles, grandfathers and cousins committed 22.4 per cent of the abuses. Considerably high is the percentage of abuses carried out by those who were

---

[4] Article 203(1) 'Whosoever, by lewd acts, defiles a minor of either sex, shall, on conviction, be liable to imprisonment for a term not exceeding two years, with or without solitary confinement'.

[5] Article 203(1)(c) 'if the offence is committed by any ascendant by consanguinity or affinity, or by the adoptive father or mother, or by the tutor of the minor, or by any other person charged, even temporarily, with the care, education, instruction, control or custody of the minor'.

not members of the family. In fact, 32.7 per cent of the children were subjected to sexual abuse by various persons including family acquaintances, babysitters and strangers.

All in all, these figures indicate that 'children usually are sexually abused by someone they know and often trust' (Gomes-Schwartz et al., 1991, p. 63). This would undoubtedly give rise to long-term consequences for the 'defenceless victims'. In fact, Finkelhor (1988, p. 25) maintains that research on physically and sexually abused children, together with abused wives, have shown the tendency of

> common patterns of mental health impairment. The victims suffering from long-term effects of abuse are characterized by low self-esteem, instability in their intimate relationships, anxiety, depression, suicide attempts, substance abuse, psychosomatic complaints, and poor functioning in school and work situations.

In many cases, sexual abuse and incest on children are carried out by the use of force or threat of violence. In this respect, therefore, the children involved in such relations are usually also physically battered. Giddens (1992, p. 408) identifies the latter type of domestic violence as a male domain and adds that 'studies show that the prime targets of physical abuse are again children, especially small children under the age of six'. In this respect, MPS data for the two-year period between January 1992 and December 1993, reveals that there were 19 reported cases of child battering, 10 of whom involved male children, the youngest being 4 years old. Six of the cases were reported at the police stations of Police District 4 whilst five cases were lodged at the police stations of Police District 3.

Wife / Husband Battering

Domestic violence also involves wife/husband battering. Although many believe that only husbands use violence against their wives within the family settings, it has been discovered that wives can be just as violent. However, marital violence remains primarily the female spouse's problem.

According to Gelles & Cornell (1986, p. 69), wife beating can at times follow an unfortunate pattern and, in most violent households, it is not a single and isolated event. The factors which could actually lead to wife battering are various, and these include unemployment, financial problems, sexual difficulties, low job satisfaction, and poor housing conditions, besides experiences of violence in the childhood and adolescence of the perpetrator. Rouse (1984, p. 182) observed that the experience of

> violence in childhood or adolescence was significantly associated with later use of abusive tactics in martial disputes.

All these factors are considered as inter-related issues to marital violence. However, the major factor remains alcoholism. In fact, various studies observed that between 36 and 52 per cent of wife battering cases were usually closely connected with the abuse of alcohol (Gelles & Cornell, 1986).

MPS data demonstrates that over a period of two years,[6] from January 1992 to December 1993, there were 147 reported cases of wife battering as compared to 7 cases of husband battering reported to the police (see Table 1.7). This shows that in Malta, the frequency of wife battering could very well be 95.5 per cent compared to the 4.5 per cent of husband battering incidence.

Table 1.7 Crime Location Pattern – Wife/Husband Battering cases reported to the Police (Jan 1992-May 1993)

District	Wife Battering	Husband Battering	Totals
1	0	0	0
2	11	0	11
3	66	0	66
4	37	0	37
5	5	0	5
6	2	0	2
7	23	7	30
8	0	0	0
9	2	0	2
10	1	0	1
Totals	147	7	154

---

[6] MPS have only since recently been keeping record of wife/husband/child battering.

Before analysing and interpreting this data, it is necessary to establish that like the figures previously identified in connection with child abuses, the figures related to wife batterings are likewise rather difficult to interpret since no precise measure of domestic violence can possibly be employed. In this respect, therefore, it would be wise to keep in mind that the relative data is limited only to the cases reported to the police.

As previously noted in connection with child battering, Police Districts 3 and 4 also seem to occupy the highest placings with regard to wife batterings, with 66 cases and 37 cases respectively. However, it is interesting to observe that besides the 23 reported cases of wife battering lodged at the police stations of Police District 7, all the 7 cases involving husband battering were also reported in the same Police District.[7]

Unfortunately, the ages of the battered wives whose report was lodged with the police were not always indicated in the MPS and therefore, a proper analysis of the age group involved is not possible. However, from the limited available data in the relative reports, it would appear that the age group of the female spouses concerned seemed to be between 21 years and 69 years of age. This substantiates the view that marital violence may occur at any stage of marriage and any woman of any age may be subjected to it. Gelles & Cornell (1986, p. 73) argue that it seems to be most frequent among those under 30 years of age. They remark that 'the rate of marital violence among those under thirty years of age is more than double the rate for the next older age group (thirty-one to fifty)'. In spite of more legal protection, battered wives who attempt to seek help discover that they have very restrictive options to choose from. Police intervention is more often than not, limited if not altogether ineffective. Moreover, social agencies like the *Għaqda Nies Imsawta*, a local association for battered wives, endeavour to provide the best possible refuge for battered women and their children. Many women who have

---

[7] Of the 7 husband-battering cases reported to the police, 6 reports were lodged at one specific police station in Police District 7 and therefore, it is the opinion of the author that the reports could have easily been made by the same person.

experienced violence within the family have questioned the success or failure of law in the protection of their rights. However, it is important to emphasise that, no matter the amount of legislation enacted, law is more an instrument of deterrence. It is not a solution to these issues.

Marital Rape

Closely related to domestic violence is the issue of marital rape. In a very simplistic way, it may be defined as the nonconsensual sexual intercourse by a husband with his lawful wife, usually accompanied by physical violence.

The crime of rape as defined by our Criminal Code is that act by means of which a person, using either physical or moral violence, has sexual carnal connection with another person of either sex.[8] The interpretation of the term 'another person' excludes the spouse and therefore, it ensues that in Maltese law, as in English law, a man cannot rape his wife.

The assumption that the husband cannot rape his wife owes its origin to English common law in the seventeenth century when Judge Sir Matthew Hale delivering a ruling in 1736, declared that 'the husband cannot be guilty of a rape committed by himself upon his lawful wife, for by their mutual matrimonial consent and contract the wife hath given up herself in this kind unto her husband which she cannot retract'.[9] However, it is admitted that there would still be marital rape if, amongst other circumstances,[10] there exists a judicial separation between the spouses and the

---

[8] Article 198: 'Whosoever shall, by violence, have carnal knowledge of a person of either sex, shall on conviction be liable to imprisonment for a term from three to nine years, with or without solitary confinement'.

[9] Referred to by Hale, I.M., *The History of the pleas of the Crown*, 629 Emlin ed. 1736.

[10] These would include a non-molestation injunction and a personal protection order.

man constrains the woman to have sexual intercourse. In this respect, *de facto* separated women have no legal defence against rape by their husbands.

Many refuse to believe that in certain countries marital rape is a crime. Countries like Denmark, Sweden, Norway, Canada and the USA consider rape within marriage as illegal. J.C. Barden (May, 1987) in an article entitled 'Marital Rape: Drive for tougher laws is pressed' published in *The New York Times*, maintains that 'it is now a crime in 25 states for a husband to rape his wife while the two are living together'. In fact, it was the state of South Dakota which was first to make the rape of a spouse a crime. To this effect, 'nationally, from 1978 through June 1985 ... 118 husbands were prosecuted on charges of raping their wives and 104 of them convicted' (ibid.).

Indeed, the difficulty exists how to be persuasive in explaining that rape within marriage is not a sexual crime but one of violence. In fact, underlying a number of misconceptions in the crime of marital rape is the failure to refuse to acknowledge this precise distinction.

> It is the violence, outrage and injury to the victim, not sex which demands criminal punishment...(after all) a married woman certainly relinquishes some autonomy, but she most certainly does not exchange her autonomy for a license by her husband to commit violence upon her body (Catania, 1989, p. 97).

A corollary may exist with respect to man.

Various arguments have been put forward in order to minimise this abuse within the family setting, including the attempt to justify the act of rape performed by a spouse as being less serious than that performed by a stranger. However, spousal rape can in effect be more traumatic than stranger rape. It has been argued that 'when you are raped by a stranger you have to live with a frightening memory. When you are raped by your husband, you have to live with the rapist' (Groth, 1979, p. 179).

Data on Crimes: Limitations

The local data analysis on patterns of crime referred to in this paper, was limited to the period 1982-1993 and it was primarily obtained from official statistics of the Malta Police, Data Processing Branch. No considerable difficulties were encountered in determining the regional variations in the patterns of crime according to the police districts. However, the figures published by MPS about crime and delinquency in the Maltese islands could very well be limited since they only include those reported to the police.

Sociologists are well aware that official statistics on crimes are far from being accurate since a high percentage of crimes remains unreported and therefore, unrecorded. Radzinowicz & King (1977, p. 31) remark that 'the recorded figures of crime are huge, but the reality behind them everywhere looms far larger'. This phenomenon, better known in criminological literature as the 'dark figure of crime', has haunted criminologists for many years.

In order to overcome the limitations of official statistics, victimization studies were introduced in various countries whereby individuals in a sample survey would be asked whether they had been victims of crime during the previous year and if in the affirmative, whether they had reported the crime to the police. Such studies to investigate unreported crimes have been carried out in the USA by the Bureau of the Census since 1973 and by the Home Office Research and Planning Unit in the UK since 1982.

One such victimization study was carried out in 1988 to study the amount of unreported crimes in the UK for the year 1987. In this study, a sample of 15,392 adults aged 16 years or over from Scotland, England and Wales was used. Haralambos & Holborn (1992, p.605) refer specifically to this 1988 British Crime Survey which confirmed that 'criminal statistics are highly unreliable'. In fact, this survey revealed that only 37 per cent of certain crimes like thefts from dwellings, thefts from and of motor vehicles, woundings and sexual offences, were reported to the police. This finding tends to confirm Giddens's remark (1992, p. 133) that the majority of crimes are never reported to the police.

What possible reasons could there be for this high rate of unreported crimes? The 1988 British Crime Survey found that almost half of those who failed to report the crime, did so because they believed that it was too trivial an offence to report; 32 per cent thought that the police would not have been bothered about their report, let alone interested; 2 per cent referred to the inconvenience of reporting, 1 per cent mentioned dislike of the police; and 1 per cent were afraid of retaliations if they had to report the offence to the police.

In this respect, therefore, if we want a proper analysis of the patterns of crime in the Maltese islands, we need to acquire an insight on the 'dark figure of crime' in Malta by conducting surveys similar to those referred to above. Nonetheless, although we have to admit that any survey intended to arrive at accurate estimates of unreported crimes is impossible because of the various difficulties arising from any given sampling, McClintock & Avison (1968, pp. 12-13) opine that the basic material obtainable from official publications on crime yields much information that is of considerable value to anyone concerned with furthering the knowledge about the state of crime in a given society.

References

Abela, A.M. (1992) *Changing Youth Culture in Malta*, Jesuit Publications in association with Diocesan Youth Commission, Valletta.

Catania, J. (1989) 'Marital rape: The misunderstood crime', in Tanti Dougall, M. (ed.) *Id-Dritt*, vol. 14, Malta, University of Malta, Faculty of Laws.

Central Office of Statistics (C.O.S.) (1993) *Annual Abstract of Statistics 1990*, Malta, Government Press.

Finkelhor, D. (1984) *Child Sexual Abuse: New Theory and Research*, New York, Free Press.

Finkelhor, D. (1988) *Stopping Family Violence, Research Priorities for the Coming Decade*, London, Sage.

Gelles, R.J. & Cornell, C.P. (1986) *Intimate Violence in Families*, London, Sage.

Giddens, A. (1992) *Sociology*, Cambridge, Polity Press.

Gomes-Schwartz, B., Horowitz, M. & Cardelli, C. (1991) *Child Sexual Abuse – The Initial Effects*, London, Sage.

Groth, M. (1979) *Men Who Rape: The Psychology of the Offender*, New York Plenum.

Haralambos, M. & Holborn, M. (1991) *Sociology: Themes and Perspectives*, 3e, Collins Educational.

Hotaling, G.T., Finkelhor, D., Kirkpatrick, J.T. & Straus, M.A. (1988) *Family Abuse and its Consequences, New Directions in Research*, London, Sage.

Mamo, A.J. (1972) *Notes on Criminal Law*, Malta, University of Malta.

McClintock, F.H. & Avison, N.H. (1968) *Crime in England and Wales*, Cambridge, published on behalf of the Institute of Criminology.

Radzinowicz, L. & King, J. (1977) *The Growth of Crime, The International Experience*, London, Hamish Hamilton.

Rouse, L.P. (1988) 'Conflict Tactics Used by Men in Marital Disputes' in Hotaling, G.T. et al. (1988) *Family Abuse and its Consequences, New Directions in Research*, London, Sage.

Smith, J.C. & Hogan, B. (1988) *Criminal Law*, 6e, London, Butterworth.

Tonna, B. (1993) *Malta Trends 1993: The Signs of the Times*, Institute for Research on the Signs of the Times, Malta, Media Centre.

Worsley, P. (ed.) (1987) *The New Introducing Sociology*, Harmondsworth, Penguin.

34

The Maltese Elderly: From Institutionalization to Active Participation in the Community

Joseph Troisi

Introduction

One of the most significant phenomena of the twentieth century has been the dramatic increase in the number and proportion of persons aged sixty and over. Population ageing is primarily the result of a three stage process termed by the World Health Organization as 'the epidemiological transition', whereby a population moves from high fertility and high mortality rates to low fertility and low mortality rates (WHO, 1984).

Population ageing has become a major global concern, posing unique challenges to every society. Following the Second World

War, the world's progress towards higher living standards – brought about by advances in medical science, nutrition and social conditions, and by the control of communicable diseases – has resulted in a remarkable increase in life expectancy. This, unavoidably implies both a heightened demand for existing support services as well as for new services and alternative approaches for the care of the elderly. Though the elderly have many needs which they share with the rest of the population, they have some which are specialized and age-oriented. Consequently, new approaches to medical care and to the delivery of health and social services may be required.

The issue becomes more complex because the traditional role of the Maltese family in the daily care and support of the elderly members (especially those who are frail) is currently under threat, owing to economic, social and psychological strains (Troisi, 1989), as are the families of many other countries.

Given the concurrent phenomena of industrialization, urbanization and modernization, as well as other demographic and socio-economic factors affecting the family structure, the needs of the frail elderly can no longer be met by the family alone. It cannot do without the support of specialized programmes and services often sponsored by governments. Hence, the increasing significant demand for additional services from the formal sector.

The issues related to ageing are multi-disciplinary in nature, covering such sectors as health care; education and culture; housing and environment; social assistance and family protection; recreation and rehabilitation; pension and invalidity insurance. Care of the elderly is a complex and interdependent matter. The health and happiness of the elderly is dependent upon social, emotional and psychological factors. Good health has been defined by the World Health Organization (WHO, 1984) as not merely the absence of disease and infirmity but the physical, mental and social well-being of the individual.

Although ageing does not 'cause' any disease, certain ailments, especially chronic ones, are more prevalent among the elderly, particularly among the 'old-old'.[1] As they advance in age, people

---

[1] A number of demographers and social gerontologists, among them Prof.

find themselves generally slowing down, as some of their faculties start to decline and, at the same time, certain disabilities begin to develop. These gradually limit the elderly's ability to autonomy and to undertake the normal activities of daily living. Moreover, the 'old-old' are those most likely to be widowed, living alone and to have a lesser number of supportive relatives, if any at all.

This paper proposes to identify and justify the policy shift undergone recently in looking at:

a. the relationship of the Maltese elderly to the rest of their society and
b. the responsibilities of the family, the State and other voluntary organizations towards senior citizens.

The argument defends this transition from a centralized and bureaucratic transmission of benevolent paternalism to responsible and active participation. It describes the concrete measures taken to initiate and sustain this still ongoing transition. The case is placed within the context of a statistical preamble which captures the increasing proportion of the elderly in Maltese society.

Malta's Ageing Population

A concerted assessment of demographic patterns over past decades and projected on the basis of current trends provides useful insights towards understanding the disproportionate, perhaps even alarming, share of the elderly within the Maltese population. The main demographic variables relevant to this discussion include population increase, birth rates, fertility rates, life expectancy, dependency ratios and gender differences. Each of these is reviewed below.

At the end of 1990, there were in Malta 52,536 persons aged 60 and over. Projections suggest that the number of the elderly will increase to 62,500 by the year 2002 and to 95,000 by the year 2020. (See Table 1)

Bernice Neugarten, speak about the 'young-old' and the 'old-old' to distinguish between those persons aged 60-74 and those who are 75 years and older.

Table 1. Maltese Population by Sex and Age Groups as on 31 December 1990

Age Group	Males	Females	Total
All Ages	175782	180128	355910
0-4	13811	13023	26834
5-59	138971	137569	276540
60-64	6878	8213	15091
65-69	6265	7602	13867
70-74	4204	5253	9457
75-79	2959	4063	7022
80-84	1830	2742	4572
85+	864	1663	2527

Source: (C.O.S., 1991).

During this same period, the country's population is expected to increase from 356,000 in 1990, to 383,000 by the year 2002 and to 409,000 by the year 2020. Taken together, these two statistics suggest that the proportion of the elderly within the total Maltese population is also expected to increase: From 14.8% in 1990, to 16.3% in 2002 to 23.3% – almost one out of every four Maltese – by the year 2020.

Among these elderly, the 'old-old' will register the most significant increase. As an example, the Maltese eighty-plus category will double from a figure of 7,000 registered in 1990 to 14,000 by 2020 (U.N.S.O., 1988).

Projections of changes in the proportion of the elderly primarily reflect past trends in fertility and assumptions about the future gross reproduction rate (i.e. the number of female children a woman is expected to bear in her life time). One of the combined effects of a sustained drop in the crude birth rate and of the gross reproduction rate is a marked reduction in the proportion of young people, which is expected to decline from 36.8% to 19.6% of the total population over the epoch 1960-2020. One consequence of these composite factors is an increase in the dependency ratio of the elderly on the economically active (15-59) population.

The average life expectancy has increased dramatically during the last half century, from 41.35 years for males and 43.46 years for females in 1930 to 73.70 years and 78.69 years respectively in 1985. This is projected to increase further to 74 years and 80 years by the year 2025 (C.O.S., 1986).

Each national census taken since 1842 has revealed that the Maltese population is characterized by a marked dominance of females over males. The 1985 Census recorded a sex-ratio of 967 males for every 1,000 females in the Maltese Islands (C.O.S., 1986). This 'feminization' phenomenon is expected to continue and will lead to a still higher ratio of females to males in the older age groups. In 1990, Maltese women constituted 56.2% of the elderly population. It is estimated that by the year 2020, they will constitute 54.5% of the elderly population (C.O.S., 1991). Life expectancy estimates suggest that the number of years by which on average women are expected to outlive men has thus increased from 2.11 years in 1930 to 4.39 years in 1990 (C.O.S., 1986). This dominance of women over men coupled with a higher female life expectancy, results in a high incidence of widowed women needing social support, income and health care.

Family Care

Maltese society has always been characterized by its strong family structure and ties. One may add that it has been part of Malta's social pattern that where a daughter remained unmarried or was married but bore no children, she was expected to look after her elderly parents (Busuttil, 1971). Despite recurrent misgivings about the commitment of the family to care for its elderly members, it is generally accepted that most help continues nevertheless to come from the family (Troisi, 1991). One cannot, however, deny the fact that, in recent years, as in other countries, various social and cultural changes have subjected the traditional care of the elderly provided by Maltese families to a strain.

The fall in the average Maltese family size – a fall which has occurred during the last four decades – has resulted in a reduction in the number of available family carers of the elderly kin. The gradual emergence of the two-child family and its actual acceptance as the 'standard' size of the Maltese family, had been markedly evident in the 1985 Census results (C.O.S., 1986). In 1948, there were still 7.7 persons available for each person of retirement age. This figure declined to 4.3 by 1986 and is projected to further decrease to 2.2 by the year 2020 (UN, 1984).

Moreover, the growth in opportunities for paid employment especially in light manufacturing, domestic and tourist-oriented services, together with changes towards a more materialist life-style, have caused young and middle-aged married women to be increasingly tempted to seek work outside the home. This further reduces the available time for those who are economically active, to visit and take care of their frail elderly parents. Families are becoming more and more geographically separated as younger daughters, on getting married, move into newer properties. Though distances in Malta rarely exceed a few kilometres, the married daughter living in a separate area is quite unable to render the same degree of care and support as before. Furthermore, the achieved longevity has resulted in the emergence of the multi-generational family, some families now boasting of three or even four living generations in lineal descent. With the smaller number of siblings to share the caring, the task, if not relinquished, is compounded, aggravating the family's heavy strain of care.

Formal Care

All the factors mentioned above have had the inevitable effect of increasing the difficulties that elderly persons, especially the 'old-old', experience in meeting their basic needs leading to an increased demand for statutory and voluntary services. On their part, the elderly, though by and large desirous to remain in their own homes and environment, are worried and anxious about their future especially when they reach the stage of dependency on others.

Institutionalization

In the past, as was the case in a number of Western countries, the State was more preoccupied with meeting the 'humanitarian' issues of the elderly especially the frail 'old-old', directing its programmes towards 'protecting' the elderly. It contemplated a system of care which was to a large extent restricted to medical care and physical comfort. Hardly any emphasis was put on how to 'socialize' and rehabilitate the growing population of older citizens who were no longer economically active.[2]

---

[2] Malta has one of the largest residential complexes for the elderly in Europe, housing more than a thousand persons. Formerly known as *Imgieret* it served as a Poor House where the destitute, mainly elderly persons, could find refuge.

The results of this approach was the institutionalization of the elderly who were, thus, expected to pass the last years of their life in security, if not in comfort, under the supervision of trained nursing personnel (S.A.M., 1982). Such a strategy resulted in relegating the elderly to mere passive observers and, worse still, in emarginating them from society, uprooting them from their environment, separated from their dear ones and from the customs to which they were deeply attached and from which they derived meaning, identity and purpose.

To counter-act this, the need was felt for a radical change of perspective, replacing the policy of segregation with a strategy of integration enabling the elderly to continue participating in society to the greatest extent possible. A report published in connection with an international conference, recommended that as part of an overall strategy towards best tackling this ever growing demographic challenge, policies should (a) stimulate different forms of care for older populations and (b) try as much as possible to keep elderly people living in the community (UN, 1993).

National Policies

Malta stands today at a critical turning point for confronting the challenges and issues generated by a growing, aging population. The approach to these problems and needs should, however, not be treated in isolation. It should rather form an integral part of an overall economic and social development planning programme of the country. It is equally important to carry out a re-examination of the essential aspects of social infrastructure including family types, housing, employment, income and social security. The concerted attention of planners, policy makers and the population at large to the implications arising from population ageing provides our country with a golden opportunity to be better prepared and thus hopefully avoid the situation in which events overtake history.

The Old Age Pensions Act of 1948 was the first of a sequence

In the past years, St Vincent de Paule Residence for the Elderly, as it came to be known, has incorporated a more functional organization with smaller numbers of elderly persons in each section, as part of its modernization.

of legislative measures aimed at ameliorating the standard of living of the Maltese elderly. The National Assistance Act of 1956 widened the scope of the previous Act by embracing a larger section of the elderly population. It introduced a universal contributory old age pension scheme. This act, as amended in 1979, grants the right to a two-thirds pension to all contributors to the national insurance fund. There is also a non-contributory pension scheme.

Health services in Malta are highly developed with free hospital and primary care services for all. There is also a free drugs distribution service for low income persons and for those suffering from certain scheduled diseases.

Most of the elderly in Malta own their own place of residence. Non-owners live in property with controlled rents. By and large housing is of good standard. Practically all existing housing stock has running water, electricity provision, adequate space and sanitation.

It is important to note that in the past, the social welfare policies prevalent in Malta had in turn led to the creation of a welfare state based on a complicated system of social services. These tended to replace rather than complement family policy. At the same time, it was becoming evident that it was necessary to reverse the tendency to depersonalization by offering instead a personalized social service.

It has gradually dawned on policy makers and interested pressure groups that the family environment is the one best suited to the life-style of the elderly. On the other hand, it was recognized that the family's traditional role of care-giver to its elderly members was being subjected to economic, social and psychological strain. And yet the participation of the elderly within society also basically implies their actual involvement within the family. As Shanas (1979) points out,

> old persons turn first to their families for help, then to neighbours, and finally to the bureaucratic agencies and others, because they expect families to help in case of need.

An integrated social policy with a family oriented approach thus received state priority in recent years. A plan was set in motion intending to replace the existing bureaucratic and institutional administrative system with a personalized social service policy package. This was also to be integrated as much as possible within the normal living physical and social environment of every Maltese citizen.

The guiding principle of such social policy is to strengthen the adaptability of the family to the new demands, while at the same time supporting and protecting it so as to enable it to continue responding to the specific needs of its members (NP, 1987).

Personalization in Community Care

Stamping the formulation and implementation of social service provision for the elderly with a personalized character is not to be achieved by mere cosmetic reform. Various public and private policies and programmes have been reformulated to supplement family support to the growing elderly population, enabling the latter to remain within the desirable environment of their own family and community for as long as possible. The care of the elderly, in the community has become the accepted perspective of present health and social policy in Malta. In these efforts, the initiatives of the state are significantly complemented by the sterling services provided by a number of voluntary organizations, notably those under the aegis of the Catholic Church.

During these last few years, the Maltese Government has also embarked upon and is co-ordinating a comprehensive community health and social care package best suited to the needs of the elderly especially the frail and those living alone. By providing care and support where the family and the individual are unable to manage by themselves, community care services help the elderly to maintain good health and to live independent lives in their own homes and in the community. At the same time, these services enable families to cope with caring demands of their elderly relatives. This prevents or at least defers the need for long-term institutional care. The trend is to hospitalize geriatric patients only in acute cases and to return them to their families and community as soon as possible furnishing them with appropriate follow-up home treatment and supportive services.

Apart from totally free hospitalization and complete access to public funded health centres and free prescription of drugs, the range of personalized, home-focused community care services includes, amongst others: domiciliary nursing; home help; home care and maintenance; day care centres; community hostel-type homes; meals on wheels; provision of technical aids; self health care schemes; social clubs and telecare service.

There is also free access to a specialized geriatric and rehabilitative hospital and to respite homes. Financial assistance is also given to disabled elderly persons to help them carry out adaptations in their homes so as to enable them to cope in spite of their physical disabilities. A non-contributory carers' pension is given to those family members who are looking after their elderly relatives (Troisi, 1988). All of these community based services are heavily subsidized by the State. The recurrent national expenditure on the range of services offered to elderly people has been increasing, and is likely to continue to do so, mainly because of two factors: The decreasing number of working people in proportion to the number of pensioners, and increasing longevity. Medical costs may also be projected to increase in real terms. This situation, which is also prevalent in a number of industrialized economies, needs to be tackled sooner rather than later if it is not to turn into a fiscal nightmare.[3]

The fact that most of the voluntary endeavour is under Church auspices helps to a large extent to avoid the difficulties experienced in other countries where the very plethora and variety of organizations often makes it difficult to secure effective co-ordination. Mention must also be made of a number of self-help groups – such as the Pensioners' Association – all of which contribute, through a number of programmes and activities, to ameliorate the socio-economic conditions of elderly citizens.

Government's declared objective is the integration of the network of diverse services now being implemented by the State and Non-Governmental Organizations (NGOs), in order to rationalize the use of available resources and increase the co-operation and co-ordination between the different programmes. The State recognizes the invaluable role of the non-government organizations in meeting the increasing demand for social provisions for the elderly. The expressed commitment is therefore to strengthen and provide every support to the services made available by these NGOs to society in general and to the elderly in particular. In this way these agencies will

---

[3] The United Nations Economic Commission for Europe and the United Nations Population Fund (1993) warned that the elderly would prove an ever greater economic burden if Western nations tried to maintain existing standards of social and health care.

find ampler space within which to widen their operations, while Government will adopt a more co-ordinating role – a role which is in line with the general policy of transforming the welfare state into a welfare society.

The Elderly as Active Contributors

The Vienna International Plan of Action on Ageing, strongly emphasized that while every society had a duty to maintain the elderly who were in need of support, it should also explore the possibilities of utilizing and benefiting from the varied resources of the elderly.

> The ageing population constitutes a valuable and important component of society's human resources (UN, 1983).

The Maltese elderly are, in general, well supported and the social services at their disposal are highly developed and progressive. More emphasis has, however, to be placed on their participation and contribution to the very developmental process of their country. In other words, the elderly should be regarded as contributors to and agencies of a country's developmental effort and not as mere beneficiaries. It is high time the Maltese society started paying more attention to tapping this invaluable resource to the fullest extent possible. Innovative policies and programmes for encouraging, mobilizing and securing the active participation of the elderly in development and at utilizing their contribution to the country's economy and social life should be formulated. However important the role of the State and that of organizations and agencies may be, it is equally important that the elderly themselves actively participate in the process of formulating and implementing national policies. The recent setting up of a National Council of the Elderly was certainly an important step forward in this regard.

The UN's Economic Commission for Europe strongly urged that

> the valuable contribution that the productive roles played by the elderly make to society, especially as volunteers and caregivers, should be given due recognition (UN, 1993).

In line with this, Caritas Malta – one main source of voluntary action for the elderly on the island – provides a powerful force of volunteers who are trained not only to provide a service to the elderly but, aware as they are of the latter's potential, also to encourage their very participation. In fact, a number of Caritas programmes are run by the elderly themselves.

It is interesting to note that experts from various countries attending an International Seminar convened in Malta by the United Nations, repeatedly stressed the fact that by maximizing the elderly's developmental potential, the entire nation would benefit. In this respect, it was suggested that their full participation in productive employment and economic growth should be promoted. Discussions also focused on the need to review the present practice of mandatory retirement and the provision of new jobs and retraining assistance to the elderly (UNCSDHA, 1988).

Conclusion

One of the paradoxes of the process of socio-economic development of the twentieth century is that

> as advances in medical science and technology have made it possible to prolong life, although at exorbitant costs, the provision of these resources remains a major social issue both for individual families and society at large (Chow, 1987).

If governments look at the growing proportions of the elderly within their populations from the point of view of the welfare state ideology, then the situation will become more complex for the state itself and unbearable for the elderly who, in turn, will only be looked upon as a tolerated burden. Every society is faced with a challenging situation. On the one hand, population ageing is a phenomenon which has come to stay and which will become more felt and acute with the passage of time. Its repercussions are so wide-ranging and manifold that they can only be ignored at a tremendous cost to society at large. On the other hand, to speak of an unchanging family support system is a myth.

A solution could only be found through a radical transformation. We must go from the welfare state model of social policy to the caring society model. In this model, social institutions, governmental and otherwise, along with family members, and last but not least, the elderly themselves, have an important role to play. People must show that they actually care by providing the spaces and opportunities for dignifying participation.

The participation of the elderly within society necessarily and basically implies their actual involvement within their family and community. Consequently, all matters concerning the elderly are not to be conceived of in isolation but in the wider context of a family-centred social policy. Social services for the elderly ought to be perceived and planned as networks in which the elderly themselves, their families, the community and the general public are constantly interacting. The elderly must be made aware that, as an intrinsic part of every society, they have rights and duties to uphold and exercise. Rights include those of living independently and of dying with dignity. Duties include the preparation to remain active in their society, to share their wisdom and experience, and to adapt responsibly and courageously to social change.

References

Busuttil, S.(1971) *The Aged in Urbanizing Societies*, Malta.
Central Office of Statistics (1986) *Malta Census 1985: Vol.1, A Demographic Profile of Malta and Gozo*, Malta, Government Press.
Central Office of Statistics (1991) *Demographic Review of the Maltese Islands 1990*, Malta, Government Press.
Chow, W.S. (1987) 'The urban elderly in developing East and Southeast Asian countries', in Schulz, J. & Davis-Friedman, D. (eds), *Aging China: Family, Economies and Government Policies in Transition*, Washington, D.C.
Nationalist Party (NP) (1987) *Xogħol, Ġustizzja, Libertà: Is-Sisien tal-Ġejjieni*, Malta, Progress Press.
Shanas, E. (1979) 'The family as a social support system in old age', *The Gerontologist*, vol. 19, 2.
Social Action Movement (SAM) (1982) *A Study on the Aged*, Malta, Centre for Social Research, Social Action Movement.
Troisi, J. (1988) *Organisations of Comprehensive Services for the Elderly in the Community in Malta*, Copenhagen, World Health Organisation.
Troisi, J. (1989) *The Place of the Elderly in the Changing Traditional Role of the Family*, European Federation for the Welfare of the Elderly (EURAG), Padova, Italy, September.
Troisi, J. (1991) *The Role of the Family as Care-giver to the Frail Elderly in Belgium, France, Germany, Greece, Malta and the United Kingdom*, Steering Committee on Social Policy, Council of Europe, Strasburg, June.
United Nations (1984) Department of International Economic and Social Affairs, *Periodical on Ageing*, New York, United Nations.
United Nations (UN) (1983), *Vienna International Plan of Action on Ageing*, New York, United Nations.
United Nations Centre for Social Development and Humanitarian Affairs (UNCSDHA) (1988) *Policies and Strategies for Participation of the Elderly in Development*, Malta.

United Nations Economic Commission for Europe & the United Nations Population Fund (1993) *Demographic Causes and Economic Consequences of Population Ageing*, Geneva, United Nations.

United Nations Statistical Office (UNSO) (1988) *World Demographic Estimates and Projections: 1950-2025*, New York, United Nations.

World Health Organization (WHO) (1984) *The Uses of Epidemiology in the Study of the Elderly*, Technical Report Series, No. 706.

35

Drug Abuse Among School Children

Anthony M. Abela

Over the past few years there has been a growing concern with drug abuse in Malta. The successive European Values surveys, held in Malta first in the mid-eighties and later in the early nineties give witness to an increase in public awareness against the abuse of drugs (Abela, 1991, p. 312).

The few Maltese respondents who in the eighties did not think of drugs as a very serious matter (19%) have dropped to a bare minimum (2%) in the nineties. In recent years, the vast majority think that illegal drug taking has become a very serious (71%) or quite a serious (23%) problem. There is an ever growing consensus that the abuse of drugs has become just as serious as in other European countries. Concomitant to this concern is a growing tendency among the Maltese to become less tolerant of drug abuse. In fact, the percentage of Maltese respondents who would never justify the use of 'marijuana' or 'hashish' has risen from a high of 90% in the eighties to 97% in the nineties. Again, 66% of Maltese respondents in the Values study of the nineties, contended that they would not like to have drug addicts as their neighbours (See Table 1).

Table 1. Opinion on seriousness of drug abuse.

"Do you think drug taking is a serious problem?"	EUROPE '81	MALTA '83 '91
Illicit drug taking	%	%
very serious	68	43 71
quite serious	24	32 23
not very serious	5	18 1
not at all serious	1	1 1
don't know	2	6 4
Use of marijuana is never justified*	80	90 97
Do not want drug addicts as neighbours	NA	NA 66

SOURCE: EVSSG, 1981-91.

* Percent who situate themselves on the extreme end '1' on a 10-point justification scale where '1' = 'use of marijuana is never justified' and '10' = 'always justified, NA = Not Asked.

Recent studies on youth give evidence to a relatively widespread consumption of alcohol and a certain facility for them to find drugs in places of entertainment. Three out of every ten Maltese youths were reported to be convinced that young people get drunk (30%) and that drug-pushing is a normal practice (26%) in discotheques. Quite a few also agree (29%) or are not so sure (37%) that tourism is chiefly responsible for the spread of drugs on the island (Abela, 1992, pp. 25, 69-70). Undoubtedly, drugs are not uncommon in contemporary youth culture. One cannot deny that youths are aware of the use of drugs, even though they may not know their extensive availability and abuse. It seems that youths are exposed to drugs in their places of entertainment and through their contacts with foreigners.

In order to assess the extent of drug abuse amongst Maltese youth, Caritas, a national voluntary organization, launched a survey in all secondary and post-secondary schools in Malta. Caritas set two main objectives for its project. First, it sought to investigate scientifically the validity of the data coming from its Rehabilitation

Programme, namely that 62% of ex-drug users had abused of drugs as from the age of 10 to the age of 15. Second, it sought to evaluate the effectiveness of its prevention programme.[1]

A Maltese National Survey of the total population of school-age youths (11-17 years old) was conducted for Caritas (Malta) by PRIDE, an international organization devoted to the prevention of drug abuse through education. The survey was held on 29 November 1991 with 20,815 students from Malta and Gozo completing the set questionnaire. PRIDE was assisted by local agents who helped set the questions in Maltese and to administer a standard questionnaire in the local schools. All completed questionnaires were shipped to Atlanta in the USA where they were computer processed between December 1991 and February 1992. Separate files with tabulated results for all Secondary and Sixth Form schools were produced by PRIDE and sent to Caritas in February 1992.[2]

In this paper we shall first describe the characteristics of our young respondents and report on their claimed use of cigarettes, alcohol and drugs. We shall then examine the social environment and the intoxication effects of drug abuse. Finally we evaluate the results and suggest policies for the prevention of drug abuse amongst school-age adolescents in Malta.

Characteristics of Respondents

Of the 20,815 secondary and post-secondary school students who responded the Caritas/PRIDE 1991 questionnaire, 14,522 attended 58 state schools in Malta, 1,248 came from 12 state schools in Gozo and 5,045 from 24 private schools in Malta and Gozo. At the time of the survey 76% of our respondents (11-17 years old)

---

[1] In a letter dated February 12, 1992, Mgr. Victor Grech, Director of Caritas, requested from the author: (1) a general sociological analysis of the present situation of student drug abuse in Malta as apparent in the Caritas/PRIDE 1991 Schools Survey; (2) to indicate the areas and persons most at risk; and (3) to offer guidance in planning a Prevention Programme to enable Caritas to reach these people in the most effective way possible.

[2] The final report was prepared by The Institute for Research on the Signs of the Times (Discern, 1993).

were attending a state secondary or post-secondary level school in Malta (70%) and Gozo (6%) whereas 24% were in other private secondary or sixth form schools. 53% were boys and 47% girls.

The vast majority of our respondents live in families where their fathers work for a living (95.4%) and their mothers look after the family (76%). Quite a few have mothers who work full-time (17.6%) or part-time (6.7%) outside the home. Most Maltese students (95.2%) come from families where the parents live together. A few have a deceased father (1.8%) or mother (0.7%). Very few have parents who live apart (2.3%). A considerable number have brothers and sisters: most have one (43%) or two (32.3%), others have three (14%), four (6.2%) or even more (4.6%). Overall many think that their parents are very (28%) or quite (37%) strict with them. Parents are seen to be stricter by the younger (36%) than by the older students (17%).

Generally the fathers of our respondents were found to possess higher levels of education than their mothers. Whereas 13% and 16% of all male parents received a training in skills or a higher education, only 3% and 9% of their mothers received an equivalent education, respectively.

Until the age of 15 the sexes are equally represented in secondary schools. A gender imbalance is noticed, however, for students pursuing post-secondary education. 59% of our 16 year-old respondents are male and 41% are female. This gender difference is further widened for the 17 year-olds, where 68% are males and 32% females.

On the whole, Maltese adolescents are happy (77%), go to Church regularly (74.6%) and to a lower extent practise some kind of sport (47.5%). Most never feel lonely (67%). Quite a few (30.4%) often go to parties or to discos. In particular, 47% of all post-secondary 17 year-old Maltese youths go to discos often or very often. In this age group only 5% never go to discos, 18% go rarely and 28% go occasionally. Others, especially those from the upper forms, often go out with a friend of the opposite sex (34%). Several others invite friends at home (56%). Quite a few of the older students often drive a car (22%) whereas others get a ride with their friends (25%). Very few often have trouble at school (6%) whereas many get good grades at school (43%).

When in trouble most students talk about their problems mainly with their mothers (62.4%), a few others with their fathers (33.1%), but a considerable number also do so with their friends (39.8%), a brother or a sister (20.3%), their boy- or girl-friend (17.1%) while others turn to a priest, a nun (13.1%) or a teacher (12.3%). Quite a few do not confide in anyone (11.2%).

Whereas our youngest respondents open up with their parents (70% with their mother, 42% with their father), older youths prefer to talk with their friends (52%) or a partner of the opposite sex (32%).

Cigarettes and Alcohol

In the space of a year, three out of every ten of our respondents smoked cigarettes at least once. 17% smoked less than once a week, 9% once a week or more often and 5% smoked everyday. Cigarette smoking is differentiated by sex and increases with age. Young men (38%) smoke more than women (28%). Whereas only 14% of 12 year-olds claim to have smoked at least once in the span of a year, the figure rises to 42% for 17 year-olds. Adolescents enjoy smoking with friends (25%), during the weekend (23%) but a few also do so at school (3%) before (4%) or after (7%) school hours.

There is widespread consumption of beer and wine but less of alcohol. 80% of our respondents drink beer, 75% drink wine and 44% drink whisky or alcohol. Beer and wine are very popular among young people in Malta. Adolescents mostly drink beer (59%) or wine (64%) at home possibly at table or to socialize in the family. But they also drink beer or its milder substitute 'shandy' during the weekend in the company of their friends (40%). Similar patterns are observed for the consumption of whisky by youths at home (29%) and with their friends (19%) (See Table 2).

Despite the apparent high consumption of beer and wine by Maltese youths, Adams & Gleaton (1992) observed no alarming high level of intoxication under the influence of these substances. They remarked that Maltese youths have either developed a tolerance for beer and wine or else drink it in low quantities. In contrast, some 30% reported reaching high or moderate levels of intoxication when they drink whisky – this is over twice the rate for wine and three times the rate for beer.

Table 2. Substance use by Maltese adolescents (11-17 years old) in percentages.

Total Use*		At Home	At School	During Weekend	With Friends	Friends Take	Easy To Find
%		%	%	%	%	%	%
31	Cigarettes	12	4.4	23	25	60	65
80	Beer/Shandy	59	1.0	58	40	88	81
75	Wine	64	0.5	47	17	78	77
44	Whisky/alcohol	29	0.3	29	19	57	61

Sorce: PRIDE/CARITAS Malta Schools Drugs Survey 1991. * = at least once over past year.

Apparently, as there are no enforced restrictions prohibiting the sale of cigarettes and alcohol to minors in Malta, most of our respondents (75%) find no difficulty in obtaining any of these substances. The high use of these substances reflects their availability. There appears to be a need for an education for the prevention of the early use of these substances and possibly also an enforcement of legal restrictions in the sale of cigarettes and alcohol to minors. Such efforts may need to be targeted to adults, parents, educators, shop owners, community or church leaders as well as to students.

Frequency of Drug Use

Two percent of all Maltese students between 11 and 17 years of age (Forms II-VI) who have responded the Caritas/PRIDE 1991 questionnaire have used drugs at least once during the year.

Marijuana or *ħaxixa* and downers or *kalmanti* are the most common drugs used by adolescents in Malta. Slightly more than two percent of our respondents claimed to have smoked *ħaxixa* (2.1%) or taken *kalmanti* (2.5%) at some point in their life. Less have ever taken cocaine (1.6%), steroids (0.9%), uppers or *stimulanti*

(1.0%), L.S.D. (0.5%), heroin (0.4%), or other drugs (1.5%)[3] (See Table 3).

Table 3. Substance use by school-age adolescents (11-17 year-olds) in Malta.

Type of substance:	Used at least once			
	in your life		over past year	
	N	%	N	%
Cigarettes	6634	33.8	6051	30.9
Beer/shandy	15651	80.8	15337	79.8
Wine	14418	75.6	14120	74.6
Whisky/alcohol	8436	44.9	8337	43.7
Marijuana	406	2.1	364	1.9
Downers/*kalmanti*	478	2.5	358	1.9
Uppers/*stimulanti*	181	1.0	161	0.9
Heroin	75	0.4	74	0.4
L.S.D.	90	0.5	71	0.4
Steroids	158	0.9	139	0.8
Cocaine/'coke'	256	1.4	238	1.3
Other drugs	281	1.5	241	1.3

N = Number of responses, missing cases not included. Total number of respondents = 20,815.

Not all students who have ever tasted drugs continue to do so on a regular basis. Fewer adolescents who have taken some type of drug in the past were found to have done so during the year when the survey was held.

When asked about the frequency of drug use over the past year very few of our respondents claimed to have smoked *ħaxixa*

---

[3] Marijuana is a drug made from the plant *Cannabis Sativa* and is either smoked or absorbed through the lungs. Heroin is a highly addictive white crystalline drug derived from morphine often used as a narcotic. Lysergic acid diethylamide (L.S.D.) is a powerful hallucinogenic drug. It is a synthetic white powder and is taken orally or absorbed through the skin. Steroids are organic compounds containing hormones, alkaloids and vitamins. Cocaine is a drug derived from coca or prepared synthetically. It is used as a stimulant.

every day (0.1%), more than once a week (0.2%) or more than once a month (0.3%). Over the twelve months preceding the questionnaire's administration, some had smoked once a month (0.2%), once every two months (0.3%) or just once (0.8%).

Choice of Drugs

Use of *ħaxixa* is mostly popular among 17 year old male students (7.5%) in contrast to their female peers (3.4%) and 11-13 year old students (1.0%). The PRIDE interim report observes a trend towards an increase in the smoking of *ħaxixa* by older girls. This accounts only for those girls presently attending Sixth Form schools.

Kalmanti or downers are used more by adolescent girls (4%) than boys (3.2%). The use of these mild drugs merits further investigation.

Stimulanti or uppers are mostly used by older boys. In this case Maltese youths differ from those of other countries where uppers are generally used by girls for dieting purposes.

Extremely little use is made of heroin and L.S.D. where the total consumption is less than 0.6%.

Quite a few young men (16 year-olds) use steroids (2.4%), possibly for body-building or to enhance their performance in sports. This suggests the need for a targeted education about the harmful effects of these dangerous drugs.

Results on the use of cocaine (also referred to as 'coke' in the questionnaire) have to be interpreted very cautiously as local agents have informed us that some respondents, the younger ones in particular, have confused 'coke' with a popular drink.

The few of our respondents who take drugs often do so in the company of their friends, away from the school buildings and during the weekend. Only the consumption of *kalmanti* is an exception. Post-secondary school students have become accustomed to taking *kalmanti* at home, possibly to counter the stress from conflicting demands in modern Maltese society.

Social Environment

Greatest Incidence of Drugs

The greatest incidence of drug use was found amongst older students from post-secondary schools. Over the year, 17 year-old students claimed to have taken the following drugs at least once:

6.2% ħaxixa, 3.1% kalmanti, 2% stimulanti, 0.4% heroin, 0.4% L.S.D., 0.4% steroids, 1.3% cocaine, 1.7% other drugs.

First Use

Most of our post-secondary respondents who take *kalmanti* claim to have started this practice at the age of 14 (2%) whereas most of those who take *ħaxixa* largely began to do so at the age of 16 or older (5.8%). Abuse of other hard drugs generally takes place at the age of 16 or later: Our 17 year old respondents who take drugs report having been initiated at 16 years or older to take heroin (0.4%), L.S.D. (1.1%), steroids (1.3%), cocaine (0.7%) or other drugs (1.7%). This does not exclude that a few others have been initiated into drugs at an earlier age.

Early initiation to *ħaxixa* was reported to be higher in private than in state schools. Students who smoked *ħaxixa* at least once were found to be more in private schools (12%) than in state schools in Malta (8%) or Gozo (6%). However not all students who ever tasted *ħaxixa* or any other drug continue to do so. (See Table 4).

Table 4. How old were you when you smoked *ħaxixa* for the first time?

| All schools | *first time smoked ħaxixa* | | | |
	Never	11-15	16+	N
11-17 year-olds	97.9	1.4	0.6	19,323
15 year-olds	97.9	2.1	DNA	3,547
17 year-olds	91.6	2.7	8.8	1,449
17 year-olds in				
Gozo State Schools	93.9	0.0	6.1	66
Malta State Schools	91.8	2.9	5.6	1,200
All Private Schools	88.0	3.8	8.2	158

Source: PRIDE/CARITAS Malta Schools Drugs Survey 1991.
DNA = Does not apply; N = Number of valid cases.

Drug Use in Schools

Very few students claim to consume drugs during school hours. In the 17 year-old category, where drug use is at its highest, very few report having ever smoked *ħaxixa* (0.3%), or taken kalmanti (0.3%), *stimulanti* (0.1%), heroin (0.1%), steroids (0.1%), L.S.D. (0.3%) or other drugs (0.2%) at school.

Drug Use Out of Schools

The greatest consumption of drugs takes place outside school buildings mostly during the weekend and in the company of friends. In the 17 year old category only *kalmanti* (2.8%) and, to a lower extent, steroids (0.7%) have a high incidence in the home. *Haxixa* is smoked during the weekend (3.9%) and with friends (6.3%) but not so much at home (0.5%) or at school (0.3%). *Kalmanti* are also taken during the weekend (0.8%) and with friends (0.8%). Similarly, *stimulanti* are consumed during the weekend (0.9%), in the company of friends (1.4%) and to a lesser extent at home (0.5%) but few do so at school (0.1%). The few 17-year-old students who consume heroin claim to do so equally at home (0.1%), during the weekend (0.1%), with friends (0.1%) and at school (0.1%). L.S.D. seems to have greater incidence during the weekend (0.3%) in the company of friends (0.5%) and at school (0.3%) but not as much at home (0.1%) (See Table 5).

Table 5. Drug Consumption Patterns by 17-year old students

TOTAL USE* %		At home %	At school %	During Weekend %	With Friends %	Friends take %	Easy to find %
6.3	Haxixa	0.5	0.3	3.9	6.3	8.7	24.6
3.1	Kalmanti	2.8	0.3	0.8	0.8	10.2	30.9
2.0	Stimulanti	0.5	0.1	0.9	1.4	9.0	21.4
0.4	Heroin	0.1	0.1	0.1	0.1	6.1	8.9
0.4	L.S.D.	0.1	0.3	0.3	0.5	8.1	6.3
0.4	Steroids	0.7	0.1	0.1	0.4	8.1	15.9
1.3	Cocaine	0.5	0.5	0.7	1.0	6.1	10.1
1.7	Other drugs	0.7	0.2	1.0	1.0	10.2	11.8

Source: PRIDE/CARITAS Malta Schools Drugs Survey 1991; * = at least once over preceding year.

Drug-free Schools

There are 23 drug-free secondary level schools (out of a total of 96) in Malta and Gozo, that is 24% of all schools represented in the Caritas/PRIDE 1991 survey. Only 21% of secondary-level schools in Malta are completely drug-free. In Gozo, a number of schools were found to be exceptionally clean of drugs: 6 out of 12 schools, that is 50% of secondary schools in Gozo are drug-free[4] (See Table 6).

Table 6. Distribution of Drugs in Schools

Type of drug	Private Schools Malta and Gozo %	State Schools Malta %	State Schools Gozo %	All Drug Free %	All Non-Drug Free %
Ħaxixa	21	23	55	26	74
Kalmanti	21	19	45	23	77
Stimulanti	42	39	55	41	59
Heroin	71	56	82	63	37
L.S.D.	63	56	73	60	40
Steroids	42	46	63	47	53
Cocaine/'coke'	17	26	36	25	75
Other drugs	29	30	54	33	67

Influence of Friends

Almost ten percent of our respondents (9.7%) claim to have friends who take drugs. Very few have all (0.6%) or most (1.3%) of their friends abusing with drugs. In their greatest majority,

---

[4] Here a drug-free school refers to a situation where no student claimed to have used drugs over the span of the year preceding the administration of the survey questionnaire.

Maltese youths (91.3%) mix with peers who are drug-free, but it is not completely excluded that some come into contact with youths who take drugs.

Influence of Parents

One in ten of our respondents have one or both parents who take *kalmanti* or *stimulanti*, but extremely few have parents who smoke *ħaxixa* (0.7%) or take any other drug like heroin or L.S.D. (0.2%).

Availability of Drugs

A considerable number of our post-secondary respondents think that it is quite easy to find *kalmanti* (31%),[5] *ħaxixa* (25%) and *stimulanti* (21%). Less available are steroids (16%), cocaine (10%), heroin (9%) and L.S.D. (6%).

Consciousness Against Drugs

There is a widespread consciousness amongst Maltese youths against the abuse of drugs. Amongst those who frequently speak to them on the bad effects of drugs, our respondents mention their parents (56.4%), teachers (41.3%) and to a lesser extent their friends (19.8%). Very few parents (7.2%), teachers (9.5%) or friends (24.2%) never talk to them about the bad effects of drugs.

Intoxication Effects

More than half (52.4%) of those who use *ħaxixa* or *kalmanti* (50%) report experiences of intoxication by the drug. Males and the oldest students report higher levels of intoxication than women and younger adolescents.

As the number of Maltese students claiming to use illicit drugs is extremely small, the results from the survey on drug intoxication are very unstable and inconclusive. Further analysis needs to be carried out on specific target groups which are found to be highly dependent on drugs.

---

[5] In 1991 Malta imported more than nine and a half (9.57) million pills of different types and doses of tranquillizers (Statistics obtained from the Dept of Health).

Evaluation and Policy

The Caritas/PRIDE survey has the quality of a micro-census of all secondary and post-secondary schools in Malta and Gozo. It provides a global picture of the availability and use of harmful substances by the present generation of school-age adolescents in Malta and Gozo. It furnishes a base-line for researchers to monitor future changes in drug use, thus enabling reliable comparisons between schools, social groups, regions, societies and countries over time. The near census quality of the results are of particular relevance to educational policy makers as they provide accurate information about the distribution of students, their social characteristics, their exposure and consumption of harmful substances.

Unavoidably, a survey of this kind has its shortcomings. The nature of a self-administered questionnaire and the conditions under which it was carried out call for caution in the interpretation of results and generalizations made regarding them. As the survey is representative of adolescents attending school on a particular day, the results do not account for youths in the work force, the unemployed, school dropouts, or those who were absent because of sickness or other reasons on the day of the survey.[6]

Apart from this, given the conditions and the nature of a captive audience within school classrooms, some students might have felt threatened and afraid to reveal their actual use of drugs. Again, the survey relied on the truthfulness of the students and some questions might have been deliberately left unanswered or completely falsified. Although the considerable number of no answers (missing values were a high of 10% in Malta compared to 3.5% for an equivalent national survey administered in the USA by PRIDE in 1989-90) could easily be explained by the unfamiliarity of the Maltese with multiple choice computer-processed questions, it might well be the case that some students simply refused to answer specific questions on the use of drugs.

---

[6] Absenteeism, truancy and early school-leaving is highest in trade-schools. In 1988, the Guidance and Counselling Services of the Department of Education estimated an absentee rate of 33% for girls and 24% for boys in trade-schools (Sultana, 1992, p. 358).

Substance Abuse in Malta

The main findings from the Caritas/PRIDE 1991 schools survey posit the use and availability of cigarettes and alcohol as the greatest health problem among Maltese students. Education regarding the harmful effects of cigarettes and alcohol amongst children and young adolescents needs to be made available to concerned adults and students.

Drug abuse was not reported by a large percentage of Maltese youth. The results from the survey led PRIDE researchers to observe that in Malta, 'relatively few students report use of illicit drugs, and illicit drugs are not yet widespread amongst Maltese students' (Adams & Gleaton, 1992, p. 10). The greatest abuse of drugs by school-age Maltese youths takes place during the weekend in the company of their friends and away from school and the family.

There is evidence that some Maltese youths, older male

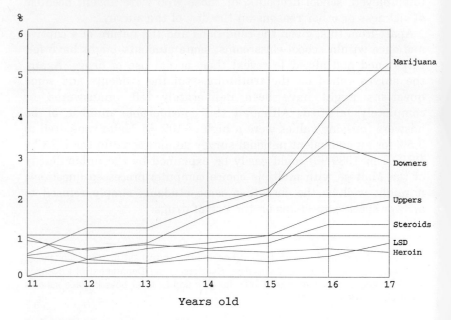

Figure 1. Drug use over past year & age for total school population in Malta.

Caritas/Pride Schools Survey 1991

students in particular, are experimenting with illicit drugs. There is also evidence that *haxixa, stimulanti* and *kalmanti* are available to one-fifth of the students over 15 years of age. In particular, a considerable number of school-age youths have no difficulty in finding downers or *kalmanti* (30.9%) and unlike other drugs, they make use of them at home (2.8%). More than a few Maltese adolescents also think that hard drugs like cocaine, heroin, and L.S.D. are easy to find. The prevalence of these drugs poses a real danger of escalation (See Figure 1). At this critical stage efforts should be addressed to prevent the spread of harmful drugs.

From the survey it emerges that initiation into drugs tends to take place in the final years of secondary schooling or even later at the time of post-secondary education. There is no evidence to support the view that most secondary school students are exposed to drugs at an early age. Nor is there sufficient evidence to support the view that students from upper forms in secondary or post-secondary schools who are presently familiar with drugs had their first experience of drugs at a much earlier age.

Such findings do not exclude the possibility as affirmed in our hypothesis that the relatively few drug addicts who over the past few years went through Caritas' Rehabilitation Programme had actually abused of drugs at an early age. Possibly, people who are initiated into drugs early in life are the ones most likely to develop a dependence on these harmful substances. In this respect, the drug problem would best be addressed right from its infancy with a strategy for the prevention of drug abuse through education.

Particular attention needs to be given to the dissemination of information in schools, families and local communities about the harmful effects of cigarettes, alcohol and drugs. It is suggested that Caritas strengthens its programmes for the prevention of drug abuse, and possibly also extend them to other addictive substances that were found to be readily accessible and a cause of intoxication for adolescents in Malta.

References

Abela, A.M. (1991) *Transmitting Values in European Malta: A Study in the Contemporary Values of Modern Society*, Malta, Jesuit Publications & Rome, Editrice Pontificia Università Gregoriana.

Abela, A.M. (1992) *Changing Youth Culture in Malta,* Malta, Social Values Studies, Jesuit Publications & Diocesan Youth Commission.

Adams, R.D. & Gleaton, T. (1992) *1991 Maltese Survey of Adolescent Drug Use: An interim report submitted to the Director of Caritas Malta,* Atlanta, PRIDE.

DISCERN (1993) *Adolescent Drug Use in Malta: A Survey Conducted by Caritas Malta in November 1990 with the Technical Assistance of PRIDE International, Report Prepared by the Institute for Research on the Signs of the Times,* Caritas, Malta.

EVSSG (European Values Survey Study Group) (1981) *Values Study European Countries Tabulations,* London, Social Surveys, (Gallup Poll) Ltd.

EVSSG (European Values Survey Study Group) (1991) *1990 Values Survey Tabulated Results,* London, Social Surveys (Gallup Poll) Ltd.

Sultana, R.G. (1992) *Education and National Development: Historical and Critical Perspectives on Vocational Schooling in Malta,* Malta, Mireva Publications.

36

Land Use:
An Account of Environmental Stewardship

Edward A. Mallia

Introduction

In the year of grace 1993 'the environment' has become a fact of social and political life in the Maltese islands. This situation has come about through a combination of strangely diverse factors, perhaps a combination unique to these islands. It all started when we raised our small voice in international bodies on what have come to be seen as environmental issues, starting with the proposal, in 1967, which led to the adoption of the Convention of the Law of the Sea by the UN in 1981. The motives may have been mixed and the results may have left much to be desired, but there can be little doubt that we had opened a window on to an area of social experience that was new to us.

Our attempts to lecture the world on environmental issues could not fail to generate domestic interest. The more so as our development of an international dimension, soon after attaining political independence from Britain, coincided with the emergence of obvious tensions between the demands of economic and social development and the limited resources of these islands. But contrary to what one might expect, this interest was not exactly encouraged by governments. Consciously or otherwise, part of the platform for our launching of global themes had been built on the thesis that our impact on the global environment was insignificant. This would be true of course only if we failed to remember that we had a duty to our own people. Close looks at our own house were therefore not encouraged; they could tarnish our international reputation.

But one result of such a close look may have taken us all by surprise. Even if rather ancient and ramshackle, there already existed a legal framework, dealing with 'environmental' matters, even though the environment had not visibly been on the social or political agenda when the various pieces had been put into place. That pleasant surprise was followed by a rude shock: whatever regulation or legislation existed was largely being observed in the breach, even by government. As a result of this, the proper development of environmental sensitivity in these islands has, until recently, depended much more on the activities of non-governmental organizations (NGOs) than on official activity.

What follows represents a look at the various strands that have gone into the making of the present situation, characterized by the concurrent emergence of environmental and ecological sensitivity on the one side and extensive destruction of the natural and built environment on the other. Population growth and economic development after 1945 are set in the legal, social and political framework, in an effort to trace the emergence of environmental issues onto the social and political scene. In conclusion, an attempt is made to determine whether or not these new sensitivities and the legal weapons that we have created can persuade us into forms of social action which go against our individualist grain. The choice lies between swimming together or sinking together.

Human Settlement and Population

A useful outline of the geography, geology and climate of the Maltese Islands has been given by Schembri & Lanfranco (1993) and Chetcuti et al. (1992)

There is no basis for any credible local estimates of population levels until the flood-tide of temple building (3500 BC – 2200 BC) some 1,500 years after the first arrivals to the Maltese Islands of neolithic people moving south from Sicily. (Renfrew, 1979, p.166) Considering the locations of temples and the work involved – work with essentially the same stone tools brought over from Sicily – Renfrew (1979) suggests a population of around 10,000 for Malta and Gozo. These would have had to be producing enough to feed themselves and to have a labour surplus which was engaged in temple building. With stories of Mġarr (Malta) church being built from the proceeds of sale of donated agricultural produce, within sight of two major Neolithic temples, one might have here a truly remarkable continuity of outlook.

The raising of a local militia (Wettinger, 1969) as some defence against incursions by corsairs, the necessity of importing subsidized grain from Sicily and, after 1563, the instruction of the Council of Trent to parish priests to keep a register of births, deaths and marriages, provide the elements of moderately reliable population estimates from the 15th century onwards (Central Office of Statistics, 1986). Jean Quintin d'Autun, (Vella, 1980), writing in 1536, reckoned the population as above 20,000, 'most of them...living beyond their 80th year'. Around 1635 the population had reached 50,000 and in 1798 the invading French estimated 114,000, a value close to that (114,500) found in the first official census carried out by the British government in 1842. This was the first in the regular series of decennial censuses which, with the two exceptions of 1941 and 1977, have been carried out since then.

This long series of censuses gives a detailed picture of population movements as well as hints of social conditions (Central Office of Statistics, 1986). Projections based on the population in mid-1955 (299,000) – with the then-current birth, death and marriage rates, with six children per marriage and no emigration – had concluded that the population would reach 469,000 by mid-1975!

Two factors intervened to upset that prediction: a marked decline in fertility consequent on changing social and religious attitudes to childbearing, and heavy emigration. The three decades after the end of the Second World War were marked by a huge migration principally to Australia but also to Canada and the UK. A Government scheme to subsidise travel costs for emigrants, introduced in 1948, proved to be the trigger. In the period 1946-1974 over 130,000 people emigrated; fewer than 5,000 returned. The peak years were 1953-4 (11,500), 1963-4 (8,500) and 1972-3 (4,000). Then, starting in 1974-5, the return current became significantly stronger than the outgoing one, although by then both were at a much lower level than the previous outflow. Parallel with this movement, in which persons of childbearing age would have predominated, there was a halving of the birth rate between 1950 and 1970. At some 1.5%, it is now at the lower end of the European range.

The combined effects of migration and declining birth rate were seen in the 1967 census which registered a drop in population from the 1957 values for both Malta and Gozo. The population appears to have peaked in 1962 at close to 333,000, dipped to 303,000 in 1967 and then resumed a slow rise after 1975. The 1985 census (1977 was missed out) found 345,000 inhabitants, including some 5,000 non-Maltese residents. Projections for future growth give 370,500 by the year 2000 and predict a levelling off at around 402,000 by the middle of the next century. A population density of 1,270 per square kilometre, compared to the present 1,095 per square kilometre, would seem to be unsustainable at present rates of consumption of resources.

Social Developments and Land Use

Together with population growth, social and economic developments condition the demands on the resources of the ecosystem. An improving basic quality of life for a generation which started off in very restricted circumstances after the 2nd World War, was bound to increase pressure on local resources; it was also likely to be accompanied by a bow-wave of rapidly rising expectations, which could well be beyond the capacity of the ecosystem to satisfy in a sustainable manner.

In 1948, the proportion of houses that were owner-occupied was just under 30%. Most families (71%) occupied rented housing and most people starting families expected to find rented accommodation. Annual rents were and still are strictly controlled. Even in 1990, most were less than three to four weeks' (minimum) wages (Zammit, 1990).

The punitive rent laws[1] persuaded landlords to leave older housing stock vacant. The housing survey conducted with the 1985 census found around 20% of all dwellings vacant. Admittedly this figure cannot be taken simply at face value. For instance, tourist accommodation which happened to be unoccupied at census time, may well have contributed significantly to the figure. Another reason for unoccupied premises lay in the fact that some 6% of families (4,500) were found to possess a summer house – this on an island where the sea is less than a 30 minute drive from anywhere. Much of the current building activity on Gozo is that of turning out holiday flats aimed at this internal tourist market; while veritable shanty towns of summer 'residences', abusively built on public land, have mushroomed in a number of bays.

All in all, about a quarter of all vacant dwellings are probably available for occupation. But unfortunately new householders cannot rent such property. Among the 5,500 vacant properties examined by the Housing Stock Survey in 1990, not one was available for renting by Maltese citizens. Nor, it must be said, are such people inclined to purchase, as the quality of such housing is generally below present expectations. Owners wanting to obtain a decent return from such property prefer to demolish it and re-develop the site. The built environment in historic town and village cores is suffering major degradation as a result (Zammit, 1990).

The supply of social housing did not keep up with demand in quantity and, equally significant, in perceived quality. The virtual disappearance of the private renting market has led to a large increase in owner-occupiers – from 28% in 1948 to 60% of all householders on Malta and Gozo in 1990. Indeed, for the past 15 years, most new householders have had to go in for the heavy capital investment involved in buying or building a house. The

---

[1] Ordinance XVI 1944 Rent Restriction (Dwelling Houses); Housing Act: Act II (1949).

financial burden has been mitigated by the provision of building plots by government and Church at subsidized prices and by low interest loans from the one local building society, but aggravated by a socially emulative approach to house size – the typical dwelling has become the three-bedroomed terrace house – and to house furnishing. Of the two paradigms of the late 1960s – the 'housing estate' with its blocks of flats and small terraced houses (Santa Lucia and San Ġwann), and the 'garden cities' of Misraħ Kola and Santa Marija Estate – the latter has proved to be much more socially influential.

The interaction of population with number of households and settlement area between 1957 and 1985 for Malta are shown in Figure 1. The number of households increased by 40% for a 10% increase in population, reflecting a distinct break from the extended family situations prevalent in the 1930s. The number of dwellings increased by 60%, but the settlement area shot up four times as rapidly – by 254%. This suggests a significant increase in the area taken up by each dwelling place. In fact it has been established that we have the largest room volume per person in Europe.

The absolute values paint an even more alarming picture. The built up area on Malta has gone from 11 square kilometre in 1957 (4.5% of the total land area) to 44 square kilometre (18%) in 1990, with another 5 square kilometre (2%) covered by roads, which have expanded from 900 kilometre to 1,500 kilometre in length over the same period. On Gozo, some 3.4 square kilometre (5%) in 1957 have expanded to 5.4 square kilometre (8%), and this against a backdrop of a declining population.

This inflation of settlement area has been accompanied by a precipitous decline in land under agriculture: from 185 square kilometre (55%) in 1960 to below 110 square kilometre (35%) in 1990. This decline has come about not just through urban sprawl and road building (190,000 registered vehicles at end 1992), but also through ribbon development (that is the siting of commercial premises along road arteries) and increases in tourist accommodation – particularly the swing towards the mass market (just over 1 million arrivals in 1992 and 1993).

The latter has led to the wholesale development of the Qawra-Buġibba peninsula, Xemxija, Marsascala and Marsalforn and Xlendi on Gozo. Major infrastructural works like the extension of

Figure 1. Development of Settlement Area, Number of Dwellings, Number of Households

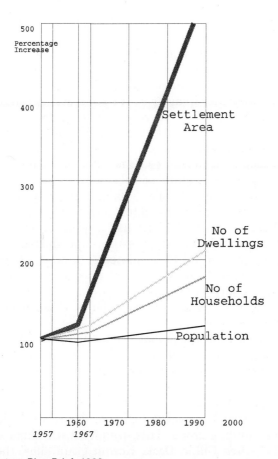

Source: Structure Plan Brief, 1989.

airport runway and the provision of a new terminal building have consumed their fair share of arable land, as have the industrial estates at Marsa, Bulebel (Żabbar), Corradino, Ricasoli, Ħal Far, San Ġwann and Xewkija (Gozo). The expansion of the three official landfills, all of it at the expense of agricultural land, has also been accompanied by indiscriminate dumping in the countryside. Significant areas of low quality arable land have been taken over by bird-trappers.

While arable land has had to satisfy the major share of the insatiable demand for building land, other types of land, of greater ecological and amenity value have not escaped lightly. Development on karst land has occurred at il-Qortin and on other parts of the Mellieħa ridge, at the back of Mellieħa Bay (the Danish holiday village), and around Dingli, Imtaħleb and Baħrija villages. Accessible coast has also suffered severely. On Malta over a third of the coastal zone is dominated by tourist activity, and a further quarter by a combination of industrial and maritime activities. The corresponding figures for Gozo and Comino are 20% and 10% (Anderson & Schembri, 1989).

The inaccessibility of most of the Gozo coastal zone has saved it from development pressures. But other areas have had to pay the price, of course. Points of relatively easy access – Xlendi, Mġarr ix-Xini, Dwejra, Ramla l-Ħamra in Gozo and the Santa Marija valley in Comino, all sites connected with rare habitat types – have come under intense pressure, while for some inaccessible coastal zones, pressure has shifted inland. The notable case here is Ta' Ċenċ plateau, between Sannat village and Mġarr ix-Xini. Here a series of development proposals are threatening the largest expanse of karstland (garigue) left on the Maltese islands – one, moreover, which is a bird nesting area of European importance.

But the effects of development are by no means confined to the land area actually taken up. There is always a strong multiplier effect. For instance, the extension of roads to previously inaccessible areas encourages settlement development away from the old nuclei. Furthermore, the production of close to 2500 dwellings per year over these last 6 or 7 years has doubled the demand for building stone. This, coupled with major infrastructural works – Red China Dock, Kordin grain silos, the Freeport at Marsaxlokk, the Delimara power station, the road network expansion – have required the mobilization of local raw materials for the construction industry on an unprecedented scale. This mobilization and its methods have proved to be major destroyers of non-arable land.

Building stone (franka) production has been concentrated at the old sources around Mqabba, Qrendi and Siġġiewi (Sammut, 1991). In Gozo the demand for building stone has led to a rapid expansion of the quarries overlooking Dwejra, where there is the only major outcrop of globigerina. Here, careless exploitation is wreaking havoc in an area of great scenic and ecological value (Schembri et al., 1987).

The huge expansion of hardstone quarrying for aggregate (żrar) has had a major impact on landscape. Most of the upland areas, with their coralline limestone, are being ruthlessly stripped. The Dingli-Ta' Żuta-Għar Lapsi area, the Naxxar-Madliena and the Mellieħa ridges have all been extensively mined, with the wanton destruction of large areas of karstland ecology by dumping of quarry spoil. On Gozo the garigue on the Għajn Abdul plateau has been virtually wiped out; the Nadur garigue has suffered severely; while on the coast east of Qala, the vast hardstone quarry, with its crushers/graders and its mounds of aggregate, has swallowed up the lower coralline coastal zone over a length of more than half a kilometer, in an area where the sea is accessible.

The Political and Legal Dimension

Social attitudes to the environment did not develop in a legislative vacuum, even if the political air must have been rather thin. While 'environment' or 'planning' legislation had not featured prominently in the post-independence parliamentary activity, some such items (e.g. The Clean Air Act, 1967) had been placed on the statute books, to add to those Acts and regulations from pre-independence days. In 1969, the Nationalist government passed The Town and Country Planning (TCP) Act; it was never promulgated and was finally repealed by a Labour government in 1981. This was a disaster of the first water, with long term effects. Had the TCP Act come into force in 1969, it could have provided a period of public education at a time when development pressures were still quite limited.

The fact is that until the early 1980s environmental issues were not really on the political agenda. Election manifestoes of the 1960s and 1970s were essentially devoid of such items. In the middle 60s there had been a couple of public campaigns concerned with specific aspects of the environment: one by Din l-Art Ħelwa directed against the building of a hotel under the Valletta bastions; and one by the proto-Ornithological Society to prevent a road being driven through the Għadira salt marsh.

Some years later the Malta Ornithological Society successfully lobbied to have Għadira declared a bird sanctuary, a status confirmed in Act XVII of 1980, which established other sanctuaries at Buskett, and at Ta' Ċenċ as well as on Filfla and Comino. Despite this, the general impression, up to the middle 70s at least, was that in Malta there were no pressure groups to mount regular campaigns of this nature. (Boissevain & Serracino Inglott, 1979)

The Labour government which took office in 1971 had no alternative to the TCP Act. During its first two terms of office (1971-81) — a period of population increase, economic expansion, improved living standards and rising expectations — there was no general policy for sane management of scarce land resource. Proposals in the 1981 election manifesto (MLP-GWU, 1981) did not even mention the central problem of land use. There was a perfunctory mention of improvement (?) of laws regulating hunting and trapping and the creation of more bird sanctuaries.

The Nationalist Party manifesto (Partit Nazzjonalista, 1981) had a lament for the TCP Act; it promised the setting up of a Planning Commission, renewed effort at soil conservation and afforestation, as well as the establishment of marine parks and bird sanctuaries. There were some of those trenchant declarations which political parties in Opposition are so adept at making, particularly at election time: the coastline should be public property; and more obscurely 'no irremedial development mistakes were to be committed, particularly in valleys or on the coast'. There was more 'environmental' material in an unofficial floating voters' election guide (Mallia, 1981) than in the publications of the two main parties.

Yet, although there had not been any hint in its 1981 manifesto, the Labour Government did make an attempt to bring the situation under control, with the passage of The Building Development Areas (BDA) Act of 1983. Unfortunately, the BDA Act vested the Minister of Public Works with wide discretionary powers, which were mainly used to satisfy demands by clients. The end result was just the opposite of the declared intention of the Act — a further surge in building sprawl with political clients as main beneficiaries.

The blatantly abusive manner in which the BDA Act was applied gave rise to some public awareness of potential and actual environmental problems. This feeling was amplified and focussed by a number of incidents which could not fail to catch the public eye. A hardstone quarry producing what was touted as 'Malta Marble' started operation on a site close to Mnajdra temples. Work was allowed to proceed even when it was evident that blasting was damaging the temple megaliths. Further 'callous' acts by government included the setting up of a road tar plant at Burmarrad with destruction of good agricultural land and widespread damage to crops from stack emissions; and the granting of an annual subsidy of several thousand pounds as well as exclusive use of Miżieb and l-Aħrax tal-Mellieħa during the open seasons to the Għaqda Kaċċaturi, Nassaba u Konservazzjonisti.[2] Other, not strictly environmental problems like water shortages acted as a catalyst to a number of public protest demonstrations. Participants were often roughed up by police, by political thugs, and in one case by members of the Għaqda Kaċċaturi (*The Times*, 6 June 1985).

The robust style – one cannot really speak of policies – of the then Minister of Public Works, flanked by equally robust police methods, led directly to the emergence of environmentalists in the European mold, quite prepared to go in for a degree of public action. An umbrella organization was formed to act as a coordinating body for the various environmental NGOs active at the time. After about a year, it was realized that there was room for a non-specialist organization which would also take up issues which did not fall within the remit of existing groups. This ensured that aspects of environment which had hitherto not received much attention – land use, air and water quality, energy policy – would be kept in the public eye as much as the traditional ones of the historical environment, hunting and trapping and general ecology.

In the final twelve months of its third consecutive term of office the Labour government created an environment division attached to the Ministry of Education. Unfortunately, the ministerial pecking order in the Cabinet ensured that Environ-

---

[2] Association of Hunters, Trappers and Conservationists.

ment was almost completely impotent against Public Works. The Minister responsible for the Environment was ignored even by the police in his attempts to have the Burmarrad road tar plant, operating without police permit, closed down (*The Times*, 16 January, 1987).

Yet even such negative attitudes may have helped to place environmental issues on the political agenda, and that in an irrevocable manner. All the 1987 election manifestoes had prominent sections dealing with environment. The MLP still seemed to be harbouring suspicions that 'the environment' was a devilish anti-worker plot. The manifesto argued for the need 'to strike a balance between the needs of the people and the protection of the environment'. It was not made clear which needs of which people were being served by poor quality water or by allowing grit blasting on ships in dock alongside residential areas in Cospicua, or by the workings of the BDA Act.[3] Even less was there any hint that protection of the environment was one of the people's long-term needs.

For the Nationalist Party, there was clearly a lot of political mileage in environmental issues, given the gross 'sins' of the government and the rising tide of public awareness. Even then, the Party did not go overboard in its electoral programme. Hunting and trapping were not even mentioned, for instance. There was much bemoaning the fact that the Labour government had repealed the TCP Act, that same Act that had been allowed to wither on the statute book by a Nationalist government. The Labour substitute, the BDA Act, got pride of place in the PN demonology. It was castigated for having hugely increased the very property and land speculation which it was meant to restrain. It was to be abolished, new schemes for land use would be drawn up and enforced 'without delay'.

---

[3] The row of unfinished houses across the Rabat Road from the psychiatric hospital was one of the last 'developments' under the BDA Act. On the other hand the block of luxury flats which mushroomed alongside the old sanctuary at Qala, Gozo were granted planning permission during the 8 month delay in abolishing the BDA Act by clause 10 of Act X (1988).

Of course, 'without delay' was a mere figure of speech. When in 1988 The Building Permits (Temporary Provisions) Act (Act X 1988) was passed through parliament by a Nationalist government, clause 10, which abolished the BDA Act was left inoperative for 8 months – long enough to allow clients to get their act together in time for the setting up of the temporary development lines required by the Act. The 'public consultation' had a very one-sided result: practically all requests to extend the lines were met while all requests to restrict lines were refused.

But Act X (1988) for all its faults did contain one radically new declaration of intent: to set up a Structure Plan (SP), defined as

> a written statement formulating a national planning policy designed to integrate in a general way the demands that economic, social, transport and environmental policies make on the use of land.

The SP was to be completed in the space of 2 years, a somewhat optimistic expectation as it turned out.

The promise to set up a Structure Plan with very wide terms of reference had one immediate beneficial effect. The foreign consultants engaged to draw up the Plan organized an extensive effort to gather basic data on all aspects of the environment. The returns of the 1985 Census had been worked up and served as a basis; various SP teams then elaborated census data and produced detailed reports on areas not tackled in the census. Paramount among these was the report on Natural Resources, (Ministry for the Development of the Infrastructure, 1991), which contained the first detailed inventory of mineral, ecological and marine resources and, equally vital, an assessment of their state.

While the SP was being drawn up government published a White Paper on a Proposed Draft Bill on Environment Protection, which was eventually approved by Parliament as The Environment Protection (EP) Act 1991. It was principally an enabling Act which empowered the Minister responsible for the environment to make regulations designed to protect the natural and human environment from pollution as well as to safeguard the natural and cultural resources of the nation from the negative effects of development. New legal notions included obligation to carry out Environmental Impact Assessments (EIA), a Review Authority to which the citizen could appeal against some Ministerial decisions, and the liability of a proven polluter to foot the bill for rehabilitation of the environment. From the first draft of the SP, published in November 1990, it was evident that there was a potential for demarcation disputes between the EP Act and the Planning Authority, established by Act I 1992, to operate the Structure Plan. These potential clashes may have been defused by the fact that development and environment were placed under one minister called the Minister for the Environment, who shepherded the Structure Plan through Parliament in July 1992. But it is more than likely that the general public has lost out in the process.

Masters or Stewards?

One may wonder how, despite the extant legal framework prior to 1990, the overall state of the environment is still little short of disastrous. It may be argued, with some justice, that the legal framework was not up to the severity of the problems. Perhaps even now, we have no very clear idea of the social forces shaping the situation. But that may suggest that the path to our environmental hell is at least lined with good intentions. Yet certain aspects of legislation, of its application, of the operation of the courts , of enforcement and of our general approach to law point to collective responsibilities for choices we have made and continue to make at least semi-deliberately.

Among the general public, a prevalent view is that law and regulation are a good thing and should be observed, most particularly by others. Those who are called to higher things, should not really be bound by such restrictions. A great amount of time and energy is devoted to finding ways and means of evading them. The large number of court cases[4] on infringement of building regulations is one manifestation of such attitudes. Some recent figures (Sammut, 1991) on illegal softstone quarrying showed that in Gozo 75% of the quarried area was operating without the necessary police permits.

---

[4] Over 500 cases in the Gozo Courts alone in 1991.

But perhaps the largest group of constant law breakers in the country are shooters, who regularly shoot at protected birds, shoot when out at sea, shoot inside bird sanctuaries and within prohibited distances of built-up areas. A comparable group are the owner-occupiers of the sea-side shanty towns, who have erected structures on public land in defiance of every known law of the land on such matters.

The police have an overwhelming share in enforcement, partly a reflection of the fact that one needs some type of police permit for nearly every imaginable activity. In situations where 'crime' is not of the obvious type, effective enforcement depends on a concerned citizenry reporting potential infringements. Such a concerned citizenry has hardly existed, and in any case the police are all too often lax in following up certain types of reports. In the smaller towns and villages, the police may be locals themselves with an extensive network of friends and relations. This is most obviously the case in Gozo. Enforcement would not come easy in such situations or in others where politicians are leaning on the police on behalf of clients.

Where building regulations are concerned, the relatively small number of building inspectors, coupled with a limited sense of duty (Falzon, 1991) leads to very patchy monitoring. When enforcement does take place there remains the further hurdle of long-winded legal proceedings, at the end of which even a conviction rarely results in a punishment to fit the crime. Fines are generally derisory, compared to the wages of sin or to the damage done to the res publica. A fine of Lm20[5] for operating a Dwejra quarry without permit for over a year does not square with the likely minimum of Lm20,000 profit and major damage to the landscape and to the ecology. To grant a permit after conviction is then to add insult to injury.

But the bitterest pill of all is that government is itself a major law breaker. One of the best known instances relates to the regulation that every house must have a well, which regulation has been completely ignored in the construction of public and

---

[5] Sentence in the Gozo Magistrates Court, 12 September 1989.

private housing. Other, less well known instances include instructions to the Marsa Power Station to make smoke only at night while, under the 1967 Clean Air Act, the authorities were busy prosecuting ship captains who made smoke in harbour (C.J. Mallia, private communication); or providing services to quarries and industrial plants operating without permits.

Clients

The power of clients has always been greatly respected in these islands. There has been strenuous and public defence of client politics (*The Malta Independent*, 23 August, 1992) and the client-dominated situation par excellence – Gozo – has been held up as a paradigm of good government (*The Malta Independent*, 6 December, 1992). The client is usually after favours, exceptions and mitigations, without too much concern as to which side of the law these may lie. Grand policy may end up as a tattered patchwork of conflicting client demands. The final version of the temporary development lines established by Act X (1988) is one example of such patchwork; so is much of the operation of the now-defunct Planning Area Permits Board.

The lines of the police – politician – client triangle stand out clearly in an interview with the then Minister for the Development of the Infrastructure, Mr. Michael Falzon (Caruana Galizia, 1989):

> ...In that particular case [a concrete ready-mix plant situated just outside Żebbuġ] there is no permit because of objections, which I agree with, from the Environment Department – because it is in the wrong place. We have not issued a permit, we have taken legal steps.
> *DCG*: So they can actually be stopped?
> *Minister*: They are, they should be stopped because they do not even have a police permit. They do not have a permit to build, and they do not have a police permit to operate.
> *DCG*: So who is responsible for stopping them, the police?
> *Minister*: If they are operating without a police permit...
> *DCG*: The police. So would not a word from you to the police stop them?
> *Minister*: That's a good question. But the police know, we have written on more than one occasion to the Commissioner of Police, to take steps to stop the work being carried out.
> *DCG*: Does government have contracts with the said Gaffarena plant?
> *Minister*: Not as far as I know...Government buys its concrete from Konkos Ltd.

Of course, the plant was connected to the public water and electricity services, the remit of Mr. Falzon's junior minister, the Parliamentary Secretary for Energy and Water. Quite by chance one of the original plant owners happened to be the junior minister's brother.

Following protests by environmentalists, the Prime Minister issued a statement to say that in future no buildings or operations without permits would be connected to services – which connections were probably being carried out at Armier shanty town, for instance, even as the Prime Minister was still hurling his anathemas. Meanwhile the plant did not lose a day's production. If it was not supplying any ready-mix to government – and ready-mix has no fingerprints – it was supplying the Nationalist Party Club a-building in Attard (Mallia, 1992). One of the owners was even allowed to damage photographs of the plant at a public exhibition, with the police and the then Parliamentary Secretary for the Environment turning a blind eye (Mallia, 1991). Some months after the 1992 general election the plant was granted all necessary permits by the new Minister of the Environment.

An equally significant case was that of persons who, despite being convicted under hunting regulations, successfully petitioned the President of the Republic to have their shotguns, confiscated by the police, returned to them (*The Malta Independent*, 16 January, 1993).

An intensely adversarial view of politics has had a pernicious effect on environment-related legislation, which by its very nature and in our case also by its timing is bound to run counter to the entrenched interests of significant numbers of voters. Despite agreement across the political divide that some piece of legislation should be enacted, government may well hold back for fear that the Opposition will make political capital out of it. The classic case is that of the rent laws which, by universal agreement, require radical revision in order to re-establish a local renting market and so cut down on the demand for building land. These laws are as yet untouched. There is, however, a White Paper about to be produced on the subject.

Partisan political restraints extend to practical situations. The parliamentary opposition voted against approval of the Structure Plan on quite trivial grounds (*The Times*, 1 August, 1992); it has given only highly equivocal support to the drive to eliminate seaside shanties; Government and Opposition have failed to propose credible measures to bring hunting laws in line with modern conservation policies; Ministers boast of the huge increase in the number of vehicles on the roads; air and water quality are only of concern to politicians when they are on the Opposition benches. There is no air pollution monitoring service; regular testing of drinking water is carried out but the results are not published. On the positive side, last year there was an extensive sampling of sea-water quality. Furthermore, our application to join the European Union has encouraged Government to be somewhat less pusillanimous about environment legislation.

Conclusion

What has been attempted in this paper is an account of the environmental stewardship of these islands. It would be a mistake to think that this stewardship has been vested solely or even in major part in those who govern us. That would lead to wrong attribution of responsibility and to mis-directed expectations of salvation. Environmental stewardship is a very democratic office. Everyone can make significant contributions to its success or failure; which is why it is also a very demanding office. Insensitivity to environmental matters has been part of the cultural backcloth. Various strands have gone into its making. Existence on a barren rock lost in the Middle Sea has never been easy. For a long while, therefore, there has been that drive for survival and for improving material conditions. Anything that was perceived as standing in the way of such 'progress' was given short shrift. This is why social reflexes continue to operate when they have outlived any original survival value and have even become positive dangers. The individual, and through him social groups, persists in relying on what have become fossil reflexes, much as the body still responds to sudden chill by 'gooseflesh' – a quite useless defence against cold in our present hairless condition. For example, the function of land and property as secure forms of wealth has generated attitudes which have outlived their usefulness.

At one level these fossil reflexes can be seen in social attitudes to law, to government and to the commonwealth; at another level, they can be seen in the notions of distance, of countryside, of wilderness, of our relation to other inhabitants of the ecosystem. Furthermore, the comparatively sudden exposure to European life-styles has been dazzling enough to blind us to the need to cut expectations down to what local conditions can yield. We have unquestioningly taken on status symbols which are unsuited to our circumstances and ultimately damaging. Large houses, palatial furnishings, over-powerful cars, and such 'sport' as bird hunting and trapping or off-road car rallies have become status symbols.

Possibly since the megalithic temple period but certainly over these last three decades, rapid economic development has been fuelled by the construction industry, directed at infrastructural works as well as at house building. We are still using the industry as a prop; the projections of the Structure Plan[6] show that quite clearly. Yet the demand for building land is in increasingly violent collision with other demands on land.

The danger lies not in the collision going unnoticed but in our tendency to accord the demand for building land supreme value while other demands are devalued to the point of extinction. A case in point is the absence of any value attached to wilderness and particularly to its place in the biological and cultural ecosystems. It is commonly accorded the derogatory description of waste land, fit only to be put to the meanest uses. Even when some hazy notion of its value does surface, impulses range from 'reclaiming' it, to quarrying it, to driving a road through it or at least to render it accessible to wheels – all good recipes for its rapid destruction. Ministers responsible for the environment who show tendencies to 'develop' anything in sight e.g. architects, civil engineers and even planners, are a menace in this respect.

There are now some 350,000 humans and around 190,00 wheeled vehicles in the republic. These two species compete fiercely for living space and breathable air. Their immediate habitat covers close to 20% of the face of the land; but their

---

[6] When production in the building industry was running at close to 3000 dwellings per year, the projected requirement for new dwellings during the 20 year life of the Structure Plan was reckoned at 60,000.

tentacles reach into every corner. Other species must struggle to find a niche. Countryside is shrinking; trees suffer constant depredations; wilderness is almost gone; most bird song comes out of cramped cages; fish populations are on the decline. Clearly we stand in some danger of being stewards no longer unless these trends are modified.

At present the Structure Plan is in place and the Planning Authority to administer it has been appointed and has started work. Some of the provisions of the Environment Protection Act have come into force. So that as far as legislation is concerned we have certainly broken new ground. There is some cause for satisfaction but not for complacency. The legislation and the Authorities concerned have yet to show that they are up to the measure of the problem. And the problem lies not in the environment but in ourselves.

References

Anderson, P.W. & Schembri, P.J. (1989) *Coastal Zone Survey of the Maltese Islands*, Floriana, Planning Services Division.

Boissevain, J. & Serracino Inglott P. (1979) 'Tourism in Malta' in de Kadt, E. (ed.) *Tourism: Passport to Development?* Oxford, Oxford University Press.

Brincat, J. M. (1991) *Malta 870-1054: Al-Himyari's Account*, Valletta, University of Malta, Foundation for International Studies.

Caruana Galizia, D. (1989) *The Sunday Times*, 29 August.

Central Office of Statistics, (1986) *Census 1985, Vol.I, A Demographic Profile of Malta and Gozo*, Valletta, Government Press.

Chetcuti D., Buhagiar A., Schembri P.J. & Ventura F. (1992) *The Climate of the Maltese Islands: A Review*, Malta, Malta University Press.

Lanfranco, E. (1990) 'The garigue: wasteland or wilderness?', *Ambjent*, Valletta, Moviment Għall-Ambjent, March.

Mallia, E.A. (1981) 'The floating voter's election guide', Oxford.

Mallia, E.A. (1991) 'Letter to the editor', *The Times*, June 1, Valletta, Malta.

Mallia, E.A. (1992) Photo-archive, Malta, Moviment għall-Ambjent.

Malta Labour Party – General Workers' Union (1981) *Mit-Tajjeb għall-Aħjar*, Valletta, Union Press.

Partit Nazzjonalista (1981) *Programm Elettorali*, Pietà, Independence Press.

Renfrew, C. (1979) *Before Civilisation*, London, Penguin.

Sammut A. (1991) *An Assessment of Globigerina Limestone Resources*, unpublished dissertation, University of Malta, Faculty of Architecture and Civil Engineering.

Schembri, P.J. & Lanfranco E. (1993) 'The effects of development on the natural environment of the Maltese Islands' in Lockhart, D.G., Drakakis-Smith, D.,

Schembri, J. (eds) *The Development Process in Small Island States*, London, Routledge.

Schembri, P.J., Lanfranco,E., Farrugia P., Schembri, S. and Sultana, J. (1987) *Localities with conservation value in the Maltese Islands*, Floriana, Environment Division, Ministry of Education.

Structure Plan Brief (1989) Floriana, Planning Services Division.

Vella, H.C.R. (1980) *The Earliest Description of Malta* (Lyons, 1536), Sliema, DeBono Enterprises.

Wettinger, G. (1969) 'The militia list 1419-20', *Melita Historica*, vol. 5, 2.

Zammit, I. (1990) Housing Stock Survey Results – 3. Rental Accommodation, *Structure Plan Newsletter*, Floriana, Planning Services Division, July/August.

Index

Abela, A.M., 96, 171, 172, 174, 255, 256, 257, 371, 448, 598, 605, 645, 669, 670
Abercrombie, N., 604
ablebodiedness, 214
abortion, 258, 314
absence, the politics of, 7
absenteeism, 383; *from schools*, 526; *at work*, 567
abused wives, 648
accommodational strategies, 19
Adams, R.D., 673
adaptive responses, 620
Addison, J.T., 48
Adorno, T., 175
adultery, 314, 636
advertisements, 167; *and drinking*, 627; *industry*,173; *and politics*, 175; *and sex*, 177
aesthetics, 177
affluence, 167; *affluent society*, 239; *affluent workers*, 484, 492
Agar, M., 619
age and social distinction, 330
ageing population, 477, 656
agency, 7
Aggleton, P., 324
Agius, J., 426
Aids to Industries Board, 66
Aids to Industry Ordinance, 64, 66
AIDS, 261, 314, 598
Air Malta, 418
alcohol, abuse of, 626; *consumption of*, 670, 673
Alexander, A., 307
Alexandria, 10
Alfaro Moreno, R.M., 315
alienation, 176; *at work*, 490
Allen, R.C., 304, 312
allophonic variation, 118
alternative social order, 621
Alternattiva Demokratika, 89
Althusser, L., 30

American civil war, 277
Anderson, P.W., 692
Ang, I., 304
anglicization, 279; *of Maltese names*, 217
Anglo-Maltese Joint Mission, 65
anomie, 240
anonymity, 375; *and microstates*, 17
anthropology, 617
anti-riformisti, 106
antitheism, 295
Anyon, J., 33, 330, 404
Apple, M.W., 323, 330, 448
apprenticeship schemes, 475
Apter, D.E., 101
Aquilina, J., 117, 121
Arabic, in schools, 109
architecture *and consumption*, 165; *and social relations*, 370, 375
Argyris, C., 496
Armier, 701
Ascher, K., 443, 446
Ashford, S., 257
Ashworth, M., 218
assembly lines, 560
atheism, 295
Attard, 36, 137-144, 147, 149, 150, 153, 154, 158, 203, 701
Attard, J., 548
Attard, L.E., 104
audience research, 311, 318
Auld, J., 620
Austin, J., 104-105
Australia, migration and, 212
authority, belief, 329; *command*, 329
autonomy, 46
Auxiliary Workers' Training Scheme, 471
avis of the European Community, 105

Avison, N.H., 654
Azzopardi, M., 630

Babuscio, J., 597, 598
Badger, G.P., 272
Baħrija, 692
Bailey, F.G., 378
Bakhtin, M., 179
balconies and social control, 375
Baldacchino, A.M., 626, 627,
Baldacchino, G., 34, 38, 44, 59, 97, 99, 487, 507, 508, 509, 511, 513, 516, 517, 574, 575, 576, 577, 578, 583, 584, 587
Baldamus, G., 558, 559
Balogh, T., 61, 62, 63, 65
Balzan, 147, 158, 203, 275
band clubs, 216, 272; *list of*, 274; *and parishes*, 272, *and political allegiance*, 279
Bandura, A., 91
Banfield, E., 236
Baran, P., 60
Barbara, A., 88, 581
Barbuto, J., 510
Barden, J.C., 652
bargaining, industrial relations as, 546
Barker, R.L., 596
Barrat-Brown, M., 58
basic needs, 163
Bates, E., 125
Baudelot, C., 47
Baudrillard, J., 180
Baumol, W.J., 474
Bayat, A., 578, 586
Bean, R., 545
Beatlemania, 425
Becker, H.S., 595, 623, 634
Beetham, D., 444
belief authority, 329
Belisle, F.J., 346
Bell, A., 436
Bell, D., 172
Belsey, A., 444
Benigni, L., 125
Bequele, A., 528, 535

Berger, P.L., 286
Bernstein, P., 582
Bertell, R., 198
Bertram, A., 108
Bestler, A., 88
Bezzina, J., 272
Big Government, 517
bigotry, 3
Bingham, C., 523
bird sanctuaries, 694
Bird, C., 405
Birgu (see Vittoriosa)
Birkirkara, 119, 147-150, 159, 203, 275, 278, 280
birth control, 235
Birżebbuġa, 147, 149, 158
Bishop, M., 446
black economy, 164, 171, 401, 466, 521; and children, 48, 521; *and tourism*, 350
black market, 620
Blondel, J., 96, 108
Blouet, B., 374
Blumberg, P., 507
Blumer, H., 630
Blumler, J.G., 303
Bocock, R., 163, 175, 180, 181
Boisgelin de Kerdu, P.M.L., 272
Boissevain, J., 134, 164, 174, 179, 181, 279, 281, 360, 375, 410, 411, 418, 584, 694
Bonavia, G., 215
Bonett, S., 513
Boorstin, D.J., 177
border crossings, 221, 374
Borg, C., 218
Borg, R., 193
Bormla (see Cospicua)
Boss, P., 599
Boswell, D.M., 6, 36, 38, 141, 153, 604
Bourdieu, P., 33, 49, 117, 181, 182, 391, 397
bourgeois democracy, 30
bourgeoisie, 31, 42, 73
Bowen-Jones, H., 235
Bowles, S., 396, 402
Boyden, J., 528, 535

Index

Brake, M., 421, 432
Brietenbach, H., 444
Briguglio, L., 165, 237, 467
Brincat, M., 59, 70
British base, 58; *colonial rulers*, 10; *Conservative Party*, 255; *defence base, closure of*, 137; *Defence Establishments*, 463; *Party*, 361; *Union Club*, 277
broadcasting authority, 311
brokerage, 351, 366
Bronner, S.E., 175
Broughton, G., 126
Brown, M.E., 307
Brown, R., 125
Bruce, S., 286, 287
Bugeja, M., 193
Bugeja, V., 278
Buġibba, 147, 149, 159, 643, 690
building, Development Areas Act, 694; *inspectors*, 699; *society*, 690
built up areas, 690
Bulebel, 691
Burawoy, M., 558, 563, 565
Burchill, J., 431
bureaucracy, 32
bureaucratization, 508
Burgess, E.W., 243
Bury, M., 619, 623
Busuttil, S., 485, 659
Byzantines, 10

cable audio systems, 359
cable television, 359
Cable, J., 507
Cacciottolo, J., 628
Cachia, J., 446
Camilleri, A., 579
Camilleri, J., 218
Camilleri, P., 511
Campbell, J.K., 372
Campbell-Johnston, M., 255
cancer, and age, 196; *and class*, 205; *and DDT*, 198; *and gender*, 194; *and locality*, 200; *and mortality rates*, 191; *and tobacco*, 200

canonical regression, 153
capital resources test, 82
capitalism, 28, 445; *and development in Malta*, 56; *international*, 50; *and labour-led development*, 70; *logic of*, 554; *and sexism*, 604; *and world system*, 579
capitalists, *domestic*, 44; *foreign*, 44
Carby, H.V., 222
Cardoso, F.H., 44, 59
career structure, 48
Caritas Malta, 87, 606, 665, 670
carnival, 179
Carnoy, M., 44
Carthaginians, 10
Caruana, J., 567
Caruana Galizia, D., 700
Carveth, R., 307
Casey, J., 622
Cassar-Pullicino, J., 272
Castagna, P.P., 272
casual labour, 530
Catania, J., 652
Catholic Church, 7, 11, 50, 173, 174, 234, 274, 369, 373; *and attendance at mass*, 293; *and dispute with the state*, 640; *and the elderly*, 663; *and gender*, xxxii; *hegemony of*, 13; *and homosexuality*, 598; *organizations of*, 12; *and privileges*, 12; *and property*, 286; *and schools*, 12, 324; *and state*, 367; *teachings of*, 605; *and women*, 90
Cattell, R.B., 153
census, 45, 135, 628, 659
central Europe, 253
Centre for Contemporary Cultural Studies, 50, 178
Ċentru Ħidma Soċjali, 601
certification, 31
Chamber of Commerce, 62, 67, 178; *and privatization*, 447
Chaplin, Charles, 623
Chetcuti, D., 687
Chilcote, R.H., 74

child abuse, 599, 601
child labour, 164, 474, 521; *and conditions of work*, 533; *and economic exploitation*, 533, 603; *in developed countries*, 523; *in developing countries*, 523; *in Gozo*, 524; *and policy-making*, 534
child care centres, 85
children's homes, 603
children's rights, 602
China, 58
Chow, W.S., 666
Christian Democracy, 71
christian democratic parties, 254
christianity and politics, 256; *and women*, 90
cigarette smoking and Maltese youth, 673
Cirillo, R., 212
city state, 133, 134
city, the, 29
civil marriage, 234
civil rights, 101
civil society, 448
Clark, A., 530
Clarke, J., 176, 182, 334
class, 27; *allegiance*, 46; *analysis*, 40-41, 50-1; *and cancer*, 205; *cartography*, xxxi, 50; *conflict*, 30, 31; *consciousness*, 30, 36, 38; *definition of*, 33; *dominant*, 43; *as economic relationship*, 28-31; *and educational achievement*, 383; *and festa partiti*, 281; *for-itself*, 35, 36, 37; *formation, in Malta*, 39; *and language*, 117; *interest*, 32; *interest of bourgeoisie*, 45; *location*, 221; *in Malta*, 33; *of-itself*, 35; *politics*, 109; *size*, 45-46; *structure*, xxxi, 7, 31; *struggle*, 30, 37
classification of occupations, 139
classificatory principles, 330
classless society, 28, 38
Clean Air Act, 693, 700
cleanliness, households and, 237

Clegg, H., 542
client politics (see patronage)
cluster analysis, definition of, 148
CMT (cut, make & trim) production, 74, 512, 555
CMTU (see Confederation of Malta Trade Unions)
co-education, 406
coalition building, 20
cock-rock, 437
code of ethics, for journalists, 365; *of honour*, 371; *of shame*, 371
coercion, 443
Cohen, P., 179, 581
collective agreements, 497, 538, 567
collective consciousness, 371
collective mobilization, 516
collective ownership, 38
colonial, *administrators*, 573; *history*, 359; *legacy*, 583; *penetration*, 15
colonialism, 350; *and identity*, 213; *and Malta*, 10, 133
command authority, 329
Commander, S., 445, 446, 447, 451
commodification of public goods, 442, 455
commodities, 177
commodity exchange, 38
common good, 256
common-sense knowledge, 340
communication and control, 564
communications media, development of, 358
communicative competence, 118
community care, personalization of, 663
community-based education, 218
competition, 333
comprador élite, 10
compulsory schooling, 522
Concilium Regionale Melitense, 273
Conditions of Employment (Regulations) Act, 548
conditions of work, 497

Index

Confederation of Malta Trade Unions, 550, 578
conflict, 4, 7, 37, 41; *of interest*, 29; *sociology*, 622
conformity, 372
Connell, R.W., 86, 88, 91, 330
conscientization, 240
consensus, 7
conservatism, 422; *and ideology*, 335
conspicuous consumption, 174
constructionist sociology, 623
consumer, *and privatization*, 446; *Protection Act*, 178; *rights*, 178
consumerism, 231, 238, 243, 254, 570; *culture of*, 164, 167
consumption, 11, 28, 32, 70, 553; *and citizenship*, 176; *and class*, 181; *conspicuous*, 174; *excessive*, 179; *and identity*, 180; *of leisure*, 422; *mass*, 570; *patterns of*, 49, 169; *pleasures of*, 174, 179; *and private education*, 181; *and religion*, 180; *and status groups*, 181; *and surplus production*, 164; *and University students*, 174
contradictory class locations, 46
contraventions, 638
control and technology, 565
control strategies, management and, 558
control strategies, schools and, 331
Cook, P., 442, 445, 446
Cooke, K., 346
Cooper, R.J., 344
cooperatives, 506; *failure of*, 508
Corradino, 691
Cork, P., 442
Cornell, C.P., 648, 650
corporate giants, 44
corporate strategies, 554, 556
corporatism, 579
Corrigan, P., 388, 405
Cospicua, 119, 121, 122, 124, 134, 145, 147, 149, 150, 201, 203, 272
cost of living, 49; *rise in*, 538

cotton industry, 277
Cottonera, 121-124, 129, 134, 135, 153, 158, 160, 624
Council of Europe, 215, 242
counter-cultures, 421
counterfeit society, 17
Cox, H., 285
Coxon, A.P.M., 154, 157
Cramp, J., 603
credentialling ideology, 401
Cremona, J., 474, 524, 525, 527, 528, 529, 531, 533
crime, 172, 636; *definition of*, 635; *and the family*, 646; *in Gozo*, 645; *location patterns*, 643; *patterns of*, 639; *and punishment*, 636; *statistics*, 637; *target patterns*, 641
Crimean war, 277
Criminal Code, 636
criminal law, 636
Critcher, C., 176, 182, 334
Critchley, F., 157
critical paradigm, 309
critical sociology, 595
Crockett, H., 119
crony capitalism, 447, 451
Crook, S., 570
crown colony status, 279
cultural, *artifacts*, 12; *capital*, 117, 391; *diasporas*, iv; *differentiation*, 239; *identity*, xxvii, 484; *imposition*, 398; *intermediaries*, 182; *lag*, 230; *pluralism*, 421; *rebel*, 422; *reproduction*, 32
culture magazines, 182
culture shock, 351
Cummins, J., 218
currency in circulation, 43
curriculum, *covert*, 323; *overt*, 323

Da Silva, T.T., 390
Dahrendorf, R., 7, 254
Darmanin, M., 40, 86, 324, 333, 442, 454
Davies, P.M., 154, 157

De Moor, R.A., 257, 264
De Rios, M.D., 618
de-traditionalization, xxviii
death duty, 43
Debono, G., 89
decentralization, illusion of, 545
decentred viewing-experience, 315
deconstruction, 4
Defence White Paper, 64
deficit theories, 387
De Kadt, E., 346
Delamont, S., 406
Delia, E.P., 171, 212, 464, 467, 468, 469, 475, 478, 521
Delimara, 692
delinquency, juvenile, 645
democracy, *bourgeois*, 30; *direct*, 38; *and the media*, 364; *western model of*, 102
demography, *changes*, 462, 477; *patterns*, 657; *trends*, 687
denationalization, 442
Dench, C., 212, 235
department stores, 166
dependency theory, 44
desacralization, 239, 291
deskilling, 565
determinism, 7
developing world, 556
development, xxix; *and the bourgeoisie*, 59; *export-led*, 56; *plans*, 58, 64, 66, 345, 468; *stages of*, 60, 64; *strategy*, 61; *theory*, 55
deviance, 605, 619, 628; *and the law*, 636; *social construction of*, 388
deviant behaviour, 378; *dialectal pride*, 124; *dialects of Maltese*, 118; *difference*, 214; *differentiation*, 288
Dimech, E., 282
Din l-Art Ħelwa, 693
Dingli, 203, 692, 693
disability, 214
discrimination, 269
disenchantment, 291
dissacration, 291

distinction, 325
divestiture, 446
division of labour, 393, 498; *international*, xxvii; *sexual*, 83
divorce, 259, 314
dockyard, towns, 135; *work*, 489; *workers*, 415
Dohnalik, J., 307, 316
domestic labour, 84
domestic violence, 605, 648
dominant class, 43
dominant ideology, 306
domination, 40
Dominelli, L., 605
Dorn, N., 622
Douglas, M., 374
Doxey, G.V., 344
Doyal, L., 196
Drache, D., 445
dress styles, 425
drug, *abuse*, 617, 669, 674; *culture*, 427; *and social class*, 622; *and schools*, 630
drunk driving, 626
Drydocks, 37
dual labour market theory, 48
Dubin, R., 493
Dubisch, J., 380
Dunlop, J., 542, 543, 544, 546, 547
Duverger, J., 102
Dwejra, 692, 699

early industrial development, 64
early school leaving, 526
eastern Europe, 103, 253
ecclesiastical tribunal, 245
Eckert, P., 381
ECLA (Economic Commission for Latin America) school, 58, 59
ecology of small states, 19
economic *activity of the State*, 463; *booms*, 485; *change and family*, 229; *cycles*, 444; *dependence*, 63, 237; *depressions*, 485; *diversification*, 476; *imperialism*, 58
economy, fortress, 346, 463, 517,

575, 577
economies of scale, 507, 573
Edelstein, J.C., 74
education, *achievement and class*, 39, 383; *and class reproduction*, 40; *and culture*, 246; *and economy*, 466; *expansion and mobility*, 40; *and meritocracy*, 39; *and privatization*, 454; *and social mobility*, 236; *and standards*, 475, 488; *and stratification*, 39; *and women*, 85
Education-Industry Unit, 467
Edwards, A.D., 397
Edwards, P.K., 558
Edwards, R.C., 559, 561, 563, 571
egalitarian society, 35
egality, 327
Egypt, 10
elderly, *care of*, 656; *and housing*, 662; *and institutionalization*, 660; *and marginalization*, 661; *as national resource*, 665; *and pensions*, 661
élite, *commercial*, 44; *in Malta*, 57, 106; *service*, 44
emigration, 143, 211, 275, 688; *and the labour market*, 467; *post-war*, 462
empirical sociology, 4
empiricism, 2
Employment and Training Corporation, 513
Engels, F., 29, 604
English language, 20; *as a second language*, 217
enterprise, *culture*, 262; *ethic*, 564; *solidarity*, 564
entrepreneur, 34, 291

environment, 266, 427, 685; *degradation*, xxx; *Impact Assessments*, 697; *and pollution*, 445; *protection*, 254; *Protection Act*, 697
epidemiology, 202, 655
Epstein, S., 188, 196
Ersson, S.O., 95

Ervin-Tripp, S., 125
essential paradigms, 56
Establet, R., 47
Estrin, S., 453
ethnic communities, 31
ethnocentricity, 213
ethnographic research, 325, 384, 619
eurocentric, 213
Europe, changes in, 254
European Commission, 105
European Community, 68, 70, 267
european domination, 214
European Union, 466, 476, 554, 702
European Values surveys, 488, 669
evolutionism, 49
Ewen, S., 177
excellence teams, 580
expertise, and microstates, 18
exploitation, 28, 40; *of female labour*, 69
export markets, 64
export-led industrial development, 62
extended family, 125, 232
externalism, 295

factionalism, 283
factor analysis, 146, 148
Faculty of Theology, 13
Fagen, R.R., 358
fairs, 179
Faletto, E., 44, 59
false needs, 176
Falzon, M., 700
familiarity, and microstates, 16
familism, 236
family, *celebrations*, 231; *changes in*, 659; *and children*, 235; *conventional*, 248; *and crime*, 646; *deprived*, 248; *and division of labour*, 250; *and economic change*, 229; *extended*, 232; *law*, 250; *and Marxism*, 250; *modernist*, 248; *nuclear*, 233; *and politics*, 96-97; *progressive*,

249; *planning*, 303; *policy*, 662; *and religion and morality*, 257; *size*, 246; *structure*, 656; *support systems*, 666; *ties*, 231; *traditional*, 247; *types*, xxxii, 247; *typologies*, 229; *unity*, 230; *and values*, 229; *violence*, 598
family-based economy, 29
fatalism, 485
feast confraternities, 278
feasts and teachers, 277
feasts, 220
Featherstone, M., 179, 180, 182
Federation of Malta Industries, 61, 63, 74; *and privatization*, 447
female culture, 312
feminism, 406
feminist sociology, 595, 605
Fenech, A., 539
Fenech, F., 1977
Fenech Adami, E., 449
Fenn, R.E., 290
fertility, *rates*, 655, 687; *decline of*, 84
festa, 179, 272, 294, 373, 626; *and factionalism*, 276; *partiti*, 271; *partiti and class*, 281
festivals, 179
feudal, *relations of production*, 41; *rent*, 29, 41; *social relations*, 34; *society*, 29
Feuer, J., 306
Fgura, 36, 137-144, 147, 149, 153, 154, 158, 160, 205
fidelity in marriage, 232, 379
Fiegehen, G., 82
Fiji, 2
film narrative, 306
Finkelhor, D., 599, 601, 646, 648
Finn, D., 521, 529
first world, 41
fiscal crisis, 450
Fishman, J.A., 117, 118
Fiske, J., 306
Fitzroy, F., 507
Flanders, A., 542
Floriana, 135, 143, 203, 279

folk sociology, 1
folklore, 378
Ford, M., 125
foreign investment, 579
foreign sociologists (in Malta), 14
foreign-owned industry, 67
Formosa, R.A., 509, 512
forms of address, 125
fortress economy, 346, 463, 517, 575, 577
Foucault, M., 221
Fox, A., 484, 494, 496, 501, 507, 541, 575
Fox, I., 327
Frank, A.G., 44, 59
Frankfurt School, the, 5, 51, 175
free market, 49
free marketeers, 444
Freedom Day, 60
freedom of speech, 265
freedom, negative concept of, 443
Frendo, H., 100, 106, 107, 108, 212, 213, 220, 279, 282
Friedman, A.L., 557
friendship, 243
Frith, S., 438
frugality, 164
Fuller, R.C., 630
functionalism, 619
fundamentalism, 294
Furlong, J., 405

Gabe, J., 619, 623
Galea, A., 171
Gallie, D., 501
Gallup, 256
Gamble, E.A., 443
game theory, 542
Garton Ash, T., 253
Gay Liberation Movement, 597
Gelles, R.J., 648, 650
gemeinschaft, 286
gender, *differentiation*, 370, 376, *discrimination on the labour market*, 259
equality, 79; *and family budgeting*, 83; *and household*

chores, 376; *identities*, 398; *and leisure*, 376; *and media*, 367; *and poverty*, 81; *gender and power*, 79; *relations*, 259; *roles*, 79, 377; *and social space*, 376
General Workers' Union, 415, 499, 511, 539, 550, 567, 576, 578, 694; *and the MLP*, 576
geographic mobility, 462
Germani, G., 56, 73
Gertler, M.S., 445
gesellschaft, 286
Għadira, 693-4
Għajn Abdul, 693
Għaqda Kaċċaturi, Nassaba u Konservazzjonisti, 695
Għaqda Nies Imsawta, 650
Għaxaq, 204, 275, 277, 278, 283
Għargħur, 201, 204, 205, 275, 283
Għar Lapsi, 693
ghetto, 218
Ghodse, A.H., 625, 626
Giahan, 272
Giddens, A., 14, 30, 32, 620, 637, 646, 647, 648, 653
Gilman, A., 125
Gintis, H., 396, 402
Giroux, H., 213, 221, 222, 323
Glaessner, V., 306
Glaser, B.G., 384, 432
Glaser, D., 429
Gleaton, T., 673
Glendinning, C., 81, 83
global, *change*, 286; *networks*, 366; *systems*, xxvii
globalization, xxvii, 686
Gluckman, M., 369
Goetz, J.P., 324
Goldthorpe, J.H., 126, 139, 484, 492
Gomes-Schwartz, B., 647
gossip, 16, 307, 358, 369, 378; *and community cohesion*, 381; *and control of sexuality*, 379; *as subversive*, 307
Gouder, A., 630
Gouldner, A., 496
Goulet, D., 507

government, *borrowing*, 450; *and environment*, 699; *and law-breaking*, 699; *and microstates*, 17; *and work*, 491
Gozo, 272, 375, 689, 690, 692, 698, 699; *and child labour*, 524; *and crime*, 645; *and drug use*, 624, 677; *and patronage*, 700; *and shrewdness*, 134; *and tourism*, 689
Graham, H., 83
Gramsci, A., 30, 448
Grand Harbour conurbation, 134
grand theories, crisis of, 349
grand traditions, xxviii
Gray, A., 312
Grech, J.C., 67, 68, 563
Grech, S., 511
Griffin, C., 526
Grima, J.F., 360
Grixti, A., 538
grounded theory, 384
Gudja, 204, 205, 275
Gulia, A., 505
Gwardamangia, 203
GWU (see General Workers' Union)
Gżira, 145-147, 149, 159

Habermas, J., 175
habitus, 397
Hale, I.M., 651
Ħal Far, 691
Hall, S., 425
Hallinan, M.T., 330
Ħamrun, 119, 135, 146, 147, 149, 159, 203, 275, 424, 425
handicapped, 48
Haralambos, M., 240, 621, 623, 637, 653
Hargreaves, A., 325
Harrison, A., 135
Harrod, J., 574
Hartley, A.W.M., 70
Hayek, F.A., 443, 454
Haywood Metz, M., 328
headbanger subculture, 428

Heald, G., 256, 257
health services, 662
hegemony, 30, 221
Held, D., 30, 32
hermeneutic circle, 5
heterosexuality, 214, 597
Hicks, J., 59
hierarchy, 402; *and schooling*, 327
high-technology industry, 72
Hilsum, L., 69
Hindess, B., 443, 444, 453
hippy culture, 621
historical agents, 213
Hobsbawm, E., 60
Hogan, B., 638
Holborn, M., 621, 623, 637, 653
home ownership, 139
home-based labour, 527
home-centred family life, 231
homophobia, 597
homosexuality, 214, 261; *and Catholic Church*, 598; *and marginalization*, 596
honour, code of, 369
Hope, K., 139
Horkheimer, M., 175
house unions, 556
household, *budgetary survey*, 168-170, 628, 629; *labour*, 372, 398
housework, 315
housing, 239; *conditions*, 649; *and elderly*, 662; *estates*, 690; *market*, 138; *rented*, 688; *social*, 689; *Stock Survey*, 689
Howieson, C., 526, 529
Hoy, D.R., 346
Hubbard, R.P.S., 135
Hudson, R.A., 118
human agency, 444
human capital theory, 581
human life cycle, 12
human needs, hierarchy of, 484
human resource management, 504
Humphreys, L., 597
hunters and law breaking, 699
hunters and trappers, Association of, 98

Huston, A.C., 91
Huyssens, A., 213
Hyman, R., 563, 564

ideal types, 232, 558
identity, *of Maltese*, 134; *social constructions of*, 2
ideological state apparatus, 30
ideology, xxviii
illiteracy, 39
image-making, 175
immigration, *illegal*, 468; *of labour*, 462
importation, *liberalization of*, 165, 538; *substitution*, 58, 70, 445, 465
importers' lobby, 63
Imtaħleb, 692
incest, 646
income, *differentials*, 37; *disparities*, 464; *per capita*, 164; *policy*, 551; *trends*, 44
Independence Day, 60
indigenous culture and tourism, 350
individualism, 240, 243
individualization, 287
industrial, *action*, 539; *capitalism*, 41; *democracy*, 507, 579; *Development Bill*, 447; *Development Board*, 65; *estates*, 137
industrial relations, 494, 504, 537, 581; *and political parties*, 551; *as bargaining*, 546; *and game theory*, 542; *and Marxist perspectives*, 541; *and systems approach*, 542; *and the Oxford School*, 542
industrial revolution, 28
Industrial Tribunal, 539
industrialization, 656; *delayed*, 56; *export-oriented*, 61
industriousness, 35
industry, clothing, 553
infidelity and social stigma, 233
informal economy, 487
information technology, 446

Index

infrastructural development, 690
Ingelhart, R., 254, 265
Inguanez, C., 467
inherited titles, 39
invisibility, of Maltese, 215
integration with Britain, 61
intellectual existentialism, 426
interactionist sociology, 49, 596, 622-3
interactive research methodology, 324
interest groups, 581
interest rates, liberalization of, 447
interest satisfaction, 37
intermarriage, 32, 219
international capitalism, 349
International Labour Organisation, 522
interpretative sociology, 4, 5
intimacy, and microstates, 16 and passim
intoxicants, 618
intrinsic gratification, 396
investigative journalism, 367
irregular economy (see black economy; twilight economy)
irritation index and tourism, 344
Isla, L- (see Senglea)
Islam, 103, 294
Isserlin, B.S.J., 117, 121
Italian language, 279
Italian party, 361
Italian printers, 360
Italy, as trading partner, 72

Jackall, R., 508
Jacquette, J.S., 87
Jameson, F., 180
Japan, 68
Jesuit College, of Malta, 13
job enlargement, 580
job satisfaction, 494
job security, 500
Jonathan, R., 454
Joppke, C., 27, 32
journalism, investigative, 7

journalism, 359, 365
juvenile delinquency, 645

Kahler, E., 291
Kalkara, 203, 205, 283
Kapferer, J.L., 335
Katz, E., 303, 305
Kautsky, K., 29
Keenan report, 279
Kellner, D.M., 175
Kerkhofs, J., 257, 264
Kerslake, A., 603
Kertzer, D., 326, 328
Kester, G., 361, 493, 577, 578, 581, 582, 583, 587, 588
Keynesian economics, 59
Killick, T., 445, 446, 447, 451
King, J., 636, 653
King, R., 212
Kinnie, N., 545
kinship ties, 233
Kirkop, 275, 278, 281-283
Kirkpatrick, C., 442, 445, 446
Kmetova, T., 118
Knapp, J.A., 59
Knights of St. John, 12
Koster, A., 50
Koziara, E.C., 462
Krugman, P.R., 476
kulturkampf, 286

labelling theory, 389, 605, 637
labour, *control of*, 38, 558, 574, 587, 588; *corps*, 468; *power*, 28; *process*, 47, 541; *statistics*, 468; *turnover*, 490, 568; *and women*, 84, 568
labour force and women, 84
labour parties, 30
Labour Party (see Malta Labour Party)
Labov, W., 118, 149, 122
Laclau, E., 56, 59, 213
Ladewig, H., 346
Lambert, W., 125
land development, 269

land use, 688
landfills, 691
landowners, 41
Lane, J., 95
Lanfranco, E., 687
language, 3, 20; *and class*, 117; *and cultural imposition*, 398; *and nationalism*, 282; *question*, 100; *and sociology*, 117; *varieties*, 118
Latin America, 58
law, *and power*, 636; *of the Sea*, 685; *and social control*, 636
Layard, R., 82
Le Grand, J., 453
Le Compte, M.D., 324
Lee, D., 230
Lee, H.A., 104, 107
Lefkowitz, J., 568
legitimation, 288
leisure, 172; *and gender*, 376; *and youth*, 422, 425, 529; *sociology of*, 334
Lenin, V.I., 29
lesbians, marginalization of, 596
less developed countries and privatization, 445
Lever-Tracy, C., 212, 467
Levi-Strauss, C., 303
Levin, H.M., 508
Levine, L., 119
Levitas, R., 443
Lewis, A., 59
Lewis, G.C., 104-105
liberalization, *of economy*, 254; *of importation*, 538; *policies*, 538
liberationism, 426
Libya, 10, 58; *and Malta*, 146, 219
Lidz, C.W., 625
Liebes, T., 303, 305
life chances, 31, 36, 51, 118
life expectancy, 656
life styles, consumption of, 32, 33, 49, 164, 182, 421, 624
life-world, 175
Lija, 147, 275
liminal space, 180
linguistic capital, 118

linguistic variation, 119
Linn, M., 119, 126
Livingstone, S.M., 307, 316, 317
local councils, 97, 450
locality differentiation, criteria for, 159
locality, occupational distribution in, 139
lock-out, teachers', 640
Lockhart, D.G., 207
Loether, H.J., 145, 149
Lopes, J., 218
lord, 28
Louvain, 13
low waged-labour, 62
Lucchetti Bingemer, M.C., 90
Luckmann, T., 289, 290
lumpen-development, 70
Luqa, 271, 275

MacBride, S., 362
MacDonald, M., 327
machine pacing, 560
machismo, 220
Mackenzie, G., 485
MacLennan, E., 523, 526
macro narratives, 5
Madliena, 693
Magro, J., 178
males and domestic work, 242
Mallia, C.J., 700
Mallia, E.A., 694, 701
Mallia, H., 562, 56, 569
Mallia, M., 330
Mallia, V., 561, 570
Malta, *and anglicization*, 106; *and Europe*, 103; *and fortress economy*, 10; *geography of*, 9; *as hub in Mediterranean*, 366; *and industrialization*, 41; *insularity of*, 9; *as intermediately developed economy*, 237; *and membership of European Union*, 105; *as micro state*, 9, 14; *and overseas investment*, 62; *and political independence*, 10; *and population of*, 9; *rentier status of*, 20;

as social laboratory, 15; *as total society*, 14; *and values*, 255
Malta Council for Economic Development, 551
Malta Development Corporation, 66, 68, 471
Malta Drydocks and worker participation, 576
Malta Investment Management Company Ltd., (see MIMCOL)
Malta Labour Movement, 42; *and industrialization*, 58
Malta Labour Party, 34, 35, 55, 56, 89, 97, 109, 164, 166, 175, 362, 410-1, 512, 694; *and environment politics*, 695; *and feasts*, 275-6; *and marxism*, 58; *and socialism*, 57; *and Structure Plan*, 701; *support for*, 281; *and welfare provision*, 49; *social measures of*, 34-35, 49
Malta Ornithological Society, 694
Malta Tourist Bureau, 347
Maltese culture as static, 221
Maltese diaspora, 211, 213
Maltese economy, *changes in*, 135; *development of*, 485
Maltese identity, 103, 212
Maltese language, 106; *regional variation of*, 121
Maltese nobility, 103
Maltese sociological discourse, 8
Maltese worker, characteristics of, 505
Mamo, A.J., 635, 636, 638
Management Systems Unit, 446, 450
management, nationalization of, 545
management-labour relations, 558
Manduca, J., 43
Mangion, A., 561
Manis, J.G., 605
manpower surveys, 462, 467
manual workers, 35, 37, 485
manufacturing industry, 486, 554
Marcuse, H., 175, 176
marginalization, xxx, 595

marital rape, 636, 651
marital violence, 648
market economy, 461; *and social justice*, 454; *and philosophy*, xxxi, 443, 454; *and socialism*, 453; *and Marxism*, 444
market research, 5, 171, 359
Market Response System, 556
market socialism, 453
Marramao, G., 286, 287
marriage, *annulment*, 244; *breakdown*, 81; *rate*, 234; *separation*, 233; *and catholic church*, 244
married women, *at work*, 241; *gainful employment of*, 242
Marsa, 137, 147, 149, 203, 691
Marsalforn, 690
Marsascala, 203, 205, 690
Marsaxlokk, 692
Martin, D., 293
Marx, K., 6, 27, 28-31, 565, 604
Marxism, *and development*, 103; *and the market*, 444; *culturalist*, 50; *structuralist*, 50; *and sociology*, 603, 622
Maslow, A.H., 484, 501
mass communication theory, 303
mass culture, 51, 176
mass media, 244, 301, 358
mass rituals, 339
materialism, 167, 254, 264, 660
materialist values, 254
Mayo, P., 218
mayor, 12
McCann, G.C., 346
McCarthy, B., 542
McClintock, F.H., 654
McKercher, W.R., 329
McKersie, R.B., 546, 548
McLaren, P., 323, 325, 329, 335, 337, 392
McLeod, E., 605
McLuhan, M., 177
McNeil, L., 325, 332
McRobbie, A., 397, 398, 399, 406
McTavish, D.G., 145, 149
Mdina, 203; *defence syndrome*, 360

means of production, 28
media, *and the business community*, 363; *and colonialism*, 351; *and democracy*, 364; *and gender*, 367; *history of*, 361; *monopoly*, 363; *and political parties*, 362; *and power structures*, 367; *research*, 358; *studies*, 302; *and traditional values*, 358
medical doctors, dispute of, 189
medical sociology, 625
medicalization, 625
Mediterranean, *culture*, 370, 371; *religions*, 373
medium of instruction, 397
medium-sized firms, 44
Meerdink, J., 70
Mellieħa, 205, 275, 280, 692, 693, 695
merchant capital, 41, 57
merchant shipping, 135
Mercieca, J., 335
merit, 37
meritocracy, 3, 39
Mermet, G., 170, 184
Merton, R.K., 620
meta narratives, 213
metropole capital, 44
metropolis, 181
Mġarr, 205
Mġarr ix-Xini, 692
Micallef, K., 558
Miceli, P., 80, 86, 90, 600
Miceli Farrugia, M., 70
micro narratives, 5
micro-status, of Malta, 9
Mid-Med Bank, 450
middle class, 119 (see also class)
Miege, M., 272
Mifsud, A., 166, 175
Mifsud, E., 324
Mifsud, J., 330
Mifsud Bonnici, R., 278, 280
migration, *internal*, 135, 150; *return*, 212
Milanesi, G., 292, 293
Miles, R., 91

Miliband, R., 29, 30, 31, 40, 42, 44, 47, 48
military base, 464
military, the, 30
Millar, J., 81, 83
Miller, A., 175
Miller, W.B., 428
Millward, R., 446
Milne, R.G., 201
MIMCOL, 451, 452
minimum wage, 68, 462, 532, 562
Mintoff Bland, Y., 198, 488, 490, 503
Mintoff, Dom, 34, 62, 409, 410, 577
Misraħ Kola, 690
Mitchell, C., 157, 159
Mitchell, J.C., 147, 153
mixed economy policy, 463
Miżieb, 695
Mizzi, S. O'Reilly, 48, 83, 84, 88, 370, 376, 377, 379, 600
mobility, *intergenerational upward*, 216; *residential*, 135
mobilization, collective, 566
modernism, 230
modernity, xxvii, 100
modernization, 230, 268, 656
Modleski, T., 306, 315
mods, 179
Moir, C., 602
monopoly, 446; *power*, 18; *and microstates*, 18
Monsarrat, N., 344
moral absolutism, 289
moral imperative of markets, 443
mortality rates, 656
Mosta, 119, 137, 201, 275, 280, 282
Mouffe, C., 213
Mount Carmel Hospital, 627
Mqabba, 134, 201, 202, 275, 280, 692
Msida, 203, 283
MSU, (see Management Systems Unit)
Mulcahy, R., 218
Mullard, M., 442
multicultural society, 221

Index

multifunctionality, of administrators in microstates, 19
multinational companies, 545; 555, 556; *and unions*, 545
Murga, F.A., 59
MUSEUM, 425
music and class location, 424
Myers, R.R., 630
myth, 303; *of sacred woman*, 374

Nadur, 693
Nani, P., 278
nation of shareholders, 447
national bourgeoisie, 43
national identity, 266
National Labour Board, 539
national reconciliation, 261
national-popular movements, 56
nationalism, xxvii, 282
Nationalist Government, 538
Nationalist Party, 49, 56, 57, 70, 89, 97, 165, 166, 175, 178, 362, 694; *and development*, 70; *and environmental politics*, 693; *and participatory economy*, 578; *and policy on elderly*, 662; *and privatization*, 448
nationalization of banks, 414
NATO, 109
Naxxar, 281-283, 693
negotiation theory, 546
neo-colonialism, 60
neo-conservatism, 448
neo-liberal philosophy, 441
neo-traditionality of Maltese, 267
network(s), 17, 37, 283, 313, 357, 359, 375, 376, 584, 608; *analysis*, 606; *and employment*, 489; *formation*, 20; *and men*, 376; *old boys*, 20; *theory*, 19; *and women*, 377
neutrality, 4
new communication technology, 366
new information technology, 366
new poor, xxxi, 49
new professions, 39

Newby, H., 230
Nichols, T., 557
Niebuhr, R., 299
Nijk, A.J., 286
Noble, G., 313
Nolan, P., 558
non-aligned movements, 58
non-governmental organizations, 664, 686
non-manual workers, 35, 485
Nozick, R., 454
nuclear bomb testing, 198
nuclear family, 236

O'Connor, J., 60
Oakley, A., 86
obesity, 628
occupational distribution, 486
occupational prestige, 36, 604
oil crisis, 414
Okuno, A., 218
oligopoly, 446
opposition, forms of, xxix
oppression, 211, 596
oppressor consciousness, 219
OPTIMA (Optimal Performance through Internal Management Action), 509, 512
Order of St John, 103
organized labour, 574
orientations to work, 483
Osborne, J., 348
outsiders, 339, 595
Owen, R.J., 58
ownership of means of production, 37
Oxaal, I., 59
Oxford, 14

Pace, G., 426
Paceville, 134, 643
Paine, R., 369
Pamos, J., 218
Paola, 119, 121, 124, 147, 149, 150, 153, 158, 424
parastatal companies, 452

parental choice and education, 442
parish, 360
parish church, 12, 218, 373
parish priest, 12, 180, 218, 614;
  role of, 373
Parker, S., 334
Parkin, F., 437
parliament, 30
parliamentary system, 32, 102
parochialism, 134
Parsons, T., 288, 289, 290, 431
part-time employment, 487, 508;
  and tourism, 350; and women,
  242
participant observation, 325, 385
participation at work, 264, 507
participative rights, 499
participatory society, 38
particularist values, 290
partit, 273
party, loyalty to political, 97
Passeron, J.C., 33
pastoral letter, 358
Pastoral Research Services, 13
Pateman, C., 508
paternalism, 516; benevolent, 564;
  and tradition, 491; and management, 585
patriarchal society, 87, 219, 307,
  399
patron saint, 220, 273
patronage, 37, 584, 700; and
  networks, 37; political, 39
Paul, St., 11
Pearce, P.L., 344
Pearson, N.G., 624
peasant revolts, 29
peasants, 42
pedagogy, and power, 330;
  pedagogy empowering, 218
performance appraisal, 561
peripherality, 215
Peristiany, J.G., 371
Perse, E.M., 307
person rights, 448
petty bourgeoisie, 31, 41, 46; new,
  47; traditional, 47
phenomenological field, 49

Phoenicia Hotel dispute, 538
piece-rate system, 561
Pietà, 203
Pinaud, H., 587
pioneer sociologists, 6
Pirotta, G.A., 104, 105, 106, 109
Pitré, G., 277
Pitt Rivers, J.H., 372
Pizam, A., 346
pjazza, 361
Planning Area Permits Board, 700
Planning Authority, 704
Plant, M., 617, 619
Plant, R., 454
polarization, 97 and passim
police force, 30, 637; and catholic
  church, 275; and environment
  protection, 699
political, centralization, 134; corruption, 98, 418; economic
  policy, of Malta, 55; economy,
  441; independence, 686; modernization, 95; parties, rise of, 32,
  99; rallies, 413; re-structuring,
  97; rhetoric, 409; sociology, 99;
  vacuum, 516
politics of pedagogy, 395
pollution, 266
popular culture, 272
popular novels, 315
popularity of soap opera, in
  Malta, 309; in UK, 317
population growth, 686
Portelli, J., 577, 583
positional goods, 118, 181
positivism, 2, 384
post-colonialism, xxix
post-communism, 254
post-industrial society, 230, 254
post-materialism, 171, 254, 264
post-modernism, xxx, 5, 213
post-traditional communities, 371
Poulantzas, N., 38, 47
poverty, 49; feminization of, 81, 83
power, xxviii; distribution of, 537;
  élite, 31, 42, 43; sharing, 582
powerlessness, 216
pre-capitalist social formations, 47

Prebisch, R., 59
Preble, E., 622
preferential option for poor, 256
pressure groups, 95, 630
price control, 265
price freeze, 70, 538
Price, C., 212, 377
Price, J.L., 568
PRIDE/Caritas survey, 671
primary sector, 48
primitive societies, 290
private education, 181, 324
private enterprise, 263; *and privatization*, 442
privatization, 441, 476; *of banks*, 451; *and education*, 454; *and the European Union*, 452; *and housing*, 455; *and less developed countries*, 445; *and social policy*, 442; *and the state*, 447
privileges, 35
production, 28; *cycle time*, 557; *process*, 553; *quotas*, 560
professional class, 44
profit, 29; *motive*, 464; *and cooperatives*, 508
proletariat, 30
proletarian movement, 37
proletarianization, 46, 575
promotion opportunities, 48
propensity for consumption, 167-8
property rights, 448
proportional representation, 134
proverbs as source of conventional wisdom, 485
psychedelic rock, 427
psychoanalysis, 2, 358
public corporations, 451, 477; *enterprises*, 43; *housing*, 137; *monopolies*, 442; *schools*, 332; *sector*, 463; *sector reform*, 580; *space*, 165
punk rock movement, 423
pupil workers, 469

Qala, 283, 693
Qawra, 643, 690
Qormi, 147, 149, 275, 276, 416, 418
Qrendi, 201, 202, 275, 692
qualifications, 400
qualitative methodology, 5, 308, 324, 384
quality circles, 580
quality control, 561
quality of life, 237
quantitative methodology, 4, 308, 359
quarrying industry, 693
quasi-groups, 20
quasi-socialism, 42
Quintin d'Autun, J., 687

Rabat, 119, 203, 272, 275, 276, 283
race, the Maltese, 100
racism, 219, 220
Radford Ruether, R., 90
radical consciousness, 34
radio stations, 359
Radway, J., 315
Radzinowicz, L., 636, 653
Ragonesi, V., 541, 545
Ratcliff, R.E., 75
rationalization, 239, 291
Rawls, J.A., 454
re-regulation of economy, 447
rebellion, 621
Rediffusion, 361
reference groups, 289
refolution, 253
reformist party, 58
register, linguistic, 410
Reid, K., 388
reification, 3
relations of production, *social*, 563; *technical*, 563; *relative deprivation*, 487
relativism, 5
reliability, 384
religion, 232; *and Maltese culture*, 294; *and hegemony*, 294
religious, *lessons and ideology*, 334; *movements*, 295, 299;

revival, 295
Renfrew, C., 687
rent laws, 689, 701
rent rates, 138
Repetitive Strain Injury, 569
Report on Natural Resources, 697
repression, 176
repressive state apparatus, 30
reproduction, 7; of élites, 340; of outcasts, 340; rate, 658
reputation, social, 372
research methodology, 2
residential, desirability, 153; dispersion, 243; inversion, 181; loyalty, 150; prestige, 36
resistance, 221, 337, 384, 421; of students, 324; to schooling, 406; of workers, 566
Retour, D., 586
retreatism, 621
revolution, 30
revolutionary action, 264
ribbon development, 690
Ricasoli, 691
Richardson, M., 135
Richter, L.K., 349
riformisti, 106
riots, tax increases and, 279
ritual(s), 179, 326, 434; escalation, 174
ritualism, 621
Rizzo, S., 509
road building, 690
Robens, Lord, 65
Roca, S., 586
rock music, 421; and ideology, 434; and politics, 435; and sexism, 434
role(s), 16; conflict, 584; confusion, 584; diffusion, 584; diversity, 19; enlargement, 19; models, 374; multiplicity, 17; performance, 290; sets, 16, 20, 397; theory, 410
Romaine, S., 119
Roman, M.P., 625
Romans, 10
Rome, 13, 14

Rosow, J.M., 545, 549
Rostow, W.W., 60, 64, 65
Rouse, L.P., 649
Roxborough, I., 59
Royal University of Malta, 410
Ruan, F.W., 104
Rubin, A., 307, 316
Rubington, E., 604
Runciman, W.G., 485
rural boundaries, elimination of, 137

sabotage, 566
Sacco, R., 60
Safi, 125-129, 205, 275
Safraz, A., 193
saints, 20
Salisbury, R.F., 283
Salter, B., 335
Sammut, A., 692, 698
Samoff, J., 44
San Ġwann, 135, 137, 147, 149, 159, 201, 203, 690, 691
Sannat, 692
San Pawl tat-Targa, 147, 149, 158
Sant, A., 164, 175, 450
Sant, C., 89
Santa Lucia, 135, 145, 147, 149, 690
Santa Marija Estate, 690
Santa Venera, 147-149, 203
Santos, T. dos, 59
Sayers, J., 602
scaling programmes, multi-dimensional, 154
scarcity, 171
scatter-diagram, 145
Schembri, P.J., 687, 692, 693
Schiavone, M.J., 97
Schildkrout, E., 522, 523
Schneider, J., 371, 519
Schranz, A.G., 628
Schroder, K.C., 305, 309
Schuster, G., 63, 65
Sciberras, L., 41
Sciberras, M., 630
Sciberras, P., 626

Index

Scicluna Calleja, S., 526
Scicluna, E., 165
Sciriha, L., 118, 122, 125, 126, 211, 215, 216, 217
Scott, M., 393
Scott, W.D., 63, 65
Scuiling, M., 70
Scullion, H., 558
Sea Malta, 418
Second World War, 55, 73, 254
secondary partit, 281
secondary sector, 48
Secretariat for the Equal Status of Women, 599
secular society, 101
secular values, 336
secularization, 238, 268, 285; *of consciousness*, 286; *as decline of religion*, 287; *as rebirth of religion*, 287; *thesis*, 287
Seditious Propoganda (Prohibition) Act, 362
Seers, D., 61, 62, 63, 65
Segalen, M., 245
selection of job, 488
self-determination, 36
semiotics, 303
Senglea, 36, 119, 121, 124, 134, 137-145, 147, 149, 150, 153, 154, 201, 203, 205, 279, 370, 371, 600
separation, 81
serf, 28
Serracino-Inglott, P., 71, 694
service labour, 350
Sette Giugno, 362
settlement areas, 690
sex ratio, 659
sexism, *and capitalism*, 604; *and rock*, 434; *in textbooks*, 85
sexual abuse, 601, 646; *of children*, 599
sexual behaviour, 372; *division of labour*, 530; *harassment*, 530, 561; *promiscuity*, 258; *revolution*, 597
sexuality and social control, 372
SGS-Thomson, 72

shame, code of, 369
Shanas, E., 662
shanty towns, 699
Shiner, L., 286, 291
shop floor, experience on the, 558
shop stewards, 557, 564
Sicilian popular culture, 277
Sicily, 10, 41
Siebert, W.S., 48
Siegel, R., 617
Siġġiewi, 147-150, 275, 692
Sik, O., 507
Sills, D.L., 246
Silverman, M., 283
Simmel, G., 180
skill bottlenecks, 475
skill, definition of, 560
Sklair, L., 57, 69
Sliema, 36, 119, 134, 135, 137-145, 147, 149, 150, 153, 154, 158, 160, 201, 203, 275, 277, 278, 280, 643
small, *industries*, 34; *nation identity*, 211, 214; *state*, 39; *size and sociology*, 370, 375
Smith, D.E., 618
Smith, G., 102
Smith, J.C., 638
Smith, V., 344
Smole-Grobovsek, V., 583
soap opera(s), 302; *and escapsim*, 316; *and female empowerment*, 307; *popularity of*, 309, 317; *reasons for watching*, 309; *and social control*, 306; *as socializing agents*, 319; *types of*, 302; *and women*, 305
Social Action Movement, 517
social assistance, gender and, 80
social brokerage, 584
social change, 286, 421
social class (see class)
social class and drug use, 622
social closure, 182
social cohesion and tourism, 352
social conflict, 2
social construction of social problems, 618-9

social control, 369; *agencies of*, 625; *and the law*, 636
social costs, 34
social distance, 181
social exclusiveness, 35
social housing, 689
social identity and work, 496
social indicators of development, 237
social justice, 615; *and market mechanisms*, 454
social map, 40
social mobility, 3, 36, 37, 51, 137, 246
social movements, 99
social network analysis, 595
social norms, 620
social objectification, 582, 586
social order, 265
social policy, 255
social prestige, of locality, 134
social problems, 3
social psychology, 302, 630
social ranking, 31
social relations of production, 31
social science paradigm, 309
social services, 263, 656
social space, 148
social status, 4
social stigma, 233
social stigmatization of linguistic variables, 123
social stratification, 7,
social welfare, 262
socialism, 42, 44, 419
socialization and schooling, 324
socially deprived areas, 246
Società Operaia Cattolica, 518
Society of Jesus, 255
sociolinguistics, 117; *descriptive*, 118
sociological, *discourse*, 8; *imagination*, 3; *space*, 145; *theories*, 595; *traditions*, 27
sociology, *of education*, 323; *of environment*, xxx; *as a field*, 6; *and generative themes in*, 6; *of health*, 187; *as narrative*, xxviii, 1
solidarity, 5, 261, 449
souks, 179
southern european identity, 219,
Soviet Union, 58; *collapse of*, 103
space analysis, 145, 157
Spain, Royal Houses of, 10
Spiteri, L., 44, 48, 63, 64, 67, 68, 69, 452
St. Julians, 125-129, 147, 149, 150, 158, 203, 643
St. Paul's Bay, 344, 643
stagflation, 445
Stallybrass, P., 179
Starr, J., 379
state, 7, 51, *apparatus*, 506; *capitalism*, 416; *employment*, 487; *enterprises*, 43; *intervention*, 42, 444; *-owned industry*, 466; *-owned manufacturing companies*, 578; *and privatization*, 447; *rolling back of the*, 478; *sector*, xxxii; *stateless society*, 38
status, *goods*, 181; *groups*, 31, 39, 181, 182; *hierarchy of localities*, 143; *and locality*, 135; *quo*, 374, 622; *symbols*, 181, 239, 703
Stephens, E.H., 579
Stephens, R., 622, 623
Stimson, G., 618
stock exchange, 451
Straits of Gibraltar, 10
Strang, J., 618
stratification, xxviii
Strauss, A.L., 384, 432
streaming, 330, 390
street culture, 375
strike, teachers', 640
structural analysis of society, 615
structuralism, 410
structuralist functionalism, 389
structure plan, 269, 697, 701
student unrest, 415
student workers, 469
Stumme, H., 117
sub-contracting, 557
sub-culture, 485, 622, 623; *and*

drugs, 621
sub-systems, 289
subculture, workers', 498
subliminal messages, 340
subordinate classes, 47
substance abuse, 618, 648
Suez canal crisis, 412
suicide, 648
Sultana, A., 627, 628, 629
Sultana, H.M., 193
Sultana, R.G., 28, 40, 73, 164, 172, 324, 334, 336, 383, 384, 390, 474, 475, 523, 524, 529, 530, 603, 681
summer residence, 689
Sunday mass, attendance of, 12
surplus labour, 40
surplus value, 29, 41
surveillance, 17
Sutcliffe, R.B., 58
Swepston, L., 522, 523
Swieqi, 158
symbolic interactionism, 389, 605, 623
symbolic violence, 390, 397
symbolic world, 326

Tabone, C., 49, 90, 96, 97, 230, 232, 235, 242, 295, 570
taboo, 180, 381
Ta' Ċenċ, 692, 694
tangenti, 99, 447
Tanner, D., 380, 381
Tapper, T., 335
Tarxien, 137, 272
Ta' Xbiex, 145, 147-149, 158
Taylor, L., 566
technological innovation, 47
technology and control, 565
telecare, 80
telenovelas, 303 (see soap operas)
television, *and meaning-construction*, 304; *and society*, 301; *viewers*, 304
temples, neolithic, 373
territoriality, 276
tertiary education, reform of, 415

textile industry, 67, 556
Therborn, G., 30, 38
third world countries, 57; *drugs and*, 620
Thompson, E.P., 50
Thorndike, T., 238
thrift, 164, 258
time discipline, 557
time-study engineers, 562
Timms, N., 257
titular saint, 272
tolerance, 258, 261
Tonna, B., 13, 165, 295, 570, 639
Tönnies, F., 286
totalitarian systems, 253
totality, and microstates, 17 and passim
totalizing discourse, 5
tourism, 137, 487; *and accomodation*, 689; *and dependence*, 349; *and economy*, 11, 343, 528, 573; *and environment*, 266; *impact of*, 344; *and indigenous culture*, 350; *and part-time work*, 350; *and social and cultural impact*, 346; *and social cohesion*, 352; *and values*, 351
Town and Country Planning Act, 693
Townsend, P., 82, 83
Tracy, E.M., 606, 608
trade fairs, 166
Trade School Research Project, 524
trade schools, 383
trade union(s), 42, 556, (see also CMTU, GWU); *activism*, 583; *affiliation*, 574; *and multinational companies*, 545
traditional, *communities*, 370; *family*, 232, 247; *values, change and*, 230; *virtues*, 486
transformation, 7, 295
transnational corporations, 56, 348
Tripp, D.H., 393
Troisi, J., 656, 659, 664
truancy, 383

Trudgill, P., 118, 122
Trump, D.H., 373
trust in institutions, 260-1
Tucker, G., 125
Tunisia, 2, 10
twilight economy, 48, 521

under-age workers, 48
underclass, xxxi, 31, 48
underground economy, (see black economy)
unemployed, 48
unemployment, 70, 263, 462, 485, 513; *rate*, 486; *structural*, 212
uni-causality, 49
unification of Italy, 360
United Kingdom, 2
United Nations, 685
United States of America, 13, 68
universalist values, 290
University of Malta, 13, 18
University of Oxford, 11
upward mobility, 37
urban expansion, 134
urban sprawl, 690
urban theft, 643
urbanization, 656
Urry, J., 43, 348
utilitarian politics, 108
utopian discourse, 57
utopian radicalism, 426

validity, 384
Valletta, 119, 135, 146-149, 158, 159, 203, 272, 275, 276, 279, 375, 424, 425, 429, 693; *employment in*, 143
value(s), 371; *changes in Malta*, 253; *and the family*, 229; *and the media*, 358; *particularistic*, 230; *and soap operas*, 314; *systems*, 216; *and tourism*, 351; *universalistic*, 230; *and youth*, 426
Vanek, J., 507
Vassalli, M.A., 117

Vassallo, M., 6, 35, 38, 39, 40, 90, 294, 373, 377
Veblen, T., 180, 181
vehicles, number of registered, 690
Veliz, C., 75
Vella, E.B., 280
Vella, H.C.R., 687
Vella, M., 34, 38, 41, 43, 47, 48, 58, 70, 71, 73
vernacular, 217
Vickers, J., 447
victimization studies, 653
Victoria, 275, 276, 278
Vigar, M., 361
villages, characteristics of, 134
Villegas, R.V., 511
violence, feasts and, 275
virginity, 379
Vittoriosa, 119, 121, 124, 134, 150, 201, 205, 272, 275, 279, 374
vocational training, 475
voting patterns, 96

WPDC, (see Workers' Participation Development Centre)
wage, *dependence*, 48; *differentials*, 35; *discipline*, 561; *as exploitation*, 3; *freeze*, 70, 164, 538; *labour*, 28; *for Maltese*, 63, 64; *policy*, 583; *spiralling*, 49
Walford, G., 335
Walls, H., 576
Walton, P., 566
Walton, R.E., 546, 548
Warrington, E., 59
WASP (white, anglo-saxon, protestant) 217
Waters, A.I., 625
wealth ownership, 446
Weber, M., 27, 31-33, 232, 286, 287, 288, 291
Wedderburn, D., 82
weekly resources test, 82
Weinberg, M.S., 604
Welch, C., 101
welfare, *goods*, 453; *officers*, 387;

programmes, 465, 477; *state*, 35, 42; *system*, 618
welfarism, attack of, 49
weltanschauung, 218, 293
western european values, 255
Westphalia, peace treaty of, 286
Wettinger, G., 687
White, A., 179
wife abuse, 599
wife battering, 600, 648
Williams, R., 33
Willis, P., 166, 167, 173, 177, 178, 324, 385, 388, 399, 401, 404, 406, 407
Wilmott, P., 182
women, *aspirations of*, 85; *authority of*, 88; *career achievements of*, 89; *and the church*, 90; *and clothing industry*, 554; *and the Curia*, 90; *demographic profiles of*, 80-81; *and education*, 85; *and employment*, 141, 477; *labour force of*, 84; *and labour turnover*, 569; *and participation in economy*, 462; *and politics*, 86-89; *priests*, 90; *sacredness of*, 369, 373; *and soap operas*, 305; *stereotypes of*, 90; *and volontary work*, 87; *and work*, 554; *at work*, 241
Woods, W., 61, 345
work, *ethic of the Maltese*, 486; *contemporary orientation towards*, 502; *extrinsic value of*, 484; *intrinsic value of*, 484; *meaning of*, 498
worker(s), *committees*, 577; *directors*, 578, 584; *empowerment*, 580; *non-industrial*, 498; *participation*, 38, 264, 493, 574; *participation and Malta Drydocks*, 576; *participation and private sector*, 585; *participation as control*, 575; *self-management*, 583; *and resistance*, 566
Workers' Participation Development Centre, 84, 85, 477, 562, 582

working class, 31, 47, 119, 281; *increase in number of*, 48; *industrial*, 47; *women*, 370
workplace culture, 554
World Bank, 445
World Health Organization, 631, 655
world views, 397
World War I, 11
World War II, 688
Worsley, P., 646
Wright, E.O., 33

Xagħra, 283
Xandir Malta, 362
Xemxija, 690
Xewkija, 691
Xlendi, 691
Xuereb, C., 426

Yanagisako, J., 377
Yorke, B., 104, 212
Young, F.W., 516
Young, J., 624
Young, M., 182
youth and values, 426
youth culture, 670

Żabbar, 146, 147, 149, 204, 275, 691
Zammit, Elias, 61, 62, 74
Zammit, E.L., 6, 33-8, 74, 108, 119, 164, 181, 216, 485, 487-8, 490-1, 493, 503, 570, 574-5, 577, 584, 604
Zammit, I., 689
Zammit, J., 509
Żebbuġ, 272, 275, 278, 283, 700
Zeitlin, M., 75
Żejtun, 119, 137, 146, 147, 149, 204, 275
Zen Buddhism, 426
Zillman, D., 313
Żurrieq, 275, 280
Zwerdling, D., 519